INTERNATIONAL COURTS VERSUS NON-COMPLIANCE MECHANISMS

This book explores the best mechanisms for helping bring about states' compliance with international treaties. Many recent treaties include non-compliance mechanisms (NCMs) to facilitate implementation and promote parties' compliance with their obligations. These NCMs exist alongside the formal dispute resolution processes of international courts and tribunals. The authors bring together a wide legal spectrum of views from different parts of the world representing novel insights into NCMs' contribution to treaty implementation and compliance. Their research has cast important light on how procedural innovations may help render NCMs more effective, as well as on the circumstances in which NCMs may be better suited than international courts to facilitate compliance. This applies in particular to issues where states share common interests, such as environmental or human rights protection, that are interdependent, and where implementation makes significant administrative, regulatory and political demands. To enable this research to make an impact around the world, this book is also available as Open Access on Cambridge Core.

CHRISTINA VOIGT is Professor of Law at the University of Oslo; Chair of the IUCN World Commission on Environmental Law; and Co-Chair of the Paris Agreement Implementation and Compliance Committee. She is a renowned expert in international environmental law and has taught and published widely in this field. She is the editor of, *inter alia*, *International Judicial Practice on the Environment: Questions of Legitimacy* (Cambridge University Press 2019) and *Courts and the Environment* (co-edited with Zen Makuch, Edward Elgar 2018).

CAROLINE FOSTER is Professor of International Law at the University of Auckland and Director of the New Zealand Centre for Environmental Law. She is the author of *Global Regulatory Standards in Environmental and Health Disputes: Regulatory Coherence, Due Regard and Due Diligence* (Oxford University Press 2021) and *Science and the Precautionary Principle in International Courts and Tribunals: Expert Evidence, Burden of Proof and Finality* (Cambridge University Press 2011).

STUDIES ON INTERNATIONAL COURTS AND TRIBUNALS

General Editors
Andreas Føllesdal, University of Oslo
Geir Ulfstein, University of Oslo

Studies on International Courts and Tribunals contains theoretical and interdisciplinary scholarship on legal aspects as well as the legitimacy and effectiveness of international courts and tribunals.

Other books in the series:

Mads Andenas and Eirik Bjorge (eds) *A Farewell to Fragmentation: Reassertion and Convergence in International Law*

Cecilia M Bailliet and Nobuo Hayashi (eds) *The Legitimacy of International Criminal Tribunals*

Amrei Müller with Hege Elisabeth Kjos, (eds) *Judicial Dialogue and Human Rights*

Nienke Grossman, Harlan Grant Cohen, Andreas Føllesdal and Geir Ulfstein (eds) *Legitimacy and International Courts*

Theresa Squatrito, Oran R. Young, Andreas Føllesdal, Geir Ulfstein (eds) *The Performance of International Courts and Tribunals*

Robert Howse, Hélène Ruiz-Fabri, Geir Ulfstein and Michelle Q. Zang (eds) *The Legitimacy of International Trade Courts and Tribunals*

Marlene Wind (ed.) *International Courts and Domestic Politics*

Christina Voigt (ed.) *International Judicial Practice on the Environment: Questions of Legitimacy*

Martin Scheinin (ed.) *Human Rights Norms in 'Other' International Courts*

Freya Baetens (ed.) *Legitimacy of Unseen Actors in International Adjudication*

Shai Dothan *International Judicial Review: When Should International Courts Intervene?*

Silje Langvatn, Mattias Kumm, Wojciech Sadurski (eds) *Public Reason and Courts*

Daniel Behn, Szilárd Gáspár-Szilágyi, Malcolm Langford (eds) *Adjudicating Trade and Investment Disputes: Convergence or Divergence?*

Sondre Torp Helmersen *The Application of Teachings by the International Court of Justice*

Daniel Behn, Ole Kristian Fauchald, Malcolm Langford (eds) *The Legitimacy of Investment Arbitration: Empirical Perspectives*

Eric De Brabandere *International Procedure in Interstate Litigation and Arbitration: A Comparative Approach*

Chiara Giorgetti and Mark Pollack (eds) *Beyond Fragmentation: Cross-Fertilization, Cooperation and Competition among International Courts and Tribunals*

Stavros Brekoulakis and Georgios Dimitropoulos (eds) *International Commercial Courts: The Future of Transnational Adjudication*

Mark Gillett *Prosecuting Environmental Harm before the International Criminal Court*

Sassan Gholiagha *The Humanization of Global Politics: International Criminal Law, the Responsibility to Protect, and Drones*

Ezgi Yildiz *The European Court of Human Rights and the Norm Against Torture: Between Forbearance and Audacity*

Christina Voigt and Caroline Foster (eds) *International Courts versus Non-Compliance Mechanisms: Comparative Advantages in Strengthening Treaty Implementation*

Luise Müller *The Right to Punish: Political Authority and International Criminal Justice*

INTERNATIONAL COURTS VERSUS NON-COMPLIANCE MECHANISMS

Comparative Advantages in Strengthening Treaty Implementation

Edited by

CHRISTINA VOIGT

University of Oslo

CAROLINE FOSTER

University of Auckland

CAMBRIDGE
UNIVERSITY PRESS

CAMBRIDGE
UNIVERSITY PRESS

Shaftesbury Road, Cambridge CB2 8EA, United Kingdom

One Liberty Plaza, 20th Floor, New York, NY 10006, USA

477 Williamstown Road, Port Melbourne, VIC 3207, Australia

314–321, 3rd Floor, Plot 3, Splendor Forum, Jasola District Centre, New Delhi – 110025, India

103 Penang Road, #05-06/07, Visioncrest Commercial, Singapore 238467

Cambridge University Press is part of Cambridge University Press & Assessment, a department of the University of Cambridge.

We share the University's mission to contribute to society through the pursuit of education, learning and research at the highest international levels of excellence.

www.cambridge.org
Information on this title: www.cambridge.org/9781009373906

DOI: 10.1017/9781009373913

First published 2024

A catalogue record for this publication is available from the British Library.

Library of Congress Cataloging-in-Publication Data
Names: Voigt, Christina, 1971- editor. | Foster, Caroline, 1962- editor.
Title: International courts versus non-compliance mechanisms : comparative advantages in strengthening treaty implementation / edited by Christina Voigt, University of Oslo; Caroline Foster, University of Auckland.
Description: Cambridge, United Kingdom ; New York, NY : Cambridge University Press, 2023.
Identifiers: LCCN 2023029660 (print) | LCCN 2023029661 (ebook) | ISBN 9781009373906 (hardback) | ISBN 9781009373920 (paperback) | ISBN 9781009373913 (ebook)
Subjects: LCSH: International courts. | Compliance. | Treaties–Interpretation and construction. | International law and human rights. | Climatic changes–Law and legislation. | Environmental law, International.
Classification: LCC KZ6250 .I579 2023 (print) | LCC KZ6250 (ebook) | DDC 341.5/5–dc23/eng/20230929
LC record available at https://lccn.loc.gov/2023029660
LC ebook record available at https://lccn.loc.gov/2023029661

ISBN 978-1-009-37390-6 Hardback

CONTENTS

CONTRIBUTORS

Editors

Caroline Foster

Caroline Foster is a professor of international law at the Faculty of Law, University of Auckland, New Zealand and Director of the New Zealand Centre for Environmental Law. She is the author of two monographs: *Global Regulatory Standards in Environmental and Health Disputes: Regulatory Coherence, Due Regard and Due Diligence* (Oxford University Press 2021) and *Science and the Precautionary Principle in International Courts and Tribunals: Expert Evidence, Burden of Proof and Finality* (Cambridge University Press 2011). Her articles appear in numerous international journals. She regularly collaborates internationally and serves on the editorial advisory boards of the *New Zealand Yearbook of International Law* and the *New Zealand Journal of Environmental Law.*

Professor Foster was formerly a legal and policy advisor at the New Zealand Ministry of Foreign Affairs and Trade. She graduated from the Andrés Bello Chilean Diplomatic Academy as a foreign diplomat and worked with the Ministry in the 1990s, where she was involved in various UN legal issues and the work of the International Law Commission. On the environmental side she advised on the negotiations for the Kyoto Protocol and the Cartagena Biosafety Protocol on the safe transfer and handling of living modified organisms. She also served as a New Zealand representative at international negotiations in a number of different areas of international law, including air services and the rights of indigenous peoples, and worked at the New Zealand High Commission in London.

Professor Foster took her LLM and PhD from the University of Cambridge and has visited the Lauterpacht Research Centre for International Law in Cambridge a number of times as a visiting fellow. She has also worked in the NGO sector in the UK and carried out research for the British Institute of International and Comparative Law. Her work spans issues of environment, health, trade, human rights and wider areas, including the law of the sea and Antarctica. Recent publications include 'Dynamics in the Relationship between International and Domestic Climate Change Law and Policy in Aotearoa New Zealand', in An Hertogen and Anna Hood (eds) *International Law in Aotearoa New Zealand* (Thomson Reuters 2021).

Christina Voigt

Christina Voigt is a full professor of law at the Department of Public and International Law, University of Oslo, Norway; Chair of the IUCN World Commission of Environmental Law; and Member of the Council of the IUCN.

Professor Christina Voigt is an expert in international environmental law. She works on legal issues of climate change, biodiversity conservation, environmental multilateralism and sustainability. She is the author of numerous academic articles, a monograph and several edited volumes, including *International Judicial Practice on the Environment: Questions of Legitimacy* (Cambridge University Press 2019), Courts *and the Environment* (with Z Makuch, Edward Elgar 2018), *Research Handbook on REDD+ and International Law* (Edward Elgar 2016) and *Rule of Law for Nature* (Cambridge University Press 2013). In 2009, she was awarded the inaugural Junior Scholarship Prize of the IUCN Academy of Environmental Law.

From 2009 to 2019, she also worked for the Norwegian government as lead negotiator on REDD+ (Reducing emissions from deforestation and forest degradation in developing countries) and as principal legal adviser in the UN climate negotiations, negotiating, *inter alia*, the Paris Agreement (2015) and the Rulebook for the Paris Agreement (2018). In 2017 and 2018, she was co-facilitator for the negotiations on the rules for the Paris Agreement's implementation and compliance committee. In June 2020, she was elected by the first Meeting of the Parties to the Paris Agreement as member and inaugural co-chair of that committee and will serve in this capacity until 2024.

From 2013 until 2023, she was on the Steering Committee of the Legitimate Roles of the Judiciary in the Global Order (Pluricourts) Center of Excellence, where she was project lead for non-compliance mechanisms. She is a member of the editorial boards of the *Journal of Human Rights and the Environment*, *RECIEL*, *Climate Law*, *Chinese Journal of Environmental Law*, *Environmental Policy and Law*, *Resource*

Management Theory & Practice and *Nordic Journal of International Law* and works as a legal consultant for UNEP, UNDP, OECD, FAO and the Council of Europe. She was a member of the International Expert Drafting Panel on the legal definition of 'ecocide' (2002–2021) and is a member of the Council of Europe Committee of Experts on the Protection of the Environment through Criminal Law (PC-ENV).

Chapter Authors

Justine Bendel

Justine Bendel is a lecturer at the University of Leeds. She was a Marie Skłodowska-Curie fellow at the University of Copenhagen from 2022 to 2024. Her project titled INTERFOR focused on the implementation of international and regional law protecting forests. Prior to this, she was a lecturer at the University of Exeter. She is the author of a monograph *Litigating the Environment: Process and Procedure before International Courts and Tribunals* (Elgar, 2023) and the co-editor of *Public Interest Litigation in International Law* (Routledge, 2023). She holds a PhD from the University of Edinburgh, obtained in 2017, as well as a Master and a Bachelor of Laws from the University of Geneva. She has also worked as a research intern at the UN Office of Legal Affairs, Codification Division, and at the environmental NGO ClientEarth.

Leonardo Borlini

Leonardo Borlini is a professor of international law at the legal department of Bocconi University and a faculty member of the PhD in Legal Studies. He is a visiting professor at the School of Transnational Law at Peking University at the Singapore Management University Yong Pung How School of Law. Apart from his academic appointments, he has served the IMF as a technical assistance specialist and authored and co-authored reports for the Council of Europe, the European Commission, the Inter-American Development Bank, the World Bank and the United Nations Office on Drugs and Crime. He is also an attorney at law at the Milan Bar.

Jonathan Brosseau

Jonathan Brosseau is a PhD/DCL candidate (full scholarship) at the Université Paris 1 Panthéon-Sorbonne and McGill University. His thesis is on the civil procedure rules shaping State immunity disputes. Jonathan is a graduate from the BCL/LLB honours programme at McGill University (Gualtieri-Doran and Cook Awards) and the LLM programme at the

University of Cambridge (Volterra Fietta and Nappert Prizes). A member of the Quebec Bar, he has practised at the global law firm Freshfields, the International Court of Justice, the United Nations and Canada's Ministry of Foreign Affairs. Jonathan has authored or co-authored more than a dozen scholarly publications on international law.

Mary Jude Cantorias-Marvel

Cantorias-Marvel received her LLM in dispute resolution with a Gibson Rankin scholarship from the University of Missouri School of Law, Columbia; her LLB from Arellano University School of Law; and her BSc in child development from the University of the Philippines. She has served as a mediator in the Better Business Bureau in New York City and as a research associate in the International Center for Cooperation and Conflict Resolution in Teachers College, Columbia University, for practical training in her Masters programme. She has authored several articles on arbitration, and has presented at international conferences in the US, Canada and China. She is admitted to the Philippine Bar.

Kathleen Claussen

Kathleen Claussen is a professor of law at the University of Miami. She has authored more than forty articles and essays concerning trade, investment and international dispute settlement, among other related research areas. She has also served as counsel or arbitrator in over two dozen international disputes. Among other leadership roles, she has served on the Executive Council and Executive Committee of the American Society of International Law and is a co-editor-in-chief of the *Journal of International Economic Law*. Prior to joining the academy, Professor Claussen was Associate General Counsel at the Office of the US Trade Representative. Earlier in her career, she was Legal Counsel at the Permanent Court of Arbitration in The Hague, covering disputes between countries and investment law arbitration. She is a graduate of the Yale Law School, Queen's University Belfast, where she was a Mitchell scholar, and of Indiana University, where she was a Wells scholar.

Carlos A. Cruz Carrillo

Carlos A. Cruz Carrillo is a PhD researcher/SNSF DocCH fellow at the University of Basel. He holds an LLM in international law from the Graduate Institute of Geneva (IHEID) and an LLB from the National Autonomous University of Mexico (UNAM). Carlos has professional experience in international law from the Ministry of Foreign Affairs of

Mexico, the International Tribunal for the Law of the Sea (ITLOS), the United Nations Division for Ocean Affairs and the Law of the Sea (DOALOS) and as an international consultant. His research and professional interests comprise ocean affairs, climate change, watercourses, energy transition, human rights, cultural heritage law and international dispute settlement.

Rukmini Das

Rukmini Das has a PhD (*summa cum laude*) in public international law from the University of Geneva. She is a guest lecturer at the Graduate Institute, Geneva, and WBNUJS, Kolkata. Her research interests include international dispute settlement, international environmental law, the law of evidence and general public international law. Rukmini has worked as a researcher at the University of Geneva, as a consultant at the United Nations and as a research fellow in an Indian legal policy organisation advising the Government of India. She is qualified as an advocate in India and as a solicitor in England and Wales.

Elena Evangelidis

Elena Evangelidis is a PhD candidate at the European University Institute. She holds an LLM in public international law from Leiden University and an LLB in Scots law from the University of Strathclyde, Glasgow. Her doctoral research explores the role of cities in transnational biodiversity law.

Alice Fabris

Dr Alice Lopes Fabris is a Marie Skłodowska-Curie Fellow at the Brussels School of Governance (Vrije Universiteit Brussel). Her project focusses on cultural rights of Indigenous Peoples and marron communities affected by environmental degradation in Brazil and Colombia. In 2023, she was a Postdoctoral Researcher at UMR 7206 Eco-Anthropologie CNRS/MNHN/Université Paris-Cité on a project on Anthropocene and the ecological dimension of environmental norms. She obtained in 2021 a PhD in Law from ENS Paris-Saclay (full scholarship from CAPES-Brazil) and her thesis on 'la notion de crime contre le patrimoine culturel en droit international' [the notion of crimes against cultural heritage in international law] received the Prix Joinet 2022 – justice pénale internationale. She holds a Bachelor of Laws at the Universidade Federal de Minas Gerais (Brazil).

Ambroise Fahrner

Ambroise Fahrner is pursuing a doctoral thesis in the field of international monetary law at Paris Nanterre University under the supervision of Professor Mathias Forteau, and at the Humboldt University in Berlin under the supervision of Professor Georg Nolte. Ambroise has taught public international law and international economic law in several French universities. His research interests include international and regional monetary law, international economic law and legal theory.

Malgosia Fitzmaurice

Malgosia Fitzmaurice holds a chair of public international law at the Department of Law, Queen Mary University of London. In 2019 she was elected an associate member of the Institut de Droit International; and in 2021 she was awarded the Doctorate Honoris Causa of the University of Neuchâtel. She specialises in international environmental law, the law of treaties and indigenous peoples. She publishes widely on these subjects. She has delivered a lecture on the international protection of the environment at the Hague Academy of International Law. Professor Fitzmaurice has been invited as a visiting professor to various universities at which she has also lectured, including Berkeley Law School, the University of Kobe and Panthéon-Sorbonne (Paris I). She is Editor-in-Chief of the International Community Law Review Journal and of a book series published by Brill Nijhoff – Queen Mary Studies in International Law.

Jean-Pierre Gauci

Jean-Pierre Gauci is an Arthur Watts Senior Research Fellow in public international law and Director of Teaching and Training at the British Institute of International and Comparative Law. In this role, among other things, Jean-Pierre leads BIICL's work in the fields of migration, trafficking and labour rights. Jean-Pierre is also a co-founder and co-director of the People for Change Foundation, a human rights think-tank based in Malta, and is a visiting lecturer in international migration law and ocean governance at the University of Malta. Jean-Pierre holds a PhD in law from Kings College London focused on trafficking-based asylum claims, and a Doctor of Laws from the University of Malta.

Noemi Magugliani

Noemi Magugliani is a lecturer in law at Kent Law School, University of Kent, and co-lead of *de:border // migration justice collective*. They are also a senior legal advisor to the United Nations Special Rapporteur on Trafficking in Persons, Especially Women and Children, and a research fellow at the British Institute of International and Comparative Law. Their research focuses on border violence, legal in/justice, transfeminism, and queer theory. Noemi holds a PhD in Law from the University of Galway, and an LLM in International Human Rights Law and Policy from University College Cork. Prior to joining Kent Law School, Noemi lectured at the University of Galway, and held positions at the Council of Europe and the International Organisation for Migration.

Laura Pineschi

Laura Pineschi is a full professor of international law at the Department of Law, Politics and International Studies (Department of Excellence 2023–2027) of the University of Parma (Italy). She has authored two monographs and edited various volumes. Results of her research activity with regard to international environmental law, peacekeeping operations, human rights and cultural heritage have also been published in academic journals or book chapters. She was the director of the Directed Studies of the Hague Academy of International Law (English speaking section) in 2015. At the University of Parma, she served as Dean of the Faculty of Law from 2009 to 2012 and as Director of the Center for Studies in European and International Affairs (CSEIA) from 2016 to 2023.

Alexander Solntsev

Alexander Solntsev is an associate professor and the Deputy Head of the Department of International Law, Peoples' Friendship University of Russia (RUDN). He has studied at RUDN and at the University of Amsterdam. He has authored more than 700 works and was co-initiator of the project of publication of international environmental agreements with comments in the Russian language. He is a member of several international organisations, including the European Society of International Law, European Environmental Law Forum and World Commission on Environmental Law of the IUCN. Alexander took part in the preparation of Russia's Voluntary National Review on the Sustainable Development Goals.

Andreas von Staden

Andreas von Staden is Excellence Strategy Manager and Deputy Team Head in the strategy department at Universität Hamburg. He previously served as assistant professor of political science, especially global governance, and as principal investigator of the research project "On the Causal (In)Significance of Legal Status: Assessing and Explaining Compliance with the 'Views' of the UN Human Rights Treaty Bodies" in the university's department of social sciences, and as acting professor of international relations and law at Universität Münster. Andreas earned his PhD from Princeton University with an award-winning dissertation subsequently published as *Strategies of Compliance with the European Court of Human Rights: Rational Choice within Normative Constraints* (2018) and holds MA degrees from Princeton University, Yale University, and Universität Hamburg.

Yusra Suedi

Yusra Suedi is a Lecturer in International Law at the University of Manchester, where her research is focused on international dispute settlement, climate/environmental law and human rights. She holds a doctorate in Public International Law from the University of Geneva for her manuscript entitled *The Individual in the Law and Practice of the International Court of Justice* (forthcoming with Cambridge University Press). Yusra has worked for the United Nations Office in Geneva, the International Law Commission, the Institut Du Droit International, the International Labour Organization Administrative Tribunal and the International Court of Justice. She has held teaching and research positions at the London School of Economics (LSE) Law School and King's College London, UK. She has assisted counsel acting for governments and organisations before the International Court of Justice and has published in journals such as *The Law and Practice of International Courts and Tribunals and the Leiden Journal of International Law.*

Jin Sun

Jin Sun is an assistant professor of sociology at the Chinese University of Hong Kong. His research received funding from the Stanton Foundation, the European Research Council and the Swiss Network for International Studies. His articles have been published in the *American Journal of Sociology*, *Global Governance*, and other peer-reviewed journals and books. His research focuses on law and global governance with regard to sanctions, environment and climate change, digitalisation and multilateral finance. He has been admitted to the Chinese Bar in Beijing and has directed studies at the Hague Academy of International Law. He obtained LLM and PhD degrees, respectively, from Harvard University and the Geneva Graduate Institute of International and Development Studies.

Maria Antonia Tigre

Maria Antonia Tigre is the Director of Global Climate Change Litigation at the Sabin Center for Climate Change Law at Columbia Law School, where she maintains the world's most comprehensive database on climate change litigation – the Climate Case Chart. Dr Tigre serves as the Deputy Director of the Global Network for Human Rights and the Environment, where she works with scholars and practitioners in the region to study the interface between human rights and the environment. In addition, Dr. Tigre is a member of the IUCN World Commission on Environmental Law. Dr Tigre has an JD from the Pontifícia Universidade Católica in Rio de Janeiro Brazil and a double LLM and an SJD from the Elisabeth Haub School of Law at Pace University.

Samuel White

Samuel White is a senior lecturer in law at the School of Business and Creative Industries at the University of the West of Scotland. He was awarded an LLB (Hons) and a PhD by the University of Dundee, where his doctoral research, funded by the Carnegie Trust for the Universities of Scotland, examined the impact of incorporation of the European Convention on Human Rights on human rights protection in the UK. He currently leads a Royal Society of Edinburgh-funded project studying the use of human rights treaties in the decision-making of Scottish courts.

FOREWORD

When Weakness Is Strength: Why Non-Compliance Mechanisms Are Not Just Second Best

A frequent lament concerning international courts is that they are ineffective, lacking coercive measures against non-compliers. Even States that will generally comply may more likely refuse if they suspect that unwilling States shirk their obligations without consequence.

Not so, argue Caroline Foster and Christina Voigt, editors of this fascinating collection of essays on 'in-house' non-compliance mechanisms. Sanctions often do not enhance compliance, for States are often willing to comply with their international legal obligations but find themselves uncertain or unable to do so. A range of 'weak' non-compliance mechanisms can foster compliance not by punishing but by facilitating compliance. They help clarify treaty obligations, provide authoritative interpretations, render advisory opinions, uncover and alleviate compliance challenges – and may help resolve disputes among States.

The chapters combine to move the research frontier forward. The intriguing questions concern not only whether States comply absent sanctions, but why and when they do – and how non-compliance mechanisms may contribute to these processes. This volume by Foster and Voigt brings attention to these important issues of comparative institutional analysis, drawing on a range of specialists who supplement their own widely recognised expertise.

Foster and Voigt use the case studies to suggest thought-provoking hypotheses prone for further testing. For instance, non-compliance mechanisms are more likely to contribute to compliance towards global public goods. Indeed, States may prefer non-compliance mechanisms when the interests are more broadly shared, rather than agree to more independent courts and tribunals. Other factors that may render non-compliance mechanisms beneficial are when there are sufficiently powerful domestic 'compliance constituencies', and when public, trustworthy information about other States' compliance is decisive.

Foster and Voigt underscore the need to better understand how non-compliance mechanisms and more formal international courts or tribunals may interact to promote – but also hinder – compliance. And paradoxically, they observe that non-compliance mechanisms may sometimes be more effective than more formal international courts and tribunals, precisely because the procedures are less adversarial, and obligations are not legally binding. Sometimes weakness is strength.

Andreas Føllesdal and Geir Ulfstein, series editors

Introduction

1

Non-Compliance Mechanisms or International Courts: How to Increase Treaty Compliance?

CAROLINE FOSTER AND CHRISTINA VOIGT

International courts are traditionally seen as 'guardians' of the international treaty regimes by which they were established and over which they have jurisdiction.[1] However in recent years many international treaties have established 'in-house' non-compliance mechanisms (NCMs) or other treaty bodies to facilitate implementation and promote Parties' compliance with their obligations.

Implementation and compliance committees are best known in international environmental law.[2] Certain treaty regimes have complaint procedures and dispute resolution bodies to hear claims by Parties, private entities or affected non-Party stakeholders, such as individuals and communities. Others have facilitative committees that aim to help Parties to overcome implementation or compliance challenges. Multilateral environmental treaty (MEA) regimes with established NCMs include, for example, the Montreal Protocol on Substances that Deplete the Ozone Layer,[3] the Convention on International Trade in

[1] Von Bogdandy, *In Whose Name? A Public Law Theory of International Adjudication* (Oxford University Press 2014); KJ Alter, *The New Terrain of International Law* (Princeton University Press 2014); C Voigt (ed.), *International Judicial Practice on the Environment: Questions of Legitimacy* (Cambridge University Press 2019); T Squatrito, OR Young, A Føllesdal and G Ulfstein, *A Framework for Evaluating the Performance of International Courts and Tribunals* (Cambridge University Press 2018).

[2] T Treves, A Tanzi, C Pitea, C Ragni and L Pineschi (eds), *Non-Compliance Procedures and Mechanisms and the Effectiveness of International Environmental Agreements* (TMC Asser Press 2009); MA Fitzmaurice and C Redgwell, 'Environmental Non-Compliance Procedures and International Law' (2000) 31 *Netherlands Yearbook of International Law* 35; C Godsfriend, 'Comparing Environmental Dispute Management Compliance Mechanisms in International Environmental Treaties and Traditional Dispute Resolution Mechanisms in the Search for Effective Implementation' (2020) 7 SOASLJ 74; J Brunnée, M Doelle and L Rajamani (eds), *Promoting Compliance in an Evolving Climate Regime* (Cambridge University Press 2012).

[3] Montreal Protocol on Substances that Deplete the Ozone Layer, signed 25 November 1992, entered into force 14 June 1994, 1785 UNTS 517, available

Endangered Species of Wild Fauna and Flora,[4] the Rotterdam Convention on the Prior Informed Consent Procedure for Certain Hazardous Chemicals and Pesticides in International Trade,[5] the Kyoto Protocol to the United Nations Framework Convention on Climate Change,[6] the Paris Agreement,[7] the Basel Convention on the Control of Transboundary Movements of Hazardous Wastes and their Disposal,[8] the Minamata Convention on Mercury,[9] the United Nations Economic Commission for Europe (UNECE) Convention on the Protection and Use of Transboundary Watercourses and International Lakes,[10] the Aarhus Convention on Access to Information, Public Participation in Decision-Making and Access to Justice in Environmental Matters[11] and the Espoo Convention on Environmental Impact Assessment in a Transboundary Context.[12]

at https://treaties.un.org/doc/publication/unts/volume%201522/volume-1522-i-26369-english.pdf

4 Convention on International Trade in Endangered Species of Wild Fauna and Flora, signed 3 March 1973, entered into force 1 July 1975, 1453 UNTS 243, available at https://cites.org/eng/disc/text.php.

5 Rotterdam Convention on the Prior Informed Consent Procedure for Certain Hazardous Chemicals and Pesticides in International Trade, signed 10 September 1998, entered into force 24 February 2004, 2244 UNTS 337, available at www.pic.int/TheConvention/Overview/TextoftheConvention/tabid/1048/language/en-US/Default.aspx.

6 Kyoto Protocol to the United Nations Framework Convention on Climate Change, signed 11 December 1997, entered into force 16 February 2005, 2303 UNTS 162, available at https://unfccc.int/resource/docs/convkp/kpeng.pdf.

7 Paris Agreement signed 12 December 2015, entered into force 4 November 2016, 1673 UNTS 125, available at https://unfccc.int/sites/default/files/english_paris_agreement.pdf.

8 Basel Convention on the Control of Transboundary Movements of Hazardous Wastes and their Disposal, signed 22 March 1989, entered into force 5 May 1992, 1673 UNTS 57, available at www.basel.int/TheConvention/Overview/TextoftheConvention/tabid/1275/Default.aspx.

9 Minamata Convention on Mercury, 10 October 2013, entered into force 16 August 2017, available at www.mercuryconvention.org/en/resources/minamata-convention-mercury-text-and-annexes.

10 UNECE Convention on the Protection and Use of Transboundary Watercourses and International Lakes, signed 17 March 1992, entered into force 6 October 1996, 1936 UNTS 269, available at https://unece.org/DAM/env/water/pdf/watercon.pdf.

11 Convention on Access to Information, Public Participation in Decision-Making and Access to Justice in Environmental Matters, signed 25 June 1998, entered into force 29 October 2001, 2161 UNTS 447, available at https://unece.org/DAM/env/pp/documents/cep43e.pdf.

12 Convention on Environmental Impact Assessment in a Transboundary Context, 25 February 1991, entered into force 10 September 1997, 1989 UNTS 309, available

What is perhaps less well known is the extent to which highly developed NCMs are increasingly found across a wide spectrum of international law, with more non-compliance processes under negotiation as we write. Implementation and compliance machinery is found in various fields of international law including trade; international finance, including the work of the World Bank and the International Monetary Fund (IMF); disarmament; international criminal law and cultural heritage law. While scholarship has so far largely focussed on NCMs in international environmental law[13] and human rights law,[14] mechanisms operating in these other contexts also merit scholarly and comparative analysis. At the same time, the way in which NCMs operate within international environmental law has continued to evolve, taking on a range of features distinguishing a new generation of MEAs. In particular, recent NCMs in MEAs, such as the Paris Agreement Implementation and Compliance Committee, are losing their hard quality and becoming increasingly facilitative.[15] Multilateral environmental treaty NCMs have also become more sophisticated, taking on new processual elements such as that seen in the UNECE Water Convention, where an advisory opinion may now be sought through the Convention's NCM.

All these 'quasi-judicial' NCMs are designed to exist alongside formal dispute resolution processes, including through international courts and tribunals (ICTs).[16] Yet their functions in some cases overlap with those of

at https://unece.org/fileadmin/DAM/env/eia/documents/legaltexts/Espoo_Convention_authentic_ENG.pdf.

13 See, for example: Treves et al. (n 2).

14 S Atapattu, *UN Human Rights Institutions and the Environment, Synergies, Challenges, Trajectories* (Routledge 2023).

15 See, for example: M Doelle, 'In Defence of the Paris Agreement's Compliance System: The Case for Facilitative Compliance' in B Mayer and A Zahar (eds), *Debating Climate Law* (Cambridge University Press 2020); C Voigt, 'The Compliance and Implementation Mechanism of the Paris Agreement' (2016) 25 *Review of European, Comparative & International Environmental Law* 161; C Voigt and G Xiang, 'Accountability in the Paris Agreement: The Interplay between Transparency and Compliance' (2020) 1 *Nordic Journal of International Law* 31; G Zihua, C Voigt and J Werksman, 'Facilitating Implementation and Promoting Compliance with the Paris Agreement: Conceptual Challenges and Pragmatic Choices' (2019) 9 *Climate Law* 65; C Campbell-Duruflé, 'Accountability or Accounting? Elaboration of the Paris Agreement's Implementation and Compliance Committee at COP 23' (2018) 8 *Climate Law* 1; S Oberthür and E Northrop, 'Towards an Effective Mechanism to Facilitate Implementation and Promote Compliance under the Paris Agreement' (2018) 8 *Climate Law* 39.

16 T Squatrito, OR Young, A Føllesdal and G Ulfstein, *A Framework for Evaluating the Performance of International Courts and Tribunals* (Cambridge University Press 2018); C

ICTs, ranging from clarifying treaty obligations and providing authoritative interpretations, rendering advisory opinions, inquiring into Parties' compliance challenges and providing suggestions for addressing them, to the resolution of disputes between Parties.[17] The relationship between compliance mechanisms and international courts is complex and not clear cut – and this book has set out to explore this relationship. To this end, the book's comparative institutional and empirical analyses examine the design of NCMs, their importance for advancing and protecting shared international interests and matters influencing their legitimacy and effectiveness. Overall, the book aims to improve the understanding of which processes and institutions enhance States' compliance with their international obligations and for what reasons.

The book's first aim is to generate a greater understanding of the often-overlooked NCMs operating in diverse areas of international law, considering the prompts for the setting up of NCMs and factors influencing their design, including subject-specific trajectories. We investigate the nature of the processes employed under these compliance mechanisms and treaty bodies, and investigate their advantages and disadvantages by juxtaposing punitive versus facilitative measures, reactive versus proactive initiatives, and procedures promoting implementation versus addressing non-compliance. An emerging conclusion is that there is a significant spectrum of legal effects, depending for instance on whether mechanisms involve facilitative engagement with the Party concerned, rendering an advisory opinion or resolving a contentious case, and the level of transparency and third-party access to proceedings. Importantly, the book's analyses are forward looking, embracing discussions on novel NCMs like those in Chapter 5 (water law), Chapter 8 (trade) and Chapter 9 (finance). The exploration of new ways in which existing mechanisms may be used is also an emerging trend as discussed in Chapter 6 (State-to-State triggering of NCMs), Chapter 16 (human rights and environment) and Chapter 7 (science-based treaties). Authors

Lutmar, CL Carneiro and SM Mitchell, 'Formal Commitments and States' Interests: Compliance in International Relations' (2016) 42(4) *International Interactions* 559–64.

17 C Voigt (ed.), *International Judicial Practice on the Environment: Questions of Legitimacy* (Cambridge University Press 2019); C Foster, *Science and the Precautionary Principle in International Courts and Tribunals: Expert Evidence, Burden of Proof and Finality* (Cambridge University Press 2011); C Foster, *Global Regulatory Standards in Environmental and Health Disputes: Regulatory Coherence, Due Regard and Due Diligence* (Oxford University Press 2021).

engage specifically with the development of new compliance processes in current treaty negotiations in fields including international pandemic law, biodiversity on the high seas and plastics pollution as seen in chapters including Chapter 2 (health).

Second, the book investigates the working hypothesis that there is an 'interest-outcome' correlation: the more broadly that legal interests are shared among States (e.g., global public goods, common concerns),[18] the less beneficial may be a narrow legal result particular to a specific situation and the more instrumental it may be to employ a more far-reaching process in which all with a legal interest have a degree of ownership. For broadly shared interests, NCMs may provide a more fruitful avenue for States to address concerns, compared to confrontational, contentious litigation or arbitration. Non-compliance mechanism proceedings may be pursued either in place of or alongside proceedings in ICTs. The authors' research supports the hypothesis that non-compliance machinery is particularly well suited and important for addressing broadly shared international legal interests affecting common concerns and global public goods. This is brought out in the research presented for instance in Chapter 2 (health), Chapter 4 (watercourses), Chapter 6 (State-to-State triggering of NCMs), Chapter 10 (economic law) and also in Leonardo Borlini's work in Chapter 17 (international criminal law), the latter a field of densely interdependent and shared interests.

Third, in analysing the legitimacy of NCMs, the authors consider firstly procedural challenges such as consent, participation, representation and reliance on NGOs and human rights organisations, including problems with funding, technological organisation and capacity but also mandate, legitimacy and selective political orientation, representation by lawyers, the independence of the members of NCMs, the independence of secretariats supporting them, the role of scientific bodies, the need for technical expertise and assistance, public involvement and the provision of triggering information. The legitimacy of NCMs with reference to

[18] J Brunnée, 'International Environmental Law and Community Interests: Procedural Aspects' in E Benvenisti and G Nolte (eds), *Community Obligations in International Law* (Oxford University Press 2018); see also KN Scott 'Non-Compliance Procedures and Dispute Resolution Mechanisms under International Environmental Agreements' in D French, M Saul and ND White (eds), *International Law and Dispute Settlement: New Problems and Techniques* (Hart 2010).

their outputs is then considered, including the prevention of harm versus the remedying of harm; stewardship of common versus individual interests; multilateral versus bilateral effects, and containing the unilateral exercise of power.

Chapter 3 (environment) helpfully sets a baseline in relation to these analyses of legitimacy, with the environmental field having been considered the core field in recent decades for the establishment of non-compliance machinery. Malgosia Fitzmaurice underlines the emergence of facilitative compliance and the foundational requirement here of procedural legitimacy. This theme is taken up in subsequent chapters such as Chapter 4 (watercourses) which highlights the importance of representation and participation by all actors, a commitment properly to take into account the public interest and also the importance of scientific and technical expertise, a matter also addressed in Chapter 7 (science-based treaties). Chapter 12 (right to a healthy environment) goes on to discuss the importance of public participation under the Escazú Agreement, while Chapter 20 (law of the sea) also highlights the important role of public opinion in bringing about compliance and opening co-operative horizons.

Finally, the book considers the relative effectiveness of non-compliance machinery and the factors that may help make NCMs work best. The book looks into whether and why in some circumstances the use of informal NCMs may be more effective in helping to bring States into compliance with their treaty obligations or to address situations of non-compliance than recourse to an ICT for breach of a treaty. Factors differentiating NCMs from ICTs include the mode of initiation of procedures, non-adversarial procedures, largely the absence of punitive sanctions, the need for more follow up and less timebound decision-making and the absence of legal bindingness. Non-compliance mechanisms' complementarity and synergy with ICTs are addressed, as well as their complementarity and synergy with other NCMs, and situations that fall between the mechanisms. The relationship between NCMs and between NCMs and ICTs is a fascinating topic, including the cross-referencing and communication among NCMs, as well as cross-referencing and communication between NCMs and ICTs; the potential for strategic litigation; the value of diversity in available fora, but also the danger of 'forum shopping' and the relationship to national decision-making and the work of domestic courts, especially regarding the exhaustion of domestic remedies, as well as margins of appreciation and subsidiarity.

The book's chapters reveal important complementarity and synergies between and among mechanisms.[19] This ranges from the insight by Laura Pineschi in Chapter 4 (watercourses) that all available means must be used to achieve full implementation, to the analysis from Alice Fabris in Chapter 19 (cultural heritage) where the combined contribution of compliance mechanisms still leaves a need for further action as problems of cultural protection in armed conflict continue to fall between the gaps. In the case of Sun's analysis in Chapter 18 (disarmament) it is clear that the interplay between mechanisms becomes important when some of these mechanisms fail, including at times of change in political leadership, and that a balance of procedural options can help achieve positive outcomes. The combination of judicial, non-traditional specialised bodies is important in diverse fields, especially when used strategically, as seen in the contributions from Noemi Magugliani and Jeanne-Pierre Gauci in Chapter 15 (human trafficking). Civil society actors have learnt how to switch between NCMs and ICTs for best effect in some areas, as analysed by Elena Evangelidis in Chapter 11 (wildlife conservation). However certain advantages of NCMs remain clear, with this type of machinery tending to be quicker and less expensive, helping avoid costly long-running disputes and promoting co-operation, and providing access to support and constructive engagement in solving the compliance issue at stake. Emerging new mechanisms and innovations will help capitalise on this promise as seen in the analyses by Carlos Cruz Carrillo in Chapter 5 (water law) and Jonathan Brosseau in Chapter 9 (finance).

There are also tensions in the books' findings, with the pieces by Andreas von Staden in Chapter 13 (human rights) and Samuel White in Chapter 14 (human rights) complementing one another with contrasting conclusions from differently configured studies, raising questions for future consideration. Andreas von Staden comments on the jurisdictional overlap in the human rights domain which results in a growing body of decisions coming from different institutions that address the same or related rights with respect to the same States. This raises, among other things, the question of their comparative effectiveness in resolving disputes and providing remedies to victims of human rights violations. In his view, the legal status of the output of individual complaints procedures is, by itself, determinative neither of compliance nor of

[19] See, previously A Cardesa-Salzmann, 'Constitutionalising Secondary Rules in Global Environmental Regimes: Non-Compliance Procedures and the Enforcement of Multilateral Environmental Agreements' (2011) 24(1) *Journal of Environmental Law* 103.

non-compliance. Samuel White, on the other hand, suggests, based on an analysis of the UK's experience with the European Convention on Human Rights on the one hand, and the International Covenant on Civil and Political Rights (ICCPR) on the other, that the former, characterised by a strong, judicial compliance mechanism, can be linked with better human rights outcomes. By contrast, the ICCPR, with its weaker, reporting-based compliance monitoring and opt-in right of individual petition has, in his view, not had the same impact.

This book represents a rich body of work where the complexity of the issues and interconnection of the themes involved becomes apparent, adding to previous valuable scholarly contributions in the field. An edited collection, it is the result of work carried out by the selected pool of authors following their constructive discussions at a workshop titled 'International Courts versus Compliance Mechanisms' held in October 2021 under the auspices of PluriCourts, the Center of Excellence for the Study of the Legitimacy of the International Judiciary hosted by the University of Oslo, Faculty of Law and administered by Professor Dr Christina Voigt. The authors represent different international legal fields; among them are prominent scholars and practitioners in these areas. Importantly, however, they bring together a wide legal and geographical spectrum of views from researchers in different parts of the world at different stages in their careers. Authors were invited to develop their work for publication and the editors worked closely with many of the authors on their individual chapters to bring the project to fruition. The novelty of the developments discussed, the depth of the authors' legal analyses and the quality of their contributions, were key factors in the inclusion of the chapters in this book.

The editors are hopeful that the book will inform and enlighten academics working at all levels on the topics of international courts and tribunals, governance structures and international governance and compliance, as well as conflict resolution; officials and analysts working for international environmental, human rights, development, trade and investment-related institutions and organisations; legal practitioners, lawyers, advisors and governmental consultancies including in environmental, social and trade ministries; judges, arbitrators and clerks at courts and tribunals; attorneys in the areas of international environmental, human rights, trade, economic and development law; the members of secretariats supporting NCMs under various international treaty regimes; and civil society organisations and foundations working on issues relating to global governance and compliance.

In sum, the research for the book has revealed, as expected, greater complexity in interactions between reliance on NCMs and ICTs, as well as a wide variety of factors regarding their design, legitimacy, effects, outcomes and the conceptual underpinnings of their work. This research has cast an important light on how procedural innovations may help render NCMs more effective as well as on the circumstances in which they may be needed, including particularly where States share common interests, populations are interdependent, and implementation makes significant administrative, regulatory and political demands.

Producing the book has been a fruitful exercise in exchanging views and ideas on strengthening protection for fundamental interests through the rule of law. The ultimate starting point for the deliberations in the book is the importance of treaty compliance. International law abounds with treaties; yet effective implementation and compliance are recurring challenges. However, both are crucial for the effectiveness of any given treaty and the international legal order.

PART I

General and Conceptual Issues

2

Lessons from the Paris Agreement for International Pandemic Law and Beyond

CAROLINE E. FOSTER

2.1 Introduction

Populations around the world today are physically and economically interdependent. They share a global economy, they share supply chains, they share the global environment, they share the earth's resources, they share the air that we breathe, they share contagious diseases and they share a reliance on nature's well-being. In this world of shared interests, conceiving of implementation and compliance primarily through a dispute settlement lens has become more outdated than ever before. Dispute settlement machinery deals with often bilateral individual disputes, and it deals with them once they have crystallised, and often retrospectively. Even in multilateral settings, it is likely to be focussed on a relatively narrow range of issues identified by the litigants in light of their immediate and longer-term strategic interests. In contrast, today's international problems increasingly require addressing *ex ante*, at times before major concerns become apparent. They call for dynamic processes that will review and re-review compliance. They correspond to a broad agenda calling for contemporaneous action by multiple Parties across multiple interrelated policy spheres. They require significant information flow, including scientific, technical and economic and social information.

Facilitative implementation and compliance processes like those found mainly in multilateral environmental agreements (MEAs) have the potential to help address this set of needs if we bring them into wider use across international law, and this chapter advocates their more widespread adoption in treaty regimes across diverse fields of international law. Provision for these processes should specifically be included in the expected treaty on pandemic preparedness and response, to which this chapter devotes its main attention, and the intended international legally binding instrument under the United Nations Convention on the Law of the Sea on the Conservation and Sustainable Use of Marine

Biological Diversity of Areas Beyond National Jurisdiction (BBNJ),[1] as well as the plastics pollution treaty presently under negotiation.[2]

Frequently contrasted with formal international dispute settlement, such non-compliance mechanisms (NCMs) are generally characterised as providing a softer option. Indeed, a 'new generation'[3] of MEAs, including the Paris Agreement,[4] the Rotterdam Convention on the Prior Consent Procedure for Certain Hazardous Chemicals and Pesticides in International Trade as it now operates[5] and the UNECE Convention on the Protection and Use of Transboundary Watercourses and International Lakes[6] now leave aside the enforcement elements seen in the non-compliance arrangements under earlier regimes like the Montreal Protocol on Substances that Deplete the Ozone Layer (Montreal Protocol),[7] the Convention on International Trade in Endangered Species of Wild Fauna and Flora (CITES),[8] the Convention on Access to Information, Public Participation in Decision-Making and Access to Justice in Environmental Matters (Aarhus Convention)[9] and

[1] International legally binding instrument under the United Nations Convention on the Law of the Sea on the Conservation and Sustainable Use of Marine Biological Diversity of Areas Beyond National Jurisdiction, UNGA Res 72/249, 24 December 2017, UN Doc A/RES/72/249.

[2] UNEP/EA.5/L.23/Rev.1 United Nations Environment Assembly of the United Nations Environment Programme, 2 March 2022; CA Cruz Carrillo, 'The Advisory Procedure in Non-Compliance Procedures: Lessons from the UNECE Water Convention' in C Voigt and C Foster (eds), *International Courts versus Non-Compliance Mechanisms: Comparative Advantages and Shortcomings* (Cambridge University Press 2024).

[3] M Fitzmaurice, 'The New Generation of Environmental Non-Compliance Procedures and the Question of Legitimacy' in C Voigt and C Foster (eds), *International Courts versus Non-Compliance Mechanisms: Comparative Advantages in Strengthening Treaty Implementation* (Cambridge University Press 2024).

[4] Paris Agreement signed 12 December 2015, entered into force 4 November 2016, 1673 UNTS 125.

[5] Rotterdam Convention on the Prior Informed Consent Procedure for Certain Hazardous Chemicals and Pesticides in International Trade, signed 10 September 1998, entered into force 24 February 2004, 2244 UNTS 337.

[6] UNECE Convention on the Protection and Use of Transboundary Watercourses and International Lakes, signed 17 March 1992, entered into force 6 October 1996, 1936 UNTS 269.

[7] Montreal Protocol on Substances that Deplete the Ozone Layer, signed 25 November 1992, entered into force 14 June 1994, 1785 UNTS 517.

[8] Convention on International Trade in Endangered Species of Wild Fauna and Flora, signed 3 March 1973, entered into force 1 July 1975, 1453 UNTS 243.

[9] Convention on Access to Information, Public Participation in Decision-Making and Access to Justice in Environmental Matters, signed 25 June 1998, entered into force 29 October 2001, 2161 UNTS 447; also with punitive elements see the Regional

the Kyoto Protocol to the United Nations Framework Convention on Climate Change.[10] These 'new generation' regimes emphasise the practical facilitation of compliance, increasingly omitting sanctions for non-compliance and taking an explicitly non-confrontational approach.[11] The focus and the terminology being employed have both shifted towards implementation as well as compliance. We can arguably now talk of 'implementation and compliance mechanisms' rather than non-compliance mechanisms, but for simplicity the more general term 'non-compliance mechanisms' will continue to be used in this chapter.

Pursuing the argument that including facilitative NCMs in international pandemic law and beyond could help meet the needs of an increasingly interdependent world, this chapter is divided into four parts. The first part introduces the chapter. The second part considers the value that an NCM could add to the international law on pandemic preparedness and response. As negotiations for a new pandemic treaty progress, there are important opportunities to adopt machinery that will help ensure its better implementation. The third part investigates whether aspects of the facilitative compliance and accountability machinery in the Paris Agreement – as perhaps the most recent, sophisticated and universal of the NCMs in the various MEAs – could potentially be transferable to international pandemic law. While we have still to see the Paris Agreement's compliance and accountability machinery in operation over time in order to evaluate its strengths and weaknesses, the Paris model provides much food for thought. It is not too early to suggest that reflections on the Paris model can helpfully inform negotiations on compliance in new instruments across other fields of international law.

The fourth part underpins these practical discussions with an investigation of developments in the theoretical basis for NCMs, explaining

Agreement on Access to Information, Public Participation and Justice in Environmental Matters in Latin America and the Caribbean, known as the Escazú Agreement; MA Tigre, 'The Right to a Healthy Environment in Latin America and the Caribbean: Compliance through the Inter-American System and the Escazú Agreement' in C Voigt and C Foster (eds), *International Courts versus Non-Compliance Mechanisms: Comparative Advantages and Shortcomings* (Cambridge University Press 2024).

[10] Kyoto Protocol to the United Nations Framework Convention on Climate Change, signed 11 December 1997, entered into force 16 February 2005, 2303 UNTS 162. J Brunnée, 'Promoting Compliance with MEAs' in J Brunnée, M Doelle and L Rajamani (eds), *Promoting Compliance in an Evolving Climate Regime* (Cambridge University Press 2011) 38.

[11] G Handl, 'Compliance Control Mechanisms and International Environmental Obligations' (1997) 5 *Tulane Journal of International and Comparative Law* 29, 34.

that, in today's interdependent world, managerial and rationalist theories of compliance converge to support the adoption of facilitative implementation and compliance machinery. At the same time, facilitative implementation and compliance mechanisms will work in complement with the occasional exercise of international courts' and tribunals' jurisdiction and formal dispute settlement processes more generally. The chapter concludes with comments on associated questions of State responsibility as well as an update on relevant negotiations.

2.2 An NCM for International Pandemic Law?

International law on pandemic preparedness and response has not had a strong focus on the development of non-compliance machinery. Yet compliance with the central legal instrument, the International Health Regulations (IHR), is critical. The IHR concern matters including sanitary and quarantine requirements and other procedures designed to prevent the international spread of disease. They were adopted by the World Health Assembly in 1969 under Article 21 of the WHO's Constitution.[12] They are binding on WHO member States by virtue of Article 22 of the Constitution and were reviewed in 1983 following the eradication of smallpox and in 2005 after the defeat of the novel coronavirus SARS-CoV (Severe Acute Respiratory Syndrome).

The IHR 2005 revolve around a set of concrete requirements relating respectively to capacity[13] and to notification and information sharing.[14] As to capacity, the key provisions in Article 5 and Article 13 require States to develop, strengthen and maintain respectively the surveillance capacity to detect, assess, notify and report events; and the public health response capacity to respond promptly and effectively to public health risks and public health emergencies of international concern. The WHO is to assist on request.[15] Eight inferred core capacities are in the areas of

[12] The IHR 2005 were adopted by the Fifty-eighth World Health Assembly on 23 May 2005. They entered into force on 15 June 2007.

[13] IHR 2005, Articles 5, 13 (n 12).

[14] IHR 2005, Articles 6–10 (n 12).

[15] In response to the call for a globally agreed minimum standard, the Parties added an Annex to the IHR in 2005 that sets out States' required capacities. See, G Bartolini, 'The Failure of "Core Capacities" under the WHO International Health Regulations' (2021) 70 *International and Comparative Law Quarterly* 233, 234. See respectively Annex 1(A) and (B): 'Core Capacity Requirements for Surveillance and Response'; and 'Core Capacity Requirements for Designated Airports, Ports and Ground Crossings'.

national legislation, policy and financing; coordination and national focal point communications; surveillance; response; preparedness; risk communication; human resources and laboratory services.[16] As to notification, the IHR call for notification by a WHO member State to the WHO within twenty-four hours of assessment of public health information of any event which may constitute a public health emergency in its territory, as well as the response and support received.[17] Further provisions of the Regulations deal with matters including the declaration of public health emergencies of international concern, the WHO adoption of temporary and standing recommendations, measures to be taken at points of entry, travel and transport-related public health measures, travel documentation, charges, additional health measures, collaboration and assistance, and further matters relating to administration and review of the regulations.

Public debate on the IHR's effectiveness has tended to focus on the emergency provisions, neglecting the underpinning significance of the capacity provisions and mechanisms to help ensure implementation.[18] The Review Committee on the Functioning of the International Health Regulations (2005) during the COVID-19 Response observed that the IHR 2005 'do not contain a clear mechanism to monitor compliance with the many obligations of WHO and States Parties' other than a 'static self-assessment report on core capacities' and a WHO secretariat annual implementation report to the World Health Assembly.[19] Under Article 54(c) of the IHR 2005, States Party and the Director-General are to report to the Health Assembly on the implementation of these

[16] These eight core capacities are inferred in the WHO Secretariat's 'Checklist and Indicators for Monitoring Progress on the Development of IHR Core Capacities in States Parties', previously used for States' annual reports to the WHO on their implementation of the regulations. Bartolini (n 15) 238, citing WHO/HSE/IHR/2010.1.Rev.1 (2010) and following revision in 2013 WHO/HSE/GGR/2013.2 (2013).

[17] IHR 2005, Article 6 (n 12). See also Annex 2: 'Decision Instrument for the Assessment and Notification of Events That May Constitute a Public Health Emergency of International Concern'.

[18] GL Burci and M Eccleston-Turner, 'Preparing for the Next Pandemic: The International Health Regulations and World Health Organization during COVID-19' (2021) 2 *Yearbook of International Disaster Law* 259, 270.

[19] 'WHO's Work in Health Emergencies, Strengthening Preparedness for Health Emergencies: Implementation of the International Health Regulations (2005)', Report of the Review Committee on the Functioning of the International Health Regulations (2005) during the COVID-19 Response, 30 April 2021, A74/9 (Review Committee on the COVID-19 Response), para 121.

Regulations as decided by the Health Assembly.[20] Historically, Article 54 reports were required to align with the indicators, scoring system and topics found in the WHO's 2010 IHR Core Capacity Monitoring Framework. However, since 2018 a self-scoring quantitative questionnaire has been used, known as the State Parties Self-Assessment Annual Reporting (SPAR) tool.[21] The number of States submitting annual reports has increased.[22] However, it has been argued that under the new model, the required content does not contribute effectively to identification of what is expected of States in terms of core capacities.[23] Furthermore, although the scores submitted by States in their reports may be made public, there is no subsequent critical review process.[24] Neither is there a clear adverse consequence in case of non-submission, late submission or incomplete reporting.[25] The processes used are evidently insufficiently focussed: '[t]hese reports, and the tools used to produce them, do not assess how well individual countries have performed on specific IHR functions and obligations.'[26]

The annual reporting process is the main feature of the WHO's 2016 IHR Monitoring and Evaluation Framework, also embracing three processes introduced in response to a call to move away from the self-evaluations on which Article 54 reports rely. These three processes are: voluntary joint external evaluations (JEEs); after-action reviews; and simulation exercises,[27] all of which remain voluntary. Figures published

[20] This takes place annually in accordance with World Health Assembly Resolution WHA61.2 (2008).

[21] A Berman, 'Closing the Compliance Gap: From Soft to Hard Monitoring Mechanisms under the International Health Regulations' (2021) 20 *Washington University Global Studies Law Review* 593, 598–99; Bartolini (n 15) 233, 239.

[22] Bartolini (n 15) 240, reports a rise from 127 reports in 2016 to 189 in 2018 and 173 in 2019, observing that greater detail is required on IHR 2005 core capacities under the 2019 WHO Benchmarks for International Health Regulations (IHR) Capacities, which the Secretariat drafted to help States in developing a Voluntary National Action Plan for Health Security. Citing WHO, 'NAPHS for ALL: A Country Implementation Guide for NAPHS' (2019) WHO/WHE/CPI/19.5.

[23] Bartolini (n 15) 240, observing that greater detail is required on IHR 2005 core capacities under the 2019 WHO Benchmarks for International Health Regulations (IHR) Capacities, which the Secretariat drafted to help States in developing a Voluntary National Action Plan for Health Security. Citing WHO, 'NAPHS for ALL: A Country Implementation Guide for NAPHS' (2019) WHO/WHE/CPI/19.5.

[24] Bartolini (n 15) 240.

[25] Ibid.

[26] Review Committee on the COVID-19 Response (n 19), para 121.

[27] Ibid., para 21.

in 2021 suggest that 112 on-site JEE missions had taken place, 64 reviews following public health action under the IHR, and 128 simulation exercises.[28] Refined in 2018,[29] the JEE process involves a State's preliminary self-assessment with subsequent on-site visits and reviews by a combined group of external and local experts.[30] Reliance within the JEE process on States' self-assessment is considered a weakness of the JEE process.[31] States' self-assessments are said to be an estimated 20 per cent higher than estimates of their capacity in JEE reports.[32] States' agreement is required for the experts' selection and methodology, and any publication of a JEE report.[33]

COVID-19 revealed critical gaps in pandemic preparedness, including gaps in governance, subnational gaps and capacity, essential public health functions, such as diagnosis/testing, contact tracing and treatment capacities.[34] According to the data reported to the WHO by State Parties, as at 2021 the vast majority of countries still had low or moderate levels of national preparedness.[35] The Review Committee also found that weak capacities were reported for emergency preparedness and response at points of entry.[36] Confounding matters, IHR core capacities alone did not prove to be a good predictor of pandemic response in respect of COVID-19.[37] COVID-19's magnitude and challenges overwhelmed many countries, including countries with high assessment scores.[38] There was 'a significant disconnect between the actual and perceived levels of preparedness'.[39] Compliance problems had, though, previously been fully apparent. Too many countries had missed the five-year deadline for development of the requisite capacities, even with second

[28] Bartolini (n 15) 243–44.

[29] WHO, 'Joint External Evaluation Tool: Second Edition' (2018).

[30] Berman (n 21) 599. JEEs focus on 19 technical areas using 49 indicators and approximately 200 technical or contextual questions. Bartolini (n 15) 244, though noting there has been criticism of quality and accuracy of some indicators.

[31] Bartolini (n 15) 244.

[32] Berman (n 21) citing the work of the 2015 Review Committee on Second Extensions for Establishing National Public Health Capacities in IHR Implementation.

[33] Bartolini (n 15) 244.

[34] Review Committee on the COVID-19 Response (n 19), para 25.

[35] Ibid., para 23.

[36] Ibid.

[37] Ibid.

[38] Ibid., para 27

[39] Member States Working Group on Strengthening WHO Preparedness for and Response to Health Emergencies (WGPR), 'Preliminary Findings From COVID-19-Related Recommendation Mapping', A/WGPR/2/3, 26 August 2021, para 11.

extensions.[40] Reviews of the functioning of the IHR following past disease outbreaks including H1N1 and Ebola had provided relevant readings on the state of under-preparedness and the under-implementation of the IHR.[41] And, to be fair, two thirds of States' own annual reports to the WHO indicated only a poor or modest preparedness, at a level of 1 to 3 out of 5.[42] Even with progress in the evaluation of core capacities from 2016 to 2018,[43] the compliance problem had attracted serious concern to the point where the WHO had identified protection from health emergencies as one of three strategic priority areas for the World Health Organization in the 2019–2023 period.[44]

Strengthening the effectiveness and implementation of, and compliance with, the IHR 2005 is now a clear area of priority for all member States.[45] Improved compliance with the international law on pandemic preparedness and response is central to preventing fresh iterations of the experience with COVID-19, or worse, in the case of future emerging pandemics, and clearly requires greater attention. Initially a 2021 World Health Assembly mandate tasked the WHO Member States Working Group on Strengthening WHO Preparedness and Response to Health

[40] IHR 2005 Articles 5(2) and 12(2) and Annex 1(A) para 2 provided for two-year extensions subject to States' development and implementation of action plans.

[41] e.g., Report of the Review Committee on the Functioning of the International Health Regulations (2005) in relation to Pandemic (H1N1) 2009, WHO (2011), available at https://apps.who.int/gb/ebwha/pdf_files/WHA64/A64_10-en.pdf. Summary at https://theindependentpanel.org/wp-content/uploads/2020/10/IndependentPanel_Mapping-Exercise.pdf, para 26.

[42] Bartolini (n 15) 241, citing WHO, 'Thematic Paper on the Status of Country Preparedness Capacities', 25 September 2019.

[43] O Jonas, R Katz, S Yansen, K Geddes and A Jha, 'Call for Independent Monitoring of Diseases Outbreak Preparedness' (2018) 361 *British Medical Journal* 361, mapping completion of States' joint external evaluations in partnership with the WHO.

[44] WHO, 'Thirteenth General Programme of Work 2019–2023' WHO/PRP/18.1, approved by the Seventy-first World Health Assembly in Resolution WHA71.1 on 25 May 2018, 7. See also 'Five-Year Global Strategic Plan to Improve Public Health Preparedness and Response 2018–2023' adopted by the World Health Assembly in 2018, WHA 71(15), 26 May 2018.

[45] Bureau's Summary Report of the Second Meeting of the Working Group on Strengthening WHO Preparedness and Response to Health Emergencies, 1–3 September 2021, A/WGPR/2/4, 1 October 2021, para 2(a). See also Zero Draft, 'Report of the Member States Working Group on Strengthening WHO Preparedness for and Response to Health Emergencies to the special session of the World Health Assembly', Report of the Fourth Meeting of the Working Group on Strengthening WHO Preparedness and Response to Health Emergencies, A/WGPR/4/3, 28 October 2021, (Zero Draft) para 3.

Emergencies (WGPR) to assess the benefits of developing such a convention, agreement or instrument on pandemic preparedness and response.[46] On 1 December 2021 the WHA established a new Intergovernmental Negotiating Body to work on the intended instrument, with the WHO secretariat tasked in March 2022 to prepare a draft text, in an open and inclusive manner. In parallel the WGPR continued to consider improvements to the IHR 2005. In July 2022 governments decided that the new instrument would be legally binding and would be adopted under Article 19 of the WHO Constitution. It has remained unclear whether improved compliance and implementation procedures will be elaborated in the context of the expected new instrument.[47] However, during the period this book was being produced, governments began to turn their attention more closely to this question.

The reports and reviews on which the intergovernmental negotiations and WGPR are drawing have addressed implementation and compliance in broad terms only. These reports and reviews have included reports of the Independent Global Preparedness Monitoring Board,[48] the WHO's Review Committee on the functioning of the IHR 2005 during the COVID-19 Response,[49] the Independent Panel for Pandemic Preparedness and Response (IPPR)[50] and the WHO's Independent Oversight Advisory Committee.[51]

2.2.1 *Proposals for Compliance Mechanisms*

2.2.1.1 Global Preparedness Monitoring Board

The Global Preparedness Monitoring Board, an entity comprising political leaders, agency principals and experts co-convened by the Director-General of the World Health Organization and the President of the

46 'Special Session of the World Health Assembly to Consider Developing a WHO Convention, Agreement or Other International Instrument on Pandemic Preparedness and Response', Resolution WHA74 (16), 1 May 2021.

47 See, in 2021, Bureau's Summary Report of the Second Meeting (n 45), para 2(a). See also Zero Draft (n 45), para 3, paras 22(d) and 26.

48 In particular, 'From Worlds Apart to a World Prepared', Global Preparedness Monitoring Board Annual Report 2021 (GPMB 2021).

49 Review Committee on the COVID-19 Response (n 19).

50 Report of the Panel for Pandemic Preparedness and Response (IPPR), 'Make it the Last Pandemic', May 2021, 52, available at https://theindependentpanel.org/.

51 'From Worlds Apart' (n 48); Report of the Independent Oversight and Advisory Committee for the WHO Health Emergencies Programme, A74/16, 5 May 2021 (IOAC 2021).

World Bank, emphasised the critical importance of strengthened independent monitoring to incentivise action and engender greater mutual accountability.[52] Independence is key; a monitoring body must be 'autonomous, unconstrained by political, organizational, operational or financial considerations'.[53] Objectivity is essential, assessments must be evidence-based, transparent and independently verifiable.[54] For monitoring to generate accountability, assessments and recommendations must then be expected to lead to action.[55]

2.2.1.2 Review Committee on the Functioning of the International Health Regulations (2005)

The Review Committee on the Functioning of the International Health Regulations (2005) convened by the WHO Director-General under the IHR to review the Regulations' functioning during the COVID-19 Response recommended that the WHO 'should continue to review and strengthen tools and processes for assessing, monitoring and reporting on core capacities, taking into consideration lessons learned from the current pandemic, including functional assessments, to allow for accurate analysis and dynamic adaptation of capacities at the national and subnational levels'.[56] Practical exercises may be necessary to gauge as well as to improve capacity and functioning. The Review Committee suggested that '[a] combination of static measurements of capacities scores, and dynamic assessments through external evaluations, simulation exercises and after-action reviews, were found to provide a more complete overview of both the existence and functionality of capacities'.[57] The Committee also recommended that 'WHO should work with States Parties and relevant stakeholders to develop and implement a universal periodic review mechanism to assess, report on and improve compliance

[52] 'From Worlds Apart' (n 48), 5, 9, 12, 38, referring also to collective financing, echoing the Paris Agreement where accountability and compliance mechanisms embrace obligations to report on finance flows. See also GL Burci, S Moon, ACR Crosato Neumann and A Bezruki, 'Envisioning an International Normative Framework for Pandemic Preparedness and Response: Issues, Instruments and Options', Institutional Repository, Graduate Institute Of International And Development Studies, University of Geneva, 2021, available at https://repository.graduateinstitute.ch/record/299175?ln=en, 18.

[53] 'From Worlds Apart' (n 48) 38.

[54] Ibid. The GPMB has said it is developing a Monitoring Framework as a robust platform for monitoring the world's pandemic preparedness.

[55] Ibid.

[56] Review Committee on the COVID-19 Response (n 19) 25.

[57] Ibid., para 26.

with IHR requirements, and ensure accountability for the IHR obligations, through a multisectoral and whole-of-government approach'.[58] The Committee noted that as it operated in the human rights arena, universal periodic review had helped foster intersectoral coordination, whole-of-government approaches and civil society engagement, as well as encouraging participation and good practices, with implementation of its recommendations linked to the Sustainable Development Goals and other government agendas.

2.2.1.3 Independent Oversight and Advisory Committee for the WHO Health Emergencies Programme

The Independent Oversight and Advisory Committee for the WHO Health Emergencies Programme was established in 2016 with an advisory and oversight function in respect of the WHO's work in disease outbreaks and emergencies and necessarily has a collaborative relationship with the WHO secretariat. The Committee's 2021 report iterated that the COVID-19 pandemic has exposed failings in pandemic preparedness and response across the world, with national and international systems struggling and health systems overwhelmed, highlighting shortcomings in the IHR 2005 and their application by member States and the WHO secretariat.[59] Stricter compliance with the IHR 2005, together with stronger international solidarity, was of the utmost importance in facing future pandemic threats.[60] The Committee aligned itself with the Review Committee's recommendation to introduce a mechanism to foster whole-of-government accountability,[61] and sought a review by the secretariat of the existing tools and framework for national and international preparedness, including JEEs and national action plans. The Committee intends to keep this area of work under close review.[62]

2.2.1.4 Independent Panel for Pandemic Preparedness and Response

The IPPR, co-chaired by Helen Clark and Ellen Johnson Sirleaf, was convened by the World Health Organization (WHO) Director-General in response to 2020 World Health Assembly (WHA) Resolution

[58] Ibid., 54.
[59] Report of the Independent Oversight and Advisory Committee (n 51), para 7.
[60] Ibid., para 22.
[61] Ibid., para 19.
[62] Ibid., para 21.

WHA73.1 to evaluate the world's response to the COVID-19 pandemic. The IPPR's Report (i) called for immediate action to alleviate the devastating reality of the COVID-19 pandemic, and (ii) set out a roadmap for fundamental transformation in the international system for pandemic preparedness and response.

Centrally for present purposes, the report recommended investment in preparedness now, and not when the next crisis hits, with critical accountability mechanisms to spur action. The report also recommended stronger leadership and better coordination at national, regional and international level, including a more focussed and independent WHO, a pandemic treaty and a senior Global Health Threats Council; an improved system for surveillance and alert at a speed that can combat viruses like SARS-CoV-2, and new authority for the WHO to publish information and dispatch expert missions immediately; a pre-negotiated platform for production and equitable distribution of vaccines, diagnostics, therapeutics and supplies; and access to financial resources as a vital investment in preparedness and for immediate availability at the onset of a potential pandemic.[63] Highlighting the failure to take pandemics seriously, the report emphasised that the world had attended insufficiently to accumulated warnings following the 2003 SARS epidemic, the 2009 H1N1 influenza pandemic, the 2014–2016 Ebola outbreak in West Africa, Zika and other disease outbreaks, including Middle East respiratory syndrome (MERS).[64] In the Report's own words, the majority of pandemic preparedness and response recommendations had not been implemented.[65] National pandemic preparedness was vastly underfunded,[66] and too many national governments lacked solid preparedness plans and core public health capacities.[67]

The Panel incorporated a central focus on the question of accountability, capacity building and access to finance in its section on leadership. In recommending that States establish a Global Health Threats Council, the Panel intended to secure high-level political leadership for pandemic preparedness and response, and ensure the subject would gain

[63] Report of the Panel for Pandemic Preparedness and Response (n 50), 45. For summary and analysis, C Foster, 'Report of the Panel for Pandemic Preparedness and Response (IPPR), "Make it the Last Pandemic"' (Oxford International Organizations 2022).

[64] Ibid., 15.

[65] Ibid., 16.

[66] Ibid., 17.

[67] Ibid., 18.

sustained attention.[68] This body would monitor progress towards the goals and targets to be set by the WHO, as well as against new scientific evidence and international legal frameworks, and report on a regular basis to the United Nations General Assembly and the WHA. Actors would be held accountable including through peer recognition and/or scrutiny and the publishing of analytical progress status reports.[69] This would operate in a context of coordinated leadership from the WHO, the International Monetary Fund (IMF), the World Bank and the United Nations Secretary-General, as well as regionally.[70]

The Panel proposed incorporation of relevant pandemic considerations into existing instruments used by the IMF and World Bank, as well as the amalgamation of disaster risk reduction capacity building which has largely been separated from health sector pandemic preparedness efforts.[71] The Panel recommended further that the WHO set new and measurable targets and benchmarks for pandemic preparedness and response capacities against which all national governments should update their national preparedness plans within six months.[72] The Panel recommended formalising universal periodic peer reviews of national pandemic preparedness and response capacities against the WHO's targets as a means of both accountability and learning between countries. The Panel suggested also that, as part of its regular consultation with member countries under Article IV of the IMF's Articles of Agreement, the IMF should routinely include a pandemic preparedness assessment, including an evaluation of economic policy response plans. Five-yearly Pandemic Preparedness Assessment Programs should also be instituted in each member country, in the same spirit as the Financial Sector Assessment Programs, jointly conducted by the IMF and the World Bank.[73] Incentivising speedy action on outbreaks to reward early and precautionary response action will be key.[74]

[68] Ibid., 46.
[69] Ibid., 47.
[70] Ibid., 46.
[71] Ibid., 50.
[72] Ibid., 51.
[73] Ibid.
[74] Ibid., 52. See, proposing the establishment of a specific instances enquiry mechanism to provide accountability for trade restrictions, C Foster, 'Disease Outbreak Disclosure and Trade in Goods: A Specific Instances Inquiry Mechanism?' (2020) 18 *New Zealand Yearbook of International Law* 3.

2.2.2 *Evaluating the Proposals*

An appropriate NCM supported by the secretariat of the WHO has the potential to add value to all the options contemplated above, helping bridge the gaps in the presently contemplated IHR 2005 compliance and implementation processes, and assisting the international community in meeting on an enduring basis the imperative need for robust pandemic preparedness and response. This would involve a shift away from viewing compliance as a matter of setting up a layer of '[i]ndependent monitoring, evaluation and oversight',[75] to the expectation of a more engaged form of ongoing member State accountability. Although peer recognition, public scrutiny and transparency will be significant motivators for compliance, many of the proposed mechanisms are not closely enough focussed on an on-the-ground engagement with realities of public health and communications systems in each WHO member State. Prior experience suggests that such proposals are likely to remain insufficient, given the ongoing difficulties and wide gap between capacity required under the IHR 2005 and WHO member States' actual capacity to deal with contagious disease outbreaks. The inter-linkage of implementation and compliance with questions of equity, finance and capacity building also calls for hands-on practical and informed country- and case-specific attention.

The proposed Global Health Threats Council also differs from an NCM in that it would be high level only, and the idea does not initially appear to have met with strong support from member States.[76] World Health Organization targets for achievement of core capacities would help reinforce resolve and political will. However, target-setting arguably needs to be accompanied by means of differentiating the challenges faced by different populations, communities and bureaucracies with a view to close-range analysis and assistance. The IPPR's suggested IMF and World Bank procedures may serve as pragmatic planks for the development of pandemic preparedness and response capacity. Yet these are financial institutions. Although pandemic preparedness and response is a whole-of-government endeavour and economic concerns are central,

The idea of recognising a disclosing country's 'right' to assistance has also been considered. '2022 Beeby Exchange, "Prospects for a Global Pandemic Treaty"', Wellington, 3 March 2022.

75 Member States Working Group on Strengthening WHO Preparedness for and Response to Health Emergencies (n 39) Annex.

76 See, e.g., Zero Draft (n 45) para 22(h).

there is a strong case that compliance machinery for aspects of pandemic preparedness and review relating directly to health systems should be housed in an institution experienced in health policy.

The idea of a universal periodic review (UPR) would go some way towards reinforcing compliance needs and identifying implementation gaps, but does not appear to offer the schematic complexity or focussed expert attention, support and communication that an NCM could bring to bear. The UPR model seen in the human rights field is set up to provide a review of all States' fulfillment of human rights commitments once every four and a half years, through a series of three two-week periods annually where a State's representatives are interviewed by other States' representatives. This is combined with a country visit by experts from the roster of the Office of the High Commissioner for Human Rights. A working group proposes a set of recommendations and the State concerned then decides which recommendations merely to note and which to accept and implement.[77]

Conceptually, the UPR seems in certain respects an unusual fit for pandemic preparedness law. The UPR concept brings with it overtones of the special sensitivity of States to potential criticism of their human rights records. Reflecting this orientation, the description of the UPR process on the website of the Office for the High Commissioner of Human Rights refers to it as 'a State-driven process, under the auspices of the Human Rights Council, which provides the opportunity for each State to declare what actions they have taken to improve the human rights situations in their countries'.[78] Yet, because pandemics affect all countries, and in such serious ways, it seems inappropriate to carry such a sensitivity over to the field of pandemic law. There is also the risk that the idea of a UPR, drawing inspiration from the human rights domain,[79] will reinforce the idea that the implementation of the IHR 2005 is essentially for the well-being of a State's own citizens, even though in the context of contagious diseases, reviews of any one State are critical for all States. There are elements in common with Trade Policy Reviews in the World Trade Organization (WTO).

The adjusted denominator 'Universal Health Preparedness Review' (UHPR) has been employed to describe a pilot process in the WHO, for which WHO member States from all regions have expressed

[77] Review Committee on the COVID-19 Response, (n 19) 53.

[78] www.ohchr.org/en/hr-bodies/upr/upr-main.

[79] Review Committee on the COVID-19 Response, (n 19) para 123.

appreciation.[80] It will be interesting to see the results of the WHO UHPR which is described as involving a 'Member State-driven intergovernmental consultative mechanism' involving 'volunteer and peer-to-peer' (i.e., State-to-State) reviews of States' preparedness capacities.[81] Even if States decide that a UHPR is the best way forward for helping ensure compliance with international pandemic law, it would be valuable to see the UHPR process evolve in ways that incorporate various of the independent, expert, tailored and facilitative elements of the type we see in the non-compliance machinery of the Paris Agreement and elsewhere.

The next section of this chapter examines the Paris Agreement model more closely, including features to consider for transfer to international pandemic law and beyond.

2.3 The Paris Agreement's Compliance and Accountability Machinery as a Model for International Pandemic Law

The Paris Agreement is of a particular character in that participating States' emissions reductions targets or Nationally Determined Contributions (NDCs) are self-specified. There is no obligation in the Paris Agreement compelling their realisation (although NDCs are subject to the Agreement's requirements that each Party's successive nationally determined contribution will represent a progression beyond the Party's then current nationally determined contribution and reflect its highest possible ambition).[82] Accordingly the Paris Agreement's accountability and compliance arrangements focus on a range of other administrative and procedural obligations and processes intended to help bring about the Agreement's effective implementation.

Compliance with the Paris Agreement is encouraged through several overlapping mechanisms including: accountability in relation to NDCs, an enhanced transparency framework and the work of the Implementation and Compliance Committee. In addition, there is the

[80] Zero Draft (n 45) para 20(b).

[81] https://apps.who.int/gb/COVID-19/pdf_files/2021/25_11/Item2.pdf.

[82] Paris Agreement, Article 4(3). See L Rajamani, 'The 2015 Paris Agreement: Interplay between Hard, Soft and Non-Obligations' (2016) 28(2) *Journal of Environmental Law* 337; and earlier C Voigt and F Ferreira, '"Dynamic Differentiation": The Principles of CBDR-RC, Progression and Highest Possible Ambition in the Paris Agreement' (2016) 5 *Transnational Environmental Law* 2, 285–303.

Global Stocktake, and additionally the possibility of dispute settlement.[83] Communication, reporting and accounting requirements for NDCs are central.[84]

The Enhanced Transparency Framework (ETF) is established under Article 13. The ETF involves compulsory submission of national greenhouse gas inventory reports (NIRs) and information necessary to track progress in implementing and achieving a Party's NDC.[85] The transparency framework is to be implemented in a facilitative, non-intrusive, non-punitive manner, respectful of national sovereignty, avoiding placing an undue burden on the Parties.[86] Biennial transparency reports (BTRs) are expected, and NIRs may also be provided as stand-alone documents for developed countries reporting annually. For developed country Parties, the BTR must also contain information on finance provided and mobilised, as well as on technology transfer and capacity building for developing country Parties. Each report goes through an independent Technical Expert Review (TER). The Technical Expert teams review the consistency of the information submitted with requirements in the ETF's Modalities, Procedures and Guidelines (Article 13 MPG).[87] The review also requires consideration of the Party's implementation and achievement of its NDC, consideration of the Party's support provided, identifying areas of improvement for the Party relating to the implementation of Article 13, and, for those developing country Parties that need it in the light of their capacities, assistance in identifying capacity-building needs.[88] A report is prepared containing recommendations with respect to these mandatory reporting requirements. The TER

[83] C Voigt and G Xiang, 'Accountability in the Paris Agreement: The Interplay between Transparency and Compliance' (2020) 1 *Nordic Environmental Law Journal* 31–57; see also C Voigt, 'Accountability in the Paris Agreement (Transparency and Compliance)', 9 April 2021, The Road to COP 26/CMA 3 Preparatory Lecture Series.

[84] See Paris Agreement, Article 4.8, 4.9, 4.13.

[85] Article 13(7), see also Article 13(8) on adaptation and Article 13(9) on finance flows.

[86] Article 13(3); Decision 18/CMA.1, Modalities, Procedures and Guidelines for the Transparency Framework for Action and Support Referred to in Article 13 of the Paris Agreement, FCCC/PA/CMA/2018/3/Add.2 (19 March 2019) (Article 13 MPG), Annex, para 148.

[87] Article 13 MPG (n 86), and Decision 5/CMA.3, Guidance for Operationalizing the Modalities, Procedures and Guidelines for the Enhanced Transparency Framework Referred to in Article 13 of the Paris Agreement.

[88] Article 13 MPG (n 86), para 146; H van Asselt and K Kulovesi, 'Article 13: Enhanced Transparency Framework for Action and Support' in G van Calster and L Reins (eds), *The Paris Agreement on Climate Change: A Commentary* (Edward Elgar 2021) 302, 319–22.

is followed by a Facilitated Multilateral Consideration of Progress (FMCP).[89] This is a plenary dialogue which involves a biennial question-and-answer session and then a working group session.[90]

The Paris Agreement's Implementation and Compliance Committee was established under Article 15(1) as part of a 'mechanism to facilitate implementation of and promote compliance with the agreement' and the Conference of the Parties to the UN Framework Convention on Climate Change (UNFCCC) serving as the Meeting of the Parties to the Paris Agreement (CMA) adopted the Committee's rules of procedure in 2021[91] and 2022.[92] Article 15(2) specifies that the mechanism 'shall consist of a committee that shall be expert-based and facilitative in nature and function in a manner that is transparent, non-adversarial and non-punitive' and that the Committee is to pay particular attention to the Parties' respective national capabilities and circumstances. The Committee is a standing body with geographically and politically representative composition. Its mandate is discrete from that of the other bodies and elements of the Paris Agreement's overall accountability and compliance scheme previously discussed.[93] The Committee is to address individual Party's performance within the parameters of the modalities and procedures (MP) adopted by the CMA in 2018 to guide the Committee's work.[94]

[89] van Asselt and Kulovesi (n 88), 322–23; G Zihua, C Voigt and J Werksman, 'Facilitating Implementation and Promoting Compliance with the Paris Agreement: Conceptual Challenges and Pragmatic Choices' (2019) 9 *Climate Law* 65, 90, citing Article 13 MPG (n 86) Annex, ch. VIII.

[90] Zihua, Voigt and Werksman (n 89), 79, citing Article 13 MPG (n 86) Annex, paras 191–99.

[91] Decision 24/CMA.3, Rules of Procedure of the Committee to Facilitate Implementation and Promote Compliance Referred to in Article 15, paragraph 2, of the Paris Agreement.

[92] Report of the Committee to Facilitate Implementation and Promote Compliance Referred to in Article 15, paragraph 2, of the Paris Agreement, Decision -/CMA.4, Rules of Procedure of the Committee to Facilitate Implementation and Promote Compliance Referred to in Article 15, paragraph 2, of the Paris Agreement, 14 November 2022, available at https://unfccc.int/sites/default/files/resource/cma4_auv_16_PAICC.pdf

[93] Zihua, Voigt and Werksman (n 89).

[94] Decision 20/CMA.1, Modalities and Procedures for the Effective Operation of the Committee to Facilitate Implementation and Promote Compliance Referred to in Article 15, paragraph 2, of the Paris Agreement, FCCC/PA/CMA/2018/3/Add.2, Annex (19 March 2019) (MP).

Consideration of a Party's situation by the Committee may be initiated in three different ways depending on the issues of concern.[95] Firstly, as seen in many MEAs including the Montreal Protocol, a State may refer issues related to its own implementation or compliance to the Committee of its own motion.[96] Secondly, consideration of a Party's situation by the Committee may be initiated automatically as a matter of course in certain types of situation where non-compliance is apparent on the face of the public record, as provided for under the Agreement in relation to a Party's non-fulfillment of its obligation to communicate or maintain an NDC, its reporting obligations[97] or non-participation in the FMCP.[98] Thirdly, with a Party's consent, the Committee may deal with cases involving significant and persistent inconsistencies between the information a State has submitted within the ETF and Article 13 MPG.[99] Additionally, the Committee has a role, as seen in MEAs, including the Minamata Convention on Mercury[100] and the Basel Convention on the Control of Transboundary Movements of Hazardous Wastes and their Disposal[101] in identifying and making recommendations to the CMA on issues of a systemic nature, at its own initiative or on the request of the CMA.[102]

The Committee is to constructively engage a Party at all stages, remaining in regular contact or making all efforts to do so.[103] The MP recognise several types of action that the Committee may take in order to help bring about a Party's compliance with the Paris Agreement.[104] Firstly, the Committee may engage in a dialogue with the Party, to identify the challenges the Party is facing in implementing the Paris Agreement and make recommendations as well as share information

[95] L Benjamin, R Haynes and B Rudyk, 'Article 15: Compliance Mechanism' in G van Calster and L Reins (eds), *The Paris Agreement on Climate Change: A Commentary* (Edward Elgar 2021) 347, 356.

[96] Para 20. Zihua, Voigt and Werksman (n 89), 83–85.

[97] MP (n 94), para 22(a).

[98] Ibid.

[99] Ibid., para 22(b). See also MPGs (n 86).

[100] Minamata Convention on Mercury, signed 10 October 2013, entered into force 16 August 2017.

[101] Basel Convention on the Control of Transboundary Movements of Hazardous Wastes and their Disposal, signed 22 March 1989, entered into force 5 May 1992, 1673 UNTS 57.

[102] Zihua, Voigt and Werksman (n 89) 94–96.

[103] Benjamin, Haynes and Rudyk (n 95) 355.

[104] Zihua, Voigt and Werksman (n 89) 80–83.

on how to access support, thus acting as a 'source of advice and assistance'.[105] Secondly, the Committee may assist the Party in its engagement with institutions that may be able to help meet its needs in relation to finance, technology and capacity building to help it better implement its obligations.[106] The Committee may make recommendations in this regard to the Party concerned, and communicate those recommendations to the relevant institutions. Thirdly, as in the case of compliance committees operating under other MEAs, the Committee may recommend a Party's development of an action plan, providing assistance on request, and encourage a Party that has developed a plan to inform the Committee of its implementation progress.[107] Fourthly, in readily identifiable circumstances, the Committee may issue findings of fact regarding a Party's non-participation in the FMCP,[108] or a Party's non-submission of particular communications and reports.[109] These communications and reports comprise the communication (and maintenance) of an NDC,[110] NIRs,[111] information necessary for tracking progress in implementing and achieving NDCs[112] and, in the case of developed country Parties, information on support provided or mobilised to developing country Parties, as well as communication of finance to be provided (*ex ante*) to developing countries.[113]

The Implementation and Compliance Committee's work has to be considered in the context of the Paris Agreement's accountability and compliance scheme as a whole. The Committee's work complements the TER. The Committee provides a backstop in cases of repeated inaction, while the TER also performs aspects of a facilitative role. The FMCP that follows the TER process provides a plenary inter-State process enabling all States to take partial ownership of the drive for compliance. The Paris Agreement's Global Stocktake, also mentioned, enables the efforts of all to be evaluated against appropriate benchmarks. Global Stocktakes will take place every five years, beginning in 2023, as a way to consider the combined, collective performance of all Parties. The Global Stocktake

105 MP (n 94) para 30(a).
106 Ibid., para 30(b) and (c).
107 Ibid., para 31.
108 Ibid., para 22(a)(iii).
109 Ibid., para 30(e).
110 Ibid., para 22(a)(i); see Article 4(2) Paris Agreement.
111 Ibid., para 22(a)(ii); see Article 13(7) Paris Agreement.
112 Ibid., para 22(a)(ii); see Article 13(7)(b) Paris Agreement.
113 Ibid., para 22(a)(ii); see Article 13(9), 9(5), 9(7) Paris Agreement.

process collects and assesses technical information, leading to a discussion of the findings that will inform all Parties' actions under the Agreement on an ongoing basis.[114]

The value added to the Paris Agreement by its combined accountability and compliance arrangements is clear. They can be expected to make a significant difference to the Agreement's implementation. Their standout features include the way they embrace global and technical processes, including with plenary participation, as well as Party-specific compliance committee processes involving a higher level of facilitative engagement. Parties to the Paris Agreement will be able to turn to the Implementation and Compliance Committee to gain access to increased assistance with implementation, and for support in the adoption and rollout of action plans where needed. The Committee's power to make findings of fact will also be significant for formal transparency as well as constituting a partial sanction for certain of States' implementation failures.

Like the Paris Agreement, the IHR 2005 represent a body of international law where interdependence is strong and coordinated regulation is essential. The regulatory and administrative actions taken by States to give effect to their commitments will be crucial. Yet in the WGPR there appears to be as yet an insufficient focus on how new compliance arrangements could assist with helping ensure the implementation of international law on pandemic preparedness and response 'on the ground'.

In summary, what does the Paris Agreement model offer in relation to the development of compliance machinery for the IHR and potentially more widely? Of all the features of the Paris regime, aspects of the Implementation and Compliance Committee's role may be the most valuable to consider for transfer, combined with an appropriate form of prior technical review like the FMCP, which has some similarities with the idea of universal periodic reviews already under discussion and trial in the WHO. The Implementation and Compliance Committee is an independent standing body mandated to take an objective perspective.[115]

[114] Zihua, Voigt and Werksman (n 89) 79.

[115] Even though she considers standing review bodies to fall at the high end on a spectrum of possible mechanisms arranged according to intrusiveness, Berman recommends for the IHR 2005 both stronger, mandatory reporting and an independent standing review body, together with external inspections subject to oversight and incorporating an element of potential support. Bartolini also recommends mandatory independent evaluations. Cf Lin, who also envisages a 'compliance and accountability' committee but envisages a quasi-adjudicatory body whose focus is on a pandemic response rather than

Concepts of dialogue, support and potentially ongoing processes underpin how the Committee will function. The CMA's modalities and procedures specifically envisage this idea of dialogue,[116] in which there is an exchange of communications elucidating a Party's situation and the challenges it faces. The Committee's independent status and express mandate to make recommendations and to share information on how to access support is important, together with the capacity to recommend a Party develop an action plan and to assist with this on request, also looking at a Party's progress under the plan where a Party accepts the Committee's encouragement to keep the Committee informed.[117]

The Committee's power to make findings of fact is also potentially transferable, as is its systemic role, which could be valuable in the IHR 2005 and similar contexts to help identify needs for targeted multi-jurisdictional implementation assistance programmes. There is merit, too, in potentially transferring the global stocktaking notion to the IHR 2005, even taking into account that managing a diminishing planetary carbon budget is naturally different to preparations for preventing the international spread of diseases. Processes that will catalyse political motivation at the highest level have an important role to play.[118] Global stocktaking in the pandemic context could embrace both States' individual domestic pandemic readiness and the extent to which countries have jointly engaged in the necessary level of planning for international co-operation on all aspects of disease outbreak and pandemic management.

An overarching difference remains between the Paris Agreement and many international agreements, including the IHR 2005: States' substantive emissions reductions targets in the Paris Agreement are not binding and indeed are individually determined by States themselves. The Paris Agreement's compliance and accountability machinery is oriented around ensuring implementation of the Parties' reporting obligations, although there is also potential for a Party to seek the Implementation and Compliance Committee's engagement when struggling to meet its NDC target. In contrast, the IHR 2005 set down the substantive capacity

preparedness. C Lin, 'Covid-19 and the Institutional Resilience of the IHR (2005): Time for Dispute Settlement Redesign?' (2020) 13 *Contemporary Asia Arbitration Journal* 269.

116 MP (n 94) para 30(a).

117 Bartolini recommends that compliance machinery for the IHR 2005 should likewise help in the provision of financial or technical assistance, and also recommends greater use of action plans under the IHR 2005.

118 Bartolini (n 15) 249.

outcomes that Parties are to achieve. This is a case of a fixed floor. Retaining such binding substantive legal commitments in the IHR 2005 and elsewhere makes sense, on balance. However as indicated in the next section of this chapter, for facilitative implementation and compliance machinery to work effectively in such contexts it may need to be taken as written that States' underperformance will be indulged while they continue to make appropriate progress towards better implementation, keeping the spectre of State responsibility at a distance.

2.4 Convergence in the Application of Managerial and Enforcement Theory

In addition to the practical considerations addressed in the previous part of this chapter, the extent to which States' populations are now physically, economically and legally dependent on one another also strengthens the theoretical basis for more widespread facilitative implementation and compliance procedures.[119] In situations of intensified interdependence, the previously opposing managerial and rationalist theories of compliance converge to support reliance on facilitative compliance mechanisms. Rather than having to be forced to do so, it becomes increasingly rational for each State to change its conduct and comply as fully as possible with its international commitments. When a treaty addresses internationally shared regulatory and policy problems, it will be in a State's own interests to comply thoroughly. Compliance by a State will directly reduce the threat posed to it, by reducing the scale of the problem. Compliance by a State will also indirectly reduce the threat posed to it because it will help induce compliance by others and encourage their full participation to protect internationally shared interests.

In sum, the world's situation as contemplated by Abram Chayes and Antonia Handler Chayes' seminal 1995 work on the managerial approach, *The New Sovereignty*,[120] has since moved on, into an era of intensified interdependence. Today, the reasons that States may do their best to comply with relevant obligations may include not only normative considerations such as their desire for good standing internationally as emphasised by the Chayes, but increasingly also a rational appreciation

[119] C Foster, *Global Regulatory Standards in Environmental and Health Disputes: Regulatory Coherence, Due Regard and Due Diligence* (Oxford University Press 2021)

[120] A Chayes and A Handler Chayes, *The New Sovereignty: Compliance with International Regulatory Agreements* (Harvard University Press 1995) 22.

of their physical needs in an interdependent world. International compliance machinery employing a facilitative approach can assist States in meeting these combined goals.

2.4.1 Managerial Theory

The Chayes' work in the 1990s captured vital insights into how compliance with international regulatory systems is effective when a 'managerial' model is adopted rather than an enforcement model. Consistent with the Chayes' insights into the nature of implementation challenges in international regulatory systems, deficits in the implementation of the IHR 2005 are not, in general, caused by willful political decisions to go against States' commitments but rather by insufficient capacity and prioritisation.[121] As the Chayes saw it, in these circumstances, the complaint that international legal regimes 'have no teeth'[122] is likely to be misplaced; and an approach that seeks primarily to facilitate compliance rather than enforce it may be most productive.[123] Capacity is indeed the overarching problem in compliance with pandemic preparedness law, twinned with prioritisation issues.

Accompanying this insight is the understanding that levels of compliance and implementation will vary. In complex international regulatory systems, compliance is not an 'on-off' phenomenon; States' conduct within a certain penumbra or zone will often be accepted as adequately conforming with their obligations.[124] Compliance and implementation become an activity to manage, or, from today's perspective, to facilitate. What will keep treaty implementation and compliance at acceptable levels will be

> For the most part, compliance strategies seek[ing] to remove obstacles, clarify issues, and convince parties to change their behaviour. The dominant approach is cooperative rather than adversarial. Instances of apparent non-compliance are treated as problems to be solved, rather than

[121] Bartolini (n 15) 241. In the context of the Paris Agreement see similarly Benjamin, Haynes and Rudyk (n 95) 350, 363.

[122] e.g., in the WHO, Committee members' repeated observations that the IHR 2005 lacks enforcement mechanisms and 'has no teeth'. Review Committee on the COVID-19 Response (n 19) para 121.

[123] Chayes and Chayes (n 120) 2.

[124] Ibid., 17. See also at 20.

> wrongs to be punished. In general, the method is verbal, interactive, and consensual.[125]

Bringing about improved implementation and compliance will involve a series of measures and activities, usually starting with the data and its verification and then moving into more active management, identifying behaviour that raises significant compliance questions.[126] The process is initially exploratory, seeking to clarify the nature of the behaviour and surrounding facts and circumstances.[127] The next step in cases of persistent concern may be a diagnosis of the causes for non-implementation and non-compliance, and the aim here is to identify an obstacle that could be removed or solve problems standing in the way of implementation and compliance, such as capacity issues and the need for technical assistance or access to resources.[128] The process will be interactive.[129] This compliance and implementation model ties into the importance of justification and discourse as crucial elements in how international norms operate to control conduct, with questionable action to be explained and justified.[130] While the foundation of compliance remains the normative framework in the relevant treaty,[131] transparency is core.[132]

All these elements of the Chayes' theory have provided valuable insights for the design of NCMs. However, at the same time, the globe is in a fundamentally different position to that of twenty-five years ago. Populations' increasingly shared physical dependence on the health of Earth's planetary systems has become starkly apparent, and now successive novel diseases frequently crossing species from animals to humans, reveal our vulnerability also in terms of collective health. The application of managerial theory increasingly overlaps with the application of rationalist theory.

[125] Ibid., 109, albeit adding that 'In some cases ... the regime may have benefits it can withhold'.
[126] Ibid., 110.
[127] Ibid., 110.
[128] Ibid., 110, 25, 197.
[129] Ibid., 110.
[130] Ibid., 118.
[131] Ibid., 110.
[132] Ibid., 22, 162. Consistent with this, see, on the purposes of the Paris Agreement's ETF, van Asselt and Kulovesi (n 88) 304.

2.4.2 Rationalist Theory

Political economists, led by George Downs and others, have traditionally insisted on the importance of enforcement, emphasising a rationalist approach.[133] Enforcement rather than management is the key to compliance, they say, in situations where there are strong incentives to depart from compliance, where treaties require States to pursue conduct themselves differently from that they would have pursued in the absence of the treaty, and where deep co-operation is lacking. This may initially appear to be the case in respect of pandemic preparedness and response, climate change and also problems such as the management of biodiversity on the high seas. But additional, competing, rationalist considerations increasingly logically feed into States' assessment of the degree to which they will comply with such bodies of law. In circumstances of vital physical interdependence like those in which the world now clearly finds itself, sanctions for non-compliance are to a degree inbuilt insofar as a Party's non-compliance will leave that Party more exposed to the global threats now faced. Experiences with the COVID-19 pandemic and severe weather events are illustrative. Depending on the Party's profile relative to the threat, the increased exposure may be greater or lesser. And each Party needs also to reckon with the question of whether its non-compliance will encourage others' non-compliance, ratcheting up the threat. Contrastingly, a State that adopts a policy of close compliance with relevant international legal obligations will rationally derive a range of direct and indirect benefits. By modelling good conduct for others, it will help bring about better compliance and better results globally, as well as enhancing the State's reputation and political influence in ongoing negotiations to address critical problems.[134]

[133] GW Downs, DM Rocke and PN Barsoom, 'Is the Good News about Compliance Good News about Cooperation?' (1996) 50 *International Organization* 379. For discussion, J Brunnée and SJ Toope, 'Persuasion and Enforcement: Explaining Compliance with International Law' (2002) 13 *Finnish Yearbook of International Law* 273, 282; M Doelle, 'Non-Compliance Procedures' in L Rajamani and J Peel (eds), *The Oxford Handbook of International Environmental Law* (2nd ed, Oxford University Press 2021) 972.

[134] C Foster, 'Dynamics in the Relationship between International and Domestic Climate Change Law and Policy in Aotearoa New Zealand' in A Hertogen and A Hood (eds), *International Law in Aotearoa New Zealand* (Thomson Reuters 2021) 433.

2.4.3 *Convergence of the Theories*

The realities on which the theory in *The New Sovereignty* was built have evolved to embrace circumstances of deepened global interdependence. At this point in history, it is becoming increasingly rational for States to comply as a matter of self-interest with treaties designed to address pressing problems of global interdependence like the problems we see in the areas of climate change, pandemic prevention and high seas biodiversity. This means that facilitative, non-punitive compliance machinery, or 'new' generation compliance machinery, has a stronger theoretical basis now than before. Non-compliance mechanisms increasingly take the form of 'facilitated implementation and compliance' as with the Paris Agreement.[135] Getting to this point has not been straightforward. The adoption of the reporting and review processes for all Parties to the Paris Agreement represented a significant shift, given the previous ongoing resistance of developing countries including China and India.[136] However, all this strengthens the case for States to consider transferring appropriately adapted elements of the Paris Agreement's facilitative compliance scheme both to international pandemic law and beyond.

2.4.4 *International Courts and Tribunals and Questions of State Responsibility*

At the same time, international courts' and tribunals' (ICTs) role as avenues for possible formal dispute settlement also continues to be valuable.[137] Adjudication remains available, where there is jurisdiction, in respect of States' general obligations under customary international law regarding the prevention of harm as well as in accordance with the dispute settlement provisions of applicable treaties. And adjudication

[135] M Doelle, 'In Defence of the Paris Agreement's Compliance System: The Case for Facilitative Compliance' in B Mayer and A Zahar (eds), *Debating Climate Law* (Cambridge University Press 2020). Cf the Kyoto Protocol's double-branched 'facilitative' and 'enforcement' machinery, differentiating between developed and developing countries.

[136] Van Asselt and Kulovesi (n 88) 319.

[137] For the IHR 2005 dispute settlement provisions, see Article 56. Lin (n 115) at 278, observes that Article 56 has never been invoked. Article 24 of the Paris Agreement applies *mutatis mutandis* the dispute settlement provisions in Article 14 of the United Nations Framework Convention on Climate Change.

may lead to sanctions including modes of collective enforcement.[138] Adjudication is clearly still on the 'menu',[139] though as a side rather than a main course. It is understood that the operation of facilitative compliance systems and multilateral review processes is unlikely to be enough all the time on its own to persuade powerful countries to comply with all of their commitments. Access to dispute settlement will remain important as a broader aspect of compliance schemes.[140]

Further, ICTs' contribution to the authoritative clarification of international law is helpful. This may take place in contentious or advisory proceedings. The expected International Court of Justice[141] and International Tribunal for the Law of the Sea[142] advisory opinions on climate change are examples. The development of new advisory

138 Brunnée and Toope (n 133), 294.

139 Z Savaşan, *Paris Climate Agreement: A Deal for Better Compliance?* (Springer Nature 2019) 253; as Brunnée and Toope put it: '[i]ncentives and disincentives, formal dispute settlement provisions processes, and enforcement through sanctions all have a role to play in shaping the behaviour of international actors.' J Brunnée and SJ Toope, 'Persuasion and Enforcement: Explaining Compliance with International Law' (2002) 13 *Finnish Yearbook of International Law* 273, 294.

140 Chayes and Chayes (n 120) 24, 197.

141 The draft resolution circulated to UN Members by Vanuatu on 29 November 2022 requested the Court to give its opinion on the questions:

(1) What are the obligations of States under the above-mentioned body of international law to ensure the protection of the climate system and other parts of the environment for present and future generations;

(2) What are the legal consequences under these obligations for States which, by their acts and omissions, have caused significant harm to the climate system and other parts of the environment, with respect to:

(a) Small island developing States and other States which, due to their geographical circumstances and level of development, are injured or specially affected by or are particularly vulnerable to the adverse effects of climate change?

(b) Peoples and individuals of the present and future generations affected by the adverse effects of climate change?

Available at www.vanuatuicj.com/resolution, accessed 13 December 2022.

142 The Commission of Small Island States' Request for an Advisory Opinion of 12 December 2022 asks: What are the specific obligations of State Parties to the United Nations Convention on the Law of the Sea (the 'UNCLOS'), including under Part XII:

(a) to prevent, reduce and control pollution of the marine environment in relation to the deleterious effects that result or are likely to result from climate change, including through ocean warming and sea level rise, and ocean acidification, which are caused by anthropogenic greenhouse gas emissions into the atmosphere?

procedures within certain multilateral institutional frameworks, examples of which are discussed in later chapters of this book, are also a promising mechanism.[143] Such procedures may help bring about greater compliance by clarifying States' or others' obligations. In the meantime, traditional non-compliance procedures help to prevent breaches and harm in advance and 'can be considered to work alongside and complement traditional dispute settlement processes rather than replace them'.[144] Today's international legal regulatory problems should also be viewed in the broader context of reliance on 'mosaic' enforcement including through domestic administrative and judicial processes.[145] Flanking tools and principles may helpfully be brought to bear in all these contexts, including impact assessment, the precautionary principle and a dedication to greater equity within and across generations.

However, it is clear that NCMs have the potential to perform a special function in international law as it reconfigures itself in the course of the twenty-first century. They provide a shortcut to enhanced compliance in relation to the advancement or protection of shared international interests in an interdependent world. They are both less confrontational than inter-State procedures, and less beset by hurdles relating to standing. Where NCMs are relied on, the rules relating to the invocation of State responsibility move back-of-picture and the specific rules on initiation of non-compliance proceedings in the regime in question come to bear. There is no need to determine whether an individual State is an injured State or otherwise entitled to invoke the rules with which compliance is to be assessed and whether these rules are for instance obligations *erga omnes partes*. In this respect the advent of an era of greater reliance on

(b) to protect and preserve the marine environment in relation to climate change impacts, including ocean warming and sea level rise, and ocean acidification?

Available at: www.itlos.org/fileadmin/itlos/documents/cases/31/Request_for_Advisory_Opinion_COSIS_12.12.22.pdf.

143 See in particular Cruz Carillo (n 2).

144 J Mossop, 'Dispute Settlement in Areas beyond National Jurisdiction' in V De Lucia, L Ngoc Nguyen and A Oude Elferink (eds), *International Law and Marine Areas beyond National Jurisdiction: Reflections on Justice, Space, Knowledge and Power* (Brill 2021), available at https://ssrn.com/abstract=3885272. Cf L Lijnzaad, 'Dispute Settlement for Marine Biodiversity beyond National Jurisdiction: Not an Afterthought' in H Ruiz Fabri, E Franckx, M Benatar and T Meshel (eds), *A Bridge over Troubled Waters* (Brill 2020) 147.

145 C Redgwell, 'Facilitation of Compliance' in J Brunnée, M Doelle and L Rajamani (eds), *Promoting Compliance in an Evolving Climate Regime* (Cambridge University Press 2012).

NCMs would be an appropriate response to international law's entwinement with increasing global interdependence.

What is the relationship, though, between the use of non-compliance procedures on the one hand and on the other hand dispute settlement in ICTs and State responsibility?[146] Generally it appears that the law on State responsibility will continue to apply where a State is not complying with its international obligations. Certain legal consequences attach including in respect of reparation to other affected States. And generally, it appears that it will remain open to States to go to international dispute settlement even while compliance procedures may be underway if there is an international court or tribunal with jurisdiction. States are slow to invoke the responsibility of other States and are even slower to seek formal international dispute settlement. But there is a palpable tension here. Non-compliance procedures in effect ask of States that they acknowledge their implementation of treaty commitments which leaves something to be desired, in order that this non-compliance machinery can be used to get help to these States so that they can achieve better implementation. So are States admitting to treaty breaches when they seek or receive help in the context of working with a compliance committee?

Martii Koskenniemi, who was with the Foreign Ministry of Finland at the time the Montreal Protocol negotiations took place, wrote then that non-compliance procedures could constitute specialised systems of State responsibility which would replace the general international law on State responsibility, in effect taking the question off the table for practical purposes.[147] But this feels unintuitive, because with the fuller range of NCMs now operating in international environmental law, we can see that

[146] Scholars have addressed various versions of this question since the Montréal protocol negotiations. M Koskenniemi, 'Breach of Treaty or Non-Compliance? Reflections on the Enforcement of the Montreal Protocol' (1992) 3(1) *Yearbook of International Environmental Law* 123–62; T Treves, L Pineschi, A Tanzi et al. (eds), *Non-Compliance Procedures and Mechanisms and the Effectiveness of International Environmental Agreements* (TMC Asser Press 2009); K Scott, 'Non-Compliance Procedures and Dispute Resolution Mechanisms under International Environmental Agreements' in D French, M Saul and N White *International Law and Dispute Settlement: New Problems and Techniques* (Hart 2010); P Sands, 'Compliance with International Environmental Obligations: Existing International Legal Arrangements' in J Cameron, J Werksman and P Roderick (eds), *Improving Compliance with International Environmental Law* (Earthscan 1996).

[147] Koskenniemi (n 146).

it is possible there may be inbuilt limits on their reach and effect within each regime.[148] Scholars since have, in any event, tended not to endorse Koskenniemi's view.[149]

In closing, a few thoughts on the question of State responsibility are as follows. First, we should welcome the sense of flexibility-in-the-system that accompanies more widespread reliance on non-compliance machinery, and the indulgence of concerted efforts to improve implementation for the benefit of all in an interdependent world in which timely, preventive action to help protect shared interests is more valuable than remonstration *post hoc*. Second, given that non-compliance procedures will generally help address shared public interests, could we view the current situation as the blending of aspects of a more public or administrative law dimension into the international legal order, layering onto the more traditional, bilateral conceptions of international law as analogised with the private law of contract and tort?[150] Third, it may be possible to create semi-formalised safe zones around non-compliance processes, for instance agreeing clearly that the findings of compliance committees will not constitute the equivalent of *res judicata* or will be without prejudice to the findings made in any subsequent international dispute settlement proceedings. Fourth, we may find that States will be careful to try and ringfence the scope of the issues that they ask NCMs to address, although where issues are interlinked, there is likely always to be scope for a certain overlap with matters of State responsibility. States may be more comfortable if such committees are referred to as 'implementation and compliance' committees rather than NCMs. This allows scope for views that the improved conduct requested of States through such machinery may or may not relate to failed compliance attracting State responsibility. Depending on the circumstances it may be a matter only of improving States' implementation of their obligations.

2.5 Conclusion

A world in which international law continues to grapple with the prevention of some of the greatest threats humanity has known to date is a

[148] Their remits will probably not cover all legal issues potentially arising under a given treaty.

[149] e.g., Scott (n 146).

[150] B Simma, 'From Bilateralism to Community Interest in International Law' (Receuil des Cours de L'Academie de Droit International, 1994) 250.

world in which facilitative compliance linked with targeted support and capacity building must surely play a central role. Compliance machinery needs to be built on a supportive but serious ethos, enabling a well-informed and realistic approach, and taking into account the limitations of actors in situations where compliance is a challenge and equity an important consideration. Negotiating governments should consider the Paris Agreement's compliance machinery (and the accumulated practice of reliance on NCMs under MEAs), when they consider the types of mechanism that could be put in place to help improve compliance with various relevant bodies of international law.

In international pandemic law and in other international legal contexts, States could do well to consider the way in which Paris Agreement-style accountability and compliance arrangements need to go beyond declaratory processes presenting States' progress and involve independent, expert engagement with individual States' implementation needs, including taking concrete steps to assist with requests for resources, capacity and remedial planning. These are crucial factors that will need to be seriously considered for introduction into implementation and compliance procedures if international law on pandemic prevention preparedness and response is to be sufficiently effective.

At the time this chapter was initially drafted, in January 2022, and informally circulated, negotiations on both the intended treaty on pandemic preparedness and response and on the BBNJ instrument were mid-stream. As part of its participation in the pandemic treaty negotiations, New Zealand put forward the suggestion in April 2022 that the Paris Agreement could be used as a model for non-compliance procedures under the new treaty.[151] At the same time, the text of the expected BBNJ instrument was also evolving. Initially it was envisaged simply that the BBNJ agreement's Conference of the Parties might in due course adopt co-operative procedures and institutional mechanisms to promote

[151] New Zealand submitted: 'There are different ways to achieve this objective. One option would be a Universal Periodic Health Review process, similar to that operating under international human rights Instruments (building on the WHO Universal Heath Preparedness Review currently being trialed). Option two would be a facilitative compliance committee, similar to that operating under the Paris Agreement on Climate Change.' Aotearoa New Zealand Submission to the Intergovernmental Negotiating Body, April 2022, available at www.health.govt.nz/system/files/documents/pages/new-zealand-submission-to-the-inb-april-2022.pdf.

compliance and address cases of non-compliance.[152] This text was itself in square brackets and at least one delegation (the United States) requested its deletion.[153] Nevertheless, the President of the negotiations, Ambassador Rena Lee of Singapore, retained the provision in the draft text, produced in July 2022, adding as an alternative a more extended five-paragraph compliance provision which would establish a compliance committee based closely in part on the Paris Agreement.[154] At the negotiations in August 2022 in New York, where New Zealand chaired the talks on the compliance issue, States refined this provision.[155]

The non-compliance provision in the BBNJ text is likely to be of particular value within the BBNJ regime because the instrument's practical effect will depend closely on compliance with procedural obligations, including commitments on information flow. Equity and environmental protection can best be assured with the necessary transparency and accountability, whether this be in the accessing of marine genetic resources or the conduct of appropriate environmental impact assessment in zones abutting the Area. An appropriate NCM will complement existing law of the sea dispute settlement machinery, facilitating provision of assistance to States who may be facing technical and political implementation challenges and enabling the international community to

152 UN, *Revised Draft Text of an Agreement under the United Nations Convention on the Law of the Sea on the Conservation and Sustainable Use of Marine Biological Diversity of Areas Beyond National Jurisdiction* (Draft text 2020), UN Doc A/CONF.232/2020/3, Article 53(3). Available at https://undocs.org/en/a/conf.232/2020/3. For discussion, see Mossop (n 144).

153 Article-by-article compilation of textual proposals for consideration at the fourth session dated 15 April 2020.

154 *Further Revised Draft Text of an Agreement under the United Nations Convention on the Law of the Sea on the Conservation and Sustainable Use of Marine Biological Diversity of Areas Beyond National Jurisdiction: Note by the President* (now available in all official languages), 20 July 2022.

155 Article 53 ter, *Further Refreshed Draft Text of an Agreement under the United Nations Convention on the Law of the Sea on the Conservation and Sustainable Use of Marine Biological Diversity of Areas Beyond National Jurisdiction*, UN Doc A/CONF.232/2022/CRP.13, 26 August 2022. The author attended and participated actively in a series of workshops and informal consultations with the New Zealand Ministry for Foreign Affairs and Trade in the lead up to and during the negotiations led by the New Zealand Government's chief international legal advisor, Victoria Hallum. At the August 2022 negotiations, Hallum took on the role of chairing/facilitating the negotiations on the instrument's non-compliance provisions. See also High Seas Alliance, *Cross-Cutting Briefing #2 Effective Implementation and Compliance under the BBNJ Agreement through an Implementation and Compliance Committee*, available at www.highseasalliance.org/resources-category/policy-recommendations-and-briefs/.

better protect populations' mutually important interests for the long term. Inclusion of an appropriate NCM in the new pandemic treaty instrument, and in the negotiations for the new international legally binding instrument on plastic pollution, would be a similarly valuable step. Governments must be prompted more actively to ensure they adopt appropriate NCMs, sooner rather than later, in all relevant spheres.

3

The New Generation of Environmental Non-Compliance Procedures and the Question of Legitimacy

MALGOSIA FITZMAURICE

3.1 Introduction

This chapter will explore the evolution of Non-Compliance Procedures (NCPs). NCPs are designed in principle to facilitate and assist the compliance of States Parties with obligations deriving from Multilateral Environmental Agreements (MEAs), but potentially trigger harsher means to elicit compliance, such as suspension of a Party's rights under an MEA. The chapter will begin by analysing the classical NCPs such as the NCP in the Montreal Protocol on Substances That Deplete the Ozone Layer (Montreal Protocol),[1] Convention on International Trade in Endangered Species of Wild Fauna and Flora (CITES),[2] the UNECE Convention on Access to Information, Public Participation in Decision-Making and Access to Justice in Environmental Matters (Aarhus Convention),[3] and the Kyoto Protocol.[4] The chapter will then analyse new NCPs such as those established in the Paris Agreement[5] and the Rotterdam Convention on the Prior Informed Consent Procedure for Certain Hazardous Chemicals and Pesticides in International Trade

[1] Montreal Protocol on Substances That Deplete the Ozone Layer, signed 25 November 1992, entered into force 14 June 1994, 1785 UNTS 517.

[2] Convention on International Trade in Endangered Species of Wild Fauna and Flora, signed 3 March 1973, entered into force 1 July 1975, 1453 UNTS 243.

[3] Convention on Access to Information, Public Participation in Decision-Making and Access to Justice in Environmental Matters, signed 25 June 1998, entered into force 30 October 2001, 2161 UNTS 447.

[4] Kyoto Protocol to the United Nations Framework Convention on Climate Change, signed 11 December 1997, entered into force 16 February 2005, 2303 UNTS 162.

[5] Paris Agreement signed 12 December 2015, entered into force 4 November 2016, 1673 UNTS 125.

(Rotterdam Convention)[6] and the UNECE Convention on the Protection and Use of Transboundary Watercourses and International Lakes (Water Convention).[7] This chapter also takes a new look at classical NCPs in the Montreal, CITES and Aarhus Conventions and at whether, in the years since they were established, compliance has been ensured by more facilitative than coercive methods.

NCPs' functions raise questions of legitimacy; likewise, the powers of Conferences or Meetings of the Parties (COPs/MOPs) which decide ultimately on non-compliance in the majority of cases. Thus, the next step of the analysis will be the issue of the legitimacy of the functions of NCPs and COPs/MOPs in both old and new regimes. As will be further explained, the premise on which the legitimacy of the new generation of NCPs is hinged is the concept of facilitative compliance, and the exclusion of the possibility of far-reaching and radical measures of suspension in the rights of a Party to an MEA.

3.2 The Question of Legitimacy: General Introduction

The general question of the definition of legitimacy and its link to legality in international law is a subject which is still debated and largely unresolved. An in-depth discussion of this topic exceeds the framework of this chapter. As it has been aptly observed,

> [l]egitimacy is often criticised as a notoriously slippery concept. It is defined in a myriad of ways by many different authors … Yet it is a meaningful concept because it seeks to explain why these addressed by an authority should comply with its mandates in the absence of perceived self-interest or brute coercion. A legitimate power is broadly understood as to mean one that has the 'the right to rule'.[8]

According to Wolfrum,[9] there are different elements which may legitimise authority. These elements include source-based legitimisation, procedure-based legitimisation and result-based legitimisation, or a

[6] Rotterdam Convention on the Prior Informed Consent Procedure for Certain Hazardous Chemicals and Pesticides in International Trade, signed 10 September 1998, entered into force 24 February 2004, 2244 UNTS 337.

[7] Convention on the Protection and Use of Transboundary Watercourses and International Lakes, signed 17 March 1992, entered into force 6 October 1996, 1936 UNTS 269.

[8] N Grossman, H Grant Cohen, A Follesdal and G Ulfstein, 'Legitimacy and International Courts: A Framework' in N Grossman, H Grant Cohen, A Follesdal and G Ulfstein (eds), *Legitimacy and International Courts* (Cambridge University Press 2018) 4.

[9] R Wolfrum, 'Legitimacy in International Law from a Legal Perspective. Some Introductory Considerations' in R Wolfrum and V Roeben (eds), *Legitimacy in International Law* (Springer 2008) 1–24.

combination thereof.[10] In relation to source-based legitimisation, the classical view is that this derives from the consent of States. This is most pronounced in the case of treaties, in which international law obligations are legitimised through national institutions. Questions do remain in connection with the chain of legitimacy, such as the situations when some of the participating States are not democratically structured, but it is beyond the scope of this chapter to discuss these issues in depth.[11] Consent-based legitimacy is more complex in the case of customary international law in which the legitimising role of consent is less clear-cut than in relation to treaties. However, if customary international law is understood as a tacit agreement of States concerned, 'then its ultimate source is the consent of States'.[12] More problematic is the view according to which the source of customary international law is the fictitious consent of States. In this view, customary international law is based on the voluntary acts of States 'which they undertake in the awareness of their implications for the possible development of customary international law'.[13] Finally, an important element of consent-based legitimacy is the form in which it is accorded by States. Consent can be given to one act, which results in a singular international obligation (static), or can conversely be accorded as a general authorisation for the exercise of a dynamic (evolutionary) function setting up a regime of governance, consisting of a series of acts, based on a single, general authorisation by States. Such a regime may modify the regime of governance.[14]

Authority can secondly be legitimised through adequate and fair procedures (such as the rules concerning the composition of an institution, or the rules relating to its decision-making procedures and participation).[15] Public participation and transparency, according to Bodansky, are fairly weak forms of legitimation as they merely accord an opportunity for the public to communicate their views to relevant officials rather than enabling the public to participate in decision-making.[16] Nevertheless, as will be analysed further, public participation and transparency play a pivotal role in NCPs' legitimacy.

[10] Ibid., 6.

[11] Ibid., 7.

[12] Ibid., 8.

[13] Ibid., 8.

[14] Ibid., 8.

[15] Ibid., 6.

[16] D Bodansky, 'The Legitimacy of International Governance: A Coming Challenge for International Environmental Law' (1999) 93 *American Journal of International Law* 596, 619.

Outcome is the third and the last element potentially legitimising authority. This basis for legitimacy is more vague and less tangible than source and procedure-based legitimisation. In broad brushstrokes, if an institution acting on the basis of an established procedure does not achieve the expected results, then this may lead to the erosion of legitimacy.[17]

Wolfrum's analysis of legitimacy is highly positivistic. In fact, the concept of legitimacy has not only a normative but also a sociological aspect. On the one hand, in its sociological aspect, it refers to popular attitudes about authority. As Bodansky writes, '[a]uthority, has popular legitimacy if the subjects to whom it is addressed accept it as justified'. Bodansky observes that 'the more positive the public's attitudes about an institution's right to govern, the greater its popular legitimacy'. On the other hand, 'legitimacy' can have a normative meaning, referring to whether a claim to authority is well founded; and to 'whether it is justified in some objective sense'.[18] These two aspects of legitimacy are conceptually distinct.[19] Bodansky has also opined that legitimacy in the context of international environmental law developed 'through a consensual rather than an authoritative process' and the phenomenon of authority plays only an ancillary role.[20]

The next issue, which is subject to ongoing debate, is the question of the link between legality and legitimacy. There are highly divergent views on this subject and there does not exist one single approach which would gain general approval. It may be said that, as argued by Bodansky, legality plays a fundamental role in ensuring that the exercise of authority by an international institution can be connected to its treaty basis, which in fact is consent.[21] However, Bodansky is also of the view that legitimacy is a broader concept than that of legality. For example, legality is not the only criterion for assessing legitimacy and the justification for exercising authority may also be based on wider extra-legal considerations and not be limited to legally binding rules.[22]

The general notion of legitimacy adopted in this chapter will be grounded in the concept of legitimacy as based on consent accorded as a general authorisation for the exercise of a dynamic (evolutionary)

[17] Wolfrum (n 9) 7.

[18] Bodansky (n 16) 604.

[19] Ibid., 602.

[20] Ibid., 604.

[21] Ibid., 311.

[22] Ibid., 311–18.

function, setting up a regime of governance which consists of a series of acts based on a single, general authorisation by States. As mentioned, in Wolfrum's analysis, such a general consent may modify the regime of governance. This form of consent is particularly apt in relation to environmental dispute settlement and the establishment and operation of NCPs. COPs/MOPs adopt decisions (most commonly on the basis of so-called enabling clauses contained in an MEA) to set up NCPs, which through a series of decisions, may contribute to the implementation of State Parties' obligations, influencing the regime of governance. However, it may be added that legitimacy in relation to the operation of NCPs sits at the nexus of consent-based and procedural legitimacy. Procedural legitimacy (transparency, public participation) will be discussed further.

3.3 Conferences of the Parties/Meetings of the Parties: General Considerations

COPs and MOPs play a pivotal role in the functioning of NCP regimes. They ultimately decide on non-compliance and the measures which are to be imposed in the event of non-compliance. They are well placed to manage non-compliance. As the highest organs of an MEA, they exercise all-encompassing functions relating to the MEA, adopt the most important decisions and have an overview of the whole agreement.

There is a plethora of bodies established by various multilateral treaties whose functions go beyond just managing the treaty regime. However, it was the advent of MEAs in particular that initiated a fertile legal (if inconclusive) debate on the nature of the functions of COPs. When MEAs began to be established after the 1972 Stockholm Conference on the Human Environment, COPs were created in order to make the management of MEAs more efficient and flexible, in contrast to previous bureaucratic arrangements. The functions of COPs have evolved beyond those of the early, basic COP with limited powers as in the Ramsar Convention on Wetlands of International Importance.[23] The COP of the Ramsar Convention today enjoys wide powers, as do other COPs. The term 'Conference of the Parties' was first used in the 1973 Convention of Trade in Endangered Species of Wild Fauna and Flora (CITES). The original Article 6 of that Convention provided that the COP would 'as the necessity arises, convene Conferences on the

[23] Ramsar Convention on Wetlands of International Importance, signed 2 February 1971, entered into force 21 December 1975, 996 UNTS 245.

Conservation of Wetlands and Waterfowl'. It also stated that the COP had an advisory character. This Article was amended in 1986 in order to create a Conference of the Contracting Parties, tasked with the oversight and promotion of the Convention's implementation. The reference to the COP's advisory character was deleted. The 1972 London Convention on the Prevention of Marine Pollution by Dumping of Wastes and Other Matter[24] created a body (the Consultative Meeting of States Parties) that enjoyed more powers. This body, however, lacked any express authority to establish subsidiary bodies and had very limited powers of supervision.

The powers of COPs today vary. Camenzuli, however highlights one common trend among contemporary COPs; namely that their powers are very broad, including their law-making powers. She has identified the following general powers: setting priorities and reviewing the implementation of the relevant convention based on reports submitted by governments; consolidating and analysing information from governments, NGOs and individuals to make recommendations to the Parties on the implementation of the convention; making decisions necessary for promoting the effectiveness of the convention; revising the convention when necessary; and acting as a forum for discussing matters of importance.[25] As a rule, the powers of COPs are set out in the referent treaty. However, certain treaties define COPs' powers in an open-ended fashion. For example, the London Convention provides that COP is 'to consider any additional action that may be required' (Article XIV(4)(f)). The 1979 Convention on Long-range Transboundary Air Pollution[26] provides that the COP can '[f]ulfil such other functions as may be appropriate under the provisions ... of the Convention' (Article 10(2)(c)). The UNFCCC states that the COP is to '[e]xercise such other functions as are required for the achievement of the objective of the Convention' (Article 7(2)). COPs often have the mandate to keep the implementation of the treaty 'under regular review' and make, within their mandate, the

[24] London Convention on the Prevention of Marine Pollution by Dumping of Wastes and Other Matter, signed 29 December 1972, entered into force 30 August 1975, 1046 UNTS 120.

[25] LK Camenzuli, 'The Development of International Environmental Law at the Multilateral Environmental Agreements Conference of the Parties and Its Validity', available at www.ecolex.org/details/literature/the-development-of-international-environmental-law-at-the-multilateral-environmental-agreements-conference-of-the-parties-and-its-validity-mon-085461/.

[26] 1979 Convention on Long-range Transboundary Air Pollution, signed 13 November 1979, entered into force 16 March 1983, 1302 UNTS 217, Article 17.

decisions necessary to promote effective implementation (see e.g., the Paris Agreement, Article 16, paragraph 4).

COPs' functions cover both external and internal matters. Several of their functions can develop international law. They are the following: (i) powers of decision-making on the amendment and modification of conventions and the adoption of new protocols; (ii) decision-making and resolution powers; (iii) supervisory powers; (iv) interpretative powers; (v) powers in respect of the establishment of non-compliance mechanisms (vi) keeping under regular review the implementation of the treaty (e.g., Article 16(4) of the Paris Agreement). Through the reviewing process COPs may 'examine specific difficulties of compliance and consider measures aimed at improving it'.[27] As previously observed, there is no uniform and consistent view on the legal nature of the COPs in scholarship. The most prevalent view is that they are of a hybrid character, positioned between issue-specific diplomatic conferences and the permanent plenary bodies of international organisations, and that they exercise their functions at the interface of the law of treaties and the law of international organisations.[28] They constitute useful fora for State Parties to evolve treaty regimes and co-operate. They are treaty bodies in the sense that they are created on the basis of a treaty, but they should not be equated with bodies that comprise independent experts or bodies with a limited membership.

The extensive range of functions of MEAs is an example of so-called creative legal engineering. The powers of the organs established by MEAs, in particular COPs, gave rise to varying views regarding the nature of convention organs and bodies endowed with decision-making powers According to one view, they can be seen as free-standing entities, involving institutional arrangements, or structures, which are independent from the Parties, and having, at least to a certain extent, an autonomous character in the sense of having (i) their own law-making or rule-making powers (or at least, the power to generate or alter obligations) and (ii) the power to formulate, or operate, mechanisms within the treaty regime, such as compliance mechanisms, which may have effects that are binding on the

[27] UNEP Training Manual on International Environmental Law, available at https://autlawiel.files.wordpress.com/2014/10/unep-tm-ch-4-compliance-and-enforcement-of-multilateral-environmental-agreements.pdf.

[28] G Nolte, 'Third Report on Subsequent Agreement and Subsequent Practice of States Outside of Judicial and Quasi-Judicial Proceedings' in G Nolte (ed.), *Treaties and Subsequent Practice* (Oxford University Press 2013) 365.

Parties. The Kyoto Protocol[29] granted a very broad functional remit to its MOP: 'The Conference of the Parties shall define the relevant principles, modalities, rules and guidelines, in particular for verification, reporting and accountability for emissions trading. Any such trading was to be supplemental to domestic actions for the purpose of meeting quantified emission limitation and reduction commitments.' It is clear that the MOP of the Kyoto Protocol was empowered to fill in the gaps in the text of the treaty and it has been the MOP that has also set out the modalities for the operation of the treaty's mechanisms such as emissions trading, joint implementation and the clean development mechanism.

Churchill and Ulfstein refer to institutions such as COPs and MOPs as 'autonomous institutional arrangements' (AIA).[30] Alternatively we could adhere to the view that COPs can be seen as no more than a form of diplomatic conference providing a continuous, or at least regular, context within which decisions can more readily be made than through the calling of *ad hoc* diplomatic conferences. In fact, it is submitted that COPs /MOPs may take on the character of either an AIA or a diplomatic conference, depending on both the substantive nature of what is discussed, and on whether or not their decisions will require subsequent validation to become binding on the Parties.

3.4 Non-Compliance Procedures: General Considerations

This section will deal with so-called non-compliance procedures, which concern measures directed at the Parties to MEAs in cases of non-compliance with treaty provisions or the decisions of COPs. Non-compliance procedures can be considered *quasi*-legal, as they, with the possible exception of the Enforcement Branch of the non-compliance mechanism established under the Kyoto Protocol, do not result in formally binding decisions. Non-compliance procedures do, though, uniformly address deficits in the implementation of MEAs. It has been said that they 'counteract, by means of cooperative approaches, the symptoms and causes of failure by Parties in the implementation of, and compliance

[29] Kyoto Protocol, Article 17. The Parties included in the Kyoto Protocol's Annex B were permitted to participate in emissions trading for the purposes of fulfilling their commitments under Article 3.

[30] R Churchill and G Ulfstein, 'Autonomous Institutional Arrangements in Multilateral Environmental Agreements: A Little-Noticed Phenomenon in International Law' (2000) 94 *American Journal of International Law* 623–59.

with, their obligations'.[31] Frequently, non-compliance is not the result of wilful disobedience, but due to a lack of capacity to implement a treaty. Therefore, NCPs also address the root causes of failure to implement a treaty, such as the need for capacity building and reduction of compliance costs; the functions of the Paris Agreement's Compliance Committee provide a good example.[32]

However, NCP decisions on non-compliance carry great weight and they have proven to be a very effective mechanism of engendering compliance. Not all decisions on non-compliance are referred to COPs/MOPs. For example, the Paris Agreement's Compliance Committee reports annually to the Conference of the Parties serving as the meeting of the Parties to the Paris Agreement (CMA) but adopts it decisions autonomously. Further, in its decisions '[t]he Committee may identify issues of a systemic nature with respect to the implementation of and compliance with the provisions of the Paris Agreement faced by a number of Parties and bring such issues and, as appropriate, any recommendations to the attention of the CMA for its consideration'.[33]

[31] L Pineschi, 'Non-Compliance Mechanisms and the Proposed Center for the Prevention and Management of Environmental Disputes', available at http://dadun.unav.edu/bitstream/10171/22204/1/ADI_XX_2004_05.pdf, 242.

[32] X Wang and G Wiser, 'The Implementation and Compliance Regimes under the Climate Change Convention and Its Kyoto Protocol' (2002) 11 *Review of European, Comparative & International Environmental Law* 181, 182. See e.g., functions of the Compliance Committee of the Paris Agreement: 'With a view to facilitating implementation and promoting compliance, the Committee shall take appropriate measures. These may include the following: (a) Engage in a dialogue with the Party concerned with the purpose of identifying challenges, making recommendations and sharing information, including in relation to accessing finance, technology and capacity-building support, as appropriate; (b) Assist the Party concerned in the engagement with the appropriate finance, technology and capacity-building bodies or arrangements under or serving the Paris Agreement in order to identify possible challenges and solutions; (c) Make recommendations to the Party concerned with regard to challenges and solutions referred to in paragraph 30(b) above and communicate such recommendations, with the consent of the Party concerned, to the relevant bodies or arrangements, as appropriate; (d) Recommend the development of an action plan and, if so requested, assist the Party concerned in developing the plan'; (e) Issue findings of fact in relation to matters of implementation and compliance referred to in paragraph 22(a) above': 20/CMA.1, para 30, FCCC/PA/CMA/2018/3/Add.2, 19 March 2019, available at https://unfccc.int/sites/default/files/resource/cma2018_3_add2_new_advance.pdf.

[33] Modalities and procedures for the effective operation of the Committee to facilitate implementation and promote compliance referred to in Article 15, paragraph 2, of the Paris Agreement, see in depth: G Zihua, C Voigt and J Werksman, 'Facilitating Implementation and Promoting Compliance with the Paris Agreement under Article 15: Conceptual Challenges and Pragmatic Choices' (2019) 9 *Climate Change Law* 65.

Since the establishment of a Non-Compliance Committee under the Montreal Protocol in 1992, it has been a common practice of States Parties to MEAs to create treaty bodies, called 'Compliance' or 'Implementation Committees' (or both) which have the function of determining a State Party's compliance with its international obligations. NCPs may be established in the treaty itself (e.g., the Paris Agreement) or on the basis of so-called enabling clauses in MEAs, which provide for the establishment of such a procedure by a decision of the relevant COP. An example of this is found in Article 8 of the Montreal Protocol.[34] However in a few cases such NCPs have been established without such an authorisation. For example, the NCP in the Basel Convention on Transboundary Movement of Hazardous Wastes,[35] was established without an enabling clause in the Agreement. NCPs are designed to respond to a breach of environmental obligations in the multilateral, not bilateral, context. The multilateral context is capable of accommodating the type of obligations which are of a character relevant to community interests in a truly satisfactory manner. Environmental obligations, in particular obligations relating to global issues, are not reciprocal in nature. For this reason, the classical settlement of dispute procedures as envisaged by Article 33 of the UN Charter, which are bilateral in nature, are perhaps less suitable for addressing non-compliance in a multilateral context and remedying non-compliance in respect of global issues such as climate change, and the protection of biodiversity or the ozone layer.

Legal procedures such as judicial and arbitration are different in nature, as they are adversarial, rendering binding decisions, based on third-party application of the law, and their legitimacy has its roots in different justifications. The (quite extensive) judicial practice in environmental matters before courts and tribunals has generated some critical comments. The judicial settlement of environmental disputes has been mostly focussed in the International Court of Justice (ICJ) and the International Tribunal for the Law of Sea (ITLOS). It may be said that there have been certain environmental considerations in the jurisprudence of the World Trade Organization, but they have essentially been analysed from the point of view of a limitation to the liberalisation of

[34] The Montreal Protocol on Substances That Deplete the Ozone Layer, signed 16 September 1987, entered into force 1 January 1989, 26369 UNTS 28.

[35] Basel Convention on the Control of Transboundary Movements of Hazardous Wastes and Their Disposal, signed 22 March 1989, entered into force 5 May 1992, 1673 UNTS 57.

trade.[36] The European Court of Human Rights (ECtHR) has dealt with a number of cases where environmental harm was interfering with private and family lives (Article 8 of the European Convention on Human Rights (ECHR)).[37]

There has been some support in the literature for the view that environmental disputes are amenable to judicial settlement partly due to the 'hardening' of the fabric of international environmental law.[38] This view is not entirely shared by the author of this chapter. The existing jurisprudence of international courts and tribunals has admittedly relied to some extent on principles of international environmental law and in some instances even clarified and developed them. However, international courts and tribunals (in particular the ICJ) prefer to apply well-tested principles of general international law and their attempts to venture into the realm of pure international environmental law have often been subject to severe criticism. An example is the ICJ's pronouncements in *Costa Rica v Nicaragua* regarding compensation for environmental damage which demonstrate that the Court has not entirely grasped the particularities of international environmental law.[39] It was stated in this regard that 'overall, the judgment demonstrates that the law on this topic may not be completely settled and there is plenty to argue about in future cases'.[40]

36 See e.g., WTO, EC Measures Concerning Meat and Meat Products (Hormones) AB-1997-4, Report; EC Approval and Marketing of Biotech Products DS291, available at www.wto.org/english/tratop_e/dispu_e/cases_e/ds26_e.htm.

37 T Stephens, *International Courts and Environmental Protection* (Cambridge University Press 2009); 'The Settlement of Disputes in International Environmental Law' in S Alam, JH Bhuiyan, TMR Chowdhury and EJ Techera (eds), *Routledge Handbook of International Environmental Law* (2013) 175; 'International Environmental Disputes: To Sue or Not To Sue?' in N Klein (ed.), *Litigating International Law Disputes: Weighing The Options* (Cambridge University Press 2014) 284; A Boyle and J Harrison, 'Judicial Settlement of International Environmental Disputes' (2013) 4 *Journal of International Dispute Settlement* 245; M Fitzmaurice, 'The International Court of Justice and International Environmental Law' in C Tams and J Sloane (eds), *The Development of International Law by the International Court of Justice* (Oxford University Press 2013) 353; Y Tanaka, *The Peaceful Settlement of International Disputes* (Cambridge University Press 2018) 65.

38 Stephens, *Routledge Handbook* (n 37) 175–6.

39 *Certain Activities Carried Out by Nicaragua in the Border Area* (*Costa Rica v Nicaragua*). *Compensation Owed by the Republic of Nicaragua to the Republic of Costa Rica* [2018] ICJ Rep 1.

40 See critical comments by D Desierto, 'Environmental Damages, Environmental Reparations, and the Right to a Healthy Environment: The ICJ Compensation Judgment in Costa Rica v. Nicaragua and the IACtHR Advisory Opinion on Marine Protection for the Greater Caribbean', EJIL: Talk !, 14 February 2018, available at www.ejiltalk.org/environmental-damages-environmental-reparations-and-the-right-to-a-healthy-environment-the-icj-compensa

The Court was much more comfortable in invoking within the framework of international environmental law the classical *Chorzow Factory* pronouncement according to which a responsible State has to 'wipe out all consequences of a wrongful act'.[41]

There are also alternative explanations as to why NCPs are more suited to deal with environmental non-compliance than traditional dispute settlement procedures. It may be that States prefer NCPs due to the fact that they exercise more control over the whole process and its result compared to third-party mechanisms, such as judicial or arbitral procedures. NCPs have less stringent effects; decisions are not final in the form of *res judicata* and are less intrusive. NCPs also favour prevention by relying on monitoring, verification or reporting which better suits the aims of international environmental law.[42] NCPs' character is well defined by reference to the Mechanism for Promoting Implementation and Compliance with the Basel Convention.[43] In its Objectives it is stated that

> The objective of the mechanism is to assist Parties to comply with their obligations under the Convention and to facilitate, promote, monitor and aim to secure the implementation of the compliance with the obligations under the Convention.[44]

The mechanism's nature is described in the following terms:

> The mechanism shall be non-confrontational, transparent, cost-effective and preventive in nature, simple, flexible, non-binding and oriented in the direction of helping parties to implement the provisions of the Basel Convention. It will pay particular attention to the special needs of developing countries and countries with economies in transition, and is intended to promote cooperation between all Parties. The mechanism should complement work performed by other Convention bodies and by the Basel Convention Regional Centres.[45]

tion-judgment-in-costa-rica-v-nicaragua-and-the-iacthr-advisory-opinion-on-marine-protec tion/, accessed 11 October 2020.

41 *Case Concerning the Factory at Chorzow* (Merits) (*Germany v Poland*) [1928] PCIJ (Series A, No 9) 47.

42 See M Koskenniemi, 'Breach of Treaty or Non-Compliance? Reflections on the Enforcement of the Montreal Protocol' (1992) 3 *Yearbook of International Environmental Law* 123–62.

43 The Mechanism for Promoting Implementation and Compliance with the Basel Convention, available at www.basel.int/TheConvention/ImplementationComplianceCommittee/Mandate/tabid/2296/Default.aspx.

44 Objectives, para. 1, www.basel.int/TheConvention/ImplementationComplianceCommittee/Mandate/tabid/2296/Default.aspx.

45 Article 2 NCP Basel Convention.

There are several NCP mechanisms which follow more or less the classical mechanism set out under the Montreal Protocol. The main features of the NCP of the Montreal Protocol are its facilitative character and transparency. In addition, the NCP under the Montreal Protocol follows the requirements of due process: notification, the right to a fair hearing and impartiality. Although the NCP is not a judicial procedure, it has certain characteristics, such as the right to a fair hearing, which according to paragraph 10 of the NCP, ensures that a Party potentially in non-compliance has the right to participate in the consideration by the Committee of relevant submissions.

However, although the main feature of the Montreal Protocol NCP is its facilitative character, one of the measures that may be adopted in cases of non-compliance is the suspension of a State Party's treaty rights. In the case of the Kyoto Protocol, in particular, the consequences of a finding of non-compliance through the NCP were onerous when a State Party had failed to comply with its emissions reduction target. Yet it may be said that the far-reaching powers of the NCP mechanism under the Kyoto Protocol are unique and in the view of the author are not representative when it comes to drawing conclusions concerning the legitimacy of NCPs in general, also taking into account previous (older) generation mechanisms.[46]

This controversial aspect of non-compliance under the Kyoto Protocol is excluded from the regime of the Paris Agreement.[47] Article 15 of the Paris Agreement establishes a Compliance Committee as a mechanism to facilitate implementation and promote compliance with the Agreement. The task of the Committee is explicitly facilitative: 'The Committee is expected to enhance the effective functioning of the Paris Agreement both by encouraging parties to implement the Agreement and by holding them accountable for aspects of their performance. This should build confidence and trust among the parties.'[48] The Committee is a standing, expert body with a mandate to address situations related to the performance of individual Parties. The procedure under the Paris Agreement has been agreed as follows:

[46] See Compliance under the Kyoto Protocol, available at https://unfccc.int/process/the-kyoto-protocol/compliance-under-the-kyoto-protocol.

[47] Paris Agreement, signed 22 April 2016, entered into force 4 November 2016, UNTS 3156, available at https://treaties.un.org/Pages/showDetails.aspx?objid=0800000280458f37&clang=_en.

[48] C Voigt, 'The Compliance and Implementation Mechanism of the Paris Agreement' (2016) 25 *Review of European, Comparative & International European Law* 1.

1. The mechanism to facilitate implementation of and promote compliance with the provisions of the Paris Agreement established under Article 15 of the Agreement consists of a committee (hereinafter referred to as the Committee).
2. The Committee shall be expert-based and facilitative in nature and function in a manner that is transparent, non-adversarial and non-punitive. The Committee shall pay particular attention to the respective national capabilities and circumstances of Parties.
3. The Committee's work shall be guided by the provisions of the Paris Agreement, including its Article 2.
4. In carrying out its work, the Committee shall strive to avoid duplication of effort, shall neither function as an enforcement or dispute settlement mechanism, nor impose penalties or sanctions, and shall respect national sovereignty.[49]

The functions of the Committee are elaborated in paragraphs 20 to 27, as well as paragraphs 32 to 34 (Consideration of Systemic Issues) of the Annex to Decision 20/CMA.1, titled 'Modalities and Procedures for the Effective Operation of the Committee Referred to in Article 15, paragraphs 1-3'. Paragraph 22(a) of the Modalities and Procedures provides that the Committee will initiate consideration of issues which relate to the core legally binding obligations under the Paris Agreement. These are cases where a Party has not:

(a) Communicated or maintained a nationally determined contribution (NDC) under Article 4 of the Paris Agreement, based on the most up-to-date status of communication in the public registry referred to in Article 4, paragraph 12, of the Paris Agreement;
(b) Submitted a mandatory report or communication of information under Article 13, paragraphs 7 and 9, or Article 9, paragraph 7, of the Paris Agreement;
(c) Participated in the facilitative, multilateral consideration of progress;
(d) Submitted a mandatory communication of information under Article 9, paragraph 5, of the Paris Agreement.[50]

49 Modalities and Procedures for the Effective Operation of the Committee Referred to in Article 15, paragraphs 1–3 of the Paris Agreement, FCCC/PA/CMA/2018/3/Add.2 Annex (19 March 2019), available at https://unfccc.int/sites/default/files/resource/CMA2018_03a02E.pdf.

50 Modalities and Procedures for the Effective Operation of the Committee to Facilitate Implementation and Promote Compliance Referred to in Article 15, paragraph 2, of the Paris Agreement, FCCC/PA/CMA/2018/3/Add.2, Annex (19 March 2019).

The innovative nature of the measures which may be adopted by the Compliance Committee under the Paris Agreement merits attention.

The view has been expressed that the Committee's architecture and functions 'are designed in such a way as to provide for the legitimacy, continuity, stability, and predictability of its activities' and that '[i]ts operation will be an important cornerstone of the Agreement's legitimacy, effectiveness, and longevity'.[51]

According to paragraph 30 of the Modalities and Procedures, 'the Committee shall take appropriate measures'. These may include the following:

(a) Engage in a dialogue with the Party concerned with the purpose of identifying challenges, making recommendations and sharing information, including in relation to accessing finance, technology and capacity-building support, as appropriate;
(b) Assist the Party concerned in the engagement with the appropriate finance, technology and capacity-building bodies or arrangements under or serving the Paris Agreement in order to identify possible challenges and solutions;
(c) Make recommendations to the Party concerned with regard to challenges and solutions referred to in paragraph 30(b) above and communicate such recommendations, with the consent of the Party concerned, to the relevant bodies or arrangements, as appropriate;
(d) Recommend the development of an action plan and, if so requested, assist the Party concerned in developing the plan;
(e) Issue findings of fact in relation to matters of implementation and compliance referred to in paragraph 22(a) . . . .[52]

The list of measures is a result of long and complex negotiations; thus, their application requires caution from the Committee. The Committee has discretionary powers to apply the measures. However, when doing so, 'its decision is to be informed by the legal nature of the relevant provisions of the Agreement and the comments received from the party concerned, and the Committee "shall" pay particular attention to the national capabilities and circumstances of the party concerned.[53] Special circumstances of LDC [Least Developed Countries] and SIDS [Small Island Developing States], as well as situations of *force majeure*, are to be

[51] Zihua, Voigt and Werksman (n 33) 79.

[52] Modalities and Procedures for the Effective Operation of the Committee to Facilitate Implementation and Promote Compliance Referred to in Article 15, paragraph 2, of the Paris Agreement, FCCC/PA/CMA/2018/3/Add.2, Annex (19 March 2019), para 30.

[53] Zihua, Voigt and Werksman (n 33) 80.

recognized, 'where relevant'.[54] Under clauses (b) and (c) the Committee fulfils a facilitative role and under clause (d), similarly to other MEAs, it may recommend the development of an action plan.[55] Measure (e) only relates to the matters referred to in paragraph 22(a). This measure was the subject of much debate. The measure sits in contrast with the facilitative nature of the mechanism and has the potential to be confrontational.[56] A compromise was reached that under paragraph 22(a), any 'finding of fact' 'would relate to readily identifiable circumstances of non-compliance with a binding obligation, such as the non-submission of a report . . . ' and that 'such a finding would lead to the logical conclusion that the party was in non-compliance, but without a formal finding of non-compliance by the Committee'.[57] There are two interesting features of this measure: it is based on the legal nature of the provisions concerned; and

> the Committee could issue findings of fact in various ways. 'Issuing' could, for example, take the form of a public statement, or a letter to the party, or be included in the Committee's annual report to the CMA, or a combination of the above. This step remains to be clarified.[58]

As we can see from the Paris Agreement NCP regime, very harsh measures of suspension have been abandoned. There is a marked evolution in the recent NCPs, departing from the 'classical' regimes based on hard measures. This is not the only recent NCP which has abandoned harsh measures in cases of non-compliance and replaced them with a facilitative approach. The Rotterdam Convention has also elaborated an NCP where the possibility of a suspension in the rights of a Party to a treaty has been eradicated. Both the Compliance Committee and the Conference of the Parties will have recourse in cases of non-compliance to measures which offer assistance rather than punish.[59] A similar soft approach has been adopted by the Implementation Committee of the

[54] Ibid., 80.
[55] See in depth, ibid., 80–82.
[56] Ibid., 83.
[57] Ibid., 83.
[58] Ibid., 83.
[59] Rotterdam Convention on the Prior Informed Consent Procedure for Certain Hazardous Chemicals and Pesticides in International Trade, signed 10 September 1998, entered into force, 24 February 2004, 2244 UNTS 337; paras 19 and 20 of the Procedures and Mechanisms on Compliance with the Rotterdam Convention, www.pic.int/TheConvention/ComplianceCommittee/Overview/tabid/8446/language/en-US/Default.aspx.

Water Convention.[60] This Convention also defines its compliance procedure as facilitative, supportive and collaborative in nature (Articles I and XI). The means to suspend a Party's rights exist but have never been used. The Committee has the jurisdiction to render Advisory Opinions, which are outside the remit of compliance ('The advisory procedure is aimed at facilitating implementation and application of the Convention through the provision of advice by the Committee and shall not be regarded as alleging non-compliance . . . ' (Article V)). Such a procedure may be requested by the Parties in respect of difficulties in implementing the Convention *vis-à-vis* each other, and/or non-Parties (subject to their consent) or by a Party in respect of its own compliance difficulties. The Parties or non-Parties considered to be potentially concerned and which choose not to participate in the advisory procedure will be kept informed of its progress. The Committee provides advice and assistance for individual Parties and groups of Parties in order to facilitate their implementation of the Convention.[61] Such a procedure is an entirely unique and new way of solving disputes between States in the most non-confrontational manner.[62]

It may be added that the International Law Commission in its Guidelines on the Protection of the Atmosphere has included a provision on non-compliance, which follows the patterns set out in other MEAs.[63]

[60] Convention on the Protection and Use of Transboundary Watercourses and International Lakes, signed 17 March 1992, entered into force 6 October 1996; 1936 UNTS 269.

[61] This procedure was used for the first time in 2021: 'Albania and Montenegro have agreed to establish a joint technical working group on "Monitoring & assessment" and to develop and implement an information exchange protocol to operationalize their cooperation on the shared Cijevna/Cem River basin.' . . . 'The Committee is assisting Albania and Montenegro as part of an advisory procedure – a unique tool, which distinguishes this body from other similar mechanisms and enables it to engage with countries seeking to resolve water issues in a non-confrontational manner.' https://unece.org/environment/press/water-conventions-implementation-committee-provides-advice-albania-and-montenegro.

[62] See Chapter 5, this volume.

[63] Guideline 11 Compliance

1. States are required to abide with their obligations under international law relating to the protection of the atmosphere from atmospheric pollution and atmospheric degradation in good faith, including through compliance with the rules and procedures in the relevant agreements to which they are parties. 2. To achieve compliance, facilitative or enforcement procedures may be used, as appropriate, in accordance with the relevant agreements: (a) facilitative procedures may include providing assistance to States, in cases of non-compliance, in a transparent, non-adversarial and non-punitive

However, it is worth noting that Special Rapporteur Murase explained that he 'favoured cooperative compliance mechanisms, meant to give assistance to a non-compliant party, over punitive or enforcement mechanisms, which were based on the responsibility of States and intended to place penalties on the non-compliant party'.[64]

3.5 Legitimacy and NCPs

Addressing the question of legitimacy of NCPs, Savaşan refers to the legal basis of their establishment, that is, whether an enabling clause in the primary treaty was the basis of the NCP; or whether they were established without such a clause.[65] According to Savaşan, the problem of legitimacy only arises when such a clause is absent and a COP decision establishes a 'hard' NCP with binding outcomes imposing obligations that go beyond the applicable treaty.[66] Such an approach would eliminate from the category of objectionable NCPs the new generation of 'soft' NCPs (which do not include far-reaching measures in relation to a non-compliant State), as represented by the NCP in the Paris Agreement. Savaşan is of the view that the application of punitive measures applied in NCPs (e.g., under the far-reaching regime of the Kyoto Protocol) may enhance the deterrent effect of an NCP mechanism but also challenge their legitimacy and therefore 'should be applied in line with the rules of international law'.[67] It may be argued that in the event of very harsh and binding measures under NCPs, only the amendment of the treaty may justify them.[68]

Only if such measures are applied in accordance with international law will compliance be enhanced without compromising legitimacy. Such an application of punitive measures would be in accordance with determinacy (clear rule of law) and fairness.

manner to ensure that the States concerned comply with their obligations under international law, taking into account their capabilities and special conditions; (b) enforcement procedures may include issuing a caution of non-compliance, termination of rights and privileges under the relevant agreements, and other forms of enforcement measures.

64 International Law Commission, Seventieth Session New York, 30 April–1 June and Geneva, 2 July–10 August 2018, A /CN.4/L.909.

65 Z Savaşan, 'Legitimacy Questions of Non-Compliance Procedures: Examples from Kyoto and Montreal Protocols' in C Voigt (ed.), *International Judicial Practice on the Environment: Questions of Legitimacy* (Cambridge University Press 2019) 377.

66 Ibid.

67 Ibid., 386.

68 Ibid., 377.

As mentioned above, procedural safeguards are also elements of legitimacy. As persuasively argued by Savaşan, within NCP regimes, procedural safeguards protect legitimacy. These safeguards may include a preliminary phase of prior consultation between the Parties concerned; due process; and transparency of proceedings. Rights of confidentiality and transparency are guardians of fairness in these mechanisms.[69] However, there are also some procedural elements of legitimacy which can be improved. For example, the role of civil society in the Montreal Protocol NCP does not meet the element of transparency. Civil society can take part in the proceedings as observers only if the secretariat notifies this and no Party objects. Contrastingly, under the UNECE Convention on Access to Information, Public Participation in Decision-making and Access to Justice in Environmental Matters (Aarhus Convention)[70] NCP, any member of the public, that is, any natural or legal person, may submit a communication to the Committee, which definitely enhances legitimacy.[71]

Questions regarding other aspects of the legitimacy of NCPs should not detract from the general issue of their usefulness in protection of the environment, that is, the outcomes. What is the relationship between the general usefulness of NCPs and their legitimacy? It appears that the procedural aspects of legitimacy (which have been mentioned), play a dominant role in their usefulness (outcomes). For example, the participation of civil society undoubtedly enhances the overall effectiveness of these mechanisms. However, the issue of the legitimacy of NCPs remains a broader one, encompassing all constitutive elements that is, substantive and procedural aspects and the outcomes, all entwined. The theory of consent-based legitimacy alone does not fully reflect the nature of legitimacy in these procedures, which is constituted of various elements, all of equal importance.

In the view of the author, the multilateral system on which NCPs are based makes them much better suited to address the issues concerned than classical settlement of disputes predicated upon bilateralism. NCPs indeed serve a common interest of States in the protection of the environment. That said, the UNECE Water Convention Implementation Committee, within the paradigm of its advisory function, can also, for instance, facilitate assistance within the bilateral context. This function co-exists with the NCP, which is based on multilateralism.

[69] Ibid., 381.

[70] UNECE Convention on Access to Information, Public Participation in Decision-making and Access to Justice in Environmental Matters (Aarhus Convention) UNTS 2161 447

[71] Ibid., 382.

It may be added that NCPs, which at present are based on providing assistance rather than on imposing stricter measures in cases of non-compliance, are also better equipped to fulfil environmental aims than adversarial mechanisms. However, in this context, the empowering of the Paris Agreement Compliance Committee to make 'findings of fact' should be recalled. The Paris Agreement's system of compliance and the role of the Committee has been aptly described in the following way: 'The Committee can only apply facilitative measures, and cannot impose penalties, fines, fees, sanctions, or enforcement measures of any kind. However, there will be an element of public and political accountability associated with the Committee's recommendations, including the "findings of fact", as these relate to the non-performance of the relevant provisions.'[72]

The adoption of harsh measures in case of non-compliance raises questions. However, NCPs in modern practice in general either do not include such measures or refrain from applying them. For example, the main measure employed by the Committee and the MOP in the Aarhus Convention to ensure improvement in compliance (as applied in 41 per cent of cases) has been the 'recommendation' (paragraph 37(b)). A review of practice up to 2019 indicates the MOP has issued just one 'caution' (paragraph 37(f)). Cautioning, together with suspension (but not withdrawal) of special rights and privileges[73] is considered a 'more confrontational' means of enforcing compliance.[74] The contemporary practice of the Montreal Protocol NCP evidences that indicative measure 'c' has not been resorted to but rather the provision of encouragement and facilitation to States in non-compliance. There is not a strict adherence to ascending order of the measures, as assistance (indicative measure 'a') is linked with caution (indicative measure 'b'), thus applying a mild 'carrot and stick' approach. However, the harshest indicative measure 'c' has not been applied, thus softening the measures. While the MOP in its decisions refers to the possibility of recourse to indicative measure

[71] Zihua, Voigt and Werksman (n 33) 99.

[72] Aarhus Convention, 'C. Suspension, in accordance with the applicable rules of international law concerning the suspension of the operation of a treaty, of specific rights and privileges under the Protocol, whether or not subject to time limits, including those concerned with industrial rationalization, production, consumption, trade, transfer of technology, financial mechanism and institutional arrangements.'

[73] G Samvel, 'Non-Judicial, Advisory, Yet Impactful? The Aarhus Convention Compliance Committee as a Gateway to Environmental Justice' (2020) 9(2) *Transnational Environmental Law*, 232.

'c', it has never applied this measure in contemporary practice. These examples clearly indicate that in the classical NCP under the Montreal Protocol there is a noticeable trend to avoid withdrawal of a Party's rights and privileges.[75]

In respect of measures under the NCPs leading to assistance (providing that all procedural safeguards are upheld) rather than punishment, the question of legitimacy in a traditional sense (based on consent) may not arise. The modern trend is exemplified by the NCP in the Paris Agreement, the Rotterdam Convention and the approach of the International Law Commission's (ILC) special rapporteur, Shinya Murase, with the focus on co-operative efforts combined with procedural safeguards.

Savaşan has observed that the concept of legitimacy is very complex, consisting of a multitude of diverse elements. It may be that such complexity commands further detailed examination and empirical studies 'on the distinctive characteristics of different institutions and to develop legitimacy perspective for each one of these'.[76] There is a great variety at present of these mechanisms that require case-by-case studies of legitimacy, based on theory and practice. It may be observed, however, that even if various NCPs merit a divergent analysis, there is a visible and common trend towards the adoption of softer measures, influencing the calculus of legitimacy.

[74] For example, in relation to non-compliance on the part of Argentina, MOP of the Montreal Protocol decided as the first measure upon the provision of assistance (indicative measure 'a'): 'To the degree that Argentina is working towards and meeting the specific Protocol control measures, Argentina should continue to be treated in the same manner as a party in good standing. In this regard, Argentina should continue to receive international assistance to enable it to meet these commitments in accordance with item A of the indicative list of measures that might be taken by a Meeting of the Parties in respect of non-compliance.' Interestingly this was combined with an indicative measure 'b' (caution) and the MOP added that: 'In the event that the country fails to return to compliance in a timely manner, the parties shall consider measures, consistent with item C of the indicative list of measures. These measures may include the possibility of actions available under Article 4, such as ensuring that the supply of CFCs (that is the subject of non-compliance) is ceased and that importing parties are not contributing to a continuing situation of non-compliance.' The MOP also decided: '3. To request that Argentina submit to the Implementation Committee a plan of action with time-specific benchmarks to ensure a prompt return to compliance. Argentina may wish to consider including in its plan actions to establish production quotas that will freeze production at baseline levels and support the phase-out.'

[75] Savaşan (n 65) 382.

3.6 Conclusions

The legal character and the different objectives of NCPs have evolved and fundamentally changed. Previous, classical procedures relied frequently on harsh methods, such as the CITES NCP regime under which States face suspension of trade rights. The new generation of NCPs have a different *ethos* and *telos*. Their structure, functions and measures are different and are based on the premise of facilitation. Such an evolution warrants a different approach in ascertaining the legitimacy of decisions adopted by compliance bodies, and COPs/MOPs, which have all become more facilitative bodies. In calculating the legitimacy of such new generation NCPs, procedural aspects come to the fore, focussing on transparency, and the participation of civil society, and so on, rather than more exclusively on State consent.

It is submitted that the diametrically different character of the new generation of NCPs should also be reflected in the change of the names of 'Non-Compliance Committees' into 'Implementation Committees' (a nomenclature already used in many MEAs). The new generation of NCPs are in fact implementation and facilitation bodies, whose functions are very different from the classical ones. A new classification of NCPs should be established, as the traditional approaches do not reflect the substantively divergent phenomenon of the new and facilitative NCPs. It may also be noted that despite the quite detailed and at times far-reaching obligations imposed on States by certain MEAs (such as the Montreal Protocol and the Aarhus Convention), COPs/MOPs have refrained from the imposition of harsh measures to ensure compliance, thus confirming the general trend of co-operation and understanding.

4

International Courts versus Compliance Mechanisms through the Lens of the *Gabčíkovo-Nagymaros* and *Bystroe Canal* Cases

LAURA PINESCHI

4.1 Introduction

Recent developments in international environmental law are increasingly characterized not only by the concern to ensure the effectiveness of existing international environmental obligations, but also by a growing awareness of the need to adopt a comprehensive and integrated approach to the management of natural resources. The latter implies the consideration of environmental protection as a collective interest, having due regard to the interdependence between local and global ecosystems, on the one hand, and to the integration of community legal interests into the management of natural resources shared by two or more States, on the other.

Non-compliance mechanisms (NCMs) are generally assumed to be a better mechanism than judicial settlements for achieving both the above-mentioned aims. This chapter intends to assess the correctness of this assumption through the analysis and comparison of two cases, which are characterized by some common features: the *Gabčíkovo-Nagymaros* (*G/N*) and the *Bystroe Canal* cases. Both relate to the planning of great infrastructure projects (the construction of a dam and a canal, respectively) with a possible environmental impact on the same water system (the River Danube and the Danube Delta, respectively). Both gave rise to international disputes, that, despite a judgment of the International Court of Justice (ICJ) (in the *G/N* case)[1] and the triggering of

[1] ICJ, Case concerning the *Gabčíkovo-Nagymaros Project* (*Hungary v Slovakia*), judgment of 25 September 1997 (hereinafter: ICJ Judgment), ICJ Reports 1997, 7.

non-compliance procedures (NCPs) under the Espoo[2] and the Aarhus Conventions[3] (in the *Bystroe Canal* case),[4] are still pending or have remained substantially unsettled. Accordingly, certain lessons may be learned from an analysis of these proceedings.

This chapter will compare the approaches adopted by the ICJ in the *G/N* case and by competent monitoring bodies dealing with the *Bystroe Canal* case, with the aim of evaluating their respective contributions to: balancing the Parties' conflicting interests; stimulating a meaningful and fruitful co-operation of the Parties towards an agreed solution; and integrating the interests of the Parties concerned with the interests of other States, individuals or group of individuals and the global environment. Some remarks will follow on the lessons learned from the two cases, drawing some general conclusions on the effective advantages of the mechanisms employed in each case.

4.2 The *Gabčíkovo–Nagymaros* Case

The ICJ judgment on the *G/N* case is one of the ICJ's decisions most quoted and debated by international environmental scholars. Suffice here to recall that the Parties to the dispute – Hungary and Slovakia – strongly disagreed on the implementation of a bilateral treaty, concluded by Czechoslovakia and Hungary in 1977, that provided for a joint investment for the construction of 'a single and indivisible' barrage system on the Danube River[5] consisting of two systems of locks: one at Gabčíkovo (on the Czech side) and one at Nagymaros (on the Hungarian territory).[6]

Divergences of the Parties in the implementation of the 1977 Treaty emerged from the very beginning. While Czechoslovakia was determined to pursue the project, Hungary was very reluctant. In particular, the latter contended that the aquatic environment of the Danube, the water volume and quality and the biodiversity of the region risked being severely jeopardized by the project.[7] After the suspension (and subsequently, the abandonment) of the works by Hungary in 1989 and the undertaking

[2] Convention on Environmental Impact Assessment in a Transboundary Context, Espoo, 25 February 1991, entered into force 10 September 1997, 1989 UNTS 309.

[3] Convention on Access to Information, Public Participation in Decision-Making and Access to Justice in Environmental Matters, Aarhus, 25 June 1998, entered into force 30 October 2001, 2161 UNTS 447.

[4] See Section 4.3.

[5] The Danube flows across ten European States (Germany, Austria, Slovakia, Hungary, Croatia, Serbia, Bulgaria, Romania, Moldova and Ukraine) for about 2,850 km.

[6] Treaty Concerning the Construction and Operation of the Gabčíkovo–Nagymaros System of Locks, Budapest, 16 September 1977 (1993) 32 International Legal Materials 1247, Article 1.1.

[7] ICJ Judgment, para 40.

of an alternative solution by Czechoslovakia (including the so-called 'Variant C', entailing a unilateral diversion of the Danube on its territory),[8] on 7 April 1993, Hungary and Slovakia[9] turned to the ICJ, acknowledging that 'differences have arisen' regarding the implementation and termination of the 1977 Treaty and that the Parties 'have been unable to settle these differences by negotiation'.[10]

The ICJ ruled in 1997 that Hungary was not entitled to unilaterally suspend the 1977 Treaty; the Treaty was still in force and the joint regime for its implementation was a basic element of the agreement. The Parties were thus required to 'negotiate in good faith in the light of the prevailing situation and … to take all necessary measures to ensure the achievement of the objectives of the Treaty of 16 September 1977'.[11] In particular, Hungary and Slovakia had 'to find an agreed solution within the co-operative context of the Treaty',[12] taking into account, on the one hand, 'the objectives of the Treaty, which must be pursued in a joint and integrated way' and, on the other hand, 'the norms of international environmental law and the principles of the law of international watercourses'.[13]

Nearly a quarter of a century after the judgment, the negotiations between Hungary and Slovakia are pending[14] and no agreed solution is expected in the short term.[15]

[8] Ibid., para 23.

[9] Slovakia succeeded to Czechoslovakia as a contracting party to the bilateral Treaty of 1977, after its dissolution in 1992.

[10] ICJ Judgment, paras 1 and 2.

[11] Ibid., para 155.

[12] Ibid., para 142.

[13] Ibid., para 141.

[14] On the negotiations between Hungary and Slovakia, see e.g., H Fürst, *The Hungarian–Slovakian Conflict over the Gabčíkovo–Nagymaros Dams: An Analysis* (Institute for Peace Research and Security Policy 2003); S Deets, 'Constitutional Interests and Identities in a Two-Level Game: Understanding the Gabčíkovo–Nagymaros Dam Conflict' (2009) 5 *Foreign Policy Analysis* 37; M Szabó, 'Gabčíkovo–Nagymaros Dispute: Implementation of ICJ Judgment' (2009) 39 *Environmental Policy and Law* 97; M Szabó, 'The Implementation of the Judgment of the ICJ in the Gabčíkovo–Nagymaros Dispute' (2009) 1 *Iustum, Aequum Salutare* 15; M Szabó, 'The Implementation of the Judgment of the ICJ in the Gabčíkovo–Nagymaros Dispute' (2009) 1 *Iustum, Aequum Salutare* 15; G Baranyai and G Bartus, 'Anatomy of a Deadlock: A Systemic Analysis of Why the Gabčíkovo–Nagymaros Dam Dispute Is Still Unresolved' (2016) 18 *Water Policy* 39; B Nagy, 'The ICJ Judgment in the Gabčíkovo–Nagymaros Project Case and Its Aftermath: Success or Failure?' in H Ruiz-Fabri, E Franck, M Benatar and T Meshel (eds), *A Bridge over Troubled Waters: Dispute Resolution in the Law of International Watercourses and the Law of the Sea* (Brill Nijhoff 2021) 21.

[15] '[T]he two sides cannot even agree on what the decision said.' Deets (n 14) 37 at 38.

4.2.1 *Balancing Conflicting Interests and Supporting the Parties' Co-operation*

The ICJ judgment in the *G/N* case is considered a 'balanced solution' by some scholars. Looking more closely, however, this expression has been used in its most extreme meaning ('[n]either side can claim a victory')[16] or in a meaning different from the legal one (a '"politically" palatable decision').[17]

More generally, serious doubts remain as to whether the Court fully exercised its function. First, the judgment has received much criticism for failing to clarify the obligations of the Parties[18] or, at least, for omitting 'to define the rights and obligations of the Parties with sufficient precision'.[19]

Notably, it has been observed, on the one hand, that the special role attributed by the Court to the principle *pacta sunt servanda* 'legitimized the status quo that emerged as a result of the mutual non-performance of [the bilateral Treaty of 1977]'.[20] On the other hand, the Parties themselves could be blamed for the continued non-resolution of the dispute. However, the 'condemnation' of the Parties to co-operation ('go back and negotiate in good faith')[21] has been regarded as a major cause for the 'ossification'[22] of the dispute. The judgment 'in a way exacerbated rather than help[ing] to solve the underlying conflict'.[23]

Second, it has been remarked that the Court did not sufficiently assess the relevance and the weight of the evidence submitted by the Parties. Indeed, while ensuring that 'most careful attention' had been given to the 'impressive amount of scientific material' submitted by both States with the aim of 'reinforcing their respective arguments ... as to the ecological consequences of the project', the Court concluded that 'it [was] not

[16] A Boyle, 'The Gabčíkovo–Nagymaros Case: New Law in Old Bottles' (1997) 8 *Yearbook of International Environmental Law* 13 at 14. See also Nagy (n 14) 55 ('the judgment was Solomonic, allowing a face-saving outcome for both parties') and S Stec, 'Do Two Wrongs Make a Right? Adjudicating Sustainable Development in the Danube Dam Case' (1999) 29 *Golden Gate University Law Review* 317 at 356 ('the Court reached ... an uncomfortable compromise').

[17] H Lammers, 'The *Gabčíkovo-Nagymaros* Case Seen in Particular from the Perspective of the Law of International Watercourses and the Protection of the Environment (1998) 11 *Leiden Journal of International Law* 287 at 316.

[18] See e.g., P Sands, 'International Environmental Litigation and Its Future' (1999) 32 *University of Richmond Law Review* 1619.

[19] Baranyai and Bartus (n 14) 46.

[20] See e.g., Nagy (n 14) 24–25 and Deets (n 14) 47 ('at first the court's entire approach to the case is more notable for what it did not decide than what it did').

[21] Baranyai and Bartus (n 14) 45.

[22] Ibid., 45. See also Stec (n 16) 356.

[23] Baranyai and Bartus (n 14) 45.

necessary . . . to determine which of [their] points of view [was] scientifically better founded'.[24] The 1977 Treaty contained the mechanisms for the Parties to co-operate to address environmental considerations. The Court relied also on the assumption that the dangers invoked by Hungary were mostly of a long-term nature and uncertain. Accordingly, these perils, 'without prejudging their possible gravity, were not sufficiently established . . . nor were they "imminent"'[25], as required by the plea of necessity under the ILC Draft Articles on State responsibility.[26]

It is certainly worth noting that the Court made a site visit in April 1997, between the two rounds of oral pleadings.[27] In addition, due to the technical issues at stake, the tensions between the Parties and the polarization of their respective positions, it would have been desirable for independent experts to assist the Court before it delivered its judgment. Regrettably, the ICJ's reluctance to appoint independent experts under Article 50 of its Statute and Article 67 of the Court Rules is well known and it is still a matter of extensive debate and criticism.[28]

Third, negotiations have also been affected by ambiguities in the Court's ruling. Accordingly, some controversial interpretations of the

[24] ICJ Judgment, para 54.

[25] ICJ Judgment, para 57.

[26] See Article 25.1(a) (State of Necessity), Responsibility of States for Internationally Wrongful Acts, adopted by the International Law Commission (ILC) in 2001, *Yearbook of the International Law Commission* (2001) vol. II (Part Two).

[27] ICJ Judgment, para 10. For more details see A Pellet, 'The *Gabčíkovo-Nagymaros* Case: A Personal Recollection' in S Forlati, MM Mbengue and B McGarry (eds), *The Gabčíkovo-Nagymaros Judgment and Its Contribution to the Development of International Law* (Brill Nijhoff 2020) 3 at 7–9; J-M Thouvenin, 'La descente de la Cour sur le lieux dans l'affaire relative au projet Gabčíkovo-Nagymaros' (1997) 43 *Annuaire français de droit international* 333.

[28] See e.g., ICJ, *Pulp Mills on the River Uruguay* (*Argentina v Uruguay*), Judgments, ICJ Reports 2010, Judges Al-Khasawneh and Simma joint Dissenting Opinion, para 5; C Foster, 'The Consultation of Independent Experts by International Courts and Tribunals in Health and Environment Cases' (2009) 20 *Finland Yearbook of International Law* 391; C Foster, *Science and the Precautionary Principle in International Courts and Tribunals: Expert Evidence, Burden of Proof and Finality* (Cambridge University Press 2011), in particular 136 ff.; C Foster, 'New Clothes for the Emperor?' (2014) 5 *Journal of International Dispute Settlement* 139; M Bennouna, 'Experts Before the International Court of Justice: What For?' (2018) 9 *Journal of International Dispute Settlement* 345; J Devaney, 'Reappraising the Role of Experts in Recent Cases Before the International Court of Justice' (2019) 62 *German Yearbook of International Law* 337; T Kanhanga, 'Scientific Uncertainties: A Nightmare for Environmental Adjudications' in C Voigt (ed.), *International Judicial Practice on the Environment: Questions of Legitimacy* (Cambridge University Press 2019) 121.

judgment[29] allowed both Parties to '... find sufficient legal ammunition to preserve their respective pre-litigation positions'.[30]

As to the promotion of the Parties' co-operation, only scant indications were provided by the Court to help the two governments to achieve an agreed solution. Starting from the assumption that '[i]t is not for the Court to determine what shall be the final result of these negotiations to be conducted by the Parties. It is for the Parties themselves to find an agreed solution',[31] Hungary and Slovakia were required to 'look afresh at the effects on the environment of the operation of the Gabčíkovo power plant' and to 'find a satisfactory solution for the volume of water to be released into the old bed of the Danube and into the side-arms on both sides of the river'.[32]

Some general principles were explicitly mentioned by the Court to guide the Parties' negotiations. First, good faith, which is inherent to the general duty *pacta sunt servanda* and to the duty of co-operation. The Parties were also required to find an agreed solution, taking into account the norms of international environmental law and the principles of the law of international watercourses.[33]

Regrettably, however, the Court was unwilling to dwell upon on the existence and exact content of these principles, although this was one of the reasons for the lengthy dispute between the Parties.[34] The Court mentioned the obligation of prevention[35] and invoked the concept of

[29] See e.g., Szabó (n 14), 'The Implementation of the Judgment', 19 (who focusses, in particular, on the meaning of the term 'when' at para 136 of the judgment), and Baranyai and Bartus (n 14) 45 (who consider obscure and contradictory the operative parts of the judgment relating to the future of the unfinished installations in the Hungarian territory). See also Stec (n 16) 356.

[30] Baranyai and Bartus (n 14) 45.

[31] ICJ Judgment, para 141.

[32] Ibid., para 140.

[33] See n 13.

[34] See B Fuyane and F Madai, 'The Hungary–Slovakia Danube River Dispute: Implications for Sustainable Development and Equitable Utilization of Natural Resources in International Law' (2001) 1 *International Journal of Global Environmental Issues* 329 at 340 (although these principles ' . . . formed the essence of the protracted dispute [between Hungary and Slovakia] . . . the Court responded to them only in *obiter dicta*'). See also the expectations emerging from a contribution published two years before the ICJ Judgment: E Hoenderkamp, 'The Danube: Damned or Dammed? The Dispute between Hungary and Slovakia Concerning the Gabčíkovo–Nagymaros Project' (1995) 8 *Leiden Journal of International Law* 287 at 308–9.

[35] For a thorough analysis, see: L-A Duvic-Paoli, 'Vigilance and Prevention: The Contribution of the Gabćikovo–Nagymaros Judgment' in S Forlati, MM Mbengue and B McGarry (eds), *The Gabčíkovo–Nagymaros Judgment* (Brill 2020) 193. When the judgment was delivered, various principles contained in the two declarations had already

sustainable development as aptly expressing the need to reconcile economic development with protection of the environment.[36] It declined, however, to explain its opinion with regard to the legal content of the latter, which is still one of the most controversial issues in international environmental law.[37] With regard to environmental impact assessment (EIA), the ICJ did not mention this term in its ruling. Neither did it assist the Parties in the reconciliation of their scientific and technical divergences.[38] Hungary and Slovakia agreed on the need to submit the joint project to EIA but disagreed on the substance of this decision-making process.[39] The failure by the Court to uphold the principle of precaution was also blamed by various scholars. In particular, the 'state of ecological necessity' – invoked by Hungary for justifying the suspension or termination of the 1977 Treaty – was considered by the Court exclusively from a legal perspective, that is, according to the parameters of the state of necessity under the law of State responsibility.[40] As a result, the Court imposed a much higher threshold[41] than the one required by the precautionary principle, which relies on a basic assumption: scientific uncertainty.[42]

been incorporated into various binding and non-binding instruments at the international level. Some of them were also considered customary international legal obligations by a number of prominent scholars.

36 ICJ Judgment, para 140.

37 See e.g., Sands (n 18) 1633.

38 As has rightly been highlighted: 'This was a rather curious position to adopt since the environmental effects of the project were central to the arguments advanced by both parties and were in fact the essence of the dispute.' PN Okowa and M Evans, 'Case Concerning the Gabčíkovo-Nagymaros Project (*Hungary/Slovakia*)' (1998) 47 *International and Comparative Law Quarterly* 688 at 695. For further considerations, see: EL Preiss, 'The International Obligation to Conduct an Environmental Impact Assessment: The ICJ *Case Concerning the Gabčíkovo-Nagymaros Project*' (1999) 7 *New York University Environmental Law Journal* 307.

39 See Preiss (n 38) 325 ff.

40 See text corresponding to n 25 and n 26.

41 'The Hungarian argument on the state of necessity could not convince the Court unless it was at least proven that a real, 'grave' and 'imminent' 'peril' existed in 1989', ICJ Judgment, para 54.

42 See e.g., Sands (n 18) 1631–32; S Stec and GE Eckstein, 'Of Solemn Oaths and Obligations: The Environmental Impact of the ICJ's Decision in the *Case Concerning the Gabčíkovo-Nagymaros Project*' (1997) 8 *Yearbook of International Environmental Law* 41 at 49; A A-Khavari and D Rothwell, 'The ICJ and the *Danube Dam* Case: A Missed Opportunity for International Environmental Law? (1998) 22 *Melbourne University Law Review* 507 at 529 ff.; D Dobos, 'The Necessity of Precaution: The Future of Ecological Necessity and Precautionary Principle' (2002) 13 *Fordham Environmental Law Review* 375; C Foster, 'Necessity and Precaution in International

As to the duty of co-operation in good faith, the Court observed – quoting its famous dictum in the *North Sea Continental Shelf* case[43] – that '[the Parties] are under an obligation so to conduct themselves that the negotiations are meaningful, which will not be the case when either of them insists upon its own position without contemplating any modification of it'.[44] Leaving aside any discussion on the effective compliance of the Parties with the duty to co-operate in good faith, the exact content of this obligation, as codified by Principle 19 of the 1982 Rio Declaration on Environment and Development,[45] remains controversial.[46]

4.2.2 Integration of the Interests of the Parties Concerned with the Interests of Other States and of the Global Environment

One of the most remarkable aspects of the judgment in the *G/N* case is to be found in the special role that the rules on interpretation played in the legal reasoning of the Court. It was in fact through the method of evolutionary interpretation that the ICJ established a dynamic inter-relationship and integration between the bilateral treaty obligations undertaken by the Parties in 1977 and the general principles of international environmental law that had been developed after that date. Accordingly, sustainable development was integrated into the scope of the obligations that the Parties had undertaken under their bilateral agreement.

The management of the Danube was not handled, however, as a matter transcending the interests of single riparian States. The ICJ judgment focussed strictly on the rights and obligations of the litigating States *inter partes*.[47] No explicit mention of the interests of other riparian

Law: Responding to Oblique Forms of Urgency' (2008) 23 *New Zealand Universities Law Review* 265.

43 ICJ, *Case Concerning the North Sea Continental Shelf* (Federal Republic of Germany/ Denmark; Federal Republic of Germany/Netherlands), Judgment of 20 February 1969, ICJ Reports 1969, 3.

44 ICJ Judgment, para 141.

45 UN Doc A/CONF.151/26 (Vol I), 12 August 1992.

46 For a thorough analysis of internal judicial bodies' evaluation of States' conduct in complying with the duty to co-operate in good faith, see K Hagiwara, 'Sustainable Development before International Courts and Tribunals: Duty to Cooperate and States' Good Faith' in C Voigt (ed.), *International Judicial Practice on the Environment* (Cambridge University Press 2019) 167.

47 Only an indirect reference to the 'community interest in a navigable river' was made, through the quotation of the famous dictum of the Permanent Court of International Justice in its decision on the *River Oder* case ('[the] community of interest in a navigable river becomes the basis of a common legal right, the essential features of which are the perfect equality of all riparian States in the user [sic] of the whole course of the river and

States or to the preservation of vulnerable ecosystems as an interest of the international community as a whole can be found in the Court's ruling. Unfortunately, these considerations are also missing in more recent ICJ environmental jurisprudence.[48]

It should finally be recalled that the representation of community interests through NGOs was only partially possible in the *G/N* case, due to the very limited role that NGOs can play in the context of contentious proceedings before the ICJ. An *amicus curiae* brief was prepared by two NGOs, but no reference was made to this brief in the judgment.[49] In any case, absent specific provisions in the Court Rules, no NGOs would have been entitled to make more than this indirect contribution.[50]

4.2.3 Assessment

The previous remarks confirm the limits of traditional dispute settlement generally highlighted by international scholars. It has been observed, for instance, that '[i]nternational adjudication is supposed to be slow, cumbersome, expensive and, ultimately, ineffective'.[51] Indeed, the judgment on the *G/N* case was rendered four years after the deposit of the special

the exclusion of any preferential privilege of any one riparian State in relation to the others', *Territorial Jurisdiction of the International Commission of the River Oder, Judgment No 16, 1929, PCIJ, Series A, No 23*, 27, ICJ Judgment, para 85). It has rightly been observed, however, that 'the ICJ endorses the PCIJ's statement without making an effort to clarify what it understands by the COI [community of interest] of riparian States and how this becomes a common legal right'. J Gjørtz Howden, *The Community of Interest Approach in International Water Law: A Legal Framework for the Common Management of International Watercourses* (Brill Nijhoff 2020) 27.

48 See e.g., ICJ, *Whaling in the Antarctic (Australia v Japan: New Zealand Intervening)*, Judgment of 31 March 2014, ICJ Reports 2014, 226. For further considerations see L Pineschi, 'Inter-Legality and the Protection of Marine Ecosystems' in J Klabbers and G Palombella (eds), *The Challenge of Inter-Legality* (Cambridge University Press 2019) 188 at 191 ff.

49 National Heritage Institute and International River Network; for more information see: A Wiik, *Amicus Curiae before International Courts and Tribunals* (Nomos and Hart Publishing 2018) 96, n 99. See also *Excerpts from Position Taken by WWF (World Wild Fund) with Regard to the Gabčíkovo Barrage Project*, in Counter Memorial Hungary 5 December 1994, vol. IV, Annexes, Part I, 349 ff.

50 On the indirect role played by NGOs in contentious cases in the ICJ see: E Valencia-Ospina, 'Non-Governmental Organizations and the International Court of Justice' in T Treves, A Fodella, A Tanzi and M Frigessi di Rattalma (eds), *Civil Society, International Courts and Compliance Bodies* (TMC Asser Press 2005) 227, at 228 ff.

51 AL Paulus, 'Dispute Resolution' in G Ulfstein, T Marahun and A Zimmermann (eds), *Making Treaties Work: Human Rights, Environment and Arms Control* (Cambridge University Press 2007) 351.

agreement between the Parties. This is 'not a speed record for a case without procedural difficulties';[52] it must be acknowledged, however, that among the reasons that '[t]he Court was not quick to organize hearings', was the fact that the ICJ was simultaneously dealing with other cases.[53] However, this is still a very long delay, when addressing significant environmental problems.

As mentioned, the judgment on the *G/N* case also confirms, on the one hand, that 'judicial pronouncements serve rather to elucidate important principles than to achieve a concrete and detailed settlement by themselves'.[54] On the other hand, highly technical issues can hardly 'be decided by lawyers. Allocation of responsibility for harm to specific actors is difficult, if not impossible … Problem-solving thus requires a less confrontational, more co-operative approach'.[55]

It would be misleading, however, to conclude that the abovementioned failures derive exclusively from structural limits of the judicial settlement of disputes or from its inadequacy in discharging a function for which it is not fully equipped. On the one hand, it could be argued that 'by asking the Parties to negotiate a solution … the Court was abdicating the very responsibility that the Parties had assigned to it'.[56] On the other hand, the actions and omissions of all the Parties directly or indirectly concerned in the *G/N* case cannot be ignored. In particular, the slow development of fruitless negotiations between the two contending States is largely due to the high politicization of their dispute.[57] In addition, the lack of transparency that characterizes the ongoing negotiating process does not seem to be fully consistent with the general principles of international environmental law and, notably, with the principle of access to information.[58]

The modest role played by other riparian States or international institutions in the solution of the conflict is also striking. Apparently, neither the European Union (which had been actively involved in the

[52] Pellet (n 27) 4.

[53] The advisory opinions on Nuclear Weapons and the jurisdiction in the Genocide and Oil Platform cases; Pellet (n 27) 5.

[54] Paulus (n 51) 363; see also C Romano, *The Peaceful Settlement of International Environmental Disputes: A Pragmatic Approach* (Kluwer Law International 2000) 323–24.

[55] Paulus (n 51) 365.

[56] Okowa and Evans (n 38) 697.

[57] See e.g., RD Lipschutz, 'Damming Troubled Waters: Conflict over the Danube 1950–2000' (1997) 1 *Intermarium*.

[58] See e.g., Principle 10 of the Rio Declaration on Environment and Development.

negotiations preceding the ICJ judgment)[59] nor the permanent bodies established under the Convention on Co-operation for the Protection and Sustainable Use of the River Danube (hereinafter: Danube River Protection Convention)[60] have significantly supported or facilitated the bilateral negotiations subsequent to the ICJ judgment.

Obviously, it can hardly be said that these entities or other riparian States are under a legal duty to intervene in the negotiating process. However, the issue clearly transcends the individual rights and duties of the Parties to the dispute due to the dramatic impact that the failure of their bilateral negotiations may have on the management of shared natural resources and the preservation of vulnerable ecosystems. A more proactive role in defence of a community interest should thus have been played by other riparian States or international institutions entrusted with specific competences in environmental matters.

4.3 The *Bystroe Canal* Case

The second case deals with NCPs and concerns the (re)construction[61] of the Bystroe Canal in the Ukrainian sector of the Danube Delta. The Delta covers an area of approximately 5,800 km^2, shared by Romania (86 per cent of the area), Ukraine and Moldova – ensuring a connection for Ukraine to the Black Sea, as an alternative to the two existing routes

[59] See ICJ Judgment, paras 24–25. Both Hungary and Slovakia have been member States of the European Union since 2004; accordingly, the EU legislation applies to the Danube River basin, including the EU Water Framework Directive (WFD) (Directive 2000/60/EC of the European Parliament and the Council on 23 October 2000 establishing a framework for community action in the field of water policy, OJ L 327 of 22 December 2000, 1), that focuses on the sustainable development of water systems, considered geographical and hydrological units, according to a combined approach and a common implementation strategy. It has been remarked, however, that neither political pressure nor infringement procedure have ever been undertaken by the EU Commission to induce Slovakia and Hungary to find a solution consistent with their EU obligations; see Nagy (n 14) 56.

[60] Convention on Co-operation for the Protection and Sustainable Use of the River Danube, Sofia, 29 June 1994, entered into force 22 October 1998, available at www.icpdr.org/flowpaper/app/#page=14. It includes fifteen parties: Austria, Bosnia and Herzegovina, Bulgaria, Croatia, Czech Republic, Germany, Hungary, Moldova, Montenegro, Romania, Slovakia, Slovenia, Serbia, Ukraine and the European Union. For further information on the effective involvement of the ICPDR in the implementation of the ICJ Judgment, see A Haefner, *Negotiating for Water Resources: Bridging Transboundary River Basins* (Routledge 2016) 97.

[61] After the Soviet Union's fall, the waterways used by Ukrainian vessels were no longer navigable by large ships due to the natural accumulation of sediments and lack of proper maintenance.

through Romania. Romania is obviously concerned about the implications of the project for its economic and social system, but also about its impact on an area characterized by particularly vulnerable ecosystems. Due to its special features, the Danube Delta was included in the list of wetlands of international importance under Article 2.1 of the Ramsar Convention[62] in 1991[63]. It was also inscribed on the World Heritage List in the same year[64] and designated as a Biosphere Reserve under UNESCO's Man and the Biosphere (MAB) Programme in 1998.[65]

Ukraine notified Romania of its intention to develop the Bystroe Canal Project (BCP) in 2002, but it did not provide Romania with the information required under the Espoo Convention, including an EIA, which was completed after the project had already started.[66] Ukraine was also considered to be in breach of its obligations under the Aarhus Convention for not having informed the public of the project and of its related decision-making process.[67] The first phase of the BCP was completed in 2004; the final decision to continue with Phase II was taken in 2007, and in 2010 works related to its full-scale implementation started.[68]

The actions and omissions of Ukraine in respect of its international obligations have been brought to the attention of (and monitored by) almost all institutional mechanisms established under the various international treaties and multilateral environmental agreements (MEAs) applicable to the area. The Danube Delta falls within the scope of four world treaties (the 1971 Ramsar Convention;[69] the World Heritage Convention;[70] the Convention on the Conservation of Migratory

[62] Convention on Wetlands of International Importance Especially as Waterfowl Habitats, Ramsar, 2 February 1971, entered into force 21 December 1975, 996 UNTS 245.

[63] See www.ramsar.org/sites/default/files/documents/library/sitelist.pdf.

[64] See https://whc.unesco.org/en/list/588/.

[65] See https://en.unesco.org/biosphere/eu-na/danube-delta.

[66] See submissions by Romania under the Espoo Convention of 26 May 2004 (EIA/IC/S1) and 23 January 2007 (EIA/IC/S1bis).

[67] For more details see this chapter, 23–24.

[68] Standing Committee of the Bern Convention, Doc T-PVS/Notes (2015) 2, 2.

[69] The BCP was considered under Article 3.2 of the Ramsar Convention (human interference) by the IX MOP in 2005. See Resolution IX.15, paras 14, 16 and recommendations under para 27. The file was closed in 2012, on the basis of the information submitted by Ukraine and 'on the consideration that the Ramsar Administrative Authority in Kyiv took the responsibility to declare publicly that no negative change will occur through the planned works', information provided by the Secretariat of the Ramsar Convention to the Secretariat of the Bern Convention (Standing Committee, Doc T-PVS/Notes (2015) 2, 5).

[70] Convention Concerning the Protection of the World Cultural and Natural Heritage, Paris, 16 November 1972, entered into force 17 December 1975, 1037 UNTS 151.

Species of Wild Animals (Bonn, 23 June 1979);[71] and the Convention on Biological Diversity[72]) and five regional agreements: the Convention on the Conservation of the European Wildlife and Natural Habitats (Bern, 19 September 1979);[73] the Danube River Protection Convention; the Convention on the Protection and Use of Transboundary Watercourses and International Lakes (Helsinki, 17 March 1992);[74] as well as the already mentioned Espoo and Aarhus Conventions.[75]

In this context, suffice here to recall that two NCPs under the Espoo Convention[76] were triggered by Romania in 2004 and 2007.[77] The latter complaint was submitted after the carrying out of an inquiry procedure

[71] Entered into force 1 November 1983, 1651 UNTS 356.

[72] Convention on Biological Diversity, Rio de Janeiro, 5 June 1992, entered into force 29 December 1993, 1760 UNTS 79.

[73] Entered into force 1 June 1982, 1284 UNTS 209 (hereinafter: Bern Convention). In 2004, the Standing Committee of the Bern Convention recommended Ukraine not proceed with phase II of the BCP until certain conditions were met (Recommendation No. 111 (2004)). The case was closed in 2016, considering 'the constant, fruitful and promising co-operation' of the parties, that were invited to 'report every two years on the progress achieved in solving the remaining issues'; Standing Committee 36th Meeting, Strasbourg, 15–18 November 2016, *List of Decisions and Adopted Texts*, Doc T-PVS (2016) Misc, 12.

[74] Entered into force 6 October 1996, 1936 UNTS 269.

[75] For a survey of the actions undertaken under the aforementioned Conventions, see M Koyano, 'Effective Implementation of International Environmental Agreements: Learning Lessons from the Danube Delta Conflict' in T Komori and K Wellens (eds), *Public Interest Rules of International Law: Towards Effective Implementation* (Routledge 2009) 259 at 271 ff.

[76] On the trigger mechanism under the Espoo Convention, see Decision III/2, Appendix, paras 5–6. For further details see E Fasoli, 'Procedures and Mechanisms for Review of Compliance under the 1991 Espoo Convention on Environmental Impact Assessment in a Transboundary Context and its 2003 Protocol on Strategic Assessment' in T Treves, L Pineschi, A Tanzi and C Pitea (eds), *Non-Compliance Procedures and Mechanisms and the Effectiveness of International Environmental Agreements* (TMC Asser Press 2009) 181 at 184 ff.

[77] See n 66. The Espoo Convention does not explicitly provide for a compliance procedure. However, at their second meeting, the Parties established an ad hoc body, the Implementation Committee, 'for the review of compliance by the Parties with their obligations under the Convention with a view to assisting them fully to meet their commitments' (Decision II/4, Doc MP.EIA/2001/4, 6 December 2000). The Implementation Committee (composed of eight States Parties) reports to the MOP and makes recommendations regarding compliance with the Convention (Decision III/2, Doc MP.EIA/2004/3, 26 March 2004). In 2007, the Implementation Committee agreed that the second submission by Romania superseded its first submission, which was considered closed (Doc ECE/MP.EIA/WG1/2007/4, 12 March 2007, para 23). All documents available at https://unece.org/environment-policy/environmental-assessment/eiaics1-ukraine.

on the request of the same country under Article 3.7 of the Convention.[78] The Inquiry Commission (a body composed of three independent experts appointed by the Parties concerned)[79] unanimously concluded that the BCP was likely to have a significant adverse transboundary impact in Phase I and that an even greater impact was expected in Phase II of the project.[80] In 2008, the Meeting of the Parties (MOP) declared Ukraine non-compliant with its international obligations and decided to issue a caution unless the Government of Ukraine stopped the works, repealed its final decision of 28 December 2007 concerning the BCP and took steps to comply with the relevant provisions of the Espoo Convention and the relevant decisions of the MOP.[81] The Ukrainian government was also requested to fully implement the Convention's provisions through: a revision of its legislative and administrative measures; the adoption of a strategy to be submitted to the Espoo Convention's Implementation Committee by the end of 2009; and the negotiation of agreements and arrangements with neighboring countries under Article 8 of the Convention.[82]

The above-mentioned caution to the Government of Ukraine became effective on 31 October 2008; nevertheless, no steps (or limited steps) have been taken to bring the project into full compliance with the Convention.[83] In 2021 the MOP welcomed various positive steps

[78] All documents concerning the inquiry procedure are available at https://unece.org/environment-policyenvironmental-assessment/inquiry-commission.

[79] Appendix IV to the Espoo Convention, para 2, provides that: 'if two or more States Parties to the Espoo Convention cannot agree whether a proposed activity is likely to entail a significant adverse transboundary impact, any such Party may submit that question to an inquiry commission, established under Appendix IV of the Convention, with the mandate 'to advise on the likelihood of significant adverse transboundary impact' (Article 3.7). The final opinion of the inquiry commission is based on 'accepted scientific principles' (Appendix IV, para 14).

[80] *Report on the Likely Significant Adverse Transboundary Impacts of the Danube–Black Sea Navigation Route at the Border of Romania and the Ukraine*, July 2006, available at https://unece.org/DAM/env/eia/documents/inquiry/Final%20Report%2010%20July%202006.pdf, para 6.8.

[81] Fourth MOP of the Espoo Convention, Bucharest, 19–21 May 2008, Decision IV/2, Doc ECE/MP.EIA/10 of 28 July 2008, 81 ff.

[82] Decision IV/2, paras 11, 12 and 14. Appendix VI of the Espoo Convention, under para 2 contains a detailed list of possible elements that can be included in bilateral and multilateral agreements to implement the Convention.

[83] See Decisions V/4, para 17, Doc ECE/MP.EIA/15, 16 August 2011; VI/2, para 20, Doc ECE/MP.EIA/20/Add.1–ECE/MP.EIA/SEA/4/Add.1, 15 July 2014; IS/1f, para 6, Doc ECE/MP.EIA/27/Add.1–ECE/MP.EIA/SEA/11/Add.1, 9 April 2019. Some positive steps undertaken by Ukraine were however mentioned by MOP under Decision V/4, paras

undertaken by Ukraine, including: the adoption of national measures on EIA, aimed at 'fully align[ing]' its national legislation with the provisions of the Convention;[84] an assessment of the environmental damage and the preparation of a draft plan of compensatory and mitigatory measures; the development of a new 'Bystroe Route' project and its notification to Romania.[85] However, the MOP has expressed deep concern as Ukraine has not yet fulfilled all its obligations under decisions IV/2, V/4, VI/2 and IS/1f.[86] Accordingly, the caution issued in 2008 is still effective.[87] The MOP has also reiterated that the continuation of dredging activities constitutes a further breach of the Convention.[88]

An NCP was also triggered under the Aarhus Convention,[89] on the basis of a communication from the public[90] and a submission by Romania[91]; in 2005 the MOP found Ukraine non-compliant by failing to provide for access to information and public participation under Articles 4 and 6 of the Convention.[92] After three cautions issued by the MOP in 2008, 2011 and 2014 for persistent non-compliance with its

20–22 (i.e., notification of the project and transmission of the EIA documentation to Romania; the holding of a public consultation; start of negotiations for the conclusion of bilateral agreements with neighboring countries).

84 The law on EIA was approved on 4 October 2016 and revised in 2017. The law on strategic environmental assessment was enacted in April 2018.

85 Decision VIII/4d, paras 2 and 3, Doc ECE/MP.EIA/30/Add.2–ECE/MP/EIA/SEA/13/Add.2, 11 February 2021.

86 Ibid., para 9.

87 Ibid., para 10.

88 Ibid., para 11. See also Implementation Committee, Doc ECE/MP.EIA/IC/2016/4, 13 October 2016, para 13.

89 The non-compliance procedure is provided for under Article 15 of the Aarhus Convention – requiring the Parties to set up 'arrangements of a non-confrontational, non-judicial and consultative nature' for reviewing compliance with the provisions of the Convention – a Compliance Committee was established by the first MOP (Lucca 2002, Decision I/7). The main function of the Compliance Committee (composed of eight members, serving in their personal capacity) is to consider issues of non-compliance by a Party with any provision of the Convention and to make recommendations to the MOP. On the trigger mechanism, see Decision I/7, paras 15–24. For further details, see C Pitea, 'Procedures and Mechanisms for Review of Compliance under the 1998 Aarhus Convention on Access to Information, Public Participation and Access to Justice in Environmental Matters' in Treves et al., *Non-Compliance Procedures* (n 76), 221 at 224 ff.

90 See Communication ACCC/C/2004/03 of 5 May 2003 and additional information of 1 December 2004 submitted by Ecopravo-Lviv, an NGO based in Ukraine (now Environmental People (EPL)), in (2004) 34 Environmental Policy and Law 39–42; 54–56.

91 Submission ACCC/S/2004/01 of 7 June 2004.

92 Second Meeting of the Parties to the Aarhus Convention, Decision II/5b, Doc ECE/MP.PP/2005/2/Add.8, 13 June 2005.

decisions,[93] Ukraine enacted the above-mentioned EIA provisions in 2016.[94] Accordingly, the Compliance Committee, having found that the country had adopted the necessary measures to bring its legislation into compliance with the Convention, concluded that the caution should be lifted and that Ukraine's special rights and privileges under the Convention should not be suspended.[95]

No doubt, a positive result has been achieved. It cannot be overlooked, however, that Ukraine has never abandoned the Bystroe Canal Project and that the case has been pending before the Implementation Committee and the MOP of the Espoo Convention for about eighteen years.

4.3.1 Balancing Conflicting Interests and Supporting the Parties' Co-operation

The classical bilateral structure of traditional inter-State dispute settlement procedures is lacking under NCMs. The main concern of non-compliance bodies established under MEAs is to prevent non-compliance (or to bring a State back into compliance) with certain treaty obligations, acting in the common interest of all Parties to the MEA. This aim is pursued through a pragmatic approach and a procedure that is mainly characterized by an interactive dialogue, usually based on discussion of data, persuasion and international assistance for capacity building.[96]

Indeed, the interactive dialogue promoted by the Espoo Convention's monitoring bodies in the *Bystroe Canal Project* case was based on the findings of the Espoo Inquiry Commission[97] as well as on information provided for and comments made by both Parties. Persuasion has also been exercised through consultations and exchanges of letters between relevant institutions and Ukraine. International assistance has also been provided. First, the MOP requested the Implementation Committee to

[93] Decision III/6f, Doc ECE/MP.PP/2008/2/Add.14, 26 September 2008. The action plan submitted by Ukraine in May 2008 was insufficient; Decision IV/9h, Doc ECE/MP.PP/2011/2/Add.1, 1 July 2011; Decision V/9m, Doc ECE/MP.PP/2014/2/Add.1, 14 October 2014.

[94] See this chapter, 22, and *supra* text corresponding to n 84.

[95] Doc ECE/MP.PP/2017/45, 2 August 2017, paras 65–66.

[96] See e.g., Koyano (n 75) 275 and A Tanzi and C Pitea, 'Non-Compliance Mechanisms: Lessons Learned and the Way Forward', in Treves et al., *Non-Compliance Procedures* (n 76) 569 at 579.

[97] See the Inquiry Commission Report (n 80).

assist Ukraine in complying with its obligations, notably offering technical advice in bringing Ukraine's domestic legislation into line with the Convention's provisions.[98] Second, the MOP invited both Parties to seek advice from the Secretariat to help them develop bilateral agreements or other arrangements.[99] Third, international funding and other support to Ukraine for the revision of its national legislation[100] and for bilateral co-operation was also provided through the Secretariat. A similar approach was undertaken under the Aarhus NCP.

It is also worth noting that the promotion of an interactive dialogue does not exclude the adoption of more stringent measures in the context of NCMs, such as the cautions issued by the monitoring bodies of the Aarhus and the Espoo Conventions. Cautions are not expressly envisaged under the latter's NCP. Nevertheless, their legitimacy can hardly be denied, as they are the result of a negotiating process and a final agreement of all contracting Parties in the context of one of their periodic meetings. Some decisions have also been considered severe, if not confrontational. For instance, as mentioned, Ukraine was urged by the decision of the MOP of the Espoo Convention 'to repeal without delay the final decision of 28 December 2007 concerning the implementation of the [BCP] and not to implement Phase II of the project before applying fully the provisions of the Convention'.[101] Also in this case, however, the MOP's decision can be considered consistent with general principles of international environmental law and, in particular, with the principles of prevention and precaution.[102]

4.3.2 *Integration of the Interests of the Parties Concerned with the Interests of Other States and of the Global Environment 245*

Under NCMs, bilateral conflicts are managed by a collective body that interacts with the Parties directly concerned, acting in the common

[98] Decision IV/II, para 26. An independent review of the Ukraine legislation was undertaken by a consultant, nominated by the Implementation Committee in 2009; see Doc ECE/MP.EIA/IC/2009/5, 2 July 2009.

[99] Doc ECE/MP.EIA/2008/4, paras 9, 11, 12.

[100] See n 84.

[101] Decision IV/2, para 9. See also the recommendations made by the Implementation Committee to the MOP in Doc ECE/MP/EIA/10, 95–96.

[102] M Koyano, 'The Significance of the Convention on Environmental Impact Assessment in a Transboundary Context (Espoo Convention) in International Environmental Law: Examining the Implications of the Danube Delta Case' (2008) 26 *Impact Assessment and Project Appraisal* 299 at 306.

interest of all contracting Parties. Accordingly, it can be assumed that under NCMs dealing with the BCP, not only the interests of Romania, but also those of other Parties to the relevant MEAs have been taken into account or, at least, all the contracting Parties have had the opportunity to represent their interests. The interconnection between different ecosystems has also been safeguarded.[103]

It is also noteworthy (and far from obvious) that the simultaneity of proceedings relating to the BCP under different multilateral treaties has not hindered, but rather strengthened a co-operative approach by promoting joint and complementary actions. Positive co-operation between various institutional systems is evidenced, for instance by the exchange of information on their respective activities;[104] the undertaking of joint fact-finding;[105] and the organization of multilateral consultations, such as the international conference held in Odessa in 2006 involving representatives of States, international institutions and one NGO,[106] and the informal meeting held in Geneva in 2008 by representatives of institutions established under relevant international treaties and MEAs.[107]

It should also be highlighted that, contrary to the *G/N* case, where the International Commission for the Protection of the Danube River (ICPDR) played a limited role, the ICPDR has actively contributed to fostering the dialogue between the Parties directly involved in the *Bystroe Canal* case and to sharing relevant information with other Parties to the

[103] Suffice here to mention the impact upon other European or extra European ecosystems due to the modification of migratory species routes.

[104] See e.g., Standing Committee of the Bern Convention, Doc T-PVS (2016) 25, 11 ff.

[105] See e.g., the joint mission carried out by UNESCO, under the MAB Programme and the Ramsar Secretariat in October 2003. The purpose of the mission was to examine alternative choices to the BCP and their impact on the Ukrainian Biosphere Reserve, i.e., an area that covers the most pristine part of the Danube Delta. The area was also included in the list of wetlands of international importance under the Ramsar Convention in 1995. Report available at www.ramsar.org/sites/default/files/documents/library/ram53_ukraine_kyliiske.pdf.

[106] Conference for the sustainable development of the Danube Delta (Romania, Moldova, Ukraine, ICPDR, UNESCO, Council of Europe, Ramsar Convention, European Union and WWF). Information on the outcome of the Conference and its follow-up available at www.icpdr.org/icpdr/static/dw2006_1/dw0106p16.htm.

[107] ICPDR, Secretariat of the Bern Convention, Secretariat of the Ramsar Convention, UNESCO MAB and World Heritage Convention, UNECE Secretariat of the Espoo Convention, Aarhus Convention and Water Convention. More information available at www.ramsar.org/news/bystroe-canal-project-under-international-scrutiny.

Danube River Protection Convention.[108] An integrated approach has been promoted by the ICPDR, since the BCP has been considered 'as a basin-wide threat and as a test case for the ICPDR on whether it was able to stand up for the environment and the basin'.[109]

With regard to the European Union, which is a party to all the aforementioned treaties,[110] except the Ramsar and the World Heritage Conventions, an active engagement was shown, in particular, when the EU promoted bilateral talks with Ukraine (2004–2005) and when it funded a project, consisting of an independent review of Ukraine's legislation and recommendations to ensure a correct implementation of the Espoo and Aarhus Conventions.[111]

A final remark concerns NGOs, who can be regarded as key players in many respects. The participation of NGOs (or independent individuals with an NGO background within the independent Committees) can significantly strengthen the representation of public interest in the context of NCMs.[112] On the one hand, the NGO Environmental People (EPL) filed complaints under the Espoo Convention,[113] the Aarhus Convention,[114] the

[108] For more details see: Haefner (n 60) 108 and 110; S Schmeier, *Governing International Watercourses: River Basin Organizations and the Sustainable Governance of Internationally Shared Rivers and Lakes* (Routledge 2013) 171 ff.; S Schmeier and I Zavadsky, 'Managing Disagreements in European Basins: What Role for River Basin Organizations in Water Diplomacy?' in A Kittikhoum and S Schmeier (eds), *River Basins Organizations in Water Diplomacy* (Routledge 2021) 275 at 281–83.

[109] Haefner (n 60) 107.

[110] See *supra* Section 4.3.

[111] *Support to Ukraine to Implement the Espoo and Aarhus Conventions, Draft Final Report*, EuropeAid Development and Cooperation, European Commission, August 2010, prepared by NIRAS A/S, Denmark. For a general assessment, see Koyano (n 75) 274, 279–80.

[112] For further considerations on the role played by NGOs in the context of NCMs, see C Pitea, 'NGOs in Non-Compliance Mechanisms under Multilateral Environmental Agreements: From Tolerance to Recognition?' in T Treves et al., *Civil Society* (n 50), 205; C Pitea, 'The Legal Status of NGOs in Environmental Non-Compliance Procedures: An Assessment of Law and Practice' in P-M Dupuy and L Vierucci (eds), *NGOs in International Law. Efficiency in Flexibility?* (Edward Elgar 2008), 181.

[113] EPL submitted a complaint to the Secretariat of the Espoo Convention in 2003, one year before the submission of Romania, prior to the construction of the BCP (text available in (2004) 34 *Environmental Policy and Law* 54 ff.). The complaint was dismissed for lack of standing, because ' … unsolicited information from NGOs and the public relating to specific cases of noncompliance was not within the Committee's existing mandate'. Doc MP.EIA/WG.1/2004/4, 8 April 2004, para 7.

[114] See *supra* note 91.

Bonn Convention[115] and the Danube River Protection Convention.[116] On the other hand, NGOs, including the World Wildlife Fund (WWF) and the Danube Environmental Forum (DEF), actively supported various international monitoring bodies, providing information or technical advice.[117]

4.3.3 *Assessment*

As the previous remarks clearly show, the main strength of the *Bystroe Canal* case is to be found in the continuous monitoring of the situation by competent treaty bodies and their concrete support, as well as in the active involvement of intergovernmental and non-governmental organizations and their mutual co-operation. This was a hard and lengthy process, but, in the end, a significant result was achieved: the reform of Ukraine's legal system in the field of EIA, providing for the participation of the public in the decision-making process through public hearings, in accordance with Ukraine's international obligations under the Espoo and the Aarhus Conventions.

The pragmatic and flexible approach characterizing NCMs has also facilitated a dialogue that takes into account both the interests of the Parties directly concerned and the interests of other States. The achievement of this goal has been strengthened through the promotion of inter-institutional co-operation.

A few challenges nonetheless remain. First, one of the major strengths of NCMs that is generally emphasized is their preventive approach, aimed at avoiding the infringement of international environmental obligations and the occurrence of huge or irreversible damage.[118] In the present case, it cannot be overlooked that the relevant NCMs were put into motion only after the BCP had already started. Further, monitoring

[115] EPL notified the Secretariat of the Bonn Convention alleged violations by Ukraine in 2004, http://epl.org.ua/en/law-posts/biodiversity-conservation-2/.

[116] In May 2004 EPL filed a complaint with the Secretariat of the Danube River Protection Convention for alleged violations by Ukraine of its treaty obligations. For further details on this and aforementioned complaints see http://epl.org.ua/en/law-posts/biodiversity-conservation-2/. For an overall assessment of actions undertaken by NGOs in this case, see TD Sobol, 'An NGO's Fight to Save Ukraine's Danube Delta: The Case for Granting Nongovernmental Organizations Formal Powers of Enforcement' (2006) 17 *Colorado Journal of International Environmental Law & Policy* 123 and Koyano (n 75) 276–77.

[117] For further details see Koyano (n 102) 308.

[118] See e.g., Paulus (n 51) 355.

bodies have been apparently more focussed on the consistency of the Ukrainian authorities' actions with their procedural obligations rather than on the BCP's conformity with the purposes of the applicable MEAs, which has been considered a 'delicate issue'.[119] As a result, no international proceeding prevented Ukraine from completing its project, which indeed took place before the proceedings had been completed.

Second, the very long time frame that elapsed between the initiation of compliance procedures and the enactment of legal measures by Ukraine cannot go unnoticed. Various reasons may explain the length of the process. It has also been contended, however, that Ukraine contributed to the procrastination of international procedures with a view to advancing its project and confronting the international community with a *fait accompli.*[120]

Third, reliance on NCMs can have negative effects. For instance, some doubts have been expressed with regard to certain measures adopted by the MOP of the Espoo Convention in the *Bystroe Canal* case. It is in fact unclear whether the caution issued to Ukraine, consisting of 'repealing without delay' its final decision of December 2007 and not implementing Phase II of the project 'meant cancellation [of the BCP] ... or not'.[121] Indeed, ambiguity can be fostered by the political character[122] and the 'hybrid' nature of compliance mechanisms. In fact, NCMs 'have at their disposal a variety of tools that enable them to better tailor their responses to a specific case',[123] being based on 'combinations of good will, cooperation, political handling of matters, technical expertise and the prudent recourse to incentives and disincentives which include the possibility of declaring non-compliance'.[124] In the end, however,

[119] K Wellens, 'Concluding Remarks' in Komori and Wellens (eds), *Public Interest Rules* (n 75) 459 at 461–62.

[120] S Urbinati, 'La contribution des mécanismes de contrôle et de suivi au développement du droit international: le cas du Projet du Canal de Bystroe dans le cadre de la Convention d'Espoo' in N Boschiero, T Scovazzi, C Pitea and C Ragni (eds), *International Courts and the Development of International Law: Essays in Honour of Tullio Treves* (TMC Asser Press 2013), 457 at 471.

[121] Koyano (n 102) 307. Indeed, cancellation 'seems to imply something beyond suspension'.

[122] G Ulfstein, 'Dispute Resolution, Compliance Control and Enforcement in International Environmental Law' in G Ulfstein, T Marahun and A Zimmermann (eds.), *Making Treaties Work: Human Rights, Environment and Arms Control* (Cambridge University Press 2007) 115 at 132.

[123] *Gaps in International Environmental Law and Environment-Related Instruments: Towards a Global Pact for the Environment. Report of the Secretary-General*, UN Doc A/73/419*, 30 November 2018, para 92.

[124] T Treves, 'Introduction', in Treves et al. (eds), *Non-Compliance Procedures* (n 76), 1 at 8.

> [w]hether the combination of all these elements, legal and not, succeeds in obtaining the result desired has to be assessed on a case-by-case basis. The right combination of good will, political finesse, legal and technical expertise, whatever the provisions to be applied, depends on the political situation of the moment and on the quality of the men and women engaged in the proceedings.[125]

4.4 Concluding Remarks

Both the *G/N* and the *Bystroe Canal* cases are particularly complex, as the legal and political issues involved are closely interrelated and inextricably linked. It would also be an overly ambitious task to claim to draw overall conclusions in respect of a hypothetical competition between adjudicative bodies and NCMs from the comparative analysis of only two cases. Accordingly, some general remarks will be tentatively developed strictly on the basis of the findings in the previous sections.

The judgment in the *G/N* case is rightly considered 'one of the most interesting judgments ever rendered by the International Court of Justice',[126] for 'the outstanding contribution given by the Court to the clarification of core issues of international law',[127] in particular the law of treaties, the law of international responsibility and their mutual relationship. The same judgment also represented a decisive step in the evolution of international environmental law. The formal recognition of the principle of prevention[128] and the 'irruption' of sustainable development in the jurisprudence of the ICJ[129] are among the most quoted parts of the judgment. The judgment confirmed the outstanding contribution that may be made to the development of international law through the case law of the Court. It should also be acknowledged that the role of the Court is 'not that of a ground-breaking body but rather that of a stock-taking institution or, to put [it] in [a] somewhat more colorful term, that of being the gate-keeper and guardian of general international law'.[130]

If, however, the same judgment is considered from the perspective of the main function generally ascribed to the Court, the judicial settlement of international disputes, it must be regrettably concluded that this

125 Ibid.

126 Pellet (n 27) 3.

127 Nagy (n 14) 24.

128 ICJ Judgment, para 140.

129 Ibid.

130 JE Viñuales, 'The Contribution of the International Court of Justice to the Development of International Environmental Law: A Contemporary Assessment' (2007/2008) 32 *Fordham International Law Journal* 232 at 258.

function was not fulfilled. The dispute in the *G/N* case was decided but not settled by the Court. Obviously, we will never know whether Hungary and Slovakia would have reached an agreement if the Court had provided them with more guidance. However, the 'condemnation' of the Parties to negotiation and the absence of supporting indications as to how they might proceed at the legal and technical level contributed to radicalizing the dispute.

More generally, with regard to the integration of the interests of the Parties to the disputes with the interests of other States and of the global environment, the right direction is the one indicated by Judge Weeramantry in his Separate Opinion in the *G/N* case:

> We have entered an era of international law in which international law subserves not only the interests of individual States, but looks beyond them and their parochial concerns to the greater interests of humanity and planetary welfare. In addressing such problems, which transcend the individual rights and obligations of the litigating States, international law will need to look beyond procedural rules fashioned for purely *inter partes* litigation.[131]

It can hardly be said, however, that substantive progress was made in this direction as a result of the ICJ judgment in the *G/N* case.[132]

As to the *Bystroe Canal* case, its main strength lies in the constant promotion of an interactive dialogue and in the effective involvement in the NCMs and in other international monitoring mechanisms of all main stakeholders, including other riparian States, intergovernmental organizations and NGOs. Positive results were also achieved in restoring Ukraine to compliance with some of its international obligations, through substantive reforms within the Ukrainian domestic legal system. In sum, if the issue at hand were considered from the perspective of an abstract competition between international courts and compliance mechanisms, the NCMs would win the game. Innovative mechanisms, like NCPs, appear more effective than traditional tools in managing new causes of conflicts.

A more cautious conclusion might be drawn, however, if attention is focussed on the concrete outcome achieved through the NCMs dealing with the BCP. First, it can hardly be said that legality has been fully restored: Ukraine is still considered to be non-compliant with some of its treaty obligations after decades of discussions and negotiations. Second, and above all, the different approach adopted by the monitoring bodies

131 ICJ Judgment, Separate Opinion of Vice-President Weeramantry, 118.
132 See this chapter, 13.

in assessing Ukraine's conduct with respect to the implementation of its procedural and substantive obligations may have serious implications for the effectiveness of the entire process.

More generally, if one considers the efficacy of the relevant international procedures in the *G/N* and the *Bystroe Canal* cases from the perspective of the protection of the environment as a common concern, there are no real winners but certainly one loser: the ecosystems directly or indirectly affected by the two projects and, notably, the Danube River basin's and the Danube Delta's ecosystems.

Against this backdrop, the obvious conclusion that could be drawn would be that very little can be done, within the limits of a decentralized legal order, whatever procedure is adopted to settle an international environmental dispute. The international legal system seems in fact structurally unsuited to cope with the equitable management of shared natural resources, where two fundamental principles, with formal equal rank – territorial sovereignty and sovereign equality – inevitably are in tension or even collide.[133] It should also be added that the international legal order lacks effective tools against the lack of political will, the persistent unwillingness of States or their dubious, if not bad faith.[134] In the end, it cannot be overlooked that international courts and non-compliance bodies dealing with environmental disputes are required to interpret very vague rules and principles, with serious implications both for international courts and NCMs. The former are composed of legal experts, impartial and independent, but they are obviously reluctant to play a law-making role.[135] The latter are extremely flexible and pragmatic, but their political nature tends to prevail over a legal approach.[136]

[133] See *Certain Activities Carried out by Nicaragua in the Border Area* (*Costa Rica v Nicaragua*) and *Construction of a Road in Costa Rica along the San Juan River* (*Nicaragua v Costa Rica*), Separate Opinion of Judge Donoghue, ICJ Reports 2015, 783, section 5.

[134] Suffice here to recall that the authorization and initiation of a project without waiting for the end of the negotiations between the parties concerned are a clear violation of the duty to co-operate in good faith; see ICJ, *Pulp Mills* case (n 28), para 147.

[135] See P Sands, 'Litigating Environmental Disputes: Courts, Tribunals and the Progressive Development of International Environmental Law' in TM Ndiaye and R Wolfrum (eds), *Law of the Sea, Environmental Law and Settlement of Disputes: Liber Amicorum Judge Thomas A. Mensah* (Martyinus Nijhoff Publishers 2007), 313 at 315.

[136] See J Klabbers, 'Compliance Procedures' in D Bodansky, J Brunnée and E Hey (eds), *Oxford Handbook of International Environmental Law* (Oxford University Press 2007) 995 at 1002–3.

Nevertheless, a more optimistic outlook can also be suggested. As much of the academic literature has rightly emphasized, both adjudicative bodies and treaty-based institutions are imperfect, but can play a complementary role in the settlement of international environmental disputes and in restoring legality.[137] It should also be added that their contribution can be remarkable, provided that international environmental disputes are understood in correct terms, that is, not because of the 'environmental' character of the legal rules at issue, but because they relate to the alleged detrimental impact of certain human activities on natural environmental systems.[138] To this end, some essential conditions will have to be met: all available means under international environmental law must be effectively used; the representation or participation of all key actors in the process must be assured; all possible alternative solutions must be carefully considered with the assistance of independent experts in the evaluation of scientific evidence; and, above all, the public interest in the conservation of the environment as a common concern must be duly taken into account through a genuinely integrated approach.

[137] See e.g., G Handl, 'Compliance Control Mechanisms and International Environmental Obligations' (1997) 5 *Tulane Journal of International and Comparative Law* 29 at 46; Romano (n 54) 332–34.

[138] A Boyle and J Harrison, 'Judicial Settlement of International Environmental Disputes: Current Problems' (2013) 4 *Journal of International Dispute Settlement* 245 at 247–50.

PART II

Specific Procedures

5

The Advisory Procedure in Non-Compliance Procedures

Lessons from the UNECE Water Convention

CARLOS A. CRUZ CARRILLO

5.1 Introduction

The advisory function of international judicial bodies remains an important judicial tool to elucidate the scope and content of international obligations. Today, many international judicial bodies are entrusted with an advisory function under different architectures.[1] As is well known, advisory opinions are not binding but do entail legal effects in the interpretation and application of law.[2] Recently, the advisory function is likewise permeating some compliance mechanisms established by multilateral environmental agreements (hereinafter referred to as 'MEAs'). This chapter examines the novelty of the advisory procedure envisaged in the mandate of non-judicial bodies as a new development in the implementation and compliance of MEAs.

The author wishes to thank Professor Christina Voigt, Professor Caroline Foster, Professor Attila Tanzi and Professor Martins Paparinskis for their insightful commentaries on previous versions of this chapter; and to PluriCourts, University of Oslo for their kind support. The views expressed remain my own.

[1] For a comparative study on the advisory jurisdiction, see A Sandoval Bernal, *La Jurisdicción Consultiva de las Cortes Internacionales* (Tirant lo Blanch 2019); M Runavot, *La competence consultative des jurisdictions internationals: Reflet des vicissitudes de la foncion judiciaire internationale* (LGDJ 2009).

[2] See *Delimitation of the Maritime Boundary in the Indian Ocean (Mauritius/Maldives)*, Preliminary Objections, Judgment, ITLOS Reports 2020–2021, 17, para 203; S Rosenne, *The International Court of Justice: An Essay in Political and Legal Theory* (A.W. Sijthoff 1957) 492–93; L Boisson de Chazournes, 'Advisory Opinions and the Furtherance of the Common Interest of Mankind' in L Boisson de Chazournes, C Romano and R Mackenzie (eds), *International Organizations and International Dispute Settlement: Trends and Prospects* (Transnational Publishers 2002) 107.

Since the second half of the twentieth century, many MEAs have created an institutional framework to foster compliance with the agreement in question.[3] Particularly, MEAs usually provide for the establishment of compliance or implementation committees (hereinafter referred to as 'CCs') aimed at facilitating and monitoring compliance with the agreement in question.[4] Such compliance review bodies are mandated to carry out procedures that are mostly non-adversarial and non-punitive in nature. Yet the outcome of these procedures may in some cases entail the adoption of sanctions for Parties found to be in non-compliance, directly by said bodies, or by the Meeting of the Parties (hereinafter referred to as 'MoP' or 'CoP') on the recommendation of CCs. Few MEAs add a so-called 'advisory procedure' to these procedures. This chapter argues that an advisory procedure fosters effective implementation by offering tailored technical and legal advice to States, attending to their particular circumstances, without confrontation and intrusive sanctions. Drawing on the advisory procedure of the UNECE Convention on the Protection and Use of Transboundary Watercourses and International Lakes (hereinafter referred to as 'UNECE Water Convention'), this chapter identifies areas of opportunity for enhancing implementation and compliance with current and future MEAs.

This chapter will be organized as follows. First, it will give a brief overview of the nature of non-compliance mechanisms (hereinafter referred to as 'NCMs'). Second, it will examine the advisory procedure specifically provided for the Implementation Committee of the UNECE Water Convention (hereinafter referred to as 'IC'). Third, it will identify areas of opportunity for adoption of a similar advisory procedure to help improve the implementation of other existing and future multilateral agreements.

5.2 Non-Compliance Procedures in a Nutshell

As anticipated, many MEAs envisage the possibility of establishing CCs managed by the CoP/MoP or by specialized subsidiary bodies. Their

[3] See n 11–14, 17–19, 21–24.

[4] See UNEP, *Compliance Mechanism under Selected Multilateral Environmental Agreements* (UNEP 2007); T Treves, L Pineschi, A Tanzi, et al. (eds), *Non-Compliance Procedures and Mechanisms and the Effectiveness of International Environmental Agreements* (TMC Asser Press 2009); M Fitzmaurice, *Environmental Compliance Control* (Max Planck Encyclopedia of Public International Law 2021).

main objective is to foster the implementation of and compliance with an MEA, and prevent environmental damage.[5] According to the United Nations Environment Programme (UNEP), 'compliance' is the fulfilment by the contracting Parties of their obligations under a MEA, whereas 'implementation' refers to the measures that contracting Parties adopt to meet their obligations.[6] In this context, CCs have particular common features that may attract the interests of Parties as a venue to tackle their implementation issues. The first is their non-judicial and non-confrontational nature. Second, these mechanisms aim at facilitating compliance rather than stigmatizing the concerned Party with measures or sanctions. A third common feature is the relevance of the duty of Parties and the treaty bodies to co-operate as a cornerstone of these mechanisms.[7]

Compliance or implementation committees' procedures can be seen as a public interest process where great attention is paid to due process and independence as a guarantee of legitimacy.[8] Further, the options to trigger a non-compliance procedure reflect the Parties' common interest in protecting the object of an MEA (watercourses, public participation, ozone layer, climate action, etc.).[9] The only precondition for triggering a compliance procedure is being a Party to the treaty and complying with the procedural requirements established to that end. Commonly, non-compliance procedures can be triggered by States and by particular bodies (e.g., CoP/MoP, implementation bodies). However, a few compliance mechanisms allow for broad public participation. For example,

[5] J Viñuales and P Marie Dupuy, *International Environmental Law* (2nd ed., Cambridge University Press 2018) 343–51; M Fitzmaurice, *Environmental Compliance Control* (Max Planck Encyclopedia of Public International Law 2021) paras 52–55; P Sands, J Peel, A Fabra and R Mackenzie, *Principles of International Environmental Law* (4th ed., Cambridge University Press 2018) 172–78; A Boyle, C Redgwell and P Birnie, *International Law and the Environment* (4th ed., Oxford University Press 2021) 254–60.

[6] UNEP, *Manual on Compliance with and Enforcement of Multilateral Environmental Agreements* (UNEP 2006) 59.

[7] A Tanzi and C Pitea, 'Non-Compliance Mechanisms: Lessons Learned and the Way Forward' in T Treves, L Pineschi, A Tanzi, et al. (eds), Non-Compliance Procedures (n 5) 569–70; Viñuales and Dupuy (n 6) 343–44.

[8] Cf. A Boyle, C Redgwell and P Birnie, *International Law and the Environment* (4th ed., Oxford University Press 2021) 255; M Doelle, 'Non-Compliance Procedures' in L Rajamani and J Peel (eds), *The Oxford Handbook of International Environmental Law* (Oxford University Press 2021) 982.

[9] On this point, see J Brunnée, 'International Environmental Law and Community Interests' in E Benvenisti, G Nolte and K Yalin-Mor (eds) *Community Interests across International Law* (Oxford University Press 2018) 172–74; Viñuales and Dupuy (n 6) 347.

in the mechanisms established by the UNECE Aarhus Convention,[10] the Escazú Agreement[11] the UNECE Water Convention[12] or the Protocol on Water, and Health[13] members of the public can actively participate in non-compliance procedures, either by triggering a procedure or by submitting information. Some authors also consider CCs an effective alternative to a judicial dispute settlement mechanism, which could entail a long process before a judgment or award is rendered.[14] Moreover, the outcome of these mechanisms does not result in *res judicata*, which makes them a less intrusive procedure in terms of state sovereignty.[15]

One of the very first NCMs to appear was that of the 1987 Montreal Protocol on Substances That Deplete the Ozone Layer.[16] Article 8 provided for the Parties to consider and approve mechanisms for determining non-compliance, which led to the establishment of the Implementation Committee in 1992.[17] A Party to the Protocol can trigger a procedure with respect to its non-compliance, or with respect to another Party. The Secretariat can also trigger the procedure. The Committee can adopt facilitative measures such as providing financial and technical assistance to foster the compliance of the concerned Party. However, the Committee can also adopt measures such as declarations of non-compliance, cautions and even the suspension of rights and prerogatives.[18]

[10] The Aarhus Convention enables NGOs to initiate a procedure against a Party. See UNECE, *Decision 1/7: Review of Compliance*, UN Doc ECE/MP.PP/2/Add.8, 2 April 2014, para 18.

[11] ECLAC, *Decision I/3: Rules Relating to the Structure and Functions of the Committee to Support Implementation and Compliance*, Doc 22-00344, 22 April 2022, Rule V(1).

[12] The Water Convention enables members of the public to submit information concerning the non-compliance of a Party. See UNECE, *Support to Implementation and Compliance, Decision VI/1*, UN Doc ECE/MP.WAT/37/Add.2, 2012, para 28.

[13] UNECE, *Annex to Decision I/2: Review of Compliance*, UN Doc ECE/MP.WH/2/Add.3, 3 July 2007, para 16.

[14] E Milano, 'The Outcomes of the Procedure and Their Legal Effects' in T Treves, L Pineschi, A Tanzi, et al. (eds), Non–Compliance Procedures (n 5) 413.

[15] G Ulfstein, T Marauhn and A Zimmermann (eds), *Making Treaties Work: Human Rights, Environment and Arms Control* (Cambridge University Press 2007) 10.

[16] Montreal Protocol on Substances That Deplete the Ozone Layer, signed 25 November 1992, entered into force 14 June 1994, 1785 UNTS 517, 3.

[17] UNEP, *Decision IV/5*, 4th Meeting of the Parties to the Montreal Protocol on Substances That Deplete the Ozone Layer (1992).

[18] For a detailed overview of the Implementation Committee of the Montreal Protocol, see O Yoshida, *The International Regime for the Protection of the Stratospheric Ozone Layer* (Brill 2018) 209–85; E Barratt-Brown, 'Building a Monitoring and Compliance Regime

While the Implementation Committee of the Montreal Protocol stands as the model from which later NCMs were established,[19] one may refer also to the latest generation of such mechanisms provided for in the 2015 Paris Agreement,[20] the 2013 Minamata Convention[21] and the 2018 Escazú Agreement.[22] The institutional and functional architecture of CCs under these agreements follows that of the Montreal Protocol, with some procedural adjustments concerning the actors entitled to initiate a procedure, or pertaining to the outcome of the procedure. For example, one may note the twofold CC established under the Kyoto Protocol, which comprises a facilitative and an enforcement branch. In certain circumstances, the outcome of the Kyoto Protocol procedures can result in binding recommendations.[23]

This chapter proposes the following taxonomy of functions ascribed to CCs among MEAs:

- **Reporting/Monitoring procedure**. This function is a traditional implementation technique used across MEAs and draws on the obligation of States to periodically report on the measures they have adopted to implement their obligations under the MEA in question.[24] Periodic reports enable the CoP or the CCs to foresee a State's difficulties in

under the Montreal Protocol' (1991) 16(2) *Yale Journal of International Law* 519–70; M Koskenniemi, 'Breach of Treaty or Non-Compliance? Reflections on the Enforcement of the Montreal Protocol' (1992) 3(1) *Yearbook of International Environmental Law* 123–62.

19 Viñuales and Dupuy (n 6) 334, M Fitzmaurice, *Environmental Compliance Control* (Max Planck Encyclopedia of Public International Law 2021) para 56.

20 UNFCCC, *Modalities and Procedures for the Effective Operation of the Committee to Facilitate Implementation and Promote Compliance Referred to in Article 15, paragraph 2, of the Paris Agreement*, Decision 20/CMA.1, UN Doc FCCC/PA/CMA/2018/3/Add.2, 19 March 2019. See C Voigt, 'The Compliance and Implementation Mechanism of the Paris Agreement' (2016) 25(2) *Review of European, Comparative and International Environmental Law* 1–13.

21 See UNEP, *MC-2/4: Rules of Procedure for the Implementation and Compliance Committee of the Minamata Convention on Mercury*, UN Doc UNEP/MC/COP.2/Dec.4, 6 December 2018. For an overview on this Committee, see J Templeton and P Kohler, 'Implementation and Compliance under the Minamata Convention on Mercury' (2014) 23(2) *Review of European, Comparative and International Environmental Law* 211–20.

22 ECLAC, *Decision I/3: Rules Relating to the Structure and Functions of the Committee to Support Implementation and Compliance*, Doc 22-00344, 22 April 2022.

23 UNFCCC, *Procedures and Mechanisms Relating to Compliance under the Kyoto Protocol*, Decision 27/CMP.1, Doc FCCC/KP/CMP/2005/8/Add.3, 9–10 December 2005, 94–96.

24 UNEP, *Compliance Mechanism under Selected Multilateral Environmental Agreements* (UNEP 2007) 9–10; Viñuales and Dupuy (n 6) 294–96.

complying with certain obligations of the MEA. In these cases, the CoP or the CC of an MEA may ask the Party concerned for additional information and decide whether to trigger a non-compliance procedure. Moreover, if a Party fails to comply with the obligation to report, the CC may trigger a non-compliance procedure.

- **Triggered by the Committee.** The CC can initiate *motu propio* a compliance procedure against a member State when the Committee has knowledge that the Party is failing to comply with its obligations under an MEA. As a basis for its decisions, the Committee can rely on the national reports submitted by the Parties under a monitoring procedure, or on information submitted by bodies of an MEA or by members of the public.
- **Submission procedures.** This procedure enables the mechanism to analyze particular non-compliance situations submitted by a Party with regard to its own performance (self-triggering); by a Party with regard to the performance of another Party; by the CoP; or by members of the public.[25] The outcome of a submission procedure generally entails facilitative measures such as technical and financial assistance to enhance compliance by the Party concerned. In a few cases, MEAs allow punitive measures, such as the suspension of rights and prerogatives.[26] The case law produced under this procedure is significant within the Aarhus Convention, mainly triggered by individuals and non-governmental organizations.[27] Similarly the case law of the Montreal Protocol,[28] the Espoo Convention[29] or the Kyoto Protocol.[30]

[25] Particularly, the mechanisms of the Aarhus Convention and the Escazú Agreement provide for this option.

[26] For example, the mechanisms of the UNECE Aarhus Convention, Espoo Convention and Water Convention include the suspension of rights and prerogatives as a measure in response to non-compliance.

[27] See UNECE, *Compilation of Findings of the Aarhus Convention Compliance Committee adopted 18 February 2005 to date*, 5 February 2021.

[28] See UNEP, *Implementation Committee Recommendations*, Implementation Committee of the Montreal Protocol, available at https://ozone.unep.org/list-of-implementation-committee-recommendations.

[29] UNECE, *Submissions Overview: Implementation Committee of the Espoo Convention*, available at https://unece.org/submissions-overview; UNECE, *Opinions of the Implementation Committee of the Espoo Convention* (2001–2020), (2020). Available at https://unece.org/sites/default/files/2021-02/Implementation%20Committee%20opinions%20to%202020_MOP-8_2020.pdf.

[30] UNFCCC, *Compliance under the Kyoto Protocol*, available at https://unfccc.int/process/the-kyoto-protocol/compliance-under-the-kyoto-protocol.

- **Advisory procedure.** The advisory procedure enables a CC to deliver legal and technical advice upon the request of a CC Party, the CoP or other organs of an MEA. The ultimate goal of this procedure is to facilitate the compliance with and implementation of an MEA. Thus, the procedure results in advice with recommendations for the Party, or Parties, concerned, but without measures stigmatizing any Party, as may be perceived in a submission procedure.

This chapter will focus on examining the advisory procedure as one of the most recent procedures formally established as a means to provide facilitative assistance to the Parties of an MEA. The chapter looks particularly at the advisory procedure under the UNECE Water Convention, examining the architecture of this procedure and analyzing the potential benefits of employing similar procedures as part of implementation and compliance procedures across MEAs more widely.

5.3 Advisory Opinions in the UNECE Water Convention

5.3.1 *General Overview of the Water Convention's Compliance and Implementation Machinery*

The UNECE Water Convention was adopted in 1992 and entered into force in 1996.[31] The main objective of the UNECE Water Convention is promotion of the sustainable management of transboundary waters, surface waters and ground waters. In order to help achieve that aim, the Convention sets out substantive and procedural obligations based on the principle of prevention, the obligation to co-operate, the principle of reasonable and equitable use and the no harm principle.[32] Moreover, this treaty includes a series of principles to be considered by the Parties when adopting measures to comply with and implement its obligations, namely, the precautionary principle, the polluter-pays principle and the

[31] UNECE Convention on the Protection and Use of Transboundary Watercourses and International Lakes, signed 17 March 1992, entered into force 6 October 1996, 1936 UNTS 269 (hereinafter referred to as 'UNECE Water Convention').

[32] UNECE Water Convention, Articles 2 to 6; A Tanzi, A Kolliopoulos and N Nikiforova, 'Normative Features of the UNECE Water Convention' in A Tanzi, O McIntyre, A Kolliopoulos, A Rieu-Clarke et al. (eds) *The UNECE Convention on the Protection and Use of Transboundary Watercourses and International Lakes* (Brill Nijhoff 2015) 11.6; L Boisson de Chazournes, *Fresh Water in International Law* (Oxford University Press 2013) 33–37.

principle of inter-generational equity.[33] Initially, this treaty remained a regional instrument for the European region. However, following a proposal by Switzerland, the Meeting of States Parties to the Convention adopted *Decision III/1*, allowing all United Nations member States to accede to the Convention.[34] Following this amendment, a number of countries from the African[35] regions acceded.

As to implementation and compliance, Article 17(2)(f) of the UNECE Water Convention enabled the MoP to create an Implementation Committee, which was established in 2012 with the adoption of *Decision VI/1* of the MoP.[36] The IC aims at facilitating, promoting and safeguarding the implementation and application of and compliance with the UNECE Water Convention.[37] The nature of the mechanism is non-confrontational, non-adversarial, transparent, supportive and co-operative.[38] The IC has an interdisciplinary composition of nine members with legal and scientific expertise.[39]

The IC is entrusted with a submission procedure, a procedure triggered by the IC to request further information and an advisory procedure. The submission procedure[40] can be triggered by any Party to the Convention with regard to its own issues of non-compliance (self-referral), by a Party with regard to issues of another Party or by the IC initiative in the absence of submissions. The procedure triggered by the IC *motu proprio* operates when the IC is aware of difficulties in the implementation of or non-compliance with the Convention.[41] In making a determination on whether to trigger a procedure, the IC should consider the source, content and relevance of the information submitted to it, including information submitted by the public.[42] This factor may be regarded as an indirect

[33] *UNECE Water Convention*, Article 2(5). Although the intergenerational equity principle is not expressly included, the elements of this obligation are referred to in Article 2(5)(c) of the Convention.

[34] UNECE, *Decision III/1: Amendment to the Water Convention*, adopted on 28 November 2003, UN Doc ECE/MP.WAT/14, Annex; for an overview of this amendment, see I Trombitcaia and S Koppel, 'From a Regional towards a Global Instrument: The 2003 Amendment to the UNECE Water Convention' in A Tanzi et al (eds) UNECE Convention (n 33) 15–31.

[35] Cameroon, Gambia, Namibia, Nigeria, Chad, Ghana, Guinea-Bissau, Senegal and Togo.

[36] UNECE (n 13).

[37] Ibid., para 1.

[38] Ibid., para 2.

[39] Ibid., paras 3 and 4.

[40] Ibid., paras 24–27.

[41] Ibid., paras 28–29.

[42] Ibid., paras 28 and 29.

substitute for procedures allowing for submissions, or referrals, from the public as in the Aarhus Convention or the Protocol on Water and Health.[43] The advisory procedure will be explained in a further section.

The outcome of a submission procedure is the adoption of facilitative measures aimed at supporting implementation of and compliance with the obligations in the Convention. In this regard, the IC can adopt one or more of the following measures:

I. Provide advice and facilitate assistance to the concerned Parties, including:
   (i) Suggesting or recommending that domestic regulatory regimes be set up or strengthened, and relevant domestic resources be mobilized as appropriate;
   (ii) Assistance in establishing transboundary water cooperation agreements;
   (iii) Facilitating technical and financial assistance;
   (iv) Assistance in seeking support from specialized agencies and other competent bodies, as appropriate.
II. Request and assist the concerned Parties in elaborating an action plan to facilitate implementation and compliance, within a time frame agreed by the Parties and the Committee;
III. Request the submission of progress reports.[44]

Furthermore, the IC can recommend the MoP adopt one or more of the above-mentioned measures or take other restrictive measures, including: issuing a statement of concern; issuing a declaration of non-compliance; issuing cautions; or the suspension of rights and privileges accorded to the Party concerned.[45] For this purpose, the MoP should consider the cause, type, degree and frequency of the Party's difficulties with implementation and/or non-compliance.

5.3.2 *Comparing the Water Convention's Advisory Procedure with Implementation and Compliance Procedures in Other MEAs*

As mentioned, the architecture of the NCM of the UNECE Water Convention follows the same pattern as the Montreal Protocol.

[43] UNECE, *Annex to Decision I/2 Review of Compliance*, UN Doc ECE/MP.WH/2/Add.3, 3 July 2007, para 16.

[44] UNECE (n 37) para 41.

[45] Ibid., para 42.

However, the IC of the Water Convention has an advisory function, which is unusual when compared with the more standard procedures employed by other NCMs. The advisory function is implicitly included in many implementation mechanisms. For instance, CCs operating under the Nagoya Protocol,[46] the Cartagena Protocol[47] and the London Protocol[48] among others, deliver advice and recommendations, but only as a measure following a non-compliance procedure.

Other CCs can deliver advice as a separate procedure. For example,[49] the CC of the Protocol on Water and Health has a consultation process to facilitate and support implementation by issuing technical, scientific and legal advice.[50] This procedure only operates if a Party requests it or if the CC proposes it. The case of the compliance mechanism of the Aarhus Convention is distinct. The Convention and *Decision I/7* (which establishes the Structure and Functions of the CC) did not include *ab initio* an advisory function for the CC.[51] Yet following a request for advice filed by Belarus, the MoP and the CC delineated such an advisory function. First, the Secretariat prepared a draft response which was circulated for the consideration of the CC and the Party concerned.[52] Afterwards, the CC adopted its recommendation *ACCC/A/2014/1 with respect to Belarus.*[53] In a second request for advice by Kazakhstan, the CC, without the support of the Secretariat, set out more clearly that its advisory function was founded in accordance with paragraphs 14, 36(a) and 37(a) of the

[46] CBD, *Cooperative Procedures and Institutional Mechanisms to Promote Compliance with the Nagoya Protocol and to Address Cases of Non-Compliance*, Decision NP-1/4, UNEP/CBD/NP/COP-MOP/DEC/1/4, 20 October 2014, Section F(2)(a).

[47] CBD, *Establishment of Procedures and Mechanisms on Compliance under the Cartagena Protocol on Biosafety*, Decision BS-1/7, 2004, Section VI(1)(a).

[48] IMO, *Revised 2017 Compliance Procedures and Mechanisms Pursuant to Article 11 of the 1996 Protocol to the London Convention 1972*, Doc LC 39/16/Add.1, 2017, Section 5.1.1.

[49] Other examples include the Facilitative Branch of the Kyoto Protocol, which provides advice to the Parties.

[50] UNECE, *Annex: Consultation Process of the Compliance Committee under the Protocol on Water and Health*, as amended by the Committee at its tenth meeting, UN Doc ECE/MP.WH/C.1/2014/2, 17 December 2014, para 1.

[51] UNECE, *Decision 1/7: Review of Compliance*, MoP of the Aarhus Convention, UN Doc ECE/MP.PP/2/Add.8, 2 April 2004.

[52] See the procedure proposed by the MoP: UNECE, *Report of the Fifth Session of the MoP*, UN Doc ECE/MP.PP/2014/2, 11 October 2014, para 53.

[53] UNECE, *Recommendations with Regard to Request for Advice ACCC/A/2014/1 by Belarus*, Compliance Committee of the Aarhus Convention, UN Doc ECE/MP.PP/C.1/2017/11, 18 June 2017, para 3.

annex to *Decision I/7*.[54] In both decisions, the outcome of the request for advice entailed recommendations with regard to the meaning and scope of particular terminology in the Convention, as well as a recommendation for the requesting Party to pursue certain measures at the domestic level. A third request for advice was filed by Ukraine and is pending.[55] What is uncertain in this new procedure is whether the requesting Party can become the object of measures by the CoP should it fail to implement the recommendations of the CC, and whether it remains potentially subject to a submission procedure in respect of the concerns addressed through the advisory function.

The UNECE Water Convention advisory procedure derives from the constitutive Decision by the MoP, which provides explicitly for it and underscores that the advisory procedure 'shall not be regarded as alleging non-compliance'.[56] Therefore, as will be explained in detail, the outcome of the advisory procedure is legal and technical advice without the possibility that the Committee might suggest the MoP take action in respect of relevant concerns.[57] Another noteworthy aspect of the Convention's advisory procedures is the clarity of the process regarding who can request an advisory opinion and the effects of an advisory opinion for the requesting entity. The scope of the advisory procedure embraces two situations. First, when a Party seeks advice on its difficulties in implementing the UNECE Water Convention. Second, when a Party or Parties seek advice on how to implement the Convention with respect to another Party and/or with non-Parties to the Convention. Thus, the advisory procedure has a facilitative and preventive dimension inasmuch as it seeks for the Parties to identify potential issues of non-compliance, request guidance to resolve them and, at the same time, prevent further disputes with other Parties or non-Parties with a legal interest.

The advisory procedure produces advice tailored to the needs of the requesting Party for the purposes of implementing the Water

[54] UNECE, *Recommendations with Regard to Request for Advice ACCC/A/2020/2 by Kazakhstan*, Compliance Committee of the Aarhus Convention, UN Doc. ECE/MP.PP/C.1/2021/6, 1 July 2020, para 14.

[55] UNECE, *Request for Advice by Ukraine ACCC/A/2022/3*, Letter of the Secretary of the CC of 21 July 2022.

[56] UNECE (n 37) para 18.

[57] This feature is also present in the advisory procedure/consultative process of the Protocol on Water and Health and the Facilitative Branch of the Kyoto Protocol.

Convention. According to its constitutive Decision, the Committee may include *inter alia* the following in its advisory opinion:

- Advice and assistance to an individual Party or group of Parties to facilitate the implementation of the Water Convention. The Committee can particularly recommend the enhancement of domestic regulatory regimes; provide assistance in establishing transboundary water co-operation agreements; facilitate technical and financial support, including information and technology transfer and capacity building; or provide assistance to seek support from specialized agencies;
- Requesting and assisting the Party or Parties concerned to develop an action plan to facilitate implementation, within a timeframe agreed between the IC and the Parties;
- Inviting the Party concerned to submit progress reports on the efforts that it is making to implement the Convention.[58]

These suggestions are similar to the facilitative measures that the IC can adopt in the context of a submission procedure. However, it is not contemplated that, in the context of the advisory procedure, the Committee would recommend to the MoP the adoption of measures such as issuing statements of concern or a declaration of non-compliance, cautions or the suspension of rights and privileges. Therefore, an advisory opinion seems to be a way for States to seek guidance in the implementation of the Convention without being subject to such measures. Nevertheless, nothing prevents the Committee using the information derived from an advisory procedure to act *motu proprio* with regard to the same State, or States concerned, under a more stringent procedure.

In terms of standing, the advisory procedure is open to States Parties to the Water Convention, with regard to their own actions or those of other Parties, and to non-States Parties. In the case of non-States Parties, their participation in the advisory procedure is subject to their consent.[59] The opening of the Water Convention to all UN member States in 2003 has enabled the IC to expand its functions to regions beyond Europe. For example, if Ghana,[60] which recently acceded to the Water Convention, decides to request advice from the Committee on activities

[58] UNECE (n 37) para 22.
[59] Ibid., para 19–20.
[60] Ghana acceded to the Water Convention on 22 June 2020.

conducted on the Black Volta River, the Committee could consider inviting Burkina Faso or Côte d'Ivoire to participate in the advisory procedure as riparian States. However, since the latter two States are non-Parties to the Water Convention, their consent to participation is essential. In fact, the Committee is obliged to explain the advisory procedure to those Parties and suggest their participation.[61]

Finally, public participation is possible within the functions of the IC and other mechanisms in at least in two ways. First, members of the public can transmit information to the Committee on a Party's non-compliance, on the basis of which the Committee may initiate *motu proprio* a procedure against the concerned Party.[62] Second, during the advisory and submission procedures the Committee shall take into account the information submitted by the public.[63]

5.3.3 *An Example of the Water Convention's Advisory Procedure: The Cijevna/Cem River Advisory Procedure (WAT/IC/AP/1 – Montenegro and Albania)*

The Cijevna/Cem River advisory procedure provides a good example of the effectiveness of the Water Convention advisory procedure. On 22 November 2019, Montenegro filed a letter to the Secretariat of the UNECE Water Convention, afterwards circulated to the IC of the UNECE Water Convention. In its letter, Montenegro expressly requested the involvement of the IC in relation to the construction of small hydro-power plants on the Cijevna/Cem River in Albania.[64] Montenegro was not clear as to the procedure under which it was approaching the IC, which appeared to fall somewhere between a submission and a request for the advisory procedure. The IC analyzed Montenegro's letter and considered it a request for the exercise of its advisory function. Yet it also left open the possibility of initiation at a later stage of a *motu proprio* procedure.[65] In accordance with the established process, the IC invited

61 UNECE (n 37) para 23.
62 Ibid., paras 28 and 29.
63 Ibid., para 31.
64 UNECE, *Report of the Preparatory Meeting for the Eleventh Meeting of the Implementation Committee*, UN Doc. ECE/MP.WAT/IC/2020/2, 13 October 2020, para 6.
65 UNECE, *Report of the Implementation Committee on Its Tenth Meeting*, UN Doc ECE/MP.WAT/IC/2019/2, 27 May 2020, paras 7–8.

Albania to participate in the advisory procedure. Albania agreed to do so on 31 January 2020.[66]

The situation at Cijevna/Cem River is also the object of a submission procedure before the Implementation Committee of the Convention on Environmental Impact Assessment in a Transboundary Context (Espoo Convention). Montenegro instituted proceedings under the Espoo Convention on 11 September 2019,[67] and Albania replied on 30 December 2019, asserting compliance with its obligations under this treaty.[68] At the moment of writing this chapter, the procedure is ongoing and has not yet led to an outcome. In this context, an interesting preliminary aspect of the procedure is the co-ordination between the implementation committees of the UNECE Water Convention and the Espoo Convention,[69] who agreed on sharing information related to the matter through their secretariats.[70] A similar situation is less likely to occur among judicial and arbitral bodies.

The Committee held several information-gathering and consultation sessions with Albania and Montenegro. The Committee decided to adopt a two-track approach: to facilitate the exchange of information between both countries and to assist in the establishment of a joint monitoring and assessment framework for surface waters, groundwater and ecosystems in the Cijevna/Cem River.[71] During the process, Albania proposed the existing bilateral commission established under the 2018 Framework Agreement on Mutual Relations in the Field of Management of Transboundary Waters as a forum for consultations with Montenegro. The Committee proposed a joint technical working group within the framework of this bilateral commission. Albania underscored the importance of avoiding duplication with the existent mechanisms, such as the efforts adopted in the framework of the mechanism governing the Drin River basin.[72] The Committee clarified the scope of the

[66] UNECE (n 65) para 7.

[67] UNECE, *EIA/IC/S/7 Albania*, Submission by Montenegro to the Implementation Committee of the Espoo Convention, 11 September 2019.

[68] UNECE, *EIA/IC/S/7 Albania*, Response from Albania, 30 December 2019.

[69] UNECE (n 66) para 7 to 10.

[70] UNECE (n 65) para 11.

[71] See UNECE, *Report of the Implementation Committee on its Twelfth Meeting*, UN Doc ECE/MP.WAT/IC/2021/1, 18 March 2021, para 7.

[72] Adopted by the riparian states Albania, Greece, Montenegro, North Macedonia and Kosovo.

advisory procedure as limited to the Cijevna/Cem River and not the Drin River.[73]

The Committee delivered its legal and technical advice in March 2021.[74] The Committee held that due to the absence of sufficient monitoring information and data, it was unable to confirm or deny the likelihood of a cumulative transboundary impact caused by the planned construction.[75] However, the Committee elaborated on the potential difficulty of implementing certain obligations of the Water Convention. In this regard, the Committee recognized that the Convention's procedural obligations are instrumental in operationalizing substantive obligations such as the obligations to prevent, control and reduce transboundary impact. The Committee examined the matter of the Cijevna/Cem River in the context of the procedural obligations of establishing joint bodies, concluding transboundary water agreements, holding consultations, joint monitoring and assessment and exchanging data and information.

Particularly, the Committee advised Albania and Montenegro to enhance their efforts in implementing the obligation of carrying out joint monitoring and assessment by establishing a joint or co-ordinated monitoring and assessment framework. Similarly, the Committee advised the Parties on developing a practice of exchanging information and data, and procedures in pursuit of that aim.[76] Albania and Montenegro engaged in a joint effort to implement the Committee's advice. In particular, both countries are working on establishing the joint technical working group for monitoring and assessment of the Cijevna/Cem River. The Parties submitted to the IC a first briefing on the implementation on 20 May 2021.[77] The IC continues to assist Albania and Montenegro.

5.3.4 *Contributions of the Advisory Procedure to the Implementation of MEAs*

This section of the chapter will elaborate on three valuable dimensions of the Water Convention's advisory procedure. First, the role of the

[73] UNECE (n 72) paras 11–14.

[74] For the summary of the legal and technical advice provided by the Committee, see UNECE, *Annex to the Report of the Implementation Committee on its Twelfth Meeting*, UN Doc ECE/MP.WAT/IC/2021/1, 18 March 2021.

[75] UNECE (n 75) 6.

[76] Ibid., 6–8.

[77] See UNECE, *Report of the Implementation Committee on Its Thirteenth Meeting*, UN Doc ECE/MP.WAT/IC/2021/3, 21 July 2021, para 7.

advisory procedure in water diplomacy and the prevention of further disputes. Second, the importance of having a tailored legal and technical advisory opinion to assist in the implementation of an MEA. Third, the areas of opportunity where the advisory procedure may enhance the implementation of current and future MEAs.

5.3.4.1 The Conciliatory Role of the Advisory Procedure in the Context of Water Diplomacy

Water diplomacy mainly hinges on co-operation agreements such as the recent co-operation framework on the Senegal–Mauritanian Aquifer Basin.[78] In the absence of co-operation agreements and the will to implement them, States may engage in long-lasting and costly disputes such as the dispute relating to the Gabčíkovo–Nagymaros Project or the 'Dispute over the Status and Use of the Waters of the Silala',[79] both before the ICJ. In this context, the first remarkable feature of the advisory procedure is its role in fostering water diplomacy to help prevent long-lasting and costly disputes.

In particular, the advisory procedure provides alternative ways forward to two or more States with competing interests in a shared resource. This feature is not present in other non-compliance procedures, and it is unique because its main objective is to explore potential solutions with the concerned Parties and non-Parties, without triggering a confrontational judicial or quasi-judicial procedure. This may prove to be attractive to States. Arguably, the advisory procedure offers a cheaper way forward than recourse to judicial or arbitral proceedings. One could assert that the advisory procedure is a conciliatory way to prevent a dispute, and to prevent environmental damage[80] or, as expressed by some former judges, it is a form of 'advisory arbitration'.[81] Indeed, the engagement of the IC

[78] UNECE, *The Gambia, Guinea Bissau, Mauritania and Senegal Commit to Cooperate on Shared Groundwater as Foundation for Regional Stability, Sustainable Development and Climate Adaptation*, Press Release, 29 September 2021.

[79] Currently under deliberation. ICJ, 'Dispute over the Status and Use of the Waters of the Silala (Chile v. Bolivia) – Conclusion of the Public Hearing', Press Release 2022/13, 14 April 2022.

[80] For some considerations on conciliation and NCMs, see M Fitzmaurice, 'The Potential of Inter-State Conciliation within the Framework of Environmental Treaties' in C Tomuschat and M Kohen, *Flexibility in International Dispute Settlement: Conciliation Revisited* (Brill Nijhoff 2020) 95–110.

[81] Judges Lapradelle and Negulesco coined the term: 'The procedure which allows States to apply to the Court through the Council for an opinion constitutes a new dispute settlement mechanism. This mechanism differs from the opinion properly provided for

in facilitating a solution among the Parties makes of the advisory procedure a new development among non-compliance procedures. The Cijevna/Cem River advisory procedure is a clear example of this. The Parties consented to participating in the procedure and are currently working together to prevent environmental damage in this watercourse.

If the Parties fail to reach an agreement through the advisory procedure, they may resort to other means of dispute settlement. Most MEAs are clear in recognizing the independence of the non-compliance procedure from dispute settlement processes.[82] For example, the UNECE Water Convention recognizes that the procedure to facilitate and support implementation and compliance shall be without prejudice to Article 22 of the Convention on the settlement of disputes.[83] The next question is whether the advisory opinion rendered by the IC has any value in a further judicial or non-judicial proceeding. To contextualize this point, let us go back to the Cijevna/Cem River advisory procedure, where the IC was unable to confirm or deny the likelihood of cumulative transboundary impact caused by the planned hydropower plants.[84] What would have been the legal consequence of a determination confirming cumulative environmental impact? A first point to remember is that non-compliance procedures, even if some of them entail sanctions, are not judicial processes. Therefore, the principle of *res judicata* cannot be invoked as a basis to request a tribunal not to exercise its jurisdiction over a dispute.[85] However, the findings of the IC can assist a judicial/ arbitral organ in adopting an interpretation of the treaty and may

in Article 14 of the Covenant, in that it is similar to arbitration, but has certain features peculiar to it. It could be called advisory arbitration.' MA Lapradelle and D Negulesco, 'Rapport sur la nature Juridique des Avis Consultatifs de la Cour Permanente de Justice Internationale - leur valeur et leur portée positive en droit International' (1928) 34 *Annuaire Institut de Droit International* 453.

82 See T Treves, 'The Settlement of Disputes and Non-Compliance Procedures' in T Treves, L Pineschi, A Tanzi et al. (eds), Non–Compliance Procedures (n 5) 505–11.

83 UNECE (n 13) para 45.

84 UNECE (n 75) 6.

85 For a punctual discussion on the interlinkage between NCMs and dispute settlement, see P Sands, 'Non-Compliance and Dispute Settlement' in R Wolfrum, P-T Stoll and U Beyerlin (eds) *Ensuring Compliance with Multilateral Environmental Agreements: A Dialogue between Practitioners and Academia* (Brill 2006) 356–58; T Treves, 'The Settlement of Disputes and Non-Compliance Procedures' in T Treves, L Pineschi, A Tanzi, et al. (eds), Non–Compliance Procedures (n 5) 505–11.

provide elements of fact-finding.[86] For example in the *Diallo* case, the ICJ ascribed great weight to the interpretation of the International Covenant on Civil and Political Rights (ICCPR) adopted by the Human Rights Committee, as an independent body that was established specifically to supervise the application of the ICCPR.[87] Yet the facilitative nature of the advisory procedure differs from the advisory function of a judicial body. The goal of judicial advisory proceedings is delivering an authoritative statement of law on a legal question requested by an entity (international organizations, States or NGOs[88]) for the fulfilment of its obligations and/or functions. An advisory opinion constitutes a source of international law and entails legal effects for the requesting entity and the legal system.[89]

5.3.4.2 Tailored Technical and Legal Advice

One of the most crucial roles of a CC is identifying the main reasons why a Party is failing to implement its obligations under an MEA. The reasons for non-compliance can go beyond a problem with political will. Instead, a Party might be in the position of lacking the technical and financial capacity to implement its obligations. For these reasons, States need an IC from which they can request technical and legal advice without being accused of non-compliance by another Party, the public or the CC. Submission, reviewing and self-trigger procedures generate a certain level of stigmatization against the concerned Party, which may help tackle the absence of political will to implement an MEA. However, despite the recommendations that may follow these procedures, States may be reluctant to implement them because of their confrontational and punitive nature.[90] As underscored by Judge Buergenthal, 'it is easier for

[86] See the replies of the IC to questions received from Latin American countries: UNECE, *Annex to the Report of the Implementation Committee on its Fourteenth Meeting*, UN Doc ECE/MP.WAT/IC/2022/2, 24 May 2022, 7.

[87] *Ahmadou Sadio Diallo (Republic of Guinea v Democratic Republic of the Congo)*, Merits, Judgment, ICJ Reports 2010, 639, para 66.

[88] Only possible at the African Court of Human and People's Rights. *Protocol to the African Charter on Human and People's Rights on the Establishment of an African Court on Human and People's Rights*, 10 June 1998, Article 4(1).

[89] See *Delimitation of the Maritime Boundary in the Indian Ocean (Mauritius/Maldives)*, Preliminary Objections, Judgment, ITLOS Reports 2020–2021, 17, paras 203–5.

[90] See F Romanin Jacur, 'Triggering Non-Compliance Procedures' in T Treves, L Pineschi, A Tanzi, et al. (eds), Non-Compliance Procedures (n 5) 375–77.

governments to comply with advisory opinions because such rulings do not stigmatize them'.[91]

In this context, the advisory procedure, as envisaged in the UNECE Water Convention, goes beyond the traditional role of ICs by offering a procedure to those Parties with the political will to implement an MEA but with a lack of capacity to do so. Under the advisory procedure, a Party can have recourse to the IC to expose its situation and to request financial, technical or legal advice. On this point, the IC has underscored the benefit of the Committee's interdisciplinary composition.[92] As explained, the outcome of an advisory procedure entails recommendations aimed at enhancing domestic regulatory regimes or facilitating technical and financial support for the requesting Party. Furthermore, the IC can bring to the attention of the CoPs/MoPs the financial and technical difficulties of a Party with the aim of seeking support among other Parties.

5.3.4.3 Assessing the Utility of Employing an Advisory Procedure in other MEAs

As discussed, the advisory procedure has emerged within an IC of an MEA governing the management of international watercourses and lakes. Yet, this procedure can be easily adapted for use under other MEAs addressing the management of common/shared resources or addressing a common concern. The inclusion of a similar procedure in other compliance mechanisms could foster a more active engagement in the implementation of the related treaties and ensure the prevention of environmental damage and health risks. This improvement could be made in existing compliance mechanisms among MEAs by vesting in them the power to conduct an advisory procedure. For example, the CC of the Protocol on Water and Health adopted in 2014 a consultation process to facilitate and support implementation by issuing technical, scientific and legal advice.[93] Like the advisory procedure of the Water Convention, the consultation process is not a compliance review

[91] T Buergenthal, 'The Inter-American Court of Human Rights' (1982) 76(2) *The American Journal of International Law* 245. See also *Interpretation of Peace Treaties*, Advisory Opinion, ICJ Reports (1950) 65, para 71.

[92] UNECE, *Report of the Implementation Committee to the MoP and Draft Decision on General Issues of Implementation*, UN Doc ECE/MP.WAT/2021/5, 6 July 2021, paras 13–31.

[93] UNECE (n 51) para 1.

procedure and, thus, it doesn't establish whether a Party is non-compliant.[94] The consultation is requested by a Party or by invitation from the CC.[95] To date, the CC of the Protocol on Water and Health has dealt with seven consultation processes.

The second pathway of opportunity for introducing an advisory procedure is in the context of negotiations on compliance mechanisms of new multilateral treaties. This chapter underscores three of them:

- **BBNJ Agreement.**[96] The draft text of the international legally binding Instrument on the Conservation and Sustainable Use of Marine Biological Diversity of Areas Beyond National Jurisdiction (BBNJ), would establish in Article 53 ter an Implementation and Compliance Committee to facilitate and review the implementation of the agreement. The modalities and procedures would be adopted during the first CoP.[97] In this scenario, the advisory procedure could be a function considered by the CoP when establishing the Implementation and Compliance Committee. It should be noted that the draft text includes a proposal for the CoP to request advisory opinions from the International Tribunal for the Law of the Sea.[98] Establishing advisory procedures to be conducted, respectively, by a non-compliance body and a judicial body may complement authoritative statements of law with tailored facilitative advice for implementing the treaty.
- **Plastic pollution Treaty**. In March 2022, the United Nations Environment Assembly (UNEA) decided to convene an intergovernmental negotiating committee to develop a binding instrument on plastic pollution.[99] Despite its early stage of development, it is probable that the Intergovernmental Negotiating Committee (INC) will be considering the appropriate mechanisms to address compliance with the

[94] Ibid., para 4.

[95] Ibid., para 5.

[96] International legally binding instrument under the United Nations Convention on the Law of the Sea on the Conservation and Sustainable Use of Marine Biological Diversity of Areas Beyond National Jurisdiction, UNGA Res 72/249, 24 December 2017, UN Doc A/RES/72/249.

[97] UN, *Revised Draft Text of an Agreement under the United Nations Convention on the Law of the Sea on the Conservation and Sustainable Use of Marine Biological Diversity of Areas Beyond National Jurisdiction*, UN Doc A/CONF.232/2022/5, Articles 53 and 53 ter.

[98] Ibid., Article 55 ter.

[99] UNEA, *End Plastic Pollution: Towards an International Legally Binding Instrument*, UNEP/EA.5/L.23/Rev.1, 2 March 2022, Operative 1 and 3.

treaty.[100] Stakeholders have expressed the importance of adopting an instrument that takes into account countries' different capacities, as well as their need for financial and technical assistance.[101] In this context, the INC might draw on the advisory procedure under the Water Convention.

- **Pandemic Treaty.** In December 2021, the World Health Organization agreed on establishing an intergovernmental negotiating body to negotiate a binding instrument to strengthen pandemic prevention, preparedness and response.[102] Given the preventive nature of the upcoming instrument, an IC or similar body will be useful to implement the treaty.[103]

In sum, the advisory procedure established in the UNECE Water Convention and other MEAs constitutes a truly facilitative non-compliance procedure capable of offering advice to tackle technical and financial implementation issues, to prevent environmental damage and to help prevent further disputes. The advisory procedure could prove to be an efficient tool in the implementation of multilateral treaties addressing common concerns or the management of shared resources.

5.4 Conclusions

This chapter has explored the potential of the advisory procedure in CCs by drawing on the advisory procedure employed by the IC of the UNECE Water Convention and recent experience with this procedure. The chapter has highlighted the benefits of non-confrontational and non-punitive NCMs and procedures. While most of these procedures can be useful to address the lack of political will to implement MEAs, it is true that they may be more limited in their contribution to addressing other

[100] UNEA (n 100) para 3(p); UNEP, *Note by the Secretariat*, UNEP/PP/INC.1/5, 14 October 2022, para 22.

[101] UNEP-IISD, 'Marine Litter and Plastic Pollution Bulletin', *Earth Negotiations Bulletin*, September 2021, 4; Ministerial Calls for Global Agreement on Marine Litter, Plastic Pollution, International Institute for Sustainable Development, 7 September 2021.

[102] WHO, *The World Together: Establishment of an Intergovernmental Negotiating Body to Strengthen Pandemic Prevention, Preparedness and Response*, World Health Assembly, Second Special Session, Doc SSA2(5), 1 December 2021.

[103] H Nikogosian, *A Guide to a Pandemic Treaty: Things You Must Know to Help You Make a Decision on a Pandemic Treaty* (The Graduate Institute of International and Development Studies – Global Health Centre 2021) 23–24; See Chapter 2, this volume.

compliance issues, such as lack of capacity or the emergence of a dispute. The chapter draws the following conclusions on the advisory procedure:

(1) The tailored and technical advice offered through an advisory procedure stands out as one of the unique features of the advisory procedure as compared with the outcome of a submission, reporting or self-triggered procedure. This feature may prove to be attractive for States willing to implement an MEA but struggling to do so for technical or financial reasons. Moreover, the interdisciplinary composition of non-compliance bodies enables the production of advisory opinions with technical and legal recommendations, tailored to the specific needs of the requesting Party.

(2) The advisory procedure offers a conciliatory avenue for the prevention of potentially long-standing and costly disputes before judicial or arbitral bodies. Relying on the principle of cooperation, the concerned States can request an advisory opinion from the IC to obtain guidance on how to implement treaty obligations in respect to a particular project or a situation that may entail environmental harm. On the one hand, the advisory procedure seeks to prevent a dispute, and on the other, it offers alternatives to prevent further damage.

(3) The non-inquisitorial nature of the advisory procedure fosters a more facilitative approach across MEAs. Bearing this in mind, existing CCs should consider the establishment of an advisory procedure, adopting a similar architecture to that in the UNECE Water Convention. Furthermore, the advisory procedure could be considered for inclusion in designing compliance and implementation mechanisms in the course of the negotiation of new treaties such as the BBNJ Agreement, the Plastic Pollution Treaty or a new treaty on pandemic preparedness and response.

6

State-to-State Procedures before Environmental Compliance Committees: Still Alive?

JUSTINE BENDEL AND YUSRA SUEDI

6.1 Introduction

Many multilateral environmental agreements (MEAs) have established committees that monitor compliance and/or facilitate State parties' implementation.[1] They offer an alternative to traditional judicial dispute settlement and are designed with a slightly different purpose in mind. One of the ways they are different from international courts is the way in which a procedure can be triggered.[2] Indeed, there are many ways such committees may be triggered to take action: the committee could act *proprio motu* (committee trigger), or any State party could trigger the committee with respect to its own compliance or implementation (self-trigger) or sometimes an NGO or member of the public can trigger the committee (third-party trigger). However, most compliance committees also have a more 'traditional' way to initiate a procedure before them, reminiscent of a judicial procedure: a State party may seize the committee concerning the compliance or implementation of another State party.[3] This type of trigger has only been used a handful of times across the existing

[1] The difference between implementation and compliance is defined clearly by C Voigt, 'The Compliance and Implementation Mechanism of the Paris Agreement' (2016) 25(2) *Review of European Community and International Environmental Law* 161–73, 166.

[2] While 'trigger' is the most common term used in literature, States have also used 'referral' and 'initiation' in negotiations. See S Oberthür and E Northrop, 'Towards an Effective Mechanism to Facilitate Implementation and Promote Compliance under the Paris Agreement' (2018) 8(1–2) *Climate Law* 39–69, 53, fn 44; Ad-hoc Working Group on the Paris Agreement, Third Part of the First Session, Bonn, 8–18 May 2017, Agenda Item 7: Modalities and Procedures for the Effective Operation of the Committee to Facilitate Implementation and Promote Compliance Referred to in Article 15.2 of the Paris Agreement, Informal Note by the Co-Facilitators, Final Version, available at https://unfccc.int/files/meetings/bonn_may_2017/application/pdf/apa_item7_informalnote_provisional_17may2017@1100_final.pdf.

[3] For an overview of existing triggers, see J Bendel, *Litigating the Environment: Process, and Procedure before International Courts and Tribunals* (Edward Elgar 2023) 218–22.

environmental committees that provide for it, most famously in the context of the Aarhus Convention. However, this trigger has deliberately not been included in the list of the various options triggering the Paris Agreement Implementation and Compliance Committee (PAICC). It is also interesting to see that, in the human rights context, the UN Convention on Racial Discrimination's Committee has been triggered only twice.

One may ask: What is to be achieved through State-to-State triggers that is not achieved through other triggers? Why should they exist? Arguments for their existence and added value are twofold. The main objective of State-to-State triggers is to give responsibility to States themselves to make sure that every party implements the treaty, and to reinforce norms as community interests. Many rules contained in MEAs are arguably obligations *erga omnes partes*, which can and should be implemented and complied with by all parties to the treaty. While compliance committees are tasked with monitoring States' compliance with such obligations, State-to-State triggers reflect States' primary role in their implementation and compliance. The existence of State-to-State triggers is also justified as it creates another means, alongside other types of triggers, to implement and ensure compliance with a multilateral treaty. Having multiple ways to access the compliance mechanism of a treaty is beneficial, as more actors can be involved in the compliance process.

As a result, this chapter explores the following question: What are the challenges and obstacles of State-to-State triggers that can explain their sparse use? Focussing on compliance committees for MEAs, we identify two types of challenges faced by State-to-State triggers: challenges related to the perception and behaviour of States *vis-à-vis* State-to-State triggers (Section 6.3) and challenges related to the institutional design and procedural mechanisms of State-to-State procedures (Section 6.4). While the methodology is doctrinal in essence, we also conducted interviews with three negotiators of the Paris Agreement, in order to better understand the process that led to the creation of the PAICC. We also refer to examples in the human rights context where relevant. Before delving into the challenges identified, we first explain how State-to-State triggers were established (Section 6.2.1) and describe the instances in which they have been used (Section 6.2.2).

6.2 Overview of State-to-State Compliance Procedures

In order to understand the challenges faced by State-to-State triggers, we first explain the negotiation process leading up to their creation and present the instances in which they have been employed.

6.2.1 *Establishment*

The inclusion of State-to-State triggers as a means to encourage compliance with MEAs has historically been a contentious matter. Indeed, there has long been an ideological conflict within the international community about the best approach to guarantee States' compliance with their international environmental obligations. The adversarial approach, on one hand, is typically where one State will 'sue' another for non-compliance in a confrontational manner. The State-to-State trigger is representative of this approach. The facilitative approach, on the other hand, involves 'non-confrontational means to persuade State parties into compliance, through technical and financial assistance, aid with reporting requirements, advice, technology transfers and capacity building'.[4]

Such tension is reflected in the negotiation processes to establish a number of MEAs. During negotiations on the compliance committee for the 1989 Basel Convention on the Control of Transboundary Movements of Hazardous Wastes and Their Disposal (Basel Convention), for instance, Australia argued that 'a right to raise the performance of other parties would not be consistent with the consultative, non-confrontational nature of the mechanism',[5] and that 'compliance should not be secured through threats or by creating a mechanism equipped with strong enforcement procedures'.[6] The draft decision from the *ad hoc* Legal Working Group that established the compliance mechanism was a matter of lengthy and heated debate,[7] resulting in a consensus that was not satisfactory to all States.[8] Similarly, provisions on the State-to-State trigger in MEAs such as the 1998 Rotterdam Convention on the Prior

[4] N Goeteyn and F Maes, 'Compliance Mechanisms in Multilateral Environmental Agreements: An Effective Way to Improve Compliance?' (2011) 10 *Chinese Journal of International Law* 36.

[5] Monitoring the Implementation of and Compliance with the Obligations set out by the Basel Convention, comment submitted by Australia, UNEP/CHW/LWG/2/3/Add.1, 2000.

[6] A Shibata, 'The Basel Compliance Mechanism' (2003) 12(2) *Review of European, Comparative & International Environmental Law* 183–98, 184, citing Draft Decision for the Sixth Meeting of the Conference of the Parties Establishing a Mechanism for the Basel Convention, Rome, 15–17 October 2001, available at www.basel.int/meetings/LWG/index.html.

[7] UNEP, Conference of the Parties to the Basel Convention on the Control of Transboundary Movements of Hazardous Wastes and Their Disposal, Geneva, 9–12 December 2002, Report of the Conference of the Parties to the Basel Convention on the Control of Transboundary Movements of Hazardous Wastes and Their Disposal, UNEP/CHW.6/40, para 57, available at www.basel.int/TheConvention/ConferenceoftheParties/Meetings/COP6/tabid/6149/Default.aspx.

[8] Ibid., para 65.

Informed Consent Procedure for Certain Hazardous Chemicals and Pesticides in International Trade (Rotterdam Convention) and the 2001 International Treaty on Plant and Genetic Resources were enclosed in square brackets during the drafting process 'as no agreement [had] been reached on this issue between the Parties'.[9]

The tension was particularly high in the context of the Paris Agreement. This was considered to be more 'more sensitive'[10] than other MEA negotiations due to the high political implications, the focus on the complex matter of climate change and a wide range of issues covered in the Agreement (such as mitigation, adaptation, finance, transparency and technical support). The mere inclusion of a compliance mechanism was difficult to negotiate in the first place, but certain States managed to convince the majority that the inclusion of a compliance committee would add value and guarantee accountability to the world.[11] However, reluctance remained regarding the acceptable ways to trigger such a committee. While many were initially willing to retain only a self-trigger,[12] a committee trigger was eventually added.[13] Unfortunately, State-to-State triggers were 'shut down immediately by some parties'.[14] Deemed 'impossible to include' and 'something parties would never agree

[9] Rotterdam Convention on the Prior Informed Consent Procedure for Certain Hazardous Chemicals and Pesticides in International Trade, signed 10 September 1998, entered into force 24 February 2004, 2244 UNTS 337, para 12(b). S Bugnatelli, 'The 1998 Rotterdam Convention on the Prior Informed Consent Procedure' in T Treves, L Pineschi, A Tanzi et al. (eds), *Non-Compliance Procedures and Mechanisms and the Effectiveness of International Environmental Agreements* (TMC Asser Press 2009) 93; L Crema, 'The 2001 International Treaty on Plant and Genetic Resources' in Treves et al. (eds.), *Non-Compliance Procedures* (n 9) 147.

[10] Participant 2, question 1.

[11] Participant 1, question 2: 'We insisted that this shouldn't be an ATM machine, where you say "I have problems, give me money" – it should add value in the context of the whole Paris Agreement'; 'Listen, when you go back home, you will have journalists, academia and students asking you this one question: "What happens if a state doesn't comply?" If we don't have this body, your answer will be extremely complicated! But with Article 15 of the Paris Agreement establishing a compliance committee, you will have a straightforward answer.'

[12] The committee trigger was successfully included after difficult negotiations in Katowice. Participant 1, question 1: 'The options were secretariat: that didn't work either; the Committee itself, which is what it is there in the text. And other triggers were not even considered, like NGOs. That was completely unacceptable for many.' Informal note, May 2017, 4: 'Other referrals would risk the Committee becoming politicized, adversarial, intrusive and redundant.'

[13] Participant 3 questions 3 and 4.

[14] Participant 3, question 1; participant 2, questions 2 and 3.

to', this proposal was abandoned by its negotiators in favour of other ideas that could be more readily accepted.[15]

Today, most MEAs contain many features that lean towards a facilitative rather than an adversarial approach. This facilitative approach is the essence of environmental compliance procedures, within which more adversarial State-to-State triggers can exist. While some may believe that an adversarial approach to non-compliance is more efficient, most opine that the facilitative approach characterising compliance procedures is 'better suited to promoting compliance' in this context, particularly as it is 'easier to sell to states'.[16] It can therefore be said that the facilitative approach is at the core of the existence of compliance procedures.[17] However, compromises have been reached in some MEAs to allow a State party preferring a more adversarial approach to seize the compliance committee against another State party if so desired. When featured, the State-to-State trigger has therefore found itself incorporated as a concession; a square peg in a round hole.

6.2.2 Practice

This context indicates why the facilitative approach has become the preference in the majority of MEAs. To date, only three compliance committees have been triggered for review by a State against another State: the Aarhus Compliance Committee (twice), the Espoo Implementation Committee (nine times) and the Kyoto Protocol Facilitative Branch (once).

The Aarhus Convention Compliance Committee saw its first State-to-State procedure in 2004 when Romania triggered a non-compliance procedure against Ukraine, in relation to the Bystre Canal project in

[15] Participant 2, question 2.

[16] D Bodansky, J Brunnée and L Rajamani, *International Climate Change Law* (Oxford University Press 2017) 68 ' . . . One might add that this "softer touch" on compliance has also been easier to sell to states than a harder-edged approach would have been.'; M Doelle, 'In Defence of the Paris Agreement's Compliance System: The Case for Facilitative Compliance' in B Mayer and A Zahar (eds), *Debating Climate Law* (Cambridge University Press 2021) 86–98; J von Stein, 'The International Law and Politics of Climate Change: Ratification of the United Nations Framework Convention and the Kyoto Protocol' (2008) 52(2) *Journal of Conflict Resolution* 243–44.

[17] J Klabbers, 'Compliance Procedures' in D Bodansky, J Brunnée and E Hey (eds), *The Oxford Handbook of International Environmental Law* (Oxford University Press 2007) 1004; A Chayes and AH Chayes, *The New Sovereignty: Compliance with International Regulatory Agreements* (Harvard University Press 1995).

the Danube Delta.[18] It alleged that the Ukrainian authorities had not complied with the obligations of public participation and had not let various local and international NGOs participate throughout the planning of the project. The second procedure triggered before the Aarhus Convention Compliance Committee was submitted by Lithuania against Belarus in 2015 with regard to the construction of a nuclear power plant in Belarus. Lithuania claimed that Belarus had denied the right to access detailed information of citizens to Lithuania during the preparatory and project implementation phases of the construction of the nuclear power plant.[19]

The Espoo Implementation Committee has seen nine procedures initiated by a State party against another, making it the most successful to date. They are all related to large projects with transnational effects, such as nuclear power plants, oil and gas projects, mining, hydropower plants or modifications to river waterways.[20] In these cases, the triggering parties argued that the transboundary environmental impact assessments were not carried out in accordance with the Espoo Convention.

Another interesting procedure was triggered before the Kyoto Protocol Facilitative Branch in 2006 by South Africa. In this case, South Africa made a submission, in its capacity as Chairman of the Group of 77 and China and on their behalf, about State parties' non-compliance with Article 3.1 of the Kyoto Protocol.[21] The alleged non-compliance concerned the submission of national progress reports, as several countries had not submitted theirs six months after the set deadline.

There is further evidence of a sparing use of State-to-State procedures even beyond MEAs. For instance, before the UN human rights treaty bodies, the first inter-State communications ever to be submitted both occurred in 2018 before the Committee on the Elimination of Racial

[18] Aarhus Convention's Compliance Committee, 'Findings and Recommendations with Regard to Compliance by Ukraine with the Obligations under the Aarhus Convention in the Case of Bystre Deep-water Navigation Canal Construction', Doc ECE/MP.PP/C.1/2005/2/Add.3, 18 February 2005 (14 March 2005), available at https://unece.org/DAM/env/documents/2005/pp/c.1/ece.mp.pp.c1.2005.2.Add.3.e.pdf.

[19] Ministry of Environment of Lithuania, 'Submission to the Compliance Committee by the Republic of Lithuania Requesting to Investigate the Compliance of the Republic of Belarus', 25 March 2015, available at https://unece.org/DAM/env/pp/compliance/S2015-02_Belarus/Submission/Submission_by_Lithuania_concerning_Belarus_27.03.2015.pdf.

[20] All submissions can be found at https://unece.org/submissions-overview.

[21] Submission by South Africa, CC-2006-1-1/FB, available at https://unfccc.int/files/kyoto_mechanisms/compliance/application/pdf/cc-2006-1-1-fb.pdf.

Discrimination (CERD).[22] The CERD dealt with an inter-State communication submitted by Qatar on 8 March 2018 against Saudi Arabia and the United Arab Emirates (UAE), and an inter-State communication submitted on 23 April 2018 by the State of Palestine against Israel.

There are several reasons that could explain the very sparing use of State-to-State triggers, despite their appearance in the guidelines or rules of procedure of all compliance committees. We identify two types of challenges: challenges related to the perception and behaviour of States vis-à-vis State-to-State triggers and challenges related to the institutional design and procedural mechanisms of State-to-State procedures.

6.3 Reluctance of States to Use Compliance Procedures

Although it is not within the scope of this chapter to empirically assess why States are reluctant to use State-to-State triggers, we identify two circumstances that may make State-to-State compliance procedures seem undesirable to States. First, State-to-State compliance procedures can be perceived as hostile mechanisms by States (Section 6.3.1). Second, States may lack the motivation to defend communal interests through State-to-State triggers (Section 6.3.2).

6.3.1 Hostile Perception of State-to-State Compliance Procedures

The principal reason States may be discouraged from using State-to-State procedures is the adversarial and hostile perception of those State-to-State triggers, as mentioned in Section 6.2.1. This hostile perception means that States may think that triggering a compliance procedure against another State may be perceived as an escalation of tensions in their diplomatic relations. This is because the process of one State complaining about another State before a third party (judicial, quasi-judicial or non-judicial) is perceived negatively in international relations. Indeed, while the judicial avenue is theoretically an equal alternative to other forms of peaceful dispute settlement provided in the UN Charter,[23] it tends to be a last resort in practice. Certain MEAs or international human rights conventions even provide that a court (most commonly, the International Court of Justice (ICJ)) may only be seized once negotiations

[22] OHCHR, 'Inter State Communications: Committee on the Elimination of Racial Discrimination', available at www.ohchr.org/en/treaty-bodies/cerd/inter-state-communications.

[23] See Article 33(1) UN Charter.

have been exhausted.[24] This indicates that States may turn to a third party when they are unable to communicate successfully between themselves, or, worse, when they have reached a political 'boiling point' or deadlock.[25] In the context of human rights compliance committees, notable examples include the Israeli–Palestinian dispute before the CERD as part of a decades-long historical conflict with deadlocked negotiations.[26] The other dispute before the same committee between Qatar and the UAE is also in the context of an important political conflict between these two countries which also made its way onto the ICJ's docket.[27]

Tensions that lead to the triggering of a State-to-State procedure escalate more easily between neighbouring countries. In addition to the two disputes between neighbouring countries before the CERD, all procedures before the Espoo Implementation Committee have involved neighbouring States, where projects have had clear transboundary effects. Obligations around transboundary environmental impact assessments lend themselves naturally towards a bilateral and adversarial conflict, as they are easily 'bilateralisable'. For instance, in 2019, Montenegro started a procedure against Albania regarding the ongoing build of a small hydropower plant on the Cijevna River, which is shared with Montenegro. It alleged that Albania had not considered the potential adverse impacts of the project on Montenegrin territory and people.[28] This is a clear case of a 'bilateralisable' and adversarial problem arising

[24] See, for example, Article 20 of the Basel Convention. In another instance, the ICJ declared the *Georgia v Russia* dispute inadmissible as Georgia had made no attempt at negotiations prior to *Case Concerning Application of the International Convention on the Elimination of All Forms of Racial Discrimination (Georgia v Russian Federation)*, Preliminary Objections, Judgment, 1 April 2011, para 182.

[25] For example, in *Obligation to Negotiate Access to the Pacific Ocean (Bolivia v Chile)*, Judgment, ICJ Reports 2018, 507.

[26] On 30 April 2021, the CERD declared Palestine's submission admissible. See 'Inter-State Communication Submitted by the State of Palestine against Israel: Decision on Admissibility', CERD/C/103/4, available at https://documents-dds-ny.un.org/doc/UNDOC/GEN/G21/150/90/PDF/G2115090.pdf?OpenElement.

[27] *Application of the International Convention on the Elimination of All Forms of Racial Discrimination (Qatar v United Arab Emirates)*, Preliminary Objections, ICJ Reports 2021.

[28] 'Submission by Montenegro having concerns about the Compliance of the Republic of Albania with Its Obligations under the Convention on Environmental Impact Assessment in a Transboundary Context: Espoo and the Protocol on Strategic Environmental Assessment (SEA) in Respect of the Activity of the Construction of the Small Hydropower Plants on the Cijevna River', 11 September 2019 (submission was received by the secretariat on 25 September 2019), available at https://unece.org/DAM/env/documents/2019/ece/IC/Submission/Albania/Submission_to_the_Implementation_Committee__Espoo_11._IX_2019.pdf.

within a multilateral treaty, where Montenegro is using similar rhetoric and seeking a similar outcome to what it would use, and seek, in a judicial procedure.

Any compliance arrangements in general may already be viewed as hostile, discouraging States from setting ambitious environmental targets or even joining the MEA altogether.[29] However, State-to-State triggers would naturally be seen as particularly undesirable. One participant recalled that 'parties are very reluctant to be pointed the finger at. They want to avoid that'.[30] This could, at least partly, be due to the disclosure of sensitive information or the attraction of potentially negative public opinion during proceedings.[31] It could also be due to costs associated with such proceedings where relevant. Another reason could be the risk of a 'boomerang effect', whereby the initiating State may be under closer scrutiny from the alleged non-complying State, who is looking for retaliation. The latter may become vindictive and look into whether the triggering State is also complying. Such a 'boomerang effect' could also take place with respect to another MEA, as there are chances that both States are parties to multiple treaties. States could even bring other issues beyond the scope of the MEA in question to the forefront. The committee would be 'open to misuse',[32] creating a space for political issues other than the compliance with the treaty in question. However, such risks can and will be mitigated by the committee itself, which will decide on its jurisdiction and the scope of its work. Unfortunately, this was not a sufficient guarantee in the negotiations of the PAICC, possibly because of the high political stakes under the Paris Agreement.

The hostile perception of State-to-State triggers could also explain why the dispute settlement mechanisms featured in MEAs are rarely used.[33] Indeed, a few MEAs feature a clause giving State parties the option to

29 Voigt (n 1) 162.

30 Participant 1, question 1.

31 State-to-State triggers are by default closed to the public: see Section 6.4.3. See also F Romanin Jacur, 'Triggering Non-Compliance Procedures' in Treves et al. (eds), *Non-Compliance Procedures* (n 9) 374.

32 Participant 3, question 1; Participant 1, question 3; Participant 2, question 3; Informal note May 2017 (n 2) 4; Draft Elements for APA Agenda Item 7: Modalities and Procedures for the Effective Operation of the Committee to Facilitate Implementation and Promote Compliance Referred to in Article 15.2 of the Paris Agreement, Informal note by the Co-facilitators, Final Version, 13 November 2017, 7.

33 Notable exceptions include cases brought before the ICJ regarding the Genocide Convention, the CERD and the Whaling Convention.

resort to the ICJ or possibly arbitration if a dispute arises about the interpretation, application of or compliance with the relevant convention.[34] Therefore, in theory, a State could resort directly to judicial bodies as opposed to non-compliance procedures on a matter of another State's non-compliance with their shared convention. These procedures are separate.[35] However, 'there appears to be widespread avoidance of resort to third-party dispute resolution'.[36] This may in part be due to the fact that most non-compliance is due to capacity issues as opposed to the legal interpretation of a provision in an MEA.[37] It is however mainly due to the confrontational nature of dispute settlement, requiring the existence of a dispute where States 'hold clearly opposite views concerning the question of the performance or non-performance of certain international obligations',[38] with one party's claim being 'positively opposed' by the other.[39] It is also likely due to the binding nature of dispute resolution procedures, disliked by States who prefer more flexibility with regard to their environmental commitments.[40]

[34] See, for example, Basel Convention Article 20; Rotterdam Convention Article 20; Stockholm Convention on Persistent Organic Pollutants, signed 22 May 2001, entered into force 17 May 2004, 2256 UNTS 119, Article 18.

[35] See, for example, Cartagena Protocol on Biosafety to the Convention on Biological Diversity, signed 29 January 2000, entered into force 11 September 2003, 2226 UNTS 208, Article 34.

[36] U Beyerlin, P-T Stoll and R Wolfrum, 'Conclusions Drawn from the Conference on Ensuring Compliance with MEAs' in U Beyerlin, P-T Stoll and R Wolfrum (eds), *Ensuring Compliance with Multilateral Environmental Agreements: A Dialogue between Practitioners and Academia* (Brill 2006) 369.

[37] Goeteyn and Maes (n 4) 37–38, para 43.

[38] *Application of the Convention on the Prevention and Punishment of the Crime of Genocide (The Gambia v Myanmar)*, Provisional Measures, Order of 23 January 2020, ICJ Reports 2020, 10, para 20; *Application of the International Convention for the Suppression of the Financing of Terrorism and of the International Convention on the Elimination of All Forms of Racial Discrimination (Ukraine v Russian Federation)*, Provisional Measures, Order of 19 April 2017, ICJ Reports 2017, 115, para 22; *Interpretation of Peace Treaties with Bulgaria, Hungary and Romania*, First Phase, Advisory Opinion, ICJ Reports 1950, 74.

[39] *Application (The Gambia v Myanmar)* (n 37); *South West Africa (Ethiopia v South Africa; Liberia v South Africa)*, Preliminary Objections, Judgment, ICJ Reports 1962, 328.

[40] United Nations Environmental Programme (UNEP), *Compliance Mechanism under Selected Multilateral Environmental Agreements*, available at https://wedocs.unep.org/bitstream/handle/20.500.11822/7507/-Compliance%20Mechanisms%20under%20selected%20Multilateral%20Environmental%20Agreements-2007761.pdf?sequence=3&amp%3BisAllowed=, 119.

6.3.2 *Lack of Motive to Defend Communal Interests*

Many of the obligations contained in MEAs are arguably obligations *erga omnes partes*. This means that a State party owes such obligations towards all the other States parties to the same treaty, due to the treaty's protection of collective interests. Therefore, all State parties have their own interests on the one hand and communal interests on the other hand.[41] By ratifying those treaties, they have agreed that the protection of environmental rights is worth joint efforts. The pursuit of this 'common good', however, does not seem to have inspired many States to date. They may lack motivation to pursue such proceedings due to both the absence of perceived personal gain and the novelty of the practice itself. Indeed, from a jurisdictional perspective, States have a legal interest in safeguarding community interests before a judicial body or a compliance committee, if such obligations are *erga omnes partes*. However, international jurisprudence has recently distinguished between specially affected States – directly and tangibly impacted by the breach of an obligation – and non-specially affected States that may be concerned about ensuring respect for the *erga omnes partes* obligation but are not directly and tangibly impacted by its breach.[42] While States occasionally demonstrate altruism in international relations,[43] they may generally hesitate to start a procedure against another State if they are not specially affected by the breach in question. This may particularly be the case as the practice is quite novel.

As much as this can explain some of the reasons States are reluctant to use State-to-State compliance procedures, it does not make such procedures redundant. Contrary to the common perception that State-to-State proceedings are hostile, it can be argued that they were designed to allow for collegial co-operation and solidarity between States. Indeed, a State-to-State compliance procedure is communal in nature.[44] Even if the

41 A Fodella, 'Structural and Institutional Aspects of Non-Compliance Mechanisms' in Treves et al. (eds), *Non-Compliance Procedures* (n 9) 366; Romanin Jacur (n 31) 376; L Pineschi, 'Non-Compliance Procedures and the Law of State Responsibility', in Treves et al. (eds), *Non-Compliance Procedures* (n 9) 494; T Treves, 'The Settlement of Disputes and Non-Compliance Procedures', in Treves et al. (eds), *Non-Compliance Procedures* (n 9) 513–14.

42 *Application (The Gambia v Myanmar)* (n 38) paras 41–42.

43 J Rudall, *Altruism in International Law* (Cambridge University Press 2021).

44 U Fastenrath, D E Khan, R Geiger, A Paulus and S von Schorlemer (eds), *From Bilateralism to Community Interest: Essays in Honour of Bruno Simma* (Oxford University Press 2011).

procedure itself opposes two parties, the purpose of the procedure has a larger communal objective. In this sense, it is possible to view such procedures not as hostile, but as co-operative, aspiring towards a 'common good'.

On one hand, there are many instances where the initiating State is specially affected by another State's non-compliance, and therefore communal obligations can be 'bilateralisable' such as the case of the Espoo Convention on Transboundary Environmental Impact Assessments. On the other hand, there are instances where a State can be non-specially affected by another State's non-compliance with communal obligations, such as in the case of the Kyoto Protocol. In both types of cases, a shift in States' understanding of State-to-State procedures may be used as is necessary: individual adversarial procedures can be conducted for the defence of community interests. Although the more bilateral nature of a State-to-State procedure may be at odds, from the perspective of State parties, with the communal spirit of the treaties under review, they are not incompatible.

6.4 Procedural and Institutional Challenges

Since State-to-State compliance procedures are adversarial in nature, opposing two States, the type of procedural rules applicable become central to the conduct of such procedures. Certain well-established procedural principles developed in the judicial context become essential to the State-to-State compliance procedure, such as questions of jurisdiction (Section 6.4.1), evidence (Section 6.4.2), expertise (Section 6.4.3), independence and impartiality (Section 6.4.4), participation and transparency (Section 6.4.5) and outcomes (Section 6.4.6). This section will argue that the design and practice surrounding these identified procedural and institutional features of State-to-State triggers can contribute to their scarce use by States.

6.4.1 Jurisdiction

Questions such as when a compliance committee should pursue a State-to-State procedure are worth exploring, as they show that it is not only States that can be the reason why State-to-State procedures do not proliferate, but it is also committees themselves that can prevent procedures from being heard. This means that even when State-to-State triggers are initiated, the process can be impeded by a hesitant committee.

The case submitted by South Africa to the Kyoto Protocol Facilitative Branch – one of the two branches of the Protocol's compliance committee – shows that the committees themselves may not be as familiar as expected in dealing with State-to-State compliance procedures. Potential reasons for this may be that they have so little prior experience. In this case, as soon as the submission was not exactly in line with the set procedures, the committee decided to end the procedure altogether.

As mentioned, the submission by South Africa was made, on behalf of the Group of 77 and China, against various parties for failure to communicate national reports. The Facilitative Branch dismissed the submission on procedural grounds. Indeed, two questions needed to be answered: Can a party submit on behalf of a group, and can a party submit against multiple other parties? These questions were not answered clearly in the Branch's rules of procedures. Therefore, the committee decided the procedure could not continue. In only two instances, concerning Slovenia and Latvia, the Branch closed the procedure, as these two countries had in the meantime complied with their obligations, making the compliance procedure redundant.[45]

The fact that the Branch did not engage with the merits of the claim brought by South Africa shows a strict application of the rules of procedures, despite there being easily justifiable grounds to continue the procedure. Indeed, the committee decided that South Africa did not name the States against which it was making its submission, but South Africa stated clearly that those States who were six months late in submitting their reports were the object of the submission, and sent the submission to the relevant fifteen States. Therefore, despite the fact that it did not clearly name the parties against which it was initiating the procedure, it was in fact clear who it was aimed at. This level of respect for the procedural rules may be seen as contrary to the Kyoto Protocol's objective to, *inter alia*, '[c]ooperate with other . . . Parties to enhance the individual and combined effectiveness of their policies and measures'.[46] The decision shows great commitment to the wording of the rule, which could be explained by a lack of confidence on the part of the committee in its own 'jurisdiction' to rule on such matters. It also shows an

[45] Goeteyn and Maes (n 4) 33.

[46] Article 2(1)(b) Kyoto Protocol to the United Nations Framework Convention on Climate Change, signed 11 December 1997, entered into force 16 February 2005, 2303 UNTS 162. See also Article 18.

unwillingness on the part of the committee to take matters into its own hands. An explanation for this behaviour may be that the committee does not have a traditionally 'judicial' mandate as do international courts and tribunals, and may have hesitated to take action without such traditionally understood 'judicial' legitimacy. This may contribute to an unclear institutional framework for the use of State-to-State procedures.

6.4.2 *Evidence*

Another procedural hurdle contributing to the scarce use of State-to-State triggers is the requirements for and handling of evidence during a State-to-State procedure. State-to-State triggers in MEAs allow for a State party to seize another State party before the compliance committee on the grounds of concern alone. In the 1972 London Convention on the Prevention of Marine Pollution by Dumping of Wastes and Other Matter the party must have an interest where it is affected or likely to be affected.[47] In the 2000 Cartagena Protocol on Biosafety and in the Rotterdam Convention it must be '*directly* affected or likely to be *directly* affected'.[48] The Basel Convention Compliance Mechanism is the most demanding in this respect, requiring a specific, bilateral relationship between the two parties involved in order to be triggered.[49] In all other MEAs, however, State parties may trigger this procedure without having to prove involvement or interest.[50] The benefit of this is that it facilitates the ability for States to easily trigger the procedure.

However, non-specially affected States may have more difficulty obtaining evidence that a certain State has violated an obligation in their shared convention. Indeed, States are still required to provide evidence of their claim in the form of an informational report. However, there are two obstacles to fulfilling this requirement.

[47] LC 39/16/Add.1 Annex 5, para. 4.1.3, available at https://wwwcdn.imo.org/localresources/en/OurWork/Environment/Documents/Revised%202017%20CPM.pdf.

[48] Cartagena Protocol, available at https://bch.cbd.int/protocol/cpb_art34_cc.shtml; Rotterdam Convention, Article 12(b) (emphasis added).

[49] A Fodella, 'Mechanism for Promoting Implementation and Compliance with the 1989 Basel Convention on the Transboundary Movements of Hazardous Wastes and their Disposal' in Treves et al. (eds), *Non-Compliance Procedures* (n 9) 40; A Shibata, 'Ensuring Compliance with the Basel Convention: Its Unique Features' in Beyerlin et al. (eds), *Conclusions* (n 36) 81.

[50] VI.1(b) Kyoto Protocol; Montreal Protocol; LRTAP; Kyoto Protocol; Aarhus Convention; Espoo Convention; Water Protocol para 12(b); Rotterdam Convention.

First, it is perhaps difficult to imagine how a State would substantiate its claims in such a report if it were not directly affected. It is easier to substantiate claims and provide information for a matter that is of direct relevance to a State, as more information about the effects of the non-compliance is in the country itself. This closely mirrors traditional judicial inter-State disputes before international courts and tribunals.

Second, it is generally difficult for State parties to be aware of the level of compliance of other States. This would not be as much of a problem before international courts and tribunals because, at the ICJ for instance, proceedings involving *erga omnes partes* obligations have tended to be high-profile cases where evidence has already been collected by UN fact-finding missions or media outlets.[51] Therefore, even if the effects of the violation could not be measured on the State's territory, it could still obtain enough evidence to support its claim.[52] States' compliance with MEAs, however, does not garner the same level of publicity.

It is therefore more difficult for States who are not directly affected to corroborate their claims before compliance committees. This could explain why, in practice, only specially affected States have resorted to State-to-State triggers to date.[53] Regarding the attempt made by South Africa before the Kyoto Protocol Facilitative Branch, its submission was also rejected because it 'was not supported by corroborating information and did not substantiate how the question related to any of the specific commitments of the relevant parties under the Protocol'.[54]

6.4.3 *Expertise of Members of Compliance Committees*

State-to-State procedures would also benefit from clearer rules surrounding the appointment and expertise of compliance committee members, if

[51] For example, in *Armed Activities on the Territory of the Congo (Democratic Republic of the Congo v Uganda)*; *Application of the Convention on the Prevention and Punishment of the Crime of Genocide (Bosnia and Herzegovina v Serbia and Montenegro).*

[52] *Application (The Gambia v Myanmar)* (n 38) paras 71–72.

[53] For example, Aarhus Convention Decision *Romania v Ukraine*, available at https://unece.org/DAM/env/documents/2005/pp/c.1/ece.mp.pp.c1.2005.2.Add.3.e.pdf; Aarhus Convention Decision *Lithuania v Belarus*, available at https://unece.org/env/pp/cc/accc.s.2015.2_belarus.

[54] S Oberthür and R Lefeber, 'Holding Countries to Account: The Kyoto Protocol's Compliance System Revisited after Four Years of Experience' (2010) 1 *Climate Law* 138–39; *Report of the Compliance Committee on the Deliberations in the Facilitative Branch Relating to the Submission*, FCCC/KP/CMP/2006/6, 22 September 2006, available at http://unfccc.int/kyotoprotocol/compliance/plenary/items/3788.php.

their use is to be enhanced. The range of expertise needed in order to be able to sit on a compliance committee is a point of contention, as the technical nature of a compliance committee may require non-legal skills, yet legal knowledge is essential to make adequate decisions. In order to make a decision on compliance, compliance committees need to rely on both legal and scientific or technical knowledge. This is often reflected in the rules, which might say for example that members 'shall have expertise relating to the subject matter of the Convention in areas including scientific, technical, socio-economic and/or legal fields', in the case of the Basel Convention Implementation and Compliance Committee.[55] Similar language is used for the PAICC.[56] This is an advantage that compliance committees may have over international courts, as the latter are often criticised for their lack of ability to handle scientific evidence.[57] One of the challenges of international adjudication, especially in an environmental context, is how judges handle complex facts, especially when they involve complex science, and how that affects their decision-making.[58]

However, it is not always clear whether the requirements concerning the legal and/or scientific skills of the committee members are fulfilled in practice. Before the Montreal Protocol Implementation Committee, member States of the Montreal Protocol appoint their representatives. This means there is no requirement to co-ordinate between member States, and therefore no guarantee that the committee itself will be composed of individuals with balanced and complementary expertise.[59] Even in the human rights context, the CERD stated explicitly in the *Qatar v Saudi Arabia* case that it initially could not take any decisions

[55] Sixth Meeting of the Conference of Parties to the Basel Convention, Decision VI/12, Terms of Reference, UNEP/CHW.6/40, para 5. Available at www.basel.int/Portals/4/Basel%20Convention/docs/meetings/cop/cop6/english/Report40e.pdf#page=45.

[56] ' . . . members with recognized competence in relevant scientific, technical, socioeconomic or legal fields'. Decision 20/CMA.1, FCCC/PA/CMA/2018/3/Add.2, para 5. Available at https://unfccc.int/sites/default/files/resource/cma2018_3_add2_new_advance.pdf.

[57] MM Mbengue, 'International Courts and Tribunals as Fact-Finders: The Case of Scientific Fact-Finding in International Adjudication' (2011) 34 *Loyola of Los Angeles International and Comparative Law Review* 53.

[58] K Sulyok, *Science and Judicial Reasoning: The Legitimacy of International Environmental Adjudication* (Cambridge University Press 2021); C Foster, *Science and the Precautionary Principle in International Courts and Tribunals* (Cambridge University Press 2011).

[59] F Romanin Jacur, 'The Non-Compliance Procedure of the 1987 Montreal Protocol to the 1985 Vienna Convention on Substances That Deplete the Ozone Layer' in Treves et al. (eds), *Non-Compliance Procedures* (n 9) 17.

due to 'the legal complexity of the issues broached and a lack of resources'.[60]

6.4.4 *Impartiality and Independence of Members of the Compliance Committees*

Another difficulty in relation to the members of the compliance committees contributing to the limited use of State-to-State triggers relates to their impartiality and independence. An important procedural safeguard that ensures a fair procedure is to separate the relationship between the individual members and the State(s) of which they are citizens. Guaranteeing that the members are not influenced or manipulated by outside forces, especially by potential parties to a compliance procedure, is a key element to achieving a fair outcome. It is a well-established rule in the judicial context and has also been integrated into the provisions and rules governing most compliance committees.[61] The reason why the two notions of impartiality and independence are especially important in State-to-State compliance procedures is that the role of the compliance committee is more akin to that of an arbiter between two parties in such a procedure. This role requires the committees to show fairness and equality in the process, and this is ensured, *inter alia*, by having impartial and independent members.

In order to ensure independence, a lot of compliance committees require that their members act in their personal capacities, and not as representatives of their member States.[62] Indeed, once they have been elected, often according to rules of geographical and/or gender representation, they need to be able to decide in their own name, separately from the States that nominated them. An example of how to operationalise the concept of impartiality can be seen in the context of the PAICC, where '[m]embers and alternate members shall perform any duties and exercise any authority in an honourable, independent, impartial and

[60] OHCHR (n 22); OHCHR, 'Committee on the Elimination of Racial Discrimination Concludes its Ninety-Eighth Session' (10 May 2019), available at www.ohchr.org/EN/NewsEvents/Pages/DisplayNews.aspx?NewsID=24601&LangID=E.

[61] R Mackenzie and P Sands, 'International Courts and Tribunals and the Independence of the International Judge' (2003) 44 *Harvard International Law Journal* 271; D Shelton, 'Form, Function, and the Powers of International Courts' (2009) 9 *Chinese Journal of International Law* 537, 545.

[62] A few examples can be found in the Cartagena Protocol (2000), the Aarhus Convention (1998), the Paris Agreement (2015) and the Rotterdam Convention (1998).

conscientious manner',[63] and they have to confirm in writing that they will do so at the beginning of their mandate.[64] They also have to 'disclose immediately any interest in any matter under discussion before the Committee that may constitute a real or apparent, personal or financial conflict of interest or that might be incompatible with the objectivity, independence and impartiality expected of a member', which then prevents them from being involved in matters related to the issues they disclosed.[65]

However, not all compliance committees are structured in the same way, and some important committees still have their members sit as representatives of parties, such as the Montreal Protocol and CITES.[66] When rules on impartiality and independence are not as clear, it can negatively affect the functioning of the committee. For instance, issues may arise when a member of the committee has a duty, as a civil servant, to relay information to its State.[67] This can impact the procedures and decision-making processes of the committee, as States before the committee may not feel free to share all necessary information for the committee to decide in the best possible way.

These guarantees of impartiality and independence may not be as essential in other roles performed by the compliance committees, especially as facilitators in compliance processes. However, when they act as arbiters in adversarial procedures, these guarantees are necessary and when they are lacking, this seriously undermines the State-to-State compliance procedures.

6.4.5 *Participation and Transparency*

Another procedural challenge in State-to-State procedures is the transparency of proceedings from the moment a State triggers the procedure against another State. While the State whose compliance is being called into question fully partakes in the proceedings and has the right to be

[63] Decision 24/CMA.3, Annex, 'Rules of Procedure of the Committee to Facilitate Implementation and Promote Compliance Referred to in Article 15, paragraph 2, of the Paris Agreement', FCCC/PA/CMA/2021/10/Add.3, Rule 3.3, para 1.

[64] Ibid., para 3.

[65] Ibid.

[66] Montreal Protocol MOP Decision X/10, Annex II: 'Non-Compliance Procedure (1998): Tenth Meeting of the Parties'; CITES Resolution Conf 18.2 Establishment of Committees, available at https://cites.org/sites/default/files/document/E-Res-18-02.pdf.

[67] Participant 2, question 4.

heard, the same cannot systematically be said for the State who initiated the procedure. Typically, the latter State will be excluded from the procedure going forward and will have no opportunity to take stock of matters with which it was initially concerned. In fact, meetings between the compliance committee and the party whose compliance is in question are closed to the public.[68] This is possibly favourable towards the party in question who can avoid public scrutiny, potential embarrassment and the divulging of sensitive information. However, it does an injustice to the State triggering the procedure who has expressed concern.

This is particularly so in instances whereby the State triggering the procedure is required to be affected or have an interest of some sort. For instance, regarding the 2001 Stockholm Convention on Persistent Organic Pollutants, one author has observed a contradiction between the fact that a party must be particularly affected in order to trigger the procedure – reflective of a more 'traditional, bilateral, state-to-state dispute approach' – but cannot participate in the consequent proceedings.[69] Similarly, transparency before the Basel Convention has been described as 'remarkably poor as far as … the Party triggering the mechanism [is] concerned'.[70]

Before international courts and tribunals, State litigants are given equal rights of participation. Third States making requests for intervention are likewise fully integrated in written and oral proceedings if their request is granted.[71] Transparency is also an important feature of proceedings before international courts and tribunals. Before the ICJ, for example, written parties' submissions may be made public on or after oral proceedings with the parties' consent,[72] while oral hearings are made open to the public[73] and streamed live online.[74] At the International Tribunal for the Law of the Sea (ITLOS), written pleadings of the parties are publicly accessible even before oral pleadings commence.[75] The World Trade Organization (WTO) Dispute Settlement Mechanism's contrasting practices (confidential submissions by parties and closed oral hearings) have

68 See for example, the Stockholm Convention, Terms of Reference para 16.

69 Fodella (n 49) 40.

70 Ibid., 40.

71 Articles 62 and 63 ICJ Statute.

72 Rules of the Court, 14 April 1978, entered into force 1 July 1978, Article 53(2).

73 Unless the Court or both parties decide otherwise. See Article 46, ICJ Statute; Article 59, Rules of the Court.

74 They are streamed on UN Web TV, available at http://webtv.un.org/.

75 Rule 67(2) ITLOS Rules of Procedure.

been widely criticised, demonstrating the increasing importance that transparency yields in international law.[76] Generally, participation and transparency have become increasingly significant in international judicial processes.

Greater transparency and participation are certainly imaginable before non-compliance procedures,[77] without jeopardising their facilitative spirit. In the case of the 1987 Montreal Protocol on Substances That Deplete the Ozone Layer, for example, '[a]lthough [it] is based on facilitative and amicable principles, it also envisages principles of due process, such as notification, right to a fair hearing and impartiality, which are usually found in traditional dispute settlement mechanisms'.[78]

6.4.6 *Outcomes of State-to-State Compliance Procedures*

The lack of clarity in the outcome that States can get from triggering such procedures may further discourage their use. Indeed, the political cost of triggering a compliance procedure may not justify such an uncertain outcome. The question States may ask is: What can they get out of a State-to-State compliance procedure? The answer to this question is twofold and can partly explain why State-to-State compliance procedures have not been popular so far.

First, the fact that the decisions are not final and binding renders the overall effect of the decisions weaker. Indeed, the decisions taken by compliance committees 'generally do not possess any legally binding force. Even if a non-compliance procedure results in giving an appropriate response to non-compliance, such a response would still be of only a preliminary nature, because it is up to the Conference of the Parties to take a final decision'.[79] The decisions taken by compliance committees

[76] S Charnovitz, 'Transparency and Participation in the World Trade Organization' (2004) 56 *Rutgers Law Review* 927; G Villalta Puig and B Al-Haddab, 'The Transparency Deficit of Dispute Settlement in the World Trade Organization' (2011) 8 *Manchester Journal International Economic Law* 2; G Marceau and M Hurley, 'Transparency and Public Participation: A Report Card on WTO Transparency Mechanisms' (2012) IV(1) *Trade, Law and Development*; L Wallach, 'Transparency in WTO Dispute Resolution' (1999-2000) 31 *Law & Policy International Business* 773; see also A Bianchi and A Peters (eds), *Transparency in International Law* (Cambridge University Press 2013) 4.

[77] G Handl, 'Compliance Control Mechanisms and International Environmental Obligations' (1997) 5 *Tulane Journal of International and Comparative Law* 29–49, 42–43.

[78] Romanin Jacur (n 59) 21.

[79] Beyerlin, Stoll and Wolfrum (n 36) 369.

are mostly endorsed by the Conference of the Parties – the governing body of the treaty – but theoretically the latter could depart from the initial decisions, or only adopt a part of them. In many instances, the compliance committee can take some decisions that are facilitative in nature, but when more punitive measures have to be taken, or those with financial consequences, the Conference of the Parties is the body that will take this type of decision.[80] This is contrary to judicial decisions rendered by international courts and tribunals, which are binding and final.

Second, the range of options available to compliance committees is also uncertain, rendering the outcome less predictable. Some measures that can be decided upon by compliance committees may also not necessarily suit a State-to-State compliance procedure. Facilitative measures include providing advice and information about how to facilitate compliance and requesting special reporting or action plans from the non-complying party. These may not be the desired outcome of a State-to-State compliance procedure.

Some potential outcomes could be more suitable from the perspective of a State triggering a non-compliance procedure, such as a declaration of non-compliance or a suspension of specific rights under the treaty. For instance, in the case between Lithuania and Belarus concerning Belarus' non-compliance with the Aarhus Convention, the Committee was able to conclude that Belarus had 'failed to comply' with a number of provisions of the Convention[81] and therefore recommended that 'the Party concerned takes the necessary legislative, regulatory and administrative measures and establishes practical arrangements'.[82] This type of decision raises a number of questions pertaining to the law of State responsibility and the law of treaties, which have been the object of debate.[83] The lack

80 This separation exists for instance in the Basel Convention (1989), the Cartagena Protocol (2000), CITES (1973) and the Nagoya Protocol (2010). For a detailed list, see the overview provided by the Compliance Committee under the Cartagena Protocol on Biosafety, UNEP/CBD/BS/CC/13/INF/2, Annex I, 22 January 2016, 29–35.

81 'Findings and Recommendations with Regard to Submission ACCC/S/2015/2 Concerning Compliance by Belarus', para 161. Available at https://unece.org/sites/default/files/2021-07/S2_Belarus_findings_advance_unedited.pdf.

82 Ibid., para 162.

83 See for instance, M Fitzmaurice and C Redgwell, 'Environmental Non-Compliance Procedures and International Law' (2000) 31 *Netherlands Yearbook of International Law* 52–62; M Koskenniemi, 'Breach of Treaty or Non-Compliance? Reflections on the Enforcement of the Montreal Protocol' (1992) 3(1) *Yearbook of International Environmental Law* 123–62.

of clarity on these points may contribute to a misunderstanding of the role of State-to-State compliance procedures.

In sum, it is not the case that compliance committees do not have the means to address State-to-State requests, as shown in the Aarhus Committee decision regarding Belarus' compliance, but their role encompassing a broad range of actions may deter States from triggering them. Moreover, the frameworks within which compliance committees operate may prevent the latter from being more assertive in their decision-making, since they can only make recommendations that have to be adopted by the Conference of the Parties, which is constituted of States parties to the treaty in question. In other words, compliance committees may not have the tools necessary to make bolder decisions, as their overarching aim is still only facilitative – even in a more adversarial procedure – and their decisions are not final.

6.5 Conclusion

This chapter has sought to shed light on the reasons why State-to-State triggers are seldom used by State parties to MEAs. The reluctance of States is due firstly to the hostile perception of State-to-State compliance procedures and States' lack of motivation to defend communal interests in the environmental context. A number of procedural and institutional challenges were additionally identified, such as issues with jurisdiction, evidence, participation, impartiality and independence, the expertise of such compliance committees, and the outcomes of proceedings.

The chapter observed that, regarding procedural and institutional challenges, international courts and tribunals have more rigorous and effective practices than compliance committees. Not only do international courts and tribunals perform better in many of these respects, but their decisions generate a higher level of authority in the international legal system.[84] Therefore, a combination of the efficient procedural practices of international courts and tribunals and their authority make them a more suitable venue for States to take environmental disputes. This can partly explain why there is an undeniable increase in

[84] F Zarbiyev, 'Saying Credibly What the Law Is: On Marks of Authority in International Law' (2018) 9(2) *Journal of International Dispute Settlement* 291–314; AV Huneeus, 'Compliance with International Court Judgments and Decisions' in KJ Alter, C Romano and Y Shany (eds), *Oxford Handbook of International Adjudication* (2013) 437–63.

inter-State environmental disputes before international courts and tribunals.[85]

In an international legal system abundant with choices to keep States accountable to their obligations, compliance committees complement international courts and tribunals: compliance procedures provide a soft way to advise, encourage and influence States to comply with their obligations through assistance, aid and capacity building.[86] They are also helpful where State responsibility is difficult to establish in the environmental context. As Klabbers stated, 'there is ... often no real wrongfulness at issue – causality between behaviour and environmental degradation is frequently difficult to establish with the degree of precision that the law would insist on'.[87] Judicial procedures, on the other hand, through binding judgments, force States into compliance where State responsibility for environmental degradation can be established. Non-compliance procedures may also be viewed as instruments of 'political rationality' or a 'symbolic exercise' attempting to demonstrate effort to address an issue, while judicial enforcement embodies an 'instrumental rationality' attempting to achieve a desired result.[88] Both may be used concurrently[89] and both, in different yet complementary ways, push States to respect their international environmental obligations.

Where, in the midst of this, does this leave State-to-State triggers? They have certain judicial or quasi-judicial features, but the procedures they trigger under MEAs will take place before compliance committees rather than in international courts or tribunals. They are also part of a menu of other triggers designed to be facilitative and to provide support

[85] For example, Obligations of States in respect of climate change (Request for an Advisory Opinion), ICJ, Order of 20 April 2023; Request for an Advisory Opinion submitted by the Commission of Small Island States on Climate Change and International Law (Request for Advisory Opinion submitted to the Tribunal), ITLOS, 12 December 2022; *Certain Activities varied out by Nicaragua in the Border Area (Costa Rica v Nicaragua)*, Compensation, Judgment, ICJ Reports 2018, 15; *Dispute Concerning Delimitation of the Maritime Boundary between Ghana and Côte d'Ivoire in the Atlantic Ocean* (Ghana/Côte d'Ivoire), Provisional Measures, Order of 25 April 2015, ITLOS Reports 2015, 146 (on the marine environment).

[86] Goeteyn and Maes (n 4) 36.

[87] Klabbers (n 16) 1001. See more generally, M Bowman and A Boyle (eds), *Environmental Damage in International and Comparative Law: Problems of Definition and Valuation* (Oxford University Press 2002).

[88] Klabbers (n 17) 1005.

[89] P Sands, 'Non Compliance and Dispute Settlement' in U Beyerlin, P-T Stoll and R Wolfrum (eds), *Ensuring Compliance with Multilateral Environmental Agreements: A Dialogue between Practitioners and Academia* (Brill 2006) 353–58.

for capacity issues impeding States' compliance with MEAs – but are perceived to be more confrontational as opposed to facilitative in their nature. State-to-State triggers therefore sit in between judicial and non-judicial procedures, and between facilitation on one hand and enforcement on the other.

There is, however, room for State-to-State triggers to evolve out of this supposed identity crisis. This could involve mirroring judicial procedures to align more with the practices of international courts and tribunals. This may not be appealing to States but would give more teeth to environmental obligations. Especially in light of current global environmental crises, we believe that this direction is the most desirable for the future of our planet.

7

Compliance with Science-Based Treaties

RUKMINI DAS

7.1 Introduction

International law, from its very origins, has developed without a central authority. Consequently, mechanisms for settling disputes or for ensuring compliance with international treaties have not been uniform or even coordinated. There is a wide array of courts and tribunals for judicial settlement of international disputes. There are also multiple non-judicial mechanisms to address treaty breaches or non-compliance, to interpret treaty provisions, or for dispute prevention. Judicial dispute settlement is thus not the only means of ensuring adherence to treaty provisions.

International legal agreements in recent times, especially those on various environmental or other technical or scientifically complex subject matters, envisage mechanisms for facilitating, promoting, and enforcing compliance with the commitments undertaken by the parties to these treaties.[1] Such mechanisms for assessing the compliance of parties with their obligations under that treaty have been referred to as non-compliance mechanisms (NCMs). Such NCMs are usually non-confrontational. As such they are markedly different from judicial dispute settlement, which is adversarial or confrontational by its very nature. For this reason, these NCMs may provide innovative alternatives to traditional dispute resolution procedures.[2]

[1] See, e.g., Convention on International Trade in Endangered Species of Wild Fauna and Flora, signed 3 March 1973, entered into force 1 July 1975, 1453 UNTS 243 (CITES); Convention on Biological Diversity, signed 5 June 1992, 1760 UNTS 79; Cartagena Protocol on Biosafety to the Convention on Biological Diversity, signed 29 January 2000, entered into force 11 September 2003, 2226 UNTS 208; United Nations Framework Convention on Climate Change 1992, signed 9 May 1992, entered into force 21 March 1994, 1771 UNTS 107; Kyoto Protocol to the United Nations Framework Convention on Climate Change, signed 11 December 1997, entered into force 16 February 2005, 2303 UNTS 162.

[2] Y Lador, 'Access to Justice and Public Participation in the Water Sector: A Promising Legal Development' in M Tignino and K Sangbana (eds), *Public Participation and Water*

Another kind of treaty body often seen in international instruments of this nature is the Scientific Committee. Scientific committees have varying names under different treaty regimes.[3] This kind of committee, often with an advisory role, exists in treaty regimes related to, for example, environment and health, where scientific research is critically important to establishing agreed procedures and for effectively administering the treaty regime. Though not specifically established for the purposes of bringing about treaty compliance, these committees may make pronouncements that assist States to implement provisions of treaties or ascertain whether treaty obligations have been violated. This has the potential to go beyond mere application of treaty provisions, leading to the interpretation of certain (usually scientific) aspects of the treaty, thus overlapping to an extent with the powers of international courts or tribunals (ICTs) or avoiding recourse to them by pre-empting a dispute. The work of such committees and their impact is also examined in this chapter, along with NCMs and ICTs.

The focus on 'science-based' treaties in this chapter stems from the unique nature of the compliance issues that may arise in the context of treaties that govern complex technical or scientific subject matters. In the context of compliance with treaty obligations, a single treaty might provide for an NCM, provide for recourse to an ICT as a dispute settlement forum, and might also have a scientific committee whose role may involve indirectly interpreting treaty provisions. This chapter therefore analyses the various institutional contributions towards implementation and compliance of science-based treaties made through NCMs, other treaty bodies including scientific committees and dispute resolution before an ICT. The focus is on how best to address potential or actual treaty breaches, and the possible interactions among these different bodies.

Considering the evidently disparate natures of these processes – NCMs, the activities of scientific committees, and ICT dispute settlement – concerns exist with respect to the selection of members serving on the relevant bodies, their qualifications, expertise, and independence. Some of these concerns may arise out of a perception that scientific committees of a treaty would tend to be biased in favour of conservation

Resources Management: Where Do We Stand in International Law? International Conference, Geneva 13 December 2013 Proceedings (UNESCO 2015) 147–53, 150.

3 These include the Scientific Committee of the International Whaling Commission (IWC) and the Commission on Conservation of Southern Bluefin Tuna (CCSBT). See Section 7.3.

or protection of the environment, while on the other hand, judges of ICTs may be considered less qualified to rule on matters involving scientific issues. The way in which judicial decision-making works, as distinct from a scientific body feeding its views into issues of treaty compliance, may also lead to particular questions of legitimacy of the outcome. It is however unclear which options may lend themselves to greater legitimacy. Would a judicial process with all its trappings of due process and reasoned decision-making, or the recommendation of a group of individuals with technical expertise in the relevant subject matter be more legitimate? Is it perhaps a combination of both?

This chapter takes a look at the various modes of enhancing the compliance of State parties with treaty obligations – whether with the aid of ICTs, scientific committees, or NCMs. In doing so, the chapter examines how procedures in NCMs, scientific committees, and international courts relate to each other and how they may operate in conjunction with one another. Scientific committees, on the one hand, and ICTs, on the other, are not presented as two dispute settlement choices emanating from a fork-in-the-road clause. Their spheres of influence may operate independently of each other in the treaty system. They may also be arranged sequentially with a committee serving as a first step in efforts to clarify facts about obligations and facilitate compliance, or to address a difference before it becomes a dispute.

A question that arises in this context is whether a judicial body should decide a case in the situation where there exists an expert scientific body under the relevant treaty, such as the International Whaling Commission (IWC) or the Commission on the Limits of the Continental Shelf (CLCS) under the UN Convention for the Law of the Sea (UNCLOS). Should an ICT necessarily defer to a competent scientific body, or can it decide not to rule on the issue?

It could be argued that in the *Whaling* case,[4] the definitive assessment of Japan's actions should have been undertaken by the Scientific Committee of the IWC, a body truly competent to do so.[5] Similarly, in the *Bay of Bengal* delimitation case, the International Tribunal for the Law of the Sea (ITLOS) determined that it was able to delimit the continental shelf between the parties in the area beyond 200 nautical

[4] *Whaling in the Antarctic (Australia v Japan: New Zealand intervening)*, Judgment [2014] ICJ Reports 226.

[5] *Whaling in the Antarctic (Australia v Japan: New Zealand intervening)*, Judgment, Dissenting Opinion of Judge Bennouna [2014] ICJ Reports 341, 346.

miles ('nm') from the respective States' coasts, notwithstanding the role of the CLCS in issuing recommendations to States regarding the outer limits of the continental shelf.[6] The International Court of Justice (ICJ) adopted a similar approach in *Delimitation of the Continental Shelf between Nicaragua and Colombia beyond 200 Nautical Miles.*[7] In this context it is useful to remember the words of Arbitrator Wolfrum in the *Chagos* arbitration, in the context of leaving matters of scientific debate to scientists – 'lawyers can do nearly everything'.[8] It is clear from the jurisprudence, and it is also the author's opinion, that a judicial body is well within its jurisdictional limits to decide a legal dispute having scientific aspects.[9] It is indeed a fulfilment of its judicial function.

This chapter first examines NCMs (Section 7.2) and scientific committees (Section 7.3) in a range of treaties that cover environmental or other issues of a scientific character. This is followed by an examination of reference to ICTs for dispute settlement in the context of violations of treaties that also have an NCM alternative or a scientific committee making pronouncements on overlapping issues (Section 7.4). Thereafter, the chapter engages in a further discussion with specific case studies involving the crossing of paths between ICTs and certain scientific committees (Section 7.5). The chapter ends with concluding observations arising out of this analysis (Section 7.6).

7.2 Non-Compliance Mechanisms and Their Contribution to Compliance

This section provides an overview of compliance mechanisms (NCMs),[10] their working methods generally and in specific contexts, the scope of

[6] *Delimitation of the Maritime Boundary in the Bay of Bengal (Bangladesh/Myanmar)*, Judgment [2012] ITLOS Reports 4, 107.

[7] *Question of the Delimitation of the Continental Shelf between Nicaragua and Colombia beyond 200 Nautical Miles from the Nicaraguan Coast (Nicaragua v Colombia)*, Preliminary Objections, Judgment [2016] ICJ Reports 100, 137.

[8] *Chagos Marine Protected Area Arbitration* (*Mauritius v United Kingdom*), Hearing Transcript Day 11, available at pcacases.com/web/sendAttach/1581 (accessed 22 November 2022) 1344.

[9] Scientific aspects would include those issues that involve diverging views on science and may require specialised scientific knowledge for their resolution.

[10] See, e.g., T Stephens, *International Courts and Environment Protection* (Cambridge University Press 2009) 81–89; T Treves, L Pineschi, A Tanzi et al. (eds), *Non-Compliance Procedures and Mechanisms and the Effectiveness of International Environmental Agreements* (TMC Asser Press 2009); M Fitzmaurice and P Merkouris,

their powers, and the nature of their pronouncements, that is, the outcome of the compliance procedure.

NCMs in the form of compliance committees (with some having wider powers) can often be found in treaties, conventions, or protocols relating to the environment, or scientific issues generally (such as technical aspects of health, food, and agriculture). These include, *inter alia*, the Aarhus Convention,[11] the Kyoto Protocol,[12] the Kiev Protocol,[13] the London Protocol on Water and Health,[14] the Convention on the Conservation of Antarctic Marine Living Resources,[15] the Basel Convention on Transboundary Movement of Hazardous Wastes,[16] the Paris Agreement,[17] and the International Treaty on Plant Genetic Resources for Food and Agriculture.[18]

Non-compliance committees such as those under the above-mentioned conventions and protocols are generally established to review compliance under that protocol or treaty. An NCM commonly goes through the following steps. Review of a party's compliance may be

'Environmental Compliance Mechanisms' (*Oxford Bibliographies Online*, 2021) http://doi.org/10.1093/obo/9780199796953-0010.

11 Convention on Access to Information, Public Participation in Decision-Making and Access to Justice in Environmental Matters, signed 25 June 1998, entered into force 29 October 2001, 2161 UNTS 447.

12 Kyoto Protocol to the United Nations Framework Convention on Climate Change.

13 Protocol on Pollutant Release and Transfer Registers to the Convention on Access to Information, Public Participation in Decision-Making and Access to Justice in Environmental Matters, signed 21 May 2003, entered into force 8 October 2009, 2626 UNTS 119.

14 Protocol on Water and Health to the 1992 Convention on the Protection and Use of Transboundary Watercourses and International Lakes, 17 June 1999, entered into force 4 August 2005, 2331 UNTS 202.

15 Standing Committee on Implementation and Compliance, established by the Commission for the Conservation of Antarctic Marine Living Resources (CCAMLR) with terms of reference available at www.ccamlr.org/en/system/files/e-pt8_0.pdf (accessed 11 November 2022). The CCAMLR was established under Article VII, Convention for the Conservation of Antarctic Marine Living Resources, signed 20 May 1980, entered into force 7 April 1982, 1329 UNTS 47.

16 Implementation and Compliance Committee, established by the Conference of Parties under Article 15, Basel Convention on the Control of Transboundary Movements of Hazardous Wastes and Their Disposal, signed 22 March 1989, entered into force 5 May 1992, 1673 UNTS 57.

17 Paris Agreement, signed 12 December 2015, entered into force 4 November 2016, UNTS 3156, UN Doc FCCC/CP/2015/L.9/Rev/1.

18 Compliance Committee, established under Article 21 of the International Treaty on Plant Genetic Resources for Food and Agriculture, signed 3 November 2001, entered into force 29 June 2004, 2400 UNTS 303.

triggered usually in several ways: by a submission to the treaty committee from another party, or from the party itself concerning its own compliance, or by referrals from the secretariat of the treaty body, or by the committee itself. In case of the Aarhus Convention, submissions may even come from members of the public.[19] Non-compliance committees are empowered and required to examine the question of non-compliance before them. However, they cannot issue binding decisions. Instead, these committees make 'recommendations' to the parties collectively, or to individual parties. The members of these NCMs are appointed in their personal capacity and are therefore expected to remain independent as opposed to being State representatives. This should depoliticise their work and give them greater independence and credibility. Unlike ICTs,[20] such NCMs tend to include in their membership technical or scientific experts as well as lawyers or diplomats.

Pursuant to an NCM's recommendation, the final output is often a decision by the Conference of Parties to the treaty. Substantively, an NCM procedure could lead to financial or technical incentives to assist the party concerned in becoming compliant, or it could lead to penalties, sanctions, or suspension of privileges. Despite these possible consequences, the procedures before NCMs remain less adversarial and thus non-confrontational.[21]

One of the earliest NCMs can be seen within the framework of the Montreal Protocol.[22] It may be triggered by any party, or the secretariat.[23] Once the NCM is invoked, the Implementation Committee, a standing body elected by the Meeting of the Parties, considers the

[19] UNECE, 'Guidance Document on the Aarhus Convention Compliance Mechanism', 2, available at www.unece.org/fileadmin/DAM/env/pp/compliance/CC_GuidanceDocument.pdf (accessed 2 October 2021).

[20] See, e.g., referring to dispute resolution by the ICJ: Convention on Biological Diversity, Art 27(3)(b); United Nations Framework Convention on Climate Change, Article 14(2)(a); UNECE Convention on Environmental Impact Assessment in a Transboundary Context, signed 25 February 1991, entered into force 10 September 1997, 1989 UNTS 309, Article 15(2); Protocol on Further Reduction of Sulphur Emissions to the 1979 Convention on Long-Range Transboundary Air Pollution, Article 9.

[21] For the issue of State-to-State triggers, see Chapter 6.

[22] Montreal Protocol on Substances That Deplete the Ozone Layer, signed 16 September 1987, entered into force 1 January 1989, 1522 UNTS 3, Article 8.

[23] Decision IV/5, Report of the Fourth Meeting of the Parties to the Montreal Protocol on Substances That Deplete the Ozone Layer, UN Doc UNEP/Oz.L.Pro.4/15 (1992) (as revised by Decision X/10, Report of the Tenth Meeting of the Parties to the Montreal Protocol on Substances That Deplete the Ozone Layer, UN Doc UNEP/OzL.Pro.10/9 (1998)).

situation of non-compliance, with a view to securing an amicable solution. Recommendations of this committee can be adopted as decisions of the Meeting of the Parties. The Kyoto Protocol's comprehensive compliance mechanism includes an enforcement branch that determines non-compliance followed by a consequent course of action.[24]

The compliance committee under the Aarhus Convention has been established pursuant to Article 15 of the Convention, which requires the Meeting of the Parties to establish 'optional arrangements of a non-confrontational, non-judicial and consultative nature for reviewing compliance with the provisions of the Convention'. On the recommendations of this committee, parties to the Convention adopt decisions on general issues of compliance as well as compliance by individual parties. Under the Escazú Agreement, a Committee to Support Implementation and Compliance is established[25] as a subsidiary body of the Conference of Parties to promote the implementation of the treaty and to support the parties in that regard. The nature and role of this committee is clarified in this provision itself, as 'consultative and transparent', 'non-adversarial, non-judicial and non-punitive', while it reviews compliance with treaty provisions and makes recommendations. Its functioning is further defined by the rules promulgated at the first meeting of the Conference of Parties to this treaty.[26] Similar to the Aarhus Convention, here too, members of the public have the option to file communications regarding non-compliance by a treaty party.[27] Article 15 of the Minamata Convention on Mercury establishes an Implementation and Compliance Committee as a subsidiary body of the Conference of Parties. It functions according to its own rules of procedure, drawn up

[24] See UNFCCC, 'An Introduction to the Kyoto Protocol Compliance Mechanism', available at http://unfccc.int/process/the-kyoto-protocol/compliance-under-the-kyoto-protocol/introduction (accessed 15 April 2022). See also Chapter 3. The course of action depends on the nature of non-compliance and could take the form of making up the difference in emissions exceeding the assigned amount, or suspension of eligibility to make transfers under emissions trading.

[25] Regional Agreement on Access to Information, Public Participation and Justice in Environmental Matters in Latin America and the Caribbean, 4 March 2018, Article 18.

[26] Rules Relating to the Structure and Functions of the Committee to Support Implementation and Compliance of the Regional Agreement on Access to Information, Public Participation and Justice in Environmental Matters in Latin America and the Caribbean, Annex 1 of Decision I/3, First Meeting of Conference of Parties.

[27] Ibid., Rule V(1).

at its first meeting.[28] The Espoo Convention has an Implementation Committee, established by a Meeting of the Parties,[29] to review party compliance with treaty objectives. The procedures of this committee have been referred to as non-adversarial and assistance-oriented,[30] and they are without prejudice to provisions for dispute settlement under the Convention.

Most recently, the Paris Agreement, under Article 15, established the Committee to Facilitate Implementation and Promote Compliance, whose role is to function in a transparent, non-adversarial, and non-punitive manner. It will function according to its rules of procedure, adopted at CMA4 in Egypt,[31] and the committee's work is guided by the modalities and procedures for its effective functioning.[32]

A potential weakness of compliance committees is that the committee decisions cannot have the same legal weight as those of judicial bodies. However, this may also be viewed instead as an advantage. The procedures of compliance committees are still too often considered only in comparison to those of judicial organs, leading to the conclusion that they are similar to judicial bodies, but without the same capacity for action.[33] A number of them are composed of legal, as well as other expert members, with recognised competence in the field to which the treaty or protocol relates. Yet they have distinct procedures for determining facts and for discussing different points of view. And, in essence, a compliance

[28] Decision Adopted by the Second Conference of the Parties to the Minamata Convention on Mercury, Second Meeting, Geneva, 19–23 November 2018, UNEP/MC/COP.2/Dec.4.

[29] Decision II/4 of the Second Meeting of the Parties, revised as Decision III/2.

[30] Structure and Functions of the Implementation Committee and Procedures for Review of Compliance, Decision III/2, Appendix (ECE/MP.EIA/6) as Amended by Decision VI/2 (ECE/MP.EIA/20/Add.1– ECE/MP.EIA/SEA/4/ Add.1), Article 14, available at http://unece.org/DAM/env/eia/documents/ImplementationCommittee/2014_Structure_and_functions/Implementation_Committee_structure_functions_procedures_rules.e_2014.pdf (accessed 6 February 2022).

[31] Decision 24-/CMA.4, Rules of Procedure of the Committee to Facilitate Implementation and Promote Compliance Referred to in Article 15, paragraph 2, of the Paris Agreement, UN Doc FCCC/PA/CMA/2022/L.1.

[32] Decision 20/CMA.1, available at http://unfccc.int/process-and-meetings/bodies/constituted-bodies/committee-to-facilitate-implementation-and-promote-compliance-referred-to-in-article-15-paragraph-2 (accessed 15 April 2022). See also, 'Report of the Conference of the Parties Serving as the Meeting of the Parties to the Paris Agreement on the Third Part of Its First Session, Katowice 2–15 December 2018, UN Doc FCCC/PA/CMA/2018/3/Add.2 (19 March 2019).

[33] M Tignino, 'Quasi-Judicial Bodies' in CM Brölmann and Y Radi (eds), *Research Handbook on the Theory and Practice of International Law-Making* (Edward Elgar 2016) 242–61.

committee often provides a non-confrontational means of preventing and addressing situations of non-compliance, with legal as well as technical expert involvement.

Due to their quasi-judicial nature, compliance committees are halfway between scientific committees and ICTs from an institutional perspective.[34] However, they are suitable for minor breaches,[35] especially when the party in breach is willing to comply, or for serious issues of non-compliance in the first instance (before seeking recourse to an ICT), in cases involving systemic concerns, or when penalties for non-compliance are severe. In the case of serious breaches or when it is foreseen that a treaty party may be unwilling to comply, ICTs have the advantage of providing a more public forum of redress, bringing widespread attention to the non-complying party's infractions.

7.3 Scientific Committees and Their Contribution to Compliance

Scientific committees contribute to treaty compliance in a number of ways, although their primary role can be seen as an advisory one, on scientific and technical matters, usually advising a treaty's Conference of Parties. This function helps in strengthening the treaty regime, making it more robust, defensible, and progressive. There are, however, other ways in which scientific bodies could contribute to treaty compliance. This may take the form of contributions to treaty interpretation, or even determining treaty infractions,[36] though such roles are rarely seen.

Scientific committees are a sub-class of a wider range of treaty bodies. Under various treaties with environmental or scientific subject

[34] See V Roben, 'Institutional Developments under Modern International Environmental Agreements' in JA Frowein and R Wolfrum (eds), *Max Planck Yearbook of United Nations Law* (Kluwer Law International 2000) 363–443; G Samvel, 'Non-Judicial, Advisory, Yet Impactful? The Aarhus Convention Compliance Committee as a Gateway to Environmental Justice' (2020) 9 *Transnational Environmental Law* 211–38; C Zengerling, *Greening International Jurisprudence: Environmental NGOs before International Courts, Tribunals, and Compliance Committees* (Brill 2013) 1, 4, 9–10.

[35] As opposed to a serious, significant, or material breach; or in other words, a breach that can be remedied without much difficulty. A minor breach by its nature would not be the subject of much disagreement that may otherwise necessitate recourse to ICTs.

[36] For example, special permit whaling, in compliance with Article VIII of the Whaling Convention, is regularly reviewed by the Scientific Committee established under the International Whaling Commission. See e.g., Scientific Committee, 'Report, Annex P: Process for the Review of Special Permit Proposals and Research Results from Existing and Completed Permits' (2015) 16(Suppl) *Journal of Cetacean Resource Management*, 349.

matters, as under certain other treaties, there are often treaty bodies which effectively monitor implementation of or compliance with the treaty (such as the IWC Infractions Sub-Committee),[37] or provide advice or recommendations on the interpretation[38] or application of the concerned treaty (such as the CLCS).[39] Treaty bodies may be legal or technical depending on the body. The Infractions Sub-Committee of the IWC is an intergovernmental body, while the CLCS is a technical body. Examples of other intergovernmental treaty bodies include fisheries commissions such as the Commission for the Conservation of Southern Bluefin Tuna (CCSBT)[40] or regional seas bodies such as the OSPAR Commission.[41] These latter treaty bodies are advised in turn by scientific committees established under these treaties.

Undoubtedly, the role of scientific committees is distinct from that of other treaty bodies as well as from both NCMs and ICTs. Scientific committees exist to ensure smooth and uniform functioning of the treaty regime, along with pushing forward the growth of scientific knowledge in the specific field pertaining to the treaty. For selected examples of scientific committees, we can refer to the scientific committees under the IWC[42] or the Convention for the Conservation of Southern Bluefin Tuna, the Scientific Committee of which performs an important role in advising the intergovernmental CCSBT.[43]

However, as in other regional fisheries management organisations, it is the intergovernmental Commission that is the decision-making organ under the Convention. The CCSBT exists to ensure the conservation and optimum utilisation of Southern Bluefin Tuna. Similar to the IWC, the CCSBT is responsible for setting a total allowable catch and its allocation among the members, it can administer regulatory measures to meet

[37] International Whaling Commission, Infractions Sub-Committee, available at http://iwc.int/index.php?cID=html_513 (accessed 15 April 2022).

[38] See S Suarez, *The Outer Limits of the Continental Shelf: Legal Aspects of Their Establishment* (Springer 2008) 122.

[39] Commission on the Limits of the Continental Shelf (CLCS): Purpose, Functions and Sessions, available at www.un.org/depts/los/clcs_new/commission_purpose.htm (accessed 15 April 2022).

[40] See Commission for the Conservation of Southern Bluefin Tuna, available at www.ccsbt.org/ (accessed 15 April 2022).

[41] See Ospar Commission, available at www.ospar.org/about/how/ (accessed 11 November 2022).

[42] Established by the IWC under Article III(4) of the ICRW.

[43] Established by the CCSBT under Article 9 of the Convention for the Conservation of Southern Bluefin Tuna, 10 May 1993, 1819 UNTS 359.

Convention objectives, and also take decisions to support and implement fishery management. The CCSBT has also adopted a compliance plan, providing a framework for States to improve compliance. Moreover, non-compliance with the total allowable catch attracts 'corrective action'. The compliance plan includes policy guidelines such as the Corrective Actions Policy, which sets out a framework to respond to evidence of non-compliance by a treaty party.[44] This includes details of the decision-making process of the compliance committee of the CCSBT and a list of corrective actions that the committee may recommend. As in the IWC, the Commission's Scientific Committee acts as an advisory body and makes recommendations to the CCSBT.

We likewise see both non-scientific and scientific treaty bodies under the Convention on International Trade in Endangered Species (CITES), which has a Standing Committee, Secretariat, and two scientific committees – the Animals and Plants Committees – who all play their roles in ensuring treaty implementation and compliance. The Standing Committee provides policy guidance to the Secretariat concerning the implementation of CITES, while also co-ordinating the work of the other committees. The two scientific committees are composed of scientific experts and were established at the sixth meeting of the Conference of Parties in 1987. Their function is to provide technical support to decision-making about species of plants or animals that are or may become subject to CITES trade controls. They provide scientific advice and guidance to the other bodies involved in ensuring compliance, and their membership ensures geographic diversity.

Scientific committees, as distinguished from NCMs and other treaty bodies, are usually composed of scientific members,[45] and their working procedures vary. Their strength lies in providing authoritative pronouncements on scientific issues. Their recommendations may be used by another treaty body (such as a commission) in arriving at its decisions (as is the case with the IWC relying on its Scientific Committee's reports in making recommendations and the CCSBT drawing on its Scientific Committee's advice).

[44] Corrective Actions Policy, Compliance Policy Guideline 3 (updated at the Twenty-Fifth Annual Meeting, 18 October 2018), available at www.ccsbt.org/sites/default/files/userfiles/file/docs_english/operational_resolutions/CPG3_CorrectiveActions.pdf (accessed 15 April 2022).

[45] It must be noted that while the SBSTTA of the CBD is composed of parties, specific committees are composed of individuals.

The IWC is composed of Commissioners, one from each party to the International Convention for the Regulation of Whaling (ICRW). Its tasks include designating whale sanctuaries, setting catch limits on whales by species and area, and imposing restrictions on hunting methods. In the absence of any explicit compliance mechanism under the ICRW, the IWC has established an Infractions Sub-Committee. Breaches of the Convention must be reported to the IWC and are discussed by this Sub-Committee. It is not always easy to determine the existence of an infraction, due to 'wider issues within the Commission'.[46] Infractions within a country's national jurisdiction are dealt with by that nation itself, and these countries often impose penalties in the form of fines or imprisonment. The Scientific Committee of the IWC provides scientific advice to the Commission on matters under the Convention. Its tasks have included, for example, review of the second phase of Japan's Whale Research Programme under Special Permit in the Antarctic (JARPA II),[47] which was the subject matter of a dispute before the ICJ,[48] discussed in Section 7.5.1. Thus, a scientific review of whaling research programmes such as JARPA II falls within the purview of the Scientific Committee. The IWC, on the advice of its Scientific Committee, has the power to amend the schedule to the ICRW by adopting regulations with respect to the conservation and utilisation of whale resources.[49] The Commission may also make recommendations to the State parties.[50]

Established under the UNCLOS is the CLCS. The CLCS is a *sui generis* body. Like scientific committees under the various conventions, it is comprised of technical experts. It is composed of twenty members, experts in the fields of geology, geophysics, or hydrography, who are elected by States parties to the Convention from among their nationals.[51] They serve in their personal capacities.[52] Yet its role differs markedly

[46] International Whaling Commission (n 37).

[47] Report of the Scientific Committee (n 36).

[48] *Whaling in the Antarctic* (n 4).

[49] International Convention for the Regulation of Whaling, 2 December 1946, 161 UNTS 72, Article V(1). See Art V(2): 'based on scientific findings.'

[50] ICRW, Article VI.

[51] UNCLOS Annex II, Article 2. See also, Commission on the Limits of the Continental Shelf (CLCS): Members of the Commission, available at www.un.org/depts/los/clcs_new/commission_members.htm (accessed 15 April 2022).

[52] See UNCLOS Rules of Procedure of the Commission on the Limits of the Continental Shelf, 17 April 2008, UN Doc CLCS/40/Rev.1, Article 11: Duty to Act Independently.

from that of scientific committees. The primary function of the CLCS is to implement Article 76 of UNCLOS, dealing with the definition of the continental shelf, and to establish the outer limit of the continental shelf beyond 200 nautical miles (nm). More specifically, the CLCS considers data from coastal States (UNCLOS parties) concerning the outer limits of the continental shelf beyond 200 nm, provides scientific or technical advice to the State if so asked during preparation of this data, and makes recommendations on the same. The CLCS also has detailed rules of procedure governing not just its composition, conduct of business, and voting, but also the procedure to be followed when receiving submissions from a coastal State and in giving advice to such States.[53] It is important to note that the limits of the continental shelf beyond 200 nm established by coastal States based on CLCS recommendations are final and binding.[54] This is an important distinguishing feature of this body, and is one of the features setting it apart both from traditional scientific committees and from the NCMs discussed so far.

7.4 Recourse to ICTs

Apart from the above-mentioned non-judicial, non-confrontational mechanisms to ensure compliance, many of the treaties or protocols also envisage the option for dispute settlement before an ICT. As the following discussion reveals, these could be the same treaties that also include NCMs. This section looks at the dispute settlement clauses in these kinds of treaties and how ICTs may therefore contribute to treaty compliance, focussing on the examples of the ICRW, UNCLOS, and the CCSBT.

ICTs are certainly not incapable of resolving disputes involving complex scientific issues. An advantage of resorting to judicial means would be that judges have fresh eyes on the matters which treaty bodies deal with on a daily (or at least annual) basis. Judges would thus have some distance and an independent perspective on the matter. This perceived independence also arises out of a perception that scientific committees of a treaty system would tend to be biased in favour of conservation or protection of the environment.

[53] UNCLOS, Rules of Procedure of the Commission, available at www.un.org/depts/los/clcs_new/commission_rules.htm (accessed 15 April 2022).

[54] UNCLOS, Article 76(8).

Apart from the IWC and its various committees keeping a check on compliance by treaty parties, there is no dispute resolution clause in the ICRW, providing for recourse to arbitration or judicial settlement by the ICJ, for example. The dispute between Australia and Japan under this Convention was brought before the ICJ through the optional clause of the Statute of the ICJ, that allows States to opt into accepting the compulsory jurisdiction of the ICJ.[55]

On the other hand, the UNCLOS has a robust system of compulsory dispute settlement laid out in Part XV of the Convention. This Part provides a number of options to Contracting Parties, after attempting to settle a dispute through peaceful means, negotiation, or conciliation: recourse to either the ICJ, ITLOS or arbitration under Annex VII or Annex VIII of the Convention. All matters covered by the UNCLOS fall within the jurisdiction of these courts and tribunals. A few specific matters may be expressly excluded by a Contracting Party, as listed in Section 3 of Part XV. UNCLOS tribunals will otherwise have jurisdiction over disputes relating to the continental shelf, and indeed a number of disputes have come up, as discussed in Section 7.5.2.[56]

Parties to the Southern Bluefin Tuna Convention may submit any dispute concerning its interpretation or application, that is not settled amicably to the ICJ or to arbitration under the Annex to the Convention.[57] However, prior consent of all parties concerned is required before resorting to either of these judicial means of dispute settlement. In the *Southern Bluefin Tuna* cases,[58] the Tribunal established under Annex VII of UNCLOS declined jurisdiction since it found that these provisions of the Southern Bluefin Tuna Convention excluded dispute settlement under UNCLOS.

The treaties and conventions discussed in Section 7.2, all possessing NCMs to oversee compliance with treaty obligations, also provide for dispute settlement through ICTs, as in the Southern Bluefin Tuna Convention. Under the Aarhus Convention, parties, after attempting to resolve a dispute by negotiation, have the option to accept the compulsory jurisdiction of the ICJ or of arbitration[59] for disputes arising under

[55] Statute of the International Court of Justice (1945) 33 UNTS 993, Article 36(2). See also *Whaling in the Antarctic* (n 4) 234.

[56] *Question of the Delimitation* (n 7); *Delimitation of the Maritime Boundary* (n 6); *Dispute Concerning Delimitation of the Maritime Boundary between Ghana and Côte d'Ivoire in the Atlantic Ocean (Ghana/Côte d'Ivoire)*, Judgment [2017] ITLOS Reports 4.

[57] Convention for the Conservation of Southern Bluefin Tuna, Article 16(2).

[58] *Southern Bluefin Tuna Cases (New Zealand v Japan; Australia v Japan) (Award on Jurisdiction and Admissibility)* (2000) XXIII UNRIAA 1.

[59] In accordance with the procedure set out in Annex II of the Convention.

this treaty.[60] The Escazú Agreement[61] and the Espoo Convention[62] follow an identical procedure to the Aarhus Convention. The CITES follows a similar route, however including only the possibility of arbitration at the Permanent Court of Arbitration, if negotiations fail.[63] The Convention on Biological Diversity envisages a few more amicable means of resolving disputes. Failing resolution through negotiations, parties in dispute could jointly seek good offices or mediation.[64] Failing both these stages, the modes of ICT dispute settlement as in the Aarhus Convention are also envisaged here.[65]

7.5 Relationship between ICTs and Scientific Committees

The preceding sections have mapped broadly three kinds of mechanisms that operate simultaneously towards treaty implementation and compliance: NCMs, treaty bodies including scientific committees, and ICTs. This chapter now focusses on the latter two mechanisms. This section investigates the relationship between the work of scientific committees and ICTs through a focus on two examples: the Japanese whaling programme in the Antarctic, and selected disputes regarding continental shelf delimitation beyond 200 nm.

First, examining the dispute over the Japanese whaling programme in the ICJ, a proposal is made for the greater involvement of scientific treaty bodies in decision-making by ICTs. Second, examining the selected continental shelf disputes, we look at situations where a specialised scientific body (the CLCS) may issue its recommendations on matters before they proceed to an ICT. This is a unique situation and in the author's opinion deserves a brief discussion.

7.5.1 Whaling in the Antarctic: The ICJ and IWC's Scientific Committee

The preceding sections have examined the contributions of different international bodies to treaty compliance. In focussing this section on the relationship between two of these fora (scientific committees and

60 Aarhus Convention (n 11) Article 16.

61 Escazú Agreement (n 25) Article 19.

62 Convention on Environmental Impact Assessment in a Transboundary Context, Article 15.

63 CITES, Article XVIII.

64 Convention on Biological Diversity (n 1) Article 27(1) and (2).

65 Convention on Biological Diversity (n 1) Article 27(3).

ICTs), a case study on the *Whaling* case before the ICJ leads to a proposal to involve scientific treaty bodies in the decision-making of ICTs.

In the *Whaling* case, Australia brought a dispute against Japan (with New Zealand intervening) under the ICRW before the ICJ claiming that Japan's whaling programme was in breach of its obligations under the Convention.[66] Although twelve judges were in favour of the majority in its final decision on the merits, eleven judges appended separate or dissenting opinions to the judgment. A reading of these opinions indicates that judges were divided on whether it was the Court's task to judicially review the Japanese whale research programme, and decide whether the same was 'for the purpose of scientific research', or whether it could only be subject to scientific review by the IWC.[67] According to Judge Xue, the question whether activities under Japan's whaling research programme , 'JARPA II', involved scientific research was a matter of fact rather than a matter of law, and thus should be subject to scientific, not judicial review.[68] On the other hand, Judge Keith's declaration emphasised the ICJ's power to judicially review a State's granting of special permits under the ICRW.[69] Judge Bennouna raised the issue that perhaps instead of the ICJ sitting in judgment over such matters of science, these issues could best be left to the IWC and the Scientific Committee to determine at the appropriate times, as determined by the ICRW.[70] In Judge Bennouna's opinion, the Court had usurped the powers of these treaty-based bodies. Judge Owada agreed with this proposition,[71] though he further argued that certain aspects of these issues were subject to legal scrutiny – such as whether procedural requirements were followed, or whether the activities in question met the

[66] *Whaling in the Antarctic* (n 4).

[67] MM Mbengue and R Das, 'The ICJ's Engagement with Science: To Interpret or Not To Interpret?' (2015) 6 *Journal of International Dispute Settlement* 568, 573–74; J Morishita, 'IWC and the ICJ Judgment' in M Fitzmaurice and D Tamada (eds), *Whaling in the Antarctic: The Significance and the Implications of the ICJ Judgment* (Brill 2016) 238–67, 253.

[68] *Whaling in the Antarctic (Australia v Japan: New Zealand intervening)*, Judgment, Separate Opinion of Judge Xue [2014] ICJ Reports 420, para 15.

[69] *Whaling in the Antarctic (Australia v Japan: New Zealand intervening)*, Judgment, Declaration of Judge Keith [2014] ICJ Reports 336, para 7.

[70] *Whaling in the Antarctic (Australia v Japan: New Zealand intervening)*, Judgment, Dissenting Opinion of Judge Bennouna [2014] ICJ Reports 341, 346: 'In engaging in an evaluation of the programme, the Court has, in a sense, substituted itself for these two bodies.'

[71] *Whaling in the Antarctic (Australia v Japan: New Zealand intervening)*, Judgment, Dissenting Opinion of Judge Owada [2014] ICJ Reports 301, 312.

'general accepted notion of scientific research'.[72] In the context of adherence to procedural requirements, the Court ruled that Japan had complied with the obligations under paragraph 30 of the Schedule to the ICRW, that is, submitting proposed scientific permits for review by the Scientific Committee. It is interesting to note the interaction between the Court and the Scientific Committee in this analysis, in the sense that the Court went into detail regarding the Committee's practice and arrived at its decision on this point based on that practice.[73]

Thus in the *Whaling* case, although parties presented expert witnesses who testified and were cross-examined in the oral proceedings, a few judges were of the opinion that the expertise most suited to decide these scientific issues was situated outside the Court.[74] It is important to note that in accordance with its Statute, the ICJ Registrar had notified the IWC of the proceedings before the Court; however, the IWC chose not to submit any observations.[75] The Court also noted that the Scientific Committee of the IWC is not empowered to make binding assessments on special whaling permits, the subject of contention before the Court.[76] Rather, the Committee sends 'recommendations' to the IWC regarding its views on programmes for scientific research. The Court considered that Japan should have given 'due regard' to the Scientific Committee's recommendations since States parties to the treaty had a duty to co-operate with the IWC and Committee.[77] However, a point of contention in this dispute included an assessment of whether all the required reviews had been conducted by the Scientific Committee.

The dissenting judges' critiques raise important questions regarding the processes most suited to resolve disputes of a scientific nature, especially in the context of treaties which have constituted scientific bodies to advise and provide recommendations on the same scientific issues. One may even consider how ICTs could benefit from the expertise

72 Ibid.

73 *Whaling in the Antarctic* (n 4) 297.

74 *Whaling in the Antarctic*, Separate Opinion of Judge Xue (n 70) 420, 425; *Whaling in the Antarctic (Australia v Japan: New Zealand intervening)*, Judgment, Separate Opinion of Judge Sebutinde [2014] ICJ Reports 431, 433; *Whaling in the Antarctic*, Dissenting Opinion of Judge Bennouna (n 72) 341, 346–47.

75 *Whaling in the Antarctic* (n 4) 234.

76 *Whaling in the Antarctic* (n 4) 248.

77 *Whaling in the Antarctic* (n 4) 257, 271. The Court noted that by using lethal methods and not assessing the feasibility of non-lethal alternatives in its new proposed research programme, Japan was clearly not giving due regard to the IWC and scientific committee recommendations calling for an assessment of non-lethal alternatives.

of scientific bodies in their decision-making. The involvement of scientific bodies could be envisaged in two ways: either as consultants involved in the selection of court-appointed experts, or as experts themselves, advising the court or tribunal. Such involvement would provide the dual benefits of uniform treaty compliance and enhanced legitimacy of the judicial decision.

The question of legitimacy of outcome hinges on the legitimacy of the judicial process versus the legitimacy of scientific findings. An ICT could combine the two if it involved the relevant scientific bodies in its decision-making process, perhaps through seeking expert opinions from these bodies. Dispute settlement panels of the World Trade Organization receive advice from international organisations that have the necessary expertise on the subject in dispute before them.[78] They may also rely on international organisations to suggest names of experts who could aid in fact-finding.[79] At the same time, certain scientific bodies have often been criticised as being politicised. Some disputing parties may also be of the opinion that scientific committees will always have a bias in favour of the treaty's objectives (not necessarily a disadvantage). If there is merit in these arguments, it may be better for ICTs to go through their own processes of seeking expert advice (or relying on parties' expert evidence) and reaching a decision.

7.5.2 Delimitation of the Continental Shelf: Judicial Bodies and the CLCS

This section looks at a specific scientific treaty body, the CLCS, and how its activities intertwine with those of ICTs. In examining selected decisions by the ICJ and ITLOS, this section proposes that for a specialised scientific body like the CLCS, it may be more conducive to compliance if the parties were to wait until the CLCS issues its recommendations prior to initiating dispute settlement proceedings before an ICT.

[78] See e.g., *Saudi Arabia – Protection of IPR* (DS567) (consulting WIPO); *Korea – Radionuclides* (DS495) (consulting Codex Alimentarius Commission, IAEA, and International Commission on Radiological Protection); *Australia – Tobacco Plain Packaging* (DS435, DS441, DS458, DS467) (consulting, among others, the WHO Framework Convention on Tobacco Control).

[79] See e.g., *Russia – Pigs* (DS475) (consulting FAO and World Organisation for Animal Health – OIE); *India – Agricultural Products* (DS430) (consulting the WHO, FAO, and OIE); *Australia – Apples* (DS367) (consulting the Secretariat of the International Plant Protection Convention).

A series of cases before different ICTs have highlighted the interactions between these judicial bodies and the CLCS. Before the ICJ, in the case concerning *Delimitation of the Continental Shelf between Nicaragua and Colombia*,[80] Colombia made a preliminary objection to admissibility of the dispute on the ground that Nicaragua had not obtained the requisite recommendation from the CLCS. While the Court decided on this point that it could undertake the delimitation of the continental shelf beyond 200 nm independently of a recommendation of the CLCS,[81] Judge Bhandari's declaration on this issue is also interesting to note. In his opinion, the CLCS, a specialised agency with a specific mandate to investigate and pronounce upon continental shelf claims, consisting of members who are world-renowned experts in such relevant fields as geology, geophysics, and hydrology, are better equipped to resolve a continental shelf dispute such as the one before the ICJ. He was not in favour of relying on expert testimony from the parties either, since that would not only constitute an

> inefficient use of valuable Court resources, but … Parties would bring witnesses most likely to advance their respective and competing claims, whose opinions could … be at odds with those of the expert members of the CLCS. This, in turn, could potentially lead to the uneasy situation wherein the CLCS and the Court reach incompatible conclusions regarding Nicaragua's continental shelf claim.[82]

While Judge Bhandari's comment brings forth the general question of the ICJ being able to adjudicate scientific claims, in this particular instance, it must be read with Article 9 of Annex II to UNCLOS, which states that the 'actions of the Commission shall not prejudice matters relating to delimitation of boundaries between States with opposite or adjacent coasts'. This could, however, lead to conflicting pronouncements from two different authorities. Scholarly opinion leans towards the Court appointing experts under Article 50 of its Statute, for a transparent evaluation of the scientific evidence.[83]

[80] *Question of the Delimitation* (n 7) 100.

[81] *Question of the Delimitation* (n 7) 100, 137.

[82] *Question of the Delimitation of the Continental Shelf between Nicaragua and Colombia beyond 200 Nautical Miles from the Nicaraguan Coast* (*Nicaragua v Colombia*), Preliminary Objections, Declaration of Judge Bhandari [2016] ICJ Reports 204, 206.

[83] X Liao, 'Evaluation of Scientific Evidence by International Courts and Tribunals in the Continental Shelf Delimitation Cases' (2017) 136(48) *Ocean Development & International Law* 150–51.

In another ICJ dispute between Somalia and Kenya, the Court noted unequivocally that

> a lack of certainty regarding the outer limits of the continental shelf, and thus the precise location of the endpoint of a given boundary in the area beyond 200 nautical miles, does not, however, necessarily prevent either the States concerned or the Court from undertaking the delimitation of the boundary in appropriate circumstances before the CLCS has made its recommendations.[84]

This pronouncement is a step towards embracing the legal aspect of scientific issues and responds to the challenge to the ICJ's capability to evaluate the scientific evidence supporting a claim of continental shelf beyond 200 nm.[85] Thus, issues of maritime delimitation require international tribunals 'to make a conclusive decision as to whether the continental shelves beyond 200 nm exist and to what extent they are overlapping'.[86]

Like the ICJ, the ITLOS has also faced the question of its competence to decide technical questions of boundary delimitation as opposed to the CLCS. While the Tribunal decided that it is competent to decide the legal aspects of these issues, strong opposing views contend that the CLCS being an expert body would be best placed to ascertain the scientific facts, perhaps in contradiction to uncontested evidence before the ITLOS. The significance of the *Bangladesh/Myanmar* case[87] lies in the examination of the relationship between the dispute-settling role of the Tribunal and the recommendatory (though almost decision-making) role of a body composed of scientific experts, the CLCS.[88] The determination of entitlement on the continental shelf beyond the 200 nm limit requires interpretation of Article 76 of UNCLOS, which, *inter alia*, defines the continental shelf and its limits. It is with respect to this task that the judgment made important remarks regarding the Tribunal's authority to interpret and

84 *Maritime Delimitation in the Indian Ocean (Somalia v Kenya)*, Preliminary Objections, Judgment [2017] ICJ Reports 3, 38.

85 G Vega-Barbosa, 'The Admissibility of Outer Continental Shelf Delimitation Claims before the ICJ Absent a Recommendation by the CLCS' (2018) 49 *Ocean Development & International Law* 103, 111.

86 Liao (n 85) 139; Vega-Barbosa (n 87) 112.

87 *Delimitation of the Maritime Boundary (Bangladesh/Myanmar)* (n 6).

88 T Treves, 'Law and Science in the Interpretation of the Law of the Sea Convention: Article 76 between the Law of the Sea Tribunal and the Commission on the Limits of the Continental Shelf' (2012) 3 *Journal of International Dispute Settlement* 483, 484.

apply Article 76, relying on scientific evidence as appropriate. The ITLOS noted that

> as this article contains elements of law and science, its proper interpretation and application requires both legal and scientific expertise. While the CLCS is a scientific and technical body with recommendatory functions entrusted by the Convention to consider scientific and technical issues arising in the implementation of article 76 on the basis of submissions by coastal States, the Tribunal can interpret and apply the provisions of the UNCLOS, including article 76. This may include dealing with uncontested scientific materials or require recourse to experts.[89]

Moreover, since the question before the Tribunal regarding the parties' entitlement to a continental shelf beyond 200 nm was largely legal in nature, the ITLOS ruled that it 'can and should determine entitlements of the Parties in this particular case'. However since the application of Article 76(4) required scientific and technical expertise, the ITLOS considered that it 'would have been hesitant to proceed with the delimitation of the area beyond 200 nm had it concluded that there was significant uncertainty as to the existence of a continental margin in the area in question'.[90] Due to the 'uncontested scientific material' before it (Bangladesh's expert reports that Myanmar did not challenge), it could proceed to decide the legal question, by interpreting Article 76.[91] It would have been interesting to see the steps taken by the Tribunal if there were no such uncontested scientific evidence before it.[92] The facts of this case also raise the question as to whether uncontested scientific evidence should in principle relieve the ITLOS of its obligation to evaluate the evidence on its merits.

An interesting aspect of this unchallenged acceptance of scientific evidence comes to light from Judge Ndiaye's Separate Opinion in *Bangladesh/Myanmar*.[93] He notes that under UNCLOS the power to assess the scientific and technical data submitted by a coastal State to the CLCS is vested exclusively in the CLCS. According to him, an 'exercise in maritime delimitation consists of applying the natural

89 *Delimitation of the Maritime Boundary (Bangladesh/Myanmar)* (n 6), 107.
90 Ibid., 115.
91 Liao (n 85) 144.
92 Treves (n 90) 491.
93 *Delimitation of the Maritime Boundary in the Bay of Bengal (Bangladesh/Myanmar)*, Judgment, Separate Opinion of Judge Ndiaye [2012] ITLOS Reports 151.

sciences to ascertain the extent of the natural prolongation under the sea of each of the two States and of making a finding on – not awarding – the extent of the submarine basement nature has placed before each of the two States.'[94] While it is true that under Article 9 of Annex II to UNCLOS, actions of the CLCS do not prejudice matters regarding delimitation of coastal boundaries between States, according to Judge Ndiaye, the subject matter of this dispute called for a factual determination, rather than the Tribunal's acceptance of 'uncontested scientific evidence'. The CLCS, conducting an independent, objective analysis,[95] might have found the uncontested scientific evidence to be incorrect. This reasoning goes a step further than that of Judge Bhandari in *Nicaragua v Colombia* before the ICJ.

More recently, in the maritime boundary dispute between Ghana and Côte d'Ivoire, the CLCS had already made its recommendations in respect of Ghana, thus there was no risk that a judicial pronouncement would interfere with the functions of the CLCS. The Special Chamber of the ITLOS constituted to deal with the dispute, following the Tribunal in the *Bangladesh/Myanmar* case, also decided that it had the jurisdiction to delimit the continental shelf beyond 200 nm.[96] In this case, it justified its decision in light of the circumstances of the case: 'there [was] no doubt that a continental shelf beyond 200 nm exists in respect of the two Parties.'[97]

The exercise of delimitation of the continental shelf has both legal and scientific components. Although scientifically based,[98] it is legal in nature since it prescribes the entitlement of coastal States to the continental shelf.[99] Conversely, although legal in nature, the establishment of entitlement to the continental shelf beyond 200 nm involves evaluation of

[94] Ibid., 172.

[95] Ibid., 183.

[96] *Dispute Concerning Delimitation (Ghana/Côte d'Ivoire)* (n 58) 136.

[97] Ibid., 138: '. . . the Special Chamber has no doubt that a continental shelf beyond 200 nm exists for Côte d'Ivoire since its geological situation is identical to that of Ghana, for which affirmative recommendations of the CLCS exist.'

[98] RW Smith and G Taft, 'Legal Aspects of the Continental Shelf' in PJ Cook and C Carleton (eds), *Continental Shelf Limits: The Scientific and Legal Interface* (Oxford University Press 2000) 17.

[99] *Delimitation of the Maritime Boundary in the Gulf of Maine Area (Canada/United States of America)*, Judgment [1984] ICJ Reports 246, 296: 'Legal title to certain maritime or submarine areas is always and exclusively the effect of a legal operation.'

scientific evidence from geology or geomorphology or both. While Article 76 of the UNCLOS sets out specific criteria for the determination of the outer edge of the continental margin and the outer limits of the legal continental shelf, the task of application is not straightforward. Although Article 76 uses scientific terminology, the terms do not necessarily have the same meaning as in science. As pointed out in the Scientific and Technical Guidelines adopted by the CLCS, '[t]he Convention makes use of scientific terms in the legal context which at times departs significantly from accepted scientific definitions and terminology'.[100]

Two main options are thus presented to disputing parties: first, if States dealing with a continental shelf delimitation were consistently to follow a sequence of approaching the CLCS before resorting to ICTs (if necessary), these courts and tribunals would have the benefit of a CLCS recommendation before issuing their decisions. It is in States' interests to avoid inconsistency between recommendations and rulings in these different fora. Second, in the event that such disputes are brought before ICTs, if the courts' decision-making involves assessment of scientific evidence, the use of experts by ICTs could grant greater legitimacy to their decisions and might increase the possibility of the courts' operating in harmony with the recommendations of the CLCS. Of course, it must be borne in mind that, thus far, consultation of experts by the ICJ has been sparse, and by the ITLOS non-existent.[101]

7.6 Conclusion

This chapter has examined how treaty compliance could be strengthened through the spectrum of a variety of fora – NCMs, scientific committees, and ICTs. The goal has been to examine their roles in treaty compliance both separately and in conjunction with each other. The chapter concludes that, to the extent possible, treaty parties should aim for a

[100] Commission on the Limits of the Continental Shelf, 'Scientific and Technical Guidelines of the Commission on the Limits of the Continental Shelf, CLCS/11', adopted 13 May 1999, para 1.3, available at www.un.org/depts/los/clcs_new/commission_documents.htm#Guidelines (accessed 19 October 2021).

[101] MM Mbengue and R Das, 'Experts' in *Max Planck Encyclopaedia of International Procedural Law* (2022); C Foster, 'Court-Appointed Expert' in *Max Planck Encyclopaedia of International Procedural Law* (2019).

sequential approach, with ICTs being the last resort. This would provide the ICTs with the technical expertise of the scientific committees, and could enhance the legitimacy of the judicial decision, also avoiding inconsistencies between the outcomes of different fora. States parties should operate on a basis informed by the advice of scientific committees and the guidance of NCMs and thereafter, if necessary, an ICT could rely on this Scientific Committee's findings or recommendations in arriving at its decision.

PART III

Trade, Finance and Investment

8

Trade's Enforcement Conundrum

KATHLEEN CLAUSSEN

8.1 Introduction

International law scholars have spilled much ink on questions of institutional design surrounding dispute settlement. Commentators over the last forty years have praised the concept of third-party dispute settlement as a great achievement in our sovereigntist discipline.[1] Yet, reviews of "dispute settlement mechanisms" tend to concentrate on courts on the one hand and on tribunals on the other. These are typically State-to-State mechanisms, although not exclusively so. Thus, when we consider "compliance" in international law, most questions of design concentrate on these institutions in which one State maintains that another has violated the latter's commitments.

Today, however, the targets of international legal obligations are changing and with them, the concept of compliance, especially in trade law on which this chapter concentrates. By focusing on dispute settlement as the primary means by which to achieve compliance, the literature tends to constrain the sources it consults and the range of devices that may be appropriate to achieve its predetermined goals. It is overly limited to these now widely shared ideals about dispute resolution, operating within a closed set of options.

That our ideas of compliance are limited to settlement of disputes is the consequence of another limitation in thinking: that of the purpose and aims of international law more generally. We examine State behavior because one of the primary goals of international law is to shape that

Many thanks to PluriCourts for the invitation to be a part of this volume. I am also especially grateful for comments on an earlier draft from colleagues in the International Economic Law and Policy Workshop.

[1] See e.g., A Keck and S Schropp, "Indisputably Essential: The Economics of Dispute Settlement Institutions in Trade Agreements" (2008) 42 *Journal of World Trade* 785; T Schoenbaum, "WTO Dispute Settlement: Praise and Suggestions for Reform" (1998) 47 *International & Comparative Law Quarterly* 647.

behavior. That is true likewise in trade: commitments made in trade agreements seek to install reciprocal behavioral constraints. The primary mechanism for holding States accountable in trade is, like elsewhere, third-party dispute settlement. The culmination of that exercise is license to a State to impose economic penalties (often in the form of suspension of concessions) on the party that has acted in breach of the agreement.

The "compliance" story is complicated by the terminology that practitioners and scholars apply. Trade officials and other stakeholders regularly call for greater "enforcement." By that, they mean holding other States accountable when those other States act in a way believed to breach a trade agreement.[2] But recent innovations in trade agreements have concentrated on how to enhance compliance with agreement norms by both State actors and especially non-State actors. In these new iterations, "compliance" appears to encompass ideas beyond individual State action in dispute settlement, unlike "enforcement," although they are not used precisely. Few have studied these innovations in detail and those that have tend to concentrate on the substance of the commitment or the procedures behind the tool.[3] This chapter, in contrast, queries how these evolving concepts of trade "enforcement" might enhance "compliance" by diverse stakeholders – some of whom may not be readily identifiable by the governments that negotiate these agreements in the first place. It peels back the layers of the trade agreement compliance apparatus.

Recently, and as will be discussed further, some of these innovative mechanisms for compliance have gained considerable public attention. They have garnered notice for their innovativeness as well as for their considerable reach and emphasis on "trade-plus" as seemingly more important than "ordinary trade" matters. They have altered the conversation on the meaning of "compliance" and "enforcement." These recent mechanisms have implications for how we think about trade agreements as instruments and the power of States to precipitate change behind the border.

The chapter proceeds in three parts. First, it analyzes the trade enforcement/compliance conundrum through examples arising under these

[2] In fact, the term "enforcement" is used indiscriminately by many political actors as part of a "be tough" campaign. See e.g., K Claussen, "Arguing about Trade Law beyond the Courtroom" in I Johnstone and S Ratner (eds), *Talking International Law* (Oxford University Press 2021).

[3] See e.g., M Bronckers and G Gruni, "Retooling the Sustainability Standards in EU Free Trade Agreements" (2021) 24 *Journal of International Economic Law* 25.

innovative mechanisms in recent trade agreements. Second, it turns to an assessment of trade non-compliance mechanisms (NCMs) and argues that they both exhibit significant potential for an expansive reach and also suffer from shortcomings. Finally, the chapter closes by mapping these normative evaluations onto conventional compliance theories to draw conclusions about those theories' resilience and flexibility before making recommendations both for trade law and international law more generally.

8.2 Trade's Enforcement/Compliance Conundrum: The Mechanisms

Apart from international criminal law that seeks to hold individuals accountable for their actions in contravention of international law, international law focuses largely on State behavior. Central to that enterprise is the law on State responsibility which sets out generalized norms for appropriate responses to breaches of international law by States. To supplement those amorphous norms, treaties and other forms of agreements often develop their own closed set of responses to breaches of an individual agreement. Those mechanisms are most robust in international economic law where both individuals and other States have means by which to hold States accountable to their commitments under trade agreements and investment treaties. In these contexts, where the emphasis has been on securing State compliance with obligations made by States in those agreements, "enforcement" and "compliance" were often viewed as synonymous, and those terms were in turn synonymous with "dispute settlement," even though in common parlance they are undoubtedly not synonyms. States could invoke the dispute settlement chapter of a trade agreement as a means by which to ensure that other States were complying – in effect, to enforce the agreement.

Traditionally, trade agreements have relied on adjudication for enforcement, where they have had any enforcement mechanism at all. The trade "enforcement" system is generally one of State-to-State dispute resolution carried out by a neutral panel which makes a recommendation that then must be adopted by a larger community of States or by the parties, at risk of economic penalty. In recent years, trade agreements have expanded their scope both in substance[4] and in terms of their

[4] See e.g., C Ryngaert, "EU Trade Agreements and Human Rights: From Extraterritorial to Territorial Obligations" (2018) 20 *International Community Law Review* 374; K Milewicz,

enforcement mechanisms.[5] The reach of traditional adjudicatory mechanisms has been extended from, originally, economic measures to what some have called "trade-plus" measures: areas with an impact on and part of trade broadly defined such as intellectual property, labor, environment, sustainable development, and more. Consequently, trade agreement NCMs have begun to shift the compliance landscape not just on trade but also in trade-adjacent areas as will be described. Central to this thesis is that new moves in the trade law and policy space are changing how we think about compliance, and the central actors behind the agreements.

While trade negotiations have always reflected a cacophony of views and interests, the issues surrounding enforcement of trade-plus matters are even more muddled than those generally complex debates. Actors from various political backgrounds have advocated for different institutional structures to address complications in supply chains, migration, the perceived effects of globalization, and domestic economic policies. Many States still do not subject the bulk of those "trade-plus" measures to ordinary dispute settlement, making their enforceability seem elusive to some advocates.[6] In other instances, however, States have gone beyond ordinary State-to-State dispute settlement in their trade agreements on these "trade-plus" matters.

8.2.1 *Innovations in Trade-Plus Enforcement*

New mechanisms seek to shift the enforcement effort toward other actors including but not limited to the State. Most of these come from the US experience where the voices of advocates for greater domestic penetration by trade agreements are loudest. The most recent and most celebrated example of this move comes from the 2020 economic agreement signed by the North American countries known as the United States–Mexico–Canada Agreement (USMCA) which launched a new tool: the

J Hollway, C Peacock and D Snidal, "Beyond Trade: The Expanding Scope of the Nontrade Agenda in Trade Agreements" (2016) 62 *Journal of Conflict Resolution* 743.

5 See generally, JB Velut, D Baeza-Breinbauer, M de Bruijne, M Garnizova et al., "Comparative Analysis of Trade and Sustainable Development Provisions in Free Trade Agreements", LSE Trade Policy Hub, February 2022.

6 These examples are discussed in the LSE Trade Policy Hub report (n 5) as well as in the ILO's database on Labor Provisions in Trade Agreements, available at www.ilo.org/global/research/projects/trade-decent-work/publications/WCMS_835562/lang–en/index.htm.

"Facility-Specific Rapid Response Labor Mechanism" (RRM).[7] This tool was the product of an intense deliberation between the Democrats in the US Congress and the Trump Administration in which the former sought greater labor protections in the USMCA text.

The RRM is a novel compliance tool and a supplement to the State-to-State dispute settlement system. Operating in addition to the traditional adjudicatory mechanism for disputes about the interpretation and application of the labor chapter, the RRM is a unilateral means for any of the parties to seek to force individual worksites in the territory of another party to comply with domestic law.[8] It has a relatively straightforward aim: to ensure remediation of a denial of collective bargaining rights. Contrast this with one of the primary aims of most other labor chapters in US trade agreements to date: to ensure that each party does not fail "to effectively enforce labor laws through a sustained or recurring course of action." Rather than hold governments accountable for the administration of their domestic law, the RRM is a way to handle a specific denial of the right of free association and collective bargaining by a private entity at a *particular worksite*. It still turns on engagement between the relevant two governments and the use of an arbitral panel, but it is far more incident-specific than the traditional adjudicatory labor compliance mechanisms.

Another feature of the USMCA trade-plus compliance machinery is similar to that used in other US trade agreements: public engagement. As in the context of other US trade agreements, each of the three governments in the USMCA has devised a system for receiving information about possible denials of rights at worksites, although at the time of writing, the governments had not committed to making publicly available information they received. This mechanism expands the reach of each of the governments, allowing individual actors and civil society to bring to the attention of the authorities problems of which they are aware.

Following a multi-step investigation process, governments can prompt the constitution of a neutral panel of labor experts to make a determination on whether workers are being denied their rights at the factory in

[7] United States–Mexico–Canada Agreement, entered into force July 1, 2020, Annex 31-A.

[8] There are in fact two annexes here with Rapid Response Mechanisms: one to address issues between the United States and Mexico and another to address issues between Canada and Mexico. The two annexes are the same with only the smallest of adjustments in the footnotes to accommodate the two countries' different domestic processes.

question.[9] Where the panel identifies that the factory is denying workers' rights, the responding government may choose to hold consultations with the complaining government before the complainant then "impose[s] remedies."[10] Importantly, those "remedies" or penalties are not against the respondent but rather against the worksite company itself. The complainant can choose a remedy which "may include" suspending preferential tariff treatment for the goods made at that worksite or other "penalties" on the goods.[11] At the least, the agreement text specifically notes that the complainant may deny entry to goods from the company in question in instances of repeat offenses. The complainant is limited only by some imprecise principles of proportionality. The "remedy" continues to be applied until the denial of rights has been "remediated."[12]

But relatively broad language in the agreement suggests the complaining government is not limited in its choice of remedies other than in their magnitude. That is, the agreement provides a non-exhaustive list of possible "remedies" against a worksite or the home government and only requires that the complaining government's selection be proportional. As of the time of writing, there had been no test of the panel or remedies aspect of the RRM.

The United States activated the RRM tool twice during the summer of 2021 and once more in May 2022. In the first instance, it reached agreement with Mexico on how to remediate the situation. In the second, the United States reached out directly to the company and its US parent company to develop a means to address the worksite issues. The third remains ongoing at the time of writing.

A second innovative and recent model for trade-related compliance may be found in the United States–Peru Trade Promotion Agreement (PTPA) which entered into force in 2009.[13] The PTPA contains a unique Environment Chapter and Annex on Forest Sector Governance, which includes a requirement for Peru to conduct audits of particular timber producers and exporters, and upon request from the United States, perform verifications of shipments of wood products from Peru. The United States may then take action directly against the shipment that is subject to the verification if it is not satisfied with the results. The purpose

[9] USMCA, Article 31A-4.
[10] Ibid.
[11] Ibid., Article 31A-10.
[12] Ibid.
[13] United States–Peru Trade Promotion Agreement, entered into force February 1, 2009.

of this Annex is to protect against illegal logging that threatens to deplete forests and exacerbate climate change. The Annex also creates an Interagency Committee on Trade in Timber Products from Peru to monitor Peru and its companies' actions in this respect.

The PTPA Forest Annex was and remains the first of its kind, although some of the aspects of the USMCA RRM resemble its features. The PTPA offers an illustrative list of actions the United States may take with respect to the shipment or enterprise that is the subject of the verification. For example, the United States may deny entry to certain products for up to three years, or until the Timber Committee determines that the company in question has complied with all applicable laws, regulations, and other measures of Peru governing the harvest of and trade in timber products, whichever is shorter.

The company-specific aspect of the Annex was tested first in October 2017 when the Trump Administration denied entry of timber products and exports by a Peruvian company. Peru was unable to verify that the shipment complied with all applicable Peruvian laws and regulations. Again, in July 2019, the US Trade Representative directed US Customs and Border Protection to block future timber imports from a different Peruvian exporter based on illegally harvested timber found in its supply chain. The Trump Administration characterized this move as a way to "ensur[e] that [US] trading partners live up to their [trade agreement] obligations" by not allowing illegally harvested timber to be exported to the United States.[14]

8.2.2 Drivers of Change

What has motivated these shifts in the US trade agreement compliance context? To be sure, examining the wide variety of motivations from multiple sectors and among multiple actors exceeds the scope of this chapter. But when we ask where these moves come from and why they have emerged, there appear to be two important features: first is a frustration with trade liberalization and second is recognition that existing or traditional means to countervail what many see as the

[14] Office of the United States Trade Representative, "USTR Announces Enforcement Action to Block Illegal Timber Imports from Peru," July 26, 2019, available at www://ustr.gov/about-us/policy-offices/press-office/press-releases/2019/july/ustr-announces-enforcement-action (accessed 20 January 2020).

negative effects of liberalization have failed to do so.[15] Thus, the obligations have shifted and the NCMs have followed. It is a two-step design story. The agreement provides for the home State to ensure the State maintains certain domestic commitments, often modelled after international standards, such as those found in the International Labor Organization Conventions. Where the State cannot deliver on those, the new mechanisms allow the other State to exact demands on private actors within the territory of the other State. While States still enter into reciprocal commitments in these trade-plus areas, they do not rely on State action to ensure those commitments are upheld.

One can again trace this two-step move in the debates surrounding the mechanisms for enforcing labor commitments in the USMCA leading to the RRM. Some lawmakers insisted that the US Government devise a unilateral enforcement mechanism such as that which emerged; others argued for an inspection system through which US officials would visit Mexican factories; some sought third-party dispute settlement with enhancements of various types; and still others preferred the status quo.[16] It was one of the most exploratory and expansive debates on institutional design for labor since the development of the original North American Free Trade Agreement (NAFTA) labor protections in the early 1990s.

The final product of the RRM and likewise the United States–Peru logging arrangement seek to replicate and supplement the domestic enforcement chain by outsourcing the ultimate compliance pressure to the complaining State. These mechanisms that reach beyond the border into the territory of a trading partner extend the traditional trade law institutional design questions from actions taken by that trading partner to actions taken by private actors on the ground. They empower the receiving or complaining State to penalize firms that are violating domestic law. By shifting the roles and responsibilities through these NCMs, these developments have upended the traditional discussions on enforcement institutional design in trade law and called into question whether the field has a reliable and consistent theory of compliance at all.

[15] See generally T Meyer, "Free Trade, Fair Trade, and Selective Enforcement" (2018) 118 *Columbia Law Review* 491 (collecting views).

[16] See M Curi, "Neal: USTR 'Favorably' Received USMCA Working Group's Counterproposal" (*Inside U.S. Trade*, October 4, 2019).

8.3 Assessing these New Tools: Costs, Benefits, and the Space Between

Trade NCMs like public complaint processes regarding labor rights violations or environmental abuse are not a new concept, but their latest experimental forms advance their promise. While these advances have benefits, they also have shortcomings. This section briefly assesses the behind-the-border direct compliance obligations along two dimensions. First, it will evaluate the practical consequences of such a scheme. Second, it will turn to the transformative power of this approach.

8.3.1 Practical Problems

There are at least seven issues that behind-the-border compliance schemes raise and that some critics have noted as creating potential problems for the legitimacy of such tools: transparency, predictability, selection bias, irony or hypocrisy, aggrandizement of authority, extraterritoriality, and judicial review. I will take up each in turn.

First is transparency. The present iterations of these tools are largely internal guiding schemes, but they do little to require governments to make publicly available the documentation or reasoning behind the steps taken. Transparency is not a problem unique to behind-the-border schemes in trade law[17] but the problem is surprisingly acute in these new tools – perhaps as a result of their newness.

Second is predictability. These tools do not create any degree of consistency in outcome. While there are some guidelines and the commitments are articulated to a limited degree, some private companies have noted that there is not enough information available to them to be able to comply effectively with the substantive and procedural requirements involved. They have raised questions of due process and coordination which they claim mechanisms lack.

Third is selection bias and power differentials. Although the tools are reciprocal,[18] the expectation, and so far, the practice, has been one-sided. That is, in the case of the RRM, only the United States has taken action against companies operating in Mexico, rather than the other way

[17] See e.g., K Claussen, "Trade Transparency: A Call for Surfacing Unseen Deals" (2022) 122 *Columbia Law Review Forum* 1.

[18] Not all tools are reciprocal. There is no power for Peru to regulate US logging, for example.

around, consistent with the expectation of many. The reasons for this lopsided situation include (1) the United States has limited the scope of actions that Mexico could take toward US companies to a very limited set;[19] (2) the power dynamics of the unions in the United States; and (3) power dynamics between the countries. While these are still instruments to which States agree, the bargains are not always reciprocal. The result is often advanced and wealthy economies pursuing compliance by not just developing States but now entities in developing States, including multinationals from the wealthy State. These are tools through which the United States and other countries can exert force directly on companies operating in places like Mexico and Peru and not because of any characteristic of the product that those companies seek to import, but rather based on their behavior behind the border in those other States.

Fourth is irony, or what some would call hypocrisy. Concern about the operation of the RRM is not just limited to the selection of what might be subject to the RRM. It is also a bias in result – what some would call hypocrisy or irony. This is where considerable criticism has been raised about the application of the RRM to date. The mechanism permits US Government actors to demand of companies operating in Mexico labor practices that it cannot demand from US companies operating just a few kilometers across the border.[20] A related point is the selection bias in the types of societal problems these US-designed tools are intended to solve. One does not see – yet – similar tools focused on private action to address carbon emissions, for example.

Fifth is aggrandizement of authority. The experience of the United States with its second RRM situation at a company called Tridonex in Mexico has led to some criticism about the possible aggrandizement of authority on the part of US authorities. In that context, rather than reach agreement with Mexico about a course of remediation as provided by the agreement, the US Trade Representative entered into an agreement with the company, in which the company promised to take certain actions in the interests of the workers at the identified worksite. Nothing about the RRM language or the United States implementing legislation provides authority to the US Trade

[19] The United States has limited the range of circumstances to which the RRM extends in a footnote in the Agreement. For a discussion and explanation of how this limitation operates, see D LeClercq, "Biden's Worker-Centered Trade Policy: Whose Workers?" (*International Economic Law and Policy Blog*, May 16, 2021); K Claussen, "A First Look at the New Labor Provisions in the USMCA Protocol of Amendment" (*International Economic Law and Policy Blog*, December 12, 2019).

[20] LeClercq (n 19).

Representative to enter into agreements with companies. Thus, this agreement, apart from raising questions of legality, has also suggested to some outsiders that these compliance moves are means through which US executive branch agencies may grow their authority.

Sixth is extraterritoriality. In the State-to-State context, some governments have traveled to the other State to carry out in-person investigation of the measure or practice, or they have relied on their government officials already on the ground in those places. Indeed, as noted, for some trade-plus areas, public submission or consultation opportunities have allowed foreign civil society actors to provide information from inside the breaching State to the complaining government to expand their reach. But the RRM and the Peru mechanism go still further in two respects. One way is by targeting individual companies not operating in the United States. Second is by taking action against companies for their violations of domestic labor law in Mexico (and likewise for their violation of domestic law in Peru).

And seventh, finally, is judicial review. Although one of the aforementioned mechanisms (the RRM) involves the possibility for review by a neutral panel, the actions undertaken by the US agencies involved in raising these accusations and taking such actions are not subject to review. Although their actions are regulatory, much like anti-dumping and countervailing duty actions taken by US Customs and Border Protection or the US Department of Commerce, companies affected do not have means to challenge their targeting. They cannot bring claims to a judicial body to raise concerns about the process through which they have been prosecuted.

8.3.2 *Achievements*

Despite these criticisms, advocates celebrate the new compliance tools for making positive change in the lives of many workers, as well as in combatting climate change in the case of the Peru logging situation. Further, we can respond to each of the criticisms above to defend the deployment of these tools. Some of the criticisms are about the application of the tools to date rather than the existence of the tools themselves, for example. To take one, the hypocrisy critique may be seen as shortsighted, given that these tools may assist with norm-building at the international level, even if US institutions will not permit those norms to be entrenched at home. Like elsewhere, we may be able to achieve internationally what we cannot achieve domestically due to political constraints. Similarly, the extraterritoriality claims are somewhat tempered by the fact that these do not involve US authorities arriving at Mexican companies or at Peruvian logging sites and arresting people. The action that the US Government can take is limited to that which it can exert at its borders. In theory, companies that come into focus for compliance may direct their goods elsewhere.

In sum, while these new mechanisms create some problems, they also may make positive changes toward broader goals. It is too early to draw conclusions in evaluating these tools. Further, measuring success in these trade-plus NCMs is just as difficult as it is in measuring success in other areas. A wide range of metrics may be appropriate. One metric that is often raised is increased use: the more we use an NCM, the more successful it is, according to some lawmakers. But for tools that are intended to create penalties for bad behavior, the better metric may be that there are no instances of bad behavior and therefore the NCM has effectively created a deterrent effect. Likewise, an application of the tools is hardly a sign of success. Counting up their uses does not begin to take into account the possible ancillary effects they may have on communities or within workplaces and in other respects. In the case of the RRM, some commentators have raised concern about how the US engagement with the targeted worksites may exacerbate other local problems, whether related to violence or otherwise. There are not simply winners and losers in these stories; the impact is far more textured than meets the eye.

8.3.3 In Between

These tools have also precipitated ideological shifts and normative changes that are difficult to square as criticism or achievement, as cost or benefit. Those sorts of assessments shift easily with one's perspective. For example, some proponents of free trade have seen these tools as advancing protectionism, and have suggested that in so doing, they create avoidable costs for all. These critics argue that the creators and users of these tools aim to discourage US investment in Mexico and encourage US and multinational companies to invest instead in the United States. Through a combination of tariff tools and these behind-the-border mechanisms, the United States is seeking to ensure that US and other companies will not choose Mexico over the United States.[21] Others would say this is not just about keeping US businesses at home. To these

[21] It is not just the RRM that suggests this but also other changes made to what was formerly the NAFTA.

advocates, helping Mexican workers is paramount and these sorts of tools permit the US Government to help the Mexican Government achieve that goal, particularly in areas where the Mexican Government is constrained from making progress. In both camps are those for whom the best way to promote US economic competitiveness is by making sure competitors in Mexico are held to the same standards.

At the least, these tools recognize that changing State behavior is challenging and that States' comparative advantage, or at least that of the United States, may be in changing company behavior. That is a typical domestic law function. These tools position States to achieve these goals in new ways, to decide that certain types of trade are good and other types are bad, and to put a thumb on that scale. Thus, we can evaluate these tools as a matter of policy, and as a matter of practicality, but we might also consider whether one can judge the achievements of these new institutions merely by their concrete outcomes. We can likewise examine these tools based on principles about how laws are designed to operate, where the power lies, or the value of this particular legal practice.

The operation of these new compliance tools has multifaceted effects that space does not permit me to explore here, but we might ask the following questions as a means of further evaluation from either a trade perspective or a compliance perspective: Are they redistributive or wealth-producing? Do they produce better governance? Are they norm-enhancing? Are they gap-filling or capacity-building? Are they hand-tying (self-regarding or other-regarding)? These questions and others like them require greater exploration before we can draw conclusions about trade NCMs.

8.3.4 *Lessons for Compliance Theories in International Law*

The new trade NCMs with their behind-the-border compliance focus also offer lessons for compliance theories more generally in international law. I highlight just a handful here for further exploration in later work.

First, behind-the-border NCMs adjust the levers in the conventional compliance stories that have dominated international law scholarship.[22]

[22] See e.g., O Ben-Shahar and A Bradford, "Reversible Rewards" (2012) 15 *American Law and Economics Review* 156; O Hathaway and S Shapiro, "Outcasting: Enforcement in Domestic and International Law" (2011) 121 *Yale Law Journal* 252; RE Scott and PB Stephan, *The Limits of Leviathan* (2006); A Guzman, "A Compliance-Based Theory of International Law" 90 *California Law Review* 1826; B Simmons, "Compliance with International Agreements" (1998) 1 *Annual Review of Political Science* 75; B Kingsbury,

In addition to focusing largely on State compliance with agreements or with dispute settlement reports, prior scholars have sought to explain how international law serves as a constraint on behavior. The trade NCM experience of recent years aligns the features of our international law compliance story in different ways. The ordinary touchpoints of the realist or rational functionalist literature are not salient here. For example, reputation – a key input in the functionalist compliance theory – has a diminished role in the operation of trade NCMs. Rather, the trade NCM developments purport to align more with normative theories and identify normative aims of the States involved. But that analogy is likewise strained. The shifting targets are part of the categorization issue: there is no common view on the problem these tools are intending to solve, making the compliance discussion much harder to formulate.

Second, rather than look at trade NCMs as dispute resolution or "enforcement" tools for States, we might characterize this activity as "regulation." Then we might ask: What are the options, values, and scholarship that we might seek to integrate in examining such moves? What are the implications of characterizing them as one or the other? In the existing literature on compliance, some scholars have considered the role of sanctions and incentives when comparing an "enforcement model" with a "management model." Here, we are somewhere between those poles. Again, this comparison is constrained by the differences in levels of actors involved in this story and the regulatory nature of some of them. While the literature to date has looked at first and second-order compliance, these trade NCMs might be properly characterized as third-order, given bureaucratic attention to private actors. In third-order compliance, the bureaucracy deepens as trade agencies move from negotiation and litigation to regulatory monitors.[23]

Third, these NCMs often try to replicate the domestic enforcement chain through new institutions. They do not rely on domestic actors as in a complementary system, but they include multiple steps of review by

"The Concept of Compliance as a Function of Competing Conceptions of International Law" (1998) 19 *Michigan Journal of International Law* 345; A Chayes and A Chayes, *The New Sovereignty* (Harvard University Press 1995). Rachel Brewster and Adam Chilton have looked at second-order compliance in trade, namely US compliance with World Trade Organization Dispute Settlement Body reports, but here I am referring principally to first-order compliance issues. R Brewster and A Chilton, "Supplying Compliance: Why and When the United States Complies with WTO Rulings" (2014) 39 *Yale Journal of International Law* 200.

[23] I borrow the term from R van Loo, "Regulatory Monitors: Policing Firms in the Compliance Era" (2019) 119 *Columbia Law Review* 369.

bureaucratic actors. Putting bureaucrats at the center of these mechanisms may enhance their legitimacy in the eyes of a domestic public. This approach also allows that government to retain control over the process and its outcome, as compared to using international adjudicators. In these ways, these mechanisms go beyond what other scholars have tracked in international law, blurring the lines between domestic and international authority.

Fourth, trade theories usually instead speak in terms of remedies rather than sanctions and they do so with little emphasis on deterrence given that "dispute settlement" language conveys a sense of misunderstanding rather than bad behavior. This distinction is more than a matter of semantics. Rather, the new compliance models operate within this trend and foundational understanding of how States ought to interact with one another. It becomes impossible to isolate the impact of these new tools and norms from the broader backdrop on remedies rather than the typical punitive action. There are, in fact, multiple layers of compliance at work in ways not seen before.

Fifth, the trade NCM experience demonstrates how control has shrunk in importance while cooperation is more prominent. Query then, whether cooperation can constitute compliance. In each of the aforementioned tools, the States must cooperate, and ultimately the companies likewise. Even if they are not aimed at correcting State conduct that diverges from the text of international obligations, can they still qualify as compliance mechanisms? When the US Government works with companies to fix problems abroad, is that a matter of compliance? These trade NCMs do not rely on either dispute settlement, or domestic adjudication, or entities that use force as we can see in other areas of government and international law. Rather, the trade NCMs reconsider the dynamics among the parties and expand the meaning of "party" broadly, again making traditional compliance theories more difficult to apply here.

This review of the contributions made by trade NCMs to compliance theory suggests that these may merit a "new category" of transnational compliance ideas or theory that forces a reevaluation of the *structure* of the compliance problem. If that is so, then it is worth complicating the analysis somewhat further by examining whether the parties involved in shaping this mechanism have a shared understanding of its goals and objectives.

8.4 Conclusion

The conundrum of trade-plus enforcement is the absence of a shared understanding of what enforcement is for and what institutional designs serve those likely diverse ends. Rather, the system has marched toward making commitments enforceable through third-party dispute settlement across a wide array of issue areas. For nearly twenty-five years, as free trade agreements have proliferated, most trade-plus advocates and members of civil society have advocated for third-party dispute settlement and the availability of the same remedies for trade-plus disputes, as for conventional commercial disputes as a means to serve their ends.[24] Opposition to this now-establishment view has manifested not based on effectiveness of the third-party mechanism, but rather based on concerns that the concrete remedies obtained through these types of mechanisms could create additional barriers to trade – direct and indirect. The result has been a narrow two-sided conversation about the range of possibilities for trade-plus enforcement.

This binary representation of trade-plus enforcement has diminished the relevance and prominence of a more fulsome conversation about institutional design. Today, the growing prevalence of trade NCMs pushes the boundaries of that conversation and opens a field for research in compliance theory that this chapter has sought to begin.

[24] e.g., W Krist, "The Labor Dilemma," in *Trade Policy in Crisis, The Wilson Center White Paper* (2007).

9

How the World Bank's Dispute Resolution Services Should Benefit Affected Persons and Borrower States

JONATHAN BROSSEAU

9.1 Introduction

Members of the Kawaala community in Kampala, Uganda, report that the Kampala Capital City Authority and armed guards woke them in the early hours of 4 December 2020, and began destroying their homes and farmlands.[1] Kawaala community members allege that their eviction and the ensuing destruction paved the way for the World Bank-funded Lubigi drainage channel project. They claim that the project began without proper consultation or plans for compensation and resettlement, and compromises their livelihoods and well-being, in violation of the Bank's Environmental and Social Framework (Framework) policies.[2] In turn, Bank management claimed that the project-level grievance mechanism should handle most of the Kawaala community's concerns about resettlement and that it is working with Kampala Capital City Authority to strengthen the resettlement plan related to the channel project.[3] Dissatisfied with the World Bank's (Bank) solution to their concerns,

This chapter was funded through a Research Fellowship at the United Nations University, and a version of it was first published in its Working Paper series. The chapter is published here with authorisation.

[1] Witness Radio Uganda, 'Request for Inspection by the World Bank Inspection Panel in Kampala Institutional and Infrastructure Development Project', 17 June 2021, available at www.inspectionpanel.org/sites/www.inspectionpanel.org/files/cases/documents/151-Request%20for%20Inspection-17%20June%202021.pdf.

[2] World Bank, *Environmental and Social Framework*, 4 August 2016 (Framework), available at https://thedocs.worldbank.org/en/doc/837721522762050108-0290022018/original/ESFFramework.pdf.

[3] Bank Management, 'Response: Second Kampala Institutional and Infrastructure Development Project (P133590)', 24 August 2021, available at www.inspectionpanel.org/sites/www.inspectionpanel.org/files/cases/documents/151-Management%20Response-24%20August%202021.pdf.

Kawaala community members filed a complaint to the Inspection Panel (Panel) in June 2021 with the support of local and international civil society organisations. The Panel subsequently recommended to the Bank's executive directors that the complaint be investigated.[4]

Upon the executive directors' approval of the Panel's recommendation for inspection,[5] the Kawaala community and Uganda were offered the opportunity to pursue dispute resolution rather than to go forward with the compliance review conducted by the Panel, a first in the Bank's history. Indeed, the executive directors had only approved the updated Inspection Panel Resolution[6] and the Accountability Mechanism Resolution,[7] which established the new Dispute Resolution Services (DRS) in September 2020.[8] Under the DRS, those affected by Bank-funded projects (affected persons, also referred to as requesters once they submit a request for inspection to the Panel) and the borrower State can now resolve a complaint before the Inspection Panel through joint fact-finding, mediation, and other similar approaches, where both agree to this process. In the autumn of 2021, the DRS was staffed and published its Interim Operating Procedures to implement dispute resolution processes. The Kawaala community and Uganda agreed to pursue dispute resolution shortly thereafter.[9] According to a civil society organisation supporting the Kawaala community, the dispute resolution process

[4] Inspection Panel, 'Report and Recommendation: Second Kampala Institutional and Infrastructure Development Project (P133590)', 4 October 2021, available at www.inspectionpanel.org/sites/www.inspectionpanel.org/files/cases/documents/151-Uganda-KIIDP2-Inspection%20Panel%20Report%20and%20Recommendation-4%20October%202021.pdf.

[5] World Bank, 'Parties in Uganda Infrastructure Case Agree to Pursue Dispute Resolution', 7 December 2021, available at www.worldbank.org/en/programs/accountability/brief/parties-in-uganda-infrastructure-case-agree-to-pursue-dispute-resolution.

[6] Inspection Panel Resolution (8 September 2020), Resolution No. IBRD 2020-0004 and Resolution No. IDA 2020-0003 (2020 Panel Resolution), available at www.inspectionpanel.org/sites/www.inspectionpanel.org/files/documents/InspectionPanelResolution.pdf.

[7] Accountability Mechanism Resolution (8 September 2020), Resolution No. IBRD 2020-0005 and Resolution No. IDA 2020-0004 (2020 Accountability Mechanism Resolution), available at www.inspectionpanel.org/sites/www.inspectionpanel.org/files/documents/AccountabilityMechanismResolution.pdf.

[8] While the DRS is a plural noun, this chapter treats it as a singular noun for ease of reading, as the Bank does in its publications.

[9] Accountability Mechanism Secretary, 'Notice of Agreement to Pursue Dispute Resolution: Second Kampala Institutional and Infrastructure Development Project (P133590)' (2 December 2021), available at www.inspectionpanel.org/sites/www.inspectionpanel.org/files/cases/documents/151-Notice%20of%20Agreement%20to%20Pursue%20Dispute%20Resolution-2%20December%202021.pdf.

would provide an 'appropriate forum' for the community to raise their demands, which include 'a new, proper land survey and identification of project affected persons, provision of adequate compensation, and adequate time to resettle.'[10] At the time of writing, two more cases have also begun dispute resolution process.[11]

In July 2022, the accountability mechanism published a second version of the DRS' operating procedures, on which it sought comments from any interested individuals and organisations.[12] An earlier form of the present chapter was therefore sent to the accountability mechanism, recommending amendments to the procedures similar to the ones set out below. Accountability Counsel and fifty-six other civil society organisations also submitted substantial joint comments on the procedures.[13] In December 2022, the accountability mechanism published the third and final version of the DRS' operating procedures: the 2022 Accountability Mechanism Operating Procedures. In contrast to other multilateral development banks, the World Bank did not make public the comments it received, simply noting they were from civil society organisations, other accountability mechanisms, former Panel members, and scholars. As will be explained, the revision in the accountability mechanism operating procedures that strengthens requesters' protection the most is that the requirement that additional advisers may be engaged by one Party *only* subject to the other Party's consent, which was present in the first two versions of the procedures, was

[10] RC Mosenda and C Daniel, 'World Bank Board Approves Investigation into Community Concerns of Forced Eviction by the Lubigi Drainage Channel' (*Accountability Counsel*, 27 October 2021), available at www.accountabilitycounsel.org/2021/10/world-bank-board-approves-investigation-into-community-concerns-of-forced-eviction-by-the-lubigi-drainage-channel-first-case-in-the-newly-established-dispute-resolution-service/.

[11] See Cameroon: Nachtigal Hydropower Project (P157734) and Hydropower Development on the Sanaga River Technical Assistance Project (P157733), available at www.inspectionpanel.org/panel-cases/nachtigal-hydropower-project-p157734-and-hydropower-development-sanaga-river-technical; Nepal: Nepal–India Electricity Transmission and Trade Project (P115767) and its Additional Financing (P132631), available at www.inspectionpanel.org/panel-cases/nepal-india-electricity-transmission-and-trade-project-p115767-and-its-additional.

[12] Accountability Mechanism, 'Accountability Mechanism Secretary Invites Comment on the Draft Accountability Mechanism Operating Procedures', 18 July 2022, available at www.worldbank.org/en/programs/accountability/brief/accountability-mechanism-secretary-invites-comment-on-the-draft-accountability-mechanism-operating-procedures.

[13] Accountability Counsel and others, 'Joint Comments on AM & Panel Procedures' (9 September 2022) (Joint Comments), available at www.accountabilitycounsel.org/wp-content/uploads/joint-comments-on-am-panel-procedures.pdf.

removed. As also explained below, the revision that weakens requesters' protection the most is that, while the first version required that dispute resolution agreements be consistent with *Bank policies* and domestic or international law, the final accountability mechanism operating procedures requires that the Accountability Mechanism Secretary requests the Parties 'to make appropriate modifications' if she believes there are inconsistencies with domestic or international law only.

Given the novelty of the DRS, this chapter examines how the dispute resolution process offered by the Bank should benefit affected persons and borrower States (together, the Parties). The chapter also critically evaluates the dispute resolution process in light of the mandates of the Inspection Panel and the DRS, as well as best practices concerning the right of access to a remedy under international law. In particular, it considers the strengths and weaknesses of the current dispute resolution process and suggests how the Bank should improve this process when it revises the Accountability Mechanism Resolution in late 2023[14] or the accountability mechanism operating procedures in the future. By noting how the DRS procedures have been reformed through the three versions, the chapter also records the evolution of the DRS, which includes identifying whether civil society organisation-suggested revisions have been incorporated into the procedures and whether the revisions implemented are more or less protective of affected persons. As such, the chapter seeks to contribute to the global administrative law scholarship.

The task of evaluating the DRS as part of the Bank's accountability system matters for several reasons. First, it will enable the Parties to understand better whether the DRS is indeed the 'appropriate forum' for resolving the complaint in each case, and whether they should therefore consent to it or opt instead for the compliance review process undertaken by the Panel. Further, the Bank, its executive directors, and its accountability mechanism could consider this evaluation when revising the DRS. The nearly twenty other multilateral development banks, which have been influenced by the Bank's practices on accountability in the past,[15]

[14] World Bank, 'Report and Recommendations on the Inspection Panel's Toolkit Review' (March 2020) para 37, available at https://documents1.worldbank.org/curated/en/972351583772786218/pdf/Report-and-Recommendations-on-the-Inspection-Panel-s-Toolkit-Review.pdf.

[15] R Mackenzie, CPR Romano, Y Shany, and P Sands, 'The Inspection Panel of the World Bank' in *The Manual on International Courts and Tribunals* (2nd ed., Oxford University Press 2010) para 17.29.

could also consider the parts that apply to them when revising their respective dispute resolution processes.

Overall, the chapter suggests that the DRS, as it is now designed, has the *potential* to enhance the right to access a remedy of affected persons. By emphasising party-led dispute resolution, it provides affected persons with the assistance of an independent third party, the opportunity to participate in the determination of remedial measures, and the chance to receive effective remedies beyond those envisaged by Bank policies. The heavy reliance of the DRS on the consent of both Parties may also serve to preserve a significant role for the Inspection Panel, because the Parties may not come to an agreement through dispute resolution in most cases. At the same time, this reliance on consent also enables affected persons to agree to remedies to some degree inferior to those envisaged by Bank policies. This is a real possibility, particularly where affected persons continue to bear the adverse material effects of violations of Bank policies while the dispute resolution process runs its course, and are typically vulnerable populations with fewer resources and less expertise on Bank projects than borrower States. Moreover, as Bank management is involved in the dispute resolution process only if the Parties consent to it and as a technical observer, management cannot ensure that affected persons obtain a meaningful remedy. Given that the DRS does not fully address these concerns at the moment, the question arises as to whether it will *actually* enhance the access to a remedy of affected persons, and whether it may instead prejudice the Panel's mandate to provide access to a remedy to these persons. Against this backdrop, the Bank should consider altering the dispute resolution process to better address the inequality of power between affected persons and borrower States, such as by entrenching certain minimal safeguards for affected persons, to ensure that they make informed decisions on remedies.

The chapter proceeds in two sections. Section 9.2 examines the mandates of the World Bank's three avenues for a remedy as they pertain to the right of access of affected persons. These avenues are the Inspection Panel, the Grievance Redress Service, and the DRS. This section shows that the Panel and Grievance Redress Service have succeeded in performing their respective functions of providing independent compliance review and management-led solutions. However, because they did not offer independent dispute resolution, a gap nevertheless remained in the Bank's accountability system. The establishment of the DRS filled that gap by offering affected persons access to independent dispute resolution processes. It did so while enhancing the three pillars of the Panel, which can be identified as: effectiveness, accessibility, and independence.

Section 9.3 then proposes three areas of improvement to the DRS that the Bank should consider to comply with the mandate of the Inspection Panel and best practices related to accountability mechanisms. To enhance accessibility, the Bank should consider strengthening the procedural protections and opportunities for participation afforded to affected persons in the dispute resolution process, notably by providing a minimum standard of access to project-related materials. To enhance effectiveness, it should consider clarifying the minimum threshold for remedies that affected persons can accept and provide for the mandatory verification of the implementation of the Parties' agreement. Finally, to enhance independence, the Bank should consider offering affected persons more options regarding the sequencing of compliance review and dispute resolution to protect the mandate of the Inspection Panel, and offer them funding to get support from professionals during the dispute resolution process.

9.2 The Mandates of the Bank's Three Avenues for a Remedy

Section 9.2 provides an overview of the three avenues for a remedy within the World Bank that enables the Bank to meet its moral and legal obligations to provide affected persons the right of access to a remedy, given its immunity from suit in national courts.[16] This serves to identify

[16] See Articles of Agreement of the International Bank for Reconstruction and Development, opened for signature 27 December 1945, 60 Stat 1440 (1946), HAS No. 1502, 2 UNTS 134, as amended 16 December 1965, 16 UST 1942, TIAS No 5929, Article VII, § 1 (Articles of Agreement). In the *Effects of Awards of Compensation* Advisory Opinion, the International Court of Justice held that it would 'hardly be consistent with the expressed aim of the Charter to promote freedom and justice for individuals ... that [the United Nations] should afford no judicial or arbitral remedy to its own staff for the settlement of any Accountability Mechanism which may arise between it and them'. [1954] ICJ Rep 47, 57. In the same way, it would be 'hardly consistent' with the Bank's mandate of ending extreme poverty and boosting shared prosperity, as set out in its Articles of Agreement, not to afford people affected by its funded projects the right of access to a meaningful remedy. Moreover, if the right to a remedy is determined to exist under customary international law, this would imply that the Bank is bound, as an international organisation, to ensure the realisation of this right under international law: see *Amicus Curiae* of Daniel Bradlow, *Jam v International Finance Corp.*, August 2016 (DC Circuit Court of Appeals), available at https://earthrights.org/wp-content/uploads/2016-08-17_amicus_for_appellant_dckt_.pdf.

the legal and policy standards against which the avenues for a remedy provided by the Bank should be evaluated.[17]

9.2.1 *Inspection Panel: Panel-Led Compliance Review*

The Inspection Panel was established in 1993 as the first independent accountability mechanism at an international financial institution. The Panel's mandate is to determine whether the Bank complies with its operational policies and procedures in any particular case. While the Panel thus has a compliance function and adopts a fault-finding approach, it also provides affected persons with a basic right of access to a remedy.[18] It is also a quasi-judicial body: as described below, the executive directors of the Bank cannot change its findings, but they retain the power to decide on the outcome of requests at key stages of the process. For example, the Panel cannot issue binding orders, whether interim or final, as courts can.

The right of access to a remedy provided by the Inspection Panel can be distilled into three pillars, which are at once procedural and substantive.[19] The first pillar is *effectiveness*, which is limited in practice by the Panel's mandate. Once it receives a complaint, the Panel first issues its

[17] The Resolution establishing the Inspection Panel had created in 1993 legal standards applicable to the Bank in terms of providing access to a remedy. Although multilateral development banks may resist referring to their constitutive instruments and resolutions as legal standards and may prefer referring to them as administrative standards instead, these instruments and resolutions are multilateral development banks' internal law, while domestic and international law are their external law. See P Sands and P Klein, *Bowett's Law of International Institutions* (6th ed., Sweet & Maxwell 2009) 448.

[18] Inspection Panel, Operating Procedures (1994), Purpose (1994 Panel Operating Procedures), available at www.inspectionpanel.org/about-us/panel-mandate-and-procedures. Yet, the Panel's purpose of providing access to a remedy to affected persons has sometimes been questioned. For instance, the World Bank's General Counsel in the 1990s, Ibrahim Shihata, had opined that lifting the harm 'is certainly a noble function, but it is not the function of the Panel' (quoted in D Van Den Meerssche, *The World Bank's Lawyers: The Life of International Law as Institutional Practice* (Oxford University Press 2022) 56, fn 100). But see, more recently, the 2014 and 2022 Inspection Panel Operating Procedures, para 2.a., noting that the Panel's 'two important accountability functions' are assessing compliance with Bank policies *and* 'provid[ing] a forum for people . . . to seek recourse for harm which they believe result[s] from Bank-supported operations'.

[19] These three criteria are derived from the main themes in the Panel's mandate as set out in its 1993 Resolution. Others have identified similar themes, but have broken them down into a larger number of criteria. see e.g., V Richard, 'Independent Accountability Mechanisms as Guardians of a Kaleidoscopic Legal Accountability' in O McIntyre and S Nanwani (eds), *The Practice of Independent Accountability Mechanisms (IAMs): Towards Good Governance in*

recommendation to the executive directors on whether a full investigation should be carried out.[20] If the executive directors approve an investigation, then the Panel submits its findings of facts regarding the Bank's compliance with its operational policies and makes any related findings of harm.[21] Although these findings are non-binding, they enable Bank management to propose remedial actions to prevent any non-compliance and harm from continuing. The Inspection Panel itself does not recommend remedial actions.

The second pillar is *accessibility*. The Panel has broad eligibility criteria, according to which any two or more affected persons may submit a request.[22] The opportunity for procedural participation afforded to affected persons is also relatively broad, as they can provide information about the facts underlying the complaints during the investigation.[23] They are also 'consulted' on the plan of action agreed between the Bank and the borrower State on remedial efforts, but do not have decision-making power.[24]

The third pillar of the right is *independence* and *impartiality*.[25] The Panel must be independent not only from Bank management, but also from the borrower States and requesters. The Panel must also be impartial to the merits of the complaints, meaning it should deal thoroughly and fairly with the requests brought to it. On this basis, the Panel is required to give reasons based on the evidence and facts supporting its recommendations and findings.[26]

Development Finance (Brill Nijhoff 2019) 330–37 (setting forth ten criteria of international accountability mechanisms generally).

20 In the early days of the Panel, 'only two of the first 15 cases resulted in Panel investigations, with the Board rejecting Panel recommendations to investigate in four cases. . . . The Second Clarification [in 1999] eased the procedural impasse, with the Board approving all 20 Panel recommendations to investigate over the following decade'. See Inspection Panel, *The Inspection Panel at 25 Years* (World Bank 2018) 33, available at www.inspectionpanel.org/publications.

21 1994 Panel Operating Procedures (n 18) paras 16, 52, and 54.

22 Inspection Panel Resolution (1993), Resolution No. IBRD 93-10 and Resolution No. IDA 93-6, para 12 (1993 Panel Resolution), available at www.inspectionpanel.org/sites/ip-ms8.extcc.com/files/documents/Resolution1993.pdf.

23 1994 Panel Operating Procedures (n 18) paras 47–49.

24 Inspection Panel, Updated Operating Procedures (April 2014), available at www.inspectionpanel.org/sites/ip-ms8.extcc.com/files/documents/2014%20Updated%20Operating%20Procedures.pdf, paras 68, 70.

25 LT Preston, 'The World Bank Inspection Panel' (World Bank, 24 September 1993); 1993 Panel Resolution (n 22) para 4.

26 1993 Panel Resolution (n 22) para 22; 1994 Panel Operating Procedures (n 18) para 37.

Best practices have developed in the three decades since the establishment of the Panel, suggesting today that the right of access to a remedy provided by international organisations, including multilateral development banks, should include access not only to a compliance review process but also to a dispute resolution process. Notably, the 2011 UN Guiding Principles on Business and Human Rights (UNGPs) identify best practices regarding access to a remedy, and in particular to dispute resolution functions. While most relevant for States, the UNGPs also set, by analogy, a benchmark to assess how multilateral development banks should provide access to a remedy.[27]

Two of the dispute resolution mechanisms envisaged by the UNGPs are particularly relevant to multilateral development banks like the Bank. The first is 'effective *operational-level* grievance mechanisms', which should remedy complaints early and directly.[28] The second is 'effective and appropriate *non-judicial* grievance mechanisms', which must be part of a comprehensive system to address complaints.[29] These two types of mechanisms complement, but do not substitute, each other.[30] In terms of an effective remedy, both mechanisms must 'ensur[e] that outcomes and remedies accord with internationally recognised human rights'.[31] This criterion, among others, has been endorsed by a Bank publication on the evaluation of grievance mechanisms.[32]

In response, in part, to the development of best practices concerning the right of access to a remedy, twenty multilateral development banks have established accountability mechanisms similar to the Inspection Panel to provide access to remedies through a compliance review process. Many of these banks have also included dispute resolution processes to increase the effectiveness of access.[33] All multilateral development banks

[27] See, similarly, M van Huijstee, K Genovese, C Daniel, and S Singh, 'Glass Half Full? The State of Accountability in Development Finance' (2016) 14, available at www.ciel.org/wp-content/uploads/2021/06/Glass-half-full.pdf, using the UNGPs as an assessment framework to evaluate international accountability mechanisms.

[28] UNHCR, *Guiding Principles on Business and Human Rights*, UN Doc HR/PUB/11/04, Principle 29 (emphasis added).

[29] Ibid., Principle 27 (emphasis added).

[30] Ibid., Commentary to Principle 29.

[31] Ibid., Principle 31(f).

[32] World Bank, 'Evaluating a Grievance Redress Mechanism' (2014), available at https://documents.worldbank.org/en/publication/documents-reports/documentdetail/431781468158375570/evaluating-a-grievance-redress-mechanism.

[33] Mackenzie, Romano, Shany, and Sands (n 15) para 17.29.

similar to the Bank in terms of size and function, for instance, provide access to dispute resolution processes today.[34]

The Inspection Panel has successfully exercised its mandate, even if it has not provided an effective remedy to affected persons through dispute resolution in line with best practices. The Bank receives complaints yearly on about 3 per cent of its 250 ongoing projects, and of that 3 per cent of projects, the Inspection Panel investigates about a third.[35] Most complaints concern environmental assessment, investment project financing, consultation/disclosure, and involuntary resettlement.[36] In terms of its fault-finding approach, the Panel has generally been very successful in holding the Bank accountable and promoting institutional learning.[37] It has also been moderately successful in preventing future harm.[38] For example, on the Uganda Transport Development Project, then-World Bank Group President Jim Yong Kim explained that '[t]he Inspection Panel's investigation into the … Project identified multiple failures, including cases of gender-based violence', which played 'an important role in the Bank canceling the project'.[39]

However, the Panel has been less successful in remedying the harm already suffered by affected persons.[40] While the result of the Panel's investigation is to bring the project back into compliance, it does not guarantee compensation for affected persons in relation to the harm that occurred.[41] Moreover, according to one study, compliance investigations at the Bank take on average fifteen months.[42] Such a delay is significant

[34] D Bradlow, 'External Review of the Inspection Panel's Toolkit' (2018) paras 64, 67, available at https://documents1.worldbank.org/curated/en/562131583764988998/pdf/External-Review-of-the-Inspection-Panel-s-Toolkit.pdf.

[35] Inspection Panel, *Annual Report* (World Bank 2021) 26, available at www.worldbank.org/en/programs/accountability/publication/world-bank-inspection-panel-annual-report-fy2021.

[36] Ibid., 27.

[37] World Bank (n 14) para 1.

[38] See e.g., LMG Ta and BAT Graham, 'Can Quasi-Judicial Bodies at the World Bank Provide Justice in Human Rights Cases?' (2018–2019) 50 *Georgetown Journal of International Law* 113, 124, Figure 2, reporting that over 30 per cent of eligible complaints at the World Bank resulted in a project change.

[39] Inspection Panel (2018) (n 20) 70.

[40] See e.g., Ta and Graham (n 38) 124–25, Figure 2, reporting that over 15 per cent of eligible complaints at the Inspection Panel and Compliance Advisor Ombudsman of the IFC/MIGA result in compensation, but even then they 'often simply enforce[d] the payment of sums which had been promised, but not delivered, to displaced communities'.

[41] van Huijstee, Genovese, Daniel, and Singh (n 27) 118.

[42] Ibid., 43.

for many affected persons, especially when investigations concern allegations of serious harm. Finally, as noted above, affected persons have no decision-making power on the remedial efforts agreed between the Bank and the borrower State. Management and the executive directors may also ignore – and in some cases have ignored – the findings of non-compliance by accountability mechanisms like the Panel.[43] In short, the Inspection Panel does not offer affected persons the same access to a remedy through a problem-solving approach as a dispute resolution process would.

9.2.2 *Grievance Redress Service: Management-Led Solution*

To bring its accountability system further in line with best practices concerning accountability mechanisms, the Bank established the Grievance Redress Service and two mechanisms related to the Inspection Panel.[44] First, the Grievance Redress Service is a complaint-handling mechanism that helps project teams broker solutions at the corporate level.[45] Established in 2015, it reports to senior Bank management. The mandate of the Grievance Redress Service is to address complaints directly and effectively with the project teams, with the purpose of '[closing] the gap between project-level grievance redress mechanisms … and the Inspection Panel in the Bank's accountability structure'.[46] Seeking resolution first through one of the recourses offered by the Bank, such as the Grievance Redress Service, is one of the preconditions for submitting a complaint to the Inspection Panel.[47]

The growing number of cases that the Grievance Redress Service receives each year demonstrates that it has effectively provided affected

[43] At the IFC/MIGA, see *Jam v International Finance Corp.*, No. 17–1011, 139 S Ct 759 (2019), 5–6 (US Supreme Court).

[44] Historically, affected persons seeking solutions to complaints through dispute resolution at the Bank only had access to project-level grievance mechanisms, and only where they were put in place by borrower States themselves: World Bank, Framework (n 2) paras 60–61.

[45] World Bank, 'Grievance Redress Service: Finding Solutions Together' (2021), available at https://thedocs.worldbank.org/en/doc/bb2e4345aa86a6e92414ce9041c3048f-0290022021/original/GRS-brochure-2021-english.pdf.

[46] World Bank, 'Grievance Redress Service: Annual Report 2015' (2016), available at https://thedocs.worldbank.org/en/doc/121911510349513569-0290022017/original/GRSAnnualReport2016.pdf.

[47] 2020 Panel Resolution (n 6) para 14. However, affected persons who submitted a complaint to the Inspection Panel could subsequently resort to the *Grievance Redress Service*, as there is no sequential relationship between the two.

persons with access to certain remedies.[48] In 2020, the Grievance Redress Service worked on 211 admissible cases at different processing stages concerning various project-related issues.[49] It has also regularly implemented changes that have enabled it to perform its mandate better. For instance, the recent addition of an 'escalation clause' in its Directives allows the Grievance Redress Service to bring high-risk complaints to senior management's attention quickly.[50] Given its features, the Grievance Redress Service, like project-level grievance mechanisms, fulfil the function of 'operational-level' grievance mechanisms envisaged by Principle 29 of the UNGPs. It has strengthened the governing framework of the Bank's accountability mechanisms in a way that has complemented the mandate of the Inspection Panel.

But while the Grievance Redress Service has been successful at resolving relatively simple disputes concerning operational issues, it has been less successful at resolving disputes concerning more complex or controversial issues. This is in part because the Grievance Redress Service does not report to the top level of the Bank and has a junior status in the Bank hierarchy, which hampers its operation for those disputes.[51] Its efficiency in resolving complex issues is also limited by its (real or perceived) lack of independence from management.[52]

The limitations of the Grievance Redress Service have questioned whether the Bank was meeting best practices on the right of access to a remedy, given that the Grievance Redress Service was the only dispute resolution mechanism offered by the Bank itself for a long time. Neither the Grievance Redress Service, nor other avenues for a remedy, then fulfilled the function of 'non-judicial' grievance mechanisms envisaged by Principle 29 of the UNGPs. This has had implications for the credibility and reputation of the Bank, since all other multilateral

48 Bradlow (n 34) 14, para 56.

49 World Bank, 'Grievance Redress Service: Annual Report 2020' (2021), available at https://thedocs.worldbank.org/en/doc/735981610131855597-0290022021/original/GRSAnnualReportFY20.pdf.

50 World Bank, 'Bank Directive: Grievance Redress Service' (5 May 2021), available at www.worldbank.org/en/projects-operations/products-and-services/grievance-redress-service.

51 Bradlow (n 34) 14–15, para 57.

52 Accountability Counsel, 'Civil Society Statement on the October 31 Decision of the World Bank's Board of Directors on the Review of the Inspection Panel's Toolkit' (14 January 2019), available at www.accountabilitycounsel.org/2019/01/ac-submits-joint-statement-to-wb-board-on-panel-toolkit-review/.

development banks have been offering dispute resolution at the top level of the institution.[53]

As mentioned, the Bank also introduced a second set of options to settle the complaints of affected persons. This came in the form of two mechanisms related to, but formally outside of, the Inspection Panel's process. The first mechanism was a 2013 pilot project in which the Inspection Panel was empowered to postpone its decision on *registration* of a request, and thereby delay triggering the twenty-one-business day period for management to provide its response.[54] The second mechanism was based on the Inspection Panel's 2014 Operating Procedures and entailed that the Panel delayed making a recommendation on *investigation* for a stipulated period.[55] Both mechanisms aimed to provide affected persons and management with more time to develop early solutions to complaints without a formal investigation by the Inspection Panel, to improve the 'effectiveness' of the access to a remedy of affected persons, while simultaneously adhering to the mandate of the Inspection Panel.[56]

Despite the objective of these dispute resolution mechanisms, their success in practice was doubtful. The mechanisms were only employed in a few cases, which meant neither was subject to a systematic review of its effectiveness. A first-hand account of the only two cases that went through the first mechanism – the postponement of registration – suggests that one case was reasonably successful and the other was unsuccessful.[57]

More significantly, concerns arise as to whether the mechanisms complied with the mandate of the Inspection Panel, let alone with best practices on access to a remedy. By seeking to improve the first pillar of the Panel (i.e., effectiveness), the mechanisms may well have compromised the other two (i.e., accessibility as well as independence and impartiality). As to independence, '[t]hese mechanisms blur[red] the clear distinction between the [Inspection Panel]'s responsibilities as an

[53] Bradlow (n 34) 18, para 68.

[54] World Bank, 'Piloting a New Approach to Support Early Solutions in the Inspection Panel Process' (November 2013), available at www.accountabilitycounsel.org/wp-content/uploads/2017/08/PilotingNewApproach.pdf.

[55] 2014 Operating Procedures (n 24) para 44, fn 7.

[56] World Bank (n 54) 3; Inspection Panel, 'Inspection Panel Adopts Updated Operating Procedures' (7 April 2014), available at www.inspectionpanel.org/news/inspection-panel-adopts-updated-operating-procedures.

[57] Bradlow (n 34) 15, para 58, fn 40.

independent and objective fact finder and management's role in the [Inspection Panel] process.'[58] For instance, the mechanisms lacked a neutral mediator that would oversee the problem-solving process.[59] As to accessibility, the mechanisms did not offer affected persons a meaningful opportunity to participate in the design and implementation of measures to address their complaints, and lacked procedural safeguards to counteract the inherent power imbalance between them and Bank management.[60]

In summary, the Bank's introduction of the Grievance Redress Service, the Pilot Project, and the Operating Procedure footnote to offer affected persons with options for dispute resolution can be interpreted as an acknowledgment of the dispute resolution gaps in the Bank's accountability system. But because these mechanisms did not adequately fill the gap of an *independent* dispute resolution process, the Bank introduced a third avenue for a remedy: the DRS.

9.2.3 Dispute Resolution Services: Party-Led Dispute Resolution

The DRS was established in 2020 to increase the access to a remedy of affected persons through dispute resolution processes in addition to, but not as a substitute for, compliance review processes under the auspices of the Panel. This development was precipitated by the approval of the Bank's revised operational policies and procedures, the 2016 Framework. The Framework, among other things, aligned with the concept of due diligence promoted by the UNGPs,[61] and included the requirement that every Bank-funded project has a project-level grievance redress mechanism.[62]

Following an external review and the recommendation of Bank management, the executive directors agreed to establish the DRS along the following lines. First, the requesters must meet the eligibility criteria for submission of requests to the Inspection Panel, and the executive

[58] Ibid., iii, para 12; K Gallagher, *Tools for Activists: An Information and Advocacy Guide to the World Bank Group* (Bank Information Center 2020), Modules 5, 9, available at https://bankinformationcenter.org/en-us/update/toolkit-for-activists/.

[59] van Huijstee, Genovese, Daniel, and Singh (n 27) 67–68.

[60] Richard (n 19); van Huijstee, Genovese, Daniel, and Singh (n 27) 67–68.

[61] *Compare* UNGPs (n 28), Principles 17–21, *with* Framework (n 2), Bank Requirement C ('Environmental and Social Due Diligence').

[62] Framework (n 2), Bank Requirement I ('Grievance Mechanism and Accountability') 11, paras 60–61.

directors must approve an Inspection Panel recommendation to investigate the project. Then, should both the requesters and the borrower State voluntarily agree, they would have the opportunity to resolve their disputes through dialogue, information sharing, joint fact-finding, mediation, and conciliation. In this case, the Panel will hold its compliance process in abeyance until the dispute resolution process concludes.

While the staff of the DRS will 'administer' the proceedings, an external neutral third party will help the Parties reach an agreement. With the agreement of the Parties, Bank management may be an observer in the DRS process, although the role of management remains only technical.[63] At the end of the dispute resolution process, the DRS will issue a report to the executive directors through the Accountability Mechanism Secretary, informing them of the outcome of the process. If the Parties cannot arrive at a settlement within a year and a half, then the complaint is brought back before the Inspection Panel. Like the Panel, the DRS, which facilitates the dispute resolution process, honours requests for confidentiality from the requesters.

Given its features, the DRS offers a true problem-solving approach to the Parties. It provides affected persons a greater opportunity to have alleged harm remedied than the Bank's Inspection Panel process. Affected persons also benefit from having an additional avenue of remedy through which their concerns can be heard and addressed by borrower States. The DRS therefore fulfils the function of the non-judicial grievance mechanism envisaged by Principle 29 of the UNGPs.

At the same time, the DRS should not limit the access to a remedy of affected persons through the Inspection Panel, and it is not a substitute for the compliance review process. Indeed, the executive directors have endorsed the view that the mandate of the DRS is to 'enhance the effectiveness of the World Bank's accountability system', while being accessible and independent, as is the Panel.[64] The Accountability Mechanism Resolution and the Accountability Mechanism Operating Procedures should therefore ensure that the results of problem-solving

[63] In contrast, the IFC/MIGA, 'Independent Accountability Mechanism CAO Policy' (1 July 2021) para 75, available at www.ifc.org/wps/wcm/connect/corp_ext_content/ifc_external_corporate_site/cao-policy-consultation#:~:text=The%20IFC%2FMIGA%20Independent%20Accountability,communities%20and%20IFC%2FMIGA%20clients, provides that '[w]here appropriate and agreed by the Parties, IFC/MIGA may be invited to participate in a CAO dispute resolution process. IFC/MIGA will consider its participation on a case-by-case basis.'

[64] World Bank (n 14) 4, para 23, *and* 6, para 38.

are no less protective of requesters than the one offered by the Inspection Panel.[65]

9.3 The Compliance of the DRS with the Panel's Mandate and Best Practices

Section 9.2 identified the legal and policy standards against which the DRS must be evaluated – respectively, the 1993 mandate of the Inspection Panel and the 2020 mandate of the DRS, and best practices concerning the right of access to a remedy to be provided by accountability mechanisms. Section 9.3 proceeds to determine the compliance of the DRS with these mandates and best practices, and suggests three areas of improvement.

9.3.1 *Accessibility: Eligibility Criterion, Choice of Representatives, and Access to Information*

The first area of improvement relates to accessibility. As mentioned above, to access the DRS, requesters must meet all the eligibility criteria of the Inspection Panel.[66] Arguably, some criteria should apply to requests before both the Panel and the DRS, such as the requirement that a request must concern a Bank-funded project.

But others, such as the requirement that the harm has been caused by the Bank's violation and not the borrower State's, appear less relevant and may well reduce the accessibility of a remedy, as compared to the original mandate of the Inspection Panel. This is because one of the Panel's eligibility criteria – i.e., showing a plausible causal link between the alleged harm and the project[67] – may become more challenging under the Bank's new Framework, given that the responsibilities of the Bank are set out more clearly and narrowly therein than previously.[68] In addition, this eligibility criterion is coupled with a new feature in the eligibility determination phase, whereby Bank management can submit

[65] van Huijstee, Genovese, Daniel, and Singh (n 27) 68.

[66] 2020 Panel Resolution (n 6) paras 13–15.

[67] 2014 Operating Procedures (n 24) para 43.

[68] The shift from prescriptive standards to a 'risk management approach' makes it more difficult for the Panel to assess project compliance with the Framework: Bradlow (n 34) 16–17, para 63; Inspection Panel, 'Comments on the Second Draft of the Proposed Environmental and Social Framework' (17 June 2015) paras 10–11, available at www.inspectionpanel.org/news/inspection-panel-comments-2nd-draft-esf.

evidence of actual compliance or *intent* to comply, and requesters cannot access or respond to this evidence.[69] This lack of opportunity for procedural participation afforded to affected persons therefore also reduces their accessibility to a remedy.[70]

In the context of the Panel, it makes sense to have as one of the eligibility criteria that the harm is caused *by the Bank's violation*, because a compliance review investigation will be focussed on this issue. In the context of the DRS, however, this criterion appears unwarranted, because the goal of dispute resolution processes is *problem-solving with borrower States*. Whether the requesters suffered harm caused by non-compliance with Bank policies and procedures is typically a secondary consideration.[71]

While the criterion adopted by the Bank on the eligibility of complaints to the DRS is consistent with those of most (but not all) other multilateral development banks,[72] questions arise as to whether it complies with the Bank's commitment to increase the access to a remedy with the DRS.[73] In comparison, an approach that would increase the accessibility of the DRS would be to allow the Parties to proceed with dispute resolution if they both agreed to it, without requiring requesters to meet all the Panel's eligibility criteria additionally.[74] In such a case, the consent of borrower States would act as a sufficient barrier to prevent a potential flood of complaints to the DRS and preserve the Panel's central role in the Bank's accountability system.

For these reasons, the Bank should consider abolishing the eligibility criterion of the DRS that requires that the harm must be caused by the Bank's failure to comply with its policies. Given that this improvement

69 2020 Panel Resolution (n 6) para 19.

70 D Desierto, A Perez-Linan, K Wakkaf, R Gagnon et al., 'The "New" World Bank Accountability Mechanism: Observations from the ND Reparations Design and Compliance Lab' (*EJIL:Talk!*, 11 November 2020), available at www.ejiltalk.org/the-new-world-bank-accountability-mechanism/.

71 Bradlow (n 34) 16–17, para 63.

72 OHCHR, *Remedy in Development Finance: Guidance and Practices* (2022) HR/PUB/22/1, 117, available at www.ohchr.org/en/publications/policy-and-methodological-publications/remedy-development-finance.

73 P Woicke, D Fairman, T Salam, E Waitzer et al., *External Review of IFC/MIGA E&S Accountability, Including CAO's Role and Effectiveness: Report and Recommendations* (World Bank 2020) para 209, available at www.worldbank.org/en/about/leadership/brief/external-review-of-ifc-miga-es-accountability.

74 Inspection Panel, 'World Bank Accountability Mechanism and Inspection Panel Reforms: Virtual Discussion', available at www.youtube.com/watch?v=vhv8k Psl94, accessed 1 March 2022 (intervention of Jolie Schwarz).

concerns the Accountability Mechanism Resolution and Inspection Panel Resolution, and not the Accountability Mechanism Operating Procedures, they should be re-evaluated as part of the three-year review of the DRS.

Another proposed improvement regarding accessibility concerns the Parties' choice of representatives and advisers. Paragraph 21.2 of the Accountability Mechanism Operating Procedures requires that the appointment or change of appointment of representatives be made in 'consultation with the DRS'. Paragraph 21.2 states that the Parties can engage additional advisers but removes the requirement that this is only when 'subject to no objection of the other Party', as was present in the first two versions of the procedures. By initially requiring the Parties to agree on each other's additional advisers, the procedures risked exacerbating power imbalances that already exist between the Parties.[75] For instance, borrower States could object to requesters retaining the services of certain civil society organisations as additional advisers, because these civil society organisations would have been critical of their human rights record in the past. This could pressure requesters to 'bend' to the demands of borrower States regarding additional advisers to avoid objections concerning their choice of additional advisers.[76]

Against this backdrop, a study on the Compliance Advisor Ombudsman (CAO), the accountability mechanism of the International Finance Corporation and the Multilateral Investment Guarantee Agency, has found that when non-governmental organisations assisted complainants with dispute resolution processes, the complaints were more likely to receive a remedy or to get to compliance review.[77] It also observed that 'CAO's decision to limit the participation of civil society organisations and legal representatives during negotiation and mediation engendered

[75] See S Balaton-Chrimes and K Macdonald, *The Compliance Advisor Ombudsman for IFC/MIGA: Evaluating Potential for Human Rights Remedy* (Corporate Accountability Research 2016) 40–45. See Accountability Counsel (n 13) 14: 'On one occasion the [Civil Society Organisation] advisor to a group of requesters was completely denied entry into the mediation discussion by the bank client … even though the client was being supported by an entire legal team.'

[76] See van Huijstee, Genovese, Daniel, and Singh (n 27) 114.

[77] R Altholz and C Sullivan, 'Accountability & International Financial Institutions: Community Perspectives on the World Bank's Office of the Compliance Advisor Ombudsman' (International Human Rights Law Clinic, University of California, Berkeley 2017) 3, available at www.law.berkeley.edu/wp-content/uploads/2015/04/Accountability-International-Financial-Institutions.pdf. See also Ta and Graham (n 38) 127–29.

distrust among complainants and in some cases prompted their decision to withdraw from the [dispute resolution] process.'[78] This is sensible, because dispute resolution may not result in fair outcomes where there is inequality of power and resources between the Parties, who are often, on the one hand, local communities in developing countries, and on the other hand, State entities.[79] Therefore, removing from the final Accountability Mechanism Operating Procedures the consent of the other Party as a requirement for engaging additional advisers further protects requesters and is more in line with the DRS' mandate. Despite this positive change, the Bank should also consider revising the Accountability Mechanism Operating Procedures so that they specify what type of advice the DRS staff can give to the Parties on the choice of their representatives, and specifies that either Party can request that its representatives and advisers be copied on all communications sent to it and be present in any discussion on the complaint.

The last improvement regarding accessibility concerns the access to project information. Paragraph 12 of the Accountability Mechanism Operating Procedures does not specify the powers the neutral third party would have regarding access to materials, documents, and testimonies related to the project, leaving this issue entirely to the Parties' consent. Furthermore, paragraph 16 of the Accountability Mechanism Resolution provides that only the 'Accountability Mechanism [will] have full access to project-related information in carrying out [its] functions.' In contrast, the Inspection Panel receives all available project documentation from Bank management.[80] The result of these provisions is that the Parties engaged in the dispute resolution process could, in principle, agree that the requesters may access an amount of information that is (much) lower than that provided to the Panel. It is not an unlikely outcome, because often in practice, the concerns about a project lead to a complaint before Panel based precisely on a breakdown in the sharing of information or adequate consultation by the borrower States. Yet this situation would be problematic, because requesters can only access limited information on the project via the World Bank Policy on Access to Information[81] to

78 Ibid., 82.

79 Desierto, Perez-Linan, Wakkaf, and Gagnon (n 70).

80 1994 Panel Operating Procedures (n 18) para 61; 2014 Operating Procedures (n 24) para 54(a).

81 World Bank, 'Bank Policy: Access to Information' (EXC401-POL01) (1 July 2015), available at https://documents.worldbank.org/en/publication/documents-reports/documentdetail/

assert their rights and interests,[82] and most of the project information is typically in the hands of borrower States. In this case, the opportunity for requesters to obtain meaningful remedies would be hampered by their lack of access to project-related materials, especially early in the dispute resolution process when requesters need the relevant project information to assess their position.[83]

Against this backdrop, the Bank should consider including in the Accountability Mechanism Operating Procedures a minimum standard of information that must be shared with the requesters, or at least a commitment from the borrower State to share in good faith information necessary to ensure the orderly conduct of the dispute resolution process. This improvement would regulate the Parties' agreement on access to information, by ensuring that access is at the very least not significantly lower in the dispute resolution process than it would be in the compliance review process. It would be in line with best practices, which opine that '[m]ember States have a *legal* duty to cooperate with [the] duly established [accountability] mechanisms.'[84] This improvement would also balance the concerns about protecting the effective access to a remedy of requesters with the potential encroachment of such measures on the sovereignty of the borrower States.

In conclusion, the DRS may enhance the accessibility of remedy by providing affected persons with an alternative to the Inspection Panel, in which they play a central role in designing remedial measures that address the harm caused to them by a Bank project. At the same time, revising the aforementioned eligibility criterion, most notably, would better empower the Bank to achieve this goal.

9.3.2 *Effectiveness: Types of Complaint, Content of Agreements, and Verification of Implementation*

The second area of improvement relates to effectiveness of the right to access a remedy. Under the Accountability Mechanism Resolution and

391361468161959342/the-world-bank-policy-on-access-to-information. See also 2022 Accountability Mechanism Operating Procedures, para 8.

[82] M McDonagh, 'Evaluating the Access to Information Policies of the Multilateral Development Banks' in O McIntyre and S Nanwani (eds), *The Practice of Independent Accountability Mechanisms (IAMs): Towards Good Governance in Development Finance* (Brill Nijhoff 2019) 135–36; Altholz and Sullivan (n 77) 82.

[83] See also Desierto, Perez-Linan, Wakkaf, and Gagnon (n 70).

[84] M Shaw and K Wellens, *Accountability of International Organisations* (International Law Association, Berlin Conference 2004) 45 (emphasis added).

the Accountability Mechanism Operating Procedures, complaints concerning serious human rights violations, such as those related to torture, may be brought to the dispute resolution process. Yet, the violation of some of these human rights, such as the prohibition of torture, have *jus cogens* status.[85] This means that they are fundamental principles of international law that must be upheld in all circumstances, and no one may ever derogate from them. International organisations like the Bank are bound by these prohibitions, as they themselves acknowledge.[86] The Bank has a responsibility under international law to end any violation of a *jus cogens* norm that it may enable. When complaints at the Bank concern violations of *jus cogens* norms, it is therefore doubtful whether continuing a Bank project according to its original terms, scope, and specifications for up to a year and a half while the dispute resolution process is underway complies with internationally recognised human rights.

In comparison to the DRS, at the Compliance Advisor Ombudsman, a case can be transferred to compliance appraisal in response to an internal request from the Compliance Advisor Ombudsman director general (i.e., the equivalent to the Accountability Mechanism Secretary), the president, the board, or management.[87] This request may be made when 'concerns exist regarding particularly *severe harm*'.[88] However, such a possibility for internal requests does not exist at the Bank.[89] In fact, the DRS cuts the dialogic function with Bank management and the executive directors. According to paragraph 22.1 of the Accountability Mechanism Operating Procedures, management can only be an observer in the dispute resolution process with the Parties' agreement, and is constrained to a technical role.[90] Yet, the practice shows that Bank management engagement has proven critical to resolving disputes effectively.[91] Given its obligation to uphold *jus*

[85] D Tladi, *Fourth Report on Peremptory Norms of General International Law (Jus Cogens)* (UN International Law Commission 2019) 31–35, 63, available at https://digitallibrary.un.org/record/3798216?ln=en.

[86] K Daugirdas, 'How and Why International Law Binds International Organizations' (2016) 57 *Harvard International Law Journal* 325, 377–80.

[87] CAO Policy (n 63) para 81.

[88] Ibid., 82 (emphasis added).

[89] Only an executive director 'may in special cases of serious alleged violations of [Bank] policies and procedures ask the Panel for an investigation', subject to the Panel's eligibility requirements: 1993 Panel Resolution (n 22) para 12; 2020 Panel Resolution (n 6), para 13.

[90] See also World Bank (n 14) para 34.

[91] Accountability Counsel (n 13) 18 (describing how management involvement brought positive results in a case at the Inter-American Development Bank involving the Haitian Government).

cogens norms, the Bank should revise the Accountability Mechanism Operating Procedures and Accountability Mechanism Resolution to ensure that allegations of violation of these norms are investigated promptly by the Panel instead of moving forward with a dispute resolution process.

Another improvement concerns the content of dispute resolution agreements. According to paragraph 16 of the first version of the procedures, 'Dispute Resolution Agreements should be consistent with World Bank policies and relevant domestic and international law.'[92] This provision is in line with that of other international accountability mechanisms.[93] It only requires ascertaining whether agreements are 'consistent' (and not fully 'compliant') with Bank policies, and therefore does not call for conducting a process similar to a compliance review in parallel to the dispute resolution process. In fact, the Parties can even voluntarily agree to *some* deviations from the policies under this provision. As Professor Bradlow noted in his external review,

> [t]his could happen, for example, if the complainants decide to accept less compensation than they may be entitled to under the policies because they believe that it is more useful to obtain certain compensation now rather than the possibility of more compensation in the future or they could agree to accept less compensation than the policies stipulate in return for access to other project benefits.[94]

In contrast, the revised version of the provision, paragraph 23.1 of the Accountability Mechanism Operating Procedures, provides that, '[i]f the DRS has reason to believe that the Parties intend to include anything in a Dispute Resolution Agreement that is inconsistent with relevant domestic or international law, the [Accountability Mechanism] Secretary will request the Parties to make appropriate modifications.' This provision makes two significant changes as compared to its previous iteration. First, it removes

92 Accountability Mechanism Interim Operating Procedures (13 October 2021) para 16, available at https://thedocs.worldbank.org/en/doc/eb47509513bb29ab629f64450c465351-0330032021/original/DRS-Interim-Operating-Procedures.pdf.

93 African Development Bank's Independent Recourse Mechanism, 'Operating Rules and Procedures' (2015) para 49, available at www.afdb.org/en/documents/independent-recourse-mechanism-operating-rules-and-procedures-january-2015-updated-june-2021. See also the provision applicable to the Compliance Advisor Ombudsman, which was revised in July 2021 – after the judgment of the US Supreme Court in *Jam v International Finance Corp* – to add that it will not 'knowingly' support agreements contrary to the bank's policies: CAO Policy (n 63) para 67.

94 Bradlow (n 34) 13, para 51.

the requirement of consistency of dispute resolution agreements with Bank policies. Yet, under the Articles of Agreement[95] and the Inspection Panel Resolution,[96] the executive directors have an institutional responsibility to ensure the Bank's observance of its operational policies and procedures, an international legal obligation the Bank has no power to modify unilaterally, let alone relinquish. It is therefore doubtful that the Bank would comply with its international obligation should any agreement reached through the dispute resolution process it established be inconsistent with the policies. Second, the provision shifts from an objective requirement of consistency of dispute resolution agreements with domestic and international law, to a subjective requirement that the DRS doubts such consistency. It therefore waters down an obligation of result into an obligation of means, without imposing any burden of investigation on the DRS to absolve itself of this obligation. This change significantly weakens the protection of affected persons.

More broadly, given the inequality of power and resources between the Parties, the procedural protections afforded – or rather, not afforded – to the requesters that were examined in the previous subsection 9.3.1 are all the more important to ensure that requesters do not feel pressured to agree to a remedy that is substantially less than the one to which they are entitled under Bank policies and that would normally be assessed by the Inspection Panel. As a United Nations report noted, 'in many situations, complainants may legitimately feel that partial redress is their only feasible option.'[97] According to best practices, the DRS must ensure at least that its 'outcomes and remedies accord with internationally recognised human rights'.[98] Therefore, the Bank should revert to a provision similar to paragraph 16 of the Interim Operating Procedures, which requires consistency with Bank policies.

The last improvement regarding effectiveness concerns the verification of the implementation of the Parties' agreement. While the Accountability Mechanism Resolution states that the Parties should agree on a 'time-bound implementation schedule for agreed actions',[99] it is silent on how compliance with this implementation is monitored. Paragraph 24.1 of the Accountability Mechanism Operating Procedures

95 Articles of Agreement (n 16) Article V, § 4, (a).
96 1993 Panel Resolution (n 22) para 12; 2020 Panel Resolution (n 6) para 13.
97 OHCHR (n 72) 60.
98 UNGP (n 28), Principle 31(f).
99 2020 Accountability Mechanism Resolution (n 7) para 13(b).

adds that the DRS will monitor implementation subject to the Parties' agreement. It is therefore allowed for the Parties to agree to a relatively weak provision on implementation, whereby compliance with the agreement and the agreed remedial actions are not effectively monitored.

This provision is compatible with the 1993 mandate of the Inspection Panel, because the Panel was not originally granted monitoring powers. In the three decades following the inception of the Panel, intense public scrutiny was often helpful for the actual implementation of an agreement to occur.[100] Best practices have since evolved in parallel to the point where it has become widely accepted that the effectiveness of a dispute resolution process depends on the implementation of agreed remedial actions being monitored.[101] This is because monitoring dispute resolution agreements has proven to be a key factor in ensuring that affected persons achieve a remedy. For instance, as part of a complaint before the accountability mechanism of the Inter-American Development Bank, the monitoring of the dispute resolution agreement signed between the Haitian government and local farmers has shown that implementation remained partial and has proposed solutions to live up to the commitment made of restoring the livelihoods of displaced farmers.[102] Against this background, the executive directors have allowed the Inspection Panel in recent years to monitor compliance on a case-by-case basis.[103] The Inspection Panel Resolution went a step further: it required verification by management, and in some specific cases by the Inspection Panel and the Bank Audit Unit, of the action plan's implementation.[104]

Given that the mandate of the Inspection Panel is to provide affected persons with *basic* access to a remedy, while the mandate of the DRS is to provide them an *additional* path of access, it is unclear why management

[100] Gallagher (n 58) Modules 5, 9.

[101] M Tignino, 'Human Rights Standards in International Finance and Development: The Challenges Ahead' in O McIntyre and S Nanwani (eds), *The Practice of Independent Accountability Mechanisms (IAMs): Towards Good Governance in Development Finance* (Brill Nijhoff 2019); van Huijstee, Genovese, Daniel, and Singh (n 27) 114.

[102] Accountability Counsel, 'The Strength of a Community: Haitian Farmers Request Final Push to Receive Full Compensation' (28 January 2022), available at www.accountabilitycounsel.org/implementation-status/haiti/.

[103] Inspection Panel, 'Overview of Status of Implementation of Management Action Plans Prepared in Response to Inspection Panel Investigation Reports' (2016), available at https://documentos.bancomundial.org/es/publication/documents-reports/documentdetail/298441514906310793/overview-of-status-of-implementation-of-management-action-plans-prepared-in-response-to-inspection-panel-investigation-reports.

[104] 2020 Panel Resolution (n 6) paras 47–53.

(and the Panel) now have monitoring authority with regards to compliance review, but the DRS does not have such authority with regards to dispute resolution. In fact, all international accountability mechanisms currently have monitoring authority regarding dispute resolution, except for the DRS.[105] For example, the Compliance Advisor Ombudsman will monitor the implementation of the Parties' agreement, and a complaint will be transferred to the compliance review process if the Parties fail to implement this agreement.[106] As noted in the external review, failing to ensure that agreements are implemented may have 'adverse reputational consequences' for the Bank.[107] The Bank should therefore consider revising the DRS to require monitoring of implementation. Since this change is significant, it may be best addressed through the three-year review of the DRS in the Accountability Mechanism Resolution.

In short, whether the DRS strengthens or weakens the effectiveness of the right to access a remedy depends on whether the Parties agree to a remedy that is superior, equal, or inferior to the one mandated by Bank policies. In a few cases, affected persons and borrower States may arrive at a win-win agreement, where their respective interests align, and no compromise is needed. But it seems unlikely that in all complaints the borrower State will agree to a remedy that significantly advantages affected persons,[108] given that affected persons will only have brought their complaint before the Panel after their efforts to resolve it with the borrower State and management have already failed.[109] Moreover, the 'worst-case scenario' of a failed dispute resolution process for the borrower State is that the complaint will move forward with the compliance review process, whereby the remedy provided would be no more and no

[105] Bradlow (n 34) iii–iv.

[106] CAO Policy (n 63) paras 68, 70. See also European Investment Bank, 'Complaints Mechanism Policy' (November 2018) para. 5.3.1, available at www.eib.org/en/publications/complaints-mechanism-policy.

[107] Bradlow (n 34) iv, para 20.

[108] Since the DRS is currently assisting with its first complaints, there is no data yet on the percentage of complaints resolved through it. But as a comparison, an independent review in 2020 of nearly 400 complaints across all accountability mechanisms found that just over half of claims that made it to the 'facilitating settlement' phase ended up with an agreement between the parties: S Park, *Environmental Recourse at the Multilateral Development Banks* (Cambridge University Press 2020) 53. However, the fact that affected people consented to an agreement as part of a dispute resolution process does not indicate that they have received a remedy equal or superior to the one envisaged by the banks' policies: ibid., 54–57.

[109] See the eligibility criterion of the Panel: 2020 Panel Resolution (n 6) para 13.

less than the one prescribed by Bank policies. In these cases, the only disadvantage for the borrower State is that it will have to go through a lengthy and public investigation.

Affected persons, on the other hand, continue to experience the harm caused by the Bank project while the dispute resolution process and the compliance review process are ongoing, and therefore are incentivised to agree to some form of remedy quickly. In this context, it is all the more important that significant procedural protections ensure that affected persons do not feel pressured to agree to a remedy substantially less than the one to which they are entitled under Bank policies.

9.3.3 *Independence: Panel Mandate, Staff Involvement, and Party Funding*

The third area of improvement relates to independence and impartiality. As mentioned above, the DRS is independent of Bank management and the Inspection Panel. The Panel 'will not opine on policy compliance in dispute resolution or the outcome of the dispute resolution process'.[110] This firewall between the *structure* of the two mechanisms is warranted to avoid conflicts of interest, ensure that each mechanism performs its functions independently, and enable the Parties to fully engage in the dispute resolution process without fearing that the information divulged as part of it can be used in the compliance review process.

The DRS is intended to complement, not substitute, the compliance review process. In the Inspection Panel Resolution, '[t]he Executive Directors reaffirm[ed] the importance of the Panel's function, its independence and integrity'.[111] In practice, however, the *mandate* of the DRS may infringe on the mandate of the Inspection Panel. To take one example noted by commentators, a Party agreement reached through the dispute resolution process would 'forestall any Inspection Panel review or investigation of the matter and prevent any members of the affected community, who otherwise feel that their concerns were not addressed in the process … to request a new investigation'.[112] This is because the complaint on that project will be considered closed by the Panel, unless there is new evidence or circumstances unknown at the

[110] 2020 Accountability Mechanism Resolution (n 7) para 6; Accountability Mechanism Operating Procedures, para 11.6.

[111] 2020 Panel Resolution (n 6) para 2.

[112] Desierto, Perez-Linan, Wakkaf, and Gagnon (n 70).

time of the request.[113] Thus, the result of the dispute resolution process will prevent the Inspection Panel from carrying out its role of investigating compliance with Bank policies.

To address the potentially conflicting mandates of the dispute resolution and compliance review processes generally, scholars and civil society organisations have advocated that multilateral development banks like the Bank should provide more options for sequencing these processes. At most banks today, requesters typically have two options: they can either resort to dispute resolution first and then move on to compliance review if they are dissatisfied with the former, or go straight ahead with compliance review but thereby relinquish the possibility of dispute resolution.[114] Scholars and civil society organisations suggest that affected persons should be able to choose which process to undertake first and to change to the other one once, or to pursue both processes simultaneously.[115] They argue that compliance review can provide information and analysis to affected persons to which they might not otherwise have access in dispute resolution given their power imbalance vis-à-vis the borrower States; conversely, dispute resolution can highlight systemic issues relevant to compliance review that might not have become apparent without dialogue between the Parties.[116] At the United Nations Development Programme (UNDP) for example, affected persons can choose to go through compliance review[117] and dispute resolution[118] simultaneously. This shows that the concern, according to which allowing Parties to use compliance review irrespective of the outcome of the dispute resolution process would disincentivise borrower States from fully participating in the dispute resolution process,[119] may be overblown.

113 2020 Panel Resolution (n 6) para 15(d).

114 Bradlow (n 34) 17.

115 Accountability Counsel and others, *Good Policy Paper: Guiding Practice from the Policies of Independent Accountability Mechanisms* (2021) 51, available at www.ciel.org/reports/good-policy-paper/. See also OHCHR (n 72) 79: 'Allow . . . fluidity between compliance reviews and dispute resolution, in order to provide the flexibility needed to enable remedy in practice.'

116 van Huijstee, Genovese, Daniel, and Singh (n 27) 68; Richard (n 19) 338.

117 UNDP, *Social and Environmental Compliance Unit: Investigation Guidelines* (4 August 2017) para 33, available at www.undp.org/sites/g/files/zskgke326/files/2021-04/SECU%20Investigation%20Guidelines_4%20August%202017.pdf.

118 UNDP, *Stakeholder Response Mechanism: Overview and Guidance* (2014) para 18, available at www.undp.org/sites/g/files/zskgke326/files/2021-04/SRM%20Guidance%20Note%20r4.pdf.

119 D Bradlow, 'Private Complainants and International Organizations' (2005) 36 *Georgetown Journal of International Law* 403, 483.

Another improvement regarding independence and impartiality concerns the relationship between the DRS staff and the Parties. Paragraph 14.1 of the Accountability Mechanism Operating Procedures states that '[t]he DRS is impartial as between Parties and as to the merits of the dispute.' However, the Accountability Mechanism Secretary and the DRS staff are also significantly involved in the dispute resolution process. This involvement raises the question of whether they are perceived as independent of the Parties. As mentioned, paragraph 21.2 of the Accountability Mechanism Operating Procedures requires that the Parties 'consult' with the DRS staff regarding the choice of their representatives, which must be voluntary. These provisions imply that the DRS staff must determine whether this choice is in reality 'voluntary'. Meanwhile, neither the Accountability Mechanism Resolution nor the Accountability Mechanism Operating Procedures set limits on the content and means of communication to the Parties, which raises questions as to the extent of the DRS staff's influence in the Parties' decisions. For example, would the DRS staff give its opinion to the requesters on the quality of representation that different civil society organisations may offer them? Would it advise on the relation that the requesters could have with their representatives regarding the management of their complaint? The Accountability Mechanism Resolution and Accountability Mechanism Operating Procedures are silent on these issues. Rather, the Accountability Mechanism Operating Procedures should only require that the Parties 'inform' the DRS staff about their choice of representation.

The DRS staff is also involved in the very decision of the Parties to pursue the dispute resolution process. Paragraph 11.3 of the Accountability Mechanism Operating Procedures puts forward that '[i]f either of the Parties indicate, or the DRS assesses, a need for capacity building to allow them to better make an informed decision on whether to participate in a dispute resolution process, this may be offered by DRS within the resources and time frame available.' Under paragraph 21.4 of the Accountability Mechanism Operating Procedures, the Parties must bear the costs of their representation and advice during the dispute resolution process. Since requesters have fewer resources than borrower States, they are more likely to ask for, or be assessed as needing, this advice and capacity building. Although the requesters may benefit from this opportunity, the concern is that by treating them differently than it does borrower States, the DRS may be perceived as lacking independence and impartiality.[120]

[120] For clarity, the chapter acknowledges that the DRS may treat the Parties differently, to the extent this is done based on fairness and substantive equality.

The Bank should therefore consider addressing, through institutional changes, the general tension between accessibility and independence at the DRS. The World Trade Organization (WTO) is an example of how an international organisation successfully managed this tension. On the one hand, the secretariat, as the WTO administering institution, 'assist[s] panels, especially on the legal, historical and procedural aspects of the matters dealt with, and ... provide[s] secretarial and technical support'.[121] In parallel, the WTO Advisory Centre is a separate and independent institution that offers free advice and training on WTO dispute settlement proceedings to developing countries.[122] Because the secretariat cannot provide such assistance to less well-off States without risking its independence, this separate entity was established.[123] In contrast, the DRS plays the role of both the administering institution and advisory/training institution. This dual role in turn may jeopardise the perceived independence of the DRS. Further, by confirming that the choice of representatives is voluntary, or by offering guidance on disagreement as to the scope of the dispute resolution process between the Parties,[124] the DRS staff may also play a role typically reserved for third-party neutrals.

To address these concerns at the DRS, and more broadly increase the accessibility and effectiveness of access to a remedy, a pragmatic approach may be for the Bank to provide funding to affected persons to get support from professionals during the dispute resolution process. A recent UN report has suggested a range of funding mechanisms that international accountability mechanisms could set up to do so, which includes stand-alone remedy funds, escrow accounts, trust funds, insurance schemes, guarantees, and letters of credit.[125] Scholars and civil society organisations have long called for establishing such funds at the World Bank and other multilateral development banks, because civil society organisations currently supporting requesters in dispute resolution processes, free of charge, do not have the budget to assist most of them.[126] The argument is that, as part of the development mandate of multilateral development banks, they should reserve part of the project

[121] World Trade Organization, 'Understanding on Rules and Procedures Governing the Settlement of Disputes' (1994) Article 27(1), available at www.wto.org/english/tratop_e/dispu_e/dsu_e.htm.

[122] ACWL, 'Services of the ACWL', available at www.acwl.ch/acwl-mission/.

[123] World Trade Organization, 'Lamy Lauds Role of Advisory Centre on WTO Law' (4 October 2011), available at www.wto.org/english/news_e/sppl_e/sppl207_e.htm.

[124] Accountability Mechanism Operating Procedures, para 13.3.

[125] OHCHR (n 72) 88–89.

[126] van Huijstee, Genovese, Daniel, and Singh (n 27); Ta and Graham (n 38) 118.

budget to fund potential complaints launched by affected persons, who are typically vulnerable populations. Canada, for instance, sets aside a small portion of the total project budget of its large infrastructural projects to help minorities in areas covered by these projects to express their concerns about them.[127]

In sum, with its mandate of independence and impartiality, the DRS offers affected persons access to a neutral third party to access a remedy. As designed, however, it may infringe on the mandate of the Inspection Panel, and the involvement of the DRS staff in dispute resolution processes raises some concerns about its appearance of independence.

9.4 Conclusion

The Kawaala community and Uganda are now attempting to resolve the complaint concerning the Lubigi channel project amicably through the dispute resolution process offered by one of the Bank's avenues for a remedy, the DRS. At the time of writing, the Parties had asked and were granted the additional six months to pursue the dispute resolution process.[128] Only time will tell whether this new avenue will enhance the right of access to a remedy of the Kawaala community and all other requesters participating in the dispute resolution process, as the Bank sought to do by establishing the DRS.

This chapter has shown that, in the meantime, different aspects of the DRS raise the concerns of whether dispute resolution will actually enhance the right of access to a remedy, and whether it may instead prejudice the Inspection Panel's mandate to provide this right of access. Given these concerns, the chapter has set out three areas of improvement that the Bank could consider which, if adopted, would empower the DRS to better realise its mandate.

[127] Impact Assessment Agency of Canada, 'Participant Funding Program' (23 April 2021), available at www.canada.ca/en/impact-assessment-agency/services/public-participation/funding-programs/participant-funding-program.html.

[128] Accountability Mechanism, 'Accountability Mechanism Extends Mediation Deadline in Uganda Case' (5 December 2022), available at www.worldbank.org/en/programs/accountability/brief/accountability-mechanism-extends-mediation-deadline-in-uganda-case.

10

IMF Surveillance as a Non-Compliance Mechanism

AMBROISE FAHRNER

The Fund shall oversee . . . the compliance of each member with its obligations[1]

10.1 Introduction

This chapter evaluates the emergence and development of "surveillance" as the preferred non-compliance mechanism within the IMF architecture. This study highlights the specific role of international law within the field of international monetary relations, as well as illustrating how international monetary relations provide international law with original new tools and concepts.

John M. Keynes famously stated with respect to the creation of an international institution in charge of handling the international monetary system – what became the International Monetary Fund – that "(t)he most difficult question to determine is how much to decide by rule, and how much to leave to discretion".[2] For lawyers, this often-quoted sentence evokes the systemic need to combine rules of conduct, aiming at ordering States' behaviors, with adequate legal structures, aiming at ordering these rules of conduct and guaranteeing their efficiency, such as mechanisms of adjudication.[3] This chapter starts from this premise

[1] Article IV, section 3(a), IMF Articles of Agreement, available at www.imf.org/external/pubs/ft/aa/index.htm.

[2] JM Keynes, "The Keynes Plan: Proposals for an International Currency (or Clearing) Union (Version dated 11 February 1942) (1945–1965)" in *IMF History Volume 3: Twenty Years of International Monetary Cooperation Volume III: Documents* (International Monetary Fund 1969) 552. Keynes was one of the most prominent negotiators of the Bretton Woods architecture, redesigning the rules of the game in international monetary relations, and providing the world with the IMF, the international organization in charge of managing these rules of the game in a multilateral fashion.

[3] HLA Hart, *The Concept of Law* (Clarendon Press 1961) 93–120. According to Hart, "primary rules" are directed at behaviors, for instance determining that a given behaviour is allowed or forbidden, and "secondary rule," or to put it simply "rules about rules,"

that there is a specific and systemic need to efficiently link “command” to “compliance” in the field of global monetary governance. This is of a particular and concrete relevance as it is often held that the defining features of international monetary law are that it is soft by nature, that its institutional framework is loose by design, and its dispute settlement system mainly informal and political.[4] The chapter will therefore investigate the types of non-compliance options available in international monetary law which aim at the constitution of the international monetary system.

Surveillance is an original mechanism designed to ensure the conformity of countries’ behavior to the obligations set under the IMF legal regime, concerning exchange rates policies, broadly speaking.[5] Through surveillance, the IMF monitors the international monetary system, world economic health, and also the economic policies of its member countries (to the extent that they influence international monetary conditions). IMF surveillance enables the international monetary system to achieve its purposes of sustaining monetary and financial stability, as well as promoting sound economic growth by facilitating the exchange of goods, services, and capital among countries, including by monitoring compliance with exchange rate obligations.[6] This is achieved at two complementary levels: “bilateral surveillance,” bringing together, on a regular basis, the IMF and a given country; and “multilateral surveillance,” which provides an annual analysis of the international monetary system and global economic forecasts to the international community.[7] The Fund also advises countries about the necessary policy adjustments to be made to prevent potential crises.

A paradox lies nonetheless in Article IV of the IMF Articles of Agreement which enables surveillance: “The Fund shall oversee . . . the compliance of each member with its obligations.” On one hand, obligations undertaken by States under the IMF Articles of Agreement should be obeyed, as they are conventional obligations.[8] Reference to

enable the good functioning of the system, by allowing it to create, adapt, or enforce rules of conduct.

4 BA Simmons, “The Legalization of International Monetary Affairs” (2000) 54 *International Organization* 573–602 at 819–35.

5 Article IV, IMF Articles of Agreement.

6 Article I, IMF Articles of Agreement.

7 IMF Website, Factsheet, available at www.imf.org/en/About/Factsheets/IMF-Surveillance.

8 Article 26, Vienna Convention on the Law of Treaties: Every treaty in force is binding upon the parties to it and must be performed by them in good faith.

"compliance" in Article IV should therefore come as no surprise. On the other hand, the IMF must only "oversee" such "compliance" and it is usually assumed that this is the reason why the track record with respect to the non-compliance of States with their IMF legal obligations is said to be unsatisfactory.[9] And each past financial crisis has prompted heated debate among both the public and policy experts about how the international monetary system could strengthen existing mechanisms to monitor and forecast global economic and monetary developments and enforce States' obligations in this respect.[10] That surveillance is the preferred compliance mechanism in the international monetary system emphasizes the lack of actual jurisdictional venue in international monetary relations.

This chapter engages with the hypothesis that the more broadly a legal interest is shared among States, the less desirable it is that a compliance procedure should bring about a particular result; more relevant is some ownership of the process.[11] Global monetary and economic stability is, by definition, a broad objective. At the same time as constituting a direct interest for every State, it also constitutes a community interest.[12] This contribution addresses both the extent to which the surveillance mechanism set up by the IMF ensures the compliance of its members with its code of conduct and the extent to which the hypothesis above is verified in the monetary field. The success of IMF surveillance can be explained according to this hypothesis, because the IMF's surveillance involves broad flexibility in a way international adjudication does not. That IMF surveillance by essence is in the realm of flexibility does not mean, however, that the process is without rules. The fact that surveillance is meant to allow discretion for States and the IMF to achieve relevant objectives does not mean that it is a process that is unlegalized, more political or floats in a vacuum. It has developed procedural rules of its own. We will focus hereafter on its procedural characteristics. The fact that the IMF process is sustained universally and with regularity, that it is

[9] IEO IMF Performance in the Run-Up to the Financial and Economic Crises: IMF Surveillance in 2004–2007, 2011, available at https://ieo.imf.org/en/our-work/Evaluations/Completed/2011-0209-imf-performance-in-the-run-up-to-the-financial.

[10] K Shigehara and PE Atkinson, Surveillance by International Institutions: Lessons from the Global Financial and Economic Crisis (June 7, 2011). OECD Working Paper No 860.

[11] Background Paper, Conference on Compliance Mechanisms, PluriCourts, available at www.jus.uio.no/pluricourts/english/news-and-events/news/2021/290421-cfp-courts-versus-compliance-mechanisms.html.

[12] See, generally E Benvenisti, G Nolte, and K Yalin-Mor, *Community Interests across International Law* (Oxford University Press 2018).

often exposed to the changes in the economic landscape, and that it is regularly reviewed, means that it is in a constant process of refining these procedural rules.

Nonetheless, "surveillance" remains a strange word in the realm of legal notions. It sounds familiar to the lawyer's ears as it conveys a sense of discipline. However, it also sounds odd as it does not clearly express how it differs from functions, such as adjudication by international courts or political decision-making processes used to settle a disagreement. As a *sui generis* concept under IMF law, it was never explicitly defined, and evolved constantly. Interestingly, the word is also used in the World Trade Organization (WTO) or Organisation for Economic Co-operation (OECD) legal regimes.[13] IMF surveillance has never been the object of major doctrinal interest, as is the case also for international monetary law generally.[14]

The success of IMF surveillance will be examined in three ways. Firstly, it will be shown that surveillance appears to be the most successful mechanism to enforce international monetary obligations thanks to its broad flexibility and original mechanism. The nature and scope of surveillance, as well as the factors explaining its success, will be assessed. IMF surveillance contrasts positively with alternatives. International courts outside the IMF or political dispute settlement systems inside the IMF indeed offer limited options to settle States' disagreements with respect to their monetary obligations under the IMF Articles of Agreement. Finally, the chapter will underline how the legal dynamics of surveillance have provided States and the IMF with a dynamic and complete set of procedural rules addressing the process of surveillance as a transparent, rule-of-law inspired, and sophisticated procedure.

10.2 The Success of Surveillance as the Primary Compliance Mechanism in International Monetary Law

Explaining the relative success of IMF surveillance as the main non-compliance mechanism in global monetary governance[15] requires

[13] For a comparison, see M Kende, "Monetary Affairs in the WTO Trade Policy Review" in C Tietje, RM Lastra, and T Cottier (eds), *The Rule of Law in Monetary Affairs: World Trade Forum* (Cambridge University Press 2014) 384–408.

[14] M Waibel, "Two Decades Lost: Reinvigorating the Weak Cousin of WTO Law" (2011) 3 *Selected Papers from ESIL Proceedings* 353–63; M Waibel, *Financial Crises and International Law: The Legal Implications of Global Financial Crises* (Brill Nijhoff 2020).

[15] Global monetary governance refers to the governance of the operations of the international monetary system, such as exchange rates, exchange restrictions, and global

analyzing its essential features and how they constitute assets for the task of assessing international obligations regarding global monetary governance.

10.2.1 *Nature of IMF Surveillance*

10.2.1.1 Legal Basis of IMF Surveillance

Today, the legal basis for IMF surveillance is primarily rooted in Article IV, section 3(a) and (b) of the IMF Articles of Agreement and complemented by three Executive Board Decisions from 1977,[16] 2007,[17] and 2012.[18] It also draws inspiration from the 2015 Guidance Note for Surveillance under Article IV and its 2021 Supplement. With respect to its function, surveillance requires members to provide relevant and accurate information about the conduct of their policies, not only on the basis of Article IV, section 3(b), which directly addresses surveillance, but also of Article VIII, section 5. Surveillance at a basic level has three faces: bilateral surveillance – which is led on the basis of Article IV consultations; multilateral surveillance, published twice a year in two reports: the "World Economic Outlook Report" and the "Global Financial Stability Report"; and regional surveillance, when the IMF considers, for instance, the EU or the Euro area.

Surveillance's legal basis is also derived from the purposes of the IMF objectives as stated in Article I of the Articles of Agreement, and from a broader obligation to cooperate.[19] The objectives of the IMF are expressly stated in Article I of the Articles of Agreement, in terms almost unchanged since its adoption. The first of its objectives stated in Article I is "to promote international monetary cooperation through a permanent institution which provides the machinery for consultation and collaboration on international monetary problems".[20] Surveillance must be interpreted as contributing to fulfilling this objective. Historically, it was after the collapse of the Bretton Woods system of fixed (and adjustable)

liquidity (under the form of central banks' reserves or external assistance, typically from the IMF). In that respect, it is closed to, but must not be confused with global financial governance.

16 IMF Executive Board Decision No 5392-(72/63), Surveillance over Exchange Rates Policies, April 29, 1977.

17 IMF Executive Board Decision No 1319-(07/51), June 15, 2007.

18 IMF Executive Board Decision No 15203 (12/72), July 18, 2012.

19 Article X, IMF Articles of Agreement.

20 Article I(i), IMF Articles of Agreement.

exchange rates in 1971 that the surveillance function was incorporated into the Articles of Agreement through the Second Amendment.

As previously stated, the IMF enjoys a range of options to "remind" its members of their obligations as stated in its Articles of Agreement and made precise in various Executive Board Decisions.[21] Furthermore, it is expected that the nature of the IMF as an international organization informs us about the contours of this duty. In this perspective, it must be highlighted that the IMF Articles of Agreement truly constitute the world monetary constitution and, as such, create obligations of a more far-reaching kind than any other conventional monetary regime. They provide a "code of conduct" (the articles of the IMF Articles of Agreement, which refer to members' obligations to follow a given policy) concerned with exchange rates, international transfers, and liquidity assistance to its members.

In addition, IMF members also are under a general obligation to collaborate with the Fund to manage a stable system of exchange rates and exchange arrangements.[22] This duty is extended through a specific duty to consult with the Fund when requested and to provide relevant information. Against this backdrop, it is noteworthy that these obligations of collaboration, consultation, and then provision of information apply to all three core IMF functions: financial assistance,[23] technical assistance,[24] and surveillance[25] – surveillance being the monitoring of the members' compliance with their obligations under the IMF Articles of Agreement. The IMF's general functioning is thus inspired by these various duties to transparently collaborate, consult, and provide information.

10.2.1.2 Scope of Surveillance

Article IV not only sets out procedural rules as to the conduct of surveillance but also covers substantial obligations concerning exchange rate arrangements and the policies of IMF members. It is complemented by and must be read in conjunction with a set of Executive Board

[21] Additionally, under general international law, international organizations have, under certain circumstances, a duty to institute a legal framework to "remind" members of their obligations. *Reparation for Injuries Suffered in the Services of the United Nations*, Advisory Opinion, ICJ Reports 1949, 174, at 178–79.

[22] Article IV, section 1, IMF Articles of Agreement.

[23] Article V, section 3, IMF Articles of Agreement.

[24] Article V, section 2(b), IMF Articles of Agreement.

[25] Article IV, IMF Articles of Agreement.

Decisions establishing principles that guide members.[26] Yet the exact material scope of surveillance requires a careful and dynamic analysis. Article IV's history is illuminating in this respect. Whereas it was initially dedicated to the management of a system of fixed exchange rates, the demise of this system in the 1970s led to a more diffuse set of rules of conduct, allowing all types of exchange rate arrangements, including floating arrangements. Therefore, the *ratione materiae* jurisdiction of the field of surveillance must now be understood in a more dynamic way. There is an expectation that members will pursue policies favoring a "stable system of exchange rates" and "avoid manipulating exchange rates".[27] The material scope of surveillance relates not only to exchange rates, but also to other domestic or external economic and monetary policy "to the extent that they significantly influence present or prospective external stability".[28]

Obligations related to exchange rates are expressed in stronger language than those related to other fields of domestic or external policy, reflecting the dominant post-war consensus over the importance at that time of fostering effective collaboration in the field of exchange rates, while preserving the domestic policy space of members of an unprecedented international organization.[29] However, IMF surveillance focussed in the past on a wide range of sectors. For instance, it delivered prescriptions over members' financial sector policies despite the lack of a formal mandate relating to the international financial system.[30] Surveillance was also used to assess the capital flow policy of its members, despite the right of members embodied in the IMF Articles of Agreement to regulate this field according to their preference and without IMF involvement.[31] More surprisingly, as it does not seem to be directly linked to IMF goals, surveillance also addressed non-economic policies such as

[26] IMF Executive Board Decision No 15203-(12/72), July 18, 2012; Decision No 15203-(12/72), July 18, 2012.

[27] Article IV, IMF Articles of Agreement.

[28] §5, IMF Executive Board Decision No 1319-(07/51), June 15, 2007.

[29] N Rendak, "Monitoring and Surveillance of the International Monetary System: What Can Be Learnt from the Trade Field?" in C Tietje, RM Lastra and T Cottier (eds), *The Rule of Law in Monetary Affairs: World Trade Forum* (Cambridge University Press 2014) 204–31.

[30] A Feibelman, "Law in the Global Order: The IMF and Financial Regulation" (2017) 49 *New York University Journal of International Law and Politics* 687–745.

[31] M Broos and S Grund, "The IMF's Jurisdiction Over the Capital Account – Reviewing the Role of Surveillance in Managing Cross-Border Capital Flows" (2018) 21 *Journal of International Economic Law* 489–507.

environmental, labor, military, or institutional policies to the extent that they influence external stability.

The IMF considers obligations related to exchange rates to constitute obligations of result as opposed to the obligations of conduct, that prevails with respect to domestic or external policy. This dichotomy should not be interpreted as distinguishing between optional and mandatory obligations, or between political and fully legalized norms. Indeed, the asymmetry rather lies in the distinction between the obligation to *attempt* to achieve a given result, and the obligation to *achieve* the desired outcome. In the first case, it goes without saying that a breach of obligation can be found. At the same time, contrary to what is usually assumed, nothing stands in the way of finding a breach of an obligation of conduct. However, the breach will not be directly concerned with the unachieved goal, but with a failure in the means employed by the member State. The fact that the nature of members' obligations varies according to the material domain of the policy at stake constitutes a challenge for efficient IMF leadership.

10.2.1.3 Procedural Stages

Article IV consultations typically start with the annual IMF mission visit to each member State. They aim to gather relevant data for the purpose of updating analyses of members' current economic situation. They can include meetings with State officials, but also more surprisingly "other stakeholders such as parliamentarians, and representatives of business, labor unions and civil society".[32] This is followed by an "assessment" by the mission of the member's economic situation. The mission then engages in a further round of discussions to address the actual or prospective efficiency of the implemented policies. The mission closes its intervention by sending a report containing its preliminary findings, and then a final report to the Executive Board. The Executive Board discusses the findings of the final report sent by the mission and agrees with the State on specific conclusions. The Chairman of the Board provides then a Summing Up of the discussion which is formally addressed to the member's authority. This terminates the consultation phase. After consultations close, the IMF offers to publish the report. This only occurs if the State consents to it. Interestingly, whereas States' consent is typically verified at the jurisdictional phase in front of

[32] IMF FSAP Factsheet, available at www.imf.org/en/Publications/fssa/mandatory-financial-stability-assessments-under-the-fsap.

international courts, surveillance as a process is mandatory for both the IMF and States. Consent is expressed at the end of the process and relates only to publication of the result.

10.2.2 Factors Explaining IMF Surveillance Process: Scope, Normativity, and Authority

The dominant narrative identifies "surveillance" as one of the core functions of the IMF in the international monetary system, possessing characteristics that can be contrasted with formal dispute settlement mechanisms.[33] Its contours are blurred and its influence mainly political. As such, it is said to be fitted for the needs of international monetary governance. As a result, surveillance has mainly been analyzed so far through an economics lens, stressing the importance of transparency, peer pressure, or the relevant sectors to be monitored as factors explaining its relative success as an enforcement mechanism.[34] Legal considerations have been underemphasized so that its precise legal contours remain in the shadow of institutional practice. What are the legal features that explain the use of surveillance as a preferred method to achieve members' compliance with their obligations under IMF law?

Surveillance appears to be a practical procedure to monitor the global economy from a holistic perspective. This all-encompassing approach is increasingly needed in today's economy, in which international monetary and economic spillovers play a significant role. The initial Bretton Woods institutional set-up indeed conceived of global economic governance as best organized through a three-pronged scheme, dividing monetary, trade-related, and development-related issues, and allocating their management to three corresponding universal international organizations. Nonetheless, today's globalized economy differs greatly from the postwar era and the legal framework must mirror these paradigmatic shifts, including the substantial inter-linkages between the monetary, trade, and development fields. Global economic governance also increasingly requires not only a public international law understanding, but also awareness of key international economic issues and international political dynamics. Surveillance has been able to adapt to these key economic

[33] H Gherari, "La surveillance" in P Daillier, G de La Pradelle, and H Gherari (eds), *Le droit des relations économiques internationals* (A Pedone 2004) 857–59.

[34] M Breen and E Doak, "The IMF as a Global Monitor: Surveillance, Information, and Financial Markets" (2021) 30(1) *Review of International Political Economy* 1–25.

changes thanks to an evolution of its *ratione materiae* jurisdiction. IMF surveillance's *ratione materiae* jurisdiction is built around a dynamic principle: "Other policies will be examined in the context of surveillance only to the extent that they significantly influence present or prospective external stability."[35] Though this has been possible only at the cost of an asymmetry in terms of bindingness as between exchange rate-related obligations and obligations related to "other policies", this evolution was key to maintaining the IMF's relevance in global economic governance.

Whereas financial and technical assistance offered by the IMF are voluntary in nature, surveillance is mandatory and universal. As previously explained, the IMF is legally obliged to conduct surveillance proceedings and the member is legally obliged to participate and to conduct itself in certain ways during the proceedings. Nonetheless, surveillance does not aim at producing mandatory decisions of the nature an international court would. It also does not necessitate the existence of a "dispute". The political cost of engaging in a review of a member's obligation is therefore significantly lower than in an international court's typical proceedings. Regularity of the process also contributes to assuring a review of obligations, without triggering the political or economic costs a "dispute" would.

Though non-binding, IMF surveillance nevertheless offers an authoritative assessment of a member's compliance. The IMF cannot oblige members to implement assessments resulting from surveillance procedures. It can only persuade them. Persuasion can be direct and result from the intrinsic quality of the IMF assessment. A report's authority can also flow less directly from the reputational effects it creates, triggering peer-pressure mechanisms or market pressure. Markets or peers are given access to the IMF reports and will immediately reflect the IMF analysis in their own economic analysis. Non-compliance with IMF reports will lead to higher borrowing prices, lower foreign direct investment, and, generally speaking, lower trust in the country's word and ability to successfully manage its economy. In a nutshell, the procedure does not encompass rules obliging members to comply with the IMF assessment. This does not, however, mean that it does not possess any effective authority. Reputational effects fulfill a non-compliance sanction role.

The IMF surveillance procedure navigates between an initial confidential stage, and then a process of making the result of the procedure

[35] §5, IMF Executive Board Decision No 1319-(07/51), June 15, 2007.

transparent. During the consultations, the procedure requires confidentiality and informality. It allows for more space to build trust between the stakeholders. Importantly, it avoids sending adverse signals to markets, which could trigger by anticipation precisely the effects that the process aims at preventing. Some information might also be confidential. The publication of the IMF view is then critical to obtain the peer pressure and market signal effects on which compliance is based. While consent remains the rule, publication might also be decided upon under certain specific circumstances which require immediate action.[36] The balance between other members' interest in a stable international monetary environment and a member's right to confidentiality in the management of its balance-of-payments depends upon the circumstances and the adverse effects that publication might cause. And the determination of such circumstances will be made according to a political process ending with a voting procedure.

10.3 Weaknesses of Non-Compliance Alternatives to IMF Surveillance

We now turn to the existing alternatives to the IMF in order to contrast their respective features. We will focus on both internal and external alternatives.

Firstly, international courts have not played a significant role in global monetary governance. Matters relating to compliance with IMF obligations have not been brought to general international courts, or even international arbitration proceedings, in which specialists on monetary issues could have been appointed. This does not appear to be a matter of the skills of the judicial bodies with respect to specialized issues. The existence of an all-encompassing and conventionalized sub-regime explains the situation more satisfactorily. Secondly, within the IMF, options implying a withdrawal, a loss of rights by IMF members, an

[36] Article XII, section 8, IMF Articles of Agreement: "The Fund shall at all times have the right to communicate its views informally to any member on any matter arising under this Agreement. The Fund may, by a seventy percent majority of the total voting power, decide to publish a report made to a member regarding its monetary or economic conditions and developments which directly tend to produce a serious disequilibrium in the international balance of payments of members. The relevant member shall be entitled to representation in accordance with Section 3(j) of this Article. The Fund shall not publish a report involving changes in the fundamental structure of the economic organization of members."

interpretation of the Articles of Agreement, or an amendment have appeared too political.

10.3.1 *The Limited Recourse to International Courts in Global Monetary Governance*

The International Court of Justice (ICJ) (or its predecessor, the PCIJ) has, in the past, seized the opportunity to clarify significant general international monetary law issues, such as the customary international law principle of monetary sovereignty.[37] The Court has also shown its ability to deal with monetary issues in a case involving a discriminatory system of license control in respect of imports not involving an official allocation of currency.[38] However, the fact is that the ICJ has not played a regular role in solving disputes between States in relation to international monetary relations. It is generally assumed that the ICJ, as a non-specialized court, is not the most appropriate venue to deal with international economic law issues and that such issues should be scrutinized by specialized arbitral bodies like arbitral investment tribunals or the Dispute Settlement Body of the WTO. Yet, after a closer look, it appears that the explanation is not to be found in the often-alleged distinction between specialized and non-specialized issues, and the resulting ability of the respective judicial body to handle the issue at stake.[39]

A more explanatory distinction is the one between topics extensively covered by international conventions on one side, and residual, general, and systemic issues on the other side. Monetary rules are generally embodied in complex treaties, sometimes forming entire sub-regimes, and having their own dispute settlement systems, be it political, institutional, or to a certain extent judicial. Recourse has mainly been had to the ICJ to clarify architectural issues of international law external to or underpinning these treaties and regimes, but not specialized and conventionalized matters. The recent involvement of the ICJ in matters

[37] "It is indeed a generally accepted principle that a state is entitled to regulate its own currency." *Case Concerning the Payment of Various Serbian Loans Issued in France (France v Serbia)*, Judgment of 12 July 1929, PCIJ Report Series A Nos 20–21, 44; Charles Proctor, Mann on the Legal Aspect of Money (7th ed., Oxford University Press 2012) 526.

[38] *Case Concerning Rights of Nationals of the United States of America in Morocco (France v United States of America)*, ICJ Report 1952, 176–233.

[39] K Wellens, *Economic Conflicts and Disputes before the World Court (1922–1995): A Functional Analysis* (Kluwer Law International 1996) 252.

pertaining to monetary flows is only incidental and is a by-product of the embargo put in place by the United States against Iran in a broader geopolitical context.[40]

Neither has the IMF had recourse to ICJ Advisory Opinions. The IMF Articles of Agreement entered into force on December 27, 1945, two months after the UN Charter, and the IMF and the UN entered into a relationship agreement on November 15, 1947. From this perspective, it will be of no surprise that the "Agreement between the United Nations and the International Monetary Fund" offers the IMF the possibility to "request advisory opinions of the International Court of Justice on any legal question arising within the scope of the Fund's activities". It was expected that this option could prove useful where general international law became relevant in the activities of the IMF, such as State succession. In practice, the IMF has never seized the opportunity to request an Advisory Opinion from the ICJ and has handled matters of general international law independently.[41] Two points could be deduced. Firstly, the lack of expertise of the IMF in general international law has not prompted the need to resort to general international courts. Secondly, the fact that ICJ Advisory Opinions avoid the confrontational aspect of judgments has not led the IMF to resort to such opinions.

In the search for a dispute settlement alternative fitted for international monetary issues, it appears that the WTO dispute settlement panels or specialized arbitral tribunals could play such a role, as they incorporate technical expertise that the ICJ allegedly lacks in the field of economic law. In practice, the WTO and international investment tribunals have determined a certain number of disputes with a monetary component so far.[42] This apparent success comes at a cost. Monetary issues are only litigated insofar as they pose trade or investment-related issues.[43] As with the ICJ,

[40] *Certain Iranian Assets (Islamic Republic of Iran v United States of America), 2023, Judgment, International Court of Justice.*

[41] The IMF admitted Kosovo before the ICJ issued its legal opinion on its independence (members required only to be a "country"), available at www.imf.org/en/News/Articles/2015/09/14/01/49/pr09240, last accessed 21 August 2023; A Viterbo, *International Monetary Fund* (Kluwer Law International 2015) §23.

[42] See generally DE Siegel, "Legal Aspects of the IMF/WTO Relationship: The Fund's Articles of Agreement and the WTO Agreements" (2002) 96 *American Journal of International Law* 561–99; CJ Tams, SW Schill, and R Hofmann, *International Investment Law and the Global Financial Architecture* (Edward Elgar Publishing 2017).

[43] For instance, a case involving quantitative restrictions imposed by India involved questions about the exact role the IMF should play in the assessment of the balance of payments issues that caused the measure. See Panel Report, "India – Quantitative

these specialized bodies have proven capable of addressing global monetary issues, albeit from a generalist economic legal perspective rather than a specialist monetary and financial perspective. However, once again, it is not the alleged lack of capability that explains non-recourse to international investment tribunals or the WTO dispute settlement system, but more particularly the fact that monetary issues are specific and submitted to a comprehensive conventional regime.

10.3.2 The Limitations of Recourses to IMF Dispute Settlement Options other than Surveillance

The IMF possesses a range of compliance mechanisms, though many of these are political in nature and seldom explicitly identified as compliance mechanisms. Disputes as to monetary issues can firstly be solved via a political or institutional change; and where a solution is difficult to reach, there are sanctions available, such as the forced withdrawal of a State from the IMF, or the suspension of a member's benefits. Although these options are not meant to be used on a regular basis[44] to solve members' disagreements, they offer ultimate institutional and political mechanisms to settle a dispute between members. As will be discussed, IMF members have alternatively been known to amend the IMF's constitutional charter itself, the IMF Articles of Agreement, in order to settle a dispute. There is also available a sophisticated authoritative interpretation mechanism, though this is in practice no longer used. The IMF has mainly resorted to non-authoritative interpretation.

10.3.2.1 Options Involving Forced Withdrawal or Suspension of Rights

The IMF Articles of Agreement provide for a procedure to force a member to withdraw as per Article XXVI, section 2(c). The only case to date is that of Czechoslovakia in 1954.[45] It is also noteworthy that Article XXIX of the IMF Articles of Agreement provides for the

Restrictions on Imports of Agricultural, Textile and Industrial Products", WT/DS90/R, signed April 6, 1999, adopted September 22, 1999, as modified by Appellate Body Report, WT/DS90/AB/R, AB-1999-3. The consequences of the "pesification" (a change of exchange rate arrangement) of the economy in Argentina have notably given rise to many ICSID cases. None of these cases have however addressed pesification from a holistic monetary perspective.

44 Amendments entered into force in 1969, 1978, 1992, 2009, 2011, and 2016.

45 IMF Annual Report, 1954.

constitution of an "Arbitral Tribunal" to assist with the settlement of potential disputes arising from the withdrawal of a member. It goes without saying that this mechanism is only designed as a last-resort option.

A softer version of this approach consists of suspending a member's financial[46] or political[47] rights. These approaches are not, however, perfectly fitted for the compliance task as non-compliant States are precisely those requiring financial and political rights to address financial needs or to build political legitimacy in the context of complex reforms. Depriving members of the resources designed for them when they need them the most might not always be the best dispute settlement or compliance option.

10.3.2.2 Options Involving an Amendment of the Articles of Agreement of the IMF

The IMF Articles of Agreement also provide for an Amendment procedure embodied in Article XXVIII. The Second Amendment of 1978[48] testifies in a spectacular way that the inability of a member like the United States to comply with core IMF obligations concerning exchange rates can be settled through this means, providing a workaround so that US policy is not qualified as a breach of IMF obligations. The United States announced on August 15, 1971, that it would suspend the convertibility of the dollar into gold.[49] The collapse of the par-value system that resulted was only legalized thereafter by the Second Amendment.

Amendments have also from time to time contributed to strengthening rules aimed at creating discipline in the international monetary system. The First Amendment (1969)[50] improved the rules relating to an authoritative procedure for interpretation by the

[46] As was the case with Zimbabwe in 2001.

[47] For instance, Liberia's voting rights were suspended in 2003.

[48] The Articles of Agreement were amended for the second time, effective April 1, 1978, by the modifications approved by the Board of Governors in Resolution No 31–4, adopted April 30, 1976.

[49] JL Butkiewicz and S Ohlmacher, "Ending Bretton Woods: Evidence from the Nixon Tapes" (2021) 74 *The Economic History Review* 922–45; Address to the Nation by Richard Nixon Outlining a New Economic Policy: "The Challenge of Peace. August 15, 1971" (1971).

[50] The Articles of Agreement were amended for the first time, effective July 28, 1969, by the modifications approved by the Board of Governors in Resolution No 23–5, adopted May 31, 1968.

introduction of a Committee for Interpretation. The Third Amendment (1992)[51] introduced stricter rules for the suspension of voting rights of members who failed to repay the IMF. However, the amendment procedure requires a very constraining process and is therefore not fitted to settle most disagreements between States. Indeed, and it is quite unique in the world of international organizations, the procedure requires a majority of at least three-fifths of the members holding 85 per cent of IMF voting rights.[52] Compared with such radical and constraining dispute settlement options, "interpretation" offers a much more nuanced approach.

10.3.2.3 Options Involving Interpretation of the Articles of Agreement of the IMF

The IMF is the first international organization to be vested with the jurisdictional power to interpret its constitutive act, to formally "hear" and discuss complaints of its members through this means. Article XXIX (a) of the IMF Articles of Agreement provides that "any question of interpretation of the provisions of this Agreement between any member and the Fund or between members of the Fund shall be submitted to the Executive Board for its decision". This mechanism additionally sets out an appeal to the Board of Governors, which is assisted by a Committee on Interpretation of the Board of Governors. Whereas the first phase of the procedure employs the usual weighted voting procedure, the second phase of the procedure, the appeal, is conducted following its own voting system, according to which each member has one equal vote.[53] Article XXIX(b) of the IMF Articles of Agreement refers to the Decision of the Board of Governors as being "final" with respect to questions of interpretation. The mechanism under Article XXIX has been used ten times with only one appeal. The most recent use of the procedure ended in 1959.[54]

Interpretation could therefore have constituted a preferred, if unorthodox, means of dispute settlement within the IMF framework. It has indeed the advantage of bringing a potential solution to a situation

[51] The Articles of Agreement were amended a third time, effective November 11, 1992, by the modifications approved by the Board of Governors in Resolution No 45–3, adopted June 28, 1990.

[52] Article XII. 5, section 1, IMF Articles of Agreement.

[53] Article XII. 5, section 1, IMF Articles of Agreement.

[54] A Viterbo, *International Monetary Fund* (Kluwer Law International 2015) §57.

without directly highlighting a member's misconduct. This mechanism significantly evolved over time. Formal interpretations were useful in the first years of the life of the IMF, to clarify elements of such a new legal regime in a world not yet accustomed to international organizations of this kind. However, whereas in the first years of the IMF its formal interpretation mechanism was used on a regular basis, it has since disappeared to the benefit of regular interpretations made outside the formal IMF framework. Informal interpretations are adopted, leaving open the possibility of authoritative interpretation for settling any future or ongoing difficulty with respect to a previous interpretation. Both regular and authoritative interpretations are binding as they reflect the decision-making process of the Fund and members are obliged to comply by virtue of the obligation to collaborate with the Fund. But regular interpretations are not final because the possibility of a subsequent authoritative interpretation remains open. This two-tiered approach caters to IMF reluctance to issue formal interpretations that would inevitably tie its hands for the future and considerably reduce its space for discretionary measures.

10.4 The Dynamics of Procedural Rules Related to the Process of Surveillance

"Surveillance" has evolved over time, under the pressure of crises and internal reviews, or in order to adapt to joint surveillance exercises with other international institutions. One defining theoretical issue is the extent to which the IMF can draw from general principles used by international courts to develop its framework while preserving the unique and defining features that constitute IMF surveillance.

10.4.1 Dynamics of Procedural Rules: Crises, Internal Reviews, and "Joint Surveillance" with Other Institutions

Surveillance has become the main IMF instrument to oversee IMF members' compliance with their obligations. As opposed to other IMF or non-IMF existing dispute settlement methods, surveillance offers a non-compliance mechanism in large part based upon flexibility. Despite the flexibility that characterizes both the substantial and procedural aspects of its enforcement, surveillance seems to achieve compliance in an indirect way. That flexibility is the key to this mechanism does not mean, however, that it has not evolved over time or been provided with procedural rules.

Two types of factor have shaped the development of surveillance. Firstly, structure has followed substance as surveillance has had to adapt to changes in the global economy. The most spectacular case is that of financial crises. As the etymology suggests, "crises" differ from simple "difficulties" in that their nature and gravity require a change of a systemic nature. More gradual changes in the structure of the global economy have also prompted substantial changes in the IMF surveillance process. Secondly, surveillance procedures have also evolved as a result of scrutiny, through the IMF internal schemes of evaluation, or through confrontation with other international institutional fora.

In 1998, the IMF undertook an *ex-post* analysis of the causes of the Asian economic crisis and of its management by the IMF services. Previously, the Mexican crisis had also left its footprint on surveillance's procedures. The inability of the IMF to anticipate the Mexican crisis of 1993–1994 caused the IMF to review surveillance modalities. As a result, IMF surveillance procedures now encompass a stronger focus on sensitive matters, better internal coordination (information of the Executive Board), a broader scope of analysis (inclusion of data non-formally provided by the member), and more regular contact with officials of the member countries.[55] The 2008 global economic crisis prompted a paradigmatic shift as it introduced a more intensive recourse to joint surveillance with other international fora, such as the G20 through the Mutual Assessment Process (MAP)[56] or the Financial Stability Board through the IMF-FSB Early Warning Exercise.[57]

The IMF periodically reviews its activities to better adapt to changes in the global economy, which includes surveillance in all its aspects. This reviewing process has been driven by the need to face the weaknesses unveiled by various crises and the ambition to anticipate future developments in the world economy. The 2012 Integrated Surveillance Decision,

[55] S Fischer, "The Asian Crisis and the Changing Role of the IMF" (1998) 35(2) *Finance & Development*, available at www.imf.org/external/pubs/ft/fandd/1998/06/fischer.htm.

[56] G20 Mutual Assessment Process (MAP), available at file:///Users/ambroisefahrner/Downloads/G20-Mutual-Assessment-Process-MAP-SP.pdf.

[57] IMF–FSB Early Warning Exercise, available at www.imf.org/en/About/Factsheets/Sheets/2023/Early-Warning-Exercise#:~:text=The%20IMF%2DFSB%20Early%20Warning%20Exercise&text=It%20was%20created%20in%202008,lead%20to%20further%20sys temic%20shocks; 'The Acting Chair's Summing Up: IMF Membership in the Financial Stability Board,' Executive Board Meeting 10/86, September 8, 2010.

the 2014 Triennial Surveillance Review, the 2018 Interim Surveillance Review and the ongoing Comprehensive Surveillance Review (CSR)[58] have identified substantial weaknesses in the monitoring of the global economy, but also improved the modalities of the conduct of the surveillance process. The IMF also has an Independent Evaluation Office (IEO), established by the Executive Board in 2001. It is functionally independent of the IMF and establishes its own agenda. It has access to all relevant data. The IEO regularly issues reports containing surveillance-related advice.[59]

There has been some debate arising from the fact that the World Bank and the IMF's respective jurisdiction overlap from time to time with respect to States' borrowing. Overlapping conditions attached to external aid have been described as "cross-conditionality". Similar issues can be highlighted, which we will call "cross-surveillance" issues by analogy since existing terms do not fully describe the phenomenon. The Financial Sector Assessment Program (FSAP), for instance, is a joint World Bank–IMF program.[60] It functions very much like typical IMF surveillance activities, but its legal status is that of technical assistance. Previously operating on a voluntary basis, it is now mandatory for twenty-nine jurisdictions selected because of their systemically important financial sector. The G20 Mutual Assessment Process (MAP) involves the IMF and similar jurisdictions in a similar exercise. The legal basis is that of technical assistance, in conjunction with the legal framework of the IMF's ability to engage in joint activities. It is assumed that such collaborations have prompted discussion as to the methods and procedures employed by the IMF and other institutions. On this basis we can say that this joint exercise of surveillance has also contributed to an evolution in IMF procedures in exposing surveillance to the test of efficient collaboration.

10.4.2 Dynamics of Procedural Principles: Borrowing from General Principles?

Surveillance is a very demanding process: it is very broad in scope, it operates on a regular basis, and it is universal. This requires a sound and

58 www.imf.org/en/Topics/Comprehensive-Surveillance-Review.

59 https://ieo.imf.org.

60 www.imf.org/en/About/Factsheets/Sheets/2016/08/01/16/14/Financial-Sector-Assessment-Program; The IMF–World Bank Concordat (SM/89/54, Rev 1).

solid procedural framework to assure its legitimacy and efficiency. Its *sui generis* nature, the evolution of the world economy and the recurrence of crises have prompted regular review processes and resulted in densification of the rules relating to the procedural aspects of surveillance. It is submitted that the development of procedural rules fitted for surveillance can be viewed as reconciling two contradictory dynamics. Firstly, the rules draw inspiration from the general procedural principles used by international courts. Secondly, however, they do not properly borrow from this vocabulary, as they seek to underline the specificity of surveillance as a specific process. For instance, IMF surveillance must be conducted as a "dialogue,"[61] but it is not referred to as an "adversarial process." The procedure should be held in all "candor,"[62] "frankness"[63] and "openness,"[64] but the IMF does not precisely refer to the general principle of "good faith" as such. The IMF assessment must be "persuasive"[65] and "clear,"[66] but the wording of "reasoning" is not used.[67]

Yet, overall, IMF surveillance procedural rules are expressed in terms that evoke the general procedural principles of international litigation. This could imply that surveillance is considered as the exercise of a "quasi-international jurisdiction" to which general procedural principles of international litigation apply. At the same time the IMF's emphasis on using a different set of terms to those employed in respect of proceedings in international courts and tribunals must be emphasized. The matter may become important in the future development of the IMF legal framework.

[61] IMF Executive Board Decision No 1319-(07/51), June 15, 2007, §8.
[62] Ibid.
[63] Ibid.
[64] Ibid.
[65] Ibid.
[66] Ibid.
[67] Viterbo (n 54) para 131.

PART IV

Environment

11

Legal Mobilisation for Biodiversity Protection

Assessing the Complementary Potential of the Bern Convention's Case File System and the European Commission's Infringement Procedure

ELENA EVANGELIDIS

11.1 Introduction

The importance of civil society actors in ensuring that breaches of environmental law are identified and reported to the bodies responsible for their compliance is difficult to overstate. Nevertheless, civil society groups continue to face severe limitations in respect of access to justice in environmental matters.[1] In the European regional context, the literature concerning opportunities for legal mobilisation for environmental protection has long focussed on the mobilisation of citizens in relation to European Union environmental law, largely via their national legal systems or via the European Court of Justice (CJEU).[2] Relatively under-explored, on the other hand, has been the role of (non-)compliance systems outside the EU's institutional structure, operating with a similar geographical scope.[3] In particular, the potential of the 1979 Bern Convention on European Wildlife Conservation[4] and its corresponding (non-)compliance mechanism known as the 'case file system' (CFS)

[1] M van Wolferen and M Eliantonio, 'Access to Justice in Environmental Matters in the EU: The EU's Difficult Road towards Non-Compliance with the Aarhus Convention' in M Peeters (ed.), *Research Handbook on EU Environmental Law* (Edward Elgar 2020) 148.

[2] M Eliantonio, 'The Role of NGOs in Environmental Implementation Conflicts: "Stuck in the Middle" between Infringement Proceedings and Preliminary Rulings?' (2018) 40 *Journal of European Integration* 753.

[3] An exception to this is the Aarhus Convention's compliance committee. See, for example, van Wolferen and Eliantonio (n 1).

[4] Convention on the Conservation of European Wildlife and Natural Habitats 1979, European Treaty Series 104.

seems to be overshadowed by academic discourse on the mechanisms of the EU. The core point argued in this chapter is that while the looming shadow of CJEU judgments provides an indispensable lever for NGOs seeking to protect biodiversity with the help of the law, less confrontational and civil society-oriented compliance mechanisms such as the CFS also provide important avenues for legal mobilisation.

By applying a 'legal opportunity structures' approach – one of the theoretical approaches developed within scholarship on legal mobilisation – the chapter assesses the legal opportunities offered by the CFS and the European Commission's (EC) infringement procedure. The purpose of studying legal opportunity structures is to gain an understanding of why social movements turn to litigation or (non-)compliance mechanisms in their efforts to protect biodiversity. According to Evans, Case and Givens, the main factors defining the 'openness' of legal opportunity structures are 'the nature of the available legal stock, the rules governing access to the judiciary, and resources for legal advocacy'.[5] Zooming in on the question of access, this chapter compares the CFS and the EC's infringement procedure, examining the participatory rights provided by each system and their respective ability to respond effectively to concerns raised by civil society actors. It takes a broad view of 'legal mobilisation', which includes mobilisation through compliance procedures within its scope. Thus, it applies a modified understanding of the openness indicators which accommodates (non-)compliance procedures. Consequently, 'access' is understood to mean 'access to the judiciary or (non-)compliance mechanism'.

From this viewpoint, distinct benefits and drawbacks of each mechanism are brought to the surface. The chapter suggests that actors can ameliorate the shortcomings of either procedure and expand their legal opportunities by shifting between the two systems. It also argues that the pursuit of a parallel mobilisation strategy in previous cases has brought to the fore the synergistic potential between the CFS and the EC's infringement procedure. Given the limited scope of the chapter, preliminary reference procedures under Article 267 TFEU as complementary mobilisation pathways are excluded from the discussion.[6]

[5] R Evans Case and TE Givens, 'Re-Engineering Legal Opportunity Structures in the European Union? The Starting Line Group and the Politics of the Racial Equality Directive' (2010) 48 *Journal of Common Market Studies* 221, 233.

[6] For comparative analysis of opportunities of NGOs in relation to the Commission's infringement procedure and the preliminary reference procedure see Eliantonio (n 2).

In this chapter, a brief introduction to legal mobilisation is followed by a methodology section. Subsequently, the procedural rules and practice of the CFS and the EC's infringement procedure will be outlined, serving as a primer to the comparative assessment of the participatory possibilities and capacity for effective response to complaints in each system. The chapter will then trace the development of two case files (and corresponding CJEU proceedings) initiated by the NGO BirdLife International and its national partners in Bulgaria and Malta to draw out concrete instances of interaction between the CFS and the infringement procedures (including CJEU judgments).

11.2 A Brief Introduction to Legal Mobilisation

The literature has produced little consensus regarding the meaning of the term 'legal mobilisation'.[7] Frances Zemans' definition remains the most cited: 'The law is . . . mobilised when a desire or a want is translated into a demand as an assertion of rights.'[8] This traditional definition is somewhat ill-suited to legal mobilisation for biodiversity protection. Its emphasis on the assertion of 'rights' complicates the concept's application to the environmental field, where litigants may often struggle to demonstrate the existence or violation of a right. Lehoucq and Taylor employ a useful definition of the term as referring to 'the use of law in an explicit, self-conscious way through the invocation of formal institutional mechanisms'.[9] In any event, the characterising feature of applying a 'legal mobilisation' approach is the adoption of an actor-focussed perspective in the study of these mechanisms, using one or several of the key concepts developed within the scholarly field.

Mobilisation theory has elaborated several conceptual approaches useful for understanding the behaviour of actors within various legal systems. A commonly used conceptual approach focusses on 'legal opportunity structures' stressing the influence of access by social movements to legal procedures on the emergence and success of legal actions.[10] Scholars of legal mobilisation unambiguously agree that the

[7] E Lehoucq and WK Taylor, 'Conceptualizing Legal Mobilization: How Should We Understand the Deployment of Legal Strategies?' (2020) 45 *Law & Social Inquiry* 166.

[8] F Kahn Zemans, 'Legal Mobilization: The Neglected Role of the Law in the Political System' (1983) 77 *American Political Science Review* 690, 700.

[9] Lehoucq and Taylor (n 7) 168.

[10] L Vanhala, 'Legal Mobilization' in *Oxford Bibliographies* (Oxford University Press 2021) 12.

procedural rules in any given legal system influence the legal opportunities available to actors wishing to mobilise the law through institutional mechanisms. Research in this tradition particularly highlights the role of standing rules or access requirements on the ability of actors to influence policy – the relaxation or elimination of such hurdles is understood as one of the key elements for this purpose.[11] Relatedly, legal opportunities are affected by the cost of access to dispute settlement.[12] A lack of funds acts as a common deterrent to legal mobilisation through compliance systems. Finally, opportunity structures are shaped by 'the body of laws that exist in a particular field',[13] which is referred to as 'legal stock'. Far from being fixed, legal stock can develop over time, not least as a result of legal mobilisation efforts.[14]

11.3 Methodology and Case Study Selection

Both case studies trace and assess the strategic legal mobilisation of BirdLife International. This NGO stands out as the organisation involved in the highest number of complaints before the Bern Convention's CFS (see Table 11.1). It also occupies a special position in the pan-European institutional landscape in relation to nature conservation; its organisational structure comprises a network of national partners throughout Europe and the globe.[15] Thus, BirdLife benefits from a vast on-the-ground presence and from a large reservoir of financial and human resources.[16] Additionally, and as a consequence of the foregoing factors, BirdLife is an 'insider' to the Bern Convention's institutional structure. Its insider position is defined by BirdLife's engagement with institutional activities related to the Convention. For instance, BirdLife collaborates with the Convention's group of experts on the conservation of birds,

[11] R Evans Case and TE Givens, 'Re-Engineering Legal Opportunity Structures in the European Union? The Starting Line Group and the Politics of the Racial Equality Directive' (2010) 48 *Journal of Common Market Studies* 221, 224.

[12] L Vanhala, 'Is Legal Mobilization for the Birds? Legal Opportunity Structures and Environmental Nongovernmental Organizations in the United Kingdom, France, Finland, and Italy' (2017) 51 *Comparative Political Studies* 380, 406.

[13] Ibid., 384.

[14] Evans Case and Givens (n 11); Vanhala (n 12).

[15] 'About BirdLife Europe and Central Asia' (*BirdLife International*), available at www.birdlife.org/europe-and-central-asia/about-birdlife-europe-and-central-asia, accessed 9 May 2022.

[16] Birdlife International Europe and Central Asia, Annual Report 2022, 24, available at www.birdlife.org/wp-content/uploads/2023/05/BirdLife-Europe-Central-Asia_Annual-Report-2022.pdf, accessed 29 August 2023.

Table 11.1 *Bern Convention case file system data (April 2022)*

Complainant type	Number of complaints
BirdLife	24
WWF	12
MEDASSET	7
SEH	13
Other NGOs, scientific organisations, universities, law firms	74
Community, citizen activist groups, individuals	19
Political bodies, political parties, parties to the Convention, Secretariat	10
N/A (no reports indicating the complainant found)	52

which monitors the compliance of the parties with the provisions related to bird conservation and the implementation of the Convention's species action plans.[17] For the purposes of this chapter, national partners of BirdLife International are treated as part of the same organisation.[18] The chapter's two case studies were selected from the pool of CFS complaints lodged by BirdLife International. They distinguish themselves from BirdLife's other complaints, in that the issues raised were also brought to the attention of the EC and ultimately resulted in CJEU judgments.

Although many case files are available online through the Convention's database, the chronological tracing of individual case files is cumbersome. It is not currently possible to view all files pertaining to a single case in an organised manner and some documents pertaining to the case files may be either missing or classified.[19] Except for internal documentation, no systematic repository of the complaints received

[17] 'Group of Experts on Conservation of Birds' (*Convention on the Conservation of European Wildlife and Natural Habitats*), available at www.coe.int/en/web/bern-convention/on-the-conservation-of-birds, accessed 9 May 2022.

[18] Questions may arise as to whether different legal cultures in Europe influence the mobilisation strategies in different branches of Birdlife. Such questions could be addressed in future research, for example in the form of a comparative study.

[19] Since the writing of this chapter, the Bern Convention Secretariat has made available chronological timelines of some of its case files. See 'Case-Files' (*Council of Europe: Convention on the Conservation of European Wildlife and Natural Habitats*), available at www.coe.int/en/web/bern-convention/case-page, accessed 9 November 2022.

through the Bern Convention's CFS currently exists.[20] The lack of such a repository also complicates the production of a comprehensive overview of complainants involved in each case. An overview of basic facts pertaining to each file was produced in 2007 in the context of a stocktake on the rules of procedure for the CFS.[21] Naturally, this list only includes cases filed until 2007, excluding roughly 50 per cent of complaints. However, the Register of Bern Convention Complaints provides a complete list of complaints received since the establishment of the CFS, indicating the country concerned and the date of receipt.[22] With reference to this list, I searched for the complainant report attached to each individual case file with the aim of creating a general picture of the mobilisation practices of actors within the CFS. Unfortunately, the Bern Convention's database does not contain the documents for each case file and information for fifty cases overall is missing from the overview. The results are compiled in Table 11.1. Numbers are calculated on the basis of a total of 211 case files. Case files were counted twice, if submitted jointly by two complainants within different categories. For example, a complaint submitted jointly by an individual and an NGO was added as plus one to each category.

11.4 The Bern Convention and the EU Birds and Habitats Directives

The Bern Convention and the EU Birds and Habitats Directives together form the linchpin of nature protection law in the European area. The Bern Convention's overarching aim is the conservation of 'wild flora and fauna and their natural habitats, especially those species and habitats whose conservation requires the co-operation of several States'.[23] The Convention is therefore broad in focus, including not only all species but also the conservation of habitats in its scope. As an instrument of the Council of Europe, the Convention enjoys particularly wide ratification: its membership includes the Council of Europe's forty-nine member

[20] 'Case-File System: Reflections and Possible Restructuring in the Framework of the Bern Convention Vision and Strategic Plan for the Period to 2030', Secretariat Memorandum T-PVS/Inf(2021)30rev, 16.

[21] 'Analysis of the Rules of Procedure for the Case File System' (2007), Secretariat Memorandum T-PVS (2007) 6.

[22] 'Register of Bern Convention Complaints 2021', T-PVS/Inf(2021)5.

[23] Convention on the Conservation of European Wildlife and Natural Habitats.

States, five additional States and the European Union in its capacity as an international organisation.[24]

The Bern Convention was ratified in 1979, the same year as the EU Birds Directive[25] was adopted. These two instruments predate the Habitats Directive (1992) by more than a decade.[26] The Birds Directive and the Habitats Directive both essentially implement the Bern Convention into EU law, promoting a 'favourable conservation status' for species and habitat types included within their scope.[27] The relationship between the Bern Convention and the Habitats Directive has been deliberately synergetic from the start,[28] co-evolving in several ways. First, the Directive incorporated elements not included in the Convention, especially through the establishment of a co-ordinated network of protected areas throughout Europe known as the Natura 2000 network.[29] The Bern Convention Secretariat and Standing Committee responded to this development and followed suit through the establishment of the Emerald Network, which emulated Natura 2000 in the territories of non-EU member States party to the Bern Convention.[30] For EU members, the obligations relating to the networks are identical insofar as, for these States, 'Emerald Network sites are those of Natura 2000'.[31]

Given the overlap between the Convention and the Directives, the two instruments have naturally been the subject of ample comparison within academic literature. Authors often highlight the Bern Convention's reach within non-EU (and, indeed, non-Council of Europe) member States as the instrument's primary contemporary contribution.[32] Of course, it is true that the Bern Convention and its CFS constitute through their mere existence an international legal opportunity structure for citizens situated

[24] 'Details of Treaty No. 104' (Council of Europe Treaty Office).

[25] Amended in 2009, the Directive is now known as Directive 2009/147/EC of the European Parliament and of the Council of 30 November 2009 on the Conservation of Wild Birds ('Birds Directive').

[26] Council Directive 92/43/EEC of 21 May 1992 on the Conservation of Natural Habitats and of Wild Fauna and Flora ('Habitats Directive').

[27] Habitats Directive Article 2; Birds Directive Articles 1 and 2.

[28] C Coffey, 'The EU Habitats Directive: Enhancing Synergy with Pan-European Nature Conservation and with the EU Structural Funds' in S Oberthür and T Gehring (eds), *Institutional Interaction in Global Environmental Governance: Synergy and Conflict among International and EU Policies* (MIT Press 2006) 242.

[29] Ibid.

[30] Ibid.

[31] Standing Committee, 'Resolution No 5 Concerning the Rules for the Network of Areas of Special Conservation Interest' (Council of Europe 1998).

[32] See, for example, Coffey (n 28).

within the Bern Convention's reach, but outside of the EU. BirdLife primarily mobilised the CFS in relation to Convention breaches that occurred in countries not subject to the Directives. Out of the twenty-four identified case files involving BirdLife, fifteen were filed in relation to non-EU countries.[33]

The relatively low mobilisation rate under the Bern Convention in relation to EU countries may be the result of perceptions on the part of mobilising actors that the Bern Convention's CFS lacks legal 'teeth' when compared to the more legalised options available in relation to the EU Directives.[34] Although disputes concerning the application of the Bern Convention can be referred to binding arbitration by the Standing Committee (the CFS's decision-making organ),[35] at the time of writing, this has never happened in practice.[36] Instead, the CFS's process has been oriented towards the facilitation of productive dialogue and the promotion of practical solutions in the form of soft recommendations.[37]

Nevertheless, the CFS shows that actors do continue to mobilise via the CFS, even where EU membership has given them access to EU law and the corresponding dispute settlement procedures conferred thereunder. This raises questions as to why actors to whom both the procedures under the Bern Convention and the EU Directives are available choose to direct their complaint to the Commission, the CFS, or both.

11.5 Mobilising for Compliance with the EU Nature Directives: The European Commission's Infringement Procedure and Referrals to Litigation before the CJEU

The implementation of EU environmental law depends heavily on engaged civil society groups able to identify breaches of EU environmental law on the ground and motivated to report them to the bodies responsible for enforcement.[38] Despite this, it is well known that the

[33] Counted by and table on file with the author.

[34] D Pritchard, 'Review of the Case File System', T-PVS(2000)16 (Council of Europe 2000).

[35] Convention on the Conservation of European Wildlife and Natural Habitats 1979 (No 104) Article 18(2).

[36] A Trouwborst, FM Fleurke and JDC Linnell, 'Norway's Wolf Policy and the Bern Convention on European Wildlife: Avoiding the "Manifestly Absurd"' (2017) 20 *Journal of International Wildlife Law & Policy* 155, 165.

[37] Ibid.

[38] European Commission 2012a, 2; 2017b, in Eliantonio (n 2) 756.

CJEU is an inhospitable environment for legal mobilisation.[39] Non-privileged applicants (i.e., natural and legal persons) have to satisfy strict standing requirements to directly access the Court.[40] Non-State actors therefore rely on alternative mobilisation avenues. One of the main pathways in the EU context is the submission of complaints to the Commission to encourage infringement procedures.

At first glance, the initiation of infringement procedures seems to provide an exceptionally open opportunity structure for complainants. Individuals or organisations can submit complaints free of charge and without having to satisfy standing requirements via an online or physical complaints form, which is available in twenty-three languages.[41] The complaint's submission is followed by the Commission's assessment of the potential instance of non-compliance with EU law and a subsequent informal bilateral process between the Commission and the Member State known as the EU Pilot. Should the Member State fail to respond to the Commission within the ten-week deadline afforded to it under the Pilot, the Commission has the power (but no obligation) to open a formal infringement procedure under Article 258 TFEU.

Under the formal infringement procedure, the Commission may request a response from the Member State concerning its alleged failure to comply with EU environmental law by means of a letter of formal notice. Failure on the Member State's part to issue a satisfactory response within two months entitles the Commission to request the Member State to comply with EU law by sending a reasoned opinion (Article 258 TFEU). Non-compliance with the reasoned opinion triggers the Commission's discretion to refer the case to the CJEU.

Although the outcome of litigation before the CJEU is binding, financial penalties are imposed only in case of a second infringement procedure launched in response to a State's non-compliance with the Court's judgment. The second infringement procedure comprises fewer steps than the first – the Commission commences the procedure by sending a second letter of formal notice. Upon proposal by the Commission, the

[39] V Passalacqua, 'Legal Mobilization via Preliminary Reference: Insights from the Case of Migrant Rights' (2021) 58(3) *Common Market Law Review* 751.

[40] A Albors-Llorens, 'Remedies against the EU Institutions after Lisbon: An Era of Opportunity?' (2012) *The Cambridge Law Journal* 71 507, 513.

[41] 'How to Make a Complaint at EU Level' (European Commission).

Court then has the authority to impose a financial penalty in the form of a lump sum or daily payment on the Member State.[42]

11.6 Mobilising through the Bern Convention's Case File System: Access and Procedure

By comparison, in the Bern Convention's CFS, NGOs, individuals and other civil society actors can also file complaints without having to satisfy standing requirements.[43] This is done through complaint forms, which are followed up by a request for information, sent by the Secretariat to the party against which the complaint was issued. Should the government fail to respond within four months, the complaint is designated as a 'possible file'.[44] Subsequently, the case may be dropped on the basis of insufficient grounds to pursue the issue as a presumed breach or, alternatively, a case file can be formally opened, mandating special attention in relation to the case, for example in the form of on-the-spot appraisals.[45]

The body which decides on the status of files as well as recommendations for the resolution of disputes is the Standing Committee.[46] Functioning as the governing body of the Convention, the Standing Committee 'includes all contracting parties as well as observer states and organisations, both governmental and non-governmental, at the national and international level'.[47] Decisions of the Committee are taken by a two-thirds majority – parties are not in possession of veto powers.[48]

[42] Article 260, Consolidated Version of the Treaty on the Functioning of the European Union [2016] OJ C 202/47 (TFEU), for an example see *Commission v Greece* [1992] (European Court of Justice) C-45/91 and *Commission v Greece* [2000] (European Court of Justice) C-387/97.

[43] Standing Committee, 'Application of the Convention: Summary of Case Files and Complaints – Reminder on the Processing of Complaints and New On-Line Form' (Convention on the Conservation of European Wildlife and Natural Habitats 2008), Secretariat Memorandum T-PVS(2008)7, 3.

[44] Ibid., 4.

[45] Ibid., 5.

[46] Ibid.

[47] 'Institutions of the Bern Convention' (*Convention on the Conservation of European Wildlife and Natural Habitats*), available at www.coe.int/en/web/bern-convention/institutions, accessed 10 May 2022.

[48] 'Rules of Procedure of the Standing Committee', T-PVS/Inf(2013)6, Rule 8(b).

The rules concerning voting apply to decisions to initiate on-the-spot appraisals.[49] Decisions regarding proposals for mediation are taken by the Standing Committee or the Bureau.[50]

Since the Bern Convention has come into force, the Secretariat has received 211 complaints through the CFS,[51] and 37 case files have formally been opened. Case files are usually formally opened where the Standing Committee considers that a breach of the Convention provisions concerns a site or species of European importance, the scope of the threat is especially broad in character or the measures needed are of an urgent nature.[52] However, in recent years, there has been concern on the part of the Standing Committee that the opening of a case file indicates a presumption of non-compliance with the Convention. For this reason, the Standing Committee may refrain from formally opening a case file (it may, for example, be marked as 'in stand-by'), but still initiate measures such as 'on-the-spot appraisals' and other forms of dialogue.[53]

One example is the case file concerning the construction of an overhead power line in an environmentally sensitive area in the Lithuanian–Polish borderland. A local NGO argued that the construction could cause a direct negative impact on some species and habitats protected under the Bern Convention and EU Directives (the power line was to be located near an EU Natura 2000 site).[54] Rather than opening the case file, the Standing Committee referred the matter to mediation.[55] This commitment to a flexible handling of cases is explicitly written into the Convention. Article 18(1) read, 'The Standing Committee shall use its best endeavours to facilitate a friendly settlement of any difficulty to which the execution of this Convention may give rise.' Thus, the decisions of the Standing Committee are nuanced, and attention may be given even to those cases which are not formally opened.

[49] Ibid., Appendix I, para 1.

[50] Ibid., Appendix II, para 1.

[51] 'Register of Bern Convention Complaints 2021' (n 22).

[52] Standing Committee (n 43) 4.

[53] 'Improving the Case-File System of the Bern Convention', T-PVS(2011)14, 6.

[54] 'Mediation Procedure in the Frame of Complaint Number 2013/5: Presumed Impact of a Construction of Overhead Power Line (OHL) in an Environmentally Sensitive Area in the Lithuanian–Polish Borderland', Visit Report T-PVS/Files (2015) 51.

[55] The possibility to initiate mediation procedures was added to the CFS in 2015 and has so far not been used in any other cases. See Standing Committee (n 43) Appendix II.

11.7 Comparison of the Case File System and the European Commission's Infringement Procedure from a Legal Opportunity Structures Perspective

Based on legal opportunity structures theory, it is argued that CFS's structural openness to civil society participation is the primary pull for groups seeking compliance with nature protection law in Europe. Importantly, this is relevant not only as far as the initiation of the complaint is concerned. Rather, the potential for civil society participation continues to define the legal opportunity structure for NGOs at every stage of the process. Additionally, the potential for continuous participation interacts positively with the CFS's other defining features, such as procedural flexibility. Finally, the Bern Convention's 'small sibling' relationship with the EC in environmental matters means that the CFS's welcoming approach towards actor participation extends beyond the CFS. In fact, given the synergetic potential of the two systems, mobilisation at the interface of CFS and EC infringement procedures could potentially alter the legal opportunities available to NGOs.

Previous scholarship has suggested that while the Bern Convention's CFS would be suited to cases in which State and complainant are actively willing to reach a suitable solution, the EU's more coercive mechanism would be preferable where States are not willing to act on the basis of soft recommendations.[56] At a Bern Convention meeting on the Convention's implementation through national case law in June 1999, Mr Dave Pritchard, representative of BirdLife International and the Royal Society for the Protection of Birds (RSPB), noted that the RSPB is more likely to engage with the Bern CFS 'where the authorities themselves agree that an intervention would be helpful, where it's more of a "problem solving atmosphere" and where the process doesn't offer anything legally binding as an outcome'.[57] Thus, actors can strategically choose a more or less confrontational forum for the expression of a complaint. However, Pritchard added that complaints under the CFS may easily run in parallel with complaints made in front of other bodies.[58]

[56] J Dubrulle, 'The Evolving Potential of the (Non-)Compliance Mechanisms of the Bern Convention on European Wildlife Conservation' (*Tilburg University Environmental Law*, 7 August 2016).

[57] D Pritchard, 'The Example of a Non-Governmental Organisation in United Kingdom: The Royal Society for the Protection of Birds 1999' (2000) 42 *Environmental Encounters* 93.

[58] Ibid.

While the rules for the submission of complaints to the Commission offer, on paper, a promising avenue for mobilisation,[59] in reality the procedure is riddled with participatory difficulties. NGOs have long lamented the lack of participation and transparency in the Commission's complaints system.[60] After the submission of a complaint (the receipt of which will be communicated to the complainant), complainants are excluded from the pilot phase. Communication occurs between the Commission and the Member State only.[61] Even after the formal opening of a complaint, individuals (and other civil society actors) have no right to participate in procedures under Article 258 TFEU.[62]

The exclusion of the complainant from further stages in the case of the EC's infringement procedure creates uncertainties for mobilising actors when viewed in conjunction with the Commission's ability to act as gatekeeper at every stage of the procedure. Complaints by non-State actors can encourage the Commission to initiate an infringement procedure, but whether or not it is formally opened is subject to the Commission's discretion.[63] This applies even where the Commission considers that a breach of EU law has occurred. Generally, the Commission states that it chooses to initiate infringement procedures only if there is an indication of a 'systemic failure' to comply with EU law.[64] In all other cases, the Commission pursues a decentralised approach and will generally refer the complainants to mechanisms operating at the national level.[65] This also means, in turn, that the Commission is less likely to consider cases in which the legislation has been implemented, but on-the-ground implementation is lacking, unless this amounts to a general and systemic lack of enforcement in relation to an issue area. Because of the Commission's wide margin of discretion and the inability of mobilising actors to continue pushing for action on the

59 European Commission, 'EU Law: Better Results through Better Application', Communication from the Commission 2017/C 18/02 Annex, Section 2 'General Principles', available at https://eur-lex.europa.eu/legal-content/SK/TXT/?amp%3Btoc=OJ%3AC%3A2017%3A018%3ATOC&uri=uriserv%3AOJ.C_.2017.018.01.0010.01.ENG.

60 European Parliament 2013, 73–75, in Eliantonio (n 2) 756.

61 S Kingston, V Heyvaert and A Čavoški, *European Environmental Law* (Cambridge University Press 2017) 191.

62 Eliantonio (n 2) 753.

63 European Commission (n 59) section III.

64 Ibid.

65 Ibid.

part of the Commission through interventions, infringement procedures are not a reliable avenue for legal mobilisation.

These factors constitute a particularly difficult hurdle for applicants mobilising in relation to the Birds and Habitats Directives. The Commission noted in 2017 that the 'majority of complaints made in relation to the [Directives] concern threats to individual sites'.[66] Upon request, the Directorate General for Environment stated that 1,764 complaints filed under the keyword 'nature' were submitted between 2009 and 2020.[67] By contrast, 412 of those cases reached the 'formal notice' stage and 93 complaints (roughly 5 per cent) resulted in a referral to the Court under Article 258 TFEU.

The Commission's 2017 Communication goes on to elaborate that 'the centralised enforcement mechanism currently available to the Commission is unsuited to dealing with such complaints, particularly in terms of speed of response, use of experts with local knowledge, and site visits'.[68] Conversely, the use of experts to carry out on-the-spot appraisals is one of the CFS's greatest strengths. Well aware of this, the Secretariat is scaling up its efforts in this regard and has recently stated its intention to further expand its pool of experts to accommodate the widest possible range of case file processes.[69]

On top of this, even where a case makes it all the way to the litigation stage, it is far from guaranteed that a Member State will rectify the unlawful situation, as the Commission's willingness or capacity to remain active on a particular issue continues to factor into the equation. A study by BirdLife International, conducted in 2020, traced the implementation of eleven conservation-related CJEU judgments, paying particular attention to the Commission's role in following up after the court proceedings. The survey showed that the Commission followed up on the implementation of a CJEU judgment in only four of the eleven cases studied. In three of the remaining seven cases, the Commission did not follow up despite the continuation of the harmful activity in question.[70]

[66] 'Implementing Community Environmental Law', Communication from the Commission COM(96) 500 final (European Commission 1996).

[67] Email from Europe Direct to the author (7 October 2021).

[68] 'Implementing Community Environmental Law' (n 66).

[69] 'Case-File System: Reflections and Possible Restructuring in the Framework of the Bern Convention Vision and Strategic Plan for the Period to 2030' (n 20) 15.

[70] European Environmental Bureau and BirdLife International, 'Implementation of Rulings for Nature Conservation: Court of Justice of the European Union Case Studies'.

Unfortunately, because civil society actors find themselves outsiders in the process, their influence on the procedure ends at the initiation stage.

By contrast, civil society actors appear as active participants in the CFS's procedure in several ways.[71] First of all, non-governmental actors can act as observers in the Standing Committee, the body that decides on the handling of case files.[72] Secondly, complainants are welcome to submit information to the Secretariat, for example in the form of reports. Third-party interventions are also possible at all stages; reports can be received in relation to open cases as well as cases in other stages of consideration (e.g., stand-by). Thirdly, civil society actors can enter directly into dynamic and in-person conversation with member States, either through mediation or within the framework of expert group meetings and other official events held within the framework of the Bern Convention.[73] Consequently, mobilisation through the CFS allows complainants to retain a high degree of control over complaints. As a result, actors who possess the human resources to do so can continue to exert influence over the trajectory of a case from beginning to end. This is particularly helpful in light of the CFS's emphasis on flexibility, which is conducive to the elaboration of solutions that satisfy both the complainant and the government concerned.

Regarding flexibility of procedure, it also seems that the CFS may be better suited to deal with cases of individual non-compliance or failed enforcement, including those that do not concern 'systemic failures' of implementation. To this extent, a 2011 study by the Directorate General Environment pointed out that the absence of an EU inspectorate for the environment was hampering the Commission's ability to ensure the implementation and enforcement of EU law.[74] Among other options, the study explored the possibility of emulating the Bern Convention's model of experts, which consists of the selection of several pools of highly specialised experts ('expert groups') in nine distinct subject areas related to the objectives of the Convention.

[71] Standing Committee (n 46).

[72] 'Institutions of the Bern Convention' (n 47).

[73] 'Groups of Experts Set Up under the Bern Convention' (*Convention on the Conservation of European Wildlife and Natural Habitats*), available at www.coe.int/en/web/bern-convention/thematic-group-of-experts, accessed 10 May 2022.

[74] At the EU level, there exists the European Union Network for the Implementation and Enforcement of EU Environmental Law, which allows at least for the exchange of ideas and best practices. For more information, see 'Welcome to IMPEL Website' (*IMPEL Website*), available at www.impel.eu/en, accessed 9 May 2022.

Consequently, though the procedural rules of the Commission and the CFS do not preclude them from picking up the same complaints, the operational practice of these systems shows that they have developed different toolboxes for the handling of complaints. The following section illustrates this point by taking a closer look at BirdLife's interaction with the CFS and the EC in two cases of parallel mobilisation.

11.8 Wind Farms in Balchik and Kaliakra (Bulgaria)

The case of Balchik and Kaliakra concerns the Bulgarian Government's approval of the construction of wind farms within Emerald/Natura 2000 sites along Bulgaria's Black Sea Coast, affecting the *Via Pontica* migration route, one of Europe's important bird areas (IBA).[75] The initial complaint was filed in September 2004 with the Bern Convention's Standing Committee in relation to the Balchik wind farm. The case had previously undergone extensive mobilisation efforts at the national level. The Bulgarian Society for the Protection of Birds (BSPB) (in an alliance of several other NGOs) had made several efforts to prevent the acceptance of an environmental impact assessment by the public body tasked with its review (the Varna Regional Inspectorate of Environment and Water (RIEW)). This included participation in a public hearing procedure organised by RIEW[76] and the submission of a petition opposing the endorsement of the RIEW's decision to endorse the Environmental Impact Assessment (EIA).[77] Following the suspension of a case filed by the RSPB and other NGOs to challenge the RIEW's decision in July 2004, BirdLife, the RSPB and other national NGOs submitted a complaint to the Bern Convention's CFS outlining the events and inviting the Standing Committee to (a) open a file on the case and (b) adopt a recommendation annexed to the complaint, which contained detailed steps requested from the government to comply with its obligations under the

[75] The Important Bird and Biodiversity Area (IBA) concept was developed by Birdlife International. Key sites are identified through Birdlife's IBA programme and have been used in the European Union to designate Special Protected Areas (SPAs) under the Birds Directive. See 'Protecting Birds Where They Live and Migrate' (*BirdLife International*, 22 March 2021), available at www.birdlife.org/projects/ibas-mapping-most-important-places/, accessed 10 May 2022.

[76] 'Construction of the Balchik Wind Farm (Bulgaria)', T-PVS/Files(2004)6 Report by the NGO, para 6.

[77] Ibid., para 9.

Convention.[78] The Standing Committee responded by mandating an on-the-spot appraisal of the wind farm plant, conducted in September 2005, on the basis of which it adopted Recommendation No 117 on the plan to set up a wind farm near the town of Balchik and other wind farm developments on the *Via Pontica* route.[79] In the following years, BirdLife continued to monitor and report to the Standing Committee on the State's failure to implement the recommendation.

Upon Bulgaria's accession to the European Union on 1 January 2007, Bulgaria automatically became subject to the provisions of the Birds and Habitats Directives.[80] In early 2008, the BSPB submitted a complaint to the EC.[81] Within the same year, the Commission issued two formal letters of notice to the Bulgarian State.[82] A third letter of formal notice and a reasoned opinion were issued in 2011 and 2012 respectively.[83] In 2014, the Commission finally referred the case to the CJEU.[84] The judgment of the Court found Bulgaria to be in breach of the Birds and Habitats Directives in several respects. These included Bulgaria's failure to include the IBA territories covering the Kaliakra region in the Special Protection Areas Bulgaria had established under the criteria contained in the Birds Directive, approval of the implementation of several wind power and tourism development projects in the area, and failure to properly carry out an impact assessment in relation to another six of the wind farms concerned.[85]

Interestingly, the Bern Convention case file remained open during the Commission's infringement procedure and after the CJEU's judgment. During the proceedings, BirdLife continued to submit reports to the CFS on the Bulgarian Government's progress in implementing the recommendations issued by the Bern Convention's Standing Committee. The NGO also encouraged the submission of reports from other

[78] Ibid., para 2.

[79] 'Recommendation of the Standing Committee on the Plan to Set up a Wind Farm near the Town of Balchik and Other Wind Farm Developments, on the Via Pontica Route (Bulgaria)', Recommendation No 117 (2005).

[80] European Commission, 'Enlargement and Nature Law' (*European Commission Environment*), available at https://ec.europa.eu/environment/nature/legislation/enlargement/index_en.htm, accessed 7 November 2022.

[81] 'Kaliakra' (*Royal Society for the Protection of Birds*, 9 November 2022), available at www.rspb.org.uk/our-work/casework/cases/kaliakra/.

[82] Ibid.

[83] Ibid.

[84] *Commission v Bulgaria* [2016] Court of Justice of the European Union C-141/14.

[85] Ibid, para 98.

ornithological organisations.[86] In fact, mobilisation through the CFS and the consistent submission of information to the Committee has resulted in the creation of a detailed public record of the case. At the same time, BirdLife mobilised the Bern Convention's Standing Committee in its position as an insider in the international institutional structure. More specifically, a 2010 report submitted by BirdLife requests the Standing Committee to 'urge the [EC], immediately, to progress . . . the particular infringement case on lack of adequate protection of Kaliakra'.[87] This was just prior to the issuance of the Commission's additional letter of notice.

Since the 2016 judgment, regular complainant reports have been submitted to the Bern CFS, evidencing a shift from rights-claiming to monitoring the judgment's enforcement. It seems that in this case, due to its on-the-ground presence, the BSPB finds itself in a better position to monitor treaty enforcement than the treaty body itself.[88] Additionally, co-operation between the national NGO, its international network and the Bern Convention enables efficient flow of information between the local and the international or regional level.[89] Before 2016, complainant and NGO reports were submitted jointly to the CFS by the RSPB and BSPB. Since 2016, with the beginning of the monitoring period, all complainant reports have been submitted to the CFS solely by the BSPB – the Bulgarian arm of BirdLife with an active presence at the site in question.

In parallel, the RSPB continued its involvement in the case through its insider role within the institutional structure of the Convention. For example, in 2018, an on-the-spot appraisal (OSA) of Balchik and Kaliakra mandated by the Standing Committee was led by Pritchard, a key figure in the RSPB's involvement through the Bern Convention.[90] The OSA mission's report notes that the CJEU's judgment in Case C-141/14 refrains from prescribing specific remedies or outlining in detail the actions Bulgaria should take following the judgment.[91] This differs

[86] See F Liechi, 'Construction of the Kaliakra Wind Farm Parks', T-PVS/Files(2006)8.

[87] 'Wind Farms in Balchik and Kaliakra: Via Pontica (Bulgaria)', Report by the NGO T-PVS/Files(2010)22.

[88] See also J Braithwaite and P Drahos, *Global Business Regulation* (Cambridge University Press 2000) 564.

[89] ME Keck and K Sikkink, 'Transnational Advocacy Networks in International and Regional Politics' (2002) 51 *International Social Science Journal* 89, 92.

[90] 'Wind Farms in Balchik and Kaliakra (Bulgaria)' (2018), On-the-spot appraisal report T-PVS/Files(2018)25.

[91] Ibid.

starkly from the recommendations made on the basis of the OSA itself. Despite their soft character, the recommendations are very specific, including deadlines for the submission of progress reports, funding goals and the inclusion of stakeholders in the process of implementing the CJEU judgment.[92] In this case, parallel participation in the EU and Bern processes appears to have yielded valuable results for the NGO. BirdLife was provided with the opportunity to back its claim on the legal obligations contained in an authoritative judgment by the European Court of Justice, while remaining actively involved in the monitoring of enforcement through the complementary system of the Bern Convention via its local partners, thus leveraging the cumulative effect of both mobilisation strategies to exert pressure on the Bulgarian Government.

On top of this, the Bulgarian example demonstrates that the special status of some NGOs as key partners of the Convention means that some organisations, including BirdLife, are able to actively influence the Convention's policy development in ways that feed back into their mobilisation opportunities. Reports submitted by the Group of Experts on Conservation of Birds and, indeed, BirdLife International in its capacity as an individual organisation, can be adopted as recommendations by the Convention's Standing Committee.[93] Two years prior to the submission of the Balchik complaint, the Secretariat had tasked BirdLife International with the production of a report, completed in 2003, analysing the effects of windfarms on birds and providing guidance on environmental impact assessment and site selection criteria.[94]

The Bern Convention Standing Committee regularly adopts recommendations based on reports provided by BirdLife. Recommendation No 117(2005) on the plan to set up a wind farm near the town of Balchik and other wind farm developments, on the *Via Pontica* route, for example, explicitly draws on the findings contained in BirdLife's 2003 report on wind farms and birds,[95] including guidance on environmental assessment criteria and site selection issues. In the recommendation, the Standing Committee explicitly requests the Bulgarian Government to take into account BirdLife's report and to involve and

[92] Ibid., 17.
[93] Standing Committee (n 43) Rule 9(b).
[94] BirdLife International, 'Windfarms and Birds: An Analysis of the Effects of Windfarms on Birds, and Guidance on Environmental Assessment Criteria and Site Selection Issues', Secretariat Memorandum T-PVS/Inf (2002) 30 and T PVS/Inf(2003)12.
[95] Ibid.

consider the views of NGOs in the performance of future environmental impact assessments.[96] The recommendations of the Bern Convention Standing Committee, despite their 'soft' legal form and title, are important in that they provide concrete substantive content to the Convention's provisions.[97] Consequently, BirdLife's involvement through the submission of information to the Bern Convention system simultaneously allows the organisation to strengthen the legal basis on which it relies in its claims.

11.9 Presumed Illegal Killing of Birds in Malta

Bird killing in Malta has been a perpetual and notorious problem. At the time of writing, in late April 2022, yet another spring hunting season draws to a close. The issue of bird killing in Malta has been subjected to international attention for more than a decade. Several distinct issues have been repeatedly brought to the attention of the Commission and the CFS: both spring hunting of quail and turtle-dove (hereafter referred to as 'spring hunting'), and the autumn hunting and trapping of quail, turtle-dove and golden plovers, as well as song thrush (hereafter referred to as 'autumn hunting') and finch trapping.

In the context of the trapping of golden plovers and song thrush, and the trapping of finches, respectively, BirdLife Malta has contended that these practices should be addressed together, as the continuation of one practice risks its exploitation as a cover for the illegal continuation of the other.[98] While the Commission has addressed them separately, the CFS has treated all issues as part of a single case file. The following paragraphs therefore refer to the general CFS file at times, and to individual issues whenever possible.

The issue of spring hunting was first considered by the Commission in 2006. This culminated in a referral of Malta to the Court, which found the State in violation of the Birds Directive in its 2009 judgment.[99] In a separate infringement procedure opened in 2011, the Commission also

[96] 'Recommendation of the Standing Committee on the Plan to Set up a Wind Farm near the Town of Balchik and Other Wind Farm Developments, on the Via Pontica Route (Bulgaria)' (n 79).

[97] S Jen, 'The Convention on the Conservation of European Wildlife and Natural Habitats (Bern, 1979): Procedures of Application in Practice' (1999) 2 *Journal of International Wildlife Law & Policy* 224, 229.

[98] 'Presumed Illegal Killing of Birds in Malta', Report by the NGO T-PVS/Files(2015) 7.

[99] *Commission v Malta* [2009] Court of Justice of the European Union, C-557/15.

issued a formal notice and reasoned opinion addressing the issue of autumn hunting in Malta to the Maltese Government. In 2012, an individual submitted a complaint to the Bern Convention Secretariat, alleging a violation of Articles 6–9 of the Bern Convention by the Maltese Government in relation to spring hunting.[100] Following the complaint, BirdLife Malta became involved in the case by submitting a reaction to the Maltese Government's response to the complaint.[101] Two months later, the European Union submitted a report to the CFS.[102] The report first stressed the primary responsibility of the Member State and then went on to reassure the Convention's Secretariat of the Commission's continued attention towards the issue and communication with the Maltese Government. It specified that the Commission had received a detailed report on the hunting derogations in the 2013 season. The final paragraph then goes on to explain that no such reports had been received for the years 2009–2011 and that the Commission intended to formally request these reports in the following weeks. Although it is doubtful whether the exchange between Bern and the Commission had any practical effects (in fact, the Commission closed the case concerning spring hunting in 2015 and remained inactive in the procedure concerning autumn hunting until its closure in 2021), this dynamic further illustrates the potential use of the CFS in relation to the Commission. In this case, it seems that the CFS also functioned as a means to obtain and make public information on both the progress of the situation in Malta and the involvement of the Commission in bringing the State into compliance with its obligations.

Although this case file was never formally opened, the Bern Convention Secretariat remained engaged in the case by facilitating communication between the NGO and the government. Despite the file being kept in stand-by, mobilisation through the CFS enabled direct dialogue between the representatives of the State in question and non-governmental organisations acting as complainants. The 5th Meeting of the Select Group of Experts on Conservation of Wild Birds (2015), at

[100] Though initially triggered in relation to spring hunting, both hunting seasons and finch trapping are discussed in tandem in the reports submitted to the CFS in relation to the case file. See 'Presumed Illegal Killing of Birds in Malta' Report by the Complainant T-PVS/Files(2013)11.

[101] 'Presumed Illegal Killing of Birds in Malta', Report by the NGO T-PVS/Files(2013)23. Birdlife remained involved and continued to submit reports concerning this issue.

[102] 'Presumed Illegal Killing of Birds in Malta', Report by the European Union T-PVS/Files (2013)28.

which members of both the NGO and the government were present, discussed progress regarding the 2012/7 complaint concerning the presumed illegal killing of birds in Malta.[103] Thus, the Bern Convention's expert group was able to facilitate further discussion of the complaint.

Additionally, BirdLife occasionally used the CFS where action by the EC stagnated. In a presentation before the Bern Convention's Secretariat, BirdLife highlighted that the EC 'appears uninterested in challenging the derogation further' and 'needs to impose a ban on trapping'.[104] Birdlife called on the Council of Europe and the parties to the Bern Convention to continue monitoring the situation to ensure progress regarding the proper implementation of both the Bern Convention and the Birds Directive.[105] A similar interplay can be observed regarding the problem of finch trapping, which was first picked up by the Commission in 2014. Reports to the CFS by BirdLife Malta around this time make explicit mention of the infringement procedure, asking that the 'complaint on stand-by [with the Bern Convention] should remain open along the lines of the European Commission raising its concerns via an infringement process on the matter'.[106] More specifically, the NGO called on the Bern Convention to encourage the EC to stand against the Maltese Government's derogation permitting the trapping of finches.[107] Significantly, in this case, BirdLife Malta also asked the Bern Convention to conduct investigations into the consequences of Malta's derogation from the Birds Directive, precisely with a view to aiding the case pending before the European Court of Justice.[108] Arguably, this request indicates the perceived complementary value of the CFS's practically oriented approach, even where CJEU proceedings are on the horizon.

11.10 Conclusion

The Bern Convention's Secretariat is well aware of the danger posed by overlaps between the EC's activities and its own CFS and has stressed the importance of further developing existing synergies to avoid duplication.

[103] '5th Meeting of the Group of Experts on the Conservation of Birds', Meeting Report T-PVS(2015)25, 10.
[104] N Barbara and W Van Den Bosche, 'Complaint in Stand-by No 2012/7: ILLEGAL KILLING OF BIRDS IN MALTA'.
[105] Ibid.
[106] 'Presumed Illegal Killing of Birds in Malta', Report by the NGO T-PVS/Files(2015) 44, 5.
[107] Ibid.
[108] Ibid., 7.

Noting the Commission's superior position in terms of power and resources, the Secretariat expressed some concerns regarding the added value of its CFS for EU parties. At the same time, the Secretariat highlighted the potential benefit of acting as a first point of contact for claimants and promoting action on the part of its 'big brother' the Commission where it cannot facilitate resolution on its own.[109] In the future, it is expected that the Bern Convention will seek dialogue with the Commission to ascertain how synergies can be nourished.[110]

From a legal mobilisation perspective, this would be a very welcome development. The possibility of a CJEU referral and the related threat of hefty financial penalties will never be replaced by a non-coercive compliance system. Nevertheless, this chapter concludes that less coercive compliance systems are important mobilisation venues for civil society actors. The case studies indicate that the degree of participation offered to civil society by the CFS in the handling of individual complaints and in its programme of work provides NGOs with a unique structure to mobilise the law in their triple role as policymakers, complainants and watchdogs. While still far from an ideal system of access to justice in environmental matters, it appears that actors can to some extent use the CFS to fill the gaps left by the Commission's infringement proceedings.

[109] 'Case-File System: Reflections and Possible Restructuring in the Framework of the Bern Convention Vision and Strategic Plan for the Period to 2030' (n 20) 15.

[110] Ibid.

12

The Right to a Healthy Environment in Latin America and the Caribbean

Compliance through the Inter-American System and the Escazú Agreement

MARIA ANTONIA TIGRE

12.1 Introduction

Latin America and the Caribbean (LAC) is a region filled with paradoxes: it is uniquely biologically rich and relies heavily on primary products and natural resources, with economies driven by external commodity demands.[1] As LAC continues to pursue 'development',[2] important ecosystems and ecological processes are affected. It is also the deadliest region for environmental defenders, with countries consistently placing first in global rankings.[3]

At the same time, LAC is a leading region in the recognition of the right to a healthy environment, with the majority of countries having

The author would like to thank Lavinia Bhaskaruni for research assistance and Natalia Urzola, Alexandra Harrington, and Gastón Medici Colombo for helpful comments on earlier drafts of this chapter. This chapter was also significantly improved by a rich discussion at the PluriCourts Research Conference on Compliance Mechanisms, held at the University of Oslo in October 2021, the IUCN WCEL 2022 Oslo International Environmental Law Conference, held at the University of Oslo in October 2022, and discussions with the members of the task force of the GNHRE Implementing Principles of the Escazú Agreement. The author would also like to thank the editors of this publication, Christina Voigt and Caroline Foster, for helpful comments throughout the drafting of this chapter.

[1] 'Geo-6 Regional Summary for Latin America and the Caribbean', United Nations Environment Programme, available at www.unep.org/global-environment-outlook/findings-and-data/assessment-findings/geo-6-regional-summary-latin, accessed 1 October 2021.

[2] Meant here as the non-sustainable socio-economic development that is often pursued in the region.

[3] 'Defending Tomorrow' (*Global Witness*, July 2020), available at www.globalwitness.org/en/campaigns/environmental-activists/defending-tomorrow/, accessed 1 October 2021.

adopted a constitutional right.[4] Furthermore, the region is characterised by strong civil society movements, including environmental NGOs advocating for stronger environmental legislation and providing broad legal representation, stimulating the improvement of laws and regulations.[5] With LAC States' widespread constitutionalisation of environmental rights, judges are open to new and emerging legal theories, providing an expansive interpretation of existing norms, driving innovation, and challenging legal formalism. These emerging theories, grounded in the right to a healthy environment, are being used to push national governments towards increased activity in areas lacking implementation, such as climate ambition and deforestation.[6]

Following developments in national courts, the Inter-American Court of Human Rights (IACtHR) has recognised an autonomous right to a healthy environment, thus clearly stating that cases relying on the right to a healthy environment can be heard within the Inter-American System of Human Rights (IASHR). In 2017, the IACtHR issued a landmark Advisory Opinion recognising the right to a healthy environment as 'fundamental to the existence of humanity' under the American Convention.[7] The opinion is groundbreaking: it confirmed extraterritorial jurisdiction for transboundary environmental harms, the autonomous right to a healthy environment and State responsibility for environmental damage within and beyond the State's borders.[8] In 2020, the IACtHR

[4] 'Substantive Rights – Latin America & Caribbean' (Envirorightsmap), available at https://envirorightsmap.org/?s=&post_type=listing&et-listing-type=39&et-listing-location=6&et-listing-rating=none, accessed 1 October 2021; countries within LAC region that have enshrined the right to a healthy environment within their treaties: Argentina, Bolivia, Brazil, Chile, Colombia, Costa Rica, Cuba, Dominican Republic, Ecuador, Guyana, Mexico, Nicaragua, Paraguay, Peru and Venezuela.

[5] DR. Boyd, *The Environmental Rights Revolution: A Global Study of Constitutions, Human Rights, and the Environment* (UBC Press 2012) chapter 6, 143.

[6] J Peel and J Lin 'Transnational Climate Litigation: The Contribution of the Global South' (2019) 113 *American Journal of International Law* 679, 713; AP Riaño, 'Litígio Climático e Direitos Humanos' in J Setzer, K Cunha and A Botter Fabbri (eds), *Litigância Climática: Novas Fronteiras para o Direito Ambiental no Brasil* (Revista dos Tribunais 2019).

[7] Inter-American Court of Human Rights, *The Environment and Human Rights (State Obligations in Relation to the Environment in the Context of the Protection and Guarantee of the Rights to Life and to Personal Integrity), Interpretation and Scope of Articles 4(1) and 5(1) of the American Convention on Human Rights*, Advisory Opinion OC-23/17 of 15 November 2017, Series A, No 23, available at www.corteidh.or.cr/docs/opiniones/seriea_23_ing.pdf, accessed 21 March 2020.

[8] MA Tigre and N Urzola Gutierrez, 'The 2017 Inter-American Court's Advisory Opinion: Changing the Paradigm for International Environmental Law' (2021) 12(1) *Journal of Human Rights and the Environment* 24.

declared in *Lhaka Honhat Association v Argentina* that Argentina violated Indigenous groups' communal property and rights to a healthy environment, cultural identity, food, and water.[9] For the first time in a contentious case, the Court analysed these as autonomous rights, based on Article 26 of the American Convention on Human Rights,[10] and ordered specific restitution measures, including actions to provide access to adequate food and water, the recovery of forest resources and Indigenous culture. The decision marks a significant milestone for protecting Indigenous peoples' rights and expanding the autonomous rights to a healthy environment, water and food. Cases relying on these rights can now be heard and decided on the merits under the IASHR.[11]

Although limited to the legal context of the Americas, the decision further supported a broader campaign for the international recognition of the right to a clean, healthy and sustainable environment. In 2021 and 2022, the United Nations Human Rights Council (UNHRC) and the United Nations General Assembly (UNGA) adopted resolutions recognising the right to a clean, healthy and sustainable environment as a human right.[12] While this recognition resulted from a decades-long process and a wide-reaching international campaign, it also benefitted from the holistic approach adopted by the IACtHR. [13]

The developments at the IASHR fully embrace the justiciability of the right to a healthy environment at the regional level, opening doors for new cases and the use of regional non-compliance mechanisms for international environmental law (IEL). In the absence of an international environmental tribunal, human rights courts are crucial for adjudicating environmental rights at the regional level. Moreover, it provides a clear

[9] I'A Court H.R., *Indigenous Communities of the Lhaka Honhat (Our Land) Association v Argentina, Merits, Reparations, and Costs,* Judgment of 6 February 2020, Series C, No 400.

[10] American Convention on Human Rights (San Jose, Costa Rica, 22 November 1969) 9 ILM 673 (1970), entered into force 18 July 1978.

[11] MA Tigre, 'Indigenous Communities of the Lhaka Honhat (Our Land) Association v. Argentina' (2021) 115(4) American Journal of International Law 706.

[12] Human Rights Council Res 48/L.23/Rev.1, UN Doc A/HRC/48/L.23/Rev.1, 5 October 2021; United Nations, General Assembly, 'The Human Right to a Clean, Healthy and Sustainable Environment', A/76/L.75 (2022).

[13] See i.e., MA Tigre, *Gaps in International Environmental Law: Toward a Global Pact for the Environment* (ELI Press 2020); MA Tigre, 'International Recognition of the Right to a Healthy Environment: What Is the Added Value for Latin America and the Caribbean?' (2023) 117 *American Journal of International Law Unbound* 184.

path to promoting the rule of law by ensuring environmental accountability to governments in LAC.[14]

After a long negotiation grounded in an effective participatory process, the Escazú Agreement (Escazú) was adopted in 2018 and entered into force in April 2021. It is a landmark treaty for advancing environmental rights – and access rights, in particular – in LAC.[15] The Escazú Agreement has brought a myriad of environmental rights and duties for LAC. Escazú, unlike the Aarhus Convention, contains explicitly a provision adopting a substantive environmental right. Article 4.1 notes that 'Each Party shall guarantee the right of every person to live in a healthy environment and any other universally recognised human right related to the present Agreement.' The explicit recognition, paired with a positive duty of States to enforce it, is crucial to the development of environmental protection in the region.

In giving expression to the idea of environmental democracy, Escazú sits alongside the Aarhus Convention[16] – Europe's 1998 Convention on environmental access rights – in implementing Principle 10 of the 1992 Rio Declaration on Environment and Development.[17] Through three pillars of environmental democracy, Principle 10 recognised environmental procedural rights: (i) the right to public participation, (ii) access to environmental information, and (iii) access to justice.[18] However, Escazú provides a 'regional spin' to Principle 10 by recognising the regional underpinnings of the universal values it expands.[19] Furthermore, Escazú holds that environmental decision-making is rarely straightforward; essential in its implementation is recognising how Principle 10 applies to the region's social, cultural, economic and

[14] Tigre and Urzola Gutierrez (n 9) 49.

[15] Regional Agreement on Access to Information, Public Participation and Justice in Environmental Matters in Latin America and Caribbean (Escazú, 4 March 2018) C.N.195.2018, entered into force 22 April 2021, available at https://repositorio.cepal.org/handle/11362/43583 (Escazú Agreement).

[16] Convention on Access to Information, Public Participation in Decision-Making and Access to Justice in Environmental Matters (Aarhus, 25 June 1998) 2161 UNTS 447, entered into force 30 October 2001 (Aarhus Convention).

[17] Rio Declaration on Environment and Development, UN Doc A/CONF.151/5/Rev.1 (Rio de Janeiro, 13 June 1992) 31 ILM 874 (Rio Declaration).

[18] J Darpö, 'Principle 10 and Access to Justice' (2017), available at https://papers.ssrn.com/sol3/papers.cfm?abstract_id=2985277, accessed 1 October 2021.

[19] MA Tigre, 'Principle 10: What Can We Learn from Its Regional Implementation through the Escazú Agreement?' (Pathway to the 2022 Declaration), available at www.pathway2022declaration.org/article/principle-10-what-can-we-learn-from-its-regional-implementation-through-the-escazu-agreement/, accessed 1 October 2021.

environmental context.[20] Escazú, therefore, expands on the three traditional pillars of access rights by adding: (iv) the right to a healthy environment, (v) the protection of environmental and land defenders, and (vi) capacity building and co-operation.[21] These additional pillars are essential in implementing environmental democracy in LAC.

Countries in LAC now face the arduous task of implementing Escazú. Environmental decision-making faces a series of distinctive challenges due to the (i) volume and diversity of environmental interests, (ii) the plurality of environmental values involved, (iii) the uncertain nature of environmental knowledge, and (iv) the complex nature of environmental risk. States in the region must facilitate the implementation of the Escazú Agreement, keeping in mind multiple regional contradictions. This is a region filled with biodiversity and progressive environmental laws which still lacks effective implementation. As Escazú entered into force, a key question emerged: How can we ensure compliance with the new rules of Escazú? Furthermore, what are the mechanisms available in the case of non-compliance?

Importantly, in this context, the Agreement established a Committee to Support Implementation and Compliance (Committee) by Parties as a subsidiary body under the Conference of the Parties (COP).[22] The Committee shall be consultative, transparent, non-adversarial, non-judicial and non-punitive.[23] Considering the background briefly explained here, it is essential to develop a robust system for oversight and compliance at the regional level through the Committee to facilitate the Agreement's success. The first COP, which was held in April 2022, adopted both the rules of procedure of the Conference of the Parties (Article 15)[24] and the rules relating to the structure and functioning of the Committee (Article 18(2)).[25] These rules provide the first step towards the implementation of the Agreement. However, many other steps for effective implementation are still ahead.

[20] Ibid.

[21] MA Tigre, 'Six Pillars of the Escazú Agreement' (The Global Network for Human Rights and the Environment 2021), available at https://gnhre.org/community/the-six-pillars-of-the-escazu-agreement-part-1/, accessed 1 October 2021.

[22] Article 18 Escazú Agreement (n 16), para 1.

[23] Ibid., para 2.

[24] Report of the First Meeting of the Conference of the Parties to the Escazú Agreement, LC/COP-EZ.1/3, Annex I, Decision I/1 (2 September 2022).

[25] Article 18 Escazú Agreement (n 16), paras 1 and 2; Decision I/3 (n 26).

Implementation requires a series of actions at the domestic level. For example, each Party shall establish or designate one or more impartial entities or institutions with autonomy and independence to promote transparency in access to environmental information, oversee compliance with rules and monitor, report on and guarantee the right of access to information. Furthermore, each Party may consider including or strengthening, as appropriate, sanctioning powers to certain governmental entities to properly enforce the recognised rights in the Escazú Agreement within the scope of their responsibilities.[26]

Given the broad reach of the regional recognition of the human right to a healthy environment now available in LAC, what are the best mechanisms to prevent environmental harm through the enforcement of this right? This chapter compares the existing mechanisms available under the IASHR and the implementation and compliance mechanism under Escazú. Additionally, what can we learn from the non-compliance mechanism in the Aarhus Convention? To keep with the spirit of Escazú, meaningful participation must be maintained throughout the Agreement's implementation, so it remains a valuable living instrument. Specifically, the public should make use of and trigger the Committee on alleged non-compliance to ensure participation in its implementation.[27] This chapter discusses this ongoing process to increase enforcement of the right to a healthy environment in LAC. Section 12.2 discusses the right to a healthy environment in Escazú and the relevance of its express recognition. Section 12.3 debates the threat of non-compliance that may hinder the full implementation of the Agreement and the need to strengthen non-compliance mechanisms. Section 12.4 briefly goes over the newly adopted Rules of Procedure of the Committee. Section 12.5 draws lessons from the Aarhus Convention, Paris Agreement, Nagoya, and Convention on Biological Diversity (CBD) for Escazú's Committee. Section 12.6 analyses potential overlap with the mechanisms under the inter-American human rights system. Section 12.7 concludes.

[26] Article 5 Escazú Agreement (n 16), para 18.

[27] Ibid. NGOs cannot bring a claim to the European Court of Human Rights, for example, decreasing the efficacy of the Aarhus Convention and its integration with the European human rights system. See L Lizarazo-Rodriguez and J Teixeira de Freitas, 'Aarhus and Escazú: The Two Sides of the Atlantic in the Field of Public Participation in Environmental Matters' (The Global Network for Human Rights and the Environment 2021), available at https://gnhre.org/community/aarhus-and-escazu-the-two-sides-of-the-atlantic-in-the-field-of-public participation-in-environmental-matters/, accessed 1 October 2021.

12.2 The Right to a Healthy Environment under Escazú

The substantive right to a healthy environment for present and future generations is explicitly acknowledged in Escazú as an objective of the treaty[28] and one of its general provisions.[29] Grounded in the right to a healthy environment, Escazú establishes procedural environmental rights to provide tools to implement it. Environmental access rights are rooted in the rights of present and future generations to live in a healthy environment and to sustainable development.[30] Article 1 fully adopts the right to a healthy environment for present and future generations, with a positive duty of each Party to guarantee such right as recognised in the Agreement. As will be detailed below, the existence of a non-compliance mechanism and the intersection with the IASHR provide teeth to the recognition of the right. By joining the Agreement, the States which have not recognised the right already at the national level join a long list of countries worldwide who have done so. This process, as noted before, is further strengthened by the international recognition of the right to a healthy environment by the UNHRC and the UNGA.

Furthermore, the inclusion of future generations in Article 1 is significant and guarantees a commitment to their survival and well-being, dependent on environmental protection. The Agreement also explicitly addresses climate change and its related impacts and requires Parties to have environmental information systems to build national capacities, including climate change sources.[31] This is important because, considering the effects of climate change on future generations, environmental and human rights law must ensure that protection measures are in place

[28] Escazú Agreement (n 16) Article 1: 'The objective of the present Agreement is to guarantee the full and effective implementation in Latin America and the Caribbean of the rights of access to environmental information, public participation in the environmental decision-making process and access to justice in environmental matters, and the creation and strengthening of capacities and cooperation, contributing to the protection of the right of every person of present and future generations to live in a healthy environment and to sustainable development.'

[29] Escazú Agreement (n 16) Article 4(1): 'Each Party shall guarantee the right of every person to live in a healthy environment and any other universally-recognized human right related to the present Agreement.'

[30] Escazú Agreement (n 16).

[31] Escazú Agreement (n 16) Article 6(3): 'Each Party shall have in place one or more up-to-date environmental information systems, which may include, inter alia: (g) climate change sources aimed at building national capacities.'

to provide the right to a healthy environment for the future.[32] For example, it can be argued that the environmental rights of future generations must be considered in environmental policies adopted by the legislative and executive branches at the national level. Additionally, with the recognition of the human right to a healthy environment, future generations can have standing to invoke the right in national (if the provision is adequately implemented at the national level) and regional courts (through the recognition in the Advisory Opinion by the IACtHR and the Escazú Agreement). Finally, this explicit acknowledgement opens the door for other rights-based cases (broadly in climate litigation but also specifically in climate litigation and biodiversity litigation) to be brought on behalf of future generations, furthering the argument of intergenerational equity. Since the role of future generations in climate litigation remains contested,[33] the inclusion of this norm in the Escazú Agreement represents a welcome advance in access to justice. However, several questions remain about how compliance mechanisms will feature future generations. For example, how can the COP ensure that the rules of procedure address their needs? Furthermore, how do the protective mechanisms in the IASHR apply to them? These questions will likely be answered as cases of non-compliance arise.

A further significant feature of the Escazú Agreement is that throughout its text, one can easily recognise its commitment to ensuring that the rights acknowledged, whether traditional human rights, the right to a healthy environment or environmental access rights, are understood as interrelated and interdependent. This is in line with the jurisprudence of the IACtHR.[34] Giupponi notes that within LAC, scholars consider environmental information a fundamental part of the right to an adequate environment enshrined in national constitutions, downplaying the traditional distinction between 'procedural' and 'substantive' rights.[35] The

[32] J Greaves Siew, 'Facing the Future: The Case for a Right to a Healthy Environment for Future Generations under International Law' (2020) 8(1) *Groningen Journal of International Law* 30.

[33] See i.e., A Daly, Intergenerational Rights are Children's Rights: Upholding the Right to a Healthy Environment through the UN Convention on the Rights of the Child (20 June 2022), available at https://papers.ssrn.com/sol3/papers.cfm?abstract_id=4141475.

[34] I'A Court H.R., Advisory Opinion OC-23/17 of 15 November 2017 (n 8) para 47.

[35] B Olmos Giupponi, 'Fostering Environmental Democracy in Latin America and the Caribbean: An Analysis of the Regional Agreement on Environmental Access Rights' (2019) 28(2) *Review of European, Comparative & International Environmental Law* 136, 137.

different theoretical underpinnings of environmental law in LAC – environmental constitutionalism, the close intersection between the international and the domestic in protecting environmental rights and the greening of Latin American constitutions in the 1980s and 1990s[36] – reflect the integrationist approach to the different rights in Escazú.[37]

In essence, Escazú has a dual character. It is a binding multilateral environmental agreement (MEA) while also uniquely significant as a human rights instrument. Moreover, its approach to environmental access rights is distinctive as its implementation is sure to be reinforced through regional human rights law.[38]

12.3 Non-Compliance in Escazú: A Work in Progress

Given the global challenge generated by the insufficient implementation of environmental norms, which is particularly relevant in LAC, States must engage with measures to bring the Escazú Agreement to life at the national level. Ultimately, the effectiveness of an international agreement like Escazú relies on the contracting Parties to implement its norms domestically. Implementing Escazú means enacting relevant laws and regulations (formal implementation) and adopting effective policies, measures and actions for Parties to meet their obligations under the Agreement. The latter includes deploying the formal machinery established by the treaty.[39] An additional step lies in effectively implementing the treaty on the ground.[40] Can States in LAC conform to Escazú's different layers of compliance and implementation?

Moreover, what mechanisms are there in case of non-compliance? Several MEAs have implemented a system of compliance that accommodates the particular characteristics of international environmental law (IEL). Goote notes that IEL compliance requires (i) flexibility in applying rules open to diverse interpretations, (ii) operating in a dynamic regime that is unceasingly evolving, (iii) an ongoing process, (iv) sensitivity to conflicting political and economic interests, and yet (v) a certain level of

[36] JR May and E Daly, *Global Environmental Constitutionalism* (Cambridge University Press 2015).

[37] Giupponi (n 36) 138.

[38] Ibid., 140.

[39] LD Guruswamy, *International Environmental Law in a Nutshell* (4th ed., West Academic Publishing 2012) 56.

[40] B Olmos Giupponi, *International Environmental Law Compliance in Context: Mechanisms and Case Studies* (1st ed., Routledge 2021) 35.

predictability and procedural transparency to be considered legitimate and fair.[41] Non-compliance procedures in IEL attempt to find a compromise between flexibility and stability and between diplomacy and law.[42]

The Escazú Agreement envisions several mechanisms for implementation and compliance. For example, in the context of access to environmental information, Article 5(18) establishes parameters for independent oversight mechanisms within each member State 'to promote transparency in access to environmental information, to oversee compliance with rules, and monitor, report on, and guarantee the right of access to information'. While subsequent provisions create mechanisms for voluntary information sharing and assistance with implementation in developing States, overall, the Agreement leaves oversight mechanisms to the discretion of each national system.[43] Implementation of Article 5(18) is likely not going to be straightforward. Nevertheless, transparency of oversight mechanisms is essential. It has been recommended that State Parties ensure adequate transparency in compliance and oversight mechanisms under the Agreement. This can be done, for example, with a thorough explanation of how the compliance system functions, the values it enshrines and the potential remedies it offers. Furthermore, '[s]uch transparency measures should be designed with an understanding of the languages used throughout the region and in each State – including Indigenous languages – to optimise inclusion and awareness'.[44] Without further guidance from the COP, there is a danger that countries will quickly fall into non-compliance with Article 5(18). Nevertheless, future COPs may delineate parameters of compliance and best practices to facilitate implementation of these issues, rather than solely relying on

[41] MM Goote, 'Non-Compliance Procedures in International Environmental Law: The Middle Way between Diplomacy and Law' (1999) 1 *International Law Forum du droit international* 82.

[42] Ibid.

[43] A Harrington, 'Implementing the Escazú Agreement: The Need for Rapid Definition of the Committee to Support Implementation and Compliance' (The Global Network for Human Rights and the Environment 2021), available at https://gnhre.org/community/implementing-the-escazu-agreement-the-need-for-rapid-definition-of-the-committee-to-support-implementation-and-compliance/, accessed 1 October 2021.

[44] Global Network for Human Rights and the Environment, 'The GNHRE Implementing Principles for the Escazú Agreement' (April 2022), available at https://gnhre.org/gnhre-principles-on-the-escazu-agreement/.

national regimes to set up parameters of public participation in environmental decision-making and lawmaking.[45]

One core difficulty in implementing the Agreement is the access to justice problem. In LAC, a large section of the population still lacks full and equal access to justice. Despite advances in the scope and autonomy of courts with constitutional jurisdiction, rights protection remains highly uneven across geographic and social divides.[46] Citizens' perception of the justice system remains pervasively hostile, and cases sometimes take years – even decades – to reach a final decision. Comprehensive environmental protection essentially involves the representation of NGOs, civil society organisations and individuals. Escazú is already a step ahead of regional arrangements in Europe by promising civic engagement in all aspects related to compliance with the Agreement. In contrast, civic engagement in implementing the Aarhus Convention is restricted by excluding NGOs as claimants at the European Court of Human Rights (ECtHR).[47]

Transparency across the region will be crucial in helping ensure a robust implementation of the Escazú Agreement. Article 12, providing for creating a clearing house mechanism for member State laws, rules and policies on access rights, is a crucial step, as seen in the clearing house systems effectively deployed by other treaty regimes. However, this lacks an authoritative or evaluative function. Perhaps the most critical examples of how clearing houses can function as oversight tools come from the Convention on Biological Diversity (CBD),[48] where the Nagoya Protocol on Access and Benefit-sharing[49] establishes a dedicated clearing house of relevant national legislation (the Access and Benefit-sharing Clearing house). In addition, the Cartagena Protocol on Biosafety[50] establishes a similar entity for laws and rules relating to biosafety issues.

[45] Escazú Agreement (n 16) Article 8.

[46] L Hilbink, J Gallagher, J Restrepo Sanin, and V Salas, 'Engaging Justice Amidst Inequality in Latin America' (*Open Global Rights* 2019), available at www.openglobalrights.org/engaging-justice-amidst-inequality-in-latin-america/, accessed 1 October 2021.

[47] Lizarazo-Rodriguez and Teixeira (n 28).

[48] Convention on Biological Diversity, available at www.cbd.int/, accessed 1 October 2021.

[49] The Nagoya Protocol on Access to Genetic Resources and the Fair and Equitable Sharing of Benefits Arising from their Utilization to the Convention on Biological Diversity, UNEP/CBD/COP/DEC/X/1 of 29, entered into force 29 October 2010.

[50] Cartagena Protocol on Biosafety to the Convention on Biological Diversity (Montreal, 29 January 2000) Depositary Notification C.N.251.2000.TREATIES-1 of 27 April 2000, entered into force 11 September 2003.

Subsequent COPs may draw on these models to further develop the Escazú clearing house mechanism.

12.4 The Committee to Support Implementation and Compliance: Rules Relating to Its Structure and Functions

Critically, the Escazú Agreement establishes a Committee to Support Implementation and Compliance (Committee) as a subsidiary body under the COP. The parameters of the Committee's work are quite broad in that it is tasked with reviewing compliance with provisions of the Escazú Agreement. The Committee is to be 'consultative and transparent [in] nature, non-adversarial, non-judicial and non-punitive' and 'review compliance of the provisions of the present Agreement and formulate recommendations'. In addition, the Committee's structure and function are to follow the rules of procedure established by the COP, ensuring the significant participation of the public and paying particular attention to the national capacities and circumstances of the Parties.[51]

As referred to above, in April 2022, Escazú's first COP adopted the Rules relating to the structure and functions of the Committee to Support Implementation and Compliance (Rules).[52] However, the Rules represent a work in progress. Therefore, the COP requested the chair, with the support of the secretariat, to begin consultations with the States Parties, with significant participation of the public, to examine the compatibility of the proposed text of the Rules with the agreed language of the Agreement, to fine-tune the Rules relating to the structure and functions of the Committee and, as appropriate, consider them at the next COP, in order to enable the strengthened implementation of the Agreement.[53]

The Committee is composed of seven members elected by consensus and serving four years (renewable), with equitable geographical distribution (and no more than one member of the same nationality), gender parity, legal knowledge and experience.[54] The public may participate and contribute to factual or legal aspects of cases of non-compliance.[55] Deliberations on cases of non-compliance are to be held in closed sessions. In these cases, the Committee shall provide the session's

[51] Escazú Agreement (n 16) Article 18(2), see Decision I/3 (n 26).
[52] Decision I/3, Annex 1 (n 26).
[53] Decision I/3, para 3 (n 26).
[54] Decision I/3, Annex 1, I, paras 1, 3, 4 (n 26).
[55] Decision I/3, Annex 1, VI, para 1 (n 26).

conclusions 'as soon as possible'.[56] Decisions are to be made by consensus and a two-thirds majority in its absence.[57]

With respect to its functions, the Committee shall: (i) provide a report to the COP, including observations in cases of non-compliance, (ii) support the COP on implementation and compliance, including providing a systemic report on implementation and compliance and reports requested by the COP on any aspect of implementation and compliance with the Agreement, (iii) provide advice and support to Parties on implementation and compliance, including by formulating general comments on the interpretation of the Agreement, responding to queries on the interpretation of the Agreement, engaging in periodic consultations and dialogues with Parties and opening dialogues with Parties and members of the public, and (iv) examine cases of alleged non-compliance.[58]

In addition, Parties or members of the public may file communications requesting support for compliance or alleging non-compliance with provisions of the Agreement.[59] The envisaged inclusion of the Agreement's non-compliance procedures of members of the public significantly expands the scope and reach of environmental democracy. Questions of admissibility or merits may be decided without a hearing, but the Party concerned or the author of the communication may request one.[60]

Members of the public will have multiple opportunities to engage in non-compliance procedures (in addition to the other functions of the Committee), including through written observations on factual or legal aspects of a non-compliance case (including the implementation of the outcome of consultations with the Committee by the Party concerned), and participation in any public hearings on non-compliance cases.[61] The Party concerned and the author of the communication have the right to request a hearing on the admissibility of a communication and on the merits of the case, and Committee will decide whether to grant the request.[62] However, to further civil society participation, it has been recommended that members of the public and civil society organisations

56 Decision I/3, Annex 1, III, para 4 (n 26).
57 Decision I/3, Annex 1, III, para 6 (n 26).
58 Decision I/3, Annex 1, IV, para 1 (n 26).
59 Decision I/3, Annex 1, V, para 1 (n 26).
60 Decision I/3, Annex 1, V, para 4, 8 (n 26).
61 Decision I/3, Annex 1, V, para 7(a)(ii), VI, para 1 (n 26).
62 Decision I/3, Annex 1, V, para 4 and 8 (n 26).

be permitted to offer comments in the admissibility and merits, participate in the proceedings and have full access to the Committee's decisions.[63] Throughout all stages of the complaint review, evaluation and decision-making processes, the Committee should ensure adequate avenues for members of the public and civil society organisations to observe and participate.[64] The adoption of the rules of procedure fully endorsed these recommendations, as the chapter outlines further.

The Committee will deliberate on allegations of non-compliance and adopts preliminary observations on a case, including specific recommendations for the Party concerned.[65] Parties can then submit written comments on the preliminary observations, after which the Committee adopts final observations and measures, and makes recommendations.[66]

The Committee will provide reports to the COP on its activities, including its observations in cases of non-compliance.[67] After the Committee adopts certain measures and makes recommendations, it will present its conclusions to the Party concerned and the author of the communication.[68] When appropriate, the Committee will also monitor the implementation of recommendations.[69] If the Committee concludes that the Party concerned has failed to implement the Committee's conclusions and recommendations, it will report the case to the COP.[70]

In assessing and facilitating the implementation of and compliance with the Agreement, the Committee shall consider the national capacities and circumstances of the Parties. Additionally, the Committee shall consider the cause, type, severity and frequency of non-compliance.[71] Measures that can be adopted include: (i) observations on cases, (ii) recommendations to strengthen laws, measures and practices, (iii) requests for action plans on implementation, (iv) requests for a report on progress with recommendations, (v) advice and support, and (vi) recommendations to adopt measures to safeguard environmental defenders.[72] In addition, the COP may take such measures as it deems necessary

[63] GNHRE Principles (n 45) princ 25.
[64] GNHRE Principles (n 45) princ 27.
[65] Decision I/3, Annex 1, V, para 9 (n 26).
[66] Decision I/3, Annex 1, V, para 10 (n 26).
[67] Decision I/3, Annex 1, IV, para 1 (n 26).
[68] Decision I/3, Annex 1, V, para 10 (n 26).
[69] Ibid.
[70] Decision I/3, Annex 1, V, para 11 (n 26).
[71] Decision I/3, Annex 1, VIII, para 1 (n 26).
[72] Decision I/3, Annex 1, VIII, para 1 (n 26).

to facilitate implementation and compliance through (i) formulating declarations of non-compliance by a Party, (ii) facilitating support for compliance, (iii) issuing cautions, and (iv) suspending the rights and privileges of a Party, including voting rights.[73]

The Rules provide an initial framework for non-compliance, which will likely change and evolve. In any case, the Committee may not receive communications on compliance before the closure of COP2, which will likely happen in 2024 (ordinary meetings are held at least once every two years).[74] Furthermore, when the Agreement enters into force for other Parties joining, there is a one-year moratorium before a communication on a Party's compliance can be received by the Committee.[75] With the current framework and the 'learning process' frame of the institutional set-up of the Committee, there are several lessons to be learned from other non-compliance structures of existing MEAs.

12.5 The Committee to Support Implementation and Compliance: Drawing from the Aarhus Convention, Paris Agreement, Nagoya and CBD

Much of the terminology related to the Committee in the Escazú Agreement echoes existing oversight and compliance mechanisms ranging from those used for the Aarhus Convention and Minamata Convention, to the Paris Agreement on Climate Change.[76] As such, Escazú shares significant features with other agreements. Compliance procedures, including compliance committees, have become a common feature of MEAs. These represent a response to general and individual compliance issues based on problem-solving through negotiation to identify a flexible and pragmatic multilateral solution to questions of treaty interpretation and alleged breaches.[77] Compliance mechanisms are more fundamentally geared towards promoting *future* compliance rather than punishing *past* non-compliance, aiming to boost the regime's

[73] Decision I/3, Annex 1, VIII, para 2 (n 26).
[74] Decision I/3, Annex 1, XII, para 1 (n 26).
[75] Decision I/3, Annex 1, XII, para 2 (n 26).
[76] 'The Paris Agreement' (United Nations Climate Change), available at https://unfccc.int/process-and-meetings/the-paris-agreement/the-paris-agreement, accessed 1 October 2021.
[77] A Cardesa-Salzmann, 'Constitutionalising Secondary Rules in Global Environmental Regimes: Non-Compliance Procedures and the Enforcement of Multilateral Environmental Agreements' (2012) 24(1) *Journal of Environmental Law* 103–32.

effectiveness and facilitating multilateral solutions.[78] Nevertheless, compliance mechanisms provide an opportunity for the international community to put pressure on non-compliant Parties.[79]

The Aarhus Convention's compliance mechanisms have assisted Parties and their citizens in implementing rights and crafting laws and rules that comply with the treaty's terms. Aarhus' experience shows that an independent, professional compliance committee can act as an effective means for regime development.[80] Distinctive features of the compliance mechanism in Aarhus include the public trigger (i.e., the public can trigger a complaint) and the requirement of prior exhaustion of remedies (a soft admissibility requirement).[81] However, the decisions of its compliance committee are subject to consensus approval by the Convention's governing body, implicitly giving veto power to the Party whose compliance issues are at stake.[82] Escazú has significantly improved upon this provision. While decisions of the Committee are to be made by consensus, in the absence of consensus, a two-thirds majority suffices.[83]

The Paris Agreement's Implementation and Compliance Committee[84] has only recently begun to operate. Its recently established modalities and procedures exemplify how to bridge different views of multiple State Parties to craft a meaningful oversight entity even in the absence of significant treaty-based guidance.[85] As in the case of the Escazú

[78] E Morgera, E Tsioumani and M Buck, *Unraveling the Nagoya Protocol: A Commentary on the Nagoya Protocol on Access and Benefit-sharing to the Convention on Biological Diversity* (Brill 2014) 347.

[79] V Koester and T Young, 'Compliance with International Conventions: The Role of Public Involvement' (2007) 37 *Environmental Policy and Law* 399.

[80] S Stec and J Jendrośka, 'The Escazú Agreement and the Regional Approach to Rio Principle 10: Process, Innovation, and Shortcomings' (2019) 31 *Journal of Environmental Law* 533, 545.

[81] E Fasoli and A McGlone, 'The Non-Compliance Mechanism under the Aarhus Convention as "Soft" Enforcement of International Environmental Law: Not So Soft After All!' (2018) 65(1) *Netherlands International Law Review* 27–53; Aarhus Convention (n 17), Article 15; UNECE, *Guide to the Aarhus Convention Compliance Committee* (2017); UNECE, Report of the First Meeting of the Parties, Decision I/7, Annex, paras 15–18 (2004).

[82] V Koester, 'Aarhus Convention/MOP-4: The Compliance Mechanism – Outcomes and a Stocktaking' (2011) 41 *Environmental Policy and Law* 196, 197–198.

[83] Annex 1 of Decision I/3, para. III, 6 (n 26).

[84] Paris Agreement (n 17) Article 15.

[85] Report of the Conference of the Parties serving as the meeting of the Parties to the Paris Agreement on the third part of its first session, FCCC/PA/CMA/2018/3/Add.2, Decisions 20/CMA.1 (2019); Report of the Conference of the Parties serving as the meeting of the

Committee, the *Paris* Committee's function is to address implementation and compliance issues in a facilitative rather than punitive manner.[86]

The Aarhus Committee's well-established system of doing this could serve the Escazú Committee well as a model, given the sensitivity of the issues subject to its jurisdiction and the need to ensure that State Parties work with the Committee to ensure compliance rather than establishing a relationship based on antagonism. At the same time, the transparency of the Aarhus Committee's decision-making process, including making all decisions publicly available, can serve as an example of how the public can be assured that the oversight process for Escazú is focussed on ensuring that the treaty regime's terms are put into effect for the benefit of all.

The Nagoya protocol's mechanisms could also provide valuable insights, given its unique engagement with Indigenous and local communities, which is essential in the context of LAC. An innovative idea could be to establish an ombudsperson to support vulnerable persons and Indigenous and local communities in identifying breaches of rights and providing independent technical and legal support in ensuring the adequate redress of such breaches. The Global Network for Human Rights and the Environment (GNHRE) Principles have suggested inclusive and non-discriminatory participation in the development and implementation of environmental law of Indigenous communities and vulnerable communities, either directly or through representatives such as civil society organisations, legal organisations and legal representatives.[87] This emphasis on inclusivity and non-discrimination is particularly valuable given the threats faced by human rights advocates and defenders, land rights activists and Indigenous community leaders throughout LAC, coupled with the many ways in which access to justice and public participation have been hobbled throughout the region due to the Covid-19 pandemic.

Parties to the Paris Agreement, FCCC/PA/CMA/2021/10/Add.3, Decision 24/CMA.3 (2021).

86 C Voigt and G Xiang, 'Accountability in the Paris Agreement: The Interplay between Transparency and Compliance' (2020) 1 *Nordic Environmental Law Journal* 31–57; G Zihua, C Voigt and J Werksman, 'Facilitating Implementation and Promoting Compliance with the Paris Agreement: Conceptual Challenges and Pragmatic Choices' (2019) 9 *Climate Law* 65–100.

87 GNHRE Principles (n 45) princ 31.

12.6 Non-Compliance Mechanisms under the IASHR: Overlap

Another critical discussion in developing the Escazú Agreement's non-compliance machinery relates to potential overlap with the IASHR.[88] Implementing environmental access rights in LAC has primarily advanced through public interest litigation before regional human rights courts.[89] The IASHR is pledged to protect, promote and monitor human rights in the thirty-five Latin American States that comprise the Organization of American States (OAS).[90] The IASHR fulfils this responsibility through two principal bodies: the Inter-American Commission on Human Rights (IACHR)[91] and the Inter-American Court of Human Rights (IACtHR).[92] Each of these entities can hear individual complaints of alleged human rights violations and may issue emergency protective measures where the subject of a complaint risks immediate irreparable harm. In addition, an OAS organ or member State may seek the Court's advisory opinions on interpreting the IASHR instruments. The Commission undertakes human rights promotion, monitoring, established rapporteurships and publications for the region. The rules of procedure for the Escazú Compliance Committee generally reference the option of the Committee entering 'into dialogue and consultations with other multilateral agreements, institutions, and processes, at the global or regional level, to seek synergies for the full implementation of access rights and other matters covered by the Agreement'.[93] This may include synergies with the IASHR, although such synergies are in their very early stages and will likely develop in the future.

[88] Chapter 4, this volume. As indicated earlier, there are similarities here with the European system. See also below, accompanying notes 129-131?

[89] C Shall, 'Public Interest Litigation Concerning Environmental Matters before Human Rights' (2008) 20 *Journal of Environmental Law* 417.

[90] Antigua and Barbuda, Argentina, Bahamas, Barbados, Belize, Bolivia, Brazil, Canada, Chile, Colombia, Costa Rica, Cuba, Dominica, Ecuador, El Salvador, Grenada, Guatemala, Guyana, Haiti, Honduras, Jamaica, Mexico, Nicaragua, Panama, Paraguay, Peru, Dominican Republic, Saint Kitts and Nevis, Saint Lucia, Saint Vincent and the Grenadines, Suriname, Trinidad and Tobago, United States of America, Uruguay, and Venezuela.

[91] 'Inter-American Commission on Human Rights' (IACHR) (Organization of American States), available at www.oas.org/en/iachr/mandate/basic_documents.asp, accessed 1 October 2021.

[92] 'Inter-American Court of Human Rights' (Inter-American Court of Human Rights), available at www.corteidh.or.cr/index.cfm?lang=en, accessed 1 October 2021.

[93] Decision I/3, Annex 1, IX (n 26).

A significant body of jurisprudence on environmental access rights is available in the IASHR.[94] Litigation of environmental rights has seen considerable development in recent years. Significantly, the OAS was not endowed with an environmental protection role, yet the pervasiveness of environmental degradation placed the topic on its agenda.[95] One significant aspect of the agenda is the implementation of MEAs and environmental treaties, which is the focus of the OAS work programme on the Environmental Rule of Law in the Americas.[96] In addition, the IASHR has offered the possibility of discussing IEL compliance related to human rights, including concerning Indigenous peoples' rights and the protection of environmental defenders, which are at the core of Escazú. Finally, the Commission and the Court have developed a substantive case law related to the rights to consultation and – more recently – protection of the environment.[97]

Importantly for this chapter's discussion of the overlap between Escazú and the IASHR, the Inter-American Court of Human Rights has a specific rules-based non-compliance function. After the Court makes specific orders about a State in a particular case, it then tracks that State's implementation of its orders: this is the most direct example of the Court's non-compliance function.[98] Beyond this follow-up for specific cases, the IASHR also maintains an accountability function where it evaluates and monitors the human rights records of OAS member States through an independent commission that monitors whether States are complying with their international human rights obligations.[99] More broadly, the Inter-American Commission promotes the observance and defence of human rights in the Americas through country visits, thematic activities and initiatives, preparing reports on the human rights situation in a specific country or on a particular thematic issue, adopting

[94] II/A Court HR, *Case of Mayagna (Sumo) Awas Tingni Community v Nicaragua*, Judgment of 31 August 2001, Series C, No 79; I/A Court HR, *Case of Saramaka People v Suriname*, Judgment of November 28, 2007, Series C, No 185; I/A Court HR, *Case of Kaliña and Lokono Peoples v Suriname*, Judgment of 25 November 2015, Series C, No 309.

[95] Giupponi (n 41) 101.

[96] 'Environment' (Organization of Americas), available at www.oas.org/en/topics/environment.asp, accessed 1 October 2021.

[97] MA Tigre and SC Slinger, 'A Voice in the Development of Amazonia: The Constitutional Rights to Participation of Indigenous Peoples' in W Leal Filho, VT King and I Borges de Lima (eds), *Indigenous Amazonia, Regional Development and Territorial Dynamics: Contentious Issues* (Springer International Publishing 2020).

[98] Inter-American Court of Human Rights, Rules of Procedure (n 93) Article 69.

[99] Inter-American Court of Human Rights, Rules of Procedure (n 93) Article 58, 8.

precautionary measures or requesting provisional measures before the Court, and processing and analysing individual petitions to determine States' international responsibility for human rights violations.[100]

The Court's development of its practice and the granting of remedies is also significant. The Court has widely expanded its reparation orders beyond monetary compensation to victims: it has issued reparations in the form of demands for State reforms, criminal prosecution of individuals who have violated regional human rights and even symbolic reparations, such as calling for the erecting of memorials. However, some scholars argue that these non-compliance mechanisms are weak since the Court does not have a specific mandate for enforcement or political compliance mechanisms that would better hold States accountable in implementing the Court's orders.[101] As a result, compliance with the rulings and recommendations from the Commission and the Court remains low, and partial compliance is an expected outcome. The long procedural development of cases, paired with the low enforceability of decisions, also hinders hearing cases before the IASHR. All these factors limit the impact of the IASHR and undermine its legitimacy and authority. However, complaints continue to rise, reinforcing the importance of the system.

The participation of NGOs has been limited under the San Salvador Protocol, although NGOs can submit complaints to the IACHR.[102] However, individuals and regional human rights organisations' access has strengthened over time as the IASHR system has become increasingly judicialised, with a procedural focus on legal argumentation and regional human rights jurisprudence.[103] One significant limitation is that petitioners have to reasonably exhaust the remedies available within the domestic legal system, thereby limiting IASHR judicial intervention to cases where domestic laws and courts have not adequately protected rights and principles. Additionally, the IASHR has to consider where due process rights in the American Convention have been breached and at what point domestic courts have acted arbitrarily.[104]

While the possibility of direct access for the public to the Escazú Compliance Committee was envisioned in earlier drafts of the Agreement, it was deleted from the final version due to some Parties'

[100] Article 106 of the OAS, Charter of the Organization of American States, 30 April 1948.
[101] P Engstrom, 'Reconceptualizing the Impact of the Inter-American Human Rights System' (2017) 8 *Revista Direito & Práxis, Rio de Janeiro* 1250.
[102] Giupponi (n 41) 209.
[103] Engstrom (n 102).
[104] Ibid.

reluctance.[105] Nevertheless, it reappeared in the Rules of Procedure of the Committee, which established that a member of the public may file a communication requesting support for compliance or alleging non-compliance with provisions of the Agreement.[106] An analysis of experience under the Aarhus Convention shows the relevance of the public's ability to submit communications of non-compliance to the Committee. At the time of writing, over 190 communications have been presented before the Aarhus Committee by the public, while only two by States regarding other States' compliance, and one by a State regarding its own compliance.[107] This background reinforces the relevance of ensuring broad participation and the significance of the Escazú COP's decision on access to the Committee. In addition, it may be noted that a group of civil society organisations submitted recommendations for rules governing the structure and functions of the Escazú Committee.[108] Furthermore, paragraph 12(c) of said recommendations explicitly suggested the possibility of communications from the members of the public being brought regarding a Party's compliance with the Escazú Agreement. This input may have helped to bring about the COP's decision to allow public communications to the Committee.

Alongside regional bodies, other sub-regional judicial or quasi-judicial bodies created in the framework of regional integration processes, such as the Central American Court of Justice, the Andean Court of Justice or Mercosur arbitral tribunals, may offer an additional forum for the implementation of environmental access rights.[109] However, these bodies have rarely addressed environmental matters. The Caribbean Court of Justice (CCJ) could become an essential avenue for implementing environmental rights, as most Caribbean States have not accepted the jurisdiction of the IACtHR.[110]

105 G Médici Colombo, 'El Acuerdo Escazú: La implementación del Principio 10 de Río en América Latina y el Caribe' (2018) 9(1) *Revista Catalana De Dret Ambiental* 1–66.

106 Escazú Agreement (n 16), Rules of Procedure, V(1).

107 See UNECE, 'Communications from the Public', available at https://unece.org/env/pp/cc/communications-from-the-public.

108 Access Initiative, 'Recommendations of the Public on Proposals on Elements to be Considered in the Rules Governing the Structure and Functions of the Committee to Support Implementation and Compliance', available at https://accessinitiative.org/resource/proposal-from-the-public-on-the-implementation-and-compliance-committee-of-the-escazu-agreement/.

109 Giupponi (n 41) 139.

110 Caribbean Court of Justice, *Maya Leaders Alliance v The Attorney General of Belize*, Judgment of 30 October 2015, available at www.law.nyu.edu/sites/default/files/upload_documents/Final_GFILC_pdf.pdf, accessed 1 October 2021.

With the Escazú Agreement in force, there is an opportunity for the legal framework of the IASHR and Escazú to work together and strengthen the democratisation of environmental governance in LAC. Escazú reinforces principles and obligations established in the inter-American legislation and jurisprudence on the right to a healthy environment, highlighting the need to guarantee access rights to ensure their validity. However, how will these complementing regimes interact in practice? Noroña notes the risk of conflicting petitions or multiple claims in different forums, reinforcing the need to understand the Committee's consultative and transparent, non-adversarial, non-judicial and non-punitive nature, which only allows it to formulate recommendations and would, in theory, not conflict with the mechanisms in the IASHR.[111]

The Committee is not a court and does not issue binding decisions, even if its opinions, as per the example of Aarhus, provide an authoritative interpretation of its provisions. Nonetheless, as a human rights treaty, Escazú can be invoked within the human rights protection system of the OAS.[112] This means that the mechanisms within the IASHR are available to those who seek to enforce the Escazú Agreement. The relationship between the Escazú Agreement and the IASHR is similar to that between the Aarhus Convention and the European Convention on Human Rights (ECHR), including as it pertains to the jurisprudence of the European Court of Human Rights (ECtHR). Countries could thus be called on to answer for access rights within the IASHR.[113] This possibility significantly expands the available enforcement mechanisms under Escazú through reliance on an already established regional human rights system with decades of development. However, it should be noted that the expectation of vigorous enforcement of the Aarhus Convention by the European Court of Justice has not yet come to fruition.[114]

111 D Noroña, 'All Hands-On Deck: Is the Inter-American Human Rights System Compatible with the Escazú Agreement?' (The Global Network for Human Rights and the Environment 2021), available at https://gnhre.org/community/all-hands-on-deck-is-the-inter-american-human-rights-system-compatible-with-the-escazu-agreement/, accessed 1 October 2021.

112 'Organization of American States', available at www.oas.org/en/ accessed 1 October 2021.

113 'Inter-American Commission on Human Rights' (Organization of American States), available at www.oas.org/en/iachr/mandate/basic_documents.asp, accessed 1 October 2021 (IACHR).

114 J Jendrośka, 'Aarhus Convention Compliance Committee: Origins, Status and Activities' (2011) 8(4) *Journal for European Environmental and Planning Law* 301–14.

12.7 Conclusion

The Escazú Agreement was adopted based on broad and effective public participation and came into force with great fanfare. Escazú recognises explicitly the right to a healthy environment and has been lauded as a progressive Agreement, and there is much expectation that it will bring change to the region. One of the biggest challenges in implementing the Escazú Agreement will be overcoming LAC's tendency to adopt broad-minded legislation but implement it at a slow pace. This chapter advances some of the questions about how to facilitate the implementation of the rights, rules and principles included in the Agreement. Specifically, it addresses the implementation of the recognised right to a healthy environment. Building a system for oversight and compliance at the regional level is essential in ensuring compliance. This system should be flexible yet provide a reliable and stable response to claims. This chapter has highlighted the initial progress made at the first Escazú COP, including adopting the Rules for the Committee to Support Implementation and Compliance. In addition, the chapter has drawn on experience under other MEAs, analysed the potential overlap with regional human rights systems and provided suggestions for moving forward. To a certain extent, the compliance procedures and mechanisms established under Escazú share features that have become commonplace across MEAs.[115] However, some distinctive features of the Agreement – including its regional underpinnings – will likely lead Parties to consider innovative approaches to multilateral compliance procedures and mechanisms. The next few years will be essential in delineating the parameters of the Agreement so that it brings effective positive environmental human rights developments to the region.

[115] See i.e., U Beyerlin, P-T Stoll and R Wolfrum (eds), *Ensuring Compliance With Multilateral Environmental Agreements: A Dialogue between Practitioners and Academia* (Martinus Nijhoff Publishers 2006); T Treves, A Tanzi, C Pitea and C Ragni (eds), *Non-Compliance Procedures and Mechanisms and the Effectiveness of International Environmental Agreements* (Asser Press 2009); RB Mitchell, 'Compliance Theory: Compliance, Effectiveness and Behaviour Change in International Environmental Law' in J Brunnée, D Bodansky and E Hey, *The Oxford Handbook of International Environmental Law* (Oxford University Press 2007) 893; and A Nollkaemper, 'Compliance Control in International Environmental Law: Traversing the Limits of the National Legal Order' (2003) 13 *Yearbook of International Environmental Law* 165.

PART V

Human Rights

13

Institutional Overlap and Comparative Effectiveness

Compliance with Torture-Related Decisions of the European Court of Human Rights, the Human Rights Committee and the Committee against Torture in Europe

ANDREAS VON STADEN

13.1 Introduction

The international human rights regime consists of a multifaceted web of regional and global treaties, institutions, and compliance monitoring mechanisms.[1] While some elements complement each other, others create overlap and redundancy in terms of protected rights and of the institutions and mechanisms created to monitor compliance with them. Many core civil and political rights are covered by general conventions at both the regional and the global levels and are fleshed out further by additional group- or subject-specific treaties. In addition to monitoring mechanisms such as State reporting and inquiry procedures, the three regional human rights regimes in Europe, the Americas, and Africa as well as the nine core UN human rights treaties all provide for individual complaints/communications procedures (ICPs) that enable aggrieved individuals to have the merits of alleged human rights violations decided by independent institutions. One dimension along which these institutions differ is their institutional design. The three main regional human

ORCID: https://orcid.org/0000-0003-3551-6384. Research for this chapter was supported by Deutsche Forschungsgemeinschaft (DFG, German Research Foundation), project number 417704617.

[1] For an overview see e.g., G Oberleitner (ed.), *International Human Rights Institutions, Tribunals, and Courts* (Springer Nature 2018); International Justice Resource Center, Overview of the Human Rights Framework, available at https://ijrcenter.org/ihr-reading-room/overview-of-the-human-rights-framework/.

rights conventions feature full-fledged courts (in addition to human rights commissions in the African and inter-American human rights systems) that are staffed with professional judges and whose judgments are legally binding, whereas the committees established by the UN human rights treaties, while taking some design cues from judicial institutions, are composed of part-time experts and issue legally non-binding pronouncements that are called "views," "opinions," or "decisions."

A frequent assumption in the human rights domain (also elsewhere) is that courts and legally binding judgments will yield better rights protection by way of better compliance than non- or quasi-judicial institutions whose output lacks such legal status. Pierre-Henri Teitgen, one of the chief designers of the European Convention on Human Rights (ECHR), put the sentiment thus when arguing against the inclusion in the ECHR's monitoring machinery of solely a commission with only recommendatory powers: "If . . . we really wish to have collective protection in Europe of rights and fundamental freedoms, it is necessary to go beyond a simple Recommendation or the mere publication of a Report. We must refer the matter to the only force which, in these countries, has a final authority, that is justice; there must be a Court and Judges."[2] Conversely, in the context of the UN human rights treaty bodies, the lack of legally binding status of their pronouncements has been repeatedly adduced as one reason for the compliance problems encountered.[3] The suggestion is that legally binding court judgments generally have greater purchase with respect to inducing compliance than committee decisions that come without such legal status.

In this chapter I argue that the significance of legally binding or non-binding status for compliance is conditional on a number of contextual political and institutional factors, among them regime type, expected costs of compliance and non-compliance, and whether violations are isolated or occur as a result of State policy.[4] To explore my expectations

[2] Consultative Assembly of the Council of Europe, 1st Session, August 10–September 8, 1949, II *Collected Edition of the "Travaux Préparatoires" of the European Convention on Human Rights* (Martinus Nijhoff, 1975) 174.

[3] See e.g., C Heyns and F Viljoen, *The Impact of the United Nations Human Rights Treaties on the Domestic Level* (Martinus Nijhoff 2002) 29–33; L Oette, "The UN Human Rights Treaty Bodies: Impact and Future" in Oberleitner (n 1) 95, 106; T Buergenthal, "The U.N. Human Rights Committee" (2002) 5 *Max Planck Yearbook of United Nations Law* 341, 397.

[4] See similarly A von Staden, "The Conditional Effectiveness of Soft Law: Compliance with the Decisions of the Committee against Torture" (2022) 23 *Human Rights Review* 451–78.

empirically, I take advantage of the existence of significant jurisdictional overlap regarding individual complaints between the European Court of Human Rights (ECtHR), the UN Human Rights Committee (HRC), and the UN Committee against Torture (CAT) with respect to many European States. Because State responses to adverse decisions[5] can be expected to be affected *inter alia* by the specific issues and rights involved, I focus on compliance with adverse findings concerning one particular right: the core physical integrity right of freedom from torture and from inhuman or degrading treatment or punishment.[6] The analysis provides indicative evidence that compliance with so-called conditional violations – violations that have not yet occurred, but might with some probability if a State were to implement its planned course of action – concerning the *non-refoulement* norm is as high for treaty body decisions as it is for ECtHR judgments. When it comes to remedying actual past or ongoing violations, however, the ECtHR performs better overall, but with significant differences between countries with different democratic credentials. The implication is that the ostensibly institutionally weaker treaty body arrangements perform well when the political and material stakes for the respondent State are comparatively low, but when those stakes increase, a stronger institutional design performs better (if still far from perfectly). If respondent States are insufficiently or only weakly democratic, however, compliance is equally low for both types of institutions. While application numbers reveal a preference among petitioners for a judicial assessment of their grievances, the work of the treaty bodies can be consequential under certain circumstances, especially with respect to preventing violations.

13.2 Right to Freedom from Torture: Institutional Overlap

Few human rights are as widely affirmed in international instruments as the right to be free from torture and from other unduly harsh forms of treatment or punishment. The Universal Declaration of Human Rights (1948) set the precedent when it affirmed that "no one shall be subjected to torture or to cruel, inhuman or degrading treatment or punishment"

5 The term "decision" in this text refers both generically to all ICP outcomes and specifically to those of CAT which has been using it as designation for its ICP output – instead of the term "views" – since 2002 (ibid., 3).

6 For reasons of linguistic economy, I will in the following mostly refer only to "torture," it being understood that the other elements of lesser intensity are included as well.

(Article 5). The three regional human rights conventions in Europe,[7] the Americas,[8] and Africa[9] followed suit, as did the Arab League,[10] the Organisation of Islamic Cooperation,[11] ASEAN,[12] and the European Union,[13] with some regions adding further subject-specific treaties.[14] At the UN level, five of the nine core human rights treaties include provisions outlawing torture: the UN Convention against Torture (UNCAT),[15] the International Covenant on Civil and Political Rights (ICCPR),[16] and the conventions on the rights of children,[17] of persons with disabilities,[18] and of migrant workers and their families.[19] The prohibition of torture is recognized as customary international law and widely considered to be *ius cogens.*[20] The Statute of the International Criminal Court includes torture as a crime against humanity and a war crime.[21]

As of January 1, 2022, all forty-seven countries then subject to the ECHR/ECtHR[22] had ratified ICCPR, UNCAT, and the Convention on the Rights of the Child, all but one had ratified the Convention on the Rights of Persons with Disabilities, while only four were party to the

[7] ECHR (1950), Article 3.

[8] American Convention on Human Rights (1969) Article 5(2).

[9] African Charter of Human and Peoples' Rights (1981) Article 5.

[10] Arab Charter on Human Rights (2004) Article 8(1).

[11] Cairo Declaration on Human Rights in Islam (1990) Article 20; Cairo Declaration of the Organisation of Islamic Cooperation on Human Rights (2021) Article 4(b).

[12] ASEAN Human Rights Declaration (2012) Article 14.

[13] Charter of Fundamental Rights of the European Union (2007) Article 4.

[14] Inter-American Convention to Prevent and Punish Torture (1985); European Convention for the Prevention of Torture and Inhuman and Degrading Treatment or Punishment (1987).

[15] Convention against Torture and Other Cruel, Inhuman or Degrading Treatment or Punishment (1984) part I.

[16] International Covenant on Civil and Political Rights (1966) Article 7.

[17] Convention on the Rights of the Child (1989), Article 37 lit. a.

[18] Convention on the Rights of Persons with Disabilities (2006) Article 15.

[19] International Convention on the Protection of the Rights of All Migrant Workers and Members of Their Families (1991) Article 10.

[20] See e.g., NS Rodley, "Integrity of the Person" in D Moeckli, S Shah, and S Sivakumaran (eds), *International Human Rights Law* (3rd ed., Oxford University Press 2018) 165, 167–68.

[21] Rome Statute of the International Criminal Court (1998) Article 7(1) lit. f and Article 8 (2) lit. a(i).

[22] Russia was expelled from the Council of Europe on March 16, 2022 (see Committee of Ministers' Res. CM/Res[2022]2) in response to its war of aggression against Ukraine and ceased to be a party to the ECHR on September 16, 2022, in accordance with Article 58(3) ECHR; see Resolution of the European Court of Human Rights on the Consequences of the Cessation of Membership of the Russian Federation to the Council of Europe in Light of Article 58 of the European Convention on Human Rights, available at https://echr.coe .int/Documents/Resolution_ECHR_cessation_membership_Russia_CoE_ENG.pdf.

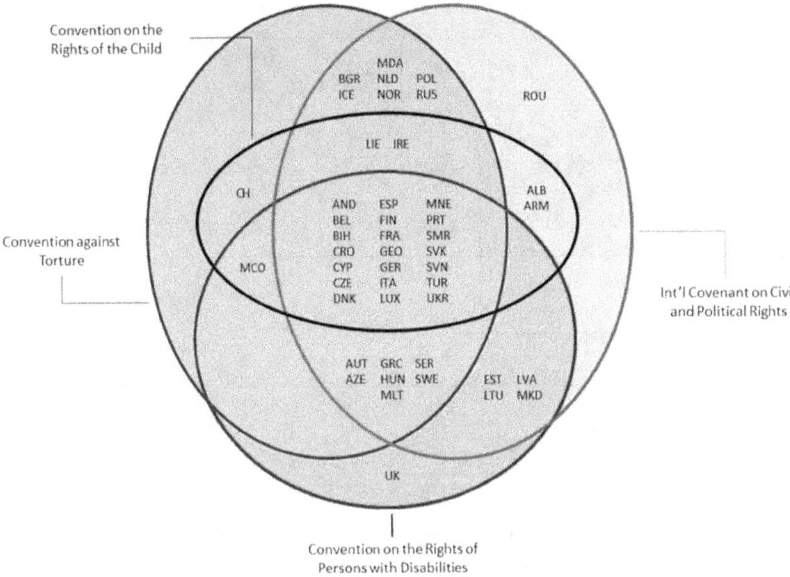

Figure 13.1 Acceptance of ICPs of relevant UN human rights treaties by ECHR parties[23]

Migrant Workers Convention. The first four treaties have active ICPs that could in some instances be used to address the same alleged violations of the prohibition of torture and of related offences.[24] Twenty-one ECHR parties have accepted all four active ICPs while two countries have accepted only one. All but three have accepted the ICCPR's ICP and thirty-nine have accepted UNCAT's.[25]

Figure 13.1 depicts ICP acceptance under the four relevant conventions. While it shows the present state of overlap, it should be noted that there have been (sometimes extended) periods of time during which countries have been subject to only a single individual complaints mechanism. One reason has to do with temporal availability: the ECtHR was

[23] See Table 13.3 in the appendix for a list of the acronyms used and the countries they refer to.

[24] The Migrant Workers Convention's ICP is not active yet and no European country has accepted it.

[25] For an exploration as to why States seek such overlap, see A von Staden and A Ullmann, "Seeking Overlap and Redundancy in Human Rights Protection: Reputation, Consistency and the Acceptance of the UN Human Rights Treaties' Individual Communications Procedures" (2022) 26 *The International Journal of Human Rights* 1476, available at https://doi.org/10.1080/13642987.2022.2036134.

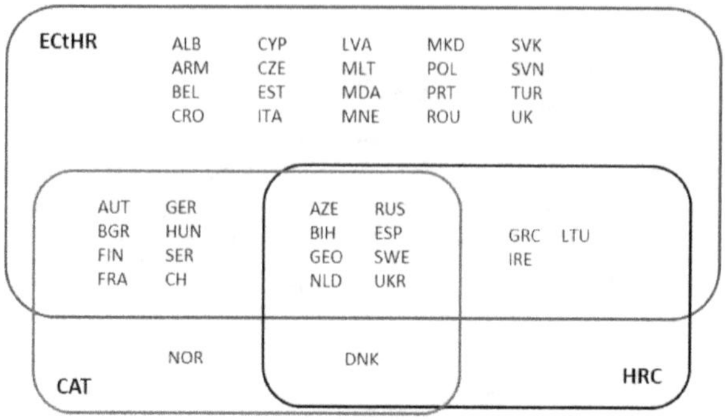

Figure 13.2 Adverse torture-related decisions by respondent State and issuing institution

set up in 1959, but the HRC's and CAT's ICP competences became operational only in 1976 and 1987, respectively, and those of the other two committees later still, in 2008 (Rights of Persons with Disabilities) and 2014 (Rights of the Child). Eastern and Central European countries only began to accept ICPs near the end of the Cold War and until that time were not subject to any of them. Even when available, States differ significantly in terms of the time between accepting the first and second of these ICPs (which are optional in the case of the treaty bodies and were so under the ECHR until 1998), ranging from less than six months for Azerbaijan, Poland, and Bulgaria to over thirty-eight years for Belgium and Germany.

Only the HRC and CAT have produced quantitatively meaningful output against ECtHR parties so far.[26] Figure 13.2 shows which States have received adverse decisions related to the prohibition of torture and from which body. Twenty States have received torture-related judgments only from the ECtHR, while two, Norway and Denmark, were until the end of 2019 – the cut-off date of the dataset used for this research – subject to adverse decisions only from the HRC and CAT. Eight countries have

[26] Violations of Article 37(a) of the Convention on the Rights of the Child have been alleged in a few communications and have been found in two decisions, see *M.K.A.H. v Switzerland*, CRC/C/88/D/95/2019 (September 22, 2021) and *D.D. v Spain*, CRC/C/80/D/4/2016 (January 31, 2019). The two communications claiming infringements of Article 15(1) of the Convention on Rights of People with Disabilities were declared inadmissible, see *L.M.L. v United Kingdom*, CRPD/C/17/D/27/2015 (March 24, 2017) and *O.O.J. v Sweden*, CRPD/C/18/D/28/2015 (August 18, 2017).

been subject to adverse decisions involving the prohibition of torture from all three bodies while six small States (Andorra, Liechtenstein, Monaco, Iceland, Luxembourg, and San Marino) have so far never been found responsible for having violated Article 3 ECHR, Article 7 ICCPR, or any UNCAT provision. In terms of the scope of the relevant treaty provisions, it is to be noted that the first two articles are single-paragraph provisions whereas UNCAT spells out rights and obligations at greater length over several articles. While the provisions and the jurisprudence based on them are not identical, there is considerable substantive overlap in terms of rights and obligations covered as a result of treaty interpretation and reading ECHR/ICCPR provisions in conjunction with other articles.[27]

Why applicants turn to the treaty bodies when they also have access to the ECtHR is worth investigating; some reasons that have been suggested in the literature have to do with the narrowing of access to the ECtHR, the (expected) shorter time to a decision, applicant-friendlier rules of evidence and different interpretive takes on certain aspects related to the prohibition of torture.[28] The question to be explored further in the following, however, is how States respond to the signals received from these two types of institutions in terms of complying, or not complying, with them and what causal factors likely play a role.

13.3 Theoretical Expectations

This section addresses from a theoretical point of view the causal factors that likely affect whether States will comply with ECtHR judgments and treaty body decisions and how such factors may play out differently with respect to the two types of decisions. I discuss the following factors: regime type and rule of law, costs of compliance and non-compliance, and systematic as opposed to isolated infringements.

[27] Cp. A Mowbray, *Cases, Materials, and Commentary on the European Convention on Human Rights* (3rd ed., Oxford University Press 2012) chapter 5 and PM Taylor, *A Commentary on the International Covenant on Civil and Political Rights: The UN Human Rights Committee's Monitoring of ICCPR Rights* (Cambridge University Press 2020) 171–217.

[28] See e.g., S Scott Ford, "Nordic Migration Cases before the UN Treaty Bodies: Pathways of International Accountability?" (2022) 91 *Nordic Journal of International Law* 44, 57–60; B Çalı, C Costello, and S Cunningham, "Hard Protection through Soft Courts? Non-Refoulement before the United Nations Treaty Bodies" (2020) 21 *German Law Journal* 355, 362.

13.3.1 *Regime Type and Rule of Law*

It is a fairly consistent finding of research on international human rights law that compliance is strongest among liberal democracies,[29] that is, States that share the values embodied in human rights and recognize them as legitimate constraints on governmental action. Liberal democracies also typically adhere to the rule of law and as such are well practised in responding to, and abiding by, the decisions of properly established monitoring and dispute settlement institutions. While all members of the Council of Europe, the ECtHR's parent institution, are nominally rule-of-law countries (a condition of membership)[30] and committed to "genuine democracy,"[31] there is variance in the strength of their rule-of-law and democratic credentials that can be expected to affect the extent of their compliance with adverse judgments and decisions. We should generally expect countries with higher scores on democracy indicators to have better compliance rates than those whose scores are lower.

To the extent that sincere commitment to human rights is the driving force behind the effects of (liberal) democracy on compliance with adverse human rights decisions, there should be no systematic difference in terms of its compliance-enhancing role with respect to ECtHR judgments and treaty body views, respectively. That commitment itself is ultimately socio-political (and not legal) in nature and there is nothing in the recognition that State action should be constrained by, and assessed in terms of conformance with, human rights norms and should give rise to remedial action in case of violations that would make it conditional on the legal status of a pronouncement. States frequently take action in the human rights and other domains in response to demands and recommendations that are legally non-binding (but may have non-legally binding quality).[32] There is no reason to expect that sufficiently well-

[29] See e.g., J von Stein, "Making Promises, Keeping Promises: Democracy, Ratification and Compliance in International Human Rights Law" (2015) 46 *British Journal of Political Science* 655, 655–56 and footnote 6; S Hug and S Wegmann, "Complying with Human Rights" (2016) 42 *International Interactions* 590, 592–94; DW Hill, Jr., and K Anne Watson, "Democracy and Compliance with Human Rights Treaties: The Conditional Effectiveness of the Convention for the Elimination of All Forms of Discrimination against Women" (2019) 63 *International Studies Quarterly* 127.

[30] Statute of the Council of Europe (May 5, 1949) Article 3 ("Every member of the Council of Europe must accept the principles of the rule of law and of the enjoyment by all persons within its jurisdiction of human rights and fundamental freedoms . . . ").

[31] Ibid., preamble (para 3).

[32] von Staden (n 4) 454–456.

reasoned decisions from the treaty bodies should be received and treated differently than ECtHR judgments solely because of their different institutional sources and legal status.

Commitment to the rule of law, on the other hand, can cut both ways when it comes to compliance with legally non-binding decisions. On the one hand, the rule of law has been linked, since A. V. Dicey gave currency to the phrase, to the possibility of resolving disputes and to obtaining redress through recourse to the courts in cases involving both civil and public law.[33] While the theoretical bond between the rule of law and "access to justice" may be weaker than often asserted, it appears that "the assumption that this connection is so obvious as to need no explication" is widespread.[34] Having a mechanism for the resolution of disputes in place in turn generates legitimate expectations of compliance on the part of its users.[35] On the other hand, the rule of law privileges the law as a specific institution over other, non-legal norms, standards, and commitments, hence the name. To allow legally non-binding decisions to trump legally binding legislation, judicial decisions or executive determinations would jar with this understanding of law as having higher normative status than non-law.

How decisions with different legal status are treated domestically differs between countries. In some States, the judicial branch in particular has emphasized that treaty body views have a subordinate and suggestive, rather than determinative role to play.[36] The Supreme Court of Ireland, for example, addressing the consequences of HRC views, stated that "[t]he notion that 'views' of a Committee, even of admittedly distinguished experts on international human rights, though not necessarily lawyers, could prevail against the concluded decision of a properly constituted court is patently unacceptable."[37] Other high courts have

[33] T Bingham, *The Rule of Law* (Penguin 2011) *passim*.

[34] W Lucy, "Access to Justice and the Rule of Law" (2020) 40 *Oxford Journal of Legal Studies* 377.

[35] A von Staden, "Ineffektivität als Legitimitätsproblem: Die Befolgung der 'Auffassungen' der Ausschüsse der UN Menschenrechtsverträge in Individualbeschwerdeverfahren" (2016) 49 *Kritische Justiz* 453, 458.

[36] See generally M Kanetake, "UN Human Rights Treaty Monitoring Bodies before Domestic Courts" (2018) 67 *International and Comparative Law Quarterly* 201; R van Alebeek and A Nollkaemper, "The Legal Status of Decisions by Human Rights Treaty Bodies in National Law" in H Keller and G Ulfstein (eds), *UN Human Rights Treaty Bodies: Law and Legitimacy* (Cambridge University Press 2012) 356.

[37] Supreme Court (Ireland), *Kavanagh v Governor of Mountjoy Prison and the Attorney General* (March 1, 2002) (2008) 132 *International Law Reports* 380, 404.

argued similarly, noting that treaty body views are not "judicial decisions" and therefore "cannot constitute the authentic interpretation of the Covenant,"[38] and do not legally bind the respondent State and its courts.[39] As a consequence, while, "domestic courts should address the view of such treaty bodies[,] they do not . . . have to endorse it."[40]

The difference in comparison to the treatment of ECtHR judgments is, however, not categorical as these judgments are typically not accorded binding effect domestically either, at least not formally, although it appears that courts tend to give greater weight to findings and arguments by the ECtHR in comparison with pronouncements by the treaty bodies.[41] The German Constitutional Court, for example, has stipulated that the effect of ECtHR judgments within the domestic legal order is not unconditional. While State authorities are under an obligation to "take into account" Strasbourg's jurisprudence in their decision-making, not only the failure to do so, but also "the 'enforcement' of such a decision in a schematic way, in violation of prior-ranking law, may . . . violate fundamental rights *in conjunction with the principle of the rule of law*."[42] At the same time, while relevant treaty body views "should" be addressed, for ECtHR judgments there is a "duty" to take them into account; they "must" be considered.[43]

[38] Constitutional Court (Spain), Sentence 70/2002 (April 3, 2002), part II, para 7 lit. (a), available at https://hj.tribunalconstitucional.es/HJ/es-ES/Resolucion/Show/SENTENCIA/2002/70.

[39] Conseil d'État (France), Juge des référés, no 238849 (October 11, 2001), available at https://juricaf.org/arret/FRANCE-CONSEILDETAT-20011011-238849.

[40] Federal Constitutional Court (Germany), Order of the Second Senate of January 29, 2019, case no 2 BvC 62/14, para 65, available at www.bverfg.de/e/cs20190129_2bvc006214en.html. See similarly *idem*, Order of the First Senate of July 26, 2016, case no 1 BVL 8/15, para 90, available at www.bverfg.de/e/ls20160726_1bvl000815en.html; see similarly C Tomuschat, "Human Rights Committee" (2019) *Max Planck Encyclopedia of Public International Law* marginal number 14.

[41] For some domestic courts' position with respect to ECtHR judgments, see C Giannopoulos, "The Reception by Domestic Courts of the *Res Interpretata* Effect of Jurisprudence of the European Court of Human Rights" (2019) 19 *Human Rights Law Review* 537.

[42] Federal Constitutional Court (Germany), Order of the Second Senate of October 14, 2004, case no 2 BvR 1481/04, para 47 (emphasis added), available at www.bverfg.de/e/rs20041014_2bvr148104en.html.

[43] Ibid., paras 67, 68; see also M Breuer, "Bundesverfassungsgericht versus Behindertenrechtsausschuss: Wer hat das letzte Wort?" (*Verfassungsblog* [*On Matters Constitutional*], February 25, 2019), available at https://verfassungsblog.de/bundesverfassungsgericht-versus-behindertenrechtsausschuss-wer-hat-das-letzte-wort/.

Elsewhere, the difference in legal status between judgments and views is diminishing or has not been a major issue to begin with. The Spanish Supreme Court's 2018 judgment declaring the views of the Committee on the Elimination of Discrimination against Women (CEDAW) to be binding on Spain is a 180-degree turn from the 2002 Spanish Constitutional Court's decision previously referenced[44] and aligns the legal status of court judgments and treaty body views.[45] In Norway, the Supreme Court in 2008 noted that "the UN Human Rights Committee's interpretation of the International Covenant must be accorded considerable weight *as a source of law*"[46] and in a recent decision concerning rights of Sami reindeer herders, the court relied heavily on the "case law" and other statements of the HRC on the scope of ethnic groups' right to enjoy their own culture as protected by Article 27 ICCPR without making an issue of their legal status.[47]

National positions on the consequences of the different legal status of ECtHR judgments and treaty body views in domestic proceedings are thus not uniform. While domestic courts, *qua* institutional identity, may be particularly concerned about issues of legal status, the same does not necessarily hold true for other governmental actors that are involved in giving effect to adverse human rights decisions. An expectation that in cases of conflict between legally binding and legally non-binding decisions, relevant actors in rule-of-law countries will, *ceteris paribus*, accord precedence to the former more often than the other way around, may appear plausible. At the same time, the different institutional actors and issue areas involved, distinct principled approaches to the implications of differences in legal status as well as areas of discretion and choice in political and legal decision-making make this a probabilistic prediction, and not one where we should expect near-consistent behaviour, one way or the other, simply as a function of legal status.

[44] See n 38.

[45] For discussion see M Kanetake, "María de los Ángeles González Carreño v. Ministry of Justice, Judgment No. 1263/2018, Supreme Court of Spain, July 17, 2018" (2019) 113 *American Journal of International Law* 586.

[46] Supreme Court (Norway), Judgment of December 19, 2008, HR-2008-2175-S, para 81 (emphasis added), available at www.domstol.no/globalassets/upload/hret/decisions-in-english-translation/case-2008-1360.pdf.

[47] Supreme Court (Norway), Judgment of October 11, 2021, HR-2021-1975-S, para 102 and *passim*, available at www.domstol.no/globalassets/upload/hret/decisions-in-english-translation/hr-2021-1975-s.pdf.

13.3.2 (Expected) Costs of Compliance and Non-Compliance

In addition to normative factors the decision whether, and how, to comply with an adverse decision is also typically affected by the expected material, political, and/or sovereignty costs of compliance and of non-compliance. When the costs of the measures necessary to bring a State into compliance with the requirements of an adverse decision are low, States will be more likely to implement them voluntarily than when they are high, especially when the likely political costs of non-compliance are minor. In an effort to minimize costs, States in some cases also adopt some, but not all of the remedial measures required, resulting in "partial compliance."[48] Existing research supports the expectation that States remain rational actors that will seek to maximize the relationship between benefits and costs of their chosen course of action and often deal with different types of remedies differently. In the context of the Inter-American and European human rights systems, States have been found to comply to greater extent with financial reparation obligations than those that require general measures such as legislative action[49] and generally appear intent on minimizing the domestic impact of adverse findings.[50] Similarly, in the case of the Court of Justice of the European Union, a routine response by States is to "contain compliance" by remedying only the violation in the decided case but refraining from drawing more general implications from it.[51]

General measures to remove systemic sources of repeat violations – such as changes in legislation, reform of administrative practices, systematic training of security personnel, or practical measures such as improving prison infrastructure – are typically the costliest, in material terms and/or with respect to their sovereignty costs, whereas the costs of individual measures, limited to the individual applicant, are in most cases lower. Where financial compensation is the only individual measure to be adopted, it is commonly the least costly remedial measure (except in instances of highly politicized cases or where compensation is exceptionally high). Most amounts are relatively small and do not constitute a

48 D Hawkins and W Jacoby, "Partial Compliance: A Comparison of the European and Inter-American Courts for Human Rights" (2010) 6 *Journal of International Law & International Relations* 35.

49 C Hillebrecht, *Domestic Politics and International Human Rights Tribunals: The Problem of Compliance* (Cambridge University Press 2014) 49–50.

50 A von Staden, *Compliance with the European Court of Human Rights: Rational Choice within Normative Constraints* (University of Pennsylvania Press 2018) 208–10.

51 L Conant, *Justice Contained: Law and Politics in the European Union* (Cornell University Press 2002).

significant financial burden, at least not for developed countries, and no additional sovereignty costs are implicated through necessary changes of substantive decisions or policies. Conditional *non-refoulement* violations have been implied to be particularly easy to remedy,[52] presumably because States primarily simply have to refrain from doing what they had planned to do. Of course, compliance with such cases is not entirely without costs – residence permits need to be issued and subsistence payments made, plus there are sovereignty costs as a result of an international expert body enjoining a State from implementing its national authorities' decisions in a domain usually viewed as a core part of State sovereignty – but none of these are beyond those that are incurred in the ordinary course of managing a State's immigration and asylum system. Compliance with decisions finding conditional violations involving the threat of torture[53] also avoids the reputational cost of being identified as a violator of a core physical integrity right and instead may generate for the complying State positive reputational capital as a State disposed to prevent grave human rights violations when able to do so.

The impact of the magnitude of the expected costs of adopting effective remedial measures when deciding whether and how to comply with adverse decisions involving the right to freedom from torture should in principle apply to ECtHR judgments and treaty body views alike. These costs arise out of the type of violation and the types of measures necessary to remedy it and their magnitude should not as such differ according to whether they follow from a judgment or a view.

The expected costs of non-compliance, however, can be expected to differ, for two reasons. First, in the case of a treaty body, the monitoring of compliance with its views is undertaken by the same treaty body that issued the decision. During the follow-up procedure the treaty bodies have no additional enforcement capabilities at their disposal other than the pre-existing power of publicizing non-conforming conduct by the respondent State in their annual and follow-up reports. In the case of the ECtHR, by contrast, supervision of the execution of the court's judgments is done by the Committee of Ministers, a political body composed of State representatives. The Committee also has no material enforcement powers other than the power of publicizing and criticizing non-compliance and the "nuclear" option of ending a country's membership in the Council of Europe and

[52] K Fox Principi, "United Nations Individual Complaint Procedures: How Do States Comply?" (2017) 37 *Human Rights Law Journal* 1, 4, footnote 26.

[53] For other rights with respect to which the *non-refoulement* norm has been applied by other treaty bodies, see Çalı, Costello, and Cunningham (n 28).

hence the Convention (which happened in the case of Russia, if for different reasons,[54] and in general tends to be rather counterproductive from the vantage point of monitoring and protecting human rights). Naming and shaming by one's peers is, however, likely more consequential than when done by the treaty bodies. Interview evidence from a study on the relative efficacy of the UN Human Rights Council's Universal Periodic Review (UPR) compared with the treaty bodies' State reporting procedure suggests that States are more sensitive to criticism from other governments than from experts without governmental authority and powers.[55] The involvement of political actors in the UPR is seen as being able to generate more political pressure than is the case for the treaty bodies. As a result of such pressure, the UPR "is perceived [by stakeholders] to be more likely to lead to actual compliance with the undertaken commitments."[56] The same logic arguably applies, *mutatis mutandis*, here as well.

Second, audience costs imposed by the larger public are likewise less likely in the case of non-compliance with treaty body decisions than they are with respect to non-compliance with ECtHR judgments, for the simple reason that the treaty bodies and their work are less known to larger publics and receive much less publicity in the media and public discourse compared to the ECtHR. In the majority of cases, knowledge about treaty body decisions is confined to experts and the applicants; as a result, political mobilization around the failure to comply with a given view is theoretically unlikely and empirically rarely seen (with occasional exceptions, e.g., when the view in question addresses an issue that is already politically salient domestically).[57] More generally, while most enforcement mechanisms available in the human rights domain – agenda setting, naming and shaming, peer pressure, electoral politics, mobilization, and lobbying – are not dependent on a decision's legal status,[58] the

[54] See n 22.

[55] V Carraro, "Promoting Compliance with Human Rights: The Performance of the United Nations' Universal Periodic Review and Treaty Bodies" (2019) 63 *International Studies Quarterly* 1079.

[56] V Carraro, "The United Nations Treaty Bodies and Universal Periodic Review: Advancing Human Rights by Preventing Politicization?" (2017) 39 *Human Rights Quarterly* 943, 969.

[57] The HRC's 2018 decisions concerning the French niqab/burqa ban (CCPR/C/123/D/2807/2016 and CCPR/C/123/D/2747/2016) come to mind.

[58] D Bodansky, "Legally Binding versus Non-Legally Binding Instruments" in S Barrett, C Carraro, and J de Melo (eds), *Towards a Workable and Effective Climate Regime* (CEPR Press and Ferdi 2015) 155, 159; A von Staden, "The Political Economy of the Non-Enforcement of International Human Rights Pronouncements by States" in A Fabbricotti

latter may affect their intensity by being interpreted by relevant audiences as signals of different normative valence and authoritativeness. If Teitgen's suggestion above is correct, then the normative signals sent by courts and their judgments may be expected to be seen by States as stronger than those of non-judicial monitoring and dispute settlement bodies. Kal Raustiala captures this effect when he notes that "the factors that push states to comply with [legally binding obligations] often apply, *albeit more weakly*, to [legally non-binding ones] as well."[59]

13.3.3 *Isolated versus Systematic Violations*

Occasional violations of physical integrity rights can and do occur even in established and otherwise well-functioning democracies, either inadvertently, through negligence, or because individual actors either intentionally commit such acts or are under the belief that their conduct does not infringe the particular rights at issue. When such violations occur in an isolated fashion, we should expect principally rights-abiding States to be willing and able to address and remedy the violations in question. The situation is different in contexts where there are patterns of recurrent violations that are either condoned or intentionally pursued as State policy. In such systemic cases, both the willingness and/or the ability to effectively end violations, prevent their recurrence, and remedy those that have already occurred, will be missing or be severely compromised. The frequency of substantively related complaints and of adverse decisions over extended periods of time is typically indicative of such systemic problems, and their implementation is impeded by having to take place in the same political and institutional environment that gave rise to the violations in the first place.

(ed.), *The Political Economy of International Law: A European Perspective* (Edward Elgar 2016) 230. Exceptions are e.g., provisions on the reopening of domestic proceedings that include as reasons adverse findings by the ECtHR but not treaty body views (see e.g., German Code of Civil Procedure (ZPO), available at www.gesetze-im-internet.de/englisch_zpo/index.html#gl_p2212, section 580, no 8, and Code of Criminal Procedure (StPO), available at www.gesetze-im-internet.de/englisch_stpo/englisch_stpo.html, section 359, no 6), although some States allow for reopening also in light of treaty body views; see K Fox Principi, "Internal Mechanisms to Implement U.N. Human Rights Decisions, notably of the U.N. Human Rights Committee" (2017) 37 *Human Rights Law Journal* 237, 241.

59 K Raustiala, "Form and Substance in International Agreements" (2005) 99 *American Journal of International Law* 581, 611 (emphasis added).

The existence of State-condoned or State-authorized systemic or repeat violations militates against the execution of adverse judgments and treaty body views alike. Because it requires changing an existing preference for the status quo, bringing about compliance in such cases typically requires more than just persuasive authority, but also some tweaking of the respondent State's cost-benefit calculations through the offer of incentives and/or the threat of sanctions. It is in this respect that the above-mentioned differences in the institutional arrangements for supervising the execution of judgments and views can be expected to be consequential, if only to an extent, in that the intergovernmental arrangement for supervising the execution of ECtHR judgments may generate some such incentives and sanctions, for example, through linking compliance to cooperation in other areas in which the respondent State has an interest. The treaty bodies, by contrast, have no such access to political incentives/sanctions that they could wield to enforce compliance against a recalcitrant State.

13.4 State of Compliance with Torture-Related Decisions

This section presents the state of compliance with ECtHR, HRC, and CAT decisions involving violations of the prohibition of torture that have been rendered until the end of 2019. Since I am interested especially in the comparative performance of the institutionally weaker UN human rights treaty bodies, only the twenty-one States that have received at least one relevant adverse HRC or CAT decision are included in the dataset, leaving out for the time being the twenty States subject only to adverse ECtHR judgments. Compliance is coded in accordance with the assessment of the body supervising the implementation of the decisions. In the case of the ECtHR, the Council of Europe's Committee of Ministers is charged with the supervision of the execution of the ECtHR's judgments (Article 46(2) ECHR). Monitoring whether States have paid the financial compensation awarded and taken individual and/or general measures to provide reparation in the applicant's case and prevent a recurrence of the violation,[60] the Committee adopts a final resolution ending supervision when it is satisfied that all measures necessary for compliance have been adopted.[61]

[60] See Committee of Ministers, "Rules of the Committee of Ministers for the Supervision of the Execution of Judgments and of the Terms of Friendly Settlements" (2017), available at https://rm.coe.int/16806eebf0, Rule 6(2).

[61] For the argument that final resolutions are a reasonable proxy for compliance see von Staden (n 50) 17–20.

HRC and CAT themselves conduct second-order compliance monitoring, having created the roles of rapporteur for follow-up of views in 1990[62] and 2002,[63] respectively. While the committees do not, for the most part,[64] use the term "compliance" but refer to "satisfactory implementation" or "satisfactory resolution," the terms of the CAT rapporteur for follow-up on decisions note the mandate to "monitor" and "encourage compliance" by examining whether respondent States have adopted "measures . . . pursuant to the Committee's decision."[65] In the case of the HRC the follow-up rapporteur is similarly charged with "ascertaining the measures taken by States parties to give effect to the Committee's Views."[66] The committees' practice shows that the standard for "satisfactory implementation" is in principle one of substantive compliance so that their assessments can be taken as reasonable indicators for this.

13.4.1 *State of Compliance: ECtHR*

The ECtHR dataset comprises 1,521 judgments involving Article 3 ECHR that the ECtHR rendered against nineteen countries between 1990 and 2019. Fourteen of these are judgments recognizing friendly settlements or solutions with an award of costs and expenses.[67] Of those on the merits, fourteen involve conditional violations whereas 1,493 find past or ongoing violations of Article 3 ECHR, alone or together with infringements of other ECHR provisions and, in fourteen instances,

[62] Report of the Human Rights Committee, UN Doc A/45740 (1990), Annex XI, para 5; see generally AM de Zayas, "The Follow-up Procedure of the UN Human Rights Committee" (1991) 47 *Review of the International Commission of Jurists* 28, 30–31.

[63] Report of the Committee against Torture, UN Doc A/57/40 (2002), para 203.

[64] For an exception, see e.g., CAT, "Follow-up Report on Decisions Relating to Communications Submitted under Article 22 of the Convention," UN Doc CAT/C/68/3 (2020), para 31.

[65] See "Terms of Reference of the Rapporteur on Follow-up of Decisions on Complaints Submitted under Article 22," Report of the Committee against Torture, UN Doc A/57/44 (2002) 220 (Annex IX).

[66] Rules of Procedure of the Human Rights Committee, UN Doc CCPR/C/3/Rev.12 (2021) Rule 106 (1).

[67] Since entry into force of Protocol No 14 in 2010, friendly settlements and unilateral declarations are endorsed by the ECtHR no longer in judgments, but in decisions (cp. Article 39(3) ECHR), the execution of which is also supervised by the Committee of Ministers. A full picture of the incidence of claims concerning Article 3 ECHR and of compliance with them would thus need to include relevant decisions as well; they are, however, not included in the present dataset.

jointly with conditional violations.[68] As of December 31, 2021, the Committee of Ministers had adopted final resolutions indicating sufficient compliance with respect to 71.4 percent of *non-refoulement* judgments and 100 percent of friendly settlements/solutions (see Table 13.1). Judgments declaring past or ongoing violations, by contrast, have been complied with at a rate of about only 36.4 percent. Since these are the most frequent type of judgment, overall compliance is, at 37.3 percent, equally low.

Judgments related to Article 3 ECHR are unevenly distributed (see Figure 13.3). Russia by far dominates the dataset with 856 observations,[69] followed by Ukraine (215), Greece (116), and Bulgaria (91); the remaining countries account for considerably fewer judgments. With a high case count and low national compliance rate of 19.2 percent, Russia drives down the overall compliance rate; without Russia, this rate increases to 54.9 percent.

[68] Addressing compliance with pronouncements involving *non-refoulement* situations under Article 3 ECHR is admittedly incomplete without considering State responses to the ECtHR's indication of interim measures as most stays of expulsion or extradition are addressed through these, rather than in judgments. The court's use of interim measures and their legal status has not been uncontested (P Leach, "Urgency at the European Court of Human Rights: New Directions and Future Prospects for the Interim Measures Mechanism?" in E Rieter and K Zwaan (eds), *Urgency and Human Rights: The Protective Potential and Legitimacy of Interim Measures* (TMC Asser Press 2021) 197, 207–9). In the absence of an express provision in the Convention, the court's authority to indicate interim measures is rooted only in its Rules of Court (Rule 39, available at https://echr.coe.int/Documents/Rules_Court_ENG.pdf). Notably, in affirming that interim measures are binding (*Mamatkulov and Askarov v Turkey* [Grand Chamber Judgment of 4 February 2005] para 128), the Court reversed itself (cp. *Cruz Varas & Others v Sweden* [Judgment of 20 March 1991] para 102). Although interim measures are also requested in the context of impending violations of other rights (ECtHR, Interim Measures (March 2022), available at https://echr.coe.int/documents/fs_interim_measures_eng.pdf), a majority of them is granted in cases of alleged threats to life and physical integrity in expulsion/extradition contexts (A Saccucci, "Interim Measures at the European Court of Human Rights: Current Practice and Future Challenges" in F Maria Palombino, R Virzo, and G Zarra (eds), *Provisional Measures Issued by International Courts and Tribunals* (TMC Asser Press 2021) 215, 220). While there are annual statistics of the number of interim measures issued and refused by the Court (see Analyses of Statistics and related files, available at www.echr.coe.int/pages/home.aspx?p=reports&c.), information on whether States complied with them is not systematically reported and is mentioned only in later judgments, if they come to pass. The absence of this data is unfortunate as the body of interim measures is voluminous – based on the numbers given in the Analysis of Statistics reports well over 5,000 of them have been issued between 2005 and 2021 – and it would be highly informative to learn to what extent States comply with them.

[69] All Russia-related data predates its expulsion from the Council of Europe on March 16, 2022 (see n 22).

Table 13.1 *Compliance status of ECtHR judgments by finding/violation type (as of December 31, 2021)*

Type of finding/violation	Final resolution adopted	Supervision pending	Sum
Conditional *non-refoulement* violation(s)	10	4	14
Past/ongoing violation(s)	544	949[†]	1,493
Recognition of friendly settlement/solution	14	0	14
Total	**568**	**953**	**1,521**

[†] Includes 14 judgments that find past/ongoing as well as conditional violations.
Source: Author's dataset based on HUDOC (hudoc.echr.coe.int/) and HUDOC Exec (hudoc.exec.coe.int/) databases

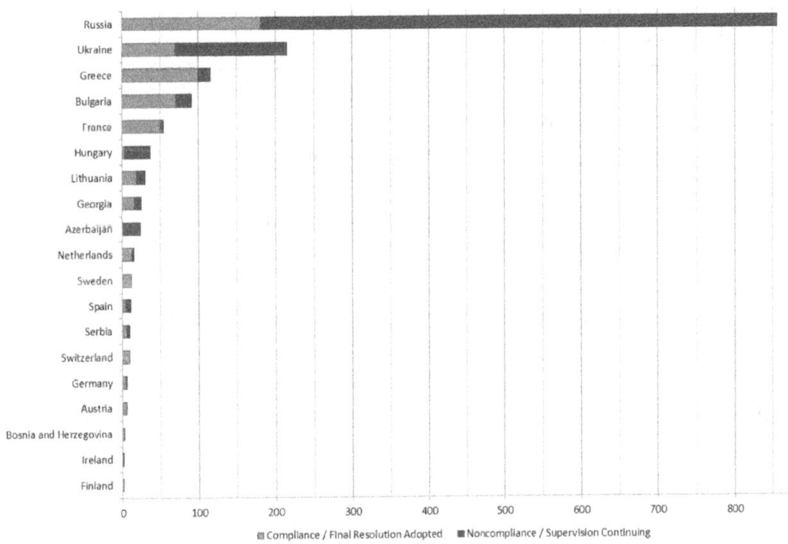

Figure 13.3 ECtHR judgments involving violations of Article 3 ECHR (–2019), by country

13.4.2 *State of Compliance: HRC and CAT*

Table 13.2 shows the compliance status for HRC's and CAT's torture-related decisions, including data from their latest available follow-up reports of 2020.[70] Until the end of 2019, the HRC had issued 242 adverse

[70] HRC, "Follow-up Progress Report on Individual Communications," CCPR/C/130/R.2 (November 19, 2020); CAT (n 63).

Table 13.2 *Follow-up assessments of HRC views and CAT decisions against ECHR parties*

	Satisfactory resolution	All other assessments*	No information	Sum
Adverse HRC views (Art. 7 ICCPR)	**14**	**39**	**22**	**75**
thereof:				
Cond. *non-refoulement* violations	10	4	13	27
Past/ongoing violations	4	35	9	48
Adverse CAT decisions	**62**	**22**	**8**	**92**
thereof:				
Cond. *non-refoulement* violations	54	5	2	61
Past/ongoing violations	8†	17††	6	31
Total HRC and CAT	**76**	**61**	**30**	**167**

* Includes e.g., findings of "follow-up ongoing," "lack of implementation" and closed follow-up due to applicants having gone missing.
† Includes five decisions with a follow-up assessment of "partially satisfactory resolution."
†† Includes one decision that found both a conditional and an actual violation.
Source: Author's dataset based on HRC and CAT annual and follow-up reports

views against 33 different ECHR parties, 75 of which involved violations of Article 7 ICCPR, by itself or in combination with other provisions. Of these, a good third concerned conditional *non-refoulement* violations while the remaining views addressed actual violations. The rate of (documented) compliance is low, at 18.6 percent, and is better for conditional violations (37 percent) than for actual ones (8.3 percent). CAT has found violations of UNCAT against 18 ECHR parties[71] in 92 decisions. CAT has assessed 88.5 percent of the 61 conditional violations as satisfactorily resolved, but only 25.8 percent of the decisions identifying past or ongoing violations. CAT's overall compliance rate is 67.4 percent. Combined, the compliance rate across the two bodies is 45.5 percent. Unlike supervision in the ECHR/ECtHR system, however, not all treaty body decisions are systematically covered by the follow-up procedures

[71] Counting as one State Serbia and Montenegro (existing as a federation until 2006) and Serbia (as successor).

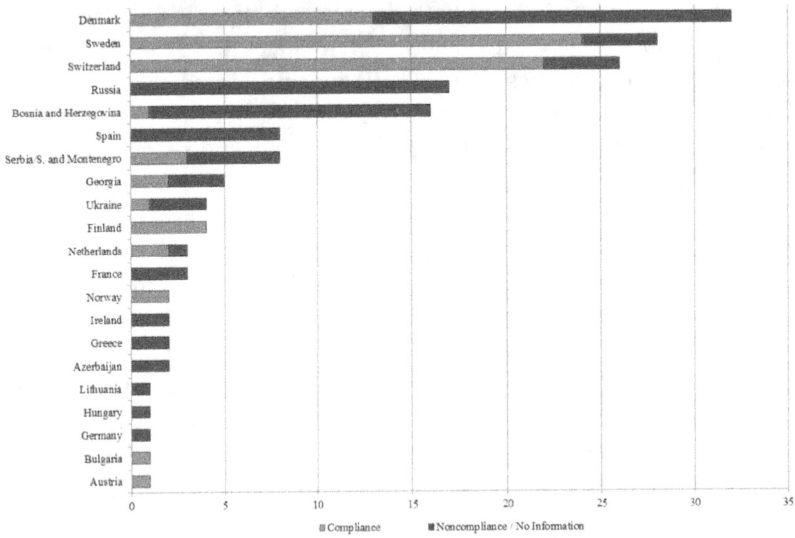

Figure 13.4 Torture-related HRC views and CAT decisions against ECHR parties (–2019) by country

and 30 decisions do not make any appearance in the follow-up reports, their implementation/compliance status thus being unknown.

As in the case of ECtHR judgments, adverse findings by the treaty bodies are unevenly distributed (see Figure 13.4). The 3 countries that top the list are unusual suspects for violations of physical integrity rights: Denmark (32 decisions), Sweden (28), and Switzerland (26). The reason behind this counterintuitive finding is the fact that all but 6 of their combined 86 adverse decisions concern conditional violations of the *non-refoulement* norm.[72]

13.4.3 Discussion

The numbers show that a clear majority of applicants with access to the ECtHR and one or both of the treaty bodies prefer a determination of alleged torture-related violations by the former, rather than the latter. The number of adverse decisions is about nine times higher for the ECtHR than for the treaty bodies (and still about 4.4 times higher when

[72] Four other countries in the dataset have received this type of decision: Finland (4), the Netherlands (2), Norway (1), and Russia (1).

excluding outlier Russia from both datasets). While this imbalance also holds for most States individually, seven States have received more adverse treaty body views than ECtHR judgments and two (Denmark and Norway) have received only adverse views, but no torture-related ECtHR judgments (see Table 13.4 in the appendix for individual country data).

The relationship between democracy and compliance with ECtHR judgments, while not determinative, is suggestive. The four countries with double-digit numbers of judgments against them and the lowest compliance rates also have the lowest average Polity IV regime scores (Azerbaijan, Russia, Ukraine)[73] or a relatively low liberal democracy score (Hungary)[74] compared with other countries in the dataset (averaged across the time period covered by the decisions against them). Conversely, respondent States with low judgment counts and high compliance rates comprise many countries with the highest Polity IV regime type score ("10"), which indicates perfect democracy (e.g., Ireland, Finland, Austria, and Switzerland). With respect to compliance with treaty body views, the patterns are not as clear-cut. While Azerbaijan, Russia, and Hungary appear not to have complied with any decision against them, this also holds true for several countries with higher regime type/democracy scores, such as Spain and Germany. That said, with case counts in the single digits, it is not possible to determine any patterns as the reasons for non-compliance may be unique to the individual case and in some cases the coding of non-compliance is due to the absence of follow-up information.

It is notable that the three countries that have complied with the highest numbers of adverse treaty body decisions (Denmark, Sweden, and Switzerland) are all consistently in the highest percentile ranks with respect to the World Bank's rule of law indicator,[75] so the expectation that commitment to the rule of law might cut against compliance with non-binding treaty body views cannot be generally confirmed. To the contrary, all three countries accord treaty body views special weight, especially in immigration and expulsion proceedings, even if they do not necessarily share the committees' *ratio decidendi*. In Sweden, legislation expressly provides that "[if] an international body that is competent

[73] von Staden (n 50) 24–26.

[74] von Staden (n 4) 468 (fn 13).

[75] Worldwide Governance Indicators, Country Data View, Indicator "Rule of Law," available at http://info.worldbank.org/governance/wgi/Home/Reports.

to examine complaints from individuals has found that a refusal-of-entry or expulsion order in a particular case is contrary to a Swedish commitment under a convention, a residence permit shall be granted to the person covered by the order, unless there are exceptional grounds against granting a residence permit."[76] The Danish Refugee Appeals Board also regularly reopens asylum cases in light of adverse treaty body decisions while in Switzerland CAT decisions can constitute "new evidence" that may result in a reassessment of an asylum seeker's application.[77] So at least in the specific area of *non-refoulement*-related cases, the lack of legally binding status does not significantly impede the treaty body views' domestic implementation.

In both institutional contexts, compliance rates differ between conditional and actual violations. With regard to the former, rates are comparably high, at 71.5 percent (ECtHR) and 72.7 percent (HRC/CAT); the rate is highest for CAT alone (88.5 percent). For actual violations, by contrast, compliance rates drop to 36.4 percent and 15.2 percent, respectively (without Russia, rates increase to 56.8 percent and 26.5 percent). In either case, the rate of compliance with ECtHR judgments finding actual past or ongoing violations is more than twice as high as the rate of compliance with comparable treaty body views. This is in line with the argument made above that conditional violations should be more straightforward and cheaper to comply with than actual violations which also carry the added moral and political opprobrium of having to recognize a violation, rather than being able to prevent one. When compliance costs increase, however, the institutionally stronger ECtHR system performs better than the treaty bodies in inducing compliance, suggesting that under these conditions differences in legal status, follow-up arrangements and mobilization are consequential.

That said, a high incidence of non-compliance often goes hand in hand with widespread, systemic patterns of violations that imply at best government indifference to violations committed in particular by the police and military, and at worst deliberate policy, neither of which is conducive to bringing about compliance. Many of the judgments and views against Russia deal with violations of this sort, for example, those concerning violations stemming from the wars in Chechnya and their

[76] Swedish Aliens Act of 2005, chapter 5, section 4, available at www.government.se/contentassets/784b3d7be3a54a0185f284bbb2683055/aliens-act-2005_716.pdf.

[77] Fox Principi (n 58) 247.

aftermaths[78] and with police brutality in different parts of the country.[79] When, in addition, a State that is being subjected to peer pressure and publicly named and shamed does not care too much about the reputation it has among those using such means, then the institutionally stronger ECtHR supervisory mechanism also reaches the limits of what it can accomplish.

13.5 Conclusion

The existence of jurisdictional overlap in the human rights domain results in a growing body of decisions coming from different institutions that address the same or related rights with respect to the same States. This raises, among other things, the question of their comparative effectiveness in resolving disputes and providing remedies to victims of human rights violations. This chapter has compared rates of compliance with adverse decisions concerning the right to be free from torture and inhuman and degrading treatment or punishment issued by three institutions with ICP jurisdiction over European States as one indicator of such effectiveness.[80] While a reliable identification of the causal factors affecting compliance and non-compliance and their relative importance in different institutional contexts requires research methods that can deal with sizable numbers of cases and variables, such as multivariate regression analysis or qualitative comparative analysis (QCA), the present text has highlighted select factors expected to be consequential with respect to furthering or inhibiting compliance with ECtHR judgments, treaty body views, or both, and taken a first look at the distribution of compliance and non-compliance across different types of decisions and countries. The empirical evidence tentatively suggests that the UN human rights treaty bodies can induce compliance equally as well as regional courts when their decisions concern conditional violations and are addressed to

[78] See the *Khashiyev* and *Akayeva* group of judgments against the Russian Federation, available at https://search.coe.int/cm/Pages/result_details.aspx?ObjectID=0900001680a3355b, and on the lack of effective execution Committee of Ministers docs CM/Del/Dec(2021)1411/H46-31 and CM/Notes/1411/H46-31.

[79] See the *Mikheyev* (2006) group of judgments against the Russian Federation, available at https://search.coe.int/cm/Pages/result_details.aspx?ObjectID=0900001680a3efc4, and on the lack of effective execution Committee of Ministers docs CM/Del/Dec(2019)1362/H46-26 and CM/Notes/1419/H46-33.

[80] On the relationship between second-order compliance and effectiveness, see von Staden (n 50) 32–34.

liberal democracies, but that the ECtHR performs comparatively better when it comes to findings of actual past and/or ongoing violations. However, when a State lacks the aspiration to adhere to the values embodied in human rights norms and in independent monitoring, both institutional settings as they currently exist are incapable of nudging such a State toward compliance with adverse decisions. Further research will need to engage in more fine-grained analysis to assess causal pathways in greater detail, but it seems clear that the presence or absence of a particular legal status of the output of individual complaints procedures is, by itself, determinative neither of compliance nor of non-compliance.

Appendix

Table 13.3 *List of country acronyms*

Acronym	Country	Acronym	Country
ALB	Albania	**LIE**	Liechtenstein
AND	Andorra	**LTU**	Lithuania
ARM	Armenia	**LUX**	Luxembourg
AUT	Austria	**LVA**	Latvia
AZE	Azerbaijan	**MCO**	Monaco
BEL	Belgium	**MDA**	Moldova
BGR	Bulgaria	**MKD**	North Macedonia
BIH	Bosnia and Herzegovina	**MLT**	Malta
CH	Switzerland	**MNE**	Montenegro
CRO	Croatia	**NLD**	Netherlands
CYP	Cyprus	**NOR**	Norway
CZE	Czech Republic	**POL**	Poland
DNK	Denmark	**PRT**	Portugal
ESP	Spain	**ROU**	Romania
EST	Estonia	**RUS**	Russia
FRA	France	**SER**	Serbia
FIN	Finland	**SMR**	San Marino
GEO	Georgia	**SVK**	Slovakia
GER	Germany	**SVN**	Slovenia
GRC	Greece	**SWE**	Sweden
HUN	Hungary	**TUR**	Turkey
ICE	Iceland	**UK**	United Kingdom
IRE	Ireland	**UKR**	Ukraine
ITA	Italy		

Table 13.4 *ECtHR judgments, HRC views and CAT decisions (–2019) finding torture-related violations and their compliance status, by country*

ECtHR Judgments Involving Article 3 ECHR against States That Also Accept HRC and/or CAT ICPs

State	Judgments finding past/ongoing violation(s)		Judgments finding conditional *non-refoulement* violations		Judgments finding past/ongoing and conditional violations		Judgments recognizing friendly settlements or solutions		All judgments		Total
	Closed	Pending	Closed	Pending	Closed	Pending	Closed	Pending	Closed	Pending	
Russia	181	659	0	3	0	13	0	0	181	675	856
Ukraine	70	145	0	0	0	0	0	0	70	145	215
Greece	99	16	0	0	0	0	1	0	100	16	116
Bulgaria	71	18	0	1	0	1	0	0	71	20	91
France	46	5	2	0	0	0	2	0	50	5	55
Hungary	3	34	0	0	0	0	0	0	3	34	37
Lithuania	19	11	0	0	0	0	0	0	19	11	30
Georgia	16	9	0	0	0	0	0	0	16	9	25
Azerbaijan	1	23	0	0	0	0	0	0	1	23	24
Netherlands	8	2	1	0	0	0	4	0	13	2	15
Sweden	6	0	3	0	0	0	3	0	12	0	12
Spain	3	7	0	0	0	0	1	0	4	7	11
Serbia/Serbia and Montenegro	6	3	0	0	0	0	0	0	6	3	9
Switzerland	4	0	3	0	0	0	2	0	9	0	9
Austria	6	0	0	0	0	0	0	0	6	0	6
Germany	3	2	0	0	0	0	1	0	4	2	6
Bosnia and Herzegovina	2	0	0	0	0	0	0	0	2	0	2
Ireland	0	1	0	0	0	0	0	0	0	1	1
Finland	0	0	1	0	0	0	0	0	1	0	1
Norway	0	0	0	0	0	0	0	0	0	0	0
Denmark	0	0	0	0	0	0	0	0	0	0	0
Sum	**544**	**935**	**10**	**4**	**0**	**14**	**14**	**0**	**568**	**953**	**1521**

CAT Decisions against ECHR Parties

State	Decisions finding past/ongoing violation(s)		Decisions finding conditional *non-refoulement* violations		Decisions finding past/ongoing and conditional violations		All decisions		Total
	Closed	Pending	Closed	Pending	Closed	Pending	Closed	Pending	
Russia	0	3	0	0	0	0	0	3	3
Ukraine	1	0	0	0	0	0	1	0	1
Greece	0	0	0	0	0	0	0	0	0
Bulgaria	1	0	0	0	0	0	1	0	1
France	1	2	0	0	0	0	1	2	3
Hungary	0	1	0	0	0	0	0	1	1
Lithuania	0	0	0	0	0	0	0	0	0
Georgia	0	1	0	0	0	0	0	1	1
Azerbaijan	0	1	0	0	0	0	0	1	1
Netherlands	0	0	2	0	0	0	2	0	2
Sweden	1	0	21	2	0	0	22	2	24
Spain	0	5	0	0	0	0	0	5	5
Serbia/Serbia and Montenegro	3	5	0	0	0	0	3	5	8
Switzerland	0	1	23	2	0	0	23	3	26
Austria	1	0	0	0	0	0	1	0	1
Germany	0	1	0	0	0	0	0	1	1
Bosnia and Herzegovina	0	1	0	0	0	0	0	1	1
Ireland	0	0	0	0	0	0	0	0	0
Finland	0	0	4	0	0	0	4	0	4
Norway	1	0	1	0	0	0	2	0	2
Denmark	0	0	5	1	0	1	5	2	7
Sum	**9**	**21**	**56**	**5**	**0**	**1**	**65**	**27**	**92**

HRC Views Involving Article 7 ICCPR against ECHR Parties

State	Views finding past/ongoing violation(s)		Views finding conditional *non-refoulement* violations		All views		Total
	Closed	Pending	Closed	Pending	Closed	Pending	
Russia	0	13	0	1	0	14	14
Ukraine	1	2	0	0	1	2	3
Greece	0	2	0	0	0	2	2
Bulgaria	0	0	0	0	0	0	0
France	0	0	0	0	0	0	0
Hungary	0	0	0	0	0	0	0
Lithuania	0	1	0	0	0	1	1
Georgia	2	2	0	0	2	2	4
Azerbaijan	0	1	0	0	0	1	1
Netherlands	0	1	0	0	0	1	1
Sweden	0	2	1	1	1	3	4
Spain	0	3	0	0	0	3	3
Serbia/Serbia and Montenegro	0	0	0	0	0	0	0
Switzerland	0	0	0	0	0	0	0
Austria	0	0	0	0	0	0	0
Germany	0	0	0	0	0	0	0
Bosnia and Herzegovina	0	15	0	0	0	15	15
Ireland	0	2	0	0	0	2	2
Finland	0	0	0	0	0	0	0
Norway	0	0	0	0	0	0	0
Denmark	1	0	9	15	10	15	25
Sum	**4**	**44**	**10**	**17**	**14**	**61**	**75**

14

The UK's Compliance with the ICCPR and ECHR: A Tale of Two Treaties

SAMUEL WHITE

14.1 Introduction

Despite the proliferation of international regimes in recent decades, compliance with treaty obligations remains a topic of much debate.[1] The field of human rights law has seen exponential growth with new treaties aimed at protecting broad categories of rights,[2] the rights of particular groups,[3] or rights within a specific geographic space.[4] With this range of protected rights has come an array of compliance mechanisms, some successful and others less so.

Scholars have sought to examine and measure the effectiveness of these mechanisms, to understand what works and what does not, as well as to understand why States bind themselves to these instruments. Many scholars look at this from a macro perspective, examining global compliance with particular rights, or using international measures to compare or rank States' compliance. Examples in this field include Hathaway,[5]

I am grateful to Susannah Paul and Sean Whittaker for their extremely helpful comments on earlier drafts of this chapter. All errors, of course, remain my own.

1 Witness the range of topics and approaches discussed at the PluriCourts Research Conference on Compliance Mechanisms in October 2021.

2 For example, the International Covenant on Civil and Political Rights, adopted 16 December 1966, entered into force 23 March 1976, 999 UNTS 171.

3 Such as the Convention on the Elimination of All Forms of Discrimination against Women, adopted 18 December 1979, entered into force 17 July 1980, 1249 UNTS 85.

4 Examples here include the European Convention for the Protection of Human Rights and Fundamental Freedoms, adopted 4 November 1950, entered into force 3 September 1953, 213 UNTS 222.

5 O Hathaway, 'Do Human Rights Treaties Make a Difference?' (2002) 111 *Yale Law Journal* 1935; O Hathaway, 'Making Human Rights Treaties Work: Global Information & Human Rights in the 21st Century' (2003) 31 *International Journal of Legal Information* 312.

Simmons,[6] and Landman and Carvalho.[7] Such works provide an important indication of levels of compliance and the differing success of various treaties in protecting the rights they secure, but they tell us very little about how particular countries experience compliance with their human rights obligations.

This chapter, therefore, examines the question of compliance with human rights treaties at a micro level, looking at the United Kingdom's (UK) experience with the International Covenant on Civil and Political Rights (ICCPR) and the European Convention on Human Rights (ECHR). The former is an important global treaty with a comparatively weak oversight model, the latter a regional example which is arguably one of the most successful human rights treaties in existence.[8] In order to carry out this examination, this chapter provides an overview of each treaty's compliance mechanism before looking at the impact each has had on the protection of human rights in the UK.

The UK has been selected as the basis of this analysis as it was heavily involved in drafting both instruments, and, whilst it has historically had a good record in relation to both, it is currently experiencing a period of significant debate around the future of its human rights protections, making questions about the protections offered by treaties timely.[9] It is hoped that the lessons learned in the context of the UK, ICCPR, and ECHR will nevertheless be relevant beyond just these contexts and will contribute to the wider debate on human rights treaty compliance. The ICCPR and ECHR have been chosen as they protect similar but not wholly overlapping sets of rights.[10] Whilst the fact that the UK is party to both may mean that the use of these instruments has developed somewhat differently than might be the case in a State which is party to just

[6] B Simmons, *Mobilizing for Human Rights* (Cambridge University Press 2009).

[7] T Landman and E Carvalho, *Measuring Human Rights* (Routledge 2010).

[8] Bates describes it as having 'created the most effective system of international protection of human rights in existence': E Bates, *The Evolution of the European Convention on Human Rights* (Oxford University Press 2010) 2.

[9] The UK's key domestic human rights legislation is currently under review and the outcome remains unclear at the time of writing. See Ministry of Justice, *Human Rights Act Reform: A Modern Bill of Rights* (CP 588, 2021).

[10] For a more detailed analysis of the divergence between the two instruments, see for example M Schmidt, 'The Complementarity of the Covenant and the European Convention on Human Rights: Recent Developments' in D Harris and S Joseph (eds), *The International Covenant on Civil and Political Rights and United Kingdom Law* (Clarendon 1995) 629.

one, the selection of these instruments allows for a direct contrast of two comparable instruments in a single jurisdiction.

This analysis demonstrates the problems with the trade-off that takes place between designing treaties to which States will be willing to bind themselves, on the one hand, and designing treaties which are possessed of strong and effective compliance mechanisms, on the other. Building on the UK experience, this chapter concludes that strong compliance mechanisms appear central to ensuring the effectiveness of human rights treaties.

14.2 The International Covenant on Civil and Political Rights

The ICCPR has been called 'probably the most important human rights treaty in the world' in recognition of its global coverage and wide range of protected rights.[11] Despite its importance, however, it serves as an excellent exemplar of the trade-offs required to secure broad global adoption of a human rights treaty. Indeed, the content, compliance mechanisms, and delayed entry into force of the ICCPR all serve to illustrate its difficult beginnings.

It had initially been intended by the United Nations (UN) that there would be a single treaty to protect both the civil and political rights and the economic and social rights contained in the Universal Declaration of Human Rights (UDHR).[12] Disagreement however meant that this was not to be, and the result was the creation of both the ICCPR and International Covenant on Economic Social and Cultural Rights (ICESCR).[13] The aim of both was to translate the UDHR into a treaty, binding on all States parties which would be 'backed up by international supervision and enforcement'.[14] There was further discord between States when it came to drafting the ICCPR and in particular its

[11] S Joseph, J Schultz and M Castan, *The International Covenant on Civil and Political Rights* (2nd ed., Oxford University Press 2005) para 1.01.

[12] S Joseph, 'Civil and Political Rights' in M Baderin and M Ssenyonjo (eds), *International Human Rights Law: Six Decades after the UDHR and Beyond* (Ashgate 2010); Universal Declaration of Human Rights, adopted 10 December 1948, UNGA Res 217A, UN Doc A/810.

[13] Joseph, Schultz, and Castan (n 11) para 1.11. International Covenant on Economic, Social and Cultural Rights, adopted 16 December 1966, entered into force 3 January 1976, 993 UNTS 3.

[14] M Hertig Randall, 'The History of the Covenants' in D Moeckli, H Keller, and C Heri (eds), *The Human Rights Covenants at 50: Their Past, Present and Future* (Oxford University Press 2018) 26.

compliance mechanism.[15] One delegate to the drafting committee described the drafting of this mechanism as 'the most difficult and controversial aspect' of the whole process.[16] It is perhaps unsurprising then that proposals for compliance mechanisms which included 'an International Court of Human Rights empowered to settle disputes concerning the Covenant' were not adopted.[17]

Whilst it may not enjoy the quasi-judicial functions some envisaged,[18] compliance with the ICCPR is overseen by the Human Rights Committee (HRC). The HRC is comprised of eighteen individuals who 'are independent members who do not represent their national states or any other entity'.[19] It has 'responsibility for monitoring [the ICCPR's] implementation',[20] a responsibility it discharges in three main ways: 'the examination of States' reports, the decision of individual communications, and the writing of General Comments.'[21]

The system of States parties' reports to the HRC is governed by Article 40 of the ICCPR. These reports provide information on how States parties 'give effect to the rights recognized in the Covenant and on the progress made in the enjoyment of those rights'.[22] The reports also 'indicate the factors and difficulties ... affecting the implementation of the [ICCPR]'.[23] This allows the HRC to focus on issues highlighted by States parties in their self-reporting to inform dialogue between the HRC

15 For discussion of the discord and geo-political divides see, for example, Hertig Randall (n 14); AWB Simpson, *Human Rights and the End of Empire* (Oxford University Press 2001).

16 Quoted in P Alston, 'The Committee on Economic, Social and Cultural Rights' in P Alston (ed.), *The United Nations and Human Rights* (Clarendon 1995) 476.

17 D McGoldrick, *The Human Rights Committee* (Clarendon 1991) para 1.19.

18 Between the plans for an International Court and the eventual agreement on the role of the HRC there were suggestions that it should have quasi-judicial status. See T Opsahl, 'The Human Rights Committee' in P Alston (ed.), *The United Nations and Human Rights* (Clarendon 1995) 371.

19 D Harris, 'The International Covenant on Civil and Political Rights and the United Kingdom: An Introduction' in D Harris and S Joseph (eds), *The International Covenant on Civil and Political Rights and United Kingdom Law* (Clarendon 1995) 22.

20 Opsahl (n 18) 370.

21 GL Neuman, 'Giving Meaning and Effect to Human Rights' in D Moeckli, H Keller and C Heri (eds), *The Human Rights Covenants at 50: Their Past, Present and Future* (Oxford University Press 2018) 33. Some add inter-State communications to the list, for example Joseph, Schultz, and Castan (n 11) para 1.3. This mechanism has never been used in relation to the ICCPR and is thus not discussed further here.

22 HRC Rules of Procedure of 11 January 2012, Rule 66.

23 Article 40(2).

and States parties.[24] Processes exist to allow the HRC to request further reports where necessary or to raise the absence of a report with individual States, but, importantly, the HRC does not have any power to force States parties to accede to such requests.[25]

The second compliance mechanism is individual communication to the HRC, provided for in the First Optional Protocol to the ICCPR.[26] Parties to the Protocol recognise 'the competence of the [HRC] to receive and consider communications from individuals'.[27] The HRC is not empowered to issue judgments, rather its decisions are referred to as 'views'.[28] These are non-binding in nature and lack the legal force of judgments; domestic courts have frequently rejected any assertion that these views are binding.[29] Nonetheless, the HRC has made apparent its opinion that States parties *ought* to comply with these views and act to remedy any violation.[30] However rates of compliance with the HRC's views are low. One study put the compliance rate at around 12 per cent, described as 'a low figure by any measure'.[31] There are 116 States parties to the Optional Protocol (from a total of 170 States parties to the ICCPR), but this does not include the UK.[32] The UK has noted that it 'remains to

[24] This is the language used by the HRC itself, see, for example, UN Human Rights Committee, 'Working Methods' (Office of the High Commissioner for Human Rights), available at www.ohchr.org/EN/HRBodies/CCPR/Pages/WorkingMethods.aspx, accessed 19 April 2022.

[25] See Opsahl (n 18) 397–419 in particular for more discussion of this.

[26] Provided for in the (First) Optional Protocol to the International Covenant on Civil and Political Rights, adopted 16 December 1966, entered into force 23 March 1976, 999 UNTS 171 (Optional Protocol 1).

[27] Optional Protocol 1, Article 1.

[28] Optional Protocol 1, Article 5(4).

[29] For example, the Supreme Court of Ireland in *Kavanagh v Governor of Mountjoy Prison* (2002) 3 IR 97.

[30] UN Human Rights Committee, 'General Comment No 33: The Obligations of States Parties under the Optional Protocol to the International Covenant on Civil and Political Rights', 5 November 2008, UN Doc CCPR/C/GC/33, para 14.

[31] DC Baluarte, *From Judgment to Justice: Implementing International and Regional Human Rights Decisions* (Open Society Foundations 2010) 119–20. This report, although from an NGO rather than the HRC, has been cited as accurate. See for example, W Sandholtz, 'Human Rights Courts and Global Constitutionalism: Coordination through Judicial Dialogue' (2021) 10 *Global Constitutionalism* 439.

[32] UNGA, 'Report of the Human Rights Committee', UN GAOR 73rd Session Supp No 40 UN Doc A/73/40, para 1. Country specific information regarding treaty status is available at http://indicators.ohchr.org/, accessed 19 April 2022.

be convinced of the added practical value to people in the United Kingdom of rights of individual petition to the United Nations'.[33]

The final mechanism at the disposal of the HRC is the issuing of General Comments. These have evolved to allow for the HRC to comment on matters which are relevant to States parties to the ICCPR, such as the interpretation of specific treaty provisions or the wider obligations of States parties. To date, thirty-seven have been issued.[34] Whilst these General Comments are not of themselves related to enforcement of the ICCPR, they 'have proven to be a valuable jurisprudential resource' when interpreting the ICCPR.[35] These are not discussed in any greater detail here as they are general in nature and are not directed at individual States' compliance.

As this shows, although there are mechanisms in place to drive compliance with the ICCPR these are limited by the fact that they are non-enforceable: they require States parties to act on the HRC's dicta, albeit with a treaty obligation to uphold and protect the rights secured by the ICCPR. Particularly for individuals within States, such as the UK, which have not accepted the right to individual petition to the HRC, there is no means by which they can bring complaints against a State. Indeed, in the UK, individuals can do nothing directly to enforce their rights under the ICCPR.

Academic commentary on the effectiveness of UN treaty bodies suggests more widely that there are concerns with the level of compliance they generate. Looking at the perception of the effectiveness of the wider UN human rights treaty body system, one study noted a widespread view 'that [UN human rights] treaty bodies are only to some extent able to generate public pressure, or even not at all'.[36] This negative outlook is further reinforced by Krommendijk's assessment of the effectiveness of treaty body recommendations, which concluded that, in the countries he surveyed, such recommendations 'largely remained ineffective … [and] have either been rejected by governments or they have been so vague and

[33] UN Human Rights Committee, 'Seventh Periodic Report of States Parties due in July 2012: United Kingdom, the British Overseas Territories, the Crown Dependencies', 29 December 2012, UN Doc CCPR/C/GBR/7, para 192.

[34] The most recent being UN Human Rights Committee, 'General Comment No 37 (2020) on the Right of Peaceful Assembly (Article 21)', 17 September 2020, UN Doc CCPR/C/GC/37.

[35] Joseph, Schultz, and Castan (n 11) para 1.42.

[36] V Carraro, 'Promoting Compliance with Human Rights: The Performance of the United Nations' Universal Periodic Review and Treaty Bodies' (2019) 63 *International Studies Quarterly* 1079, 1083–85.

broad that they simply did not elicit any follow-up measures'.[37] Against this backdrop, the UN has itself noted in respect of treaty bodies that 'While there have been many cases which could be considered as "success stories", it is clear that a large number of States fail to apply the remedies as recommended.'[38] The analysis which led to this pronouncement included an examination of compliance with the HRC's views, therefore it seems reasonable to suggest that the general trends seen in relation to the treaty bodies extend to the HRC.

14.3 The UK and the International Covenant on Civil and Political Rights

Although the UK played a significant role in the drafting of the ICCPR,[39] no steps have been taken to translate the protections afforded by the ICCPR into UK domestic law.[40] It is hard to point to any direct impact that treaty membership has had on UK legislation. In the 1980s, 'the United Kingdom Government's representative to the UN Human Rights Committee was unable to identify even one case in which the British Courts had made reference to the Covenant'.[41] A decade later, Klug, Starmer, and Weir noted that 'The United Kingdom ratified the [ICCPR] in May 1976, but has since done nothing substantial to give effect to ratification or even publicly to recognise it.'[42]

The ICCPR obliges States parties to give effect to the treaty in their own laws,[43] but how this happens is a matter for States themselves.[44]

[37] J Krommendijk, 'The (In)Effectiveness of UN Human Rights Treaty Body Recommendations' (2015) 33 *Netherlands Quarterly of Human Rights* 194.

[38] UN Human Rights Institutions, 'Follow-up Procedures on Individual Complaints', 15 December 2010, UN Doc HRI/ICM/WGFU/2011/2, para 25.

[39] This is discussed in much depth in the magisterial *Human Rights and the End of Empire*, Simpson (n 15).

[40] With the exception of section 133 of the Criminal Justice Act 1988 which gives effect to Article 14(6) of the ICCPR, there has been no co-ordinated action to give domestic effect to these rights.

[41] R Clayton and H Tomlinson (eds), *The Law of Human Rights* (2nd ed., Oxford University Press 2009) para 2.56.

[42] F Klug, K Starmer, and S Weir, 'The British Way of Doing Things: The United Kingdom and the International Covenant of Civil and Political Rights, 1976–94' (1995) *Public Law* 504. That the name of the ICCPR is incorrect in the title of this paper suggests the extent to which it has entered into legal consciousness in the UK.

[43] ICCPR Article 2(2).

[44] M Nowak, *UN Covenant on Civil and Political Rights: CCPR Commentary* (2nd rev. ed., Engel 2005) 57.

In the UK, despite suggestions to the contrary from the HRC, successive governments have been 'content to assume … no changes [to UK domestic law] were necessary because the rights and freedoms recognised in the Covenant are inherent in the United Kingdom's legal system and are protected by it and by Parliament'.[45]

The lack of mandatory oversight of individual cases by a judicial or quasi-judicial treaty body has been suggested as a reason for the UK's lack of engagement with and knowledge of the ICCPR. It has meant that 'the HRC has had no opportunity to give a ruling upon United Kingdom compliance with its obligations under the ICCPR in the context of individual communications'.[46] This in turn has deprived the UK courts of an opportunity to engage more directly with the HRC's decision-making. Although the HRC is not a court and so dialogue in the sense seen with international courts may not occur, Sandholtz has noted that in States which accept the right to individual petition, views of the HRC relating to that State are 'available to activists, advocates and courts … to support the expansion of rights' and courts have been willing to engage with the HRC's views as they would other courts' judgments.[47]

The periodic reporting structure does not appear to have spurred UK lawmakers into action when it comes to the protection of the rights contained within the ICCPR. Klug, Starmer, and Weir assert that:

> From the UK's very first report … the [HRC has] been sceptical about the ability of arrangements here to protect human rights in the absence of either constitutional [sic] guarantees of such rights or the incorporation of the Covenant in domestic law … scepticism increased when [the HRC] found that the 1979 report failed to refer to the legislative texts and judicial decisions which the government claimed gave protection to the rights and freedoms provided for in the Covenant.[48]

This scepticism has not met with any concerted action on the part of the UK's executive or legislature, despite the HRC going so far as to question whether 'the United Kingdom was in fact in a position to "ensure" that the Covenant's provisions were given proper effect'.[49] Whilst this situation may have developed to some extent since the HRC said this in

45 Klug, Starmer, and Weir (n 42) 505.

46 Harris (n 19) 46.

47 Sandholtz (n 31) 452 and generally.

48 Klug, Starmer, and Weir (n 42) 506–7.

49 UN HRC's comments on the United Kingdom's report submitted 3 September 1984, quoted in ibid. 507.

1984, the Committee has continued to raise concerns even after the UK legislated for the protection of some rights more formally in the UK via the Human Rights Act 1998 (HRA).[50]

Given the reticence of the UK to address in any depth its compliance with the ICCPR, and the lack of action to enhance compliance by means of domestic law, it is hard to point to any concrete difference made by the ICCPR to the protection of individual rights in the UK.[51] This lack of change brought about by the ICCPR within the UK is confirmed by an examination of the comments of the HRC in response to the UK's periodic reporting which consistently highlight concerns.[52] McGoldrick and Parker suggest that the ICCPR has had some limited impact in the UK,[53] but the idea that the ICCPR plays any great role is hard to square with the observations of the HRC, or with research by the author and that carried out some time ago by Klug, Starmer, and Weir.[54] Even McGoldrick and Parker themselves went on to note that 'the Covenant is yet to make a marked impact on the consciousness of the British public or on much of the government'.[55]

This general apathy towards the ICCPR in the UK is further demonstrated in the lack of reference to the treaty in domestic judgments. Thus, there were only six references in reported judgments in England and Wales which mentioned the ICCPR prior to the passage of the HRA.[56]

[50] The HRC has noted that the HRA does not offer protection for all the rights contained in the ICCPR. See UN Human Rights Committee, 'Concluding Observations of the Human Rights Committee United Kingdom of Great Britain and Northern Ireland', 30 July 2008, UN Doc CCPR/C/GBR/CO/6, para 6.

[51] The sole exception to this being the Criminal Justice Act 1988 as noted.

[52] See for example, the issues raised in the 2008 Concluding Observations (n 50) and those in 2015, UN Human Rights Committee, 'Concluding Observations on the Seventh Periodic Report of the United Kingdom of Great Britain and Northern Ireland', 17 August 2015, UN Doc CCPR/C/GBR/CO/7.

[53] D McGoldrick and N Parker, 'The United Kingdom Perspective on the International Covenant on Civil and Political Rights' in D Harris and S Joseph (eds), *The International Covenant on Civil and Political Rights and United Kingdom Law* (Clarendon 1995) 88.

[54] S White, 'Has Incorporation of the European Convention of Human Rights Secured Better Judicial Enforcement of Human Rights in England and Wales?' (PhD thesis, University of Dundee 2021). Klug, Starmer, and Weir (n 42).

[55] McGoldrick and Parker (n 53) 89.

[56] This data was collected by the author using a keyword search (for 'International Covenant on Civil and Political Rights') of published judgments of higher courts in England and Wales, the High Court, Court of Appeal, and House of Lords/Supreme Court. A wider analysis cited in Klug, Starmer, and Weir found a similar number, and showed that mentions in Parliament were even less frequent: Klug, Starmer, and Weir (n 42) 508. Hunt's research also serves to confirm this: M Hunt, *Using Human Rights in*

These six cases themselves, moreover, highlight the unwillingness of the courts to engage with the ICCPR in any depth, even when it is directly mentioned. Of the six, the case which addressed the ICCPR in the most detail related to section 133 of the Criminal Justice Act 1988.[57] The rest did not engage with the ICCPR beyond an initial mention or observation,[58] and one rejected outright the use of the ICCPR.[59]

The marked lack of engagement with the ICCPR by the UK courts prior to 1998 did not radically improve thereafter with the passage of the HRA and the creation of a greater culture of human rights literacy. In the years after 1998 the number of references to the ICCPR by the courts increased significantly. Nonetheless, these increased references did not generate any significant shift in the quality of the UK's compliance with the ICCPR.[60] Indeed, in the majority of cases, the ICCPR was only mentioned briefly and in passing and did not see the courts engaging in any depth with the protections offered. As Figure 14.1, below, shows, despite an increase in references by courts to the ICCPR there is no clear trend in use in the first twenty years after the HRA.

An examination of the HRC's two sets of concluding observations since 1998 provides examples of the areas of concern. The 2008 document noted twenty-three separate issues for concern in relation to the UK's compliance with the ICCPR.[61] These included areas such as the detention without charge of terror suspects for extended periods under the Terrorism Act 2006,[62] the control order regime restricting individual liberties without due process under the Prevention of Terrorism Act 2005,[63] and delayed access to lawyers for those detained under the Terrorism Act 2000.[64] Such concerns, and the others listed, suggest that there are areas in which the protections afforded to individuals under UK law fall short of those offered by the ICCPR. This is despite the fact that

English Courts (Hart 1997) Appendix 1. Analysis of published judgments in the other jurisdictions of the UK carried out by the author suggests that these findings are mirrored in Northern Ireland and Scotland.

57 *R v Secretary of State for the Home Department, ex p Bateman* (1995) 7 Admin LR 175.

58 For example, *Airedale NHS Trust v Bland* [1993] AC 789.

59 *R v Ministry of Defence, ex p Smith* [1995] EWCA Civ 22, [1996] QB 517.

60 This is clear from the HRC's concluding observations after 1998 which do not show a vast shift in levels of satisfaction with the UK's compliance, see for example, UN Human Rights Committee (n 52). This was the last report by the HRC in relation to the UK.

61 UN Human Rights Committee (n 50).

62 Ibid., para 15.

63 Ibid., para 16.

64 Ibid., para 19.

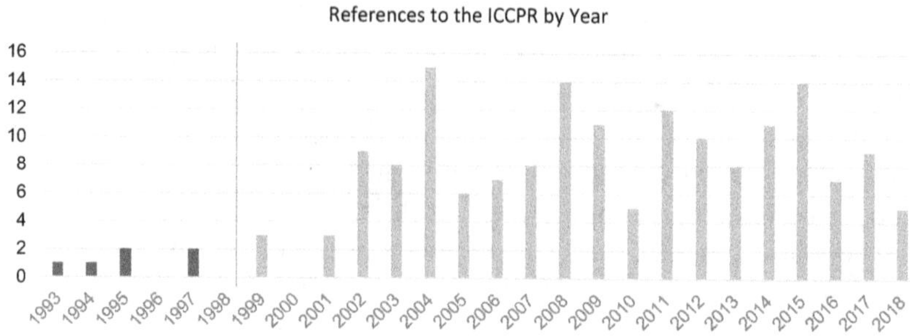

Figure 14.1 Number of cases per year in the higher courts of England and Wales making reference to the ICCPR.

the HRA translates the ECHR rights into UK law; the HRC has noted that a range of 'Covenant rights are not included among the provisions of the [ECHR] which has [sic] been incorporated into the domestic legal order through the [HRA]',[65] meaning there can be no challenge under the HRA.

In 2015 the HRC again raised concerns about the UK's compliance with the ICCPR. In its concluding observations the HRC elaborated further misgivings about the lack of direct applicability of the ICCPR in the UK.[66] The HRC additionally noted concerns about 'the lack of a comprehensive mechanism for reviewing existing gaps and inconsistencies between the domestic human rights legal framework and the rights as set forth in the Covenant'.[67] The long list of other issues suggests that although concerns had shifted slightly from those of the previous reporting cycle, there remained serious reservations on the part of the HRC about the UK's general level of compliance with its treaty obligations. Thus, for example, the HRC again highlighted counter-terrorism powers under the Terrorism Act 2000,[68] the power to deprive persons of citizenship, potentially rendering those persons stateless,[69] and the use of closed material procedures under the Justice and Security Act 2013 in civil cases where issues of national security are raised.[70]

65 Ibid., para 6.
66 UN Human Rights Committee (n 52) para 5.
67 Ibid.
68 Ibid., para 14. Including again the length of detention without charge and denial of bail for those arrested under the 2000 Act.
69 Ibid., para 15.
70 Ibid., para 22.

These two sets of concluding observations serve to highlight the range of issues of concern to the HRC in respect of the UK's compliance with the ICCPR. It is clear from the HRC's observations that it believes that the current framework of legal protection for human rights is not sufficient to protect all those rights guaranteed under the ICCPR. As this chapter goes on to argue, this is at least partially attributable to the inability of those in the UK directly to approach the HRC by means of individual petition, combined with the lack of strong enforcement powers on the part of the HRC. It also serves to show that the UK's self-assurance of compliance with the ICCPR is misplaced.

14.4 The European Convention on Human Rights

In common with the ICCPR, the UK had an important role in the development of the ECHR.[71] However, the UK's motives may at times have been questionable; Bates asserts that the main driver for the UK's entry into the ECHR system may have been 'political, "face-saving" considerations'.[72] There was opposition in the UK to the idea of individual petition with concern that it 'might be used as a weapon of political agitation'.[73] Nevertheless, although sometimes fraught, the ECHR's drafting process did not present the same levels of difficulty as had the ICCPR.[74]

The ECHR's system of protection has developed over time.[75] The early system of enforcement was complex and stemmed, at least in part, from the difficulties in securing agreement for the establishment of a judicial enforcement mechanism, to which various States, including the UK, had been opposed.[76] Some felt that the 'machinery set up for enforcing the [ECHR] should not be purely judicial but should be able and competent to give due weight to political as well as legal considerations'.[77] However, as time went on, this system was overhauled, and the original process was

[71] This role is discussed in depth in G Marston, 'The United Kingdom's Part in the Preparation of the European Convention on Human Rights, 1950' (1993) 42 *International and Comparative Law Quarterly* 796.

[72] Bates (n 8) 98.

[73] Marston (n 71) 825.

[74] See generally Bates (n 8).

[75] Whilst there is not space here to discuss the earlier system, it is examined extensively in Bates, ibid.

[76] Simpson (n 15) 655–56.

[77] UK Foreign Office minute, written after a meeting of senior officials, quoted in ibid., 701.

replaced by Protocol 11 which substituted this approach to decision-making with a permanent European Court of Human Rights (ECtHR), with the new system taking effect on 1 November 1998.

The process has since been reformed again by Protocol 14 of 2004 which Bates summarises as aiming 'to maximise economy of procedure at Strasbourg'.[78] Judgments of the ECtHR do not provide detail on the action which member States must take to address violations, where these are found: such action is at the discretion of the member State itself.[79] Where a case is 'exceptional' a reference may be made to the Grand Chamber of seventeen judges for judgment.[80] A decision of the ECtHR is binding on member States.[81] Any judgment of the Grand Chamber is final, whilst other judgments become final where the parties indicate that they do not wish to refer the judgment to the Grand Chamber, where three months have elapsed since the judgment, or where the Grand Chamber rejects a request to refer the judgment.[82]

Article 46 of the ECHR, as amended by Protocol 14, charges the Committee of Ministers, a body comprised of the foreign ministers of each member State, with overseeing the enforcement of the ECtHR's judgments. Under Protocol 14, the Committee of Ministers may now refer a member State to the ECtHR for non-compliance.[83] In addition to the Committee of Ministers and the ECtHR, the Parliamentary Assembly of the Council of Europe also plays a role in enforcement; its recommendations, resolutions, and opinions inform the work of the Committee of Ministers.[84] The ECtHR enjoys good levels of compliance with its judgments and the system as a whole has been described as 'astoundingly successful',[85] suggesting that this mix of mandatory judicial oversight

[78] Bates (n 8) 500.

[79] The ECtHR is made up of judges appointed in respect of each member State by the Parliamentary Assembly.

[80] Article 43.

[81] Article 46(1) reads: 'The High Contracting parties undertake to abide by the final judgment of the Court in any case to which they are parties.' Although 'Judgments of the [ECtHR] are not directly enforceable in a manner similar to that of judgments of domestic courts.' WA Schabas, *The European Convention on Human Rights: A Commentary* (Oxford University Press 2015) 860.

[82] Article 44.

[83] Article 46(4). Reference to other chapter/s dealing with Council of Ministers process to go here, editors can insert?

[84] B Rainey, E Wicks, and C Ovey, *Jacobs, White, and Ovey: The European Convention on Human Rights* (7th ed., Oxford University Press 2017) 5.

[85] H Fenwick, *Fenwick on Civil Liberties and Human Rights* (5th ed., Routledge 2017) 101.

(the ECtHR) combined with political supervision (the Committee of Ministers) is highly effective. Indeed, as will be argued, the relative strength of the combination of mandatory judicial oversight and individual petition is closely linked with the UK's high level of compliance with the ECHR.

14.5 The UK and the European Convention on Human Rights

Although the ICCPR has not resulted in any significant changes to the human rights landscape in the UK, the same is not true of the ECHR. Even before the ECHR was a part of the UK's domestic law, Lord Bingham asserted that it had played a role in 'the interpretation of ambiguous statutory provisions, guiding the exercise of discretions, bearing on the development of the common law'.[86] Examining these areas, it seems fair to assert that prior to the reception of the rights protected by the ECHR into UK law by way of the HRA, the ECHR's impact was already significant. Summarising the use of international human rights treaties in England and Wales prior to the HRA, Hunt suggests that 'During ... the mid-1970s, domestic judges ... not only [displayed] a willingness to interpret domestic law in the light of international human rights instruments, but often considered themselves under an obligation to do so.'[87] However, as Hunt's own analysis illustrates this willingness seems to have been almost exclusively focused on the ECHR.

Much of this development was driven by discourse between the UK courts and the ECtHR. The overall number of violations by the UK remained comparatively low during this period, but there was sufficient opportunity for the ECtHR to rule on matters of UK law, giving the UK courts the chance to engage with Strasbourg's judgments to develop their own reasoning. The judgments of the ECtHR directly impacted the UK's own relationship with the ECHR system. Thus, whilst Masterman notes that 'to think that [ECtHR] jurisprudence could be followed or applied in the manner of precedents would be a mistake',[88] Beloff and Mountfield show that UK courts set some store by the ECtHR's rulings when making

[86] *R v Lyons* [2003] 1 AC 976, para 13.

[87] Hunt (n 56) 160.

[88] R Masterman, 'Aspiration or Foundation? The Status of the Strasbourg Jurisprudence and "the Convention Rights" in Domestic Law' in H Fenwick, G Phillipson, and R Masterman (eds), *Judicial Reasoning under the UK Human Rights Act* (Cambridge University Press 2007) 64.

decisions.[89] For example, the UK courts relied directly on jurisprudence of the ECtHR in relation to freedom of expression.[90] It is therefore evident that the domestic courts were willing to look to the work of the ECtHR as part of their decision-making process, suggesting that the courts saw the benefit of dialogue with the ECtHR for the protection of human rights in the UK. This dialogue would not have been possible without the right of individual petition; a right entirely absent in the case of the protections offered by the ICCPR.

The HRA and the translation of the ECHR rights into UK domestic law marked a significant shift in the protection of human rights in the UK. Arguably, the effectiveness, in both legal and political terms of the ECtHR in identifying breaches of individual rights in the UK was a major factor in the decision to move the primary responsibility for the protection of individual rights into the domestic sphere by enacting the HRA. Indeed, concern that traditional methods of human rights protection in the UK were ineffective was 'reinforced by a perception that the European Court of Human Rights was finding the United Kingdom in violation of the [ECHR] with disquieting frequency'.[91]

The nature of the ECHR's enforcement system also appears to have been one of the reasons behind the decision to enact the HRA. The government of the day noted:

> The European Convention is not the only international human rights agreement to which the United Kingdom and other like-minded countries are party, but ... it has become one of the premier agreements defining standards of behaviour across Europe. It was also for many years unique because of the system which it put in place for people from signatory countries to take complaints to Strasbourg and for those complaints to be judicially determined. These arrangements are by now well tried and tested ... They therefore afford an excellent basis for the Human Rights Bill which we are now introducing.[92]

Since the HRA entered into force there have been increasingly few applications from the UK to the ECtHR and 'the UK has among the lowest number of applications per year allocated for a decision. It also has

[89] M Beloff and H Mountfield, 'Unconventional Behaviour? Judicial Uses of the European Convention in England and Wales' (1996) 1 *European Human Rights Law Review* 467.

[90] *Rantzen v Mirror Group Newspapers* [1994] QB 670, 696.

[91] DW Vick, 'The Human Rights Act and the British Constitution' (2002) 39 *Texas International Law Journal* 329, 348.

[92] Home Department, *Rights Brought Home: The Human Rights Bill* (1997) para 1.3.

a lower percentage of these applications declared admissible than most and loses proportionately fewer of the cases brought against it than most'.[93]

Whilst the biggest driver in the UK's increased compliance in the last two decades is undoubtedly the HRA and its translation of the ECHR rights into domestic law, a number of points should be made. First, the fact that the courts of the UK are now required to view human rights questions through the lens of the rights protected by the ECHR means that there is increased opportunity for proceedings in the national courts to address complaints under the ECHR. This in turn also allows the national courts to develop their dialogue with the ECtHR.[94] Thus, judgments of the ECtHR continue to play an important role in the protection of the Convention rights within the UK. Second, the political importance and power of enforceable judgments of the ECtHR should not be underestimated. As the row between the UK Parliament and the ECtHR on prisoner voting showed, it is very hard to face down the legal and political pressure of an adverse ruling by the Court even where political red lines have been drawn.[95]

It is clear, therefore, that the design of the enforcement mechanism of the ECHR plays an important role in the high level of compliance that the UK enjoys. The UK has developed its domestic human rights protections to reflect those envisaged under the ECHR, and the nature of the ECtHR's judgments has allowed the domestic courts to engage with their counterparts in the ECtHR on questions of law. Moreover, the success of the ECHR system, coupled with the political impact of adverse judgments of the ECtHR, was a major factor in the decision to enact the HRA and bring the rights contained in the ECHR 'home' into UK domestic law.[96]

[93] A Donald, J Gordon, and P Leach, *Research Report 83: The UK and the European Court of Human Rights* (Equality and Human Rights Commission 2012) 42.

[94] For example, this was discussed in M Amos, 'The Dialogue between United Kingdom Courts and the European Court of Human Rights' (2012) 61 *International and Comparative Law Quarterly* 557.

[95] The most recent judgment of the ECtHR in this matter, finding that there had been a violation of Hirst's right to vote, was *Hirst v United Kingdom (No 2)* (2006) 42 EHRR 41. The situation was finally resolved in 2017 when the right to vote was extended to prisoners released on temporary licence (see 'Oral Statement to Parliament: Secretary of State's Oral Statement on Sentencing' (UK Government, 2 November 2017), available at www.gov.uk/government/speeches/secretary-of-states-oral-statement-on-sentencing, accessed 19 April 2022.

[96] The White Paper which led to the HRA used this terminology, *Rights Brought Home* (n 92).

14.6 Analysis

As Heyns and Viljoen have noted, 'The success or failure of any international human rights system should be evaluated in accordance with its impact on human rights practices on the domestic . . . level.'[97] With this in mind, the wide gulf between the impact of ICCPR and ECHR in the UK suggests that the ECHR has been a much greater success.

Whilst the UK's track record at the ECtHR has improved over the past decades, an improvement which has accelerated significantly since 1998, there was already a movement towards use of the ECHR in domestic courts long before this was envisaged by domestic law. In 1998 when the HRA translated ECHR rights into UK domestic law, UK judges were empowered more overtly to have regard to the dicta of the ECtHR in their own decision-making.[98] More recently still, the UK's Supreme Court has demonstrated its willingness to keep British jurisprudence pegged to the ECtHR's interpretation of the ECHR,[99] further highlighting the continuing relevance of the ECtHR as a point of reference for domestic courts. Commentators and judges have pointed to the relatively broad impact of the ECHR on a range of areas, including in 'the interpretation of ambiguous statutory provisions, guiding the exercise of discretions [and] bearing on the development of the common law'.[100]

By contrast, the UK's compliance with the ICCPR receives little attention from the UK courts or from Parliament and this has not dramatically improved over the course of the UK's involvement with the treaty.[101] Whilst there may be a number of reasons at play for this vast disparity, given the ECtHR's role in driving compliance with the ECHR it is impossible to underplay the importance of mandatory judicial oversight of treaty bodies in ensuring that States comply with their treaty obligations. As the majority of interaction between the UK and HRC takes place quietly by means of periodic reporting and concluding observations and receives little publicity, public awareness and ownership of

97 C Heyns and F Viljoen, 'The Impact of the United Nations Human Rights Treaties on the Domestic Level' (2001) 23 *Human Rights Quarterly* 483.

98 Section 2, HRA requires the UK courts to 'take into account' decisions of the ECtHR.

99 *R (AB) v Secretary of State for Justice* [2021] UKSC 28, paras 56–59, per Lord Reed.

100 *Lyons* (n 86) para 13.

101 A review of the HRC's concluding observations shows that the only area which has seen continuous improvement is the situation in Northern Ireland, but this owes more to the peace process than attempts to secure ICCPR compliance.

the rights protected by the ICCPR are almost non-existent.[102] Moreover, the nature of periodic reports and concluding observations means that the UK courts are unlikely to engage with these in developing their own jurisprudence, preferring instead the surer ground offered by decisions of an international court.

Examining the UK experience, it seems fair to conclude that strong judicial or quasi-judicial compliance mechanisms are essential in ensuring the effectiveness of human rights treaties. However, it is acknowledged that this may deter States from becoming party to such conventions. Hathaway, drawing together empirical research on the effect of international human rights law, highlights the apparent trade-off between States' participation in and the effectiveness of human rights treaties.[103] States are more likely to participate in treaty systems with weaker compliance models. As Hathaway notes, 'Where enforcement is stronger, all else being equal fewer countries should be expected to commit. However, those fewer adherents will be more likely to comply with the treaty than they would be if the treaty were less strongly enforced.'[104]

This raises an important question: are the gains of greater compliance significant enough to justify the loss of engagement? In 'Do Human Rights Treaties Make a Difference?' Hathaway presents some concerning findings in relation to States' willingness to engage with human rights treaties: in some cases, membership of such treaty systems was shown to correlate with poorer performance in terms of compliance with the protected rights.[105] This suggests that the dichotomy might be starker than first presented. On the one hand strong compliance systems provide protection for human rights but may discourage States from becoming party to a treaty because of the risks associated with breaching treaty obligations. However, on the other hand, weaker systems allow States cynically to tether themselves to such structures to gain from the wider political and economic benefits they may bring without raising human rights standards in any meaningful way.[106] Simmons is rather more optimistic about the positive changes brought about by instruments, such

[102] A search of polling data from the polling company YouGov suggests that there is also a paucity of polling on the ICCPR in the UK.

[103] OA Hathaway, 'The New Empiricism in Human Rights: Insights and Implications' (2004) 98 *American Society of International Law Proceedings* 206, 208.

[104] Ibid.

[105] Hathaway, 'Do Human Rights Treaties Make a Difference?' (n 5).

[106] Hathaway discusses these benefits in greater detail, ibid.

as the ICCPR, believing that they can effectively empower domestic actors to bring about change.[107] Nevertheless, she acknowledges that such treaties cannot 'solve all problems'.[108] Whilst there is not enough space to explore this in greater depth here, it is a question which merits further research, particularly in the context of increasing antagonism to global institutions, such as the UN.

In any event, the UK's experience with the ICCPR and ECHR serves to underline the difference which a strong compliance mechanism (and a State's active engagement) can make to the domestic effectiveness and relevance of a human rights treaty. Given the broad range of rights protected by the ICCPR, the lack of engagement with the ICCPR and its compliance machinery represents a missed opportunity for the further development of human rights in the UK. If the pattern witnessed here is mirrored with respect to other human rights instruments in the UK, as well as in other States more broadly, it should give pause for thought about the way in which human rights are protected, and what can be done to strengthen the oversight of these protections within existing frameworks.[109]

14.7 Conclusion

This chapter has illustrated the differing outcomes brought about by differing models of compliance mechanism in human rights treaties. Using the UK's experience with the ECHR and ICCPR as a lens, it has argued that the former – characterised by a strong, judicial compliance mechanism – can be linked with better human rights outcomes. By contrast, the ICCPR, with its weaker, reporting-based compliance monitoring and opt-in right of individual petition, has not had the same impact.

Building on the UK experience it seems reasonable to conclude that strong compliance mechanisms in which all States parties are expected to participate are important in ensuring the effectiveness of human rights treaties. Whilst these findings relate to the UK, there is no reason to

[107] Simmons (n 6).

[108] Ibid., 366.

[109] Although Krommendijk points to over a decade of 'futile attempts' to strengthen the UN treaty body system, suggesting that any attempt to drive improvement will be difficult: J Krommendijk, 'Less Is More: Proposals for How UN Human Rights Treaty Bodies Can Be More Selective' (2020) 38 *Netherlands Quarterly of Human Rights* 5.

believe that the lessons learned in this context cannot be applied more widely to contribute to the debate on how human rights are best protected. A regime of human rights protection centred on strong compliance monitoring may deter States from becoming party to a human rights treaty, yet the benefits for individuals' rights protection may be enough to outweigh this.

This chapter does not seek to argue that the vast advances in rights protection since 1945 have not dramatically improved the attainment of human rights. Rather, it aims to help to safeguard the gains achieved and to allow these to be further built upon to ensure that rights protection is strengthened, and that human rights courts and treaty bodies are in a better position to ensure that the rights they steward are respected, protected, and fulfilled.

15

Exploring the Role of Decisions by Judicial, Quasi-Judicial and Specialised Non-Judicial Bodies in Advancing Anti-Trafficking Efforts

NOEMI MAGUGLIANI AND JEAN-PIERRE GAUCI

15.1 Introduction

In the last two decades, the international community has increasingly turned its attention towards the phenomenon of trafficking in human beings. Since the adoption of the 2000 Protocol to Prevent, Suppress and Punish Trafficking in Persons, Especially Women and Children (Palermo Protocol), as well as subsequent regional conventions,[1] many States have progressively sought to align their domestic legislation with the standards required by international law. Although the majority of States have adopted legislation criminalising trafficking in human beings,[2] and many have also passed legislation aimed at protecting trafficked persons, States' compliance with international and domestic standards has often been questioned.

This chapter explores proceedings before judicial, quasi-judicial and specialised non-judicial bodies[3] as determinants of advances in anti-trafficking efforts. In this context, 'determinants' are understood as

[1] Including the Council of Europe Convention on Action against Trafficking in Human Beings, signed 16 May 2005, entered into force 1 February 2008, CETS No 197; the ASEAN Convention against Trafficking in Persons, Especially Women and Children, signed 21 November 2015, entered into force 8 March 2017; and the Protocol to the African Charter on Human and Peoples' Rights on the Rights of Women in Africa, signed 11 July 2003, entered into force 25 November 2005.

[2] According to the United Nations Office on Drugs and Crime (UNODC), *Global Report on Trafficking in Persons 2020* (2020) 23: 'Twenty years [after the adoption of the Palermo Protocol], over 90 per cent of the United Nations Member States have established a specific offence for the criminalisation of trafficking, and the definition of trafficking in persons is almost universally based on the UN Protocol.'

[3] Including United Nations Special Procedures, and in particular the United Nations Special Rapporteur on Trafficking in Persons, Especially Women and Children.

factors shaping governments' anti-trafficking efforts and influencing compliance with and implementation of international standards. This contribution outlines how the role of such proceedings is perceived by anti-trafficking stakeholders, and, critically, the various ways in which proceedings influence anti-trafficking efforts. Importantly, the chapter explores how proceedings before judicial, quasi-judicial and specialised non-judicial bodies interact with other determinants in influencing anti-trafficking efforts at the domestic level.

While there is significant analysis of States' anti-trafficking efforts, it is necessary, in our view, to shift the focus of inquiry towards the determinants of anti-trafficking efforts in trying to understand *why* States adopt, or comply with, protective and progressive legislation to tackle human trafficking. While some determinants are readily identifiable (e.g., the presence of political will, the ratification of international instruments and pressure by monitoring mechanisms or external donors), others have not yet been sufficiently explored, such as the decisions of judicial, quasi-judicial and specialised non-judicial bodies. The complex, non-linear and often hidden interactions between different factors have equally not been adequately addressed. Decisions of international and regional courts and quasi-judicial bodies are relevant determinants of States' anti-trafficking efforts, as identified by, *inter alia*, the Organization for Security and Co-operation in Europe (OSCE).[4]

This chapter builds on existing literature on the role of regional courts in shaping changes in anti-trafficking action,[5] taking a step beyond the existing focus on judicial bodies and on the European Court of Human Rights (ECtHR) in particular. We have identified 19 individual communications to the United Nations Treaty Bodies,[6] 342 communications of the United Nations Special Rapporteur on Trafficking in Persons,[7] 12 judgments of the ECtHR,[8] and 2 judgments of the Inter-American

[4] See Organization for Security and Co-operation in Europe (OSCE), 'Highlights of the International Conference "The Critical Role of the Judiciary in Combating Trafficking in Human Beings"' held in Tashkent, 13–14 November 2019.

[5] See H Duffy, 'Litigating Modern Day Slavery in Regional Courts: A Nascent Contribution' (2016) 14(2) *Journal of International Criminal Justice* 375; V Milano, 'The European Court of Human Rights' Case Law on Human Trafficking in Light of L.E. v Greece: A Disturbing Setback?' (2017) 17(4) *Human Rights Law Review* 701.

[6] Available at https://juris.ohchr.org/, searched using keywords 'human trafficking'.

[7] Available at https://spcommreports.ohchr.org/Tmsearch/TMDocuments, searched filtering by mandate 'trafficking in persons'.

[8] Available at https://hudoc.echr.coe.int/, searched using keywords 'human trafficking' and filtering by language (English, French) and Article (4, 4-1, and 4-2).

Court of Human Rights (IACtHR)[9] that tackle issues related to the implementation of anti-trafficking legislation.[10] Deploying a comparative approach, this chapter evaluates four case studies (Argentina, Brazil, Cyprus and the United Kingdom) in order to assess the role of judicial, quasi-judicial and specialised non-judicial bodies, including supervisory bodies, in effecting change at the domestic level. The chapter draws on a large-scale research project exploring the determinants of anti-trafficking efforts globally.[11] The project assesses the links and sequencing of specific factors that have yielded improved political will and capacity in national governments to address trafficking in persons and which have led to sustained and comprehensive anti-trafficking efforts. It explores findings from literature reviews, expert interviews, a global survey and a series of fourteen case studies (of which the above are four).

15.2 Decisions by Judicial, Quasi-Judicial and Specialised Non-Judicial Bodies as Determinants of Anti-Trafficking Efforts

Research on human trafficking and anti-trafficking efforts highlights a broad range of factors which influence governments' anti-trafficking responses. These encompass factors instrumental in, for example, bringing about compliance and implementation of international standards, as well as causing governments to improve, hinder or regress efforts. Determinants of anti-trafficking efforts do not work in isolation. However, there is no single framework or sequencing; rather, the processes through which anti-trafficking laws, policies and measures emerge and co-exist are particular, varied and, crucially, contextual and interdependent.

A number of determinants have been discussed in the literature over the last two decades, including political will, international standards and mechanisms, structural conditions, the role of civil society organisations and funding and resource allocation. Although literature may be lacking on the role of the jurisprudence of regional and international courts and bodies due to the limited number of cases in the past two decades,

[9] Available at www.corteidh.or.cr/casos_sentencias.cfm?lang=en.

[10] The first trafficking communication before the African Commission on Human and Peoples' Rights, *J v Namibia*, is currently pending.

[11] British Institute of International and Comparative Law (BIICL), 'Determinants of Anti-Trafficking Efforts', available at www.biicl.org/projects/determinants-of-anti-trafficking-efforts.

regional and international bodies as well as some scholars have highlighted how decisions by international courts, tribunals and quasi-judicial bodies can be a decisive factor in the implementation of international standards, and in influencing national anti-trafficking responses.[12]

Crucially, decisions by domestic courts can trigger legislative change and oblige legislative compliance with international standards. For example, the general reports of the Council of Europe's Group of Experts on Action against Trafficking in Human Beings (GRETA) identify specific domestic jurisprudence which has triggered legislative change and pushed governments to adopt the advised change. They highlight, *inter alia*, *Hussein v Labour Court*,[13] which triggered legislative changes in Ireland through the enactment of the Employment Permits (Amendment) Act 2014 on 27 July 2014, and *NN v Secretary of State for the Home Department*,[14] where a United Kingdom Home Office policy was found to be unlawful and incompatible with the Council of Europe Convention on Action against Trafficking in Human Beings (ECAT) and which resulted in the introduction of a new process and guidance to assess the support needs of survivors beyond the previous exit timescales. More recently, and beyond the European context, in the case of *LVCO v AG*,[15] the Colombian Constitutional Court ordered structural measures to improve protection of trafficked persons at the national level, including: designing a protocol to identify trafficked persons; training public servants with functions related to human trafficking; and protecting the human rights of trafficked persons as soon as signs of trafficking are detected, independently of what occurs in criminal proceedings.

The OSCE has further noted that the reasoning and findings of domestic courts, for example, can be instrumental 'to ensure consistency of judicial practice and correct understanding and interpretation of anti-trafficking legislation'.[16] Interpretation and clarifications by higher courts also play an important role, especially when they are binding on lower courts.[17] Such decisions also reinforce international legal obligations and

[12] See, *inter alia*, Duffy (n 5); Milano (n 5); OSCE (n 4).

[13] *Hussein v Labour Court* [2012] IEHC 364.

[14] *NN v Secretary of State for the Home Department* [2019] EWHC 1003 (Admin).

[15] [2021] T-236-21. Available at www.corteconstitucional.gov.co/relatoria/2021/T-236-21.htm.

[16] OSCE (n 4) 8.

[17] Ibid.

encourage harmonisation and co-operation across different judicial interpretations.

With respect to the role of regional courts, an evaluation by Duffy found that courts reinforce 'duties to prevent, regulate, investigate, cooperate, criminalize and punish'.[18] Her analysis focusses on decisions by the ECtHR, the African Commission on Human and Peoples' Rights, the Court of Justice of the Economic Community of West African States, the Inter-American Commission on Human Rights (IACmHR) and the IACtHR. According to Duffy, these decisions can shed light on the shortfalls of legal frameworks and State policies, and they can be instrumental in clarifying and underlining States' positive obligations.[19] Duffy highlights four key examples:

> In some cases, such as *CN v. UK* or *Fazenda Brasil Verde*, the litigation has led to legislative changes to enhance criminal law and jurisdiction over these offences. Many other cases, however, including *Mani*, or *Periera v. Brazil*, reveal something quite different, which is laws that exist on paper but are not understood or given effect in practice, for varying reasons including the lack of capacity and knowledge of prosecutors or judges themselves, the insensitive and ineffective handling of investigations or direct corruption and collusion of state agents.[20]

The sustained impact of strategic litigation before regional courts is further explored by Milano, with specific reference to the ECtHR. Milano recognises the influence of the ECtHR's landmark case *Rantsev v Cyprus and Russia*, [21] although she is critical of the Court's ruling in *LE v Greece*, [22] which, she argues, failed to meet the expectations set out in *Rantsev* and therefore represents a regression.[23]

The role of decisions of regional courts has also been highlighted in a series of expert interviews conducted as part of the research that informed this chapter. A member of the secretariat of the ECAT emphasised how the ECtHR has triggered positive changes through the judgments of, *inter alia*, *Rantsev v Cyprus and Russia*,[24] *Chowdury and others*

[18] Duffy (n 5) 402.
[19] Ibid.
[20] Ibid. 401.
[21] App no 25965/04 (ECtHR, 7 January 2010).
[22] App no 71545/12 (ECtHR, 21 January 2016).
[23] Milano (n 5).
[24] App no 25965/04 (ECtHR, 7 January 2010).

v Greece[25] and *Siliadin v France*,[26] causing changes in national laws and the adoption of action plans.[27] The same reasoning could be applied in the future to the more recent cases of *VCL and AN v the United Kingdom*[28] and *Zoletic and others v Azerbaijan*.[29] Other participants in the research project also noted that judicial reviews have the potential to trigger direct change in obliging the enforcement of international or regional legal obligations.[30] A similar observation was made with respect to strategic litigation, which interviewees argued can be an influential tool in creating legal and policy changes.[31] With regards to the influence of UN Special Procedures, including UN Special Rapporteurs, the system of country visits and subsequent reports and recommendations have been deemed influential when rapporteurs focus on a specific policy area. Governments are responsive because country visits take place in the context of broader discussions and engagements about legislative change and improvements. Concerns of reputation and international relations are at play, but what is important to enable such influence is trust and dialogue. While there is minimal influence from governments who do not engage and co-operate with country visits, where there is a dialogue and a receptiveness to visits, changes are likely to follow.[32]

More broadly, judicial and quasi-judicial decisions can be decisive in identifying gaps in national legislation and outlining where the law needs to be improved.[33] However, the impact of litigation, and more broadly of decisions, depends on whether there is a system of precedent, or whether or not such decisions are binding. It has been noted, for example, that in Southeast Asia, court decisions are rarely written, published or translated, reducing the influence that precedent-setting may have in the region (even if influential within the specific country).[34] A similar issue was

[25] App no 21884/15 (ECtHR, 30 March 2017).
[26] App no 73316/01 (ECtHR, 26 July 2005).
[27] Interview with a member of the Secretariat of the Council of Europe Convention on Action against Trafficking in Human Beings (25 November 2020).
[28] Apps nos 77587/12 and 74603/12 (ECtHR, 16 February 2021).
[29] App no 20116/12 (ECtHR, 7 October 2021).
[30] Interview with Thomas Harré (8 April 2020); Interview with Euan Fraser (16 April 2020).
[31] Interview with the president of an anti-trafficking organisation (7 January 2020); Interview with a member of an international organisation (23 April 2020); Interview with Federica Toscano (5 March 2020).
[32] Interview with an independent expert on trafficking in human beings (16 December 2020).
[33] Interview with a member of a specialised international organisation (17 April 2020).
[34] Interview with a member of an international organisation (17 April 2020).

raised in the context of our research in Guyana.[35] In addition, integral to the influence of judicial and quasi-judicial decisions are judges', or more broadly, decision-makers', own understanding and awareness of trafficking in persons and anti-trafficking law.[36] Examples have emerged of judges having a lack of awareness and understanding of how international legal instruments ratified by their country apply,[37] as well as a lack of understanding around specific provisions (with the non-punishment principle being a key example).[38] Moreover, sight should not be lost of the fact that social and cultural contexts may influence judges and decision-makers. For example, it has been suggested that in Brazil judges and decision-makers do not always see 'the gravity of the situation' because of an underlying and embedded 'culture of exploitation',[39] a reality that would seem to normalise certain behaviours that fall within the scope of the trafficking definition. These socio-cultural contextual factors, alongside the limits to judges' understandings and the difficulties of ensuring victim co-operation in prosecutions, limit the impact of courts and judges.[40]

Indeed, judicial and quasi-judicial decisions do not operate in a *vacuum*; their influence is determined by several other factors beyond understanding of the law and social and cultural contexts. Other determinant factors identified are, for example, a State's political situation and political will to act in the aftermath of a judicial or quasi-judicial decision.[41] For example, it has been noted that the rule of law in the United Kingdom facilitates a role for court decisions, which are often based on the ECAT, in enforcing regional obligations domestically.[42] In contrast, in Moldova and Cambodia (amongst other countries), it has been noted

[35] BIICL, 'Determinants of Anti-Trafficking Efforts: Guyana Country Report' (2021).

[36] Interview with a member of an international non-governmental organisation (9 April 2020).

[37] Interview with a member of an international organisation (14 April 2020).

[38] Interview with Gary Craig (15 April 2020). See also Human Rights Council, 'Implementation of the Non-Punishment Principle: Report of the Special Rapporteur on Trafficking in Persons, Especially Women and Children, Siobhán Mullally' (17 May 2021) UN Doc A/HRC/47/34. BIICL has recently started a project together with the International Bar Association (IBA) on the application of the non-punishment principle in law and practice across different jurisdictions, available at www.biicl.org/projects/the-non-punishment-principle-in-trafficking-in-persons.

[39] Interview with a member of an international organisation (n 30).

[40] Ibid.

[41] Interview with a member of a national anti-trafficking organisation (15 May 2020).

[42] Ibid.

that the courts have minimal impact due to corruption, thus limiting their ability to trigger policy or legislative change.[43]

Against this background, however, it is relevant to note that the impact of judicial and quasi-judicial decisions, as well as of specialised non-judicial bodies' observations, can be amplified when decisions are used as levers and accountability tools by, *inter alia*, civil society and the media. This is demonstrated, for example, by the cases of fishermen from Indonesia being trafficked to New Zealand on Korean boats where 'fishing companies were bringing these migrant labourers into New Zealand under a very specific provision of the Fisheries Act'.[44] International Law Aid and the International Transport Workers' Federation, as well as other non-governmental organisations (NGOs), joined forces in pressuring the New Zealand Government to change specific provisions of the Fisheries Act 1996 – pressure that resulted in a ministerial inquiry. In parallel, the Supreme Court in New Zealand also heard cases in relation to wage claims. Together, these factors brought about significant changes in practice.[45]

15.3 The Role of Judicial, Quasi-Judicial and Specialised Non-Judicial Bodies in Argentina, Brazil, Cyprus and the United Kingdom

For the purpose of this chapter, we have selected four case studies (Argentina, Brazil, Cyprus and the United Kingdom) from amongst the fourteen undertaken as part of the broader project on determinants of anti-trafficking efforts.[46] These four were selected because they represent

[43] Ibid. See also Interview with Professor Cathy Zimmerman (14 February 2020).

[44] Interview with Thomas Harré (n 23).

[45] Ibid.

[46] In the framework of the project, fourteen case studies (Algeria, Argentina, Armenia, Bahamas, Bahrain, Brazil, Chile, Cyprus, Georgia, Guyana, Mozambique, the Philippines, Thailand and the United Kingdom) were implemented by national research consultants with expertise in trafficking frameworks and/or policymaking within the country. Each case study involved in-depth, cross-temporal, national level desk research including analysis of policy documents and (where available) *travaux préparatoires* of such policies and legislation, interviews with relevant experts and stakeholders and focus group discussions. Stakeholders consulted include people working for governments and legislatures/parliaments, academics, lawyers, criminal justice stakeholders, service providers and those working for relevant NGOs and other civil society organisations, and the private sector (if applicable and relevant), trying to maintain a 'representation balance'. Each national research consultant was provided with a literature review compiled by the BIICL team and concerned with the research question of what factors determine governments' anti-trafficking efforts. National research consultants were expected to complete

different levels of engagement of judicial, quasi-judicial and specialised non-judicial bodies across two distinct geographical areas. These are four exploratory, or hypothesis-generating, case studies, selected according to three baseline criteria: the presence of engagement of judicial, quasi-judicial or specialised non-judicial bodies; the availability of proof of such engagement; and the presence of different qualitative levels of engagement of such bodies.[47]

15.3.1 Argentina

As recognised by the United Nations Office on Drugs and Crime in its Global Report on Trafficking in Persons of 2018, Argentina reported the highest numbers of prosecution and convictions of trafficking and trafficking-related offences in the South American region.[48] By July 2020, Argentina had reported a total of 405 decisions on human trafficking and exploitation, of which 282 were convictions for human trafficking, 62 were convictions for exploitation and 61 were acquittals.[49] Argentina was one of the countries that promoted the adoption of the Palermo Protocol, driven by its political will to fight human trafficking in minors and by its strategic motivations of dealing with human trafficking as a form of transnational organised crime.[50] Argentina ratified the Palermo Protocol in August 2002 through Law 25.632,[51] and in 2008 it enshrined the crime of human trafficking in domestic law through Law 26.364.[52]

In the Argentinian context, the influence of judicial cases as determinants for public policies and legislation on anti-trafficking has always been

fifteen interviews with relevant stakeholders, trying to maintain a balance in terms of State and non-State actors. Interviews were conducted either online (including over the phone or videoconference), or in person. National research consultants also moderated focus groups, one with non-State actors, and another with State actors.

[47] J Gerring and L Cojocaru, 'Selecting Cases for Intensive Analysis: A Diversity of Goals and Methods' (2016) 45(3) *Sociological Methods & Research* 392, 399–400.

[48] UNODC, *Global Report on Trafficking in Persons* (2018) 78.

[49] Ministerio Público Fiscal, 'En Once Años Hubo 405 Sentencias en Todo el País por Trata de Personas' (31 July 2020), available at www.fiscales.gob.ar/trata/en-once-anos-hubo-405-sentencias-en-todo-el-pais-por-trata-de-personas.

[50] A Gallagher, *The International Law of Human Trafficking* (Cambridge University Press 2010) 77.

[51] Law 25.632 (2002), available at http://servicios.infoleg.gob.ar/infolegInternet/anexos/75000-79999/77329/norma.htm.

[52] Law 26.364 (2008), available at http://servicios.infoleg.gob.ar/infolegInternet/anexos/140000-144999/140100/norma.htm.

critical. Indeed, judicial cases influenced the enactment of all three of the main anti-trafficking laws, namely Law 26.364 (2008) creating the crime of human trafficking; Law 26.842 (2012)[53] modifying Law 26.364, including eliminating the 'means' element from the crime; and Law 27.508 (2019),[54] creating a fund to assist and compensate trafficked persons.

At the time of the first landmark case involving Marita Verón, Argentina did not have any criminal provision punishing human trafficking. Marita Verón was kidnapped and subjected to sexual exploitation in 2002. Through the establishment of the NGO Fundación María de los Ángeles, Marita's mother advocated for the case of her daughter and for the recognition of human trafficking in Argentina. Although the defendants were at first acquitted in 2012, the acquittal was met with widespread outrage, and on appeal the Supreme Court of Tucumán convicted ten out of the thirteen suspects (seven men and six women). The case of Marita Verón exposed the inadequacy of the Argentinian legal framework, the absence of legal provisions enabling an effective investigation into her disappearance, and difficulties in the prosecution of her alleged traffickers. Though the trial did not start until 2012, the legislators – taking into account the events of this particular case – were prompted to recognise the need to adopt provisions criminalising trafficking in persons, which led to the adoption of Law 26.364. When the first instance Court acquitted the thirteen defendants in 2012, extraordinary legislative debates were summoned, and Law 26.842 was adopted in December 2012. Amongst the modifications introduced, the law eliminated the 'means' element from the definition of the crime of human trafficking – which is now only considered to be an aggravated circumstance. According to the legislative debates, it is evident that the poor decision rendered in the case of Marita Verón was one of the main determinants for the enactment of Law 26.842.

A second landmark case, Montoya, highlighted the lack of provisions with respect to adequate redress for trafficked persons. In this case the claimant, who had been trafficked for the purpose of sexual exploitation, acted as a *querellante* (complainant) in the trial against the traffickers, seeking civil damages. She also sued the municipal State for lack of prevention and for the facilitation of the exploitation. The tribunal

[53] Law 26.842 (2012), available at www.argentina.gob.ar/normativa/nacional/ley-26842-206554/texto

[54] Law 27.508 (2019), available at www.argentina.gob.ar/normativa/nacional/ley-27508-325439/texto

sentenced three individuals to up to seven years in prison, and most notably it ruled in favour of the *querellante* in the civil damage case, ordering the municipality to pay 780,000 pesos (ca. €7,000). As in the case of Marita Verón, the Montoya case exposed gaps in the domestic anti-trafficking legal framework. Following the judgment, the Federal Council for the Fight against Human Trafficking and Exploitation and for the Protection and Assistance of Victims[55] proposed the creation of a fund to allow for the compensation of trafficked persons. In 2019, Law 27.508 was enacted, establishing a trust fund comprised of traffickers' seized assets. Notably, Law 27.508 also introduced a requirement for criminal courts to award trafficked persons restitution at the time of the traffickers' conviction and provided for the possibility of filing civil suits to receive additional restitution. In the year of its enactment, criminal courts applied Law 27.508 in seven cases, granting restitution to trafficked persons.

In 2010, the United Nations Special Rapporteur on Trafficking in Persons, Especially Women and Children, Joy Ngozi Ezeilo, conducted a country visit to Argentina at the invitation of the government.[56] The Special Rapporteur welcomed the adoption of Law 26.364 and the creation of dedicated offices within the executive to provide trafficked persons with assistance and to investigate trafficking in persons, but also observed a number of challenges. In particular, she noted the weak co-ordination of anti-trafficking activities, and the lack of identification and referral mechanisms for trafficked persons. The Special Rapporteur called on the Argentinian Government to, *inter alia*, establish:

> . . . a federal central agency to enhance coordination, not only among federal offices and units that have already been set up to combat trafficking in persons and assist victims, but also between them and authorities at the provincial and municipal levels [and to consider establishing] a special fund for the compensation of trafficked persons.[57]

UN Treaty Bodies have also raised concerns, over the years, with particular reference to the implementation of existing legislation. The Committee on the Elimination of Discrimination Against Women, in

[55] An organ established through Law 26.842 and composed of members from the executive, legislative and judiciary, as well as from international organisations and NGOs.

[56] Human Rights Council, 'Report of the Special Rapporteur on Trafficking in Persons, Especially Women and Children, Joy Ngozi Ezeilo: Addendum, Mission to Argentina' (24 May 2011) UN Doc A/HRC/17/35/Add.4.

[57] Ibid.

its 2016 Concluding Observations on the Seventh Periodic Report of Argentina, recommended that the State party '[e]stablish a referral and identification mechanism, increase funding for shelters and provide counselling, rehabilitation services and psychosocial assistance for women and girls who are victims of trafficking and exploitation of prostitution'.[58] In 2018, the Committee on Economic, Social and Cultural Rights (CESCR) made similar recommendations in the context of exploitation beyond forced prostitution, and with respect to trafficked persons regardless of biological sex. The CESCR noted that 'most of the State party's mechanisms for combating trafficking in women are geared towards emergency care and there are no programmes of sustained medium- or long-term assistance for victims'.[59] The Committee recommended 'that the State party strengthen public policies for the prevention and punishment of trafficking in persons [and] that the principle of exemption from criminal liability be respected and that, accordingly, victims of trafficking in persons not be detained or prosecuted'.[60] Similar recommendations were also made as recently as 2020 by the Committee on the Protection of the Rights of all Migrant Workers and Members of Their Families (CMW). In its Concluding Observations on the Second Periodic Report of Argentina, the CMW recommended that Argentina '[a]llocate sufficient resources in each province for the provision of psychological, legal and medical assistance to victims, in addition to shelters or specialized care centres for child, adolescent and women victims of trafficking in persons'.[61]

While the Special Rapporteur's recommendation to establish a federal central agency to enhance anti-trafficking co-ordination was addressed in 2012 through Law 26.842, a special fund was only created in 2019, following the judgment in the Montoya case, and the recommendations from UN Treaty Bodies have had limited impact, including in terms of pressure, in effecting change. The Argentinian case study highlights the

[58] Committee on the Elimination of Discrimination Against Women (CEDAW), Concluding Observations on the Seventh Periodic Report of Argentina (25 November 2016) UN Doc CEDAW/C/ARG/CO/7, para 23.

[59] Committee on Economic, Social and Cultural Rights, Concluding Observations on the Fourth Periodic Report of Argentina (1 November 2018) UN Doc E/C.12/ARG/CO/4, paras 41–42.

[60] Ibid.

[61] Committee on the Protection of the Rights of All Migrant Workers and Members of Their Families, Concluding Observations on the Second Periodic Report of Argentina (4 February 2020) UN Doc CMW/C/ARG/CO/2, paras 50–51.

role of judicial decisions in improving anti-trafficking efforts – including where a 'negative' judicial decision is reached – and it reflects both the cumulative effect of various determinants and the broader context and timescales within which determinants must be considered.

15.3.2 Brazil

Over the past two decades, Brazil has seen notable shifts in developing trafficking policy, legislation and initiatives. Brazil ratified the Palermo Protocol in 2004, through Decree n. 5.017. Upon coming into force, a series of anti-trafficking efforts were undertaken domestically. For example, in March 2005, Law n. 11.106 amended the Brazilian Criminal Code, specifically Article 231, which criminalised the 'traffic of women', and changed it to the offence of 'traffic[king] in persons for sexual exploitation'.[62] In addition, internal traffic in persons for sexual exploitation was criminalised under Article 231-A. Similarly, in 2006, Decree n. 5.948 was enacted, which approved the National Policy to Combat Trafficking in Persons and established an inter-ministerial working group to draft a proposal for a national plan.[63] The first National Plan for Combating Human Trafficking was then approved by Decree n. 6.347 in 2008.[64]

While decisions of judicial, quasi-judicial and non-judicial bodies have not been identified as key determinants of anti-trafficking efforts broadly in the Brazilian context, interviewees have highlighted the role played by such decisions in a particular sphere – that of trafficking for the purpose of forced labour. Labour trafficking is widely recognised as an issue in Brazil, so there is a pre-existing, well-developed legislative background for protecting workers' conditions,[65] in addition to an established network to tackle modern slavery (or 'work analogous to slavery', as

62 Law n. 11.106 (2005), available at https://presrepublica.jusbrasil.com.br/legislacao/96809/lei-11106-05. This was later changed by Law n. 13.344 (2016), available at https://presrepublica.jusbrasil.com.br/legislacao/392619946/lei-13344-16.

63 Decree n. 5.948 (2006), available at: https://presrepublica.jusbrasil.com.br/legislacao/95318/decreto-5948-06.

64 Decree n. 6.347 (2008), available at: https://presrepublica.jusbrasil.com.br/legislacao/94100/decreto-6347-08.

65 International Centre for Migration Policy Development (ICMPD), 'Guia de Assistência e Referenciamento de Vítimas de Tráfico de Pessoas' (2020) 41.

described by Article 149 of the Brazilian Criminal Code).[66] The underlying motivation for labour protection is rooted in Brazil's history and links with slavery,[67] and supplemented by external factors, including the IACmHR decision in *José Pereira v Brazil*.[68] As part of the amicable settlement agreement through which the government of Brazil accepted responsibility for the wrongdoings in this case, Brazil was called upon to, *inter alia*, pay financial compensation for the damages suffered by the claimant; commit to prosecute and punish the individuals responsible; and institute preventive measures, including legislative amendments, and measures to monitor and repress slave labour in Brazil. With regard to compensatory measures, the Brazilian State forwarded a bill to the National Congress which, adopted as a matter of urgency following a symbolic vote, allowed the claimant to be compensated. Through the case, it became apparent that there was a need for amendments in domestic legislation to provide a more precise definition of forced labour, which was prioritised and finally introduced through Law 10.803/2003, with the *José Pereira* case acting as a catalyst for this process.

Caso Trabalhadores da Fazenda Brasil Verde v Brazil,[69] a landmark judgment of the IACtHR, also dealt with practices of forced labour and debt bondage, but in a different context – a cattle ranch located in the municipality of Sapucaia, in the south of the state of Pará. Although the Brazilian Government made efforts to address slave labour during the 2000s, largely in response to key recommendations from the IACmHR in the *José Pereira* case, the anti-trafficking legal and policy framework in Brazil was – and remains – not fully compliant with the Palermo Protocol, nor the American Convention on Human Rights (ACHR). In 2016, the IACtHR ruled in this case that Brazil had violated the right not to be subjected to slavery, forced labour and human trafficking

[66] Interviewee BR09. Article 149 reads (in its original language): 'Reduzir alguém *a condição análoga à de escravo*, quer submetendo-o a trabalhos forçados ou a jornada exaustiva, quer sujeitando-o a condições degradantes de trabalho, quer restringindo, por qualquer meio, sua locomoção em razão de dívida contraída com o empregador ou preposto' (emphasis added). The translation of the Palermo Protocol reads, at Article 3: 'A exploração deverá incluir, pelo menos, a exploração da prostituição de outrem ou outras formas de exploração sexual, o trabalho ou serviços forçados, *a escravatura ou práticas similares à escravatura*, a servidão ou a extracção de órgãos' (emphasis added). The italicised terms are to be considered synonyms.

[67] Interviewee BR09.

[68] *José Pereira v Brazil* (IACmHR, 24 October 2003), discussed by Interviewees BR03 and BR06.

[69] *Caso Trabalhadores da Fazenda Brasil Verde v Brazil* (IACtHR, 20 October 2016).

(Articles 6(1) and 6(2) of the ACHR), among several other rights. The Court further ruled that the Brazilian government had to investigate the case, pay reparations to victims and stop applying the statute of limitations to cases that fell under the definition of slavery in international law. The decision was referred to in the context of two significant changes in anti-trafficking efforts. With respect to the duty to prosecute, following the IACtHR judgment, the Brazilian Government created a task force of prosecutors to identify and investigate situations of trafficking. With respect to the non-pecuniary measures ordered by the Court, an amendment to the Constitution was introduced in April 2017 to establish that the submission of a person to a condition analogous to slavery constitutes an imprescriptible crime. Although the owners of the cattle ranch filed a motion to dismiss in the Federal Court for the First Region, arguing that the statute of limitations had expired, in 2018 the Federal Court ruled that the statute of limitations did not apply, upholding the 2016 ruling by the IACtHR.

However, while important, the case of *Fazenda Brasil Verde* cannot be directly or conclusively linked with any substantive legislative anti-trafficking development in Brazil. Indeed, Law n. 13.344 (2016) was enacted in the same month as the IACtHR's decision, and only gave the judgment a 'symbolic weight'. There has also been very limited engagement of UN Treaty Bodies with respect to anti-trafficking efforts in Brazil. A rare instance has been the 2015 Concluding Observations on the Combined Second to Fourth Periodic Reports of Brazil by the Committee on the Rights of the Child (CRC). The CRC affirmed that it was 'deeply concerned about the trafficking in children, particularly girls, for the purposes of sexual exploitation and forced labour' and that it was 'particularly concerned about the high vulnerability of indigenous children to trafficking for the purposes of domestic labour, slave labour and sexual exploitation'.[70] Building on a recommendation issued by the Special Rapporteur on Contemporary Forms of Slavery, including its Causes and Consequences,[71] the CRC recommended that the State party 'amend its Penal Code with a view to criminalizing all forms of

[70] Committee on the Rights of the Child, Concluding Observations on the Combined Second to Fourth Periodic Reports of Brazil (30 October 2015) UN Doc CRC/C/BRA/CO/2-4, para 85.

[71] See Human Rights Council, 'Report of the Special Rapporteur on Contemporary Forms of Slavery, including its Causes and Consequences, Gulnara Shahinian: Mission to Brazil' (30 August 2010) UN Doc A/HRC/15/20/Add.4, para 118.

trafficking, including for the purpose of economic exploitation', and that it '[e]stablish specialized shelters with adequate human, technical and financial resources'.[72] Yet, it appears that the determinants that influenced the 2016 legislative process pre-dated the result in the case of *Fazenda Brasil Verde*, and were not directly related to the recommendations of UN Treaty Bodies – in contrast with the impact the IACtHR had on anti-modern slavery efforts in Brazil through the case of *José Pereira*, which was identified as a key determinant by several in-country expert interviewees. The Brazilian case study highlights how the relevance and effectiveness (level of influence) of a determinant can vary across the range of anti-trafficking efforts, including in distinct areas of anti-trafficking law and policy. Regional judicial and quasi-judicial decisions have been significant in Brazil in influencing actions against trafficking for the purpose of forced labour, arguably compensating for a lack of interest and engagement with the phenomenon on the part of law-makers and domestic courts, but less significant in actions against other forms of trafficking (although some changes achieved through decisions on forced labour have had an impact across all types of exploitation, including the establishment of a task force of specialised prosecutors).

15.3.3 *Republic of Cyprus*

The Republic of Cyprus (RoC) enacted anti-trafficking legislation criminalising all major trafficking offences in 2014 through Law 60(I)/2014,[73] which transposes European Council Directives 2011/36/EU and 2004/81/EC. The 2014 legislation includes provisions on victim protection and the establishment of a national co-ordinator for anti-trafficking efforts and a multidisciplinary co-ordination group to provide more holistic insights into the State's and civil society's anti-trafficking initiatives and co-operation. Law 60(I)/2014 was amended in 2019,[74] to increase the maximum sentences for the crime of trafficking in persons. According to interviewees in the RoC, it was international pressure, including in the form of regional courts' case law (ECtHR), that led to the 2014 legislative

[72] Committee on the Rights of the Child (n 63) para 86.

[73] Law 60(I)/2014 on the Prevention and Combating of Trafficking in and Exploitation of Persons and Protection of Victims, available (in Greek) at www.ilo.org/dyn/natlex/docs/ELECTRONIC/100603/120777/F-1323565589/CYP100603%20Grk.pdf.

[74] Law 117(I)/2019 on the Prevention and Combating of Trafficking in and Exploitation of Persons and Protection of Victims (Amendment).

changes. Increasingly, they also argued, international standards are being used to draw attention to and demand better implementation of the law.

In *Rantsev v Cyprus and Russia*,[75] in assessing Cyprus' positive obligation to put in place an appropriate legislative and administrative framework, the ECtHR noted the applicant's complaint as to the inadequacy of Cypriot trafficking legislation but did not consider that the circumstances of the case gave rise to any concern in this regard. According to the Court, Cyprus' domestic anti-trafficking legislation reflected the provisions of the Palermo Protocol, prohibited trafficking and sexual exploitation, with consent providing no defence to the offence, and provided for a duty to protect trafficked persons, *inter alia*, through the appointment of a guardian.[76] The Court, however, noted, 'as regards the general legal and administrative framework and the adequacy of Cypriot immigration policy, a number of weaknesses',[77] finding that 'the regime of artiste visas in Cyprus did not afford to Ms Rantseva practical and effective protection against trafficking and exploitation'.[78] The ECtHR's reference to 'artiste visas' relates to the existence at the time of a visa system that allowed women to come to the country and work as dancers in cabarets – although it was widely acknowledged that many of these women were forced into prostitution. *Rantsev*, which was specifically concerned with trafficking for sexual exploitation purposes, has not only sensitised the RoC authorities to this type of trafficking and its victims (almost always women),[79] but also international organisations and local NGOs are more likely to place emphasis on this issue because of the RoC's history with it.

The ECtHR's finding was instrumental in abolishing the artiste visa. When the law changed, cabarets stopped being financially viable and most of them closed, which provides an example of how one anti-trafficking determinant (international standards) contributed to another (economic conditions) in a way that had a positive impact on anti-trafficking efforts. The standards communicated to the RoC, including in the form of a decision of the ECtHR, pressured the RoC to change the

[75] App no 25965/04 (ECtHR, 7 January 2010).
[76] Ibid., para 72.
[77] Ibid para 291.
[78] Ibid para 293.
[79] This was among the conclusions of the Ombudsman's Report on the Framework for the Preventing and Combatting of Human Trafficking in Cyprus (17 October 2013). The Ombudsman stated that: 'The *Rantsev* case provided the starting point for the development of a substantially improved legislative and institutional framework on human trafficking in the last decade' (our translation, para 125).

existing legislative framework and to undertake more consistent and genuine efforts to address human trafficking. The impact of international pressure – which also continued to be exerted in the form of international reporting from the United States Department of State, GRETA and UN Treaty Bodies[80] – on the enactment and monitoring of anti-trafficking legislation was acknowledged in interviews by key stakeholders working for the government. Yet this only appears to have had a superficial or transient effect: the decrease in sexual exploitation in clubs and cabarets has been followed by an increase in prostitution and sexual exploitation in private houses and flats.[81]

While there are no individual complaints before UN Treaty Bodies with respect to the RoC and trafficking, the 2017 Law on Societies and Institutions,[82] regulating, *inter alia*, the operations of civil society organisations, was subject to scrutiny through UN Special Procedures. In March 2021, several mandates, including the mandate of the Special Rapporteur on Trafficking in Persons, Especially Women and Children, addressed with concern the information received on the deteriorating environment for civil society organisations in Cyprus in the context of a 2020 amendment to the Law on Associations and Foundations and Other Related Issues. In particular, the letter was concerned with the alleged deregistration of Action for Support, Equality and Antiracism (KISA) from the Register of Associations and Foundations on 14 December 2020.[83] KISA is an NGO that, *inter alia*, provides support to migrants,

[80] See in particular, Committee against Torture, 'Concluding Observations on the Fourth Report of Cyprus' (16 June 2014) UN Doc CAT/C/CYP/CO/4, para 10: 'The State party should: . . . (c) Monitor and assess the new visa regime to prevent its potential misuse by traffickers and urgently activate the national referral mechanism.'

[81] A Constantinou, 'Is Crime Displacement Inevitable? Lessons from the Enforcement of Laws Against Prostitution-Related Human Trafficking in Cyprus' (2016) 13(2) *European Journal of Criminology* 214; Fondation Scelles, 'Cyprus' (2019) 3, available at http://fondationscelles.org/pdf/RM5/CYPRUS_Excerpt_5th_Global_Report_Fondation_SCELLES_2019.pdf. This remains the situation despite recommendations issued by UN Treaty Bodies, including CEDAW, Concluding Observations on the Eighth Periodic Report of Cyprus (4 July 2018) UN Doc CEDAW/C/CYP/CO/8, para 29; and Committee on Economic, Social and Cultural Rights, Concluding Observations on the Sixth Periodic Report of Cyprus (28 October 2016) UN Doc E/C.12/CYP/CO/6, para 33.

[82] Law 104(I)/2017 on Societies and Institutions and Other Related Matters, available (as amended) at www.moi.gov.cy/moi/moi.nsf/pagede1a_gr/5D832FF3EA6E4154C225855F00377B3B/$file/The%20Societies%20law%20(English%20translation).pdf.

[83] Letter to the government of Cyprus from UN Special Rapporteurs (31 March 2021) AL CYP 1/2021, available at https://spcommreports.ohchr.org/TMResultsBase/DownLoadPublicCommunicationFile?gId=26312.

asylum seekers and trafficked persons. In addressing the government of Cyprus, the Special Rapporteurs drew attention to the Palermo Protocol, ratified by the RoC in 2003, which obliges State Parties to refrain from acts which would defeat or undermine the Protocol's objectives and purposes, including to prevent and combat trafficking in persons, to ensure assistance to trafficked persons and to provide effective remedies.

The Cypriot case study highlights the significant influence of regional judicial decisions in improving anti-trafficking efforts. Yet it also highlights that without a meaningful and holistic follow-up and without political will among State actors, the change(s) derived from such judicial decisions might be formalistic or superficial changes that conceal a reality of continued exploitation and weak responses in practice.

15.3.4 United Kingdom

Over the last decade, the United Kingdom's anti-trafficking response has undergone considerable development and progression. Dedicated statutes have been enacted: the Modern Slavery Act 2015 ('MSA 2015')[84] in England and Wales, the Human Trafficking and Exploitation (Scotland) Act 2015[85] and the Human Trafficking and Exploitation (Criminal Justice and Support for Victims) Act (Northern Ireland) 2015.[86] These statutes have, *inter alia*, created the role of the Independent Anti-Slavery Commissioner[87] and introduced new provisions designed to tackle labour exploitation in supply chains,[88] to place the principle of non-prosecution of trafficked persons on a statutory footing[89] and to better support child victims through the appointment of Independent Child

[84] Modern Slavery Act 2015 (MSA 2015).

[85] Human Trafficking and Exploitation (Scotland) Act 2015.

[86] Human Trafficking and Exploitation (Criminal Justice and Support for Victims) Act (Northern Ireland) 2015.

[87] MSA 2015 (n 76) Part 4.

[88] Ibid. section 54, which applies to any commercial organisation (wherever incorporated or formed) with over £36m turnover that carries on a business, or part of a business, in any part of the United Kingdom. In 2021 the government launched a central public registry for modern slavery statements, available at https://modern-slavery-statement-registry.service.gov.uk/.

[89] MSA 2015 (n 76) section 45; Human Trafficking and Exploitation (Scotland) Act (n 77) section 8; and Exploitation (Criminal Justice and Support for Victims) Act (Northern Ireland) (n 78) section 22.

Trafficking Guardians.[90] These measures are supported by statutory and non-statutory guidance.[91] Central and devolved governments have also produced modern slavery strategies[92] and published annual reports.[93]

The ratification of international and regional legal frameworks, combined with the sustained efforts of civil society organisations and survivor networks and the role of regional and domestic courts in holding the government to account, have placed significant pressure on the United Kingdom's government to develop its anti-trafficking domestic law and policy. The adoption of the National Referral Mechanism (NRM) in 2009, for example, was a result of the obligations flowing from the ECAT. The ECAT was also instrumental in the ECtHR's analysis in the case of *CN v United Kingdom*,[94] where the core of the claim was whether the absence, at the time of the events, of a specific prohibition on servitude and forced labour was at the basis of the failure to properly investigate the applicant's complaints. Indeed, although domestic authorities did investigate the applicant's complaints, it was submitted that the investigation was deficient because the lack of specific legislation criminalising domestic servitude meant that it was not directed at determining whether or not she had been a victim of treatment contrary to Article 4 of

[90] MSA 2015 (n 76) section 48 (not yet commenced); Human Trafficking and Exploitation (Scotland) Act (n 77) section 11; Exploitation (Criminal Justice and Support for Victims) Act (Northern Ireland) (n 78) section 21.

[91] Home Office, 'Modern Slavery: Statutory Guidance for England and Wales (under section 49 of the Modern Slavery Act 2015) and Non-Statutory Guidance for Scotland and Northern Ireland' (first published March 2020, latest version dated 14 June 2021); Home Office, 'Statutory Guidance: Transparency in Supply Chains: A Practical Guide' (first published in 2015, latest version dated 22 July 2021); Welsh Government, 'Code of Practice; Ethical Employment in Supply Chains' (2017); Welsh Government, 'Tackling Modern Slavery in Government Supply Chains; A Guide for Commercial and Procurement Professionals' (2019), Welsh Government, 'Tackling Modern Slavery in PPE Supply Chains': Practical Guides for Both PPE Suppliers and Public Bodies (April 2021); Home Office, 'Interim Guidance on Independent Child Trafficking Guardians' (May 2021) which should be read in conjunction with the Department for Education statutory guidance for local authorities, 'Care of Unaccompanied Migrant Children and Child Victims of Modern Slavery' (November 2017).

[92] UK Modern Slavery Strategy (November 2014), Scottish Government Trafficking and Exploitation Strategy (2017); Northern Ireland's Modern Slavery Strategies.

[93] UK Annual Reports on Modern Slavery and Scottish Government Annual Progress Reports on Trafficking and Exploitation Strategy.

[94] App No 4239/08 (ECtHR, 13 November 2012).

the European Convention on Human Rights (ECHR).[95] The ECtHR found, similar to *Siliadin v France*,[96] that the offences existing at the time of the events (trafficking, false imprisonment, kidnapping, grievous bodily harm, assault, battery, blackmail and harassment) were 'inadequate to afford practical and effective protection against treatment falling within the scope of Article 4 of the Convention'.[97] In other words, according to the Court, 'the criminal law in force at the material time did not afford practical and effective protection against treatment falling within the scope of Article 4 of the Convention'.[98] Although section 71 of the Coroners and Justice Act 2009 was enacted on 6 April 2010,[99] hence before the decision of the ECtHR in 2012, the 2013 Draft Modern Slavery Bill ECHR Memorandum confirms that the 'offence in section 71 was enacted to addresses the criticisms of the United Kingdom in the

[95] Article 4 of the ECHR provides that:

1. No one shall be held in slavery or servitude.
2. No one shall be required to perform forced or compulsory labour.
3. For the purpose of this article the term 'forced or compulsory labour' shall not include:
   (a) any work required to be done in the ordinary course of detention imposed according to the provisions of Article 5 of [the] Convention or during conditional release from such detention;
   (b) any service of a military character or, in case of conscientious objectors in countries where they are recognised, service exacted instead of compulsory military service;
   (c) any service exacted in case of an emergency or calamity threatening the life or well-being of the community;
   (d) any work or service which forms part of normal civic obligations.

[96] App no 73316/01 (ECtHR, 26 July 2005).

[97] *CN v United Kingdom* App No 4239/08 (ECtHR, 13 November 2012) para 76.

[98] Ibid., para 77.

[99] This Article provided as follows:
Slavery, servitude and forced or compulsory labour

(1) A person (D) commits an offence if –
   (a) D holds another person in slavery or servitude and the circumstances are such that D knows or ought to know that the person is so held, or
   (b) D requires another person to perform forced or compulsory labour and the circumstances are such that D knows or ought to know that the person is being required to perform such labour.
(2) In subsection (1) the references to holding a person in slavery or servitude or requiring a person to perform forced or compulsory labour are to be construed in accordance with Article 4 of the Human Rights Convention (which prohibits a person from being held in slavery or servitude or being required to perform forced or compulsory labour).

[ECtHR's] *CN v UK*'.[100] This is a situation where the filing of the case, highlighting deficiency in the law and policy, was enough to engage positive change.

Section 71 of the Coroners and Justice Act 2009 is not the only development in anti-trafficking efforts heavily influenced by decisions (and processes) of courts, tribunals or non-judicial bodies in the United Kingdom. Lawyers and the courts, in applying regional legal frameworks to enforce victim's rights enshrined in ECAT, ultimately compelled government action in several other instances. Domestic courts have also played an important role in shaping law and policy. The following are non-exhaustive examples of significant case law: *Atamewan v Secretary of State for the Home Department* led to amended guidance ensuring the proper identification of historic victims of trafficking;[101] *L v Children's Commissioner for England* resulted in new Crown Prosecution Service guidance on the non-punishment of victims provisions in ECAT and the EU Directive;[102] *Hounga v Allen* enabled some employment law rights to be applicable to irregular migrants insofar as the Supreme Court held that the doctrine of illegality arising from the employment of an 'illegal migrant' did not defeat a claim of employment discrimination brought by the same trafficked migrant worker;[103] in *Benkharbouche and Janah* the Supreme Court found the application of State immunity to employment claims brought by members of embassy staff in the United Kingdom to be incompatible with Article 6 of the ECHR, and led to the disapplication of those provisions to claims founded in EU law;[104] in *PK (Ghana) v Secretary of State for the Home Department*, the Court declared the government's policy guidance relating to the grant of discretionary leave for victims of trafficking to be unlawful for failure to give effect to the objectives of Article 14(1)(a) of the ECAT, and emphasised that new guidance should make clear that a renewal residence permit should be issued to a trafficked person where their stay is necessary, through a test that is simply one of necessity – meaning that there is no additional

[100] Home Office, 'Draft Modern Slavery Bill: European Convention on Human Rights Memorandum' (2013) para 6.
[101] *Atamewan v Secretary of State for the Home Department* [2013] EWHC 2727 (Admin).
[102] *L v Children's Commissioner for England* [2013] EWCA Crim 991.
[103] *Hounga v Allen* [2014] UKSC 47.
[104] *Secretary of State for Foreign and Commonwealth Affairs v Benkharbouche and Secretary of State for Foreign and Commonwealth Affairs and Libya v Janah* [2017] UKSC 62.

requirement for the individual to show compelling circumstances;[105] in *K and AM v Secretary of State for the Home Department* the Court found the reduction of 42 per cent in subsistence rates for trafficked persons to be unlawful, and an employment contract change which took effect on 1 March 2018 was quashed;[106] and the case of *NN v Secretary of State for the Home Department* resulted in the introduction of a new process and guidance to assess the support needs of survivors beyond the previous NRM exit timescales.[107]

As in the case of the RoC, while there are no individual complaints before UN Treaty Bodies, the UN Special Procedures have engaged with the UK Government on a number of occasions with respect to anti-trafficking efforts.[108] In May 2021, for example, the Special Rapporteurs on Contemporary Forms of Slavery, on Human Rights of Migrants and on Trafficking in Persons addressed concerns around changes to the overseas domestic worker visa and the Immigration Act.[109] Under the

[105] *PK (Ghana) v Secretary of State for the Home Department* [2018] EWCA Civ 98. Under the new guidance, '[in] seeking to [decide whether a grant of leave is necessary,] decision makers should primarily: assess whether a grant of leave to a recognised victim is necessary for the UK to meet its objective under the [ECAT] – to provide protection and assistance to that victim, owing to their personal situation'. See Home Office, 'Discretionary Leave Considerations for Victims of Modern Slavery Version 4.0' (2020) 6.

[106] *K and AM v Secretary of State for the Home Department* [2018] EWHC 2951.

[107] *NN v Secretary of State for the Home Department* (n 14). See also Home Office, 'Recovery Needs Assessment Guidance' (2019).

[108] There has only been limited engagement of UN Treaty Bodies, e.g., Committee against Torture, 'Concluding Observations on the Sixth Periodic Report of the United Kingdom of Great Britain and Northern Ireland' (7 June 2019) UN Doc CAT/C/GBR/CO/6, paras 58–59: 'The State party should: (a) Enhance its efforts to investigate claims of human trafficking and prosecute perpetrators and ensure that victims of trafficking obtain compensation, including by considering creating a civil remedy for victims of trafficking; (b) Ensure access to sufficient protection and support for all victims of trafficking and, in particular, ensure that the State party's establishment of a child trafficking protection fund results in an improvement in the availability of specialist care and support for child victims of trafficking'; and CEDAW, 'Concluding Observations on the Eighth Periodic Report of the United Kingdom of Great Britain and Northern Ireland' (26 February 2019) UN Doc CEDAW/C/GBR/CO/8, para 34: 'The Committee recommends that the State party: (a) Ensure that the definition of trafficking in persons in its national legislation is in line with the internationally agreed definition set out in the Protocol to Prevent, Suppress and Punish Trafficking in Persons, Especially Women and Children . . .; (b) Adopt a comprehensive national strategy to combat trafficking in women and girls . . .; (c) Continue to improve the national referral mechanism . . . '.

[109] Letter to the government of the United Kingdom from UN Special Rapporteurs (27 May 2021) AL GBR 6/2021, available at https://spcommreports.ohchr.org/TMResultsBase/DownLoadPublicCommunicationFile?gId=26423.

amended Immigration Rules, all migrant domestic workers were granted the option to change employer, but only for the remaining term of their six-month visa, which was non-renewable. Migrant domestic workers found to be trafficked were granted the possibility of applying for limited leave to remain in the United Kingdom for up to two years, with permission to work as domestic workers. In its response to the letter, the government acknowledged that 'the UK gives careful considerations to all recommendations by human rights bodies' and that, on the basis of such recommendations, 'officials in the Home Office are in the process of developing proposals to reform the [tied visa] route from next year'.[110]

UN Special Procedures also engaged in March 2021 with the alleged role of *Omegle*, a live video-chat website based in the United States, in facilitating self-generated and live video-streamed sexual activities and material online that depicts or otherwise represents children appearing to engage in sexually explicit conduct.[111] In June 2021, the government provided its response, mentioning the intention 'to introduce legislation on tackling online harms, including child sexual abuse' and the publication of draft legislation in May 2021 (currently under parliamentary discussion).[112]

It is also worth mentioning that in January 2021 several mandates issued a letter to, *inter alia*, the UK Government with respect to the situation of the Al-Hol and Roj camps located in north-east Syria.[113] The letter called on States to be particularly mindful of 'the potential for coercion, co-opting, grooming, trafficking, enslavement and sexual exploitation when examining [womens' and girls'] agency, or lack thereof' in the context of their association with terrorist groups. The letter further emphasised the positive obligation on States to identify

[110] UK Mission Geneva, Note Verbale No 205 (28 July 2021), available at https://spcommreports.ohchr.org/TMResultsBase/DownLoadFile?gId=36472.

[111] Letter to the government of the United Kingdom from UN Special Rapporteurs (30 March 2021) AL GBR 3/2021, available at https://spcommreports.ohchr.org/TMResultsBase/DownLoadPublicCommunicationFile?gId=26076.

[112] See Draft Online Safety Bill, available at www.gov.uk/government/publications/draft-online-safety-bill.

[113] Letter to the government of the United Kingdom from UN Special Rapporteurs (26 January 2021) AL GBR 2/2021, available at https://spcommreports.ohchr.org/TMResultsBase/DownLoadPublicCommunicationFile?gId=25972. In the past, the UN Special Rapporteur on the Promotion and Protection of Human Rights and Fundamental Freedoms while Combatting Terrorism also intervened in the Shamima Begum case. Both interventions are available at www.ohchr.org/EN/Issues/Terrorism/Pages/AmicusBriefsExpertTestimony.aspx.

trafficked persons, as 'a failure to identify a trafficked person correctly is likely to result in a further denial of that person's right'. Although the government only partially agreed with the assertions made by the Special Rapporteurs, its response provided justifications of existing practices and policies that allow for a better understanding of, and arguably provide for better counter-argumentation against, such practices and policies. The engagement by the government with these assertions also reflects the weight given to the same by the government and their potential for influencing government discussions.

The UK case study provides, amongst the four case studies presented in this chapter, the most complex and comprehensive picture of how judicial, quasi-judicial and specialised non-judicial bodies influence anti-trafficking efforts, alone or in conjunction with one another. Decisions of judicial bodies tend to result in tangible changes in anti-trafficking efforts while the engagement of specialised non-judicial bodies has been instrumental in opening and fostering dialogue with State actors on activities or developments – in policy and in law – considered at risk, or as producing risks, of trafficking and exploitation.

15.4 Conclusion

In all four case studies, decisions of judicial bodies – either domestic or regional – have played a significant role in advancing anti-trafficking efforts and protecting trafficked persons' rights. The jurisprudence of regional human rights courts has influenced both government actions and domestic courts' interpretation of anti-trafficking law, as well as human rights law provisions relevant to anti-trafficking efforts. They have resulted in the introduction of new measures, the withdrawal of existing measures and more human rights-conformant interpretations of existing legislation. Quasi-judicial human rights bodies, including the UN Treaty Bodies, are not yet consistently engaged in human trafficking cases and – in their non-judicial role, do not consistently engage with anti-trafficking concerns during periodic reviews. Yet the potential of their impact on the improvement of anti-trafficking efforts should not be ignored. Indeed, quasi-judicial bodies can be viewed as contributors to international lawmaking – influencing the interpretation, clarification and refinement of State duties and responsibilities.[114] While courts and

[114] See e.g., M Tignino, 'Quasi-Judicial Bodies' in C Brölmann and Y Radi (eds), *Research Handbook on the Theory and Practice of International Lawmaking* (Edward Elgar

quasi-judicial human rights bodies tend, by their very nature, to be reactive in nature, and the burden of initiating proceedings remains with individuals whose rights have been violated, specialised non-judicial bodies, including UN Special Procedures and Treaty Bodies in their reporting function, are, and can be, more proactive in nature. The engagement of the UN Special Rapporteurs, both in terms of country visits and thematic reports as well as through letters, has increased sharply in recent years. While responses from governments to communications of Special Rapporteurs might be circumstantial and may be labelled 'empty promises', our research has shown that the engagement that governments need to show – and for which they could be held accountable, at least in terms of international reputation – is a meaningful element in the development of anti-trafficking efforts.[115]

The analysis of decisions and observations in different contexts has shown the inter-dependence of judicial, quasi-judicial and specialised non-judicial bodies, which rely on each other – insofar as interpretation and standards are concerned – to safeguard the rights of trafficked persons and steer governments to comply with their international, regional and domestic obligations. It has also shown that the variety in the type of external pressure applied – for example, binding judgments and 'soft' pressure – can be used strategically to promote change and to ensure that change is sustainable. Because determinants of anti-trafficking efforts, understood as the factors shaping government responses, do not work in isolation, but rather are part of a broader process, it would be wrong to assume that decisions and observations of

Publishing 2016); BG Ramcharan, *United Nations Protection of Humanity and Its Habitat: A New International Law of Security and Protection* (Brill 2016) 47–53.

[115] This finding is consistent with research in other areas including in the context of economic, social and cultural rights (see C Golay, C Mahon and I Cismas, 'The Impact of the UN Special Procedures on the Development and Implementation of Economic, Social and Cultural Rights' (2011) 15(2) *The International Journal of Human Rights* 299); country-specific mandates (see M Montoya and M Limon, 'History Shows that UN Country-Specific Special Procedures are Tools for Positive Change' (2021) OpenGlobalRights, available at www.openglobalrights.org/history-shows-that-un-country-specific-special-procedures-are-tools-for-positive-change); human rights and development (see I Biglino, C Golay and I Truscan, 'The Contribution of the UN Special Procedures to the Human Rights and Development Dialogue' (2012) 9 (17) *SUR Revista Internacional de Direitos Humanos* 15; and human rights broadly (see I Nifosi Sutton, *The UN Special Procedures in the Field of Human Rights* (Intersentia 2006)).

judicial, quasi-judicial and specialised non-judicial bodies can in isolation yield the improved political will and capacity in national governments to address trafficking in persons. Yet, as demonstrated by the cases of Argentina, Brazil, the RoC and the United Kingdom, they are external points of pressure which can contribute to positive change.

16

The Growing Importance of Human Rights Treaty Bodies in Environmental Dispute Resolution

ALEXANDER SOLNTSEV

16.1 Introduction

This chapter evaluates the strengths and weaknesses of UN human rights treaty bodies (HRTB) in ensuring compliance with States' international environmental legal obligations and in resolving environmental disputes. The chapter begins with a discussion of the evolution of the "environmentalization" of international human rights law and goes on to analyze the standard functions of the HRTB as human rights treaty compliance mechanisms. Against this backdrop, the chapter considers HRTBs' contribution to ensuring compliance with States' climate-related human rights obligations, as a new trend in the greening of international human rights law and an area in which HRTB are now at the forefront of international compliance procedures. The chapter analyses HRTBs' concluding observations, general comments, and statements and specific cases dealt with by the Human Rights Committee[1] and the Committee on the Rights of the Child.[2] HRTBs' contribution to helping bring about States' compliance with international environmental legal obligations is then compared with other means of dispute resolution and compliance procedures, primarily non-compliance procedures under Multilateral Environmental Agreement (MEAs), demonstrating the positive aspects of the HRTB (the presence of a follow-up procedure, the coverage of a large number of States parties, the absence of the need to approve the decision by the Conference of the Parties), and the negative ones (the lack of legal force for the decisions).

[1] *Ioane Teitiota v New Zealand*, CCPR/C/127/D/2728/2016, UN Human Rights Committee (HRC), January 7, 2020, available at www.refworld.org/cases,HRC,5e26f7134.html, accessed 27 January 2022.

[2] *Sacchi et al. v Argentina et al.*, CRC/C/88/D/104/2019 (Argentina), CRC/C/88/D/105/2019 (Brazil), CRC/C/88/D/106/2019 (France), CRC/C/88/D/107/2019 (Germany), CRC/C/88/D/108/2019 (Turkey).

16.2 The Greening of Human Rights

Looking at the HRTB is important for a number of reasons. These include the absence of an International Environmental Court.[3] International courts' practice in environmental disputes is still in a state of evolution (for example, the unreasonably low level of compensation for environmental damage in *Certain Activities Carried Out by Nicaragua in the Border Area (Costa Rica v Nicaragua)*);[4] the procedural limitations of courts (for example, individuals cannot file a claim with the International Court of Justice (ICJ) or the International Tribunal for the Law of the Sea (ITLOS)); the lack of effective enforcement mechanisms (Japan did not comply with the ICJ's decision on Whaling in the Antarctic[5] and subsequently withdrew from the International Convention for the Regulation of Whaling);[6] and the limited practice of regional human rights courts (including in Asia, where more than 4.5 billion people do not have a regional court or human rights commission that would accept complaints from individuals or NGOs).[7] It should be clarified that, in general, regional human rights courts (the European Court of Human Rights, the Inter-American Court of Human Rights and the African Court on Human and Peoples' Rights) contribute to the

[3] A Solntsev, "The International Environmental Court: A Necessary Institution for Sustainable Planetary Governance in the Anthropocene" in M Lim (ed), *Charting Environmental Law Futures in the Anthropocene* (Springer Nature Singapore 2019) 129–38; OW Pedersen, "An International Environmental Court and International Legalism" (2012) 24.3 *Journal of Environmental Law* 547–58.

[4] ICJ, *Certain Activities Carried Out by Nicaragua in the Border Area* (*Costa Rica v. Nicaragua*), compensation owed by the Republic of Nicaragua to the Republic of Costa Rica, Judgment of 2 February 2018. See more: D Desierto, 'Environmental Damages, Environmental Reparations, and the Right to a Healthy Environment: The ICJ Compensation Judgment in Costa Rica v. Nicaragua and the IACtHR Advisory Opinion on Marine Protection for the Greater Caribbean' (*EJIL:Talk! Blog of the European Journal of International Law*, February 14, 2018), available at www.ejiltalk.org/environmental-damages-environmental-reparations-and-the-right-to-a-healthy-environment-the-icj-compensation-judgment-in-costa-rica-v-nicaragua-and-the-iacthr-advisory-opinion-on-marine-protection; J Rudall, "Certain Activities Carried Out by Nicaragua in the Border Area (Costa Rica v. Nicaragua)" (2018) 112.2 *American Journal of International Law* 288–94.

[5] *Whaling in the Antarctic (Australia/Japan, New Zealand intervening)*, Judgment [2014] ICJ Reports 226.

[6] J McCurry, 'Japan to Resume Commercial Whaling One Day after Leaving the IWC' (*The Guardian*, January 25, 2019), available at www.theguardian.com/world/2019/jan/25/japan-to-resume-commercial-whaling-one-day-after-leaving-the-iwc.

[7] D Shelton and PG Carozza, *Regional Protection of Human Rights* (Vol 1, Oxford University Press 2013).

resolution of environmental disputes. For the purposes of this chapter, I mention their practices (especially since there are currently several cases pending before the European Court of Human Rights (ECtHR)), but I do not analyze them in detail, as they do not relate to HRTB and require separate in-depth scientific research. For all these reasons, it may be helpful to evaluate the extent to which HRTB can help address compliance with international environmental law. Human rights treaty bodies offer certain mechanisms for monitoring the implementation of the main international human rights treaties, which are widely ratified.[8]

Increasingly, human rights are linked to environmental protection and the issue of combating climate change.[9] Historically, this evolved in the following way. At the 1992 Conference on Environment and Development in Rio de Janeiro,[10] the world community recognized the problems of environmental harm. The following year, the Vienna Conference on Human Rights was held, following which the UN General Assembly established the Office of the UN High Commissioner for Human Rights. However, to the great regret of environmental lawyers, the Vienna Declaration and Plan of Action[11] had only one paragraph devoted to the protection of human rights in the context of environmental protection, and only in the narrow sense in relation to dumping of toxic and dangerous products and waste: "The right to development should be fulfilled so as to meet equitably the

[8] Status of ratification available at https://indicators.ohchr.org/. International Convention on the Elimination of All Forms of Racial Discrimination – 182; International Covenant on Civil and Political Rights – 173; International Covenant on Economic, Social and Cultural Rights – 171; Convention on the Elimination of All Forms of Discrimination against Women – 189; Convention against Torture and Other Cruel, Inhuman or Degrading Treatment or Punishment – 173; Convention on the Rights of the Child – 196; Convention on the Rights of Persons with Disabilities – 184; and two less popular: International Convention on the Protection of the Rights of All Migrant Workers and Members of their Families – 56; International Convention for the Protection of all Persons from Enforced Disappearance – 65.

[9] A Boyle, "Human Rights or Environmental Rights? A Reassessment" (2007) 18(3) *Fordham Environmental Law Review* 471–511; C Voigt, "The Climate Change Dimension of Human Rights: Due Diligence and States' Positive Obligations" in N Kobylarz and E Grant (eds), *Human Rights and the Planet* (Edward Elgar 2022) 152–71.

[10] M Grubb, M Koch, K Thomson, F Sullivan, and A Munson, "The 'Earth Summit' Agreements, A Guide and Assessment: An Analysis of the Rio '92 UN Conference on Environment and Development (Vol 9, Routledge 2019).

[11] Vienna Declaration and Plan of Action adopted by the World Conference on Human Rights in Vienna, 25 June 1993, available at www.ohchr.org/Documents/ProfessionalInterest/vienna.pdf.

developmental and environmental needs of present and future generations. The World Conference on Human Rights recognizes that illicit dumping of toxic and dangerous substances and waste potentially constitutes a serious threat to the human rights to life and health of everyone . . . ."[12]

In the almost thirty years since, a great deal has changed in this area, both at the universal and regional level of human rights protection. In recent years, a number of events have taken place in the field of environmental protection through the human rights system: two important HRC resolutions[13] and a draft additional protocol to the European Convention on Human Rights (ECHR) on the right to a healthy environment[14] were adopted, the 2018 Regional Agreement on Access to Information, Participation and Justice in Environmental Matters in Latin America and the Caribbean (the Escazú Agreement)[15] was adopted and entered into force in 2021; the UN Committee on the Rights of the Child in June 2021 launched discussion on the preparation of the General Comment on Children's Rights and the Environment with Special Focus on Climate Change;[16] and in September 2019 the HRTBs issued a joint

[12] Ibid., para 11.

[13] On October 8, 2021, the UN Human Rights Council adopted Resolution 48/13 of October 8, 2021, recognizing that the right to a clean, healthy, and sustainable environment is a human right. This decision is a major step forward. Although not legally binding, its near-unanimous adoption shows consensus on the formulation, content, and importance of this human right. On the same day, the HRC adopted Resolution 48/14, establishing a Special Rapporteur on the promotion and protection of human rights in the context of climate change.

[14] Recommendation 2211 (2021), "Anchoring the Right to a Healthy Environment: Need for Enhanced Action by the Council of Europe." Appendix – Text of the Proposal for an Additional Protocol to the European Convention on Human Rights, Concerning the Right to a Safe, Clean, Healthy and Sustainable Environment, available at https://pace.coe.int/en/news/8419/pace-committee-proposes-draft-of-a-new-protocol-to-the-european-convention-on-human-rights-on-the-right-to-a-healthy-environment?s=03.

[15] Regional Agreement on Access to Information, Public Participation and Justice in Environmental Matters in Latin America and the Caribbean 2018 (Escazú Agreement), entered into force 22 April 2021.

[16] The UN Committee on the Rights of the Child commits to a new General Comment on Children's Rights and the Environment with a Special Focus on Climate Change, available at www.ohchr.org/EN/NewsEvents/Pages/DisplayNews.aspx?NewsID=27139&LangID=E (accessed on November 28, 2022). The concept note of the general comment is now available at www.ohchr.org/en/treaty-bodies/crc/concept-note-general-comment-childrens-rights-and-environment-special-focus-climate-change, accessed on November 28, 2022.

statement on human rights and climate change.[17] And finally, for the first time in the history of the UN, the UN General Assembly in its Resolution 76/300 of 28 July 2022, recognized the human right to a clean, healthy, and sustainable environment.[18] The General Assembly affirmed that the promotion of the human right to a clean, healthy, and sustainable environment requires the full implementation of the multilateral environmental agreements under the principles of international environmental law. It also recognized that the exercise of human rights, including the rights to seek, receive, and impart information, to participate effectively in the conduct of government and public affairs, and to an effective remedy, is vital to the protection of a clean, healthy, and sustainable environment.

On the one hand, international human rights law provides a limited approach to protecting the environment. By and large, the purpose of this branch of international law is to protect a particular person (or group of persons), whereas in international environmental law the goal is to protect the environment as a common good.[19] On the other hand, the cumulative effect in synergy with other international mechanisms may help to protect the environment as a whole. The environmental developments in international human rights law addressed earlier will greatly enhance this cumulative effect. These developments will mean that HRTBs play an increasingly important role in helping bring about compliance with international environmental law.

16.3 Human Rights Treaty Bodies as Compliance Bodies

Human rights treaty bodies, as examples of compliance procedures, are an opportunity to issue policy-relevant recommendations addressing specifically the shortcomings of governments' environmental or climate policies from a human rights perspective.

It is important to keep in mind that human rights law at the international level has a wide range of protection and enforcement instruments that can be used to protect environmental human rights: HRTB,

[17] See Joint Statement on "Human Rights and Climate Change," available at www.ohchr.org/en/NewsEvents/Pages/DisplayNews.aspx?NewsID=24998&LangID=E, accessed on January 28, 2022.

[18] Resolution 76/300, adopted by the General Assembly 28 July 2022. The human right to a clean, healthy, and sustainable environment.

[19] B Mayer, "Climate Change Mitigation as an Obligation under Human Rights Treaties?" (2021) 115.3 *American Journal of International Law* 409–51.

Universal Periodic Reports (UPR), Human Rights Council, Special Procedures. In this chapter, I will study the role of HRTB. When I talk about HRTB as compliance mechanisms, I should think systematically and understand that there are various forms of their activity.

Human rights treaty bodies are committees of independent experts that monitor implementation of the core international human rights treaties. As of now, ten treaty bodies have been established: the Committee on the Elimination of Racial Discrimination (CERD);[20] the Committee on Economic, Social and Cultural Rights (CESCR);[21] the Human Rights Committee (CCPR);[22] the Committee on the Elimination of Discrimination against Women (CEDAW);[23] the Committee against Torture (CAT);[24] the Committee on the Rights of the Child (CRC);[25] the Committee on Migrant Workers (CMW);[26] the Subcommittee on Prevention of Torture and other Cruel, Inhuman or Degrading Treatment or Punishment (SPT);[27] the Committee on the Rights of Persons with Disabilities (CRPD);[28] and the Committee on Enforced Disappearances (CED).[29]

It is important to emphasize that the uniqueness lies in the fact that not a single international treaty under which HRTB were established contains provisions aimed at protecting the environment. Therefore, all environmental issues are derived through a broad interpretation of the

[20] CERD monitors the implementation of the International Convention on the Elimination of All Forms of Racial Discrimination, 4 January 1969.

[21] CESCR monitors the implementation of the International Covenant on Economic, Social and Cultural Rights, 3 January 1976.

[22] CCPR monitors the implementation of the International Covenant on Civil and Political Rights, 23 March 1976, and its optional protocols.

[23] CEDAW monitors the implementation of the Convention on the Elimination of All Forms of Discrimination against Women, 1979, and its optional protocol, 3 September 1981.

[24] CAT monitors the implementation of the Convention against Torture and Other Cruel, Inhuman or Degrading Treatment, 26 June 1987.

[25] CRC monitors the implementation of the Convention on the Rights of the Child, 2 September 1990, and its optional protocols.

[26] CMW monitors the implementation of the International Convention on the Protection of the Rights of All Migrant Workers and Members of Their Families, 1 July 2003.

[27] Established pursuant to the Optional Protocol of the Convention against Torture (OPCAT), 22 June 2006.

[28] CRPD monitors the implementation of the International Convention on the Rights of Persons with Disabilities, 3 May 2008.

[29] CED monitors the implementation of the International Convention for the Protection of All Persons from Enforced Disappearance, 23 December 2010.

texts of international treaties. The only exception is the 1980 Convention on the Rights of the Child, where Article 24(2(c)) states that:

> States Parties shall pursue full implementation of this right and, in particular, shall take appropriate measures: ... To combat disease and malnutrition, including within the framework of primary health care, through, *inter alia*, the application of readily available technology and through the provision of adequate nutritious foods and clean drinking water, taking into consideration the dangers and risks of environmental pollution ....[30]

The treaty bodies perform a number of functions aimed at monitoring how the treaties are being implemented by their State parties. All treaty bodies, with the exception of the Subcommittee on Prevention of Torture, are mandated to receive and consider *periodic reports* submitted by State parties detailing how they are applying the treaty provisions nationally. The examination of a report culminates in the adoption of "concluding observations" intended to give the reporting State practical advice and encouragement on further steps to implement the rights contained in the treaty. In its concluding observations, a treaty body will acknowledge the positive steps taken by the State, but also identify areas of concern, where more needs to be done to give full effect to the treaty's provisions. The treaty bodies seek to make their recommendations as concrete and practicable as possible. In addition, each of the treaty bodies publishes its interpretation of the provisions of its respective human rights treaty in the form of "general comments" or "general recommendations." These cover a wide range of subjects, from the comprehensive interpretation of substantive provisions (the right to water or the right to adequate food), to general guidance on the information that should be submitted in State reports relating to specific articles of the treaties. Most treaty bodies may consider *complaints or communications* from individuals (or group of individuals, or entity) alleging that their rights have been violated by a State party, provided that State has opted into this procedure. Human rights treaty bodies may also consider *interstate complaints* and their views or decisions. Although these procedures are "quasi-judicial," the decisions cannot be enforced directly by the committees. In many cases, however, State parties have implemented the committees' recommendations and granted a remedy to the

[30] Convention on the Rights of the Child 1989, available at www.ohchr.org/en/professionalinterest/pages/crc.aspx.

complainants. Some HRTB may also conduct *inquiries* if they receive reliable information containing well-founded indications of serious, grave, or systematic violations of the conventions in a State party.[31]

Moreover, if the State does not comply with the recommendations, it will be reminded of this as part of the *follow-up*. It is worth emphasizing separately that the follow-up procedure is extremely important for compliance in the field of international environmental law. Environmental disputes are predominantly of a continuing nature, and it is important to monitor the extent to which the measures taken by the State helped to correct the situation and establish the possibility of taking more precise appropriate measures to resolve the environmental dispute. Thus, follow-up makes it possible to resolve environmental disputes in a continuous process of dialogue. This is something that is often lacking in international courts and is also missing under MEA non-compliance procedures. All HRTB request State parties to provide information in their periodic reports on the implementation of the recommendations contained in previous concluding observations. It is important to note that all available sources of information (other HRTB, Special Procedures, the Universal Periodic Review, the United Nations system, regional human rights mechanisms, national human rights institutions (NHRIs), and NGOs) are considered for the follow-up assessment of a State party. It is a very open and transparent procedure. It should be noted that the details and timing of the follow-up procedure vary from committee to committee.[32] Follow-up covers individual communications: (1) compliance (measures taken are satisfactory or largely satisfactory); (2) partial compliance (measures taken are partially satisfactory, but additional information or action is required); (3) non-compliance (reply received but measures taken are not satisfactory or do not implement the views or are irrelevant to the views); (4) no reply (no cooperation or no reply received). Moreover, as previously noted, the UN has a whole system of human rights bodies, and the implementation of concluding observations and HRTB opinions can also be called upon

31 See the United Nations Human Rights Treaty System Fact Sheet No 30/Rev.1., United Nations, New York and Geneva, 2012, 32–33, available at www.ohchr.org/sites/default/files/Documents/Publications/FactSheet30Rev1.pdf.

32 OHCHR, "Follow-Up to Concluding Observations, Treaty Bodies," available at www.ohchr.org/en/hrbodies/pages/followupprocedure.aspx#:~:text=What%20is%20the%20follow%2Dup,contained%20in%20previous%20concluding%20observations.&text=These%20recommendations%20are%20clearly%20identified,end%20of%20the%20concluding%20observations.

through the UPR procedure, which is an additional compliance control mechanism.

There are many examples of environmental issues under the national reports/concluding observations procedure. For example, CESCR recommended that Argentina

> reconsider the large-scale exploitation of non-conventional fossil fuels through hydraulic fracturing in the Vaca Muerta region, in order to ensure compliance with its obligations under the Covenant, in the light of the Paris Agreement commitments. It also encourages the State party to promote alternative and renewable energy sources, reduce greenhouse gas emissions and set national targets with time-bound benchmarks.[33]

Or in 2020 the Committee recommended Norway

> intensify its efforts to achieve its nationally determined contribution under the Paris Agreement to reduce emissions by at least 50 per cent and towards 55 per cent compared to 1990 levels by 2030, and to promote alternative and renewable energy sources. It also recommends that the State party reconsider its decision to increase oil and natural gas exploitation and take its human rights obligations as a primary consideration in its natural resource exploitation and export policies.[34]

For example, in its concluding observations, the Human Rights Committee recommended Cabo Verde

> (a) strengthen its public policies and strategies aimed at mitigating the impact of natural disasters and climate change on the population and reducing the vulnerability of communities, including for those whose livelihood is dependent on climatic conditions, such as farmers; (b) improve the structural safety of houses and infrastructure; and (c) regularly update its contingency and relocation plans, in consultation with the communities concerned.[35]

Quasi-judicial functions are manifested at the time of consideration of complaints (individual, collective, interstate). If earlier HRTB considered complaints in the format of an individual/group of individuals against the State, recently there has been an increase in interstate complaints. In the fifty-year history of the treaty bodies, only three interstate or

[33] E/C.12/ARG/CO/4, para 13–15: "Concluding Observations on the Fourth Periodic Report of Argentina" (2018).

[34] E/C.12/NOR/CO/6, para 11: "Concluding Observations on the Sixth Periodic Report of Norway" (2020).

[35] E/C.12/CPV/CO/1, para 9: "Concluding Observations on the Initial Report of Cabo Verde" (2018).

State-to-State complaints have been registered (admissibility accepted on its merits) by the treaty bodies, all of them in 2018 by the CERD.[36] As a comparison, interstate complaints under MEA non-compliance procedures are also rare. But it is important to understand that this is generally possible in conditions where the jurisdiction of international courts is very limited.

There were several decisions on environmental complaints in HRTB. Unfortunately, few studies are available on the analysis of these decisions.[37] For example, in 2013, the UN Independent Expert on Human Rights and the Environment, John Knox, prepared reports on the protection of environmental rights in five HRTB: CESCR, HRC, CERD, CEDAW, and CRC.[38] This chapter will highlight four recent HRTB decisions: three on climate (very interesting legal provisions were presented that might be cited by other international courts in the future[39]), and one on pesticides – a positive outcome with a wide range of measures.

The Human Rights Committee in 2019 issued an opinion in the case of the use of agrochemicals and pesticides (*Portillo Cáceres et al. v Paraguay, 2019*).[40] A farming family in Paraguay petitioned the HRC claiming the mass use of agrotoxins by nearby large agrobusinesses had poisoned many local residents and led to the death of their relative, Ruben Portillo Cáceres. The HRC found violations of the family members' rights to life; to privacy, family, and home; and to an effective remedy, noting that the State had failed to adequately enforce environmental regulations and did not properly redress the resulting harms. In connection with this decision, important strategic questions arise in

[36] See the CERD webpage on inter-state complaints, available at www.ohchr.org/EN/HRBodies/CERD/Pages/InterstateCommunications.aspx. See also D Tamada, "Inter-State Communication under ICERD: From ad hoc Conciliation to Collective Enforcement?" (2021) 12.3 *Journal of International Dispute Settlement* 405–26; G Ulfstein, "Qatar v. United Arab Emirates" (2022) 116.2 *American Journal of International Law* 397–403.

[37] S Atapattu, UN Human Rights Institutions and the Environment: Synergies, Challenges, Trajectories (Routledge 2023).

[38] Mapping Report, available at www.ohchr.org/en/issues/environment/srenvironment/pages/mappingreport.aspx.

[39] For example, the ITLOS will likely do it soon. See "Press Release. The International Tribunal for the Law of the Sea Receives a Request for an Advisory Opinion from the Commission of Small Island States on Climate Change and International Law", available at https://itlos.org/fileadmin/itlos/documents/press_releases_english/PR_327_EN.pdf, accessed on December 14, 2022.

[40] *Portillo Cáceres and Others v. Paraguay* (2021) 193 *International Law Reports* 332–60.

the context of comparison with other international legal compliance procedures: (1) in what other international body can the collective environmental rights of people be protected; (2) what other international body can deal with banned pesticides (non-compliance procedures under Article 17 of the Stockholm Convention concerned only interstate cases); and (3) in what other international body can such an effective remedy be obtained systemically?[41]

It should also be emphasized here that HRTB are more independent than non-compliance procedures under MEAs, since there is no need to wait for the final approval of all decisions by the Meetings of State Parties of the human rights treaty (while decisions adopted by the non-compliance committees under some MEAs should be approved within the CoP/MoP, for example under the Aarhus Convention).[42]

It should be noted that sometimes HRTB are at the forefront of developing environmental human rights among various international courts and compliance procedures. It may be noted that the CESCR recognized the right to water (under the International Covenant on Economic, Social and Cultural Rights) in 2002 (General Comment No 15).[43] And since that time, the Committee has had the opportunity to ask States about the protection of the right to water in the framework of periodic reports. Only in 2010, after eight years, did the United Nations General Assembly (UNGA) vote to adopt Resolution A/64/292, formally recognizing "the right to safe and clean drinking water and sanitation as a human right that is essential for the full enjoyment of life and all human rights." As human rights have expanded in scope and

[41] (a) undertake an effective, thorough investigation into the events in question; (b) impose criminal and administrative penalties on all the parties responsible for the events in the present case; (c) make full reparation, including adequate compensation, to the authors for the harm they have suffered. The State party is also under an obligation to take steps to prevent similar violations in the future; (d) receive information from the State party within 180 days about the measures taken to give effect to the Committee's Views; (e) the State party is also requested to publish the present views and to disseminate them widely, particularly in a daily newspaper with a large circulation in the Department of Canindeyú: *Portillo Cáceres and Others v. Paraguay*, paras 9–10.

[42] R Churchill and G Ulfstein, "Autonomous Institutional Arrangements in Multilateral Environmental Agreements: A Little-Noticed Phenomenon in International Law' (2000) 94.4 *American Journal of International Law* 623–59.

[43] UN Committee on Economic, Social and Cultural Rights (CESCR), General Comment No 15: The Right to Water (Articles 11 and 12 of the Covenant), 20 January 2003, E/C.12/2002/11, available at www.refworld.org/docid/4538838d11.html, accessed 27 January 2022.

influence, the UNGA's 2010 Resolution has proclaimed international political recognition of this distinct right.

HRTB have become active in the field of combating climate change. They request relevant information from States when considering periodic reports (for example, information related to what measures States are taking to protect rights affected by climate change), and if they are not satisfied with the information provided, they make relevant concluding observations (some examples have already been mentioned). In addition, HRTB approve special statements: (1) In October 2018, the CESCR adopted a statement on "Climate Change and the International Covenant on Economic, Social and Cultural Rights";[44] (2) In September 2019, the five HRTB (CEDAW, CESCR, CMW, CRC, and CRPD) issued a joint statement on human rights and climate change.[45]

The field of action against climate change is also expanded by interpreting the legal content of human rights in general comments. Regarding the last point, it should be noted that four HRTB have already done this:

- the CESCR: General Comment No 15 (2002) on the Right to Water (Articles 11 and 12 of the International Covenant on Civil and Political Rights (hereinafter referred to as the ICCPR, Covenant));[46]
- the CRC: General Comment No 15 (2013) on the Right of the Child to the Enjoyment of the Highest Attainable Standard of Health (Article 24 of the Covenant),[47] and in June 2021 work was launched on a

[44] See United Nations Committee on Economic, Social and Cultural Rights. "Climate Change and the International Covenant on Economic, Social and Cultural Rights: Statement by the Committee on Economic, Social and Cultural Rights." UN Document E/C.12/2018/1, October 31, 2018, 3. Available at https://digitallibrary.un.org/record/1651395?ln=en, accessed on January 28, 2022.

[45] See Joint Statement on "Human Rights and Climate Change". Available at www.ohchr.org/en/NewsEvents/Pages/DisplayNews.aspx?NewsID=24998&LangID=E, accessed on January 28, 2022.

[46] See United Nations Committee on Economic, Social and Cultural Rights, "Substantive Issues Arising in the Implementation of the International Covenant on Economic, Social and Cultural Rights: General Comment No. 15." UN Document E/C.12/2020/11, 20 January 2003, available at www2.ohchr.org/english/issues/water/docs/CESCR_GC_15.pdf, accessed on January 28, 2022.

[47] See Committee on the Rights of the Child, "General Comment No. 15 (2013) on the Right of the Child to the Enjoyment of the Highest Attainable Standard of Health (Article 24)." UN Doc. CRC/C/GC/15, April 17, 2013, available at https://undocs.org/ru/CRC/C/GC/15, accessed on November 28, 2021.

General Comment on Children's Rights and the Environment with Special Focus on Climate Change;[48]

- CEDAW: General Recommendation No 37 (2018) on Gender-related Dimensions of Disaster Risk Reduction in the Context of Climate Change;[49]
- HRC: General Comment No 36 (2018) on Article 6 of the ICCPR on the right to life.[50]

In this way, the treaty bodies have paved the way for concrete decisions on complaints of human rights violations due to State action/omission. Particularly relevant is the HRC General Comment No 36 on Article 6 of the ICCPR on the right to life. Attention should be paid to paragraph 62 of the document ("Relationship of Article 6 with Other Articles of the Covenant and Other Legal Regimes"), which directly links "obligations to respect and ensure the right to life" and "measures taken by States parties to preserve the environment and protect it against climate change."[51]

As a comparison with other international compliance procedures, it should be noted that the creation of such documents as general comments is very effective and useful, since it allows the generalization of extensive practice and the acceptance of a legitimate document with official interpretation. Such documents could be accepted as part of the non-compliance procedure under MEAs.

48 UN, "The UN Committee on the Rights of the Child Commits to a New General Comment on Children's Rights and the Environment with a Special Focus on Climate Change", available at www.ohchr.org/EN/NewsEvents/Pages/DisplayNews.aspx?NewsID=27139&LangID=E, accessed on November 28, 2022. The concept note of the General Comment is now available at www.ohchr.org/en/treaty-bodies/crc/concept-note-general-comment-childrens-rights-and-environment-special-focus-climate-change, accessed on November 28, 2022.

49 See Committee on the Elimination of Discrimination against Women, "General Recommendation No. 37 on Gender-Related Dimensions of Disaster Risk Reduction in the Context of Climate Change." UN Doc. CEDAW/C/GC/37, March 13, 2018, available at https://tbinternet.ohchr.org/_layouts/15/treatybodyexternal/Download.aspx?symbolno=CEDAW/C/GC/37&Lang=e, accessed on November 28, 2021.

50 See Human Rights Committee, "General Comment No. 36. Article 6: The Right to Life." UN Doc. CCPR/C/GC/36, September 3, 2019, available at https://tbinternet.ohchr.org/_layouts/15/treatybodyexternal/Download.aspx?symbolno=CCPR/C/GC/36&Lang=en, accessed on November 28, 2021.

51 Committee on the Rights of the Child, "General Comment No. 36. Article 6: The Right to Life." UN Doc. CCPR/C/GC/36, September 3, 2019, available at https://tbinternet.ohchr.org/_layouts/15/treatybodyexternal/Download.aspx?symbolno=CCPR/C/GC/36&Lang=en, accessed on November 28, 2021.

16.4 Climate Complaints in HRTB

Recently, the number of "climate" claims around the world has been growing and HRTB are no exception. It is important to note three very high-profile cases in this section. The ECtHR is also considering complaints, but has not yet ruled on climate complaints,[52] the Inter-American Commission on Human Rights has rejected a climate case,[53] but the Inter-American Court on Human Rights (IACtHR) mentions this problem in their Advisory Opinion OC-23/17.[54] On 12 December 2022, the ITLOS received a request from the Commission of Small Island States on Climate Change and International Law to render an advisory opinion.[55] Therefore, legal judgments and arguments are extremely valuable.

Important to note is the world's first international decision on climate refugees (*Ioane Teitiota v New Zealand, 2020*) by the Human Rights Committee.[56] The UN Human Rights Committee considered the "climate" claim and, refusing a specific applicant, generally recognized that, based on the non-refoulement principles and subject to a number of criteria, "climate" refugees have the right not to be sent to a country where climate change leads to such disastrous consequences that a violation of the right to life can be claimed. In this case, in the opinion of the Committee, there was no life-threatening situation for the Teitiota; also because the relevant protective measures had already been taken in the Republic of Kiribati (2007 National Adaptation Programme of Action under the United Nations Framework Convention on Climate Change

[52] *Duarte Agostinho et Autres v. Portugal et 32 Autres États etc.*, 39371/20, November 13, 2020.

[53] Petition to the Inter-American Commission on Human Rights Seeking Relief from Violations of the Rights of Arctic Athabaskan Peoples Resulting from Rapid Arctic Warming and Melting Caused by Emissions of Black Carbon by Canada, available at https://climatecasechart.com/non-us-case/petition-inter-american-commission-human-rights-seeking-relief-violations-rights-arctic-athabaskan-peoples-resulting-rapid-arctic-warming-melting-caused-emissions/, accessed on November 28, 2021.

[54] Inter-American Court of Human Rights, "Advisory Opinion OC-23/17 of November 15, 2017, Requested by the Republic of Colombia: The Environment and Human Rights (State Obligations in Relation to the Environment in the Context of the Protection and Guarantee of the Rights to Life and to Personal Integrity: Interpretation and Scope of Articles 4(1) and 5(1) in Relation to Articles 1(1) and 2 of the American Convention on Human Rights)," available at www.corteidh.or.cr/docs/opiniones/seriea_23_ing.pdf.

[55] ITLOS, "Press Release. The International Tribunal for the Law of the Sea Receives a Request for an Advisory Opinion from the Commission of Small Island States on Climate Change and International Law." Available at https://itlos.org/fileadmin/itlos/documents/press_releases_english/PR_327_EN.pdf, accessed on December 14, 2022.

[56] *Ioane Teitiota v New Zealand* (n 1).

(UNFCCC)). It turns out that the fight against climate change is a State problem and carries a threat to the entire population. However, it is extremely difficult to prove an individual threat, so most of the "climate" claims are of a collective nature. However, the HRC did not rule out that such a situation might arise in the future. The case of *Ioane Teitiota v New Zealand* has become a milestone in the development of the practice of the HRC. Thus, a new interpretation of the "real risk of irreparable harm" was given; the connection between civil rights and economic and social rights was shown within the framework of a broad interpretation of the right to life; and the "climate" component of the right to life was demonstrated in practice. Now new standards have been set that may, in the future, contribute to the favorable outcome of other climate change refugee claims. Moreover, the Committee emphasized the need for the support of countries suffering from the effects of climate change by the international community. Thus, it was recorded that the obligations for cooperation in the field of counteracting the negative effects of climate change are *erga omnes*. If decisive action is not taken at both the international and national levels, entire States may disappear under water. In this case, the threat to life will become obvious, and the host States will no longer be able to deport those who request refugee status.[57]

An important difference between HRTB and many non-compliance procedures is the fact that the decisions are not always adopted by consensus, and it is possible to find separate opinions. In *Ioane Teitiota v New Zealand*, two experts were against (Duncan Laki Muhumuza and Vasilka Sancin) and added their individual opinions by Committee members.

A second case concerns Children's Rights and Climate Change at the UN CRC. I note the Communication to the CRC concerning climate change (*16 children (including G Thunberg) v Argentina, Brazil, France, Germany, Turkey, 2019*). On 11 October 2021, the CRC published its decisions on the admissibility of complaints brought against five States – Argentina, Brazil, France, Germany, and Turkey – by the 16 child complainants under the Optional Protocol to the Convention on the Rights of the Child on a Complaints Procedure (OPIC). The Committee ultimately

[57] A Solntsev, "Priotkryvaya yashchik Pandory: analiz mneniya Komiteta po pravam cheloveka o 'klimaticheskikh' bezhentsakh 2020 goda [Half-opening Pandora's Box: Review of the Human Rights Committee's 2020 View on Climate Refugees]" (2020) 10.3 *Mezhdunarodnoe pravosudie* 41–44 (in Russian). DOI: 10.21128/2226-2059-2020-3-41-54.

declared the complaints inadmissible due to non-exhaustion of domestic remedies. However, in doing so, the Committee found that a State party can be held responsible for the negative impact of its greenhouse gas emissions on the rights of children both within and outside its territory. With regard to extraterritorial jurisdiction, the CRC endorsed the above-mentioned IACtHR Advisory Opinion OC-23/17, which clarified in paragraph 101 the scope of extraterritorial jurisdiction concerning environmental protection. As stated by I Gubbay and C Wenzler, to establish extraterritorial jurisdiction, the CRC had to consider (i) the interpretation of "control," and (ii) the significance of directness and foreseeability.[58] Under the effective control test, the State in whose territory or under whose jurisdiction the activities are carried out has effective control over them, as well as the ability to prevent transboundary harm. Potential victims of the adverse effects of a State's actions are under the jurisdiction of that State regarding its potential responsibility for failing to avoid transboundary damage. Further, under the causal nexus test, when a State's act or omission is sufficiently connected to the violation, the person suffering the violation is considered to be within the State's jurisdiction. Following the IACtHR's reasoning, then, the CRC found that every State must address climate harm outside its territory and is liable for the negative impact of its emissions on the rights of children located both within and outside its territory.[59]

The decision significantly advances international human rights law understanding of the scope of State obligations in the context of climate change – both in terms of the content of such duties and their jurisdictional application. Although greeted with understandable dismay by some climate activists, the decision is a convincingly reasoned rejection – and one that leaves the door firmly open to future child rights climate justice complaints, while according appropriate respect to domestic processes.[60] In June 2021, the CRC decided to draft a General Comment on

[58] I Gubbay and C Wenzler, 'Intergenerational Climate Change Litigation: The First Climate Communication to the UN Committee on the Rights of the Child' in I Alogna, C Bakker and J Gauci (eds), *Climate Change Litigation: Global Perspectives* (Brill Nijhoff 2021) 357–60.

[59] MA Tigre and V Lichet, "The CRC Decision in Sacchi v. Argentina" (2021) 26.25 *ASIL Insights*, available at www.asil.org/insights/volume/25/issue/26.

[60] A Nolan, "Children's Rights and Climate Change at the UN Committee on the Rights of the Child: Pragmatism and Principle in Sacchi v Argentina" (*EJIL:Talk! Blog of the European Journal of International Law*, October 20, 2021), available at www.ejiltalk .org/childrens-rights-and-climate-change-at-the-un-committee-on-the-rights-of-the-

children's rights and the environment with a particular focus on climate change, thus signaling the potential of human rights litigation to contribute to normative development beyond a specific case.

The third climate case, *Daniel Billy and others v Australia (Torres Strait Islanders Petition, 2022)*[61] is the latest in HRTB practice. The Communication was brought by eight indigenous residents of the Torres Strait Islands and some of their children to the HRC. This is so far the only decision where an international human rights body has found that a State's failure to protect people from the effects of climate change can amount to a violation of international human rights law.

In the decision, the HRC has found that Australia's failure to adequately protect indigenous Torres Islanders against the adverse effects of climate change violated their rights to enjoy their culture (Article 27 of the Covenant) and be free from arbitrary interferences with their private life, family, and home (Article 17 of the Covenant). Australia failed to adapt to climate change by, *inter alia*, upgrading seawalls on the islands and reducing greenhouse gas emissions.

However, in this case, it cannot be argued that Australia has been inactive in the fight against climate change. The HRC indicated that despite Australia's series of actions, such as the construction of new seawalls on the four islands that are expected to be completed by 2023, additional timely and appropriate measures were required to avert a risk to the Islanders' lives, since without robust national and international efforts, the effects of climate change may expose individuals to a violation of their right to life under the Covenant. This is an important conclusion-warning of the Committee for States that believe that it is possible to limit themselves to minimal actions in order to combat climate change.

As remedies, the HRC asked Australia to compensate the Indigenous Islanders for the harm suffered, engage in meaningful consultations with their communities to assess their needs, and take measures to continue to secure the communities' safe existence on their respective islands. This is

child-pragmatism-and-principle-in-sacchi-v-argentina; C Bakker, "Baptism of Fire?' The First Climate Case before the UN Committee on the Rights of the Child" (2021) 77 *QIL, Zoom-in* 5–25, available at www.qil-qdi.org/wp-content/uploads/2021/01/02_HR-in-Climate-Litigation_BAKKER_FIN.pdf.

61 *Daniel Billy and others v Australia (Torres Strait Islanders Petition)*, HRC, UN Doc CCPR/C/135/D/3624/2019, September 22, 2022.

one of the interesting points of the decision: how to calculate and make "adequate compensation, to the authors for the harm that they have suffered?"[62] How that harm will be calculated is yet unknown, not only in this decision, but in general in international climate law. The Committee left this up to Australia who has to report to the Committee on the implementation within 180 days, so there will be opportunity to analyze the further actions of the Committee at a later date.

It may also be noted that in this decision, as in the previous *Ioane Teitiota v New Zealand* the Committee ultimately dismissed the plaintiffs' claim of a violation of their right to a decent life, finding that they "did not indicate that they have experienced or are currently experiencing adverse health outcomes or a real and reasonably foreseeable risk of being physically threatened" or extreme danger likely to threaten their right to life, including their right to a life in dignity and that strong national and international efforts[63] can prevent harm that would constitute a violation of Article 6 of the Covenant. Although it was a loss for the plaintiffs in this case, it has become a roadmap for future climate cases.

Moreover, as per Voigt, "there is, however, one major shortcoming of the decision: The Committee remained silent on the need for timely and adequate mitigation measures as the 'backside of the coin' to fulfill its positive obligation towards the applicants. This is a lost opportunity."[64]

Overall, the HRC has created a pathway for individuals to assert claims where national systems have failed to take appropriate measures to protect those most vulnerable to the negative impact of climate change on the enjoyment of their human rights.

Thus, based on the method of legal forecasting, it can be said that the number of climate complaints to the HRC will grow in the near future, especially considering that 117 States of the world have recognized its jurisdiction to consider individual complaints.[65]

[62] Ibid., para 11.

[63] Ibid., para 8.6.

[64] C Voigt, "UNHRC is Turning up the Heat: Human Rights Violations Due to Inadequate Adaptation Action to Climate Change" (*EJIL:Talk! Blog of the European Journal of International Law*, September 26, 2022), available at www.ejiltalk.org/unhrc-is-turning-up-the-heat-human-rights-violations-due-to-inadequate-adaptation-action-to-climate-change/.

[65] Optional Protocol to the International Covenant on Civil and Political Rights, New York, December 16, 1966 (status as at April 12, 2022), available at https://treaties.un.org/Pages/ViewDetails.aspx?src=IND&mtdsg_no=IV-5&chapter=4&clang=_en.

16.5 Legitimacy and Citation of Decisions

All documents adopted by HRTB are soft law and are not legally binding. This has its pros and cons. However, the general comments and decisions of the HRTB are actively used in national legal systems.[66] Of course, not in all States and not in all cases, but this practice is quite common.

An important issue is that of the unification of common approaches among international courts, regional courts of human rights, and quasi-judicial bodies (mainly non-compliance procedures based on MEAs and HRTB) in terms of protecting environmental human rights. The analysis shows that HRTB in their environmental decisions repeatedly cited the decisions of the ECtHR, the African Commission on Human and Peoples' Rights and the Inter-American Court of Human Rights. For example, in *Ioane Teitiota v New Zealand*, HRC noted "that environmental degradation can compromise effective enjoyment of the right to life, and that severe environmental degradation can adversely affect an individual's well-being and lead to a violation of the right to life"[67] and cited in support the practice of European, inter-American and African human rights systems.[68]

In *Portillo Cáceres*, HRC stated that "severe environmental pollution may affect individuals' well-being and prevent them from enjoying their homes in such a way as to affect their private and family life adversely"

[66] KF Principi, "Implementation of UN Treaty Body Decisions: A Brief Insight for Practitioners" (2020) 12.1 *Journal of Human Rights Practice* 185–92; V Carraro, "Promoting Compliance with Human Rights: The Performance of the United Nations Universal Periodic Review and Treaty Bodies" (2019) 63.4 *International Studies Quarterly* 1079–93.

[67] *Ioane Teitiota v New Zealand* (n 1) para 9.5.

[68] Ibid., n 23–24: *Inter-American Court of Human Rights*, Advisory Opinion OC-23/17, 15 November 2017 on the Environment and Human Rights, Series A, No 23, para 47; *Kawas Fernández v Honduras*, judgment of 3 April 2009, Series C, No 196, para 148; African Commission on Human and People's Rights, General Comment No 3 on the African Charter on Human and Peoples' Rights: The Right to Life (Article 4), para 3 (States' Responsibilities to Protect Life "extend to preventive steps to preserve and protect the natural environment, and humanitarian responses to natural disasters, famines, outbreaks of infectious diseases, or other emergencies."); European Court of Human Rights, Application Nos 54414/13 and 54264/15, *Cordella and Others v Italy*, judgment of 24 January 2019, para 157 (serious environmental harm may affect individuals' well-being and deprive them of the enjoyment of their domicile, so as to compromise their right to private life); European Court of Human Rights, *M. Özel and others v Turkey*, judgment of 17 November 2015, paras 170, 171, and 200; *Budayeva and others v Russia*, judgment of 20 March 2008, paras 128–130, 133, and 159; *Öneryildiz v Turkey*, judgment of 30 November 2004, paras 71, 89, 90, and 118.

(paragraph 3.7) and relying upon the practice of the ECHR.[69] Also, as in the previous case, in substantiating the fact that severe environmental degradation has given rise to findings of a violation of the right to life (paragraph 7.4), HRC referred to the relevant practice of regional human rights courts. Also in evidence is that "adverse consequences of … pollution are serious because of its intensity or duration and the physical or mental harm that it does, then the degradation of the environment may adversely affect the well-being of individuals and constitute violations of private and family life and the home" (paragraph 7.8). In this, the HRC referred to the practice of the ECHR.[70]

Additionally, the ICJ has on occasion directly considered treaty body practice (Wall opinion in 2004, the *Diallo* case, the *Belgium v Senegal* (or Hissene Habre) case, *Georgia v Russia*, and the *IFAD* case).[71] Moreover, the ICJ directly stated:

> Since it was created, the Human Rights Committee has built up a considerable body of interpretative case law, in particular through its findings in response to the individual communications which may be submitted to it in respect of States parties to the first Optional Protocol, and in the form of its "General Comments." Although the Court is in no way obliged, in the exercise of its judicial functions, to model its own interpretation of the Covenant on that of the Committee, it believes that it should ascribe great weight to the interpretation adopted by this independent body that was

[69] See n 21: "paragraph 51 of *López Ostra v. Spain*, judgment of 9 December 1994; paragraphs 68 and 69 of *Fadeyeva v. Russia*, final judgment of 30 November 2005; and paragraph 105 of *Dubetska and Others v. Ukraine*, judgment of 10 February 2011".

[70] See n 51–52: "European Court of Human Rights, *Cordella and Others v. Italy*, judgment of 24 January 2019, para. 158; European Court of Human Rights, *López Ostra v. Spain*, judgment of 9 December 1994, paras. 51, 55 and 58; *Fadeyeva v. Russia*, paras. 68–70, 89, 92 and 134 and *Cordella and Others v. Italy*, paras. 173–174.

[71] Legal Consequences of the Construction of a Wall in the Occupied Palestinian Territory, Advisory Opinion, 2004, ICJ Reports 136; Diallo (*Republic of Guinea v Democratic Republic of the Congo*), Preliminary Objections, 2007, ICJ Reports 582; Ahmadou Sadio Diallo (*Republic of Guinea v Democratic Republic of the Congo*), Merits, Judgment, 2010, ICJ Reports 639; Ahmadou Sadio Diallo (*Republic of Guinea v Democratic Republic of the Congo*), Compensation, Judgment, 2012, ICJ Reports 324; Case Concerning Application of the International Convention on the Elimination of All Forms of Racial Discrimination (*Georgia v Russian Federation*), Judgment, 2011; Judgment No 2867 of the Administrative Tribunal of the International Labour Organization upon a Complaint Filed against the International Fund for Agricultural Development, Advisory Opinion, 2012, ICJ Reports 10. See N Rodley, "The International Court of Justice and Human Rights Treaty Bodies" in M Andenas and E Bjorge (eds), *A Farewell to Fragmentation: Reassertion and Convergence in International Law* (Cambridge University Press 2015), 87–108.

> established specifically to supervise the application of that treaty. The point here is to achieve the necessary clarity and the essential consistency of international law, as well as legal security, to which both the individuals with guaranteed rights and the States obliged to comply with treaty obligations are entitled[72].

The Inter-American Court of Human Rights, in its Advisory Opinion on Environmental Human Rights,[73] referred to CESCR documents, but not to decisions – only to general comments and concluding observations[74] – as well as to HRC decisions in the context of proving the existence of extraterritorial human rights obligations.[75]

Based on the method of legal forecasting, one can fairly confidently assume that the ECHR will soon quote HRTB. The HRC and CRC are the first international bodies in the world to recognize jurisdiction and adjudicate climate claims (*Ioane Teitiota v New Zealand* and five CRC claims, respectively). As noted above, HRTB denied the plaintiffs, but the rulings contained extremely important legal positions that will be useful to the ECHR, where five cases are already pending.[76] And rather than reinventing the wheel, one can rely on these legal positions of HRTB and thereby confirm their legitimacy in resolving climate disputes.

[72] Ahmadou Sadio Diallo (*Republic of Guinea v Democratic Republic of the Congo*), Merits, Judgment, 2010, ICJ Reports 664.

[73] Inter-American Court of Human Rights, "Advisory Opinion OC-23/17 of November 15, 2017, Requested by the Republic of Colombia: The Environment and Human Rights (State Obligations in Relation to the Environment in the Context of the Protection and Guarantee of the Rights to Life and to Personal Integrity: Interpretation and Scope of Articles 4(1) and 5(1) in Relation to Articles 1(1) and 2 of the American Convention on Human Rights)," available at www.corteidh.or.cr/docs/opiniones/seriea_23_ing.pdf.

[74] Ibid., fns 109–113, 185, 194, 210, 213–16, 226, 232, 234, 239, 298, 299, 344, 353. Namely: General Comment No 14: The Right to the Highest Attainable Standard of Health (Article 12 of the International Covenant on Economic, Social and Cultural Rights), UN Doc E/C.12/2000/4, August 11, 2000; General Comment No 15: The Right to Water (Articles 11 and 12 of the International Covenant on Economic, Social and Cultural Rights), UN Doc E/C.12/2002/11, January 20, 2003; Concluding Observations: Russian Federation, UN Doc. E/C.12/Add.13, May 20, 1997; General Comment No 4: The Right to Adequate Housing (Article 11.1); Concluding Observations: Madagascar, UN Doc E/C.12/MDG/CO/2, December 16, 2009, para 33; and ESCR Committee, General Comment No 21: Right of Everyone to Take Part in Cultural Life (Article 15(1)(a), UN Doc. E/C.12/GC/21/Rev.1)

[75] Ibid., fn 140: HRC, Communication No 56/1979, *Lilian Celiberti de Casariego v Uruguay*, CCPR/C/13/D/56/1979, July 29, 1981; HRC, Communication No 106/1981, *Mabel Pereira Montero v Uruguay*, CCPR/C/18/D/106/1981, March 31, 1983.

[76] Full list of cases available at https://climatecasechart.com/non-us-jurisdiction/european-court-of-human-rights, accessed 26 August 2023.

16.6 Conclusion

In general, over the years of their existence, HRTB have established themselves as an important legitimate and effective link in the resolution of international environmental disputes and as compliance "guardians." However, it should be underlined that HRTB do not actually ensure compliance with environmental obligations, but with human rights treaties, which are increasingly interpreted in the light of environmental obligations. What advantages do HRTB have in comparison with international courts? Human rights treaty bodies have developed a large regulatory framework for the consideration of environmental disputes (including special statements, general comments, and previous opinions). An analysis of decisions shows that HRTB has a wide range of remedies. It is important that the committees themselves monitor the execution of decisions based on the follow-up procedure and the request for information from States during the dialogue process when considering periodic reports; moreover, within the framework of the UPR procedure, the State may be asked about non-compliance with the decision. As quasi-judicial bodies under the UN system, HRTB are not divorced from general legal practice and refer to environmental decisions of other international courts (unlike, for example, the DSB WTO), IPCC documents, and international environmental conventions. Moreover, legal positions from their decisions are used and cited by both universal and regional human rights courts. The UN system, unlike regional human rights bodies, allows developing universal approaches to resolving environmental disputes, and a high level of ratification by States of international human rights treaties allows for the avoidance of jurisdictional restrictions (unlike, say, the Aarhus Committee or the Espoo Committee). Therefore, the world in the form of HRTB has universal legitimate mechanisms to protect the environment (and especially climate) through a link with human rights. All of this should contribute to an enhancement of the ability to protect the environment.

PART VI

Criminal Law and Disarmament Law

17

Monitoring Compliance in International Criminal Law

LEONARDO BORLINI

17.1 Introduction

The present chapter has a twofold aim. First, it maps the current state of international supervision in the area of international criminal law,[1] by looking particularly at the competence of treaty bodies and other non-compliance mechanisms (NCMs),[2] their institutional and operative differences, progressive sophistication and other developments in recent practice. Secondly, the chapter investigates the features of, and circumstances under which, NCMs established by certain international criminal law instruments are more effective than others to address situations of non-compliance and orient future actions of States.

In order to address these matters in a viable way, I plan to make four related points. First, the chapter argues that the lamented paucity of monitoring mechanisms in contemporary international criminal law does not accurately reflect the recent evolution of international

An earlier version of this chapter was presented at PluriCourts Research Conference on Compliance Mechanisms, held at the University of Oslo, on 27–28 October 2021. The discussion at this event was invaluable. I am indebted to constructive comments from Professors Malgosia Fitzmaurice, Caroline Foster, Attila Tanzi and Christina Voigt.

[1] Antonio Cassese was the first scholar to investigate international supervision (or oversight) systemically as an organizational function of the international legal system, and to illustrate the basic structural and functional differences between monitoring and judicial proceedings in international law. According to Cassese, international supervision is intended to result in "an objective evaluation of uncertain situations that has all of the moral authority of an impartial judgement." A Cassese, *Il Controllo Internazionale* (Giuffrè 1971) 310, translated into English by me.

[2] As explained in other chapters of this volume, the functions of non-compliance bodies are based on a composite notion of compliance comprising monitoring, verification and including national reporting. The term "monitoring" for the purposes of this chapter means the assessment of States' compliance with the standards or obligations implicit in adherence to international criminal law conventions.

supervision in the field.[3] Second, an important issue related to the nature of the interest to be pursued by such mechanisms is the increasing complexity of international criminal law treaties and standards. Compared to past agreements, modern international conventions aimed at the suppression of crime (*rectius:* holding criminal activities at acceptable levels), have a more prospective nature.[4] Far from being essentially reactive instruments, they are also geared towards mitigating an ongoing criminal problem, shared by different States, with a view towards achieving specific results over time. These results include the development of the rule of law, deterrence and prevention of crime, and ongoing international cooperation. Thirdly, and related, much as in the case of international human rights and environmental treaties, the mechanisms at issue are designed not to allocate legal liability, but rather to encourage States, by influence and soft power, to adopt behaviors and practices that comply with international obligations and standards. Finally, the relative effectiveness of different monitoring procedures and NCMs in the area of international criminal law depends on a variety of factors that may be identified through a comparative assessment of such instruments.

17.2 Mapping Treaty Monitoring and Non-Compliance Mechanisms in International Criminal Law

Figure 17.1 maps the range of existing mechanisms, focussing on the main treaties that oblige States Parties to criminalize specified conduct at the domestic level and cooperate internationally to prevent and prosecute those offences.

Since World War II, international criminal law has developed in a piecemeal, incremental fashion, as one, then another crime has been added to specific regimes on account of extensive treaty-making.[5]

[3] In mapping and comparing treaty monitoring and NCMs from the same era, this chapter excludes international criminal law conventions from the pre-UN Charter era and focusses on international criminal conventions that oblige State Parties to criminalize specified conduct as a matter of their domestic law without providing for individual criminal responsibility for such conduct under international law.

[4] C Rose, "Treaty Monitoring and Compliance in the Field of Transnational Criminal Law" in MJ Christensen and N Boister (eds) *New Perspectives on the Structure of Transnational Criminal Justice, Brill Research Perspectives on Transnational Crime* (Brill 2018) 40.

[5] There are various ways to define international criminal law. These include those aspects of international law involving the allocation of jurisdiction, or international cooperation in criminal matters. But the notion of international criminal law that has become widely popular among international lawyers and the public at large deals specifically with those

Through the conclusion of treaties, States have agreed to criminalize various conduct at the domestic level and to cooperate internationally to prevent and prosecute those crimes.[6] But the adoption of these treaties has not been consistently accompanied by efforts to monitor compliance with them after their entry into force. Thus, there has been a tendency by the few international lawyers who have dealt with the issue systematically to stress the scarcity of compliance monitoring mechanisms in the field.[7] My own view is slightly different. It is undeniable that the current state of

crimes that are directly criminalized by international law, which also provides for individual criminal responsibility for such conduct. Such crimes, conventionally referred to as "core crimes," are genocide, crimes against humanity, war crimes and aggression, and, along with terrorism and torture, constitute the main or exclusive ambit of investigation of well-known textbooks. See, e.g., WA Schabas and N Bernaz (eds), *Routledge Handbook of International Criminal Law* (Routledge 2011) Part II; A Cassese and P Gaeta (eds), *Cassese's International Criminal Law* (3rd ed., Oxford University Press 2013) Part II. On his part, R O'Keefe, *International Criminal Law* (Oxford University Press 2015) para 2.20, posits, following a conception advocated by Cherif Bassiouni, that an international crime is merely "a crime defined by international law, whether customary or conventional." This is, he adds, "the sole characteristic shared by every offence with a claim to the denomination 'international crime'." (Ibid.) On the grounds of such an inclusive approach to the notion of international crime, the scope *ratione materiae* of international criminal law includes, *inter alia*, crimes that in the taxonomy proposed by other scholars are defined as "transnational crimes." This is a problematic label for several reasons (Ibid., paras 2.47 and 2.48) starting from the very fact that the conduct to which it refers does not necessarily straddle state frontiers – such as drug trafficking, money laundering, trafficking in human beings and the like. More precisely, international criminal law includes offences defined by customary international law; "crimes under treaty," namely "offences, defined by international law, which give rise to the individual criminal responsibility of the perpetrator as a matter of international law itself" (specifically, by virtue of a secondary rule of customary international law); and "crimes pursuant to treaty," by which it is meant that treaties oblige States Parties "to criminalize specified conduct as a matter of their municipal law without providing for individual criminal responsibility for such conduct under international law." (Ibid. para 7.3). Interestingly, the sub-area of international criminal law under discussion has lately caught the attention of both the media and legal scholars for the cases of allegations of misappropriation of public funds by heads of States, ministers and members of their families in their country of origin (mainly African or Eastern European States), the proceeds of which had allegedly been invested in Western jurisdictions, as well as, on occasion, for the resulting application of the international rules on immunities in the context of the criminal proceedings against these persons. For a recent and remarkable example, see ICJ, *Immunities and Criminal Proceedings (Equatorial Guinea v France)*, Judgment, ICJ Reports 2020, 300.

6 Rose (n 4) 40–1; O'Keefe (n 5) chapters 4 and 7; and N Boister, *An Introduction to Transnational Criminal Law* (2nd ed., Oxford University Press, 2018) Part B, "Crimes."

7 This opinion is voiced by Rose (n 4) 41: "Most transnational criminal law treaties do not benefit from any sort of monitoring mechanism that would allow states parties or other actors to assess their domestic implementation and enforcement." From a different perspective, see also Boister (n 6) 407–11.

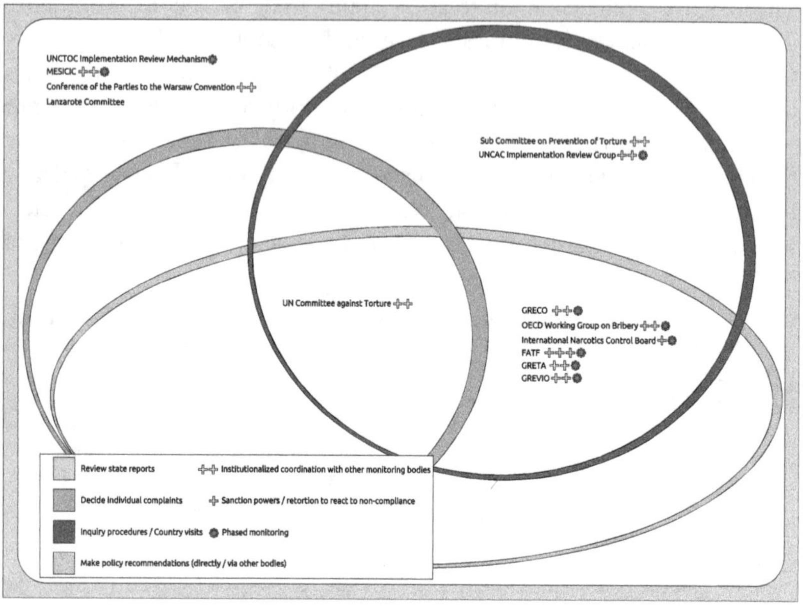

Figure 17.1 Treaty Monitoring and Non-Compliance Mechanisms - International Criminal Law

treaty monitoring in international criminal law is not as developed as in other areas of international law, such as international environmental law and human rights law.[8] However, the scarcity of sectoral international supervision seems overstated. In fact, international monitoring in international criminal law is evolving in different ways.[9] These range from the progressive development of NCMs for multilateral treaties negotiated under the auspices of the United Nations (UN), such as the review mechanisms for the UN Convention against Corruption (UNCAC)[10] and the United Nations Convention on Transnational Organized

[8] See Chapters 2, 3, 5, 6, 11, 13, 14, 15 and 16 in this book and the wide literature referred to therein.

[9] L Borlini, "Il controllo internazionale tra standardizzazione, coordinamento e 'contaminazione'" in A Annoni, S Forlati and F Salerno (eds), *La codificazione nell'ordinamento internazionale ed europeo* (ES 2019) 591, 595–8.

[10] United Nations Convention against Corruption, adopted 31 October 2003, entered into force 14 December 2005, 2349 UNTS 41 (UNCAC).

Crime (UNCTOC)[11] and its Protocols;[12] to the proliferation and sophistication of monitoring procedures established in the context of regional organizations; and the operation of fairly complex, wide-ranging and rigorous NCMs to ensure that international standards on the prevention and repression of specified international crimes such as money laundering, terrorist financing and financing of the proliferation of weapons of mass destruction (WMD) are put into effect, despite the fact that such codes are not legally binding.[13] I will now elaborate on each of these distinct developments.

17.2.1 Universal Suppression Conventions and Treaty Monitoring

UN criminal law conventions concerning torture, drug control, corruption, money laundering and different forms of organized crime – including trafficking in persons, smuggling of migrants and illicit manufacturing and trafficking in firearms – are accompanied by NCMs. There are too many instances by now for these to be discounted as constituting merely a "few exceptions" to a general absence of treaty

[11] United Nations Convention against Transnational Organized Crime and the Protocols Thereto, adopted 15 November 2000, entered into force 29 September 2003, 2225 UNTS 209 (UNCTOC).

[12] Protocol to Prevent, Suppress, Punish Trafficking in Persons, Especially Women and Children, Supplementing the United Nations Convention Against Transnational Organized Crime, adopted 15 November, 2000, entered into force 25 December 2003, 2237 UNTS 319 (Trafficking Protocol); Protocol Against the Smuggling of Migrants by Land, Sea and Air, Supplementing the United Nations Convention Against Transnational Organized Crime, adopted 15 November 2000, entered into force January 28 2004, 2241 UNTS 507 (Smuggling Protocol); Protocol against the Illicit Manufacturing of and Trafficking in Firearms, Their Parts and Components and Ammunition, Supplementing the United Nations Convention against Transnational Organized Crime, adopted 31 May 2001, entered into force June 3 2005, 2326 UNTS 208 (Firearms Protocol). Analyses of the legal framework established by these protocols are offered, by, among others, T Obokata, "Human Trafficking" in N Boister and RJ Currie (eds), *Routledge Handbook of Transnational Criminal Law* (Routledge 2015) 171; AT Gallagher and F David, *The International Law of Migrant Smuggling* (Cambridge University Press 2014); A Schloenhardt, "The UN Protocol against the Smuggling of Migrants by Land, Sea and Air 2000" in P Hauck and S Peterke (eds), *International Law and Transnational Organized Crime* (Oxford University Press 2016) 169; DL Rothe and JI Ross, "The State and Transnational Organized Crime: The Case of Small Arms Trafficking" in F Allum and S Gilmour (eds), *Routledge Handbook of Transnational Organized Crime* (Routledge 2012) 391.

[13] Borrowing from D Thürer, "Soft Law: Norms in the Twilight between Law and Politics" in D Thürer (ed.), *International Law as Progress and Prospect* (Nomos 2009) 159, at 166: "in other words: soft law is sometimes coupled with hard procedures."

monitoring in international criminal law.[14] Quite the contrary. In surveying the catalogue of international criminal treaties that aspire to attract universal participation,[15] the lack of treaty compliance monitoring mechanisms is notable only with respect to the terrorism suppression conventions. This can be ascribed to the sheer number and range of treaties in this area.[16] None of the fourteen universal terrorism suppression conventions, concluded between 1963 and 2010, creates a monitoring body, even though these agreements "were concluded under the auspices of existing international organizations that might have played such a role."[17]

14 Rose (n 4) 40.

15 This subset of crimes defined by international conventional law includes torture; drug trafficking; the different forms of terrorism that are defined by UN treaties; slavery, human trafficking and migrant smuggling; firearms trafficking; other forms of transnational organized crime; corruption and money laundering.

16 Convention on Offences and Certain Other Acts Committed on Board Aircraft, adopted 14 September 1963, entered into force 4 December 1969, 704 UNTS 219; Convention for the Suppression of Unlawful Seizure of Aircraft, adopted 16 December 1970, entered into force 14 October 1971, 860 UNTS 105; Convention for the Suppression of Unlawful Acts against the Safety of Civil Aviation, adopted 23 September 1971, entered into force 26 January 1973, 974 UNTS 177; Convention on the Prevention and Punishment of Crimes against Internationally Protected Persons, including Diplomatic Agents, adopted 14 December 1973, entered into force 20 February 1977, 1035 UNTS 167; International Convention against the Taking of Hostages, adopted 17 December 1979, entered into force 3 June 1983, 1316 UNTS 205; Convention on the Physical Protection of Nuclear Material, adopted 3 March 1980, entered into force 8 February 1987, 1456 UNTS 124; Protocol for the Suppression of Unlawful Acts of Violence at Airports Serving International Civil Aviation, adopted 24 February 1988, entered into force 6 August 1989, 1589 UNTS 474; Convention for the Suppression of Unlawful Acts against the Safety of Maritime Navigation, adopted 10 March 1988, entered into force 1 March 1992, 1678 UNTS 201; Protocol to the Convention of 10 March 1988 for the Suppression of Unlawful Acts against the Safety of Fixed Platforms Located on the Continental Shelf, adopted 10 March 1988, entered into force 1 March 1992, 1678 UNTS 201; Convention on the Marking of Plastic Explosives for the Purpose of Detection, adopted 1 March 1991, entered into force 21 June 1998, 2122 UNTS 359; International Convention for the Suppression of Terrorist Bombings, adopted 15 December 1997, entered into force 23 May 2001, 2149 UNTS 256; International Convention for the Suppression of the Financing of Terrorism, adopted 9 December 1999, entered into force 10 April 2002, 2178 UNTS 197; International Convention for the Suppression of Acts of Nuclear Terrorism, adopted 13 April 2005, entered into force 7 July 2007, 2445 UNTS 89; Convention on the Suppression of Unlawful Acts Relating to International Civil Aviation, adopted 10 September 2010, entered into force 1 July 2018, ICAO Doc 9960, DCAS Doc No 21. See MC Bassiouni, "Enslavement as an International Crime?" (1991) 23 *New York University Journal of International Law and Politics* 445.

17 Rose (n 4) 48.

The situation of other universal suppression conventions is markedly different. Granted, in adopting early treaties on crimes such as human trafficking, prostitution and slavery in the post–World War II era, States refrained from establishing monitoring bodies.[18] In fact, those conventions require States Parties to communicate implementing legislation and regulations to the UN Secretary General, but do not call for the Secretary General, or any other body, to independently monitor and review these communications. Yet, over the past twelve years, two important mechanisms have been created. The first, UNCAC's monitoring system, was established relatively recently, in 2009.[19] Specifically, UNCAC required the Conference of the States Parties to establish, if necessary, "any appropriate mechanism or body to assist in the effective implementation of the Convention."[20] Although the negotiations concerning a review mechanism for the UNCAC stretched from 2006 to 2009, they were ultimately successful. The Implementation Review Group (IRG), a subsidiary body of the Conference of the States Parties to the UNCAC, responsible for maintaining an overview of the review process and considering technical assistance requirements for the effective implementation of the Convention, began operating in 2010. Since then, the UNCAC IRG has carried out a relatively large-scale peer review process involving the treaty's nearly 180 States Parties.[21] On the basis of an extensive self-assessment checklist, a desk review and a possible country visit, each State Party is reviewed by two other State Parties, which produce a country review report with the help of the United Nations

[18] Convention for the Suppression of the Traffic in Persons and of the Exploitation of the Prostitution of Others, adopted 21 March 1950, entered into force 25 July 1951, 96 UNTS 271, Article 21; Supplementary Convention on the Abolition of Slavery, the Slave Trade, and Institutions and Practices Similar to Slavery, adopted 7 September 1956, entered into force 30 April 1957, 266 UNTS 3, Article 8. Moreover, the 1957 Abolition of Forced Labour Convention, which States concluded under the auspices of the International Labour Organization (ILO), also does not require the ILO to monitor implementation, and, in fact, the treaty does not even require States Parties to communicate their implementation efforts to the ILO. Abolition of Forced Labour Convention (International Labour Organisation Convention No 105), adopted 25 June 1957, entered into force 17 January 1959, 320 UNTS 291.

[19] For a critical assessment of this mechanism, see M Arnone and L Borlini, *Corruption: Economic Analysis and International Law* (Edward Elgar 2014) chapter 16.

[20] UNCAC (n 10) Article 63(7).

[21] P Webb and O Landwehr, "Article 63: Conference of the States Parties to the Convention" in C Rose, M Kubiciel and O Landwehr (eds), *The United Nations Convention against Corruption: A Commentary* (Oxford University Press 2019) 627, at 636–37.

Office on Drugs and Crime (UNODC). This report, however, may only be published with the consent of the Party under review.[22] The review process is phased, meaning that the IRG reviews the implementation of only a couple of chapters of UNCAC in each review cycle.[23]

Secondly, after quite a prolonged limbo, in October 2018, State Parties to the UN Convention against Transnational Organized Crime and its Protocols eventually agreed on the creation of a review mechanism (IRG) for organized crime, human trafficking, smuggling of migrants and trafficking in firearms.[24] This mechanism, established after nearly ten years of negotiation,[25] took the review mechanism for the 2003 Convention against corruption as a model: UNCTOC IRG is similar to UNCAC IRG in nearly every respect.[26] This is also because the two

[22] Arnone and Borlini (n 19) 475.

[23] Webb and Landwehr (n 21) at 636–37.

[24] Conference of the Parties to the United Nations Convention against Transnational Organized Crime, Resolution 9/1, Establishment of the Mechanism for the Review of the Implementation of the United Nations Convention against Transnational Organized Crime and the Protocols thereto, 15–19 October 2018, available at www.unodc.org/unodc/en/organized-crime/intro/review-mechanism-untoc/home.html, accessed 6 October 2021.

[25] In theory, Article 32 of UNCTOC allows for the possibility that the Conference of the Parties could gather and analyze information about implementation itself, without the help of a supplementary review mechanism. For an informed explanation of why the creation of a Review Mechanism for UNCTOC proved to be controversial, see C Rose, "The Creation of a Review Mechanism for the UN Convention against Organized Crime and Its Protocols" (2020) 114(1) *American Journal of International Law* 51.

[26] The Conference of the Parties to the UNCTOC and its Protocols ultimately settled on a twelve-year programme of reviews for all States Parties, which covers UNCTOC and the three protocols over the course of four phases. Each phase covers a particular set of provisions on topics such as criminalization, international cooperation, and so on. The phases begin with a self-assessment questionnaire to be completed by the State Party under review. States provide answers to the questionnaire via a knowledge management portal hosted by UNODC, known as SHERLOC (Sharing Electronic Resources on Laws and Crime). On the basis of this questionnaire, two peer-reviewing countries conduct a "desk-based" review of the State Party, without the benefit of a country visit. Following this desk-based review, the review team produces a country review report, which it submits to the Conference of the Parties' thematic working groups (which cover trafficking in persons, smuggling of migrants and firearms). All documents produced during this review process (i.e., the self-assessment questionnaire, the country review report and the executive summary) remain confidential unless the State under review opts to make them public. See Procedures and Rules for the Functioning of the Mechanism for the Review of the Implementation of the United Nations Convention against Transnational Organized Crime and the Protocols Thereto (UNCTOC Procedures and Rules for the Review Mechanism), esp. paras 20, 25 and 41.

treaties are comparable in terms of structure and main provisions (UNCAC was negotiated by the UN on the heels of the UNCTOC).

All this being said, the International Narcotics Control Board (Board or INCB),[27] created by the 1961 Single Convention on Narcotic Drugs, arguably represents the most significant and long-standing treaty monitoring body created by universal criminal law treaties. All three of the drug trafficking treaties concluded after World War II carve out a significant role for the Board as a body that provides technical assessments and monitors domestic implementation.[28] The Board, which describes itself as a "quasi-judicial body,"[29] periodically reviews the adequacy of domestic drug control legislation and policies, as well as measures taken by States Parties to tackle drug trafficking and abuse, the functioning of domestic drug control administrations and compliance with reporting obligations under the treaties.[30] The Board's review process comprises a limited number of "country missions" each year, which permit it to discuss drug control measures with domestic authorities and to obtain first-hand information about the drug control situation in the given State.[31] On the basis of these country missions and the information reported by States Parties, the Board makes findings and confidential

[27] International Narcotics Control Board, "About", available at www.incb.org/incb/en/about.html, accessed 10 August 2021.

[28] Single Convention on Narcotic Drugs, adopted 30 March 1961, entered into force 13 December 1964, 520 UNTS 151; Convention on Psychotropic Substances, adopted 21 February 1971, entered into force 1976, 1019 UNTS 175; United Nations Convention against Illicit Traffic in Narcotic Drugs and Psychotropic Substances, adopted 20 December 1988, entered into force 11 November 1990, 1582 UNTS 95. The latter treaty has come quite close to achieving universal participation: in January 2022, it had 191 Parties.

[29] International Narcotics Control Board (n 27). The composition of the Board is somewhat peculiar as it includes non-lawyer experts. The UN Economic and Social Council is responsible for electing the Board's thirteen members, of whom three are technical experts with medical, pharmacological or pharmaceutical experience selected from a list of persons nominated by the World Health Organization (1961 Single Convention on Narcotic Drugs, Article 9(1)(a)). The remaining ten members are nominated by UN member States and serve in their independent capacity, much like the members of the human rights treaty bodies (Ibid. Article 9(1)(b)). See B Leroy, "Drug Trafficking" in Boister and Currie (n 12) 229, 233-34.

[30] International Narcotics Control Board, "Treaty Compliance", available at www.incb.org/incb/en/treaty-compliance/index.html, accessed 26 August 2021; International Narcotics Control Board, *Report of the International Narcotics Control Board for 2015* (United Nations 2016) para 129.

[31] International Narcotics Control Board (n 30) paras 156–61.

recommendations for remedial measures.[32] Besides, it is also worth recalling that the 1988 UN Convention against Illicit Traffic in Narcotic Drugs and Psychotropic Substances was the first international instrument to require the criminalization of money laundering, albeit in the specific context of drug trafficking;[33] the same approach being then followed in the UNCTOC[34] and UNCAC.[35] And the implementation of the respective mandatory provisions on criminalization of money laundering is obviously subject to the monitoring mechanisms established under those treaties respectively.

Slightly more complicated are the UN Convention against Torture and Other Cruel, Inhuman or Degrading Treatment or Punishment[36] and its peculiar monitoring system. The Committee Against Torture (CAT) (the body of ten independent experts that monitors implementation of the Convention against Torture) and the Subcommittee on Prevention of Torture (which was created by the Optional Protocol to the Convention[37] with the mandate to visit places where persons are deprived of their liberty in the States Parties) are conventionally grouped among human rights treaty bodies. They supervise the implementation of one of "the nine core international human rights treaties,"[38] and operate much like

[32] Ibid. para 160. See also D Barrett, "Unique in International Relations? A Comparison of the International Narcotics Control Board and the UN Human Rights Treaty Bodies" (1 February 2008). Available at https://ssrn.com/abstract=1473198, accessed 12 September 2021; and Rose (n 4) 51–52.

[33] 1988 UN Convention against Illicit Traffic in Narcotic Drugs and Psychotropic Substances, Article 3(b) and (c).

[34] UNCTOC (n 11) Article 6. See also JD McClean, *Transnational Organized Crime: A Commentary on the UN Convention and Its Protocols* (Oxford University Press 2007) 76–83.

[35] UNCAC (n 10) Article 23.

[36] UN Convention against Torture and Other Cruel, Inhuman or Degrading Treatment or Punishment, adopted 10 December 1984, entered into force 26 June 1987, 1465 UNTS 112.

[37] UN General Assembly, *Optional Protocol to the Convention against Torture and other Cruel, Inhuman and Degrading Treatment or Punishment*, 9 January 2003, A/RES/57/199, entered into force 22 June 2006, available at www.refworld.org/docid/3de6490b9.html, accessed 2 February 2022.

[38] Rose (n 4) 44. The same qualification is maintained, among many, by T Kelly, "The UN Committee against Torture: Human Rights Monitoring and the Legal Recognition of Cruelty" (2009) 31(3) *Human Rights Quarterly* 777; R McQuigg, "How Effective is the United Nations Committee against Torture?" (2011) 22(3) *European Journal of International Law* 813; and G Molina, "Article 17: Committee Against Torture" in M Nowak, M Birk and G Monina (eds), *The United Nations Convention against Torture and Its Optional Protocol: A Commentary* (2nd rev. ed., Oxford University Press 2019) 475.

other well-known human rights treaty bodies, particularly the CAT.[39] Still, there is no obvious reason to exclude the same Convention from the array of multilateral treaties that oblige States Parties to criminalize specified conduct as a matter of their domestic law and to cooperate internationally to prevent and prosecute those offences.[40]

To recap, the implementation of, and compliance with, the main universal suppression conventions are now monitored by ad hoc treaty bodies and through specific review processes, the only significant exception remaining the criminal law conventions against terrorism. The composition and functions of these bodies vary, but they can be broadly grouped into three categories: subsidiary bodies of the Conference of the States Parties to the UNCTOC and UNCAC, which are responsible for the overview of the whole monitoring process; quasi-judicial bodies that periodically review the adequacy of relevant domestic legislation and policies, as well as compliance with reporting obligations under the universal treaties against drug trafficking; and in one instance a body comprising independent experts with the mandate to visit places where persons are deprived of their liberty, in States Parties to the CAT.

17.2.2 The Development of Treaty Monitoring and Non-Compliance Mechanisms in Regional Criminal Law Conventions

Non-compliance mechanisms with respect to regional and universal treaties are hardly comparable.[41] Treaties negotiated under the auspices of regional organizations, like the Council of Europe (CoE), the Organization of American States (OAS) and the African Union (AU), may lend themselves "more readily to follow-up mechanisms within the

[39] All States Parties are obliged to submit regular reports to the Committee on how the rights are being implemented. States must report initially one year after acceding to the Convention and then every four years. The Committee examines each report and addresses its concerns and recommendations to the State party in the form of "concluding observations." In addition to the reporting procedure, the Convention establishes three other mechanisms through which the Committee performs its monitoring functions: the Committee may also, under certain circumstances, consider communications from individuals claiming that their rights under the Convention have been violated, undertake inquiries and consider inter-State complaints. The Committee also publishes its interpretation of the content of the provisions of the Convention, known as general comments on thematic issues.

[40] See also O'Keefe (n 5) para 7.13.

[41] Arnone and Borlini (n 19) 474–75.

framework of an existing regional entity."[42] The problems involved in monitoring a universal treaty with nearly 200 States Parties are clearly different to those involved in monitoring conventions "with a much smaller number of relatively like-minded states that are already members of the same regional organization."[43] With that said, some meaningful developments of treaty monitoring in international criminal law have taken place in the context of regional organizations, which make the exploration of such instruments essential for the purposes of the present study. Over the last forty years criminal conventions concluded under the auspices of regional organizations, as well as sectoral intergovernmental institutions grouping like-minded States like the Organization for Economic Co-operation and Development (OECD), have proliferated.[44]

These instruments range from conventions on combating migration and exploitation crimes (human trafficking, migrant smuggling and child sex tourism); to treaties against commodity crimes (e.g., drug trafficking, weapons smuggling and cultural property trafficking); and so-called "facilitative" and organizational crime (money laundering, corruption, terrorism, cybercrimes). It is not possible, within the confines of the present chapter, to investigate this dense and complex network of rules in detail.[45] The same holds true with the panoply of monitoring mechanisms designed to elicit compliance with such rules. Without claiming to be exhaustive, one may refer to (a) the two instruments, other than the Trafficking Protocol, that encouragingly recognize the importance of victim protection in countering trafficking in human beings:[46] the Convention on the Protection of Children against Sexual Exploitation and Sexual Abuse;[47] and the Convention on Preventing and Combating

[42] Rose (n 4) 42.

[43] Ibid. 42. See also Borlini (n 9) 499.

[44] See, *ex multis*, Boister and Currie (n 12).

[45] When relevant for the purposes of this chapter, readers are referred to recent scholarly works that offer full analysis of the legal frameworks under discussion.

[46] These are the Inter-American Convention on Traffic in Minors 1994, adopted 18 March 1994, entered into force 15 August 1997, OAS Treaty Series No. 79; and, with greater force, the Council of Europe Convention on Action against Trafficking of Human Beings, adopted 16 May 2005, entered into force 1 February 2008, ETS No 197. The latter treaty aims to prevent and combat human trafficking, to protect and assist victims and witnesses of trafficking, to ensure effective investigation and prosecution and to promote international cooperation against trafficking. See Obokata (n 12) 178–79.

[47] Council of Europe Convention on the Protection of Children against Sexual Exploitation and Sexual Abuse, 25 October 2007, entered into force 1 July 2010, ETS No 201 (Lanzarote Convention). The Lanzarote Convention requires its Parties to establish specific legislation and take measures to prevent sexual exploitation and sexual abuse of

Violence against Women and Domestic Violence;[48] (b) the array of regional conventions against illicit manufacturing and trafficking in firearms, ammunitions, explosives and the like;[49] (c) the recent Convention on Offences relating to Cultural Property;[50] (d) the influential 1990 Convention on Laundering, Search, Seizure and Confiscation of the Proceeds of Crime,[51] and its successor, the Convention on Laundering, Search, Seizure and Confiscation of the Proceeds from Crime and on the Financing of Terrorism;[52] (e) the development in the

children, to protect children and to prosecute perpetrators. The Committee of the Parties to the Convention, also known as the "Lanzarote Committee," is in charge of monitoring the implementation of the Convention. It is also in charge of facilitating the collection, analysis and exchange of information, experience and good practices to enhance the capacity of Parties to prevent and combat sexual exploitation and sexual abuse of children. For a comment see K Fredette, "International Legislative Efforts to Combat Child Sex Tourism: Evaluating the Council of Europe Convention on Commercial Child Sexual Exploitation" (2009) 32(1) *Boston College International and Comparative Law Review* 8.

48 The Council of Europe Convention on Preventing and Combating Violence against Women and Domestic Violence, adopted 11 May 2011, entered into force 1 August 2014, ETS No 210 (Istanbul Convention). The Istanbul Convention places an obligation on the Parties to effectively address violence against women and domestic violence in all its forms and to take action to prevent it, protect its victims, prosecute the perpetrators and to ensure that such actions form part of a set of integrated policies.

49 Inter-American Convention against the Illicit Manufacturing of and Trafficking in Firearms, Ammunition, Explosives and Other Related Materials, adopted 14 November 1997, entered into force 1 July 1998, 37 ILM 143 (1998), (CIFTA); Protocol on Control of Firearms, Ammunition and Other Related Materials in the Southern African Development Community Region, 2001, Nairobi Protocol for the Prevention, Control and Reduction of Small Arms and Light Weapons in the Great Lakes Region and the Horn of Africa, 2004; and ECOWAS Convention on Small Arms and Light Weapons, Their Ammunition and Other Related Materials, 2006. See www.poa-iss.org/RegionalOrganizations/, accessed 17 July 2021.

50 Council of Europe Convention on Offences relating to Cultural Property, 3 May 2017, ETS No 221, not yet in force (Nicosia Convention). For a contextualization of this convention in the broader international legal framework for the protection of cultural heritage, see T Scovazzi, "International Legal Instruments as a Means for the Protection of Cultural Heritage" in O Niglio and EYJ Lee (eds), *Transcultural Diplomacy and International Law in Heritage Conservation* (Springer 2021), available at https://doi.org/10.1007/978-981-16-0309-9_11, and the literature referred to therein.

51 Council of Europe Convention on Laundering, Search, Seizure and Confiscation of the Proceeds of Crime, 8 November 1990, ETS No 141, entered into force 1 September 1993.

52 Council of Europe Convention on Laundering, Search, Seizure and Confiscation of the Proceeds from Crime and on the Financing of Terrorism, adopted 16 May 2005, entered into force 1 May 2008, ETS 198 (Warsaw Convention). See WC Gilmore, *Dirty Money: The Evolution of International Measures to Counter Money Laundering and the Financing of Terrorism* (4th ed., Council of Europe Publishing 2011) 175–95; and for the accommodation of such international instruments in the EU, L Borlini, "Regulating Criminal

late 1990s of four regional and sectoral treaties on combating bribery and corruption[53] almost in unison with the negotiations and drafting of UNCAC and the AU Convention on Preventing and Combating Corruption;[54] (f) the CoE Convention on Cybercrime;[55] (g) the so-called, "Medicrime Convention";[56] and (h) the many regional treaties on terrorism that either (1) follow the limited approach of sectoral universal treaties by proscribing certain acts or protecting certain targets[57] or declare that terrorism offences should not be regarded as political offences in extradition law, or that States must cooperate, but do not explicitly require States to criminalize the offences;[58] or (2) define

Finance in the EU in the Light of the International Instruments" (2017) 36(1) *Yearbook of European Law* 553.

53 Inter-American Convention against Corruption, adopted 29 March 1996, in force 6 March 1997, 35 ILM 724 (1996) (IACAC); OECD Convention on Combating Bribery of Foreign Public Officials in International Business Transactions, adopted 21 November 1997, entered into force 15 February 1999, 37 ILM 1(1997) (OECD Anti-Bribery Convention); Convention on the Fight against Corruption involving Officials of the European Communities or Officials of Member States of the European Union, Council Act 97/C OJ 1997 C 195/01; and Council of Europe Criminal Law Convention on Corruption, adopted 27 January 1999, entered into force 1 July 2002, ETS No 173 (CoECLCC).

54 African Union Convention on Preventing and Combating Corruption, adopted 1 July 2003, entered into force 5 August 2006, 45 ILM 5 (2003) (AUCPCC). Finally, the Arab Anti-Corruption Convention concluded under the auspices of the League of Arab States is the latest addition to the regional instruments on combating corruption. It was signed by twenty-one Arab countries on 21 December 2010 and has been ratified by more than fifteen countries to date. See www.acta.gov.qa/en/arab-anti-corruption-convention/, accessed 8 June 2021.

55 Council of Europe Convention on Cybercrime, adopted 8 November 2001, entered into force 1 July 2004, ETS No 185 (Budapest Convention).

56 Council of Europe Convention on the Counterfeiting of Medical Products and Similar Crimes Involving Threats to Public Health, adopted 28 November 2011, entered into force 1 January 2016, ETS No 211. This is the first international criminal law instrument to oblige States Parties to criminalize the manufacturing of counterfeit medical products; supplying, offering to supply and trafficking in counterfeit medical products; the falsification of documents; the unauthorized manufacturing or supplying of medicinal products and the placing on the market of medical devices which do not comply with conformity requirements.

57 Organisation of American States (OAS) Convention to Prevent and Punish Acts of Terrorism Taking the Form of Crimes against Persons and Related Extortion that are of International Significance, adopted 2 February 1971, entered into force 16 October 1973, 1438 UNTS 194; OAS, Inter-American Convention Against Terrorism, adopted 6 March 2002, entered into force 7 October 2003, available at www.refworld.org, accessed 5 June 2021.

58 Council of Europe Convention on the Suppression of Terrorism, adopted 27 January 1977, entered into force 4 August 1978, ETS No 90; Protocol amending the European

terrorism by reference to other treaties and then create preparatory or inchoate offences which States are required to criminalize;[59] or, more controversially, (3) define terrorism generally and require States to criminalize terrorist offences in domestic law.[60]

Non-compliance mechanisms established by regional criminal law conventions show great variety in structure, competence and procedures. The constellation of monitoring systems here is even more diverse than with universal treaties. Diverse monitoring systems oversee States' implementation of specific obligations under regional criminal law conventions, leaving aside those treaties that do not benefit from any such dedicated system.[61] These bodies may be intergovernmental and political (led by States),[62] or supervisory bodies made of independent experts (documenting and assessing implementation and enforcement of the supervised treaties).[63] Each of these entities was established either

Convention on the Suppression of Terrorism, adopted 15 May 2003, ETS No 190; South Asian Association for Regional Cooperation (SAARC) Regional Convention on Suppression of Terrorism, adopted 4 November 1987, entered into force 22 August 1998; Treaty on Cooperation among the States Members of the Commonwealth of Independent States (CIS) in Combating Terrorism, adopted 4 June 1999, entered into force 4 June 1999; African Union Protocol of 2004 to the Organisation of African Unity Convention on the Prevention and Combating of Terrorism 1999, 8 July 2004.

59 Council of Europe Convention on the Prevention of Terrorism 2005, adopted 16 May 2005, entered into force 1 July 2006, ETS No 196; SAARC Additional Protocol of 2004, 6 January 2004.

60 Examples include the Arab Convention on the Suppression of Terrorism, adopted 22 April 1998, entered into force 7 May 1999; the Organisation of Islamic Cooperation (OIC) Convention on Combating International Terrorism of 1999; and the Shanghai Cooperation Organization Convention on Combating Terrorism, Separatism and Extremism, adopted 15 June 2001, entered into force 29 March 2003. On the problems of defining terrorism in international law see generally B Saul, *Defining Terrorism in International Law* (Oxford University Press 2006).

61 This is the case, for instance, of the Inter-American Convention on Traffic in Minors; most of the regional conventions against terrorism; the EU Convention on the Fight against Corruption involving Officials of the European Communities or Officials of Member States, OJ C 195, 25 June 1997, 2–11.

62 CIFTA, for example, established a Consultative Committee gathering a representative for each State Party in order to guarantee its implementation, to promote the exchange of information, to facilitate cooperation and foster training between States. See www.oas.org/dsp/espanol/cpo_cifta_armas.asp, accessed on 20 September 2021. Another case in point is the Conference of the Parties to the Warsaw Convention, established as the Council of Europe monitoring mechanism for such treaty.

63 Probably the most notable case of independent expert monitoring bodies, especially for the quality of its reports is the Group of Experts on Action against Trafficking in Human Beings (GRETA), which, together with the Committee of the Parties to the Council of

directly by individual States or by groups of States, as members of intergovernmental organizations.[64] Some NCMs tasked with the

Europe Convention on Action against Trafficking in Human Beings is responsible for monitoring the implementation of the Convention. The Group meets in plenary sessions three times a year, carries out on-site visits and draws up and publishes country reports evaluating legislative and other measures taken by Parties to give effect to the provisions of the Convention. In addition, GRETA regularly publishes general reports on its activities. Article 36 of the Convention stipulates that GRETA shall have a minimum of ten and a maximum of fifteen members and stresses the need to ensure geographical and gender balance, as well as multidisciplinary expertise, when electing GRETA members. They are selected from among nationals of States Parties to the Convention on the basis of their competence in the areas covered by the Convention. Members sit in their individual capacity and must be independent and impartial in the exercise of their functions. See generally S Forlati, "Monitoring Compliance with International Obligations in the Field of Human Trafficking; Towards a 'Systemic Integration' of Control Mechanisms?" in S Marchisio, C Curti Gialdino, R Cadin and L Manca (eds), *Scritti in memoria di Maria Rita Saulle* (ES 2014). Other such organs are the Group of Experts on Action against Violence against Women and Domestic Violence (GREVIO), the independent expert body responsible for monitoring the implementation of the Istanbul Convention, whose first ten members were elected on 4 May 2015. The Group of Experts on Action against Trafficking in Human Beings works in conjunction with a body composed of representatives of the Parties to the Convention, the Committee of the Parties and with the African Union Advisory Board on Corruption, which is an autonomous organ established within the African Union (AU), in terms of Article 22 of the African Union Convention on Preventing and Combating Corruption. The Advisory Board, modelled on the African Commission on Human and Peoples' Rights, is the AU's only formal monitoring measure at the international level and at the level of the AU Commission. The follow-up mechanism provided for in Article 22 of the AUCPCC calls for an Advisory Board of eleven members, elected by the AU Executive Council and serving for a period of two years, renewable once, from among a list of experts of the highest integrity and recognized competence in matters relating to preventing and combating corruption and related offences. Board members are to "serve in their personal capacity," but the fact that they are proposed by States Parties does not help to guarantee their independence and impartiality.

64 For instance, the Lanzarote Committee (i.e., the Committee of the Parties to the Convention on the Protection of Children against Sexual Exploitation and Sexual Abuse) is the body established within the Council of Europe and composed of both present and potential representatives of the Parties to the Convention, to monitor whether Parties effectively implement the Lanzarote Convention. The Follow-Up Mechanism for the Implementation of the Inter-American Convention against Corruption (MESICIC), the Anticorruption Mechanism of the OAS, brings together thirty-three of the thirty-four member States to review their legal frameworks and institutions in the light of the IACAC. Similarly, the OECD Working Group on Bribery in International Business Transactions (WGB), established in 1994, is a peer-review monitoring system conducted in successive phases, which is responsible for monitoring the implementation and enforcement of the OECD Anti-Bribery Convention, the 2009 Recommendation on Further Combating Foreign Bribery in International Business Transactions and related instruments. The Group of States against Corruption

oversight of regional criminal law conventions perform on-site visits; others do not.[65] Monitoring may be either "vertical," that is, a single State's performance may be evaluated across a range of obligations (also known as "country-by-country" monitoring), or "horizontal," in which States' performance of a single obligation or of a group of related obligations may be compared.[66] While some procedures are based solely on periodic consultations among the Parties,[67] or the attribution of a general supervising role to the secretariat of the regional organization

(GRECO), the anti-corruption body of the Council of Europe, is peculiar in that its membership is open on an equal footing to all forty-seven member States of the organisation, as well as to non-member States, particularly those who participated in GRECO's establishment. This explains why the United States and Belarus are members and why Canada, the Holy See, Japan and Mexico could join at any time and with little formality if they wish, according to the Group's Statute.

65 On-site visits feature the work of GRECO, OECD WGB, GRETA and GREVIO. By contrast, the IACAC, AUCPCC, Lanzarote Convention and the Warsaw Convention do not foresee the possibility of on-site visits by monitoring bodies.

66 This kind of assessment is common with monitoring bodies that publish periodic general reports on their activities and/or thematic reports on specific issues. See, e.g., Council of Europe Convention on Laundering, Search, Seizure and Confiscation of the Proceeds from Crime and on the Financing of Terrorism, CETS No 198, "Third Activity Report (2018–2020)", available at www.coe.int/en/web/cop198/home, accessed on 20 September 2021. The report covers the activities of the Conference of the Parties to CETS 198 as a Council of Europe monitoring mechanism during the period 2018–2020 and provides a brief horizontal review of compliance with the provisions of international standards. For a very recent example of thematic report see Council of Europe Convention on Laundering, Search, Seizure and Confiscation of the Proceeds from Crime and on the Financing of Terrorism, "Thematic Monitoring Review of the Conference of the Parties to CETS No.198 on Article 10 (1 and 2), ('Corporate Liability')", C198-COP(2021)6_HR, Strasbourg 19 November 2021, available at https://rm.coe.int/c198-cop-2021-6prov-hr-art10-final/1680a53db0.

67 Article 30 of the Council of Europe Convention on the Prevention of Terrorism contains only a general obligation for State Parties "to consult periodically with a view to making proposals to facilitate or improve the effective use and implementation of this Convention, including the identification of any problems and the effects of any declaration made under this Convention." Similarly, the Budapest Convention foresees regular consultations of the Parties who meet at least once per year as the Cybercrime Convention Committee (T-CY). More precisely, T-CY is the mechanism "enabling" consultations in line with Article 46 of the Convention, which states that the Parties "shall consult periodically ... with a view to facilitating": "the effective use and implementation of the Convention"; "the exchange of information"; and "the consideration of possible supplementation or amendment of the Convention." The operation and activities of the T-CY are further defined by Rules of Procedure as adopted by the T-CY (Council of Europe, Cybercrime Convention Committee (T-CY), "T-CY Rules of Procedure. As revised by T-CY on 16 October 2020", T-CY (2013) (25 rev). These state in Article 1 that in pursuance of its functions, the T-CY shall, among other things, undertake assessments of the implementation of the Convention by the Parties and adopt

that originally patronized the adoption of the monitored treaties concerned,[68] certain conventions are heavily monitored with supervisory bodies working through phased reviews of the quality of implementing legislation, the application of implementing legislation, the enforcement of law and detection and other specified enforcement issues.[69] This forensic process is sometimes coupled with specific recommendations that target recalcitrant States Parties and aim to orient their future actions with regard to specific aspects of their treaty obligations.[70]

On occasion though, the same international organizations that have patronized the adoption of a given criminal law convention put out general recommendations, which, despite being related to the performance in good faith of the treaty obligations, go beyond what is strictly prescribed by the treaty regime.[71] In such cases, treaty bodies and NCMs serve also to monitor compliance with, and effective implementation of, the organization's non-binding standards, through the same type of

opinions and recommendations on the interpretation and implementation of the Convention, including Guiding Notes.

[68] Pursuant to Article 25 of the ECOWAS Convention on Small Arms and Light Weapons, Their Ammunition and Other Related Materials, the ECOWAS Executive Secretary is responsible for supporting and supervising the application of the provisions of the same treaty. Similarly, at the Third Ministerial Review Conference of the Nairobi Declaration, in June 2005, member States decided to transform the Nairobi Secretariat into a Regional Centre for Small Arms and Light Weapons (RECSA). This is now the body coordinating national efforts to implement the Protocol for the Prevention, Control and Reduction of Small Arms and Light Weapons in the Great Lakes Region and the Horn of Africa. The same Review Conference also agreed to a set of non-binding Best Practice Guidelines for the Implementation of the Nairobi Declaration and the Nairobi Protocol, which provide policy and practice recommendations on implementation of the Protocol.

[69] Cases in point are the Council of Europe Convention on Action against Trafficking in Human Beings, OECD Anti-Bribery Convention and CoECLCC.

[70] For instance, the monitoring mechanism of the Council of Europe Convention on Action against Trafficking in Human Beings consists of two distinct, but interacting, bodies: an independent expert body, the GRETA, which is composed of fifteen members who sit in their individual capacity; and a political body, the Committee of the Parties, which is composed of the representatives on the Committee of Ministers of the Council of Europe of the member States Parties to the Convention and representatives of the Parties to the Convention, which are not members of the Council of Europe. The main task of this latter body is to make specific recommendations, based on the GRETA's evaluation, to a Party concerning the measures to be taken as a follow-up to the GRETA's Report.

[71] A very recent case is given by the 2021 Anti-Bribery Recommendation adopted by the OECD Council on 26 November 2021, which puts in place new measures to reinforce the efforts of Parties to the OECD Anti-Bribery Convention to prevent, detect and investigate foreign bribery. See www.oecd.org/daf/anti-bribery/2021-oecd-anti-bribery-recommendation.htm, accessed 9 January 2022.

process of evaluation and pressure with the aim of inducing compliance with the treaty.[72] Also, certain monitoring bodies, like the Group of States Against Corruption (the anti-corruption body of the CoE (GRECO)),[73] have of late published reports with a view to disseminating information concerning bad and good practices in the implementation of supervised treaties and "derivative" recommendations (follow-up recommendations to supervised States about specific actions to undertake in order to pursue more effectively the general goals of the treaty in question).[74] Interestingly, particularly as opposed to a mixed practice of monitoring bodies established by universal suppression conventions, some recent regional criminal law conventions regulate the participation of civil society and NGOs in their monitoring process.[75]

17.2.3 A "Hard" Non-Compliance Mechanism Attached to Non-Binding Standards

In her chapter for this book, Malgosia Fitzmaurice discusses the development of non-compliance procedures in international environmental law

[72] For example, to prevent and combat corruption, the Council of Europe adopted a number of multifaceted legal instruments, including non-binding instruments such as Twenty Guiding Principles against Corruption (Resolution (97) 24); the Recommendation on Codes of Conduct for Public Officials (Recommendation No R (2000) 10); and the Recommendation on Common Rules against Corruption in the Funding of Political Parties and Electoral Campaigns (Recommendation Rec(2003)4). GRECO monitors compliance with and effective implementation of the organisation's anti-corruption standards, including non-binding codes, through the same process of mutual evaluation and peer pressure.

[73] See n 64.

[74] See, e.g., Council of Europe, "Codes of Conduct for Public Officials: GRECO Findings & Recommendations", GRECO (2019)5, Strasbourg 20 March 2019, available at https://rm.coe.int/codes-of-conduct-for-public-officials-greco-findings-recommendations-p/168094256b, accessed 29 September 2021. On this practice, see generally, R Kicker and M Möstl, *Standard-Setting through Monitoring? The Role of Council of Europe Expert in the Development of Human Rights* (Council of Europe 2012) esp. 105–15.

[75] This is the case with some of the more recent COE criminal law conventions: the Council of Europe Convention against Trafficking in Human Organs establishes in Article 23 a committee which according to Article 25 shall monitor the implementation of the Convention. Article 24, para 5 of the Convention provides that "representatives of civil society, and in particular non-governmental organisations, may be admitted as observers to the Committee of the Parties", reflecting a balanced representation of the sectors concerned. Equivalent regulations are included in Article 24 para 5 of the COE Convention on the Counterfeiting of Medical Products and Similar Crimes Involving Threats to Public Health; and in Article 39, para 3 of the Lanzarote Convention.

by looking at their recent evolution from hard to soft; that is to say, procedures based on more facilitative than coercive methods to elicit compliance with the obligations established by multilateral environmental agreements. The case I illustrate here moves in the opposite direction, with the operation of a robust (and effective) NCM to ensure that international standards on the prevention and repression of money laundering and terrorist financing are effectively put into action, despite the fact that such codes are not legally binding. I am referring to the review mechanism attached to the forty Recommendations[76] adopted by the Financial Action Task Force (FATF) in 1990.[77] This mechanism consists of mutual evaluations or peer reviews among the organization's thirty-nine members, involving also several other jurisdictions. The FATF review process involves country visits by mutual evaluators and FATF's personnel. Under the FATF review process, member States are subject to review by their peers, under ad hoc-created groups of officials from other States. The review process culminates in the publication of

[76] FATF Recommendations, available at www.fatf-gafi.org/publications/fatfrecommendations/documents/fatf-recommendations.html. FATF standards currently consist of forty consolidated recommendations comprising administrative and regulatory measures to prevent the proceeds of crime from entering into the legitimate financial system, as well as wide-ranging recommendations regarding criminal law and procedure and international cooperation. As an ad hoc intergovernmental body created in 1989 to combat money laundering in the context of drug trafficking, it produced forty Recommendations on anti-money laundering in 1990. In 2001, its remit was expanded to include CTF. Since then, FATF has periodically revised these norms, so that now they also cover the financing of proliferation of weapons of mass destruction (WMD), and have been adapted, inter alia, to financial innovations introduced by new technologies, services and products, such as virtual assets, that can attract criminals and terrorists who wish to use them to launder the proceeds of their crimes and finance their illicit activities. FATF last strengthened its standards in 2019 to clarify the application of anti-money laundering/CFT financing requirements on virtual assets and virtual asset service providers. See also Y Ishii, "Blockchain Technology and Anti-Money Laundering Regulation under International Law" 2019 23(1) *ASIL Insights*, offering a preliminary discussion of the vulnerabilities of the global anti-money laundering/CFT system to these new technologies.

[77] The FATF initially consisted exclusively of developed countries, but now includes also some emerging States. Its membership embraces thirty-seven member jurisdictions and two international regional organizations (the Gulf Cooperation Council and the EU, represented by the European Commission). FATF has expanded incrementally beyond Europe, North America, the Gulf and Japan, with the addition of Argentina, Brazil and Mexico in 2000; Russia and South Africa in 2003; China in 2007; the Republic of Korea in 2009; India in 2010; Malaysia in 2016; and Saudi Arabia in 2019. FATF has also extended observer status to a number of international organizations with financial integrity functions, including the International Monetary Fund (IMF) and the World Bank.

mutual evaluation reports.[78] The first three rounds of mutual evaluations focussed on implementation of the Recommendations, while the fourth round, which is currently ongoing, covers also the effectiveness of members' anti-money laundering and counter-terrorist financing systems.[79]

To be clear, FATF develops and produces policies, not laws.[80] However, FATF's institutional design, practices and monitoring process have contributed to the spread of its standards and their influence on domestic legislation with respect to both form and content, despite the non-binding nature of these norms. As FATF has come to serve as the international standard-setter in the anti-money laundering field, about 200 countries and jurisdictions around the world have adopted anti-money laundering policies, including States like the tiny Pacific Island nation of Nauru, with a population of 10,000, no financial institutions, significant unemployment and an external debt which amounts to 75 per cent of its GDP.[81] In the case of FATF, international financial regulation, though not emanating from traditionally binding sources, is sustained by a range of enforcement tools and consequences that make it more

[78] More specifically, under FATF's Mutual Evaluation Process, member States are subject to review by their peers, in the form of ad hoc groups of officials from other States. The process, which is formalized under a specific set of FATF rules, includes visits by the evaluation group to local officials, extensive interviews and assessment of implementation on the ground. The assessment culminates with a Mutual Evaluation Report for each State, which identifies gaps in national legislation and practice regarding money laundering and terrorist financing, and suggests corrective actions. FATF publishes the main findings of the report, as well as the overall evaluation, on its website. This means that the public can see if a country is fully or partially compliant, and what the main compliance problems are. Where a member is found only partially compliant, FATF will subsequently follow up to check whether it has taken action to remedy compliance gaps. FATF closely monitors the progress made by identified jurisdictions and reflects this in FATF's public statements at the end of each plenary meeting.

Regular members of FATF go through the Mutual Evaluation Process every few years. For a synthetic overview of the Mutual Evaluation Process and Report and preliminary information about the recent round of reviews see FATF, (n 22) 29–36.

[79] See FATF, "Procedures for the FATF Fourth Round of AML/CFT Evaluations" (2021), available at www.fatf-gafi.org/en/publications/Mutualevaluations/4th-round-procedures.html.

[80] FATF Recommendations take the form of a non-binding instrument, and the thirty-nine members of FATF have made a political rather than a legal commitment to implement the FATF Recommendations. Despite the regulatory precision of their content, the Recommendations employ hortatory language, providing "only that FATF members 'should' rather than 'shall' implement them."

[81] Republic of Nauru Department of Finance, "2021 Republic of Nauru Dept Report", 1 June 2021, 5.

coercive than traditional theories of international law might predict.[82] These include the reputational and economic consequences of non-compliance in international relations.[83] Granted, FATF has no enforcement capability. But in order to become part of FATF, a candidate country must comply with a set of legal and institutional requirements, *including the implementation* of the FATF Recommendations in the form of *hard law at the domestic level*,[84] which is a mandatory requirement to remain or become a member of FATF,[85] and the FATF can suspend member countries that fail to comply on a timely basis with its standards.

Moreover, FATF has a global reach. *International expansion* has been a key FATF goal since its inception. Rather than expanding its own membership in order to achieve this, FATF has worked together with other intergovernmental bodies, known as FATF-style regional bodies (FSRBs) to create a network of nearly 200 countries. FSRBs are made up of countries that are not necessarily FATF members. They are considered FATF "associate members" and apply their own evaluation processes, which means that FSRB member countries are subject to mutual evaluations regarding compliance with FATF standards.[86] Many countries in

[82] See generally C Brummer, *Soft Law and the Global Financial System: Rule-Making in the 21st Century* (2nd ed., Cambridge University Press 2015) 143–62. See also, with specific regard to the FATF standards, L Borlini, "Soft law, soft organizations e regolamentazione 'tecnica' di problemi di sicurezza pubblica e integrità finanziaria" (2017) 100(2) *Rivista di diritto internazionale* 356; A Rodiles, *Coalitions of the Willing and International Law: The Interplay between Formality and Informality* (Cambridge University Press 2018) 158–67; and F Ní Aoláin "'Soft Law', Informal Law-making and 'New Institutions' in the Global Counter-Terrorism Architecture" (2021) 32(3) *European Journal of International Law* 919.

[83] As C Chinkin, "Normative Development in the International Legal System" in D Shelton, *Commitment and Compliance: The Role of Non-Binding Norms in The International Legal System* (Oxford University Press 2000) 21, at 24, notes even legal norms "are not monolithic, and it is intuitively accepted that some norms are accorded greater weight than others and some are precisely framed, while others are open-ended, indeterminate, and incapable of creating precise preconditions of future behavior."

[84] The [FATF] *Handbook for Countries and Assessors on AML/ CFT Evaluations and Assessments* emphasizes that domestic measures implementing the Recommendations should impose a legal obligation. The *Handbook* specifically notes that "this standard would not be met by codes of conduct issued by private sector associations, non-binding guidance issued by a supervisory authority, or voluntary private sector behavior."

[85] Financial Action Task Force, "Process and Criteria to Become a FATF Member," available at www.fatf-gafi.org/about/membersandobservers/membershipprocessandcriteria.html.

[86] FSRBs and their members can participate in FATF meetings, provide input and engage in joint projects with FATF. When considering a revision of the forty Recommendations,

the developing world that are not members of FATF itself have become subject to FATF's standards as a result of the establishment of these regional bodies. Importantly, *FATF also holds States that are neither FATF nor FSRB members to its recommendations.* Its stated mission is to "identify national-level vulnerabilities" and, to this end, it aims to identify and engage "with high-risk, non-co-operative jurisdictions and those with strategic deficiencies in their national regimes" that pose a threat to the financial system's integrity.[87] Gadinis has convincingly argued that the *network effect* is important in anti-money efforts, because the appeal of FATF increases when new members join, as each country's addition to the FATF network increases the number of potential co-operators for countries seeking to join.[88] Also, international financial institutions' efforts to promote the stability of financial markets contribute to the reach of FATF. Recognizing the central role that FATF standards occupy in global financial regulation, influential international organizations have embraced its standards in an effort to develop robust and stable markets around the world. In their ongoing evaluation of countries' financial systems, the *International Monetary Fund (IMF) and World Bank use the FATF* standards in the context of the Financial Sector *Assessment Program (FSAP)*,[89] their joint programme aimed at providing a comprehensive framework through which assessors and authorities in participating countries can identify financial system vulnerabilities and develop appropriate policy responses.

FSRB members can offer their views but have no vote. FATF is the sole standard setter, and only FATF members vote.

87 Financial Action Task Force, "FATF Mandate" (2019), available at www.fatf-gafi.org/publications/fatfgeneral/documents/fatf-mandate.html, Article 4. Currently, only North Korea and Iran are included in what is often externally referred to as the "black list."

88 S Gadinis, "Three Pathways to Global Standards: Private, Regulation and Ministry Networks" (2015) 109(1) *American Journal of International Law* 1, esp. 28–32.

89 The FSAP is a joint programme of the International Monetary Fund and the World Bank. Launched in 1999 in the wake of the Asian financial crisis, the programme brings together Bank and Fund expertise to help countries reduce the likelihood and severity of financial sector crises. The FSAP follows a three-pronged approach when looking at the country's financial sector, examining: the soundness of a financial system versus its vulnerabilities and risks that increase the likelihood or potential severity of financial sector crises; as well as a country's developmental needs in terms of infrastructure, institutions and markets; and a country's compliance with the observance of selected financial sector standards and codes. For further information, see International Monetary Fund, "Financial Sector Assessment Program (FSAP)", available at www.imf.org/en/Publications/fssa.

Finally, FATF Recommendations are backed up by *mechanisms of "soft liability"* and *"soft sanctions"*[90] that can themselves exert discipline by generating continuous pressure for compliance.[91] FATF has a rigorous process of identifying high-risk and non-cooperative jurisdictions.[92] FATF members that do not implement FATF Recommendations effectively, as indicated in their country reports, risk losing their membership. That loss could compromise a State's participation in other international fora that include government representatives, such as the Financial Stability Board.[93] Secondly, FATF's "soft sanctions" reach not only FATF members but also countries that are members of its regional bodies or that have no relationship to FATF, but that FATF suspects of harboring money launderers. On top of that, FATF calls upon its members to severely restrict, and even prohibit fully, transactions with

[90] Some authors do not hesitate to speak of soft liability, soft dispute settlement and soft sanctions. See, among others, I Seidl-Hohenveldern, "International 'Economic' Soft Law" (1997) 163 *Recueil des cours* 165–246, and, with critical tones, J Klabbers, *The Concept of Treaty in International Law* (Kluwer Law International 1996) 158.

[91] Together with the precision of their normative content that renders them readily applicable as sufficiently identifiable prescriptive behavior, the existence of follow-up mechanisms generating pressure for compliance helps to gauge the real weight of the FATF standards and understand where they are positioned, along an ideal spectrum from soft to hard. On this continuum see O Schachter, *The Twilight Existence of Nonbinding International Agreements* (1977) 71 *American Journal of International Law* 296.

[92] As sovereign governments interested in securing one another's compliance, FATF members have mutually agreed to submit their governments' implementation efforts to periodic monitoring by foreign officials.

[93] The Financial Stability Board (FSB) was established in April 2009 as the successor to the Financial Stability Forum (FSF). At the Pittsburgh Summit, the Heads of State and Government of the G20 endorsed the FSB's original Charter of 25 September 2009 which set out the FSB's objectives and mandate, and organizational structure. The FSB has assumed a key role in promoting the reform of international financial regulation and supervision worldwide. At the Cannes Summit in November 2011, the G20 called for a strengthening of the FSB's capacity resources and governance through establishment of the FSB on an enduring organizational basis. In its Report to the G20 Los Cabos Summit on Strengthening FSB Capacity, Resources and Governance, the FSB set out concrete steps to strengthen the FSB's capacity, resources and governance and establish it on an enduring organizational footing. At the Los Cabos Summit on 19 June 2012, the Heads of State and Government of the G20 endorsed the FSB's restated and amended Charter which reinforces certain elements of its mandate, including its role in standard-setting and in promoting members' implementation of international standards and agreed G20 and FSB commitments and policy recommendations. On 28 January 2013, the FSB established itself as a not-for-profit association under Swiss law with its seat in Basel, Switzerland.

financial institutions from blacklisted jurisdictions.[94] Such limitations do not violate any international legal obligations, though they are unfriendly and thus constitute a form of retortion. FATF members control access to the most important financial markets. Shutting out countries, or persons operating from their jurisdiction, from the global financial system imposes great pressure on violators' and potential violators' governments.

All these factors taken together account for the effectiveness of the FATF review process in ensuring that international standards against money laundering and terrorist financing are complied with and put into action by States around the globe.

17.3 Nature of the Pursued Interest: Why Non-Compliance Mechanisms in International Criminal Law?

Having mapped the current state of international supervision in the area of international criminal law in Section 17.2, this section goes on to address the nature of the interests pursued by such mechanisms vis-à-vis the increasing complexity of international criminal law treaties and standards. The fragmentation and complexity of international criminal law treaties and standards is indeed key to the nature of the interest pursued by NCMs in international criminal law. International criminal law treaties concluded in the past were typically reactive in nature. These conventions mainly required the criminalization of particular conduct in

[94] See Recommendation 19 and Interpretative Note 19. Since 2000, FATF has adopted a naming and shaming approach that effectively generates a blacklist: the Non-Cooperating Countries and Territories (NCCT) process. FATF members and then controversially non-members were measured against twenty-five criteria based on the 1990 FATF Recommendations. Those that fell short were identified and classified as non-cooperative and subject to "countermeasures." The NCCT process was replaced by the International Cooperation and Review Group (ICRG) in 2006, which began operating in 2007. States revealed by this mutual evaluation process to have key deficiencies in implementation are referred for review by an ICRG regional review group and can be placed in one of two tiers either calling for consideration of the risks arising from their strategic deficiencies (the "grey" list), or the application of countermeasures by FATF members (the "black" list). Placement on the blacklist is associated with a lack of political commitment to the implementation of the Recommendations. Countermeasures include risk mitigation measures such as limiting dealings with the identified country or persons operating from that jurisdiction. For an informed introduction to this system see, among many, L de Koker and M Turkington, "Transnational Organised Crime and the Anti-Money Laundering Regime" in P Hauck and S Peterke (eds), *International Law and Transnational Organized Crime* (Oxford University Press 2016) 241.

response to ongoing problems or incidents. The terrorism suppression conventions "illustrate this point. States adopted a 'sectoral approach' to treaty-making";[95] whereby the negotiation of a treaty responded to a recent terrorism crisis or string of incidents.[96] By contrast, a number of contemporary criminal law treaties currently include a wide array of more forward-looking rules, ranging from pure criminal repression,[97] to wide-ranging preventive provisions and chapters,[98] to a cornucopia of forms of international cooperation,[99] to technical assistance rules aimed at supporting contracting Parties in the progressive fulfillment of the treaties' objectives[100] and complex rules to pursue forms of redistributive justice, epitomized by the norms on asset recovery of the UNCAC and AUCPCC.[101] In sum, modern international criminal law treaties are geared towards mitigating an ongoing criminal problem, shared by different States, with a view to achieving or maintaining a particular result in the future, including the prevention and deterrence of crime and enduring international cooperation in diverse forms.[102] Recent practice shows particularly that the "preventive component" (viz. the inclusion in the treaty regime of measures which are prophylactic in nature) is gaining importance. Obviously, the precise content of the rules on prevention varies with treaties.[103] But they have all in common that the

[95] Rose (n 4) 55.

[96] KN Trapp, "The Potentialities and Limitations of Reactive Law Making: A Case Study in International Terrorism Suppression" (2016) 39 *University of New South Wales Law Journal* 1191.

[97] Modern criminal law conventions oblige the Parties to criminalize a vast range of activities, and attach sanctions, including for legal persons.

[98] Comprehensive preventive measures occupy a significant part of a number of recent criminal law conventions and standards. Examples are the Lanzarote Convention; the Istanbul Convention; the Nicosia Convention; the Budapest Convention; UNCAC and AUCPCC; and the FATF Recommendations.

[99] Typically, State Parties also agree to treat the offences listed in the conventions as extraditable offences and commit to a cornucopia of forms of international cooperation, including measures of mutual legal assistance in investigations, prosecutions and judicial proceedings, for purposes such as, for example, taking evidence, executing searches and seizures, examining sites and providing information. These conventions also pave the way for further cooperation, including the exchange of information about suspects, the secondment of liaison officers or even the establishment of joint teams.

[100] Quite innovatively, at least for a universal suppression convention, UNCAC includes an entire chapter devoted to the regulation of technical assistance.

[101] See generally Arnone and Borlini (n 19) chapter 17.

[102] See also Rose (n 5) 56–57.

[103] Compare, for instance, the wide-array of preventive measures set in chapter 2 of the UNCAC with the detailed obligations to adopt specific legislation and take measures to

obligations they establish are not only normative, but also prospective in nature.

In order for these treaties to function properly, States Parties often require information about their current state of implementation, as well as the ability to adjust the rules accordingly. Viewed from this perspective, NCMs enable the operation of international criminal law treaties and standards. Despite their sometimes considerable differences in institutional architecture, powers and procedures, it is fair to say that all the analyzed mechanisms are designed not to allocate legal liability, but rather to encourage States, by influence and soft power, to adopt behaviors and practices that comply with international obligations and standards. Much like their well-known counterparts in the fields of human rights and environmental law, monitoring treaty bodies and NCMs dealing with international crimes are well-suited to apply measures of a *more facilitative quality* in lieu of traditional coercive approaches, consonant with the view that a cooperative and "managerial" approach, rather than an enforcement approach, may better address non-compliance issues, and, hence, favor prevention and consistency with international law, rather than reparation after a violation has occurred.[104] The *paradigmatic (or normative)* goal of modern international criminal law conventions (hence, the non-reciprocal character of the international obligations they establish), and their *forward-looking character* mean that adjudication may scarcely be appropriate. An infringement by one of the Parties might go by unheeded if it were only the other contracting State that has the right to demand compliance.

Most criminal law treaties today respond to the working hypothesis that there is an "interest-outcome" conundrum. The more broadly a (legal) interest is shared among States Parties (e.g., common concerns regarding specific forms of crime), and the less desirable a particular result (e.g., the proliferation of crime), then the more relevant is the shared ownership of the monitoring process. For broadly shared interests, such as, for instance, the rule of law, NCMs provide a "safer" avenue for States to address concerns than independent international courts. Traditional methods provided by the law of treaties or general

prevent sexual violence, and to protect child victims, established by chapter 2 and chapter IV of the Lanzarote Convention.

[104] A Cassese, "Supervision and Fact-Finding as Alternatives to Judicial Review: Fostering Increased Conformity with International Standards" in A Cassese (ed.), *Realizing Utopia: The Future of International Law* (Oxford University Press 2012) 295.

international law are likely to be of little help in ensuring effective compliance. International oversight in the field of international criminal law is designed not to assign blame, with the gravitas and severity of "Justitia's sword," but rather to encourage States to adopt desired behaviors and practices. The overall approach is not sanctions-based; it is more educative in nature, as it works through normative alignment. In this field, NCMs are functionally directed to bypass the possibility of a unilateral assessment of non-compliance with the relevant international standards by States. Quite the reverse, they operate to verify compliance with, and induce respect for, a wide array of international rules of paradigmatic, as opposed to synallagmatic, character.[105]

17.4 Qualitative Analysis: Determinants of Effectiveness in Monitoring and Addressing Situations of Non-Compliance

Suppression of crime, future deterrence and prevention are the overarching goals of the criminal law conventions and instruments discussed in this chapter. Achieving these objectives requires implementation of the rules of the relevant criminal law conventions – both substantive and procedural – in municipal law. It also requires effective compliance with these rules,[106] particularly through enforcement of national implementing legislation and international cooperation. As suggested by a commentator, the Doha Declaration,[107] adopted in 2015 at the UN Crime Congress held in Doha, "provides a convenient lens" through which to assess "the implementation of and compliance with [international] criminal law".[108] The Doha Declaration aspires to integrate crime prevention into "the wider UN agenda addressing social and economic challenges

105 The functional difference between these bodies and international courts raises questions about similarities and differences between the expectations associated with coercive justice, based on an "imperium," and the soft power that characterizes both the functions and design of international monitoring procedures.

106 On this distinction see K Raustiala and A Slaughter, "International Law, International Relations and Compliance" in W Carlsnaes, T Risse and BE Simmons (eds), *Handbook of International Relations* (Sage 2002) 538 referred to also by Boister (n 6) 401.

107 Doha Declaration on Integrating Crime Prevention and Criminal Justice into the Wider United Nations Agenda to Address Social and Economic Challenges and to Promote the Rule of Law at the National and International Levels, and Public Participation (UN 2015), available at www.unodc.org/documents/congress/Declaration/V1504151_English.pdf, accessed 6 October 2021 (Doha Declaration).

108 Boister (n 6) 402.

and promoting the rule of law,"[109] openly recognizing that "sustainable development and the rule of law are strongly interrelated and mutually reinforcing".[110]

There is a gap between suppression conventions and their implementation. These treaties "have not yielded the expected dividends in terms of effective international cooperation".[111] Boister goes further in observing that "[m]any states join these treaties, some reform their laws, but most never use them," concluding that "general support for them appears to be largely rhetorical."[112] Formal commitment is not the same as material compliance. What is undisputable is that neither implementation of, nor compliance with these treaties can be taken for granted. And States are rarely held legally accountable through international dispute settlement for non-compliance.[113]

Compliance is in fact the "product of a range of complex interactions between legal, political, social, and moral norms as well as the real advantages/disadvantages of compliance and the pressure that large powerful states and civil society exert in the promotion of compliance."[114] These relations are imponderable in the abstract. However, scholars and practitioners have identified the circumstances that, in general, favor or jeopardize implementation and compliance with

[109] Ibid. 402.

[110] Doha Declaration, para 4. As it is known, Goal 16 of the UN's post-2015 SDGs is the promotion of peaceful and inclusive societies for sustainable development, the provision of access to justice for all, and the building of effective, accountable institutions at all levels. Among the objectives indicated in Goal 16 of direct relevance to the suppression of the international crimes discussed in this chapter are the ending of child trafficking, significant reduction of arms trafficking, significant reduction of illicit financial flows, strengthening of stolen asset recovery, combating organized crime, reducing corruption and developing capacity to combat violence, terrorism and crime.

[111] Y Dandurand and V Chin, "Implementation of Transnational Criminal Law", in Boister and Currie (n 12) 437, at 440.

[112] Boister (n 6) 402.

[113] Note, for instance, the UN suppression conventions contain the standard compromissory clauses for the settlement of disputes about implementation: negotiation, arbitration and finally submission for adjudication before the International Court of Justice (ICJ). See, e.g., Article 32(4) of the 1988 Drug Trafficking Convention; Article 35 of the UNTOC; Article 66 of the UNCAC. However, as a matter of fact, the dispute resolution mechanisms established by international criminal law treaties have not been used, often because Parties to these conventions very rarely hold each other to legal account for violation of suppression conventions, preferring to deal with these matters through diplomacy.

[114] Boister (n 6) 418.

international criminal conventions.[115] Among these conditions, effective mechanisms to review implementation and incentivize compliance are usually considered critical. Gathering and reviewing information about the steps State Parties have taken to implement a suppression convention bears the potential embarrassment "of publicity about poor performance."[116] Although typically contemplated in the form of a facilitative mechanism, a finding of non-compliance may indeed be regarded *latu senso* as a "sanction," creating political discomfort for the State concerned.[117] Importantly, such a finding does not entail legal consequences. The relative effectiveness of different NCMs in international criminal law, indeed, mainly depends on operational factors.

What are the elements impacting on the effectiveness of the various NCMs? Certain elements are general and highly contextual, but, at the same time, may be decisive. By way of example, the global political climate has lately become less hospitable to internationalization efforts of the kind described in this work, with increasing tensions among global powers, nationalism on the rise and international organizations under stress. This has an effect on the operation of NCMs irrespective of their specific features. Similarly, the low cost of commitment in jurisdictions where the rule of law is not embedded encourages treaty ratification and

[115] Other than the existence and effectiveness of NCMs, a number of other factors obviously impact on compliance with international criminal law conventions, including the general reluctance of States to submit their criminal justice systems to external scrutiny; whether norms are self-executing or not; the hierarchical rank they have under national law; the quality and formulation of specific obligations (e.g., whether they set minimum standards or best practices); States Parties' actual capacity for implementation, especially developing countries; the fact that suppression conventions are not designed with a coherent system of implementation in mind and, hence, most new treaties present States with an entirely separate law reform exercise; and the persistence of the States' will to implement obligations undertaken at diplomatic conferences when the time comes. This latter determinant depends on a variety of circumstances, including the motivations driving the participation in the treaty making process – it is not infrequent that States have participated in the process of the development of the treaty for reasons other than an authentic desire to suppress the particular conduct, such as, for instance, pressure by other States or promise of aid. Also, as Boister (n 6) 406 notes, "there may have been very little agreement to take concrete steps in the first place, something usually indicated by the fragmented nature of the legal obligations in a convention (e.g., take the Firearms Protocol)."

[116] Ibid., 407.

[117] See G Ulfstein, "Treaty Bodies and Regimes" in DB Hollis (ed.), *The Oxford Guide to Treaties* (Oxford University Press 2012), 428, 441–42.

jeopardizes compliance.[118] Further, States "with integrity deficits resist being scrutinized by others."[119]

Other factors of particular interest to us here are more strictly related to the design and architecture of NCMs. Consider self-reporting in answer to a questionnaire. It is a common method,[120] especially insofar as it constitutes the first step of more sophisticated procedures. Depending on the Parties alone is,[121] however, "an invitation to abuse."[122] This is why modern suppression conventions resort to two main alternatives, by relying either on *expert review* or on *peer review* of a Party's performance. Independent expert review is epitomized by committees like GRETA, which gathers information for evaluation from Parties by questionnaire (which Parties are obliged to answer) and from civil society, and may also use in-country visits and hearings before making a report.[123] The Group's evaluation reports are rigorous and of high quality.[124] This is essential also for the accuracy of the specific recommendations the Committee of the Parties may make, on the basis of the report and conclusions of GRETA, to a Party concerning the measures to be taken as a follow-up to a GRETA Report. The precision of GRETA evaluations depends on different elements, particularly the expertise of its individual members in the areas covered by the supervised Convention; the structure of the evaluation procedures in multiple rounds; and the body's own capacity both to identify shortcomings,

118 See OA Hathaway, "The Cost of Commitment", John M Olin Center for Studies in Law, Economics, and Public Policy Working Papers No 273, available at http://digitalcommons.law.yale.edu/lepp_papers/273/ accessed 4 October 2021.

119 SM Redo, *Blue Criminology: The Power of United Nations Ideas to Counter Crime Globally* (HEUNI 2012) 189.

120 Completed questionnaires must be submitted on a periodic basis and are used by convention secretariats to compile reports for the purpose of review. As aptly remarked by Dandurand and Chin (n 111) 478, reporting is often encumbered by technical issues, lack of human and financial resources, language barriers, and complexity of, and lack of clarity about the nature and relevance of the information required.

121 The self-assessment was the primary means of review of implementation of UNCAC up until the establishment of the IRG pursuant to Article 63(5) in 2009. Initially, a Self-Assessment Checklist was created on the initiative of the Conference of State Parties (CoSP) by the secretariat so that State Parties could identify their technical assistance needs. In response, seventy-two States Parties submitted self-assessment reports to the Secretariat.

122 Boister (n 5) 407.

123 See www.coe.int/en/web/anti-human-trafficking/greta, accessed 2 January 2022.

124 See, e.g., the recent evaluation's report on Croatia. GRETA, "Evaluation Report: Croatia. Access to Justice and Effective Remedies for Victims of Trafficking in Human Beings", GRETA(2020)10, 3 December 2020.

and to take cognisance of good practices in compliance with the CoE Convention on Action against Trafficking in Human Beings. A precondition for GRETA's "effective" operation is the identification and collection of information allowing a quantitative and qualitative analysis of the effectiveness of member States' judicial systems. This is information that, like the other CoE's monitoring bodies,[125] GRETA can leverage: the work of an important late addition to the organization's institutional construction, the European Commission for the Efficiency of Justice (CEPEJ),[126] a body that has no equivalent in other international organizations.

As a second alternative to self-reporting, peer review of a Party's performance by other Parties is generally assumed to be a powerful monitoring methodology because it involves peer pressure.[127] While mutual evaluation of this kind was already used within the FATF system, it was pioneered in its treaty form under the OECD Anti-Bribery Convention and, then, by GRECO, which, as noted, was set up to complement the CoE's six anti-corruption instruments. The GRECO monitoring mechanism has two main components: an evaluation procedure which is based on on-site visits and the issuing of evaluation reports, as well as country-specific recommendations; and a fully-fledged impact assessment ("compliance procedure") designed to appraise the measures taken by its members to implement the recommendations emanating from country evaluations.[128]

Having spelled out the main alternatives for effective review, it remains to note that the form of review *per se* is no guarantee of effectiveness. As a matter of fact, poorly effective mechanisms exist among both expert- and

[125] To remain in the area of expert review, this is the case, for instance, of GREVIO and the Lanzarote Committee.

[126] A relatively late, and yet essential, initiative taken to take cognisance of good practices in compliance with the organization's *acquis juridique* dates back to 2002 when the Committee of Ministers established the European CEPEJ. Its objective is to compare judicial systems, exchange experiences and to define concrete measures to improve the efficiency and functioning of legal systems in Europe, including a better implementation of international legal standards elaborated under the auspices of the Council of Europe. See Council of Europe, CM Res (2002)12; for a detailed overview, see M Breuer, "Establishing Common Standards and Securing the Rule of Law" in S Schmahl and M Breuer (eds), *The Council of Europe: Its Law and Policies* (Oxford University Press 2017) para 28.55.

[127] This position is voiced, among others, by Boister (n 6) 408.

[128] For an informed assessment of this monitoring mechanism see W Rau, "Group of States Against Corruption" in Schmahl and Breuer (n 126) 444.

peer review-based varieties. Expert committees may be fairly powerless in some instances. The Advisory Board set up under the auspices of the AUCPCC, for example, has, virtually no role in monitoring, and is, in effect, "a toothless think tank."[129] NCMs based on peer review, too, have been criticized for their inability to orient the future conduct of States and incentivize compliance with criminal law treaties. Non-compliance mechanisms in the area of the suppression of trafficking in firearms, when existent at all, have been so far poorly effective.[130] Looking again at anti-corruption treaties, MESICIC has not been able to modify the excessive discretion the IACAC gives to States Parties as to the timetable within which they have to implement treaty obligations. And, while the OECD WGB has developed a robust peer review mechanism that adopted a four-phase review of the quality of implementing legislation, the application of implementing legislation, the enforcement of law and detection and other enforcement issues,[131] the peer review system established in 2009 by the CoSP to the UNCAC is affected by the scarcity of available information on country visits; the absence of follow-up procedures on recommendations made in country reviews; and the fact that publication of self-assessment reports and country review reports is not mandatory and depends on the authorization of States Parties.[132] Not

[129] Boister (n 6) 408. See also J Wouters, C Ryngaert and S Cloots, "The International Legal Framework against Corruption: Achievements and Challenges" (2013) 14 *Melbourne Journal of International Law* 205, 230–31.

[130] See CE Drummond and AE Cassimatis, "Weapons Smuggling" in Boister and Currie (n 12) 247.

[131] The above-described forensic process has allowed the OECD Working Group of Bribery (WGB) to target recalcitrant parties. For example, an increasingly hostile attitude from the WGB pressured the UK into adopting the Bribery Act 2010. Prior to that, the UK – a party to the convention since 1997 – had had a poor record in regard to the adoption of legal machinery to combat corruption and had failed to pass the necessary laws to prevent British companies from engaging in foreign corruption. The UK's ineffectual response drew strong criticism from the Working Group on Bribery, whose chairman, frustrated at the British Chamber of Industries' long rearguard action resisting change eventually threatened the UK with sanctions (a power the Convention did not actually provide for). See C Rose, *International Anti-Corruption Norms: Their Creation and Influence on Domestic Legal Systems* (Oxford University Press 2015), 83 et seq. For a general assessment of peer review and compliance with the 1997 OECD Convention against bribery see H Jongen, "Peer Review and Compliance with International Anti-Corruption Norms: Insights from the OECD Working Group on Bribery" (2021) 47(3) *Review of International Studies* 331–52.

[132] When a State Party refuses to authorize the publication of reports, the UNODC can only publish the executive summaries. These summaries are informative, but the relatively low number of published country review reports considerably restricts the possibility of

surprisingly, similar drawbacks seem to affect the review mechanism created to monitor the implementation of UNCTOC and its Protocols.[133]

To conclude on the point, the analysis of the NCMs discussed in this chapter shows that it is the combination of a number of legal and extra-legal factors surrounding the design and functioning of these mechanisms that most impacts on their relative effectiveness. In general, the problems surrounding the design and operation of NCMs established under regional conventions and treaties among "like-minded" States, on the one hand, and universal treaties, on the other, are hardly comparable. With the former category of treaties, the creation of robust review mechanisms that can substantially pressure States Parties into improving compliance is certainly less difficult, as implicitly confirmed by the protracted negotiations that eventually led to the creation of UNCTOC's Review System. Funding and allocation of resources are obviously critical factors and are frequently divisive issues as among the Parties to universal suppression conventions.[134]

From an institutional perspective, important elements are: (a) a balanced mix of "vertical," (i.e., a single State's performance may be evaluated across a range of obligations), and "horizontal" monitoring, (in which many States' performance of a single obligation or of a group of related obligations may be compared);[135] (b) the division of the monitoring process into phased reviews of the quality of implementing legislation, its application, enforcement of the law and detection of offences and other enforcement issues;[136] as well as (c) the institution of follow-up procedures based on full-fledged evaluation reports on implementation.[137] Even if exceptional in international criminal law, treaty bodies of a so-called "quasi-judicial" nature (bodies that are not courts, but do decide individual complaints), may help put greater

assessing the adequacy of the summaries and the availability of detailed information on the shortcomings of national implementing legislation.

133 As observed *supra* Section 17.2.1, the two treaties are closely related and UNCTOC's Review Mechanism took UNCAC's Review Mechanism as a model. Early criticism on the effectiveness of UNCTOC's Review Mechanism is expressed by Rose (n 25) 59–62. A different view is proposed by SM Redo, "The United Nations Criminal Justice System in the Suppression of Transnational Crime" in Boister and Currie (n 12) 57, esp. 62–65.

134 See further Rose (n 25) 59–60.

135 Vertical review, in particular, provides a channel to share good practices and challenges.

136 The cases of GRECO, OECD WGB, GRETA and the FATF Mutual Evaluations are most illustrative.

137 Recall again the complex monitoring mechanism of the Council of Europe Convention on Action against Trafficking in Human Beings.

compliance pressure on States.[138] As the creation of the CEPEJ shows, intra-organizational cooperation may also strengthen monitoring.[139] The same holds true with inter-organizational cooperation, especially when it is directed to channel expertise and challenges among monitoring mechanisms supervising treaties on similar/identical crimes, and, hence, also streamline burdensome reporting requirements. For instance, sharing of expertise and coordination of planning among GRECO, the WGB, MESICIC and the UNCAC monitoring system is facilitated through the close relations maintained among relevant international organizations, which have observer status within one another's NCMs.[140]

Finally, multilateral criminal treaties themselves do not commonly grant powers of sanction to monitoring bodies. The 1961 Single Convention (as amended) and the 1971 Psychotropic Conventions are the exceptions in that they grant the International Narcotics Control Board (INCB) power to impose sanctions on State Parties.[141] However, "these powers have never been used and similar powers have not been included in other treaties."[142] As explained above, a finding of non-compliance may determine only negative consequences in international relations by exposing the State concerned to political embarrassment or, as the outstanding example of the FATF standards evidences, to harsh forms of "market pressure."

[138] This is relevant for the purposes of this chapter only in relation to monitoring bodies established in human rights treaties that include also criminal law obligations, such as the international conventions against torture. See A Cassese, "A New Approach to Human Rights: The European Convention for the Prevention of Torture" (1989) 83(1) *American Journal of International Law* 128.

[139] For a discussion of other insightful examples of intra-organizational cooperation see Rau (n 127) 21.15–21.19.

[140] Cf. Conference of the States Parties to the United Nations Convention against Corruption, Resolution 7/4, "Enhancing Synergies between Relevant Multilateral Organizations Responsible for Review Mechanisms in the Field of Anti-Corruption", adopted at its Seventh Session, Vienna, 6–10 November 2017, available at www.unodc.org/unodc/en/corruption/COSP/session7-resolutions.html, accessed 31 July 2021; and GRECO, 80th GRECO Plenary Meeting, Decisions, Greco(2018)11, Strasbourg, 22 June 2018, para 35–36, available at https://rm.coe.int/decisions-80th-greco-plenary-meetingstrasbourg-18-22-june-2018-/16808b655f, accessed 31 July 2021.

[141] In terms of Article 145 of the 1961 Single Convention, for example, the INCB can call the parties' attention to breaches and call for special studies to be made. In the case of a serious endangerment of the Convention's aims or the development of a serious situation, or where these measures are most appropriate to facilitate cooperative action, it can make a report to the United Nations Economic and Social Council (ECOSOC) and recommend an embargo on the import and export of drugs to the defaulting State.

[142] Boister (n 5) 412.

18

Non-Compliance and Nuclear Disarmament

The Iran Nuclear Deal

JIN SUN

18.1 Introduction

The Treaty on the Non-Proliferation of Nuclear Weapons (NPT)[1] has been an important pillar of world peace in the international legal complex[2] of nuclear disarmament and arms control, as each non-nuclear-weapon State undertakes 'not to manufacture or acquire nuclear weapons'.[3] A constant challenge for great power rivalry and global geopolitical stability characterises States' international legal interaction in the nuclear disarmament sphere. This interaction has variously taken the form of political diplomacy, the operation of tailored non-compliance machinery, and proceedings before international courts and tribunals (ICTs) as well as most recently the negotiation of the Iran Nuclear Deal (also known as the Joint Comprehensive Plan of Action or JCPOA). The difficulty of finding a 'negotiated solution guaranteeing

This chapter is part of the author's research project funded by the European Research Council under the European Union's Horizon 2020 research and innovation programme (Grant Agreement PROSANCT, 'Bombs, Banks and Sanctions', Project 716216), and the Swiss Network for International Studies (SNIS) initiative on 'When Money Can't Buy Food and Medicine: Banking Challenges in the International Trade of Vital Goods and their Humanitarian Impact in Sanctioned Jurisdictions', both headed by Grégoire Mallard. For particularly helpful comments and edits, I would like to thank Professor Christina Voigt, Professor Caroline Foster, Professor Makane Mbengue, Even Espelid, and other participants during the conference at PluriCourts Research Centre, University of Oslo.

[1] Treaty on the Non-Proliferation of Nuclear Weapons (NPT), signed on 1 July 1968, entered into force 1970, 9 UNTS 161, available at www.un.org/disarmament/wmd/nuclear/npt/.

[2] G Mallard, 'Crafting the Nuclear Regime Complex (1950–1975): Dynamics of Harmonization of Opaque Treaty Rules' (2014) 25(2) *European Journal of International Law* 445–72.

[3] NPT (n 1) Article II.

that Iran's nuclear program is exclusively for peaceful purposes'[4] remains one of the central concerns of contemporary nuclear disarmament. The situation in relation to Iran is governed by the overarching NPT legal complex including the NPT, International Atomic Energy Agency (IAEA) Safeguards Agreements[5] and the Additional Protocol[6] (hereafter 'NPT legal complex'), as well as the Iran Nuclear Deal as mentioned above. The Iran Nuclear Deal is a detailed, 159-page agreement with five annexes which was reached by Iran and the P5+1 (China, France, Germany, Russia, the United Kingdom, and the United States) along with the European Union (EU) on 14 July 2015 through multiple rounds of negotiations which took approximately a decade.

Examining the NPT legal complex with reference to the Iran Nuclear Deal is a valuable opportunity to juxtapose and compare three types of machinery for settling disputes or bringing about compliance with international legal obligations. These three types of machinery are: political measures, non-compliance mechanisms (NCMs), and ICTs. Political measures have included unilateral sanctions efforts led by the US, the EU restrictive measures,[7] and the good offices of China, Russia, and the EU. Non-compliance mechanism was established through the NPT, enabling the IAEA to serve as a watchdog for nuclear non-compliance. When the IAEA somewhat failed to limit the Iranian nuclear program to peaceful purposes only, the UN Security Council (UNSC) 1737 Committee[8] and the

[4] UNSC Resolution 2231 (2015), S/RES/2231(2015) 1, available at https://documents-dds-ny.un.org/doc/UNDOC/GEN/N15/225/27/PDF/N1522527.pdf?OpenElement.

[5] Under Article III of the NPT, 'all non-nuclear weapons states-parties are required to conclude a safeguards agreement with the IAEA … in 1961, the IAEA's Board of Governors approved a document outlining the principles of safeguards'. For details, see IAEA, *Safeguards Implementation Practices Guide on Establishing and Maintaining State Safeguards Infrastructure*, July 2018, available at www-pub.iaea.org/MTCD/Publications/PDF/SVS_31_web.pdf; Arms Control Association, *IAEA Safeguards Agreements at a Glance*, February 2022, available at www.armscontrol.org/factsheets/IAEASafeguards.

[6] 'The Additional Protocol [for verification of IAEA Safeguards] is not a stand-alone agreement, but rather a [model] protocol … In May 1997, the IAEA Board of Governors approved the Model Additional Protocol … and requested the Director General to use this model as a standard text for … negotiations', available at www.iaea.org/topics/additional-protocol. As of 25 July 2022, Additional Protocols are in force with 139 States and Euratom. Another 13 States have signed an Additional Protocol but have yet to bring it into force.

[7] EU Council, EU restrictive measures against Iran, available at www.consilium.europa.eu/en/policies/sanctions/iran.

[8] UNSC Resolution 1737 (2006), S/RES/1737 (2006), available at www.un.org/securitycouncil/s/res/1737-(2006). The UNSC 1737 Committee ceased to operate in 2015 as part of the implementation of the JCPOA and UNSC Resolution 2231 (2015).

JCPOA Joint Commission ('the Joint Commission') were established. Last but not least, Iran has also resorted to the International Court of Justice (ICJ) and the EU courts in recent years in the hope of resolving international legal disputes arising from the effects of unilateral US and EU sanctions and other political actions in relation to Iran's nuclear activities, which Iran considers violate obligations under the NPT legal complex.[9]

This shows that the history of the NPT legal complex is a recursive process[10] in which new measures are developed to enhance compliance with the existing rules. The scope of IAEA safeguards since 1961[11] has evolved to ensure member States' fulfilment of their NPT obligations. The model Additional Protocol was approved in 1997 to increase the IAEA's ability to verify the peaceful use of nuclear material for 'exposed weaknesses'.[12] More recently, confronting the Iranian violations, a new formal non-compliance mechanism, the JCPOA, was set up in 2015 to assist further with ensuring compliance. The corresponding UNSC Resolution 2231 became a source of legal obligations for all UN member States including Iran and the US. The Joint Commission serves as the focal point for monitoring, fact-finding, and compliance by JCPOA member States. Similar to the UNSC 1737 Committee and its Panel of Experts,[13] the Joint Commission and its subordinate working groups[14] regularly review the implementation of obligations by the JCPOA member States,[15] thereby assisting the UNSC in identifying evidence of non-compliance or non-performance[16].

The Iran Nuclear Deal is an important complement to the NPT legal complex. It demonstrates how to address a 'complex global challenge'[17] through negotiations on a complementary agreement (JCPOA) when a

[9] The representative of the United States said 'our vote today demonstrates that the Council will act when countries violate their international obligations'. UN Security Council Press Release, SC/9268, 3 March 2008, available at www.un.org/press/en/2008/sc9268.doc.htm.

[10] TC Halliday and G Shaffer, *Transnational Legal Orders* (Cambridge University Press 2015).

[11] On safeguards, see n 5.

[12] Ibid.

[13] Established by UNSC Resolution 1929 (2010), S/RES/1929 (2010).

[14] JCPOA, Annex IV – Joint Commission, available at https://2009-2017.state.gov/documents/organization/245323.pdf; And two new working groups as referred to later in the chapter.

[15] JCPOA, Annex IV (n 14) 2, 'Functions', especially 2.1.14.

[16] Ibid.

[17] C Voigt, 'State Responsibility for Climate Change Damages' (2008) 77(1-2) *Nordic Journal of International Law* 1–22.

State Party (e.g., Iran) has not been fulfilling a core international treaty (here the NPT). It is also a case in which the permanent NCMs (i.e., the IAEA compliance machinery) operating under the treaty have been unable to persuade a party (Iran) to conform with its legal obligations (under the NPT). It features the establishment of a more effective non-compliance mechanism (i.e., the UNSC 1737 Committee or the Joint Commission, respectively, from 2006 to 2015 and since 2015) to resolve specific disputes with regard to compliance by relevant States (i.e., Iran from 2006 to 2015, Iran and the US since 2015). The work of the UNSC 1737 Committee, in parallel to political and diplomatic measures, contributed to the negotiations for and establishment of the JCPOA agreement as a peaceful solution to the Iranian nuclear crisis. The empirical evidence from the Iran Nuclear Deal suggests the use of mechanisms and approaches not involving recourse to ICTs can be successful in many circumstances.

Set against this positive trajectory is the decision of US President Trump in 2018 to withdraw from the JCPOA. However, this incident, too, demonstrates the effective use of mechanisms and approaches not involving recourse to ICTs. Following this decision, the United States put huge pressure on the EU to boycott international trade settlement services provided to Iran by European global banks[18] and levied tremendous pressure on China through unilateral sanctions on those Chinese multinational companies like Huawei who were claimed by the US to serve as Iran's international trade partners.[19] The strategic purposes of President Trump's pressure campaign on Europe and China were to force them to consent to the US withdrawal from the JCPOA and follow the United States in ending their obligations under the JCPOA, in addition to

[18] G Mallard, S Farzan, and J Sun, 'The Humanitarian Gap in the Global Sanctions Regime: Assessing Causes, Effects and Solutions' (2020) 26(1) *Global Governance: A Review of Multilateralism and International Organizations* 121–53.

[19] On 8 May 2018, Trump announced that the United States had unilaterally withdrawn from the Iran Nuclear Deal by reimposing the 'toughest sanctions' on Iran. In November, the United States pressured Germany, Italy, Japan, and other countries to abandon all telecom equipment from the world's largest vendor, Huawei, a private Chinese company. On 1 December, the US Department of Justice (DOJ) sent a request to Canada to arrest Huawei's Chief Financial Officer, Ms Meng Wanzhou, who was transiting in Vancouver Airport. Ms Meng was released in September 2021 after entering an agreement with DOJ. See G Mallard and J Sun, 'Viral Governance: How Unilateral US Sanctions Changed the Rules of Financial Capitalism' (2022) 128(1) *American Journal of Sociology* 144–88, available at www.justice.gov/opa/pr/huawei-cfo-wanzhou-meng-admits-misleading-global-financial institution.

obtaining more leverage in the bilateral trade negotiations with the EU and China. This violated US legal obligations under JCPOA and UNSCR 2231 to lift 'all … national sanctions related to Iran's nuclear programme, including steps on access in areas of trade, technology, finance and energy'[20] so long as Iran continued to comply with the nuclear deal. In response, alongside the negotiations in the Joint Commission, the EU and China activated a range of political mechanisms, including diplomatic good offices and various forms of persuasion or coercion, e.g., Germany, France, and the UK's Instrument in Support of Trade Exchanges (INSTEX) in January 2019, the Swiss Humanitarian Trade Arrangement (SHTA) in February 2020, and the China–Iran twenty-five-year co-operation agreement in March 2021. These efforts successfully brought the United States back to the negotiating table in Vienna and Geneva with Iran and other JCPOA member States, which led the United States into compliance with its JCPOA obligations, in addition to providing preliminary sanctions relief to Iran. In contrast with recourse to an international court or tribunal, this shows how such political processes can lead to a positive outcome. This can be achieved by creating rich incentives or rewards for a complying party (Iran). Incentives include sanctions relief, humanitarian aid, or bilateral investment and trade programmes. These incentives may need to be accompanied by substantial penalties or coercions for a defaulting party (the United States). European humanitarian payment channels (e.g., SHTA, INSTEX), in addition to serving as a reward for Iran, are an example of pressure on US foreign policy, because the European efforts frustrated the US strategy to isolate Iran from the rest of the world in international trade by helping European multinational companies to return to Iran, one of the largest consumer markets in the Middle East. As the world's largest oil consumer, China, by signing the twenty-five-year agreement with Iran in March 2021, generated a substantial penalty for the United States. Although China promised to increase energy imports from the United States in the bilateral agreement signed in January 2020,[21] China

[20] UNSC Resolution 2231 (2015), S/RES/2231 (2015) (n 4), Preamble and General Provisions, para v, and paras 18–33.

[21] China committed to an additional \$18.5 billion and \$33.9 billion of oil purchases from the United States above the 2017 baseline, respectively, in 2020 and 2021 in Article 6.2, 1 (c), Chapter 6, in the US–China phase-one trade agreement in January 2020.

cut oil imports from the United States by 42 per cent in 2021[22] and recovered substantial oil imports from Iran in the same year.[23]

Certainly, the operation of NCMs and other means of dispute resolution, including recourse to ICTs, is interconnected, as shown in the dozens of cases of Iranian banks looking for judicial review of the EU's restrictive measures, or reparations, in the EU courts. This litigation reinforced Iranian diplomatic pressure for EU action against the 2018 US decision to withdraw from the JCPOA. The overall dynamic underlines how it is important for the international community to state its respect for the principles of international law when confronted by unilateral acts on the part of a hegemon in breach of a treaty. In this case such action was key for persuading Iran to meet its obligations under the JCPOA despite US conduct. The experience in respect of the judicial cases in the EU courts in relation to the Iran Nuclear Deal may be relevant beyond the field of non-proliferation, in many other areas of compliance in international and European law, such as climate justice, environment,[24] human rights[25] and public and private actors' decarbonisation obligations.[26] Relevant too is the gradual process in which the Iranian cases show how the EU courts became willing to interpret or reinterpret the Treaty on the Functioning of the European Union (TFEU) in a direction increasingly enabling the judicial pursuit of international justice.

[22] Source of statistics: China Customs, available at https://finance.sina.com.cn/money/future/roll/2022-01-26/doc-ikyakumy2759074.shtml. 'In 2021, China's purchases of [phase-one trade agreement] covered energy products reached 52 percent (Chinese imports) or 37 percent (US exports) of the annual commitment,' available at www.piie.com/research/piie-charts/us-china-phase-one-tracker-chinas-purchases-us-goods.

[23] Experts believe Iran contributes to 6 per cent of Chinese crude oil imports, replacing the United States as the eighth largest oil importer. See www.reuters.com/article/china-oil-import-iran-020-idCNKBS2JU0C8.

[24] C Voigt and M Zen (eds), *Courts and The Environment* (Edward Elgar Publishing 2018).

[25] C Voigt and E Grant, 'The Legitimacy of Human Rights Courts in Environmental Disputes: Editorial' (2015) 1–2 *Journal of Human Rights and the Environment* 131–38.

[26] C Voigt, 'The Climate Judgment of the Norwegian Supreme Court: Aligning the Law with Politics' (2021) 33(3) *Journal of Environmental Law* 1–14; C Voigt and J Knox, 'Introduction to Symposium on Climate Change Litigation in the Global South' (2020) 114 *American Journal of International Law Unbound* 35–39. See also The Hague District Court's landmark decision in Urgenda, and a series of high-prolife cases in different places, including *Milieudefensie et al v Shell*, *Conservation Law Foundation, Inc. v ExxonMobil Corp. et al.*, *San Mateo et al. v Chevron et al.*, *Massachusetts v Exxon Mobil*, and, *Oakland, et al. v BP PLC et al.*

Section 18.1 has offered an initial discussion of the issues addressed in this chapter. Section 18.2 will provide an overview of the international legal framework with regard to Iran's obligations of nuclear non-proliferation. Section 18.3 will highlight the respective value of helping ensure Iran's compliance with its nuclear commitments to political and diplomatic mechanisms, the JCPOA as a formal non-compliance mechanism, the previous regime operating under the auspices of the UNSC, and proceedings in ICTs. Section 18.4 incorporates a discussion on the importance of fact-finding processes in this setting. Section 18.5 concludes.

18.2 The Legal Context

This section begins with a brief overview of the legal context for compliance and dispute settlement in respect of Iranian nuclear policy, on the basis that the functions, competencies, and operational mechanisms of international dispute resolution mechanisms need to be viewed from within the framework of the corresponding international law. International law plays a pivotal role here. The US Government, Iran, Israel, and the United States or its allies in the Middle East have all been required to consider the legal consequences of their potential actions.

18.2.1 The Broad Legal Framework

The broad legal framework[27] includes the Statute of the IAEA, the NPT, the Convention on Nuclear Safety (CNS), and Iran's Safeguards Agreement with the IAEA[28] and Additional Protocol[29] to the NPT, in addition to the JCPOA since 2015. In particular, Articles II and III of the IAEA Statute provide that each State Party shall establish and implement safeguards and apply safeguards to its activities with respect to atomic

[27] For a full list, see: IAEA, Country Nuclear Power Profiles, Iran (Updated 2020), Appendix 1: International, Multilateral and Bilateral Agreements, available at https://cnpp.iaea.org/countryprofiles/IranIslamicRepublicof/IranIslamicRepublicof.htm.

[28] The Agreement between Iran and the Agency for the Application of Safeguards in connection with the Treaty on the Non-Proliferation of Nuclear Weapons, INFCIRC/214, entered into force 15 May 1974.

[29] Protocol Additional to the Agreement between the Islamic Republic of Iran and the International Atomic Energy Agency for the Application of Safeguards in Connection with the Treaty on the Non-Proliferation of Nuclear Weapons, INFCIRC/214/Add.1, approved by IAEA Board 21 November 2003, and signed by Iran on 18 December 2003.

energy. Articles XVI and XVII of the IAEA Statute provide that the IAEA may 'report to the appropriate organs of the United Nations on actions taken by the Agency or its member States pursuant to this Statute … '. Article II of the NPT provides that non-nuclear States (like Iran) undertake not to develop, receive, or seek to acquire nuclear weapons, in light of which Iran is obliged to ensure its nuclear program is for peaceful purposes only, and this is subject to the IAEA's verification of fulfilment and compliance. The IAEA Safeguards Agreement and Additional Protocol with Iran set out Iran's legal obligations to provide information and additional access in a timely manner,[30] and to accept the designation of IAEA inspectors[31] in order to assist the IAEA in completing its annual conclusions.[32]

18.2.2 UNSC Resolutions, UNSC 1737 Committee and the Panel of Experts

The legal framework includes also a series of UNSC Resolutions. By UNSC Resolution 1737 (2006) of 23 December 2006, the Security Council decided to establish the 1737 Sanctions Committee to oversee and monitor UN-imposed sanctions against Iran. In 2010, the Security Council appointed a Panel of Experts to assist the Committee in its work,[33] in particular through fact-finding mechanisms, including the annual report of the Committee and the (periodic) report from the Panel of Experts.[34] In 2015, after the Iran nuclear deal was reached, the Security Council endorsed it in UNSC Resolution 2231 (2015). On 16 January 2016, the date of implementation of the Iran nuclear deal, the Council terminated the UN sanctions on Iran in accordance with the provisions of Resolution 2231 (2015). At present, although the 1737 Sanctions Committee and its Panel of Experts (POE)[35] no longer

[30] Ibid., Article 2.b(ii).
[31] Ibid., Article 11.
[32] Ibid., Article 10.c.
[33] See n 13.
[34] From 2006 to 2015, the 1737 Committee and its Panel of Experts issued ten reports. For details see Security Council Report, UN Documents for Iran: Sanctions Committee Documents, available at www.securitycouncilreport.org/un_documents_type/sanctions-committee-documents/?ctype=Iran&cbtype=iran.
[35] Although the UNSC 1737 Committee's POE was dissolved, the POE mechanism still plays an important role in other nuclear disarmament and sanctions regimes, for instance, on the DPRK nuclear ambitions. The effectiveness of this mechanism provides

exist, the UNSC remains the highest international oversight body in relation to the situation regarding Iranian nuclear activities.

18.2.3 *JCPOA and the Joint Commission*

In July 2015, Iran entered into the nuclear deal (JCPOA) with the United States, the United Kingdom, France, Russia, China, Germany, and the European Union. Under the JCPOA, Iran committed to limiting its nuclear programme to peaceful research purposes only in return for which the international community agreed to lift sanctions against Iran, including both UNSC sanctions and unilateral US and EU sanctions or restrictive measures listed in the appendix to the negotiated agreement. Paragraph ix of the preamble to the agreement provided for the establishment of a Joint Commission of the JCPOA, Article 24 of the agreement explicitly mandated the Joint Commission to address issues related to the lifting of sanctions, and Article 36 provided that if Iran believes that any party is not fulfilling the agreement, it may bring the matter to the Joint Commission for resolution. It is under this non-compliance mechanism that the current Iranian nuclear negotiations are taking place. For example, in May 2021, the two expert groups responsible for lifting sanctions against Iran and for US–Iranian measures to return to compliance submitted a draft agreement to a new round of meetings of the Joint Commission at the level of Political Director-Generals. The draft agreement essentially set out the framework for a final agreement for the United States and Iran's return to the JCPOA. The draft agreement was unfortunately not signed in Vienna in 2022 due to the Russian invasion of Ukraine.

18.2.4 *International Courts and Tribunals*

The ICJ may give its views on relevant disputes only so far as jurisdiction can be established. However, there are jurisdictional clauses in Iran's bilateral treaties with relevant countries, such as the United States (the US–Iranian Treaty of Amity of 1955) which provide for ICJ jurisdiction on certain matters. The Court of Justice of the European Union (CJEU)[36]

a concrete example to show the relevance of the expert panel as a fact-finding body in addressing complex global challenges.

36 M Lester and F Hobson, 'Targeted Sanctions and Sanctions Targeted: Iranian Banks in the European Court' (2013) May *Butterworths Journal of International Banking and Financial Law* 278–80.

has gradually expanded its jurisdiction over EU restrictive measures against individuals through its judicial precedents. Specific Iranian entities subject to EU restrictive measures, although not an individual EU citizen, can request review or annulment of the relevant restrictive measures.[37] Iranian parties have also requested the European Court of Human Rights (ECtHR) to review individual restrictive measures in accordance with the European Convention on Human Rights (ECHR) in a few cases.[38]

18.3 Comparison of Political Diplomacy, NCMs and ICTs in the Iranian Case

The previous section having introduced the relevant elements of the international legal framework, this section now moves on to evaluate their relative contribution to ensuring Iranian compliance with its nuclear commitments.

18.3.1 The Value of the JCPOA Joint Commission as a Non-Compliance Mechanism of the Iran Nuclear Deal

From 2015 to 2018, the JCPOA Joint Commission fulfilled its function of assisting Iranian efforts to comply with the JCPOA and the NPT legal complex by helping verify that the Iranian nuclear programme was restricted to peaceful purposes only. The first Joint Commission held on 19 October 2015[39] addressed measures in the nuclear field, such as the retrofitting of the Arak heavy water reactor, the military dimension of the Iranian nuclear programme, and preparations for the implementation of sanctions-lifting measures. The Joint Commission also studied the arrangements for the follow-up implementation mechanism of the agreement and made work plans for the next step in implementing the agreement. On 25 April 2017, the seventh meeting of the Joint Commission noted the continued adherence to the agreement's commitments by all participants.[40] On the signing of the first commercial

[37] Case C-548/09 P, *Bank Melli Iran v Council* (ECLI:EU:C:2011:735).

[38] *Islamic Republic of Iran Shipping Lines v Turkey* (ECHR Application No 40998/98) (2007).

[39] U.S. Institute of Peace, 'Adoption Day: Iran and P5+1 Comment', 19 October 2015, available at https://iranprimer.usip.org/blog/2015/oct/19/iran-and-p51-adoption-day.

[40] UN Security Council 7990th Meeting Press Release, SC/12894: 'Accord on Iran's Nuclear Programme Remains on Track, Political Affairs Chief Tells Security Council', 29 June 2017, available at www.un.org/press/en/2017/sc12894.doc.htm.

contract of the renovation project for the Arak heavy water reactor by Chinese and Iranian enterprises on the 23rd of that month, the parties expressed appreciation for the joint efforts of JCPOA member States.[41]

In May 2018, the Trump administration unilaterally withdrew from the Iran nuclear deal signed between Iran and the Obama Administration. This US unilateral exit from the JCPOA occurred at a time when the rest of the JCPOA member States including Iran were fulfilling their legal obligations. President Trump reimposed a series of sanctions against Iran and the European and Chinese global banks or firms, triggering the circumstances set forth in Article 36 of the Iran Nuclear Deal (as discussed). Following the US exit from the JCPOA in 2018, the Joint Commission gradually became a pivotal NCM by which the relevant parties could ensure Iran was complying with the agreement in spite of US withdrawal. However, after September 2019, Iran gradually suspended compliance with certain provisions of the Iran Nuclear Deal. Specifically, fifty-six 'centrifuges were either installed or being installed' and the piping at research and development lines was 'reinstalled' so as to restart nuclear activities in violation of the JCPOA legal obligations.[42] Meanwhile, Iran said it was committed to the 'reversibility' of the countermeasures it had taken, promising that it could return to full compliance at any time. Through the IAEA verification mechanism,[43] the international community was able to understand that Iran's countermeasures, while constituting necessary diplomatic pressure, did not yet pose an immediate nuclear security threat to regional peace and stability.

The 2020 US presidential elections brought President Joe Biden to office. Addressing the international dispute over these actions, a meeting of the Joint Commission at the level of political directors-general was held in Vienna on 6 April 2021, to discuss the resumption of US–Iranian implementation of the JCPOA. On 6 April 2021, the first round of indirect talks between the United States and Iran occurred in Vienna. Two expert working groups were formed to address the timetable to lift US unilateral sanctions on Iran and to reverse Iran's breaches of the JCPOA since September 2019. In a sign of good faith, the US State

41 Wilson Project, 'Iran Nuclear Milestones: 1967-2017', 21 June 2017, available at www.wisconsinproject.org/iran-nuclear-milestones/.

42 IAEA, 'IAEA Board Report: Verification and Monitoring in the Islamic Republic of Iran in Light of United Nations Security Council Resolution 2231 (2015)', 8 September 2019, available at www.iaea.org/sites/default/files/19/09/govinf2019-10.pdf.

43 IAEA, 'IAEA and Iran – IAEA Reports', available at www.iaea.org/newscenter/focus/iran/iaea-and-iran-iaea-reports.

Department held briefings on 6 April[44] and on 7 April[45] declaring that the United States was preparing to lift sanctions on Iran in order to restore the Iran Nuclear Deal. The Joint Commission held six rounds of talks over the following two months. On 12 June, the day before the sixth round of talks began, in another show of good faith, the United States announced the lifting of sanctions against three former Iranian officials and two companies.[46] Some experts believe that an important background factor for the US President's willingness to initiate indirect talks with Iran through the Joint Commission was China's active mediation and pressure,[47] in addition to EU pressure including through the INSTEX, its bilateral international trade settlement system with Iran, with an expectation that the US return to JCPOA would lead to Iran's full compliance. Earlier, on 27 March 2021, China and Iran had entered a twenty-five-year agreement on political, strategic, and economic co-operation, signed by Chinese State councillor and foreign minister Wang Yi and Iranian Foreign Minister Zarif in Tehran.[48] To this day, Iran maintains regular information exchange, inspection, and safeguards with the IAEA,[49] hoping that its countermeasures, which serve as pressure on the United States, will not be misunderstood as an immediate nuclear threat. The valuable work of the JCPOA Joint Commission has concluded a new draft agreement for relevant parties to resume commitments to the JCPOA. Although this draft agreement could not be signed

44 U.S. State Department, 'Department Press Briefing – April 6, 2021', available at www.state.gov/briefings/department-press-briefing-april-6-2021/. For a timeline in the negotiations played out over six rounds in Vienna from April to June 2021, see A Hanna, 'Iran Delays Return to Vienna Talks' (*The Iran Primer*, 19 July 2021), available at https://iranprimer.usip.org/blog/2021/jul/19/iran-delays-return-vienna-talks.

45 U.S. State Department, 'Department Press Briefing – April 7, 2021', available at www.state.gov/briefings/department-press-briefing-april-7-2021/.

46 The three people whose sanctions were removed by OFAC are Ahmad Ghalebani, a managing director of the National Iranian Oil Company; Farzad Bazargan, a managing director of Hong Kong Intertrade Company; and Mohammad Moinie, a commercial director of Naftiran Intertrade Company Sarl. The two companies whose sanctions were lifted used also to deal in the petrochemicals trade.

47 Reuters, 'Iran and China Sign 25-year Cooperation Agreement' (27 March 27 2021), available at www.reuters.com/world/china/iran-china-sign-25-year-cooperation-agreement-2021-03-27/.

48 '*China, Iran Sign Agreement to Map Out Comprehensive Cooperation*' (*China.org.cn*, 28 March 2021), available at www.china.org.cn/world/2021-03/28/content_77354164.htm.

49 As reflected in the 11 June 2020, 8 September 2020, and 23 February 2021 reports of the director general of the International Atomic Energy Agency (GOV/2020/30, GOV/2020/47, and GOV/2021/15) (for a full list, see n 43).

as scheduled, following the unexpected circumstance of the Russian invasion of Ukraine on 24 February 2022, the JCPOA Joint Commission did successfully help to resolve the chapter of the Iranian nuclear crisis generated by the US withdrawal from the JCPOA in 2018.

18.3.2 The Contrasting Role Played by the UNSC in the Decade Prior

The decade from 2005 to 2016 witnessed developments from the beginning of sanctions against Iran under UNSC Resolution 1737 (2006) to the termination of sanctions against Iran under Resolution 2231 (2015). It documented the rich legal practice of the UNSC in maintaining peace in the Middle East, working for regional security and stability, and defending the international nuclear security system.

An international sanctions system was constructed through successive rounds of step-by-step, courteous resolutions seeking evidence-based and fact-based compliance. With the objective of exerting the pressure necessary for nuclear diplomacy, the UNSC improved investment and trade-related compliance and monitoring procedures[50] involving restrictive measures on the arms trade; ballistic missile programmes capable of delivering nuclear weapons; financial transactions related to Iran's nuclear and missile programmes; international financial services provided to or by designated financial institutions; and the international travel of targeted sanctioned persons and their financial assets.[51] On the other hand, when Iran showed good faith in nuclear negotiations,[52] the imposition of further UNSC sanctions was held back, although high pressure remained from the major powers including the United States. When the Iran Nuclear Deal, which was eventually struck in 2015, showed Iran would conscientiously fulfil its nuclear disarmament obligations in accordance with the JCPOA agreement, the UNSC terminated the UN sanctions in accordance with UNSCR 2231.[53]

[50] UNSC Resolution 1737 (2006), S/RES/1737 (2006), paras 3, 4, and 6.

[51] Ibid., para 12.

[52] For instance, on 6 August 2013, in his first press conference, Iran's new President Hassan Rouhani called for the resumption of 'serious and substantial' talks with the P5+1 over Iran's nuclear programme. On 11 November 2013, Iran and the IAEA issued a Joint Statement on a Framework of Cooperation, aimed at resolving the IAEA's outstanding disputes about Iran's nuclear programme, and allowing IAEA inspectors broader access to nuclear sites.

[53] See (n 4).

18.3.3 *The Role of Political Measures versus Non-Compliance Mechanisms*

The handling of the Iranian nuclear crisis, which emerged around 2003, and the Iraqi issue which came to a head around the same time[54] could be used to illustrate the difference between NCMs and political measures. The Iranian nuclear issue was peacefully settled via the JCPOA agreement, while the Iraqi issue ended in a different outcome.

The 2003 Iraqi issue was a situation where political measures did not contribute to a peaceful settlement of international disputes, when there was no effective NCM or ICT.[55] The international community considered that Iraq had 'repeatedly obstructed immediate, unconditional, and unrestricted access to sites designated by the United Nations Special Commission (UNSCOM) and the International Atomic Energy Agency',[56] which constituted a serious violation of its international legal obligations. Iraq[57] failed to convince UNSC, UNSCOM, or IAEA to serve as an effective non-compliance mechanism to ensure that it would co-operate with weapons verification in good faith.[58]

Contrastingly, the Iranian nuclear crisis was settled through political measures. NCMs including the UNSC 1737 Committee and its Panel of Experts played an active role through fact-finding and the provision of good offices which helped to bring this about. The value of these processes is reflected in the IAEA report of 28 April 2006: 'Agency inspectors found no undeclared nuclear material in Iran',[59] and 'the Agency is

[54] IAEA, 'IAEA Chief Addresses Iraq, North Korea and Iran Issues' (13 December 2002), available at www.iaea.org/newscenter/news/iaea-chief-addresses-iraq-north-korea-and-iran-issues.

[55] Situations in Iraq, the Middle East, Afghanistan, Balkans, Africa Among Key Issues before Security Council in 2002, available at www.un.org/securitycouncil/content/annual-round-ups; www.un.org/press/en/2003/sc7632.doc.htm.

[56] UNSC Resolution 1441 (2002), S/RES/1441 (2002) 'condemns Iraq's repeated obstruction of immediate, unconditional and unrestricted access to sites designated by the United Nations Special Commission (UNSCOM) and the International Atomic Energy Agency (IAEA), its failure to cooperate fully and unconditionally with UNSCOM and IAEA weapons inspectors as required by resolution 687 (1991), and its eventual cessation of all cooperation with UNSCOM and IAEA in 1998'.

[57] Statement by Mr Al-Douri, Iraq's Ambassador to the UN, to the UN Security Council at the hearing on Iraqi matters on 5 February 2003.

[58] For example, Statement by Jack Straw, MP, British Secretary of State for Foreign and Commonwealth Affairs, to the UN Security Council on 5 February 2003.

[59] IAEA, 'IAEA Board Report: Implementation of the NPT Safeguards Agreement in the Islamic Republic of Iran', 28 April 2006, available at www.iaea.org/sites/default/files/gov2006 27.pdf, para 33. For a different interpretation to the report above, see P Kerr,

unable to make progress in its efforts to provide assurance about the absence of undeclared nuclear material and activities in Iran'.[60] The IAEA in effect serves as an independent fact-finding mechanism, operating as a non-compliance mechanism to show the accurate extent of Iranian breaches. It helped to maintain the confidence of the international community that the Iranian crisis could be solved or negotiated through political measures, diplomacy, and NCMs, and a war avoided. On the following day, US President George W. Bush commented that 'the diplomatic process is just beginning . . . And I've told the American people that diplomacy is my first choice'.[61] Through the active diplomatic good offices of various countries (e.g., Russia,[62] the EU, China and other P5+1 countries), peaceful measures through NCMs (e.g., UNSCRs, the UNSC 1737 Committee, and the JCPOA) remained a viable way for the international community to resolve the Iranian nuclear crisis.

18.3.4 Recourse to International Courts and Tribunals

The ICJ and the CJEU are the ICTs to which Iran and Iranians have looked for judicial remedy to settle disputes with the United States and the European Union, respectively, with regard to damages caused by unilateral actions or foreign assets targeted by unilateral sanctions. The ICJ is historically an important forum for the settlement of disputes between the United States and Iran, as the US–Iranian Treaty of Amity of 1955 has provided jurisdiction.[63] The previous cases (prior to the JCPOA) brought by Iran at the ICJ,[64] namely, the *Oil*

'IAEA Raises New Questions on Iran Program' (*Arms Control Today*, June 2006), available at www.armscontrol.org/act/2006-06/iran-nuclear-briefs/iaea-raises-new-questions-iran-program.

60 Ibid.

61 Radio Free Europe, 'U.S., Britain Seek Tough Diplomatic Action Against Iran' (*Radio Free Europe, Radio Liberty*, 29 April 2006), available at www.rferl.org/a/1068047.html.

62 Political representatives of the foreign ministries of China, France, Germany, Russia, the United Kingdom, and the United States discussed the Iranian nuclear issue in Moscow on 18 April 2006, where all participants called on Iran to make 'urgent and constructive moves' aimed at complying with IAEA decisions, starting with halting its enrichment processes. Earlier, Russia called for Iran to observe a moratorium on uranium enrichment until 28 April, when the IAEA was slated to make a report to the Security Council. For details see Radio Free Europe, 'Iran Report – April 28, 2006' (*Radio Free Europe, Radio Liberty*, 9(15), 29 April 2006), available at www.rferl.org/a/1342586.html.

63 Article 36, Statute of the International Court of Justice.

64 There were two cases in which Iran was a respondent in the ICJ, namely, United States Diplomatic and Consular Staff in Tehran (*United States of America v Iran*) in 1979 and

Platforms[65] and *Aerial Incident of 3 July 1988* cases,[66] indicate the ICJ is considered by Tehran to be an independent judicial authority with strong legal reasoning and fact-finding capability. In the *Oil Platforms* case, the Court confirmed the fact of the attacks by the US Navy on Iranian oil platforms, but also found that no direct trade relations existed between the two countries at the time of the attacks. For this reason, the US attacks were held not to violate the freedom of trade in oil guaranteed by the treaty, and there was no basis for the Iranian claim. In the *Aerial Incident* case, the ICJ verified the liability of the US Navy missile cruiser for the downing of Iran Air Flight 655, but none of the orders issued by the Court involved damages or compensation. The matter of damages was settled through bilateral negotiations.[67] The United States insisted the payment made was of an *ex-gratia* nature, refusing to acknowledge responsibility for the incident.[68]

Two cases have been brought by Iran against the United States in the ICJ in the post-JCPOA period,[69] hoping that the Court could be a source of international justice against the unilateral sanctions reimposed by the US Administration after the US withdrawal from the nuclear deal. In both cases, Iran requested the Court issue provisional measures requiring the United States to lift or suspend unliteral sanctions measures.[70] On 3 October 2018, the ICJ issued a preliminary ruling[71] requiring the United States to lift certain sanctions against Iran, mainly related to the import of food and medicines. On 13 February 2019, the ICJ

Anglo-Iranian Oil Co (*United Kingdom v Iran*) in 1951. For details see www.icj-cij.org/en/case/64; www.icj-cij.org/en/case/16.

65 *Oil Platforms* (*Islamic Republic of Iran v United States of America*).

66 Aerial Incident of 3 July 1988 (*Islamic Republic of Iran v United States of America*).

67 Settlement Agreement as of 9 February 1996, available at www.icj-cij.org/public/files/case-related/79/11131.pdf.

68 U.S. State Department, 'Iran–United States Claims Tribunal: Partial Award Containing Settlement Agreements on the Iranian Bank Claims against the United States and on the International Court of Justice Case Concerning the Aerial Incident of July 3, 1988' (1996) 35(3) *International Legal Materials* 553–602.

69 Certain Iranian Assets (*Islamic Republic of Iran v United States of America*), Judgment of 30 March 2023 [2023] ICJ Reports; Alleged Violations of the 1955 Treaty of Amity, Economic Relations, and Consular Rights (*Islamic Republic of Iran v United States of America*) Judgment of 2021 [2021] ICJ Reports 9 (hereafter 'Alleged Violations').

70 Chapter II, Memorial of the Islamic Republic of Iran, 1 February 2017, in *Certain Iranian Assets* (n 69); Chapter II, Memorial of the Islamic Republic of Iran, 24 May 2019, in *Alleged Violations* (n 69).

71 Summary of the Order of 3 October 2018 in *Alleged Violations* (n 69), VI Operative Clause (para 102).

concluded that the Court has jurisdiction to admit part of the application brought by Iran against the United States[72] in respect of Iran's claims arising from measures taken by the United States to block Iranian assets. At the time of writing, none of the orders issued by the Court in the two cases above has involved a broad lifting or suspension of unilateral US sanctions on Iranian assets.

The CJEU is where Iran has sought international justice against the restrictive measures imposed by the EU during the period from 2006 to 2015 when the JCPOA was under negotiation. Under US lobbying and pressure[73] the EU imposed unilateral and the UNSC restrictive measures on Iranian entities corresponding to UNSCR 1737 (2006) and UNSCR 1929 (2010).[74] Seventeen Iranian banks and a couple of shipping and other companies involved brought cases before the CJEU. The Court ruled early on from 2007 to 2012 that EU restrictive measures on certain Iranian entities were unlawful, as 'the Council cannot rely on a claim that the evidence concerned comes from confidential sources and cannot, consequently, be disclosed',[75] and thus, the EU Court issued decisions to annul them, after which it became a place for Iranian entities to look for international justice from the ICTs. After it became clear that Iran's nuclear programme since 2012 posed a serious threat to Europe's collective security, the EU refined its sanctions-related laws, including freezing the Iranian Central Bank's foreign exchange reserves managed in European banks and Iranian oil and gas companies,[76] and the number of cases in which the CJEU-annulled EU restrictive measures declined significantly.[77]

[72] *Certain Iranian Assets (Islamic Republic of Iran v United States of America)*, Preliminary Objections, Judgment of 13 February 2019 [2019] ICJ Reports 7 Press Release 2019/3, 13 February 2019.

[73] For instance, through 'Joint US–UK–France Demarche to Malaysia on Bank Mellat', see 'UK Requests Information on Bank Mellat to Share with Malaysia' (*The Telegraph*, 4 Feb 2011.

[74] Common Position 2007/140/CFSP; Council Decision 2008/475/EC (later amended by Council Decision 2010/413/CFSP); Council Regulation 423/2007 (later replaced by Council Regulation 961/2010).

[75] Case T-13/11, *Post Bank Iran v Council*, Judgment of the General Court of 6 September 2013, para 129.

[76] Council Decision 2012/35/CFSP; Council Decision 2012/635/CFSP (amending Council Decision 2010/413/CFSP); Council Regulation 267/2012 (replacing Council Regulation 961/2010).

[77] Mr Michael Bishop, lawyer of the EU Council Legal Service, testified in the UK House of Lords European Union Committee, 'The Legality of EU Sanctions', available at https://publications.parliament.uk/pa/ld201617/ldselect/ldeucom/102/10202.htm, para 23.

Shortly thereafter, the JCPOA was concluded and became effective in 2015, with the EU lifting all sanctions under UNSCR 2231. With the exception of human rights sanctions against Iran[78] which were not mentioned by Resolution 2231 and the Iran Nuclear Deal commitments, the EU has now completely lifted restrictive measures against Iran. Even so, after the US withdrawal from the JCPOA in 2018, many EU products including foods and medicines met with difficulties relating to bank settlements, as the global banks, including big banks in Europe, have remained concerned about US secondary sanctions.[79] The CJEU could be a potential place to settle related disputes, but proceedings in the European Court of Justice (ECJ) are now unlikely as cases concerning such matters have been ruled inadmissible, as the ECJ held in 2018 in the *Bank Mellat* case.[80] Iran has therefore lost interest in employing EU judicial procedures against the de facto European resumption of sanctions.[81]

18.3.5 Respective Strengths of the Various Compliance Mechanisms and Processes

In contrast to recourse to ICTs, NCMs show three distinct advantages. The first is timeliness. An NCM such as the Joint Commission of the JCPOA can hear complaints from relevant parties, private entities, or affected non-party stakeholders in a timely manner, and can convene expert-group-level, director-general-level, or ministerial-level meetings to promptly consider or mediate conflicts and contradictions in response to rapid changes in specific circumstances. The second advantage is

78 EU restrictive measures against Iran, Measures responding to serious human rights violations, see www.consilium.europa.eu/en/policies/sanctions/iran/.

79 G Mallard, F Sabet, and J Sun, 'The Humanitarian Gap in the Global Sanctions Regime: Assessing Causes, Effects and Solutions' (2020) 26(1) *Global Governance: A Review of Multilateralism and International Organizations*, 121–53.

80 Case C-430/16 P, *Bank Mellat v Council* (ECLI:EU:C:2018:668), para 62: 'Consequently, following the repeal of the regime at issue on 16 January 2016 within the framework of the implementation of the JCPOA, the annulment of the regime at issue by the EU Courts could no longer procure an advantage for Bank Mellat capable of justifying the retention of an interest in bringing proceedings.'

81 'Iran President Warns of "War Situation" as Sanctions Resume' (*AP News*, 6 November 2018); E Geranmayeh and J Miller, 'Iran: The Case for Protecting Humanitarian Trade' (*European Council on Foreign Relations*, 13 September 2018), available at https://ecfr.eu/article/commentary_iran_the_case_for_protecting_humanitarian_trade/.

flexibility. A mechanism such as the Joint Committee, or the UNSC Sanctions Committee or its Panel of Experts can monitor compliance and add, suspend, or lift sanctions measures in accordance with the degree of compliance observed. It is flexible enough to encourage parties with good faith in negotiations. The third advantage is that NCMs may offer 'carrots and sticks'. They may support diplomacy and reinforce the influence of major powers by identifying specific implementation or compliance challenges, improving bilateral economic and trade relations for a compliant party, while bringing condemnation, coercion, or pressure to bear on a non-compliant party.

ICTs can be employed to clarify legal obligations, provide authoritative explanations, issue an authoritative opinion on disputes between parties, and provide a voice for international justice through interim measures. The role is to reaffirm the fundamental principles of international law and to maintain the confidence of the international community that an international crisis like the new round of the Iranian nuclear crisis in 2018–2021 could be solved through peaceful means instead of any resorts to, or a threat of, use of force. Non-compliance mechanisms and ICTs can support each other where particular disputes are admissible before an international judicial body, like the CJEU in the Iranian cases prior to the JCPOA. The International Court of Justice reaffirms the applicability of international law[82] in the face of unilateral acts of major powers in violation of international treaties.[83] This has been key for the international community in convincing Iran to comply with its obligations[84] under the NPT legal complex including the JCPOA after the US withdrawal.

The judicial cases at the ICJ and CJEU indicate three weaknesses with regard to recourse to the ICTs. The first weakness is a lack of timeliness. It is unlikely that an international court will be able to act in a timely manner. International adjudication calls for due process, allowing the relevant parties to document evidence and put forward their submissions. The second weakness is a lack of flexibility. Judicially available remedies may promote the annulment of restrictive measures or the payment of damages, but it is unlikely that ICTs will be in a position to follow the logic of political diplomacy or diplomatic negotiations with variable, context-dependent sanctions calculated to influence a situation

[82] See n 72.
[83] See n 69.
[84] Ibid.

politically. The third weakness is a lack of 'carrots and sticks'. The past record of the ICTs in the above cases shows that an international court or tribunal takes a cautious approach with regard to requests for damages or reparations, especially the use of 'sticks' against major powers, and it is unlikely that ICTs will be able to provide such 'carrots' as a bilateral trade and economic co-operation agreement.

18.4 Fact-Finding Mechanism

The international legal mechanisms used to deal with the Iranian nuclear programme have most centrally involved specific forms of fact-finding, and this topic is correspondingly a final focus of reflection in this chapter. The IAEA sent experts to Iran to assist the Security Council in verifying relevant evidence or leads mentioned above, in conjunction with data collected by technical monitoring equipment installed inside Iran as the IAEA safeguards agreement[85] and Additional Protocol[86] with Iran. Serving the UNSC 1737 Committee, the Panel of Experts, composed of experts in various fields such as customs, banking, and trade, investigated the specific circumstances or extent of Iran's alleged violations of Security Council resolutions through independent sources, relying on statistics, field investigations, customs searches, and customs declarations from a global network of experts which produced periodic peer-reviewed reports on the specific facts of alleged violations.[87]

Broadly, fact-finding mechanisms make a great contribution to global governance. First, these mechanisms serve as an alternative source of legitimacy in the international community, parallel to the diplomatic endeavours of major powers or working together with international negotiations under the auspices of relevant international organisations like the UNSC or IAEA to help address complex global challenges. Second, confronting complex global challenges, fact-finding mechanisms, through science-based or fact-based policy formation processes, participate in shaping global values and the global agenda. Finally, these mechanisms assist the international community in understanding the causes of disagreement or disputes and help with the development of acceptable solutions.

[85] See n 5.
[86] See n 28.
[87] See n 13.

Fact-finding mechanisms may also work specifically to incentivise compliance with international law in situations of non-compliance. One such example is the IAEA report on 22 February 2018,[88] confirming that Iran's nuclear activities were within the standards set out in the Iran Nuclear Deal. This was embarrassing for President Trump, who had been unhappy with the Iranian nuclear deal since he took office,[89] threatening Congress and his European allies to scrap it if the 'significant flaws in the deal' were not fixed.[90] Through a periodic fact-finding mechanism, including quarterly verification reports, the IAEA encouraged Iran to continue to respect the Iranian nuclear deal and safeguards under the NPT in spite of the US withdrawal, and, in doing so, provided a strong incentive for the United States to return to its JCPOA obligations.

Fact-finding mechanisms may also help generate pressures to push relevant parties back to negotiations when needed. The report by the IAEA in September 2021 is an example. Since his inauguration as US President in January 2021, President Biden had expressed his interest in a return to the Iran Nuclear Deal. The JCPOA parties held six rounds of talks in Vienna from April to June 2021. From June to November 2021, the United States and Iran were at an impasse. It was a fact-finding mechanism that helped to break the impasse by putting pressure on the Biden administration. The IAEA report in September 2021[91] confirmed that Iran had restarted its nuclear programme, and that Iran's stockpile of enriched uranium and enrichment level exceeded the limit set by the JCPOA. Negotiations were restarted by the United States and Iran in late November 2021.[92]

18.5 Conclusion

The international community has constructed comprehensive compliance and monitoring procedures in relation to nuclear non-proliferation

[88] IAEA (n 42).

[89] J Borger, S Kamali Dehghan and P Beaumont, 'Trump Threatens to Rip Up Iran Nuclear Deal unless US and Allies Fix "serious flaws"' (*The Guardian*, 13 October 2017), available at www.theguardian.com/us-news/2017/oct/13/trump-iran-nuclear-deal-congress.

[90] S Kamali Dehghan, 'What Is the Iran Deal and Why Does Trump Want to Scrap It?' (*The Guardian*, 9 May 2018), available at www.theguardian.com/world/2018/may/08/iran-nuclear-deal-what-is-it-why-does-trump-want-to-scrap-it.

[91] See n 72.

[92] J Hansler and K Atwood, 'Iran Nuclear Talks set to Resume in Vienna at the End of November' (*CNN Politics*, 3 November 2021), available at https://edition.cnn.com/2021/11/03/politics/iran-nuclear-talks-restart-date/index.html.

compliance, in which major powers have so far retained the right to impose sanctions on Iran's nuclear programme-related investment and trade activities, as well as on the arms trade, ballistic missile programmes, nuclear programme-related financial transactions, financial assets, and international travel of designated persons. Although some of these unilateral sanctions may not have been lawful,[93] and some extra-jurisdictional measures have been used in unlawful situations, their effective deterrence may have, to a certain extent, had the objective effect of safeguarding peace and avoiding war or armed conflicts in the context of peace and stability in the Middle East.

The Iranian nuclear agreement is a result of the joint efforts of P5+1 countries and Iran, which is also a powerful example of the use of political and diplomatic measures to resolve international conflicts and disputes. The good offices, diplomacy and negotiations in which the major powers engaged to solve the Iranian nuclear crisis, as well as the NPT legal complex (e.g., NPT, IAEA safeguards, Additional Protocol, relevant UNSCRs, JCPOA) and relevant NCMs (IAEA, UNSC, UNSC 1737 Committee, POE, and the JCPOA Joint Commission) and ICTs (e.g., ICJ and CJEU), are of potentially broader significance as institutional models for global governance in fields including climate change, protection of the global environment, and the creation of a Middle East Weapons of Mass Destruction Free Zone.[94]

[93] See n 73.

[94] C Zak, F Sabet, D Esfandiar, R Einhorn, A Persbo, A Khlopkov, and G Mallard *From the Iran Nuclear Deal to a Middle East Zone? Lessons from the JCPOA for an ME WMDFZ* (UNIDIR 2021). For details see www.unidir.org/JCPOA.

PART VII

Cultural Heritage Law and Law of the Sea

19

Protecting Cultural Heritage during an Occupation

Enforcing Compliance with the 1954 Hague Convention and the Case of the Temple Preah Vihear

ALICE LOPES FABRIS

19.1 Introduction

Cultural property has always been a target in armed conflicts. From the 1870 French–German war to the recent conflict in Ukraine, cultural property has been destroyed during military hostilities, even if it is protected by international humanitarian law. To try to increase the protection of the cultural heritage of humankind, the international community has adopted the 1954 Hague Convention for the Protection of Cultural Property in the Event of Armed Conflict (the 1954 Hague Convention) in the aftermath of the Second World War. The Convention stipulates the obligation to safeguard and respect cultural property in armed conflict and during a military occupation. However, the effectiveness of this Convention is often disputed. Violations of the Convention have yet to be brought before an international court, even if courts have dealt with the destruction of historical monuments.[1]

One interesting case study on the application of the Convention concerns the Preah Vihear Temple. Situated in Cambodia near its border with Thailand, the Temple is composed of a series of sanctuaries with a complex history that can be traced to the ninth century.[2] In 1954, the

I would like to thank Professors Christina Voigt and Caroline Foster for their commentaries. I would also like to thank Professor Vincent Negri for the discussions regarding this case in the framework of my doctoral research. The opinions expressed are solely my own.

1 For instance, in the Eritrea–Ethiopia Claims Commission, even if the destruction of a cultural heritage in an armed conflict was analysed, the Convention did not apply. Customary international law was applied.

2 UNESCO, 'Temple of Preah Vihear', available at whc.unesco.org/en/list/1224/, last accessed 14 April 2022.

Temple's area was occupied by Thailand,[3] starting a fifty-five-year border dispute,[4] which almost escalated into armed conflict in 2008.[5] During this period, several international forums were seized with the protection of the Temple, including: the International Court of Justice (ICJ), United Nations Security Council (UNSC), United Nations Educational, Scientific and Cultural Organization (UNESCO) and a Joint Border Commission established by Cambodia and Thailand. This chapter will assess the contribution of all of these processes and agencies to the protection of cultural property in armed conflict with reference to this study.

Dealing with the related territorial sovereignty dispute between Cambodia and Thailand in the 1960s, the ICJ held that the Temple was in Cambodian territory and that Thailand was under an obligation to withdraw any military or police force stationed there.[6] Following this decision, UNESCO also dealt with the conflict. As the main international organisation dedicated to protecting cultural heritage, UNESCO's purposes and functions are to 'maintain, increase and diffuse knowledge by assuring the conservation and protection of the world's inheritance of books, works of art and monuments of history and science, and recommending to the nations concerned the necessary international conventions'.[7] As will be narrated later in this chapter, in April 1966, four years after the ICJ judgment, the Permanent Delegation of the Kingdom of Cambodia to UNESCO contacted the UNESCO Director-General concerning clashes at the Temple, which, according to the Cambodian Government, had damaged the historical monument.[8] Cambodia alleged that Thailand had violated the obligation to respect the Temple,[9] a customary international norm codified in the 1954 Hague Convention, and that Thailand had failed to

[3] ICJ, *Temple of Preah Vihear (Cambodia v Thailand)*, Memorial of the Government of the Kingdom of Cambodia, 20 January 1960.

[4] ICRC, *Cambodia/Thailand, Border Conflict around the Temple of Preah Vihear*, available at https://casebook.icrc.org/case-study/cambodiathailand-border-conflict-around-temple-preah-vihear, last accessed 30 November 2022.

[5] International Crisis Group, *Waging Peace: ASEAN and the Thai–Cambodian Border Conflict*, Asia Report No 215, 6 December 2011, available at www.crisisgroup.org, last accessed on 30 November 2022, 6.

[6] ICJ, Temple of Preah Vihear *(Cambodia v Thailand)*, Judgment of 15 June 1962.

[7] Constitution of the United Nations Educational, Scientific and Cultural Organization, adopted in London on 16 November 1945.

[8] Note du 2 mai 1966 de la Délégation Permanente du Cambodge auprès de l'UNESCO, UNESCO Doc DC 66/45, 2 May 1966.

[9] Letter dated 22 April 1966 from the acting Permanent Representative of Thailand addressed to the Secretary-General of the United Nations (UNESCO Archives, Press Release 17, 25 April 1966).

comply with other obligations under the Convention.[10] However, the UNESCO Director-General conveyed the view that the UN Secretary-General would provide a more adequate response.[11]

The Temple of Preah Vihear was added in 2008 to the World Heritage List established by the World Heritage Convention, following a request by Cambodia in 2007.[12] However, Thailand contested the extent to which the land around the Temple was also to be protected and claimed that the protective zone that Cambodia had established around the Temple was in Thai territory. The Temple's area as included in the World Heritage List excluded this zone. The continued conflict on the location of the Thai–Cambodian border was the object of a second ICJ judgment in 2013 interpreting the 1962 decision. In this second proceeding, the Court once more did not mention the 1954 Hague Convention and only cited the 1972 UNESCO World Heritage Convention as a reminder to the Parties that they should co-operate in matters related to World Cultural Heritage.[13]

This case study on the overlapping competence of UNESCO, the ICJ and the UN Secretary-General, highlights the shortcomings of the existing international forums as vehicles to help protect cultural property in armed conflict, and to enforce compliance with relevant international law. First, this chapter will analyse the original ICJ proceedings, including the arguments of the Parties and the law applied by the Court, to demonstrate how cultural heritage law was overlooked. Then, the chapter will examine UNESCO's actions, as the main international organisation dedicated to protecting cultural heritage. The limits of UNESCO's actions to enforce international obligations in this particular case will be demonstrated, as will the influence of international politics on the actions of international organisations. Finally, the ICJ proceedings of 2013 will be studied.

19.2 The Original Case before the ICJ

Situated on the border between Thailand and Cambodia, in a 154.7-hectare area, the Temple of Preah Vihear was dedicated to Shiva. The first

10 Thailand ratified the 1954 Hague Convention in 1958 and Cambodia in 1962.

11 The UN Secretary-General was already following the situation at the border and had sent missions to evaluate the inter-State tensions.

12 ICJ, *Request for Interpretation of the Judgment of 15 June 1962 in the Case Concerning the Temple of Preah Vihear (Cambodia v Thailand)* (Cambodia v Thailand), Judgment, 11 November 2013, para 25.

13 Ibid., para 106.

testimonies of the Temple date to the ninth century, when the monument was founded, and it was finished in the eleventh century.[14] It is composed of various sanctuaries on the edge of a plateau that dominates the plain of Cambodia. As stated by UNESCO: 'the site is exceptional for the quality of its architecture, which is adapted to the natural environment and the religious function of the temple, as well as for the exceptional quality of its carved stone ornamentation.'[15] The Temple was included on the World Heritage List in 2008 on the basis it is 'an outstanding masterpiece of Khmer architecture'. The sovereignty over the Temple's surrounding area, however, remained then still disputed.

In 1954, the year of Cambodian independence, Thailand occupied the area of the Temple. First, it should be noted that, even though Cambodia declared its independence on 9 November 1953, it became officially independent only in 1954. At the time, the Cambodian Government saw Thailand as one of the 'greatest threats to Cambodia['s] survival'.[16]

On 6 October 1959, the Cambodian Government submitted a case before the ICJ requesting (i) Thailand withdraw the armed forces that it had installed in 1954 in the ruins of the Temple and (ii) that the territorial sovereignty of the Temple belonged to Cambodia.[17] The Cambodian Government highlighted that it was

> not driven by any political, strategic or economic ulterior motive. It intends that the authentic Khmer Temple of Preah Vihear, placed by the delimitation agreements on the Cambodian side of the border, *should be piously preserved as part of the spiritual, moral, and cultural heritage of the country.*[18]

In its 1962 judgment, the Court recognised that the 1904 Franco–Siamese Treaty had established the frontier in dispute, following the work of a Mixed Delimitation Commission. According to the map used in the dispute, the Temple area was in Cambodian territory. The Court found that the map had been accepted by Thailand and concluded that the Temple was indeed situated on Cambodian territory. The Court also held that 'Thailand is under an obligation to withdraw any military or police

[14] *The Columbia Encyclopedia*, 6th ed., available at www.encyclopedia.com/reference/encyclopedias-almanacs-transcripts-and-maps/preah-vihear, last accessed on 14 April 2022.

[15] UNESCO (n 3).

[16] LC Overton and DP Chandler, 'Cambodia' in *Encyclopedia Britannica*, available at www.britannica.com/place/Cambodia, last accessed 17 April 2022.

[17] ICJ (n 4) 118–19.

[18] Ibid., 114. Emphasis added.

forces, or other guards or keepers, stationed by her at the Temple, or in its vicinity on Cambodian territory',[19] and 'is under an obligation to restore to Cambodia any objects of the kind specified in Cambodia's fifth Submission which may, since the date of the occupation of the Temple by Thailand in 1954, have been removed from the Temple or the Temple area by the Thai authorities'.[20]

In the written proceedings before the ICJ, both States argued the importance of the Temple for the cultural heritage of humanity as an example of Khmer art and heritage. It should be noted that Cambodia became a member of UNESCO on 3 July 1951, before its formal independence, but ratified the 1954 Hague Convention for the protection of cultural property in the event of an armed conflict only on 4 April 1962, after the application to the ICJ.

On the one hand, according to Cambodia's pleadings before the Court, the Temple is part of the country's spiritual, moral and cultural heritage.[21] As such, the Cambodian Government has summitted several documents that refer to the Temple as a Cambodian monument,[22] including a *Minute de la Lettre du Directeur de l'École française d'Extrême-Orient au Gouverneur Général de l'Indochine* that recognised the Temple as a Protected Monument.[23]

On the other hand, the Thai Government contested the religious importance of the Temple for Cambodians since, according to its memorial, 'the temple is a Brahminic monument, whereas Thailand and Cambodia are now both Buddhist countries'.[24] Thailand also argued that

> [i]t played so small a part in the religious life of either people that by the 19th century, it had been forgotten, and it was the Thai Prince Sanphasit who rediscovered it in 1899 . . . . Even after its rediscovery, the temple remained isolated and received only occasional visitors. Visitors from

[19] ICJ (n 7) 37.

[20] Ibid.

[21] ICJ (n 4) 114. Emphasis added.

[22] For instance, in the letter of H Parmentie of 30 January 1930 cited in ICJ, Temple of Preah Vihear *(Cambodia v Thailand)*, Reply of the Government of the Kingdom of Cambodia, 29 November 1961, 521.

[23] ICJ, Temple of Preah Vihear *(Cambodia v Thailand)*, Reply of the Government of the Kingdom of Cambodia, 29 November 1961, 527. See also ICJ, Temple of Preah Vihear *(Cambodia v Thailand)*, Reply of the Government of the Kingdom of Cambodia, 29 November 1961 at 537.

[24] ICJ, Temple of Preah Vihear *(Cambodia v Thailand)*, Counter-Memorial of the Royal Government of Thailand, 29 September 1961, at para 10.

> Cambodia were specially few, because it is difficult to get to the heights of the temple from Cambodia, there being only one very steep path up the eastern side of the cliff.[25]

Furthermore, according to Thailand, the fact that the Temple was authentically Khmer did not automatically give Cambodia sovereignty since, for instance, one can see Roman heritage throughout Europe, and not only in Italy.[26]

The Court recognised in its judgment the importance of the Temple as cultural heritage, as highlighted by both Parties:

> The Temple of Preah Vihear is an ancient sanctuary and shrine situated on the borders of Thailand and Cambodia. Although now partially in ruins, this Temple has a considerable artistic and archaeological interest and is still used as a place of pilgrimage.[27]

However, during the oral and written proceedings, the Parties invoked neither conventional nor customary international law on the protection of historical monuments against military activities to denounce or justify the presence of troops in the Temple. The pleadings focussed on the question of territorial sovereignty.[28] It should be noted that the 1954 Hague Convention could not be applied since Cambodia had ratified the Convention only in 1962. However, at the time, the protection of cultural property was established in customary international law. We might ask why the Court did not refer to this body of law when analysing the legality of Thailand's actions.

The 1907 Hague Convention (IV) respecting the Laws and Customs of War on Land and its Annex, 'Regulations Concerning the Laws and

[25] Ibid. In this sense, it was annexed to the following extract from Memoirs concerning the rediscovery of Phra Vihar in 1899 by Prince Sanphasit cited in ICJ (n 25) 242.

[26] ICJ (n 25) para 11.

[27] ICJ (n 7) 15.

[28] For instance, no reference to cultural heritage law was found in ICJ, Temple of Preah Vihear *(Cambodia v Thailand)*, Mémoire du Gouvernement du Royaume du Cambodge, 20 January 1960; ICJ, Temple of Preah Vihear *(Cambodia v Thailand)*, Contre-Mémoire du Gouvernement de Thaïlande, 29 September 1961; ICJ, Temple of Preah Vihear *(Cambodia v Thailand)*, Réplique du Gouvernement du Royaume du Cambodge, 29 November 1961; ICJ, Temple of Preah Vihear *(Cambodia v Thailand)*, Duplique du Gouvernement de Thaïlande, 2 February 1962; ICJ, Temple of Preah Vihear *(Cambodia v Thailand)*, Minutes of the Public Hearings held at the Peace Palace, The Hague, from 10 to 15 April 1961, and on 26 May 1961, the President, M Winiarski, presiding; ICJ, Temple of Preah Vihear *(Cambodia v Thailand)*, Minutes of the Public Sittings held at the Peace Palace, The Hague, from 1 to 31 March 1962, and on 15 June 1962, the President, M Winiarski, presiding.

Customs of War on Land' was also potentially applicable in the case, if the following provisions could be considered customary norms. Article 27 of the Regulations states that 'in sieges and bombardments all necessary steps must be taken to spare, as far as possible, buildings dedicated to religion, art, science, or charitable purposes, historic monuments . . ., provided they are not being used at the time for military purposes'. Moreover, Article 56 prohibits 'all seizure of, destruction or willful damage done to institutions of this character, historic monuments, works of art and science'.

The fact that the Parties did not refer to the 1954 Hague Convention, to customary international law or to the 1907 Hague Convention need not have prevented the Court from considering this body of law. According to the principle recognised in the *Lotus* case by the Permanent Court of International Justice in 1927,[29] and reaffirmed by the ICJ,[30] the Court is not limited to the arguments that the Parties to a dispute present in the written and oral proceedings. However, the Parties had made no claims to which this law might be relevant. On the merits, the Court highlighted that

> [t]he subject of the dispute submitted to the Court is confined to a difference of view about sovereignty over the region of the Temple of Preah Vihear. To decide this question of territorial sovereignty, the Court must have regard to the frontier line between the two States in this sector.[31]

[29] PCIJ, The Case of the S.S. Lotus *(France v Turkey)*, Serie A, Judgment No 9, 7 September 1927, 31.

[30] 'It being the duty of the Court itself to ascertain and apply the relevant law in the given circumstances of the case, the burden of establishing or proving rules of international law cannot be imposed upon any of the Parties, for the law lies within the judicial knowledge of the Court.' ICJ, *Fisheries Jurisdiction (Federal Republic of Germany v Iceland)*, Judgment of 25 July 1974, para 18. See also: ICJ, *Military and Paramilitary Activities in and against Nicaragua (Nicaragua v United States of America)*, Judgment of 27 June 1986, para 29.

[31] ICJ, *Temple of Preah Vihear (Cambodia v Thailand)*, Judgment of 15 June 1962, 14. According to the Judges Tanaka and Morelli's Declaration: 'The claim as it is formulated in Cambodia's Application is directed not to the return of the Temple as such, but rather to sovereignty over the portion of territory in which the Temple is situated. It is directed, further, to one of the consequences flowing from Cambodian sovereignty over the said portion of territory, that is to say, Thailand's obligation to withdraw the detachments of armed forces it had stationed there, this consequence being explicitly indicated by Cambodia in its Application', ICJ, *Temple of Preah Vihear (Cambodia v Thailand)*, Joint Declaration by Judges Tanaka and Morelli (as appended immediately after the judgment), Judgment, 15 June 1962, 38.

The Cambodian Government's claims were confined to questions of sovereignty, while also asking that the Kingdom of Thailand 'withdraw the armed forces that it has installed since 1954 in the ruins of the Temple of Preah Vihear'.[32] The law on the special protection of cultural property in the event of an armed conflict was not invoked. An additional factor at play may have been that, as Cambodia had so recently come to independence, the Court was particularly inclined to focus on the question of territorial sovereignty and take into account also the conflict in Vietnam then taking place.[33] After ratifying the 1954 Hague Convention, Cambodia, however, went on to seek from UNESCO the protection of its cultural property.

19.3 The Case before UNESCO

Thailand refused to enforce the ICJ judgment for months. However, six months after the judgment, and following a complaint by Cambodia regarding Thailand's non-compliance with the judgment, Thailand withdrew its armed forces from the Temple area.[34] However, four years later, Thailand intensified its military presence in the region. On 3 April 1966, the Cambodian Government reported that nine Cambodian guards were attacked by an estimated fifty individuals from the Thai armed forces. The site was not retaken by the Cambodian armed forces until the night of 5 to 6 April 1966. Moreover, the Thai armed forces fired against the Preah Vihear Temple almost every day from 11 April, causing considerable damage to the monument and sculptures. One month after this series of incidents in the area surrounding the Temple, Cambodia requested UNESCO protect it. Cambodia noted that 'the persistence of these facts would risk the total destruction of this jewel of Khmer art, which is at the same time a heritage of the whole humanity',[35] and made a formal request for UNESCO in the following terms:

> In order to save this temple from disaster, the Permanent Delegation of Cambodia to UNESCO, in accordance with the instructions given by its Government, would like to request the Director-General of the United Nations Educational, Scientific and Cultural Organization to

[32] ICJ (n 7).
[33] The US–Vietnam war had an impact on Cambodia, see Overton and Chandler (n 17).
[34] Note du Délégué permanant du Cambodge concernant le temple de Préah Vihéar (UNESCO Archives, 4 April 1966).
[35] Ibid.

1. communicate these facts to the States Parties to the 1954 Convention for the Protection of Cultural Property in the Event of Armed Conflict

2. assist in seeking ways and means to save the Temple of Preah Vihear from these destructive acts.[36]

The organisation's ability to respond to such a request was debated within UNESCO.[37] Even though the 1954 Hague Convention stipulated two Articles that establish procedures to assist States Parties in the protection of an endangered cultural property – the conciliation procedure provided by Article 22 and the assistance of UNESCO stipulated by Article 23 – the application of such Articles was still relatively new. Cambodia's request for assistance did not mention explicitly any Article of the 1954 Hague Convention.

19.4 The 1954 Hague Convention Procedures for Compliance

The 1954 Hague Convention was a response from the international community to the massive destruction of art and historical monuments during the Second World War.[38] The Convention aimed to establish an international regime to prevent damage to cultural property during international armed conflicts and occupation.[39]

This Convention protects, *inter alia*:

(a) movable or immovable property *of great importance to the cultural heritage of every people*, such as monuments of architecture, art or history, whether religious or secular; archaeological sites; groups of buildings which, as a whole, are of historical or artistic interest; works of art; manuscripts, books and other objects of artistic, historical or archaeological interest . . . .[40]

[36] Ibid.

[37] Ibid.

[38] For a study on the 1954 Hague Convention, see J Toman, *La protection des biens culturels en cas de conflit armé* (Éditions UNESCO 1994).

[39] According to the International Committee of the Red Cross, 'there is occupation when a State exercises an unconsented-to effective control over a territory on which it has no sovereign title'. ICRC, 'Contemporary Challenges to IHL – Occupation: Overview', available at www.icrc.org/en/doc/war-and-law/contemporary-challenges-for-ihl/occupation/overview-occupation.htm, last accessed 16 April 2022.

[40] Convention for the Protection of Cultural Property in the Event of Armed Conflict, adopted on 14 May 1954 at The Hague, 249 UNTS 215. Emphasis added.

Two main obligations are stipulated: to safeguard and to respect cultural property. The first obligation, established in Article 3, concerns the preparation in time of peace for the protection of cultural property in times of war. In addition, it concerns positive action to be undertaken by the State in which the cultural property is located. The second obligation relates to negative actions. Parties are to

> [refrain] from any use of the property and its immediate surroundings or of the appliances in use for its protection for purposes which are likely to expose it to destruction or damage in the event of armed conflict; and [refrain] from any act of hostility, directed against such property.[41]

Thus, during hostilities States must take all necessary steps to spare cultural property from destruction, to the extent military necessity allows. This includes not conducting any military activities in the vicinity of cultural property or using cultural property in a way that transforms it into a military objective.[42] Moreover, Article 5 of the 1954 Hague Convention includes obligations for an occupying State to 'support the competent national authorities of the occupied country in safeguarding and preserving its cultural property', and to 'take measures to preserve cultural property situated in occupied territory and damaged by military operations, take the most necessary measures of preservation in close co-operation with such authorities, among others'.[43]

This Convention also stipulates two procedures to assist in the protection of cultural property in the event of an armed conflict: the conciliation procedure established by Article 22 and the assistance of UNESCO as provided by Article 23. Both Articles were inspired by certain common Articles of the four 1949 Geneva Conventions, that is, the Convention (I) for the Amelioration of the Condition of the Wounded and Sick in Armed Forces in the Field of 12 August 1949, the Convention (II) for the Amelioration of the Condition of Wounded, Sick and Shipwrecked Members of Armed Forces at Sea of 12 August 1949, the Convention (III) Relative to the Treatment of Prisoners of War of 12 August 1949 and the Convention (IV) Relative to the Protection of Civilian Persons in Time of War of 12 August 1949.

41 Article 4.

42 See A Lopes Fabris, 'La notion de crime contre le Patrimoine culturel en droit international' (Institut francophone pour la justice et la démocratie, 2022).

43 Convention for the Protection of Cultural Property in the Event of Armed Conflict, The Hague, 14 May 1954.

19.4.1 *Article 22 of the 1954 Hague Convention: Conciliation Procedure*

Article 22 was established to resolve any conflict between States arising from the application of the 1954 Hague Convention. Initially, the experts drafting the 1954 Hague Convention contemplated a solution referring disputes on the Convention's application to the ICJ. However, this option was renounced since States seemed reluctant to provide for this as only a low number of States had accepted the ICJ jurisdiction.[44] In the end, States decided to adopt a provision for conciliation based on the formula for the exercise of good offices in common Articles 11/11/11/12 respectively of the four 1949 Geneva Conventions.

For analysis of Articles 11/11/11/12 of the 1949 Geneva Conventions, one can refer to the 2016 International Committee of the Red Cross Commentaries to the 1949 Geneva Convention ('2016 ICRC Commentaries'). A first version of the commentaries published in the 1950s is considered 'a major reference for the application and interpretation of these treaties'.[45] The new version of the Commentary to the First Geneva Convention, published in 2016, aims to update the 1950 Commentaries 'in order to document developments and provide up-to-date interpretations'.[46] Table 19.1 sets out the text of Articles 11/11/11/12 alongside the text of Article 22 of the 1954 Hague Convention.

According to the 2016 ICRC Commentaries,[47] in International Law, 'conciliation was originally conceived as a method of peaceful settlement of disputes between States'.[48] Thus, it 'usually involves powers of

[44] Toman (n 39) 274.

[45] L Cameron, B Demeyere, J-M Henckaerts, E La Haye and H Niebergall-Lackner, 'The Updated Commentary on the First Geneva Convention: A New Tool for Generating Respect for International Humanitarian Law' (2015) 97 *International Review of the Red Cross* 1209–26.

[46] Ibid.

[47] In the 1950s, the International Committee of the Red Cross, an impartial, neutral and independent organisation whose exclusively humanitarian mission is based on the 1949 Geneva Convention and its developments, published a set of commentaries on these Conventions, giving practical guidance on their implementation. To reflect the developments in law and practice since then, the ICRC started to publish a new set of commentaries which seek to reflect the current interpretations of the Conventions in 2016. Information available at www.icrc.org.

[48] ICRC, 'Commentary on the First Geneva Convention: Convention (I) for the Amelioration of the Condition of the Wounded and Sick in Armed Forces in the Field, 2nd edition, 2016', available at https://ihl-databases.icrc.org/ihl/full/GCI-commentary, last accessed 14 April 2022, para 1260.

Table 19.1 *Comparative table of Article 11 of the Convention (I) for the Amelioration of the Condition of the Wounded and Sick in Armed Forces in the Field of 12 August 1949 and Article 22 of the Convention on the Protection of Cultural Property in the Event of an Armed Conflict of 14 May 1954*

First Geneva Convention of 1949	1954 Hague Convention
Article 11 In cases where they deem it advisable in the interest of protected persons, particularly in cases of disagreement between the Parties to the conflict as to the application or interpretation of the provisions of the present Convention, the Protecting Powers shall lend their good offices with a view to settling the disagreement. For this purpose, each of the Protecting Powers may, either at the invitation of one Party or on its own initiative, propose to the Parties to the conflict a meeting of their representatives, in particular of the authorities responsible for the wounded and sick, members of medical personnel and chaplains, possibly on neutral territory suitably chosen. The Parties to the conflict shall be bound to give effect to the proposals made to them for this purpose. The Protecting Powers may, if necessary, propose for approval by the Parties to the conflict, a person belonging to a neutral Power or delegated by the International Committee of the Red Cross, who shall be invited to take part in such a meeting.	Article 22. Conciliation procedure 1. The Protecting Powers shall lend their good offices in all cases where they may deem it useful in the interests of cultural property, particularly if there is disagreement between the Parties to the conflict as to the application or interpretation of the provisions of the present Convention or the Regulations for its execution. 2. For this purpose, each of the Protecting Powers may, either at the invitation of one Party, of the Director-General of the United Nations Educational, Scientific and Cultural Organization, or on its own initiative, propose to the Parties to the conflict a meeting of their representatives, and in particular of the authorities responsible for the protection of cultural property, if considered appropriate on suitably chosen neutral territory. The Parties to the conflict shall be bound to give effect to the proposals for meeting made to them. The Protecting Powers shall propose for approval by the Parties to the conflict a person belonging to a neutral Power or a person presented by the Director-General of the United Nations Educational, Scientific and Cultural Organization, which person shall be invited to take part in such a meeting in the capacity of Chairman.

investigation and active participation in finding a solution to the dispute that is acceptable to all Parties to the procedure'.[49] However, it is not binding. As for the good offices to be provided on the basis of the Geneva Conventions, these do 'not necessarily suppose a disagreement between the Parties involved, but may be used, more generally, each time that it is "advisable in the interest of protected persons"'.[50] Moreover,

> The purpose of Article 11 is to determine the conditions for establishing a dialogue between Parties to an international armed conflict. Paragraph 1 invites Protecting Powers to facilitate such a dialogue through their 'good offices'. Paragraph 2 describes one possible way to proceed, namely the organization of a meeting of the representatives of the Parties to the conflict. Article 11 does not, however, suppose the creation of a panel of experts tasked with examining the dispute and proposing the terms of a settlement, as would be the case under the traditional conciliation procedure. In other words, the mechanisms established under Article 11 may involve less formal diplomatic means, as indicated by the notion of 'good offices' in paragraph 1.[51]

This type of 'good offices'[52] is also created by the 1954 Hague Convention, but this time in the best interest of the protection of cultural property. According to Jiri Toman, under Article 22, States do not interpret the Convention or the Regulations but resolve disagreements between the Parties on the application or interpretation of the Convention and the Regulations.[53]

Article 22 of the 1954 Hague Convention does not stipulate the type of good offices to be applied, with paragraph 2 only describing one example. This Article provides an avenue for belligerents to have their conflict mediated during a meeting presided over by a neutral third party, as illustrated in Figure 19.1. In this meeting, proposals can be presented to the belligerents to better protect the cultural property in question. The meeting can, for instance, be a forum to discuss the evacuation of cultural property or the establishment of safe havens.[54] This Article depends for

[49] Ibid.

[50] Ibid., para 1261.

[51] Ibid.

[52] Defined as a 'diplomatic means for the settlement of disputes'. R Lapidoth, 'Good Offices' in *Max Planck Encyclopedia of International Law*, available at https://opil.ouplaw.com/view/10.1093/law:epil/9780199231690/law-9780199231690-e31, last accessed 14 April 2022.

[53] Toman (n 39) 275.

[54] Ibid.

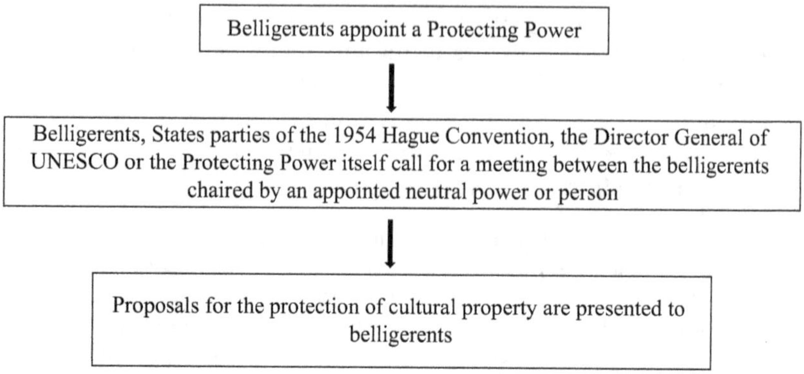

Figure 19.1 Procedure of conciliation under the 1954 Hague Convention

its operation, however, on the appointment of a Protecting Power, a neutral third party agreed by the belligerents who will preside over their negotiations.[55]

States and UNESCO might avoid the application of this Article since reliance on good offices based on the four 1949 Geneva Conventions could be more appropriate. The 1949 Geneva Conventions' good offices procedure would deal with multiple issues over a range of topics and can include the protection of cultural property – the protection of cultural property is present in the 1977 Protocols to the Geneva Conventions. However, according to the ICRC, 'the mechanism established under Article 11 has to date never been used'.[56] According to the 2016 Commentaries:

> The non-use of the conciliation procedure is a direct consequence of the lack of effectiveness of the system of Protecting Powers. Protecting Powers have been appointed on only five occasions since the adoption of the Geneva Conventions in 1949 and they have never had the opportunity to apply their formal competence based on Article 11.[57]

Similar reasoning could be applied to the system under Article 22; non-use of the conciliation procedure under the 1954 Hague Convention could be 'a direct consequence of the lack of effectiveness of the system of Protecting Powers'.[58]

55 Ibid.
56 ICRC (n 49) para 1305.
57 Ibid., at para 1306.
58 Ibid., at para 1306.

19.4.2 Article 23 of the 1954 Hague Convention: Assistance of UNESCO

Article 23 envisages UNESCO's technical assistance, broadening UNESCO's mandate to protect cultural property in the event of an armed conflict. This Article is one of the fundamental provisions on which later legal work concerning the protection of cultural property has been built. From the first propositions of an organisation or rule to protect historical monuments and works of art, the necessity of an impartial organism or State to assist belligerents is often present.[59] States and authorities have often called for the creation of a Red Cross for historical monuments and works of art.[60] According to Jiri Toman's Commentaries, the first paragraph of Article 23 is inspired by Article 9/9/9/10 respectively of the 1949 Geneva Conventions.[61] Table 19.2 sets out the text of Articles 9/9/9/10 alongside the text of Article 23.

Having again as an example the work of the ICRC, the authors of Article 23 intended to exclude any assistance from UNESCO of a political or military character:[62] UNESCO could assist States *inter alia* in the creation of National Committees for the Protection of Cultural Property; affixing distinctive signs to identify historical monuments; the construction of safe havens; and in the elaboration of protecting measures such as plans for bombardments.[63] This assistance is limited, however, to UNESCO's programme and budget. It cannot create extraordinary expenses for the organisation or State Parties. Moreover, this Article appears to exclude the belligerents from the process, which was interpreted by the UK Government during the conference for the Convention adoption as a violation of State sovereignty.[64] This exclusion was rejected by States who understood that the suggestions and proposals made by UNESCO will still depend on the approval of the concerned State.[65] Figure 19.2 illustrates the workings of the assistance procedure.

One interesting example of UNESCO assistance occurred in 1956 and 1957, when Professor Gérard Garitte, at the request of the UNESCO Member States, carried out a mission to Egypt and Israel. He prepared a

[59] Lopes Fabris (n 43).
[60] Toman (n 39) 31; for a complete analysis on the proposals, see Lopes Fabris (n 43).
[61] Toman (n 39) 284.
[62] Ibid.
[63] Ibid., 285.
[64] Ibid., 287.
[65] Ibid.

Table 19.2 *Comparative table of Article 9 of the Convention (I) for the Amelioration of the Condition of the Wounded and Sick in Armed Forces in the Field of 12 August 1949 and Article 23 of the Convention on the Protection of Cultural Property in the Event of an Armed Conflict of 14 May 1954*

First Geneva Convention of 1949	1954 Hague Convention
Article 9 The provisions of the present Convention constitute no obstacle to the humanitarian activities which the International Committee of the Red Cross or any other impartial humanitarian organization may, subject to the consent of the Parties to the conflict concerned, undertake for the protection of wounded and sick, medical personnel and chaplains, and for their relief.	Article 23. Assistance of UNESCO 1. The High Contracting Parties may call upon the United Nations Educational, Scientific and Cultural Organization for technical assistance in organizing the protection of their cultural property, or in connexion with any other problem arising out of the application of the present Convention or the Regulations for its execution. The Organization shall accord such assistance within the limits fixed by its programme and by its resources. 2. The Organization is authorized to make, on its own initiative, proposals on this matter to the High Contracting Parties.

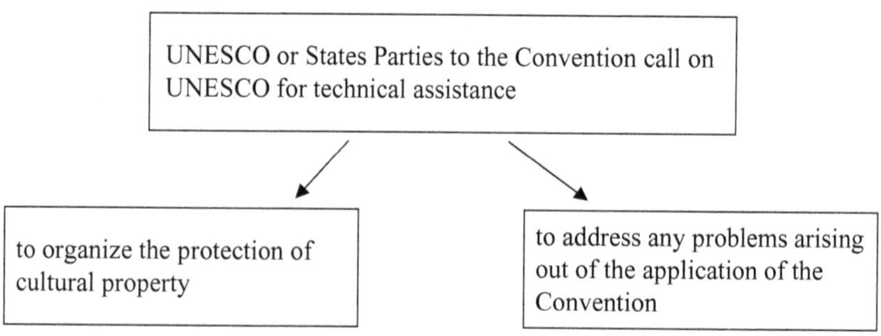

Figure 19.2 UNESCO assistance under the 1954 Hague Convention

detailed report on the state of the monastery of Saint Catherine (Sinai) and made several suggestions for its protection.[66]

It is, therefore, within this technical, even apolitical, mandate that UNESCO should seek to attempt to resolve disputes.[67] However, whereas Article 22 stipulated the possibility for a meeting between Parties presided over by a Protecting Power appointed by both Parties, Article 23 can be applied whenever UNESCO or other States have a concern for the protection of cultural property, without the necessity to appoint a neutral party – the neutral party can be UNESCO itself. A supplementary step – negotiations to agree on a Protecting Power – is thus suppressed. However, Cambodia did not invoke explicitly Article 23 of the 1954 Hague Convention when seeking assistance from UNESCO to protect the Temple of Preah Vihear. It should be mentioned that another, later convention, the Convention Concerning the Protection of the World Cultural and Natural Heritage (the 1972 World Heritage Convention), adopted on 16 November 1972, also provides for UNESCO assistance in relation to World Cultural Heritage included in the World Heritage List.[68] This UNESCO assistance is often granted.

[66] Ibid., 289.

[67] Ibid., 284.

[68] According to Article 13:

1. The World Heritage Committee shall receive and study requests for international assistance formulated by States Parties to this Convention with respect to property forming part of the cultural or natural heritage, situated in their territories, and included or potentially suitable for inclusion in the lists mentioned referred to in paragraphs 2 and 4 of Article 11. The purpose of such requests may be to secure the protection, conservation, presentation or rehabilitation of such property.
2. Requests for international assistance under paragraph 1 of this article may also be concerned with identification of cultural or natural property defined in Articles 1 and 2, when preliminary investigations have shown that further inquiries would be justified.
3. The Committee shall decide on the action to be taken with regard to these requests, determine where appropriate, the nature and extent of its assistance, and authorize the conclusion, on its behalf, of the necessary arrangements with the government concerned.
4. The Committee shall determine an order of priorities for its operations. It shall in so doing bear in mind the respective importance for the world cultural and natural heritage of the property requiring protection, the need to give international assistance to the property most representative of a natural environment or of the genius and the history of the peoples of the world, the urgency of the work to be done, the resources available to the States on whose territory the threatened property is situated and in particular the extent to which they are able to safeguard such property by their own means.

19.5 UNESCO's Response to Cambodia's Request

After receiving the Cambodian request for assistance, the UNESCO Director-General asked his legal adviser for recommendations on how to proceed. A memo dated 4 May 1966 analysed the implementation mechanism of the 1954 Hague Convention:

> The control of [the application of the 1954 Hague Convention] is entrusted, under these conditions, to authorities (protecting powers, commissioners general, etc.) which are only designated when this conflict arises. This control is carried out according to a mechanism which is only implemented at that time and which does not currently exist.
>
> Nothing in the note of the Delegation of Cambodia appears to state [the situations that may attract the application of the Convention. However, a request to safeguard the Temple] is not necessarily limited to the 1954 Convention.
>
> In any case, there is a provision in [the Convention], Article 23, which provides that the Contracting Parties may call upon the technical assistance of the Organization in respect of any problem arising from the application of this instrument.
>
> I believe that in the absence of a control mechanism provided for in the Convention, it is up to the Director-General to inform the Thai Government of the protest he has received, to express his concern for the preservation of the temple and to ask Thailand to respond to the allegations.[69]

5. The Committee shall draw up, keep up to date and publicize a list of property for which international assistance has been granted.
6. The Committee shall decide on the use of the resources of the Fund established under Article 15 of this Convention. It shall seek ways of increasing these resources and shall take all useful steps to this end.
7. The Committee shall co-operate with international and national governmental and non-governmental organizations having objectives similar to those of this Convention. For the implementation of its programmes and projects, the Committee may call on such organizations, particularly the International Centre for the Study of the Preservation and Restoration of cultural Property (the Rome Centre), the International Council of Monuments and Sites (ICOMOS) and the International Union for Conservation of Nature and Natural Resources (IUCN), as well as on public and private bodies and individuals.
8. Decisions of the Committee shall be taken by a majority of two-thirds of its members present and voting. A majority of the members of the Committee shall constitute a quorum.

[69] Memo 386, UNESCO Doc LA/Memo 386, 4 May 1966.

According to advice provided to the Director-General, a 'fact-finding' mission – that is, technical assistance with the objective of assessing the factual circumstances that endangered the cultural property – 'would go beyond the strict framework of the application of the 1954 Convention but . . . would seem to correspond to its spirit'.[70] However, after a study of the potential political consequences of UNESCO's intervention, and given that the case had been submitted to the UN Secretary-General by the Cambodian Government; the Director-General decided against UNESCO involvement.[71] Several UN missions were sent to the region between 1958 and 1968.[72] For its part, the UNSC also has appointed a special representative of the Secretary-General to both countries to review the situation and propose solutions.[73]

Thus, even if UNESCO is the specialised organisation for the protection of cultural heritage, the UNESCO Director-General understood that the UN Secretary-General had more means and tools to respond to the conflict. According to the Director-General, a more comprehensive solution that included the protection of cultural property, civilians and civilian property was preferred.

A similar decision to refer the protection of cultural heritage to the UN Secretary-General was taken during the conflicts in the Balkans:[74]

> The Director-General of UNESCO, Mr Koïchiro Matsuura, has however clearly defined on several occasions what should be the exact role of the Organization in [situations of armed conflicts]: not to intervene during the period before the conflict, to try to prevent it, or after the end of the fighting to try to rebuild a peace process between the community, throughout appropriate action in the various fields of competence of UNESCO.[75]

[70] Ibid. See also 'Political Aspects between Cambodia and Thailand Concerning the Temple of Preah Vihear' (UNESCO Archives, 4 May 1966).

[71] Lettre au Délégué permanent du Royaume du Cambodge auprès de l'UNESCO du Bureau des relations avec les États (UNESCO Archives, 23 May 1966).

[72] A first mission was sent in 1958. After the ICJ Judgment of October 1962, the UN Secretary-General requested the UNSC to send a second mission. A third mission lasted from August 1966 to February 1968. The task of this mission was to provide good offices in reducing tension between Cambodia and Thailand. KR DeRouen and P Bellamy, *International Security and the United States: An Encyclopedia* (Vol. 1, Praeger 2007) 135.

[73] Lettre datée du 16 août 1966, adressé au Président du Conseil de sécurité par le Secrétaire général UN Doc S/7486, 16 August 1966.

[74] See 'L'éclatement de la Yougoslavie et la fin de la fédération' in *Universalis*, available at www.universalis-edu.com/encyclopedie/yougoslavie/, last accessed 12 April 2022.

[75] L Lévi-Strauss, 'The Action of UNESCO in Bosnia and Herzegovina to Restore Respect and Mutual Understanding among Local Communities through the Preservation of

UNESCO has, however, granted some assistance to Cambodia in another conflict, with Vietnam. On 8 June 1970, the Permanent Delegate to UNESCO sent a letter to the Director-General expressly requesting assistance under Article 23 of the 1954 Hague Convention.[76] This time, UNESCO provided assistance to Cambodia for the protection of historical monuments. A technical mission was sent to Cambodia to assess necessary measures to protect cultural property and the following recommendations were made: (a) to send a mission to assist in the safe packing and storage of valuable objects, (b) to send a mission to advise Cambodian authorities on methods to be used to protect cultural property against fire and the effects of bombardments, and (c) to appoint a high-ranking technical adviser to supervise operations from the technical point of view. This assistance demonstrates UNESCO can sometimes intervene in ongoing conflicts, however, the assistance provided will be limited to the Party that made such a request and UNESCO should not interfere in ongoing hostilities. Thus, UNESCO has continued to preserve its position as a neutral agency.

A gap in available information about the situation of the protection of Cambodian cultural heritage follows this request. This may be due to the civil war that started in 1970, the establishment of the Khmer Rouge regime (1975–1979) and the 'tutelage' of Cambodia by the Vietnamese who withdrew their armed forces only in 1989.[77] In the ICJ reinterpretation proceedings Cambodia acknowledged that it did not protest the Thai occupation of an area surrounding the Temple 'during the period of armed conflict in Cambodia or during the succeeding years'.[78]

19.6 Request for Inscription of the Temple on the UNESCO World Heritage List

Cambodia's request for the Temple's inscription in the UNESCO World Heritage List was made in 2007 and submitted that 'the entire promontory of Preah Vihear, as well as the hill of Phnom Trap immediately to the west of the promontory', were within Cambodian territory.[79]

Cultural Heritage' in F Maniscalco (ed.), *La tutela del patrimonio culturale in caso di conflito* (Vol. 2, Massa Editore 2002) 143–48, 143.

76 UNESCO Doc 84 EX/37.

77 Overton and Chandler (n 17).

78 ICJ (n 14) para 38.

79 Ibid., para 25.

The Cambodian Government submitted that the Temple and a buffer zone – an area necessary to the application 'to give an added layer of protection to the property'[80] – were both within its territory. Thailand contested the Cambodian submission and argued that the border submitted by Cambodia was inaccurate. The Thai Government added to the listing procedure a different map that included a buffer zone on Thai territory. The International Council on Monuments and Sites (ICOMOS) study undertaken for the inscription of the Temple in the World Heritage List observed that

> the precise location of the frontier between Cambodia and Thailand to the north of the nominated site is currently the subject of a dispute between the two States Parties. The property nominated . . . and parts of its buffer zone lay partly within the disputed area.[81]

The site as inscribed in July 2008 excluded the disputed area,[82] maybe as an easy solution to assure the inclusion of the Temple without any further delay. However, following the site's inscription, several incidents took place in the area surrounding the Temple, endangering it. Two UNESCO assistances (as per Article 13 of the 1972 World Heritage Convention[83]) were approved for the Temple Preah Vihear: one assistance for the Conservation and Management of the Preah Vihear Temple adopted in 2009 and one emergency assistance for the World Heritage property 'Temple of Preah Vihear' adopted in 2011.[84]

19.7 Referral to the UN Security Council and Establishment of a Joint Border Commission

The UNSC has also been called to act in this conflict. On 18 July 2008, the Permanent Representative of Cambodia to the United Nations addressed a letter to the President of the Security Council. In this letter, the Cambodian Permanent Representative recalled the inscription of the Temple in the World Heritage List and alleged that

80 UNESCO, *Operational Guidelines for the Implementation of the World Heritage Convention*, UNESCO Doc WHC.21/01, 31 July 2021.

81 ICOMOS, *The Sacred Site of the Temple of Preah Vihear*, Advisory Body Evaluation No 1224 (2008).

82 ICJ (n 14) para 27.

83 According to Article 13(1), 'the purpose of such requests may be to secure the protection, conservation, presentation or rehabilitation of such property'.

84 UNESCO, *Assistance to the Temple of Preah Vihear*, available at https://whc.unesco.org/en/list/1224/assistance/, last accessed on 11 April 2022.

> [on 15 July 2008] about 50 Thai soldiers crossed into Keo Sikha Kiri Svara pagoda, located inside Cambodian territory, about 300 metres from the Temple of Preah Vihear. By 16 and 17 July 2008, the number of Thai soldiers on the grounds of the pagoda had increased to 480.

In a letter of 21 July 2008, the Cambodian Permanent Representative asked the President of the UNSC to convene an urgent meeting.[85] In a letter of 22 July 2008 from the Permanent Representative of Thailand addressed to the President of the Security Council, the Thai Government asked for bilateral consultations and negotiations.[86] A Joint Border Commission, created by a memorandum of understanding,[87] was thus established to survey and demarcate the entire Thai–Cambodian border.[88] However, after years of on-again-off-again talks, bilateral diplomacy met a standstill 'because the approval of the minutes, apparently a minor matter, became a highly politicised issue in Thailand'.[89]

No final and peaceful solution was achieved through this forum. In February 2011, soldiers from Thailand and Cambodia clashed once again in the area surrounding the Temple. According to a UNSC Report, 'the clashes may have been prompted by rising tensions associated with the sentencing by a Cambodian court on 1 February of two members of a Thai nationalist movement to up to eight years in prison after finding them guilty of espionage.'[90] At the same time, the UNESCO Director-General expressed concern over the escalation of violence between Thailand and Cambodia.[91] For the protection of the Temple of Preah Vihear, UNESCO sent a mission to assess the state of the Temple[92] and

[85] Ibid.

[86] Ibid.

[87] *Memorandum of Understanding between the Government of the Kingdom of Thailand and the Government of the Kingdom of Cambodia on the Survey and Demarcation of the Land Boundary*, 14 June 2000, as cited in International Crisis Group, *Waging Peace: ASEAN and the Thai-Cambodian Border Conflict*, Asia Report No 215, 6 December 2011.

[88] Letter dated 21 July 2008 from the Permanent Representative of Cambodia to the United Nations addressed to the President of the Security Council, UN Doc S/2008/475, 21 July 2008.

[89] International Crisis Group (n 88).

[90] UNSC, *Update Report No 1: Thailand/Cambodia*, 9 February 2011, available at www.securitycouncilreport.org/update-report/lookup_c_glkwlemtisg_b_6552935.php, last accessed 11 April 2022.

[91] UNESCO, 'Director-General Expresses Alarm over Escalation of Violence between Thailand and Cambodia' (*UNESCO News*, 6 February 2011), available at https://whc.unesco.org/en/news/707/, last accessed 11 April 2022.

[92] UNESCO, 'UNESCO to Send Mission to Preah Vihear' (*UNESCO News*, 8 February 2011), available at https://whc.unesco.org/en/news/708/, last accessed 11 April 2022.

convened a meeting with Thai and Cambodian prime ministers to discuss measures to protect the Temple.[93]

19.8 Request for the Interpretation of the 1962 ICJ Judgment

On 28 April 2011, Cambodia submitted to the ICJ a request for interpretation of the 1962 judgment in the *Case Concerning the Temple of Preah Vihear*. The Cambodian request concerned the meaning and scope of the 1962 judgment, particularly concerning the territorial scope of the second operative paragraph – 'that Thailand is under an obligation to withdraw any military or police forces, or other guards or keepers, stationed by her at the Temple, or in its vicinity on Cambodian territory' – namely the territorial extent of the 'vicinity' of the Preah Vihear Temple. In 1962, when Thailand withdrew its armed forces deployed in the Temple area, it built a 'barbed wire fence which divided the Temple ruins from the rest of the promontory of Preah Vihear'.[94] Such a fence was considered by the Cambodian Government as 'incompatible with the 1962 judgment'.

On 18 July 2011, the ICJ rendered a provisional measure ordering 'both Parties [to] immediately withdraw their military personnel currently present in the provisional demilitarised zone and refrain from any military presence within that zone and from any armed activity directed at that zone'.[95] On 11 November 2013 the Court gave judgment on the question of interpretation of its 1962 decision. The Court stated that 'Cambodia had sovereignty over the whole territory of the promontory of Preah Vihear … and that, in consequence, Thailand was under an obligation to withdraw from that territory the Thai military or police forces, or other guards or keepers, that were stationed there'.[96]

In the Court's judgment of 11 November 2013, the religious and cultural significance of the Temple for the peoples of the region was recognised, and the Court recalled that 'under Article 6 of the World Heritage Convention, to which both States are Parties, Cambodia and Thailand must co-operate between themselves and with the international

93 UNESCO, 'UNESCO Special Envoy on Preah Vihear to Meet with Prime Ministers of Thailand and Cambodia' (*UNESCO News*, 22 February 2011), available at https://whc.unesco.org/en/news/715/, last accessed 11 April 2022.

94 ICJ, *Request for Interpretation of the Judgment of 15 June 1962 in the Case Concerning the Temple of Preah Vihear (Cambodia v Thailand) (Cambodia v Thailand)*, Order, 18 July 2011.

95 Ibid.

96 ICJ (n 14) para 108.

community in the protection of the site since it is listed as a World Heritage'.[97] Moreover, it stated that

> ... each State is under an obligation not to 'take any deliberate measures which might damage directly or indirectly' such heritage. In the context of these obligations, the Court wishe[d] to emphasize the importance of ensuring access to the Temple from the Cambodian plain.[98]

This time round the ICJ referred to international legal obligations to protect cultural heritage and to the importance of the Temple as such. The 1954 Hague Convention is not cited, only the 1972 World Heritage Convention. Maybe the expected demarcation of the border consistent with the 1962 judgment pre-empted the idea that international law on the protection of cultural property in armed conflict, or occupation, would apply, since it is forbidden to deploy military forces in another State's territory. Judge Cançado Trindade extensively explored the cultural significance of this Temple in his Separate Opinion, demonstrating a special interest in the field, and it may be due to his interest and influence that the Court emphasized the importance of protecting the Temple as cultural heritage.[99] No more clashes between Thailand and Cambodia have been reported since 2011,[100] however, the decrease of tensions is thought to be due to the general improvement in bilateral relations.[101]

19.9 Conclusion

UNESCO is the main organisation dealing with the protection of cultural heritage; thus, States often request assistance from UNESCO in the international protection of cultural heritage in times of crisis. However, UNESCO's ability to provide a satisfactory response seems limited. Over the years, certain States have asked for UNESCO to help them ensure

97 Ibid., para 106.

98 Ibid.

99 Separate Opinion of Judge Cançado Trindade in ICJ, *Request for Interpretation of the Judgment of 15 June 1962 in the Case Concerning the Temple of Preah Vihear (Cambodia v Thailand) (Cambodia v Thailand)*, Judgment, 11 November 2013.

100 According to www.cambodia.org/Preah_Vihear/?history=timeline+of+tensions+since+2008.

101 W Nanuam, 'Thai, Cambodian Ties "Best Ever"' (*Bangkok Post*, 22 March 2018), available at www.bangkokpost.com/world/1432779/thai-cambodian-ties-best-ever, last accessed 16 November 2022; Y Soeum, 'Cambodia–Thailand Border Relationship to be Further Strengthened' (*Khmer Times*, 14 March 2022), available at www.khmertimeskh.com/501040607/cambodia-thailand-border-relationship-to-be-further-strengthened/, last accessed 16 November 2022.

compliance with the 1954 Hague Convention. Most of the steps taken by UNESCO focus on prevention rather than intervention, as implied in the Jiri Toman's Commentaries to the 1954 Hague Convention on the Procedure for Conciliation and Technical Assistance, and are employed only when States involved in the disaster, crises or conflict agree. Requests can be refused for political reasons, as was the case with Cambodia in 1966 and in the Balkans conflict.

Even if the Temple of Preah Vihear case was referred to be dealt with through the office of the UN Secretary-General and by the UN Security Council, UNESCO as the related specialised agency should have played a more important role. In this particular case, only the ICJ has been able to directly address the legal dispute on the territory sovereignty – it has ruled that the Temple is on Cambodian territory, a fact recognised by international organisations and States. However, compliance with the ICJ's decisions has also met difficulties. Despite several UN missions sent to the region and the establishment of a Joint Border Commission, no long-lasting solution has been found. The action by the UNSC and United Nations General Assembly (UNGA), through missions sent *in loco*, did not provide a permanent solution, and tensions between both States remained.

Nowadays, a synergy between organisations is proposed to provide better protection of cultural property in times of conflict. In this sense, United Nations peacekeeping forces have also acted to protect tangible and intangible cultural heritage.[102] This approach has somctimes been successful, for instance in the case of Cyprus. Though not involved in a situation of active conflict, the creation in 2009 of the Technical

[102] The United Nations Multidimensional Integrated Stabilisation Mission in Mali (MINUSMA) is one example. The protection function was even introduced into its mandate in 2013. UNSC, Resolution 2164(2014), UN Doc S/RES/2164(2014), 25 June 2014. This consists in 'assisting the Malian transitional authorities as necessary and, if possible, protecting the country's cultural and historical sites against any attacks, in collaboration with UNESCO'. UNSC, Resolution 2100(2013), UN Doc S/RES/2100 (2013), 25 April 2013, para 16(f). In 2014, this mandate was renewed in similar terms. To assist the Malian authorities, as necessary and feasible, in protecting from attack the cultural and historical sites in Mali, in collaboration with UNESCO, UNSC Resolution 2164(2014), UN Doc S/RES/2164(2014), 25 June 2014, para 14(b). In 2018, the Security Council requested: 'MINUSMA to consider the environmental impacts of its operations when fulfilling its mandated tasks and, in this context, to manage them as appropriate and in accordance with applicable and relevant General Assembly resolutions and United Nations rules and regulations, and *to operate mindfully in the vicinity of cultural and historical sites*' (emphasis added, UNSC Resolution 2423(2018), UN Doc S/RES/2423(2018), 28 June 2018, at para 67). The mission today focusses on 'ensuring security, stabilization and protection of civilians; supporting national political dialogue and reconciliation', among other things.

Committee on Cultural Heritage for the protection of cultural heritage in Cyprus is an example of an operative partnership between different actors, including the European Union and the UNDP.[103] However, once again, the main problem – how to enforce compliance in practice – was not addressed. The best answer to these difficult situations may lie in the broader context of bilateral diplomacy. For the Preah Vihear Temple case, the strengthening of Cambodian–Thai relations, notably economic relations, has stabilised the conflict, even if the two countries usually avoid addressing the issue regarding the border.[104]

[103] See *The Technical Committee on Cultural Heritage in Cyprus* (UNDP 2015), available at www.cy.undp.org/content/cyprus/en/home/library/partnershipforthefuture/the-technical-committee-on-cultural-heritage–2015-.html, last accessed 12 April 2022. See also S Hadjisavvas, 'The Destruction of the Archaeological Heritage of Cyprus' in F Maniscalco (ed.), *La tutela del patrimonio culturale in caso di conflito* (Vol. 2, Massa Editore 2002) 207–12.

[104] Nanuam (n 102); Soeum (n 102).

20

The South China Sea Arbitration

Navigating Compliance Strategies through the Lens of Raya and the Last Dragon

MARY JUDE CANTORIAS MARVEL

20.1 Introduction

This chapter offers an analysis of the South China Sea (SCS) Arbitration (*The Republic of the Philippines v The People's Republic of China*) (SCS Arbitration) and the corresponding arbitral award (the Award),[1] using a popular animated film as a lens. The film is Disney's *Raya and the Last Dragon* (Raya), which tells the story of the fictional land of Kumandra, a once-prosperous nation, and its peaceful and united people, where hundreds of years ago, magical dragons lived harmoniously amongst humans. Then evil spirits called the Druun mysteriously appeared and began to ravage the once wealthy unified nation. The people of Kumandra, distrusting each other, splintered into five warring nations/tribes: Fang, Heart, Tail, Spine, and Talon. It is against the backdrop of these fictional nations fighting each other for scarce resources that I approach this analysis. Law and Film has become a relatively mature discipline, and within the broader field of "law-in-film," there is now extensive scholarship that studies the impact of film in shaping our expectations of legal processes and how the public at large view law

I would like to thank Professor Caroline Foster and Professor Christina Voigt for their invaluable editorial comments and recommendations. All substantive views and errors are mine alone.

[1] In honor and loving memory of my husband, Simon Andrew Marvel, an audio-visual and information technology field expert, who always believed in me and understood my passion for the law. I would not have finished this chapter were it not for his inspiration. He will be forever deeply loved and missed.

and justice.[2] It has been said that film is an effective tool to communicate ideas[3] and the emotional impact of a film may shape public opinion. The conflict in Raya effectively communicates that conflict over scarce resources and overlapping territories cannot be resolved by aggression, mutual distrust, and lack of cooperation. This chapter analogizes the themes in Raya with the factual background of the SCS Arbitration with the aim of reshaping international support to help bring about compliance with the Award. While the 1982 United Nations Convention on the Law of the Sea (UNCLOS or the Convention) lacks a compliance mechanism, this chapter envisages that the Convention's conciliation procedure may offer a way forward if China does not voluntarily comply with the Award.

The first part of this chapter will introduce the SCS Arbitration, conducted under Annex VII of the UNCLOS, and discuss the enforcement of such awards. The second part of the chapter will explore further whether the Award may be capable of "enforcement," if necessary, through alternative, more practical means. The third and final part of this chapter will present a path for a cooperative process that reimagines bringing China back to the table in light of the dispute resolution strategies and tactics used in Raya and their potential to inspire renewed efforts towards a settled outcome.

20.2 The Annex VII Arbitration between the Philippines and China

As a voluntary dispute resolution mechanism where the parties submit their dispute to one or more arbitrators who render a binding arbitral award, arbitration is further distinguished by the principle of party autonomy. However, arbitration can only effectively function within the framework of a legal system establishing some "coercive" rules. In inter-State arbitration, these coercive rules will not always extend to the types of recognition and enforcement processes seen in international commercial arbitration. The Award issued in favor of the Philippines in the SCS Arbitration has yet to be enforced or even recognized by China. The Philippines finds itself in a conundrum as the recipient of a binding

[2] *South China Sea Arbitration* (*The Republic of the Philippines v The People's Republic of China*), PCA Case No 2013-19, Award of July 12, 2016, available at https://pcacases.com/web/sendAttach/2086.

[3] S Greenfield, G Osborn, and P Robson, *Film and the Law* (2nd ed., The Cinema of Justice 2010) 1–11.

arbitral award against China that, to this day, lacks an avenue of enforcement.

The Philippines initiated the SCS Arbitration proceedings on 22 January 2013,[4] invoking Article 287 of the UNCLOS, to which both the Philippines and China are party. The Convention provides compulsory third-party dispute settlement when parties cannot settle a dispute by negotiation, conciliation, or other peaceful means. States that do not make a written declaration setting out their choice of procedure for dispute resolution are deemed to have accepted Annex VII arbitration, as is the case between China and the Philippines.[5] Accordingly, the SCS Arbitration was heard by an arbitral tribunal operating under UNCLOS Annex VII.

The Philippines requested the constitution of the tribunal under Annex VII (the Tribunal) and on 22 January 2013 appointed the first Tribunal member under Article 3(b) of Annex VII of the Convention. On 23 March 2013, the International Tribunal for the Law of the Sea (ITLOS) President appointed the second Tribunal member for China upon the Philippines' request pursuant to Articles 3(c) and 3(e), which empower the ITLOS President to make such an appointment when a party fails to choose their party-appointed arbitrator within the allowed period.[6] Article 3(e) requires the ITLOS President to make such an appointment from a list of arbitrators maintained by the UN Secretary-General within thirty days of receiving such a request and in consultation with the parties. China did not participate in this process. Thereafter, the Philippines requested the President of ITLOS to appoint the three remaining members of the Tribunal under Article 3(d) and (e). On 24 April 2013, the President of ITLOS completed the constitution of the five-member tribunal, including the appointment of the Tribunal President. On 5 July 2013, the President of the duly constituted Tribunal requested the Permanent Court of Arbitration (PCA) to serve

4 A Reichman, "The Production of Law (and Cinema): Preliminary Comments on an Emerging Discourse" (2008) 17 *Southern California Interdisciplinary Law Journal* 457–506.

5 In its Notification and Statement of Claim, the Philippines appointed Judge Rüdiger Wolfrum, a German national, as a member of the Tribunal in accordance with Article 3 (b) of Annex VII to the Convention. *South China Sea Arbitration* (*Republic of the Philippines v People's Republic of China*), PCA Case No 2013-19, Award on Jurisdiction and Admissibility of October 29, 2015, available at https://pcacases.com/web/sendAttach/2579, para 28.

6 Ibid., para 109.

as registry for the proceedings,[7] which the PCA accepted, and the Philippines acceded to. Consistent with its stance that the Tribunal had no jurisdiction in the case, China neither confirmed nor refused approval of the PCA registry appointment.[8] The seat of arbitration was in the Netherlands.[9]

The Philippines filed the arbitration to address aspects of the legal dispute between the parties' respective rights and entitlements in the South China Sea after failed bilateral and multilateral negotiations (involving other Association of Southeast Asian Nations (ASEAN) member States) and consultations with China.[10] Meanwhile, the Philippines ably characterized the subject matter in these proceedings as involving only the interpretation and application of relevant UNCLOS provisions and thus falling well within the jurisdiction of the Tribunal. The Philippines argued that China's claim to "historic rights," together with China's "nine-dash line" and associated action, was effectively preventing the Philippines from exercising its rights under the Convention, to wit:

> The nine-dash line embraces over two million km[11] of maritime space, more than 60 percent of the totality of the South China Sea, one of the largest and most important semi-enclosed seas in the world, that is abutted by no less than seven coastal States. China's assertion of these purported "historic rights," and its recent efforts to enforce them, have unlawfully interfered with the enjoyment and exercise by the Philippines of its rights under UNCLOS.[12]

China, through public statements, diplomatic correspondence, and proactively, by way of China's occupation or control of eight maritime features in the SCS, had claimed "sovereign rights and jurisdiction over

[7] Ibid., paras 28 and 29.

[8] Some commentators have mistaken the PCA as the tribunal that heard the proceedings and decided the arbitration. The Award was issued by an ad hoc tribunal constituted under Annex VII of the Convention and the PCA acted merely in an administrative capacity as the Registry. Since the UNCLOS came into force in 1994, the PCA has served as the registry for thirteen arbitrations under Annex VII of UNCLOS. As the registry for the Annex VII Arbitration between the Philippines and China, the PCA performed administrative services. PCA Dispute Resolution Services, *UNCLOS Annex VII Cases Arbitrated under the Auspices of the PCA*, available at https://pca-cpa.org/en/services/arbitration-services/unclos/.

[9] Award on Jurisdiction and Admissibility of October 29, 2015 (n 5) paras 32 and 33.

[10] PCA Cases, "The South China Sea Arbitration (The Republic of Philippines v The People's Republic of China)," available at https://pca-cpa.org/en/cases/7/.

[11] *South China Sea Arbitration (Republic of the Philippines v People's Republic of China)*, PCA Case No 2013-19, *Memorial of the Philippines Volume I* (March 30, 2014) paras 1 and 28.

[12] Ibid., para 1.9.

the waters, seabed and subsoil of the South China Sea"[13] outside the entitlements allowed under UNCLOS but claimed by China to fall within its territory as encompassed by the "nine-dash line." According to China, "its 'historic rights,' which are said to pre-date and exist apart from the Convention, entitled it alone to exercise 'sovereign rights' in these areas, including the exclusive right to exploit living and non-living resources, and to prevent exploitation by other coastal States, even in areas within 200 nautical miles (nm) of their coasts."[14] The Philippines alleged that China's exaggerated maritime claims and attempts to enforce them were contrary to the Convention and without lawful effect and had violated the Philippines' rights under the Convention.[15] The Philippines went on to argue both:

> (a) that any rights that China may have had in the maritime areas of the South China Sea beyond those provided for in the Convention were extinguished by China's accession to the Convention, and (b) that China never had historic rights in the waters of the South China Sea.[16]

The Philippines expertly crafted its submission not as one concerning territorial sovereignty or maritime boundary delimitation but rather as a request for the determination of whether certain "insular features in the South China Sea were either rocks (entitled to a 12 nm territorial sea), low-tide elevations with no territorial sea, or islands (entitled to a 200 nm zone),"[17] even though sovereignty over the features in question remained disputed between the parties.

The Tribunal held it had jurisdiction to decide the South China Sea case under UNCLOS.[18] Thus, the issues raised by the Philippines were determined to be arbitrable and within the Tribunal's remit.[19] On 12 July 2016, the Tribunal issued its unanimous merits Award.

[13] Ibid., para 4.4.

[14] Ibid., at paras 3.73 and 4.4.

[15] Award of July 12, 2016 (n 2) para 112.

[16] Ibid., para 188.

[17] TL McDorman, "The South China Sea Arbitration" (2016) 20(17) *American Society of International Law*, available at www.asil.org/insights/volume/20/issue/17/south-china-sea-arbitration. See also Award on Jurisdiction and Admissibility of October 29, 2015 (n 5) para 8.

[18] Award on Jurisdiction and Admissibility of October 29, 2015 (n 5) paras 397–412.

[19] The Tribunal, however, reserved a decision on its jurisdiction with respect to some of the Philippines' submissions as they were closely linked to the merits of the Philippines' claims. Ibid., paras 398, 399, 402, 405, 406, 409, 411, and 412.

Commentators have hailed the Award as a "landmark," the most crucial part of which is the Tribunal's finding that "China's claim to 'historic rights' to the living and non-living resources within the 'nine-dash line' is incompatible with the Convention to the extent that it exceeds the limits of China's maritime zones as provided for by the Convention."[20] Interpreting the text of the Convention, the Tribunal held that the Convention grants exclusive sovereign rights in favor of the coastal State to the living and non-living resources within its exclusive economic zone and that, under the Convention, claims of sovereign rights over living and non-living resources would generally be incompatible with claims of historic rights to the same resources, specifically if such historic rights are claimed to be exclusive, as in China's case.[21] The Tribunal concluded that by its text, the Convention has comprehensively addressed the rights of other (coastal) States within the areas of the exclusive economic zone and continental shelf and leaves no space for an assertion of historic rights.[22] The Tribunal further concluded that upon China's accession to the Convention "any historic rights that China may have had to the living and non-living resources within the 'nine-dash line' were superseded, as a matter of law and as between the Philippines and China, by the limits of the maritime zones provided for by the Convention."[23]

The invalidity of China's "nine-dash line" implied a recognition of the integrity of the Philippines' full 200 nm exclusive economic zone (EEZ) in the West Philippine Sea. In effect, the Award affirms that the Philippines' maritime area is in fact bigger than the combined land area of all its islands and that all the living and non-living resources, such as fish, gas, oil, and other natural resources, in this huge maritime area belong to this archipelagic State – the Philippines.[24] Additionally, the Award would, in ordinary circumstances, also be expected to secure the freedom of the high seas in this part of the world. The waters and fish in

[20] Award of July 12, 2016 (n 2) para 261.

[21] Ibid., para 243.

[22] The Tribunal added that China even staunchly advocated for the rights of developing States over their EEZ and continental shelf as reflected in the Convention's negotiating record. Ibid., para 261.

[23] Ibid., para 262.

[24] AT Carpio (former Philippines Supreme Court Associate Justice), "Enforce Arbitral Award for Present, Future Generations" (*Thought Leaders*, July 12, 2018), available at www.rappler.com/voices/thought-leaders/207094-second-anniversary-arbitral-ruling-west-philippine-south-china-sea/.

the high seas, including the mineral resources outside the extended continental shelf, unequivocally now form part of the global commons,[25] and are therefore *res communis.*

As an offshoot of the invalidity of the "nine-dash line," the Philippines' other claims were also predominantly decided in its favor. The other salient points of the Award may be broadly categorized as involving a ruling on either "the status of certain maritime features in the South China Sea or the legality of Chinese activities in the South China Sea."[26]

The Tribunal ruled that the Spratly Islands do not generate an EEZ because they are not islands in a strict legal sense but are instead categorized as rocks[27] or low-tide elevations. The Tribunal concluded that the high-tide features in the Spratly Islands (including Itu Aba, Thitu, West York, Spratly Island, South-West Cay, and North-East Cay);[28] the high-tide features at Scarborough Shoal;[29] the high-tide features at Johnson Reef, Cuarteron Reef, and Fiery Cross Reef;[30] the high-tide features at Gaven Reef (North) and McKennan Reef, are all considered rocks.[31] They are not, in their own natural condition and without relying on external human intervention, capable of sustaining human habitation within the meaning of Article 121(3) of the Convention, nor of sustaining an economic life of their own, and thus have no EEZ nor continental shelf.[32]

Having already invalidated the "nine-dash line," the Tribunal also concluded that there is no legal basis under the Convention for China's claim of any entitlement to maritime zones in the area of Mischief Reef, Second Thomas Shoal, and Subi Reef. Being low-tide elevations, they generate no entitlement to maritime zones of their own that would overlap with the entitlement of the Philippines to an EEZ and continental shelf

[25] Ibid.

[26] C Pichel Medina, "Legal Victory for the Philippines against China: A Case Study" (Geneva Graduate Institute, *Global Challenges*, 1, February 2017), available at https://globalchallenges.ch/issue/1/legal-victory-for-the-philippines-against-china-a-case-study/.

[27] 1982 United Nations Convention on the Law of the Sea (UNCLOS), Part VII, Article 121 on Regime of Islands, December 10, 1982, available at www.un.org/Depts/los/index.htm.

[28] Award of July 12, 2016 (n 2) para 622.

[29] Ibid., para 643.

[30] Ibid., para 644.

[31] Ibid., para 645.

[32] Ibid., para 626; See also RD Williams, "Tribunal Issues Landmark Ruling in South China Sea Arbitration" (Lawfare, July 12, 2016), available at www.lawfareblog.com/tribunal-issues-landmark-ruling-south-china-sea-arbitration#3.

generated from baselines on the island of Palawan.[33] Mischief Reef and Second Thomas Shoal are well within the Philippines' 200 nm off Palawan Island. As between the Philippines and China, Mischief Reef and Second Thomas Shoal lie within the Philippines' EEZ and continental shelf.[34]

As the Convention is clear on coastal State rights in EEZs and on continental shelves,[35] the Tribunal held that China had breached UNCLOS provisions and violated the Philippines' sovereign rights to its EEZ and continental shelf,[36] as underpinned by the events and acts committed by China in the years leading up to the filing of the arbitral proceedings, such as

> interfering with the Philippine fishing and hydrocarbon exploration; constructing artificial islands; failing to prevent Chinese fishermen from fishing in the Philippines' EEZ. China also interfered with Philippine fishermen's traditional fishing rights near Scarborough Shoal ... China's construction of artificial islands at seven features in the Spratly Islands, as well as illegal fishing and harvesting by Chinese nationals, violate UNCLOS obligations to protect the marine environment. Finally, Chinese law enforcement vessels unlawfully created a serious risk of collision by physically obstructing Philippine vessels at Scarborough Shoal in 2012. China has aggravated and extended the disputes through its dredging, artificial island-building, and construction activities.[37]

Although the Award is binding,[38] the UNCLOS does not provide for an enforcement mechanism, unlike for instance, the World Trade Organization (WTO) dispute settlement mechanism, which has the WTO Dispute Settlement Body (DSB). The DSB is the official WTO body with powers to monitor disputants' compliance with dispute settlement reports/rulings and to authorize, upon request by the party invoking the dispute settlement procedures, suspension of concessions or other obligations under the covered agreements if no satisfactory compensation has been agreed within the mandated period.[39]

33 Award of July 12, 2016 (n 2) paras 631, 632, 633.

34 Ibid., para 647.

35 Ibid., paras 629 and 698.

36 Ibid., para 700.

37 Ibid., paras 702–16, 735–57, 814, 992, and 993; Williams (n 32).

38 "The award shall be final and without appeal, unless the parties to the dispute have agreed in advance to an appellate procedure. It shall be complied with by the parties to the dispute." UNCLOS (n 27) Annex VII, Article 11.

39 WTO Dispute Settlement Understanding (Annex 2 of the WTO Agreement) (DSU), Article 22.2 on Compensation and the Suspension of Concessions, April 15, 1994, available at www.wto.org/english/tratop_e/dispu_e/dsu_e.htm#22.

The UNCLOS and the WTO Agreements have notable similarities in their structure and scope in that they are both multilateral agreements having a broad mandate and reach. They both include arbitration as a dispute resolution mechanism that the parties may choose to resolve their disputes.[40] But, while these similarities exist, significant differences remain concerning enforcement. Where a dispute settlement report has been adopted, and the losing WTO Member fails to correct its breach of the relevant WTO rules, the DSB can authorize the prevailing State party to take appropriate countermeasures.[41] Disputes over the scope of such measures may themselves be the subject of Panel and Appellate Body proceedings.[42] Such measures are not made available to State parties as part of the UNCLOS dispute settlement regime,[43] although general international law will continue to apply. In respect of damage caused by pollution of the marine environment, States are to ensure the availability of compensation through their domestic legal systems[44] and to cooperate in the implementation and development of international law on liability and compensation.[45]

40 Ibid., Articles 25.1 and 25.2; "If the parties disagree on the complainant's proposed form of retaliation, arbitration may be requested." Ibid., Articles 22.6 and 22.7; See also World Trade Organization, *Dispute Settlement System Training Module. The Process: Stages in a Typical WTO Dispute Settlement Case* (2004), available at www.wto.org/english/tratop_e/dispu_e/disp_settlement_cbt_e/c6s10p2_e.htm, chapter 6.

41 DSU (n 39) Articles 3.7, 16, and 2.1; "In the event the recommendation of the DSB is not followed within the time-period specified by the panel, which shall commence from the date of adoption of the panel's report or the Appellate Body's report, the DSB shall grant authorization to the complaining Member to take appropriate countermeasures, unless the DSB decides by consensus to reject the request." (n 39) Article 4.10; "In less technical terms, the DSB is responsible for the referral of a dispute to adjudication (establishing a panel); for making the adjudicative decision binding (adopting the reports); generally, for supervising the implementation of the ruling; and for authorizing 'retaliation' when a Member does not comply with the ruling." WTO, *Dispute Settlement System Training Module. The WTO Bodies Involved in the Dispute Settlement* (2004), available at www.wto.org/english/tratop_e/dispu_e/disp_settlement_cbt_e/c3s1p1_e.htm, chapter 3.

42 "Currently, the Appellate Body is unable to review appeals. The term of the last sitting Appellate Body member expired on 30 November 2020." WTO, "Dispute Settlement, Appellate Body" (2004), available at www.wto.org/english/tratop_e/dispu_e/appellate_body_e.htm.

43 J Brower, C Koningisor, R Liss, and M Shih, *UNCLOS Dispute Settlement in Context: The United States' Record in International Arbitration Proceedings*, Yale Law (December 10, 2012), available at https://law.yale.edu/sites/default/files/documents/pdf/cglc/yale_law_school_-_unclos_and_arbitration.pdf; J Pauwelyn, "Enforcement and Countermeasures in the WTO. Rules are Rules: Toward a More Collective Approach" (2000) 94 *American Journal of International Law* 335, 336–37.

44 UNCLOS (n 27) at Part XII, Article 235, para (2).

45 Ibid., para (3).

Arbitration under UNCLOS can also be compared and contrasted with investor-state arbitration. In both UNCLOS and International Convention for the Settlement of Investment Disputes (ICSID Convention) an award of a tribunal is binding on all parties to the proceedings and each party must comply with it pursuant to its terms.[46] However, in respect of ICSID arbitration, if a party fails voluntarily to comply with an award, the other party can seek to have the pecuniary obligations recognized and enforced in the courts of any ICSID member State as though the award were a final judgment of that State's courts.[47] There is no similar mechanism available in UNCLOS.[48]

This is not however to suggest that this type of remedy (i.e., imposition of countermeasures as in the WTO) or legal process (enforcement action in respect of pecuniary obligations before a national court as in investment treaty arbitration) would be helpful or even effective in the SCS Arbitration. The latter does not involve trade issues or pecuniary obligations, and economic sanctions or judgments in respect of unmade payments do not seem appropriate.

Nevertheless, the Award in favor of the Philippines remains final and binding between the parties and must be complied with by the parties to the dispute.[49] The Award is without appeal as the parties had not agreed to an appellate procedure in advance.[50] Failure by one State party to participate does not change nor affect the final and binding nature of the Award.

20.3 Compliance Mechanisms for the SCS Arbitral Award

Years after the UNCLOS was adopted, scholars like Professor Robin Churchill have suggested that UNCLOS should have included the type of non-compliance procedure now found in several multilateral environmental agreements (MEAs).[51] Professor Churchill has further elaborated that

[46] Convention on the Settlement of Investment Disputes between States and Nationals of Other States, Section 6, Article 53(1) on Recognition and Enforcement of the Award (ICSID Convention), October 14, 1966, available at https://icsid.worldbank.org/sites/default/files/ICSID_Convention_EN.pdf.

[47] Ibid., Article 54(1).

[48] See also United Nations Convention on the Recognition and Enforcement of Foreign Arbitral Awards, June 10, 1958 (1958 New York Convention).

[49] UNCLOS (n 27), Annex VII, Articles 11 and 296.

[50] Ibid., Article 11.

[51] R Churchill, "Compulsory Dispute Settlement under the United Nations Convention on the Law of the Sea: How Has It Operated? Pt. 1." The PluriCourts Annual Lecture, June 9, 2016, available at www.jus.uio.no/pluricourts/english/blog/guests/2016-06-09-churchill-unclos-pt-1.html.

> UNCLOS suffers from widespread systemic non-compliance, e.g. illegitimate baselines, claims to coastal State jurisdiction in the contiguous zone and EEZ in excess of that permitted by UNCLOS, IUU fishing, sub-standard ships etc. The UNCLOS dispute settlement system has not (yet) really been used to address such non-compliance. To have included in UNCLOS the less confrontational non-compliance procedures (NCPs) of MEAs would have potentially been a very useful tool to address such non-compliance.[52]

In the case of the SCS dispute, would the non-adversarial nature of NCPs have led to a creative path in addressing, for example, the issues of the "nine-dash line" claim based on China's so-called "historic rights" and of China's encroachment on the Philippines' EEZ?

Non-compliance mechanisms (NCMs) may be considered a better alternative to the more traditional and adversarial dispute settlement mechanisms that may be resorted to under UNCLOS, such as the ICJ, ITLOS, and even Annex VII arbitration. Although the primary aim of NCMs is not dispute settlement, they nonetheless often produce that effect.[53] This may be attributed to the following: firstly, they provide a

[52] One of the difficult issues in UNCLOS is the matter of conservation and sustainable use of marine biological diversity of areas beyond national jurisdiction. Thus, the UN General Assembly, in its Resolution 72/249 of December 24, 2017, convened an Intergovernmental Conference to consider the text of an international legally binding instrument under the UNCLOS on the conservation and sustainable use of marine biological diversity of areas beyond national jurisdiction, with a view to developing the instrument.

The first session of negotiations was convened from September 4 to 17, 2018. The fifth session was convened in New York, in August 2022. The BBNJ Treaty is intended to build on the "vision of the Law of the Sea Convention to protect, conserve and restore marine life and sustainably and equitably use our shared ocean resources while strengthening the existing governance framework for this vast global commons." IUCN, "Looking Towards the Resumption of IGC5" (The International Union for Conservation of Nature, July 14, 2022), available at www.iucn.org/story/202207/looking-towards-resumption-igc5. The *Further Revised Draft Text of an Agreement under the United Nations Convention on the Law of the Sea on the Conservation and Sustainable Use of Marine Biological Diversity of Areas Beyond National Jurisdiction* stresses "the need for the comprehensive global regime to better address the conservation and sustainable use of marine biological diversity of areas beyond national jurisdiction . . . Respecting the sovereignty, territorial integrity and political independence of all States." UN, *Further Revised Draft Text of an Agreement under the United Nations Convention on the Law of the Sea on the Conservation and Sustainable Use of Marine Biological Diversity of Areas Beyond National Jurisdiction*, Intergovernmental Conference, Fifth Session (August 15–26, 2022), available at www.un.org/bbnj/sites/www.un.org.bbnj/files/igc_5_-_further_revised_draft_text_final.pdf.

[53] Churchill (n 51).

reportorial mechanism on how State parties implement their treaty commitments; secondly, if there are allegations of acts of non-compliance, they offer a venue for examining these incidents; and thirdly NCMs offer mechanisms for direct support to address these incidents.[54]

When the Philippines filed the arbitral proceedings in 2013, an NCM was not available. However, the Philippines' foreign policy (then led by the late President Benigno Aquino) was to obtain an unequivocal and enduring ruling that would outline the rights of the Philippines to its EEZ and its continental shelf, and recognize its citizens' unhampered rights to the fish, oil, gas, and other natural resources in these zones for its own use and benefit. The Chinese government's strategy, on the other hand, was to seek to muster international support for its stance as well as garner political capital from its own citizens.

The economic and military might of China seem daunting to a smaller developing State like the Philippines, but the SCS Arbitral Award has given the Philippines political and moral leverage. However, although the Philippines obtained the best possible outcomes from this arbitration against China, the nature of the claims raised by the Philippines lend themselves to a most difficult enforcement or compliance process: for example, in respect of the claim of sovereign rights as compared with China's "nine-dash line" claim to "historic rights"; EEZ boundaries; classification of a land feature as either an "island" or rock; the claimed violation by China of its international navigation and marine conservation treaty obligations during law enforcement and land reclamation activities;[55] illegal fishing and harvesting by Chinese nationals; and violation of UNCLOS obligations to protect the marine environment.[56] The issues raised by the Philippines did not entail trade or investment interests, but rather "largely non-economic calculations."[57] Such interests are not easily quantifiable in monetary terms, unlike for example a commercial dispute involving a mining contract and its interpretation or application, which

[54] Ibid.

[55] (n 37).

[56] Ibid.

[57] EJA Ibarra, "Probing the (Im)possibility of China's Compliance with the South China Sea Arbitration Award." Center for International Relations and Strategic Studies, The Philippine Foreign Service Institute, IV(2) (July 2017), https://fsi.gov.ph/probing-the-impossibility-of-chinas-compliance-with-the-south-china-sea-arbitration-award/.

might be unilaterally submitted to binding arbitration,[58] and dealt with through a monetary award. A claimant making these kinds of claims, as the Philippines did, is generally looking for a resumption of compliance by the other party rather than compensation. At the same time, the claims went beyond ordinary claims of maritime pollution or violations of marine conservation that might more obviously have been susceptible to multilateral NCPs, if such procedures had been available, or simply to "performance review information (self-reporting)";[59] or where improved compliance might be brought about through direct support such as by providing technical and financial assistance.[60]

As a push-back of sorts, without an outright butting of heads with China, the Philippines can and must continue to exercise its rights and jurisdiction over its 200 nm EEZ and its 12 nm territorial sea. Entering into multilateral arrangements with other neighbouring coastal States on the conservation and management of living resources in the high seas[61] could arguably be viewed as a form of unilateral "enforcement," as a confirmatory act of the ruling that China's "nine-dash line" claim is inconsistent with UNCLOS and that the high seas, as part of *res communis*, shall be enjoyed as a global commons.[62] The conclusion of a new agreement on the conservation and sustainable use of marine biological diversity of areas beyond national jurisdiction (ABNJ) emphasizes that the "high seas and marine ABNJ are open for legitimate and reasonable use by all States, and may not be appropriated to the exclusive sovereignty of any one State."[63]

Further, UNCLOS does include provisions on support for developing State parties[64] to assist them in discharging their primary marine

58 M-A Carreira da Cruz, "Deep Sea Mining, Arbitration and Environmental Rules: What Role for Standards?" (*Kluwer Arbitration Blog*, October 27, 2018), available at http://arbitrationblog.kluwerarbitration.com/2018/10/27/deep-sea-mining-arbitration-environmental-rules-role-standards.

59 GL Rose, *Report on the Comparative Analysis of Compliance Mechanisms* (University of Wollongong 2006), available at http://ro.uow.edu.au/lawpapers/36.

60 Ibid., 10.

61 Rose (n 59) Citing UNCLOS, Article 117.

62 Carpio (n 24).

63 S Hart, *Elements of a Possible Implementation Agreement to UNCLOS for the Conservation and Sustainable Use of Marine Biodiversity in Areas beyond National Jurisdiction*, IUCN Environmental Policy and Law Papers online – Marine Series No 4 (2008), available at https://portals.iucn.org/library/sites/library/files/documents/eplp-ms-4.pdf.

64 UNCLOS (n 27), PART XII, Article 202.

environmental obligations, including technical assistance.[65] Such assistance may be provided in the form of scientific, educational, and other technical assistance programmes aimed at marine environmental conservation and marine pollution control and prevention;[66] as well as "marine research and exploitation of the deep seabed; providing available scientific information relevant to the conservation of fish stocks and catch and fishing statistics."[67] This assistance could help the Philippines advance its marine science technological capacity or even strengthen the country's existing technology infrastructure for the exploration and exploitation of its marine resources,[68] its EEZ, and continental shelf. This would help the Philippines exercise its rights under UNCLOS, consistent with the SCS Arbitration Award.

20.4 Reimagining Compliance: Film and Reality

Having envisaged aspects of a unilateral "enforcement" of the Philippines' rights under the SCS Arbitral Award, we may now examine the potential for China's cooperative compliance. Reimagining even a powerful State like China voluntarily complying with the Award is not far-fetched. China has quite a history of voluntarily complying with its international obligations, and, despite appearances, still aims to be seen as a rules-based player. China is not completely immune to the reputational costs of completely disregarding the Award and "compliance with the arbitral award may also be in China's national interests."[69] China did participate in the arbitral proceedings in certain ways, despite its repeated claims that it did not recognize the Tribunal's jurisdiction and all the proceedings therein. Indeed one writer describes China's non-participation as only "nominal."[70] China's behavior during the arbitration and after the Award was issued showed China maintaining "informal communications with the tribunal to partially comply with some requirements during the proceedings."[71] For instance, although China did not submit a counter-memorial to the Tribunal, it issued a position

[65] Ibid.

[66] S Maljean-Dubois, *Chapter 16: Compliance and Implementation, Companion to Global Environmental Governance* (HAL 2020), available at https://shs.hal.science/halshs-02926756/document.

[67] Ibid.

[68] UNCLOS (n 27), PART XIV, Article 269(a).

[69] Ibarra (n 57).

[70] Ibid.

[71] Ibid.

paper (identifying what China said it believed were the reasons for the Tribunal's lack of jurisdiction) corresponding to the Tribunal's timeline on 7 December 2014. China's embassy in the Netherlands requested, by way of a *note verbale* deposited with the PCA, as the registry, that its position paper be forwarded to the Tribunal. Finally, China reiterated all of its counter-arguments in a remark by the spokesperson of the Ministry of Foreign Affairs (MFA) released on 24 August 2015.[72]

China is not oblivious to how the international community will react to a hardline stance of complete non-compliance. Proof of this is seen in China's efforts to garner international support for its claims. Indeed, public opinion has mattered to China because at the time of the proceedings, it alleged that it had the support of about sixty-five other States, of which, eventually, thirty-one would publicly confirm, and four would deny this.[73] When a ruling was issued, five States opposed the Award, and nine States would not mention the Award, but issued neutral statements. At the same time, thirty-three gave positive statements without necessarily calling for China to comply, and only seven outrightly called for the parties to comply.[74] As of 2020, Vietnam and Malaysia tacitly supported the Award by rejecting China's "historic rights," while Indonesia "endorsed" the Award, with Taiwan stating that "any claim inconsistent with international law should not be accepted."[75] As at August 2, 2021, the Asia Maritime Transparency Initiative and the Center for Strategic and International Studies had "identified 8 governments that have publicly called for the ruling to be respected, 35 that have issued generally positive statements noting the verdict but have stopped short of calling for the parties to abide by it, and 8 that have publicly rejected it."[76]

Meanwhile, the United States continues to assert a foreign policy consistent with the law as the Tribunal viewed it. The US Navy conducts ongoing freedom of navigation operations and naval exercises with allies and partners and the US Air Force has ramped up military surveillance flights in the region. India aligns with US policy, supporting freedom of navigation and overflight in the SCS and deploying its Indian Navy

[72] Ibid.
[73] Ibid.
[74] Ibid.
[75] G Grieger, "China Tightens its Grip over the South China Sea," Members' Research Service, EU European Parliamentary Research Service (February 2021), available at EPRS_ATA(2021)689338_EN.pdf.
[76] The Asia Maritime Transparency Initiative and the Center for Strategic and International Studies, *Arbitration Support Tracker* (AMTI) (August 2, 2021), available at https://amti.csis.org/arbitration-support-tracker/.

warship to the SCS. Japan has recognized the Award by performing anti-submarine drills in the SCS.[77] All these activities underscore the "geo-strategic significance"[78] of the SCS – a "strategic maritime link between the Indian Ocean and the Pacific Ocean stretching from the Strait of Malacca to the Strait of Taiwan."[79] The SCS connects the eight South-East Asian countries of Brunei, Cambodia, Indonesia, Malaysia, the Philippines, Singapore, Thailand, and Vietnam; as well as China and Taiwan "into global trade flows and is essential for their livelihoods and food security."[80] Viewed through this lens, the SCS conflict patently reflects a desire from all parties (including the nominal parties who submitted position papers or indirectly benefitted from the Award) to ensure the integrity of their territories, bearing in mind their respective national interests, as permitted under the UNCLOS.

The SCS Arbitral Award gives the disputants a reality test. The Award makes it clear that, by international law standards, the rules favor one party or are less favorable to the other, and international opinion may thus be influenced to retract or confirm public support. Therefore, public opinion (or international support) is central to a reimagined path of voluntary compliance by China with its international law obligations, or cooperation, as it were. While China has exerted certain efforts to influence international public opinion through think-tanks releasing position papers and other scholarly legal articles, there are also different modes of approach to such problems. Storytelling – compelling storytelling – can influence the discourse that shapes public perception (even international support), in general, and specifically concerning the SCS Arbitration. "The intermingling of truth and fiction in legal discourse is nothing new . . . and the best, most compelling stories are the ones that adapt familiar narrative forms featuring recognizable character types driven by ordinary feelings, motives, and desires."[81]

In Raya, the answer to the question of "How does one go back to the negotiating table?" was hardly clear-cut. Still, the film eventually reached its primary goal – to have everyone cooperate to defeat the Druuns and give everyone an acceptable and fair slice of the proverbial pie. Although

[77] Grieger (n 75).

[78] G Grieger, "China and the South China Sea Issue," Members' Research Service, EU European Parliamentary Research Service (September 2016), available at www.europarl.europa.eu/RegData/etudes/BRIE/2016/586671/EPRS_BRI(2016)586671_EN.pdf.

[79] Ibid.

[80] Ibid.

[81] R Sherwin, "Law in Popular Culture" (2004). *Articles & Chapters*, available at https://digitalcommons.nyls.edu/fac_articles_chapters/1226.

the situation in relation to the SCS Arbitration appears to be untidy, as in Raya, the Award can be used as a tool not to force "cooperation" from China but to impress upon China that it is to its best (reputational) interest to follow a path of cooperation.

In Raya, the Heart tribe and its chief became the "guardians" of the ancient Dragon Gem that not only kept evil Druuns away but also served to remind the peoples of Kumandra of their past, and of how the Druuns had ravished their lands, laying them to waste. The peace in Kumandra was fragile and kept barely intact by the Dragon Gem. Despite the advantage of having in its possession the Dragon Gem, the Heart tribe wanted to reach out to the other four tribes to ensure continuing peace in the region. The Heart tribe lowered its defenses and invited the leaders of the other tribes with their delegates to "share a meal." However, Heart trusted all the opposing parties without caution, without an exit plan, and certainly without obtaining as much information as they could about the conflict and the negotiating positions and intentions of the other tribal chiefs. While everyone was busy enjoying the festivities, the only daughter of the Fang tribe's tribal chief tried to steal the Dragon Gem from its highly secured vault. As the Heart tribe tried to stop the thief, other tribe leaders and their delegates made their own attempts to steal the Dragon Gem, which broke into pieces. This paved the way for the Druuns to resurface and lay waste to Kumandra once again.

The situation is different in the SCS dispute. The Award itself is the Philippines' "shared meal" strategy – here is a paradigm that is rooted in international law and that the (international) "public" can get behind. However, the Philippines' "shared meal" strategy is rules-based, and the Philippines is fully informed of everyone's interests and positions, unlike in the film. In effect, and ironically enough, the Award itself becomes a source of expectations for compliance with international law, now or through future legal processes. After the Award was issued, China released a statement, a portion of which stated that

> Pending final settlement, China is also ready to make every effort with the states directly concerned to enter into provisional arrangements of a practical nature, including joint development in relevant maritime areas, in order to achieve win–win results and jointly maintain peace and stability in the South China Sea.[82]

[82] China's MFA, *Statement of the Government of the People's Republic of China on China's Territorial Sovereignty and Maritime Rights and Interests in the South China Sea*, Ministry of Foreign Affairs (July 12, 2016), available at www.fmprc.gov.cn/mfa_eng/zxxx_662805/t1379493.shtml.

This statement reflects that China does understand, and indeed recognizes, that the arbitral Award forms part of a broader paradigm in the South China Sea region. Every coastal State impacted by this Award may look to it as an authoritative statement of rights and obligations.

One potential pathway forward reimagines bringing China back to the table through conciliation. Conciliation is a well-established international dispute resolution process: "The main purpose of conciliation is to lead the parties to reach an amicable settlement of their dispute; its function is not to settle a dispute by applying law per se, but rather to bring the parties to an agreement by way of negotiation and compromise."[83] Conciliation is also an UNCLOS process and in fact one of the options that other Filipino experts suggested, after the Philippines filed the arbitral claim, would have been preferable. Consider for instance the successful UNCLOS conciliation launched by East Timor with Australia,[84] that the latter opposed initially but which eventually led to an amicable agreement between the parties with the assistance of the Conciliation Commission.[85] There is nothing in the UNCLOS rules that prevents any State party from resorting to other "informal" conciliatory measures or even voluntary modes of compliance, even after a binding arbitral award has been issued, as in the case of the SCS Arbitral Award.

An audio-visual experience of a story can be an effective tool, and a film such as *Raya and the Last Dragon* may help us in distilling pathways forward to bring all concerned parties towards a settlement. A film can show heroes and anti-heroes and develop a narrative that persuades the public to choose sides. Although Raya was the apparent central character and the Heart tribe were presented as the "good side," the movie nonetheless characterized the anti-heroine (Namaari of the Fang tribe) as likeable and someone the public can also support if she chooses to do the "right" thing. In the end, both Raya and Namaari were essential cogs in the machinery that would restore Kumandra to its peoples.

83 D Tamada, "The Timor Sea Conciliation: The Unique Mechanism of Dispute Settlement" (2020) 31(1) *The European Journal of International Law* 321–44.

84 Ibid. In that case, Tamada observes: "As Australia's declaration under Article 298(1)(a)(i) 11 of 22 March 2002 excepted maritime delimitation disputes from the jurisdiction of litigation and arbitration, there was no other means open to Timor-Leste than conciliation."

85 PCA, *Conciliation Commission Constituted under Annex V to the 1982 United Nations Convention on the Law of the Sea between the Democratic Republic of Timor-Leste and the Commonwealth of Australia*, Timor Sea Conciliation (*Timor-Leste v Australia*) (April 11, 2016), available at https://pca-cpa.org/en/cases/132/.

INDEX

For EU product safety concerns, contact us at Calle de José Abascal, 56–1°,
28003 Madrid, Spain or eugpsr@cambridge.org.

www.ingramcontent.com/pod-product-compliance
Lightning Source LLC
LaVergne TN
LVHW011655200926
848484LV00004B/948
* 9 7 8 1 0 0 9 3 7 3 9 0 6 *